HISTORICAL MEMOIRS
OF THE
DUC DE SAINT-SIMON

TO
NANCY MITFORD

SYNOPSIS OF CONTENTS

1675. Birth of Louis de Rouvroy de Saint-Simon, son of Claude de Rouvroy, Capitaine de Versailles, Grand Louvetier, Premier Gentilhomme de la Chambre de Louis XIII.

1683. Saint-Simon's tutor reports that he is bad-tempered, weak in his Latin, and idle.

PART ONE
MAKING A LIFE

PART TWO

LIFE AT THE COURT

Chapter 12

1702

Saint-Simon is not promoted in the general advancement – He retires from
the army and angers the King – He owns a house at Versailles, quarrels

Chapter 19

1709

Appalling calamity of the terrible winter – Père Tellier, the King's new confessor, makes advances to Saint-Simon – He finds himself and the Duc de Chevreuse in complete agreement – Cabals against the future Dauphin (the Duc de Bourgogne) and the Duc d'Orléans; Saint-Simon defends them both – Wicked speculation in grain – Riots in Paris – The silver goes to the Mint – Saint-Simon resolves to retire from the Court – Battle of Malplaquet – Military destruction of Port-Royal-des-Champs – He seeks an audience of the King and proposes to part the Duc d'Orléans from his mistress – A year of disasters and defeats for France and Saint-Simon   402

Maps

Introduction

THE FAME of the Duc de Saint-Simon has known a curious history.
The existence of these memoirs was known by the middle of the eighteenth
century, and that he had much to say about the last years of the rule of
Louis XIV was common knowledge. Thus, we now know that Montesquieu visited the aged Duke at La Ferté-Vidame, and it is from Saint-
Simon that Montesquieu got some of the evidence to justify some of his
hostility to the absolute monarchy of Louis XIV. But the first editions of
the memoirs were truncated, badly edited, and gave a very inadequate
picture of the greatness of the Duke's achievement. He was at once
recognized, of course, as a very valuable historical source. He was, for
example, used by Macaulay for some of the most dramatic passages in his
History of England. His biases, his hostility to Louis XIV, his probity
of character with its criticism of the reign of flattery, all suited Macaulay's
own prejudices; and William III, the Stadholder who was recognized by
Louis XIV as King of England in 1697, is a kind of antithesis to his
kinsman, the 'Sun King', and that, of course, also appealed to Macaulay's
highly partisan view of history. But it was not until the middle of the
nineteenth century that anything like a respectable edition of the memoirs
was available, and in fact no edition to date—not even the admirable
Pléiade edition—can be considered quite final. A new and immense
edition is announced in Paris, and it may justify the vast expense of time
and money involved.

But since the middle of the nineteenth century interest in Saint-Simon
has been less interest in him as an historical source, or the kind of interest
provoked by the diaries of John Evelyn and Samuel Pepys or numerous
French memorialists, than interest in one of the greatest of French
writers. It was on this aspect of Saint-Simon that Sainte-Beuve insisted
in his reply to the denigratory editor Chéruel, and certainly, for the last
century, Saint-Simon has been regarded as one of the greatest if most
idiosyncratic of French prose writers and by far the greatest memoir
writer in a literature especially rich in memoirs dating back to the thirteenth
century, to Villehardouin and Joinville. None of the other memoir writers,
not even Commines, could compare for a moment with the Duke. The
very oddity of his French; the irregularity of his syntax; the originality of
his vocabulary are now seen not as reflexions of his imperfect literary
education (on which he himself comments), but as examples of his
indifference to the formal classical taste of the time and his readiness to
follow his own genius. It is a little hard to believe that Saint-Simon was

not conscious that he was doing more than telling the truth as he saw it. He was producing a work of art. It was not the art of the *grand siècle*: he was conscious of that. But the artist in him is so visible to the reader that it is hard to believe it was totally invisible to the author.

Perhaps the parallel with Boswell is worth pursuing. Macaulay saw that the numerous follies and weaknesses of Boswell were intimately connected with his greatness as a biographer. The very follies that irritated his friends and alienated his family were essential to his great work. But we now know that Boswell was a conscious artist. We now appreciate the dexterity as well as the miraculous liveliness which he revealed in his life of Johnson. Saint-Simon was not so much the professional author as was Boswell who, after all, got his first fame as the author of a book on Corsica. Saint-Simon published nothing of his memoirs in his lifetime; he did not attempt to enter the Académie Française which then, as now, welcomed literate dukes. He discussed the literary ambitions of great noblemen and great prelates with a certain amount of irony. He knew he could not write like Racine or like Bossuet—he did not try to. But the fact that he told the same story in various versions, that he went back, editing and re-editing his immense work, suggests, I think, that he was not only doing his best to tell the truth as he saw it about Louis XIV and the Court and above all to preach his own political doctrines, but was consciously creating a great work of art.

That it was a great work of art no one now doubts. The degree to which it has been parodied is proof enough of that! A good deal of Proust can be understood only as a conscious imitation of Saint-Simon. The *esprit des Guermantes* is the *esprit des Mortemart*. Some passages are lifted straight from Saint-Simon: for example, the most outrageous behaviour of Monsieur de Charlus is lifted, almost word for word, from the account of the extraordinary behaviour of the Cardinal de Bouillon. And of course Proust, long before he published his great work, had openly parodied Saint-Simon in *Pastiches et Mélanges*. If imitation is the sincerest form of flattery, Saint-Simon has been highly flattered for the last century. (He is highly flattered every week in *Le Canard Enchaîné* in the admirable parodies called *La Cour* which we owe to Monsieur Ribaud, with President de Gaulle as 'Le Roi' and Madame de Gaulle as 'Madame de Maintenant', a joke which was originally made at the expense of Madame de Maintenon). Indeed, it is not entirely paradoxical to say that Saint-Simon is among the greatest of French novelists as well as among the greatest of French memoir writers. So the job of translating him is an extremely difficult one, but it seems to me that Miss Norton has had a most agreeable success based on a sound view of how he *can* be translated into modern English.

But people who are perfectly willing to regard Saint-Simon as a great man of letters and regard him as far more important today than his kinsman, the Comte de Saint-Simon, the great Socialist theorist of the beginning of last century, still tend to carry over in their discussions of the great work some of the contempt for the author which Macaulay felt for Boswell and which Chéruel felt for Saint-Simon.

That this contempt was undeserved Miss Norton makes plain. In every sense of the term, Saint-Simon was *un honnête homme*. In a Court where mendacity, flattery, corruption were rife, he lived a life which, as Macaulay said of Cardinal Fleury's, must be considered singularly pure. His piety, narrow as it was, was genuine and not affected to attract the attention and approval of the King. Indeed, he showed his courage not only by ceasing to 'serve' in the army (a grave crime in the eyes of the King), but by his loyalty to his friends whether their stock was high or low on the great *Bourse* of Versailles. Louis XIV appreciated the honesty of this irritating, critical, censorious nobleman who felt that the King was not only in many ways a bad ruler, but a man betraying his rôle as 'the first gentleman of France'. Looking back, we can see, or think we can see, that Saint-Simon with his fatal prejudices was defending a lost cause. The cause he wanted to defend, although he may not have been quite clear about it in his own mind, was the cause above all of the higher nobility, but also the cause of the institutions of France which limited royal autocracy. Thus, while he was very hostile to the aristocratic pretensions of the *noblesse de robe*, the hereditary judges of whom Montesquieu in the next century was the most famous, some of his closest friends were, like the Chancellor Pontchartrain, members of this aspiring social group. We must remember that if Louis XIV had too sublime a confidence in his own unique position to be a snob, Saint-Simon, conscious of his rank as *duc et pair*, was also above being a snob. One of the most effective passages in the memoirs is the description of the ranker officer who was a pioneer in 'partisan' warfare. He admired bishops who were pious, who lived in their dioceses, who were soundly anti-Jesuit, who played a really pastoral rôle whatever their social origin, although he no doubt appreciated them even more if they were also great nobles.

This concentration on the small group of dukes who were peers of France (as apart from the ordinary dukes, of whom there were many more) has its comic side. It recalls Disraeli's radical duke, St. Aldegonde, who was in favour of abolishing all ranks in society, except dukes—'who were a necessity'. But Saint-Simon did, in fact, judge people by the way in which they fulfilled their own rôle in life, in that order in life to which God had called them. He was therefore peculiarly critical or censorious of Court nobles and great churchmen who did not live up to the duties of their rank and insisted only on the privileges. Perhaps it is only when he is discussing climbers; people trying to enter the sacred body of dukes and peers or the Order of the Holy Ghost, the French equivalent of the Garter, (even when they were great public servants like the Maréchal de

Villars, they were regarded as intruders whose social claims no military service could justify), that Saint-Simon is a snob. But this was not always snobbery, for Saint-Simon resisted the claims of so great a soldier, who was also so great a nobleman, as the Maréchal de Luxembourg, and his deepest hatred and scorn were for the royal bastards whom the King promoted to extremely high rank, even legitimizing them, thus insulting both the nobility of France and the sacrament of holy matrimony! Saint-Simon genuinely disapproved of adultery, a rather odd attitude at Versailles at this time, especially where royal adultery was concerned; but he especially disapproved of adultery whose fruits upset the divine order of things in the Kingdom of France. It is very hard for us at this time of day to share Saint-Simon's horror of adultery or his even greater horror of adultery breaking through the barriers of society; but this was part of the principles that made Saint-Simon so honest and upright a critic of the King.

Honest and upright: yes, but just? No. Saint-Simon too often saw the acts and attitudes of the King in terms of petty passions and petty grievances. It was not really because William III, the Stadholder, had refused to marry one of Louis's bastards that the long War of the Grand Alliance was fought. Both Louis XIV and William III had more serious matters in mind than avenging themselves for family insults. (It is often forgotten that they were cousins.) In the same way, Saint-Simon was incapable of understanding the good political reasons which Louis XIV had for using as his cabinet ministers people who had received a sound bourgeois training in business method and in hard work. Whatever chance there might have been for giving the French nobles a rôle like that of the English aristocracy, it was over by the time the farce of the Fronde had been liquidated. As Tocqueville was to point out, France no longer had an aristocracy; she had only a *noblesse*. Saint-Simon, with his schemes which he proposed to the Duke of Burgundy, the Dauphin, and then to the Regent Orléans, was looking back to a golden age which perhaps never existed, and looking forward to a reformed French monarchy which perhaps could never have come into existence even if the Duke of Burgundy had survived to succeed his grandfather. Yet ideas not very unlike those of Saint-Simon were entertained by one of the greatest French minds of the eighteenth century, Montesquieu; and it is possible that some changes could have been made, some reforms made of a Court whose debilitating effect Saint-Simon (and La Bruyère) fully understood, which might have prevented the great 'solution of continuity' of the French Revolution. Not all dreamers of possibly Utopian dreams are to be condemned as fools.

Saint-Simon knew there was something wrong, and increasingly wrong, with the government of France even if his remedy was one that could not be applied because the chance of an aristocratic monarchy had been lost, by the folly of the *noblesse*, a century before. But Saint-Simon's honesty of purpose and, probably more important, the commands of his artistic conscience saved him from being a mere denigrator of the great King. We see Louis XIV and his highly critical, fearless, upright subject as rival powers. They were not, of course, seen that way at Versailles, although Saint-Simon's appetite for gossip or, as we now think it, historical information, was noted. It was perhaps unconsciously, certainly with no desire to do so, that Saint-Simon makes the King the hero of his great book. Here we must always bear in mind, as is made clear by Miss Norton, that the great reign was past its apogee by the time Saint-Simon came to the Court, succeeded his father as Duke, and began his life-work. The first war in which Saint-Simon served, the War of the Grand Alliance, although from a military point of view it was full of brilliant French victories on sea and land, marked in fact a French defeat, because it marked the failure of Louis XIV to prevent the English Revolution, the deposition of James II, and the failure of his attempts to restore James II. Louis XIV had to accept as King of England the kinsman whom he regarded as a usurper, and that was in fact the defeat of his policy.

A few years before, the King had adopted the motto *Nec pluribus impar*, a boastful reference to the way he had faced successfully a coalition against him formed by Austria, Spain, the Dutch Republic. By the time that the King had moved into Versailles and the young Duc de Saint-Simon had begun to observe it, the King's emblem, the sun, was overcast. But it is one of the triumphs of Saint-Simon's art and one of the proofs of his probity that the King in his decline is more attractive than the King at the height of his career. Almost against his will, Saint-Simon shows us the King with his industry, his devotion to the interests of France which he identified with his own interests, often disastrously, his loyalty to often incompetent servants, his 'courage never to submit or yield' which enabled him to survive the great victories of Marlborough and Eugene, and to be in 1715 still *le grand monarque*. Saint-Simon may not have wanted to paint so impressive a picture of the King, of whom he makes so many valid and deeply felt criticisms; but his genius forced his hand. Just as Boswell could not suppress Johnson's wit even if exercised at his own expense, so Saint-Simon could not help painting Louis XIV as far superior to his ministers and marshals, to his cardinals and court abbots.

Saint-Simon wanted to write and leave to posterity a minority or dissenting report. This is especially true in his dealing with ecclesiastical questions and is made manifest in his admiration for the Abbot of La Trappe, the thundering Abbot de Rancé who gave the Cistercians their modern rigorous discipline. He had grave doubts about the Revocation of the Edict of Nantes and the imbecile persecution of the Huguenots; he had grave doubts about the campaign against the Jansenists. It may be, as Miss Norton suggests, that his hatred of the Jesuits was so excessive that it led him to side automatically with their enemies. But certainly none of the ecclesiastical views that he expresses or the ecclesiastical company that he kept could have done him any good at Court. His admiration for the two pious dukes, Beauvilliers and Chevreuse, was a genuine admiration for genuine piety. He could remain a friend and candid counsellor of the more than dissolute Duke of Orleans without ever condoning his flagrant vices. Indeed, Saint-Simon's passion for gossip, for historical truth, for his artistic conscience even made him report ill of his friends because that was the truth as he saw it, and it was the truth as he saw it that he pursued. Nothing could be more unjust than to see him as an aristocratic gossip-columnist or somebody on the level of Charles Greville in the nineteenth century.

Yet it must be candidly admitted that some of the charm and a great deal of the fascination of the book comes from its character as a *chronique scandaleuse*. While disapproving, Saint-Simon could not resist chronicling some of the more outrageous behaviour of the members of the Court. He probably preferred, in his heart of hearts, Madame de Montespan, the double adulteress, to the virtuous Madame de Maintenon. He must have taken a cruel satisfaction in his account of some of the scandals in Paris and in Versailles; and we are in his debt for the fidelity with which he reports the black as well as the brilliant side of the last years of the reign of the great King. If he was censorious, he probably felt himself bound to be censorious. Had he not condemned the vices of the great, his conscience might have forbidden him to chronicle them—to our great loss.

There are two ways to read Saint-Simon, both of them extremely profitable. One is as an historical source to be used with great care and with a full consciousness of the fact that Saint-Simon was animated, like Hilaire Belloc, by the spirit of *caritas non conturbat me*. But he could not help telling the deeper historical truths, of the greatness of the King and of the immense distress that the King's wars and the King's policies caused the unfortunate people of France.

At the same time, he was conscious of seeing a great and brilliant spectacle played out before him. Versailles was a theatre in which everyone acted a part, and the greatest of the actors was the King. Versailles was what in the theatrical jargon of the time was called 'a machine', an immensely magnified performance like one of the 'musicals', in the modern sense of the term, put on by Lully and Molière. And if we must never forget that Saint-Simon was a political chronicler of great if narrow intelligence, we must never forget he was a theatrical chronicler of genius. Perhaps we should not spend our time on the *splendeurs et misères* of the last years of Louis XIV, or perhaps we should concentrate on the sufferings of the peasantry, to which Saint-Simon was not at all indifferent.

But we are human and this, in the original sense of the term, is more a *comédie humaine* than all of Balzac—who himself was a great admirer of the great Duke.

D. W. BROGAN

Preface

THIS BOOK is intended for the pleasure of the general reader. Students, scholars, experts in theology, warfare, pedigrees, or court etiquette will go to the great original to satisfy their curiosity. That is why the notes in these volumes are intended for illumination rather than research, and why the sources of quotations are not given in detail. Quotations unacknow-ledged come from other parts of the Memoirs. This shortened version is not the true Saint-Simon. No translation, no abridgement, however loyal and sympathetic, could adequately convey the extraordinary enchantment of the whole immense work. That can easily become an addiction; Stendhal, for instance, wrote that Saint-Simon was one of his two endur-ing passions—eating spinach was the other. Taine said that reading him one lives a month in the space of an hour. But not everyone can read French; not everyone possesses the leisure, or, indeed, the endurance required to tread the whole of the desert road between the bright foun-tains, however rewarding that road may prove to be. It is to them that this book is offered as an appetizer, in the hope that they too will feel at least part of the spellbinding pleasure that reading Saint-Simon can give.

It has been my chief endeavour to preserve the flow of the history that was always uppermost in Saint-Simon's mind. Over and over again after some comical anecdote he says, 'Let us now return to the narrative'; or, 'This digression may have seemed too long [as indeed it all too often has], let us now retrace our steps to the point at which I diverged.' With this principle in mind and ever-conscious of readability, it has been easy to cast overboard the thousands of lines, the hundreds of pages devoted to the origins and nature of the French monarchy, the lengthy details of abortive diplomacy long since forgotten, the ramifications of extinct family-trees, the refinements of correct behaviour. Not that all were cast aside without a pang: for example, the ruling concerning royal and ducal coach-covers. 'Only the Queen may have pompons on her coach-covers; fastened on with nails, and of any colour that she pleases. Duchesses have blue covers. Wives of eldest sons of dukes have red covers. Widows have black velvet.'

But even with such details and longueurs jettisoned, far too much still remains to form two comfortably-proportioned volumes from the three thousand pages in minute handwriting, the approximately nine thousand of the seven-volume Pléiade edition, to which I owe so great a debt of gratitude. Much more had to be discarded. Part of the extraordinary fascination of Saint-Simon's Memoirs is that they are the record of an eye-witness who loved truth, the *Observateur Véridique* of the title-page of the 1788 edition, that may well have been the first published. 'I have preferred the truth above everything,' wrote Saint-Simon, 'I have cherished it even against myself.' He did, I am persuaded, write the truth as he saw it (what historian can do more?), but passion often blinded him, as in his loathing for Jesuits and royal bastards. I have therefore thought it not unreasonable to discard, sometimes very sadly, the events that happened before his time, which he did not know except by hearsay or his reading, the people who were dead or vanished before he arrived at the Court. Thus the Queen and the Dauphine, Mme de Montespan, Louvois, Colbert, Mansart, and Lauzun's incredible follies before he returned chastened by exile, have all been abandoned. So also have the repetitions. Some of the famous portraits are repeated two or three times; the final versions magnified and extended as Saint-Simon piled noun upon noun and added a sixth and seventh adjective on second thoughts. Some of the anecdotes he tells again and again: for example, I have found the story of Cardinal de Polignac and the dry rain at Marly appearing no less than eight times. Lastly, many of the most famous episodes have already been published in *Saint-Simon at Versailles* and may be found there. Some of these I have given here again in an extended version; as for the rest, the material of what Lytton Strachey called 'the enormous panorama, magnificent, palpitating, alive' is so extraordinarily rich that I have found little difficulty in replacing them with others equally good, and portraits just as vivid.

What then have I clung to?—the history as it unfolds, the figures that loom so large in Saint-Simon's world, the portraits that bring them alive, the comical stories that light up the past in a flash and transport it into our own century, the friends and enemies about whom he felt so passionately. Background events, such as the Spanish Court, Marlborough's wars, the quarrels of the Church, the politics, I have also retained, but only in so far as they seemed of general interest and set the stage for the great dramatic episodes. Above all, I have left in all that I could find to illuminate the character of Saint-Simon himself. What was he like as a man? Malice, always provided that it is not directed against oneself, is better fun than morals, invective than praise, quarrels than loyalty, which is why in the various selections we see only the *boudrillon*, the 'bittock', the wasplike minikin buzzing with hatred and abuse, always angry, blaming everyone, wholly engrossed in his snobbish campaign for the greater glory of his fellow ducal peers. Yet it is this same Saint-Simon of whom the King said: 'He is my nephew's intimate friend, and I wish he had had no others; for he is most upright and gives him nothing but good counsel;' this was the man whom the young Dauphin chose as his confidential assistant in forming the policies of his new reign. This was he who almost alone had the courage to stand by his friends Orléans and

Chamillar t, seeking their society when public disgrace made it positively dangerous to be seen with them. Finally, this was the great, though possibly unconscious artist who, as Montherlant describes, sustained the colossal effort 'over more than thirty years, of writing three thousand pages, with the full intention that they should be read, well knowing their extraordinary merit, yet knowing also that they would not appear in his lifetime;' and thus renouncing all hope of the personal glory for which he had longed, produced in solitude an enduring masterpiece.

As for the translation. When one sets out to translate a famous and long dead writer one accepts not one but two responsibilities, loyalty to one's author's words and style, and also to his present reputation, for what honour would it do him to reproduce him word for word, sentence by sentence, if present day readers who buy the book for pleasure found him intolerably heavy and verbose? Saint-Simon's style, based on the classical, changes from sentences three words long, stabbing the paper, to sentences that cover entire pages in the descriptions and digressions that make that desert road of which Macaulay spoke. He loved words; he gathered them from every kind of source, and when he could find none vibrant enough for his purpose he invented one. 'Patriot' and 'publicity' are supposedly his creation, a jest is a 'mouth-crumpler', 'club-bashing' means ill-treatment. He grew drunk with them, they gushed from him like water from a tap when passion or laughter seized him, or he became over-excited in revision. He used slang, he ignored grammar, he did not care for style, he is inimitable.[1] A literal translation would be unbearable, if only because slang changes so quickly that it would soon become more dated than the original. I have therefore tried above all to convey his spirit, have allowed myself to feel inspired, have tried to reproduce his racy collo-quial idiom in a style that is informal, but with as good English as I am cap-able of writing. I have never consciously changed his intentions nor put alien words into his mouth; but the demands of readability have forced me to take short cuts, to choose alternative phrases where he repeated himself, and to straighten out the parts where as he himself says at the end of the Memoirs, 'the negligences, the repetitions of the same word at close intervals, the too many synonyms, the sense obscured by long sentences, the repetitions and grammatical errors; I have felt these faults. I could not help them, for I was always carried away by the interest of the matter and was very little attentive to the manner of rendering it.' It is my great hope that readers also will be 'carried away', and that in their enjoyment they will forgive the translator her lapses and shortcomings in a task that must inevitably be a second-best, no matter how much it may have been a labour of love.

E. L. NORTON

[1] Not that Sainte-Beuve, Stendhal, Proust, Macaulay, Lytton Strachey, Winston Churchill, and Henry Adams did not all copy him.

ACKNOWLEDGEMENTS

My heartfelt thanks are due above all to Professor Sir Denis Brogan, who inspired and guided me in this complicated task and whose faith has been indestructible. Many friends have given me their untiring interest and encouragement, notably Miss Elizabeth Johnson, who has nobly sustained the company of Saint-Simon day-in, day-out, for nearly a decade. Miss Betty Askwith and Lady Shaw have special claims on my gratitude for advising me on parts of the text; Mr Derek Priestley's wise advice has been invaluable throughout. I gladly acknowledge the skill and enthusiasm of Mrs Joy Law, and of Mme Chantal Coural late of the Conservation at Versailles, in helping me to make a balanced choice of illustrations, of Mrs Ann Crawford-Jones for her work on the typescript, Miss Irene Clephane for the index, Mr H. J. Blackman for the maps. Finally, my grateful thanks to Mr Christopher Sinclair-Stevenson for the tact and patience with which he steered me safely into harbour.

NOTE ON COINAGE

1 silver livre =   1 franc (which before 1914 = 10d.)
1 écu   =   3 livres
1 gold Louis = 24 livres

BOOKS CONSULTED

Mémoires de Saint-Simon. Ed. A. de Boislisle. Paris, Hachette, 1879–1928, 43 vols.

Saint-Simon par lui-même. François-Régis Bastide. Paris, Editions du Seuil, 1953.

Saint-Simon Mémoires. Ed. Gonzague Truc. Paris, Bibliothèque de la Pléiade, Gallimard, 1953.

Saint-Simon et sa Comédie Humaine. La Varende. Paris, Hachette, 1955.

Sur Saint-Simon. Emmanuel d'Astier. Paris, Gallimard, 1962.

Introduction to Seventeenth-Century France. John Lough. London, 1954.

The Letters of Madame. Gertrude Scott Stevenson (editor). London, 1924.

Marlborough, his Life and Times. Rt Hon. Sir Winston Churchill. London, 1947.

THE ROYAL FAMILY IN 1691

Louis XIV
aged 53

His Son

Louis de France, called *Monseigneur*, *Le Grand Dauphin*, a widower, 30

His Grandsons
Children of the above

Louis de France, Duc de Bourgogne, 9
Philippe de France, Duc d'Anjou, 8
Charles de France, Duc de Berry, 6

His Brother

Philippe, Duc d'Orléans, called *Monsieur*, 51 = Elizabeth Charlotte, Princess of the Palatinate, called *Madame*, 39

His Nephew

Philippe d'Orléans, Duc de Chartres, 17, later Duc d'Orléans, later still Regent of France = Mlle de Blois

His Bastards	His Cousins the Princes of the Blood
By Mme de La Vallière	
The Dowager Princesse de Conti, 25 =	The late Prince de Conti, d. 1685
m. 1680	François Louis de Bourbon, Prince de Conti, 27, his younger brother (m. Marie de Bourbon, daughter of *Monsieur le Prince*)
	Henri-Jules de Bourbon-Condé, 48, called *Monsieur le Prince*
	Anne de Bavière, 43, his wife, called *Madame la Princesse*
By Mme de Montespan	
The Duc du Maine, 21	= Mlle de Charolais, 15, their daughter
Mlle de Nantes, 18, called *Madame la Duchesse*	= Louis III de Bourbon-Condé, 23, their son, called *Monsieur le Duc*
Mlle de Blois, 14	= The Duc de Chartres (son of *Monsieur*)
The Comte de Toulouse, 13 (m. Marie de Noailles)	

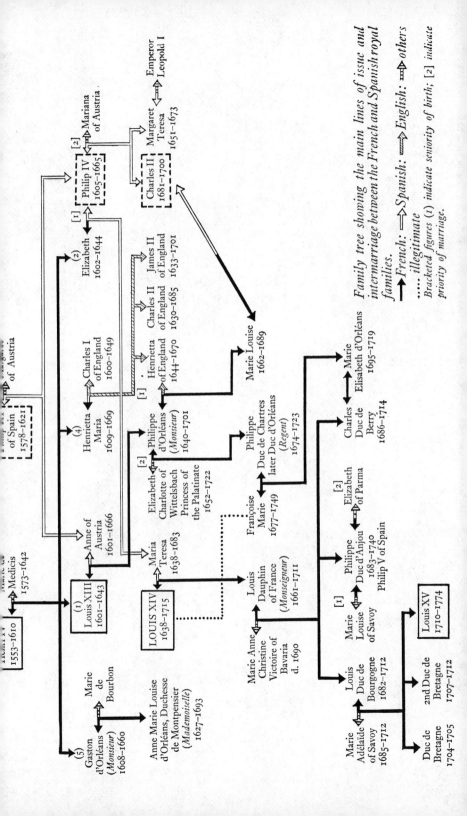

Family tree showing the main lines of issue and intermarriage between the French and Spanish royal families.

French: $\longrightarrow$ Spanish: $\Longrightarrow$ English: $\longrightarrow$ others $\Longrightarrow$

...... illegitimate

Bracketed figures (1) indicate seniority of birth; [2] indicate priority of marriage.

HISTORICAL MEMOIRS
OF THE
DUC DE SAINT-SIMON

PART I

MAKING A LIFE

CHAPTER I

1691–1692

Where and how the Memoirs were begun – My early friendship with M. le Duc de Chartres – My first campaign – The grey musketeers – The King in person lays siege to Namur – Surrender of Namur – Gunpowder concealed by the Jesuits – Naval battle off Cape La Hogue – Danger of playing with fire-arms – Death of Coëtquen

I WAS born on the night of the 15–16 January, 1675, the son of Claude Duc de Saint-Simon, Peer of France, and of his second wife Charlotte de L'Aubespine, the only child of their marriage. By his first wife Diane de Budos my father had no sons but an only daughter, whom he married to the Duc de Brissac, the Duchesse de Villeroy's only brother. She died without issue in 1684 having long lived separate from an unworthy husband, and by her will she made me her sole heir.

I bore the title Vidame de Chartres and much care and thought were lavished on my education, for my mother, a most virtuous lady endowed with remarkable intelligence and understanding, laboured continually to form me in body and mind. She feared lest I should go the way of many young men who imagine their fortunes already made when they too soon become their own masters. My father, born in 1606, would not live to spare me that misfortune, and she therefore constantly urged on me the vital need to make the most of myself, since I must enter the world alone and unprotected, the son of Louis XIII's favourite, whose friends were dead or in no position to aid me. She herself, having been brought up in the house of her kinswoman the old Duchesse d'Angoulême (maternal grandmother of the Duc de Guise) and having married an old man, knew no young persons of her own age and, what is more, had no close relatives, uncles, aunts, or cousins. I should thus be thrown entirely upon my own resources, which made it doubly necessary that I should learn to use them well, since I could expect no one else to support or advance me.

My mother at the same time tried to hearten and inspire me to overcome these major handicaps, and she did succeed in giving me a strong desire to do so. My dislike for learning and the sciences did not assist her, but I had a natural love for reading and history that made me wish to imitate the great men whom I thus encountered, and made up for my lack of enthusiasm towards the classics. I have often thought that had they not insisted on my wasting so much time with the latter, but encouraged me to make the former my serious study, I might indeed have become some-thing. This reading of history, especially private memoirs of my own period and that immediately after the reign of François I, gave me the idea of writing down my own observations, in the hope that by learning what I could of current affairs I might eventually fit myself for some high office. I foresaw the dangers, but a firm resolve to keep my undertaking secret seemed to meet all possible objections. It was in June 1694[1] that I began my memoirs, being at that time colonel of a cavalry regiment in my own name, encamped at Guinsheim in Vieux-Rhin, forming part of the army commanded by the Maréchal-Duc de Lorges.

Meanwhile, in 1691, I had been studying philosophy and equitation at the Académie des Sieurs de Mesmont et Rochefort, but had become mighty tired of masters and book-learning. I was very eager to enter the army, for the King had commanded in person at the siege of Mons earlier in that year, and most young men of my age were serving their first campaign. What moved me most, however, was the fact that M. le Duc de Chartres[2] was there also. He was my elder by eight months, we had been brought up together, and, if youth will excuse the expression between men so unequal in rank, we were friends. Such considerations had made me resolve to escape from the schoolroom, but I shall not describe all the various ruses which I employed to get my wish. I first spoke to my mother, but soon perceived that she only played for time. I then attacked my father, persuading him that as the King had laid one great siege in the present year he would not be very active in the following. I deceived my mother, who discovered my design on the eve of its execution only to find that my father was primed to resist her.

The King was strict in requiring all who entered his service, except princes of the blood and his bastards, to spend a year in one or other of his two companies of musketeers. Then, before allowing them to purchase a regiment, he obliged them to learn obedience for a certain time as cap-tains in the cavalry, or junior officers in his own regiment of artillery. My father therefore took me with him when he went to Versailles. He made his bow and presented me, as wishing to become a musketeer on the day of St. Simon and St. Jude, at half-past noon, as the King left the council. His Majesty did him the honour to embrace him three times, but when it came to me he thought me puny and delicate in appearance and said that I was still very young.[3] My father replied that I should serve him all the

---

[1] In 1699 Saint-Simon submitted his notebooks to the examination of the Abbé de Rancé, reformer of La Trappe, who was his spiritual director. It was only after receiving his approval, subject to secrecy, that the memoirs became Saint-Simon's life-work.

[2] Philippe d'Orléans (1674-1723). The King's nephew, son of 'Monsieur' (Philippe d'Or-léans). Succeeded to that dukedom 1701, Regent of France 1715.

[3] He was sixteen and tiny, people called him *le boudrillon* (the bittock). He wore the highest heels at the Court.

longer on that account. Thereupon the King inquired which of the two companies my father wished me to join, and he chose the first because his friend Maupertuis was captain and he knew that I should be well-treated. He knew also that the King carefully examined the two captains, more especially Maupertuis, regarding the young gentlemen in their companies, and that their reports influenced his first impressions, on which so much depended. As it turned out my father made no mistake, for I believe that I owe to Maupertuis the good opinion which the King at first held of me.

This Maupertuis always claimed to be one of the Maupertuis of Melun, and honestly believed himself to be so connected, for he was the very pattern of truth and honour, and had for that reason won the King's trust. In actual fact he was far short of being a Melun and was not recognized by any of that noble family. He had risen through the ranks from sergeant of the musketeers and became the general in command of them. His fairness, kindness and courage won their respect; his fussing over trifles, and his readiness to find fault, made him less popular. That, however, was the side of him most pleasing to the King, who often employed him on missions of confidence. He was, all said and done, very much the gentleman, courteous, modest, and well-mannered.

Three months after my joining the grey musketeers,[1] that is to say in March of the following year, the King went to Compiègne to review his *Maison*[2] and part of the life guards, and on one occasion I mounted guard in the King's apartments. This short military excursion gave me the excuse to mention another and more serious one to my parents. I was delighted by the prospect, but my father who had expected no such thing deeply regretted having believed me, and told me so plainly. My mother, although she had been a little sulky and vexed with my father for allowing me to enlist against her wishes, now persuaded him to be reasonable. He gave me a train of thirty-five mules and horses, and the wherewithal to eat well at my quarters every morning and evening. On the 10 May, 1692, the King set out with the ladies. I made the journey on horseback with the rest of my troop and served with the musketeers for all of the two months which that excursion lasted. I had two servants with me, one of them an old retainer who had been my superintendent, the other my mother's personal groom. The King's army was encamped at Givry with the army of

---

[1] Grey from the colour of their horses.

[2] *The Maison du Roi*, the famous regiments of the household troops, comprised, quartered in the Louvre, the four companies of the bodyguard, the *gardes de la manche* (whose duty was to follow the King's sons and grandsons closely enough to catch them by the sleeve when they were toddlers), the Hundred Swiss, the fifty *gardes de la porte* (who guarded the King's door), the *gentilshommes à bec de corbin* (who carried gilded battle-axes shaped like ravens' beaks), and the *gardes de la prévôté de l'hôtel* (the establishment of the provost-marshal). Quartered outside the Louvre were the lifeguards, the light horse, the musketeers, the mounted grenadiers, and the French and Swiss guards. A total of ten thousand men, including the sixteen companies of lifeguards.

the Maréchal de Luxembourg[1] almost adjoining. The ladies remained at Mons, two leagues[2] distant. The King invited them to visit the camp, gave them a banquet, and afterwards showed them what may well have been the most splendid review of any time, with the armies deployed in two lines, M. de Luxembourg's right touching the King's left, and the whole covering a distance of three leagues.

[*The accession of William Prince of Orange to the English throne in 1689 had destroyed Louis XIV's carefully built up alliance with England, which had been a corner-stone of his foreign policy. In 1692 King Louis was at war with the Holy Roman Empire, the Dutch Republic, Spain, England, and Sweden. Despite that formidable alliance of her enemies France won all the battles on her northern frontier until the death of the Maréchal de Luxembourg, in 1695. He was then replaced as commander by the Maréchal de Villeroy, irresistible to women but not to the enemy. The general opposing him in command of the Spanish army in the Low Countries was also a Frenchman, the Prince de Vaudémont, an illegitimate son of the House of Lorraine. The war ended in 1697 with the Peace of Ryswick, by which Louis XIV was forced to recognize the 'heretic' William as the King of England.*]

After ten days at Givry the two armies separated and marched away, and two days later the siege of Namur was proclaimed, the King having covered that journey in a five-day march. Monseigneur, Monsieur, Monsieur le Prince, and the Maréchal d'Humières, in order of rank, led the army under the King's command. The Maréchal de Luxembourg, in sole command of his army, covered the siege and took observations. Meantime the ladies removed to Dinant. On the third day of the King's march Monsieur le Prince was sent on ahead to invest Namur town, for Vauban,[3] the famous organizer of the King's sieges, had insisted on there being separate attacks for the town and the fortress. Nothing very eventful happened during the ten days of the siege; on the eleventh day of open trenches they sounded for a parley and a surrender was arranged on the defenders' terms. During all this time the King was living under canvas in very hot weather, for it had not rained since we left Paris. The army moved camp in order to besiege the fortress, and whilst that was taking

---

[1] Had been made Marshal of France in 1675. He was called 'Le Tapissier de Notre-Dame' because of all the enemy flags he had hung there. Saint-Simon was critical of him for reckoning the results of his campaign by the number of battles won.

[2] A league (*lieue*) = two kilometres.

[3] Sébastien Le Prestre, Seigneur de Vauban (1633–1707), designer of the network of fortresses covering the frontiers of France and Holland. All were constructed in the shape of a star. The procedure of attack was always the same, according to his principles. The fortress was invested. Trenches were dug at one side out of cannon-range. Zig-zag approaches were next made to within striking distance, so as to have a continuous trench line to the fortress itself. The defenders made sorties and bombarded with their cannon. The final assault was a storming of the ramparts, but this rarely occurred because a rigorous etiquette governed both sides and no governor was expected to defend a fortress over-long, nor admired for doing so. He resisted to a certain point, then surrendered, and marched out with all the honours of war, 'bag and baggage, drums beating, matches lit, bullet in the cheek, etc.' The city then passed peacefully into the hands of the besiegers and the inhabitants were usually well-treated.

place the King's own regiment of infantry found its new position held by a small detachment of the enemy digging trenches. There was a brisk engagement in which the royal troops greatly distinguished themselves, with very few losses, and the enemy were soon routed. The King was delighted by this, for he was particularly devoted to that regiment which he liked to think of as being his personal property.

The King's tents and those of his courtiers were pitched in a pleasant meadow five hundred paces from the monastery of Marlagne. By this time the weather had changed to abundant and continuous rain, such as no one in the army could remember and had thus greatly increased the reputation of St. Médard, whose feast-day is 8 June. It had poured on that day and, according to the saying, whatever the weather is then it will continue so for the next forty days, as it happened in that year. The soldiers were driven nearly to desperation by the floods, so that they cursed the saint heartily, breaking and burning his images wherever they could lay hands on them. The rain was indeed a perfect plague, and the King's tents could only be reached by laying down paths of brushwood which had daily to be renewed. The other tents were not more easily accessible and the trenches were soon full of muddy water. It sometimes took as much as three days to move a cannon from one battery to another. The waggons were unusable, and shells, cannon-balls, etc., had to be transported on mules and horses, which became the sole support of every service to the army and the Court. Without them nothing would have been possible. The flooding of the roads also prevented the army of M. de Luxembourg from using their waggons. They were near starvation for lack of fodder and would have died had not the King issued orders that detachments of his *maison* should ride each day carrying sacks of grain to a certain village where M. de Luxembourg's officers would receive and count them.

Although the *maison* had had little rest on account of carrying brushwood, mounting the various guards, and their other daily duties, they were given this additional fatigue because the cavalry also had been continuously on duty and were down to leaves for forage. That consideration aroused no sympathy in the hearts of the pampered *maison*, who were accustomed to special privileges. They complained. The King was obdurate. The task remained theirs. On the very first day, however, the lifeguards and light cavalry were openly murmuring when they reached the depot in the early morning, and they so worked upon one another that the men actually threw the sacks down and refused to pick them up again. Cresnay, my brigadier, had most courteously asked me whether I was willing to take a sack, saying that otherwise he would find me some different duty; but I had consented, hoping thus to please the King, especially in view of all the grumbling. It so happened that I arrived on the scene with my troop of musketeers at the precise moment when the red-coats were about to mutiny, and I took up my sack before them all. Thereupon Marin, a cavalry-brigadier, who was supervising the loading by the King's orders and raging at the mutineers, called out my name, exclaiming that if I did not think myself too good for such work, life-guardsmen and the light horse need not be ashamed to copy me. That argument and his stern eye had their effect; there was a rush to pick up the sacks, and never afterwards the smallest objection. Marin watched us go and then went to tell the King what had happened and the influence of my good example. That kind office resulted in the King saying some gracious things to me, and throughout the remainder of the siege he never saw me without saying something civil. I was all the more obliged to Marin because I had no acquaintance with him socially.

On Tuesday 1 July, after twenty-seven days of open trenches, the governor of the citadel sounded for a parley, which came none too soon for the besiegers, whose strength and provisions were nearly exhausted on account of the continual rain that had turned everything to a quagmire. Even the King's chargers were down to leaves for forage; indeed, none of that great array of men, horses, and waggons ever fully recovered. There would certainly have been no conclusion but for the King's presence, for his keenness kept the siege alive, and he inspired men to do the impossible without giving them orders, so eager were they to please him and earn distinction. The physical and mental hardships which he endured brought on the worst attack of gout he had hitherto experienced; but that did not prevent him from supervising everything from his bed and holding his councils as though he were at Versailles. That citadel had the reputation of being the strongest in the Netherlands and the inhabitants could not restrain their tears at the change of masters. Even the monks of Marlagne were profoundly distressed and made no effort to conceal their feelings. The King pitied them for the loss of their wheat which had been stored in Namur, and replaced it by double the amount, besides giving them generous alms. What is more, he would not allow cannon to be taken across their park, except when absolutely necessary, all the other roads being impassable. Yet despite all his goodness to them they would not so much as look at a Frenchman once the siege was over, and one monk refused a bottle of ale to an usher of the King's antechamber, even although the latter explained who he was and offered a bottle of champagne in exchange.

After the surrender an event occurred that created a fearful scandal and might have ended in tragedy with any other ruler than the King. A careful search for arms had been made in the town before his entry, although by the terms of the truce all mines, powder-magazines, and other explosives were bound to be declared. In a final examination after the fall of the citadel the Jesuits were visited, who opened bolted doors, expressing pained surprise at having their word doubted. The searchers entered none the less, and looking where least expected found the cellars to be full of gun-powder, although for what purpose it was never divulged. The explosives were confiscated, but since they were Jesuits nothing further was done.[1]

During that siege the King suffered a cruel misfortune. He had a fleet at sea commanded by the famous Admiral Tourville, and the English had another, combined with the Dutch fleet and almost twice as strong. Both fleets were in the Channel and the King of England[2] was on the coast of Normandy, waiting to cross over into England immediately after victory at Namur. King James placed such absolute reliance on the intelligence he received concerning the English sea-captains that he persuaded the King to join in battle, urging that there was no danger since more than half the English ships were preparing to desert. Tourville, renowned for his courage and ability, sent two couriers one after the other, warning the King not to rely on King James's information (for he was often deceived), stressing the vast superiority of the enemy, the lack of ports or other shelter should we be defeated, and the risk of having a large part of his fleet burned and the remainder put out of action. His arguments were useless. Weak or strong, he was commanded to attack. He obeyed and did marvels, and his seconds-in-command and junior officers did as much, but not one English vessel faltered or ran. Notwithstanding the over-whelming odds against him he saved more vessels than could have been expected, but nearly all were afterwards sunk or burned in the roadsteads of La Hogue.[3] King James, who watched the fights from the cliffs of Nor-mandy, was accused of cheering for his own people, although not one of them had kept the promise that prompted him to seek a battle.

Pontchartrain,[4] at that time secretary for the navy and controller-general of finances, was detained in Paris by the latter office and therefore sent his reports to the King through the medium of Châteauneuf, his cousin and likewise a secretary of State. He despatched a special courier with news of this disaster, which was at first kept closely secret, at the very moment when another messenger happened to be returning to Barbe-zieux[5] the war minister. This man soon overtook Pontchartrain's courier

---

[1] Dangeau wrote in his journal: 'They have found twelve hundred and fifty live bombs in the Jesuit monastery at Namur which the worthy fathers were hiding. The King, who was vexed by their behaviour, has dismissed the rector and sent him back to Dole.'

[2] James II (1635-1701) who since his abdication in 1688 had been living at Saint-Germain with his second wife Mary of Modena. Despite his recognition of William III and Mary II, Louis XIV continued to treat James as the rightful king of England. There were personal ties: both were Catholics and Monsieur's first wife had been a sister of James. They were also first cousins.

[3] The Battle of Cape La Hogue, 29 May, 1692. The burning of the French ships in the roadsteads took place on 2 June.

[4] The Comte de Pontchartrain—Louis II Phélypeaux (1643-1727). Became Chancellor of France 1699. He and his wife were Saint-Simon's firm friends.

[5] Louis François Le Tellier, Marquis de Barbezieux (1668-1701). The son of Louvois, Louis XIV's famous minister for war, he had been appointed to fill the same office early in 1691 at the age of 23.

3

who was less well mounted. They fell into conversation, and the soldier tried his utmost to extract naval information. To be brief, he spent several hours vainly pumping Pontchartrain's man. At last, weary of being questioned and never doubting but that he would be out-galloped, the latter agreed to tell all, on condition that the other promised to be silent and not ride ahead, for, said he, he wished to be first with news of a victory. Then, without more ado he described how Tourville had won a great naval battle with I know not how many enemy ships destroyed or captured. The soldier gleefully redoubled his questioning, eager to know every detail, and at the last stage before Namur set spurs to his horse and arrived there first. This was made all the easier for him because Pontchartrain's courier was in no hurry and quite prepared to let him enjoy his triumph.

On arrival the army man told his story to Barbezieux, who at once repeated it to the King. What rejoicings! But why was the news sent by such indirect methods? Châteauneuf was summoned but said that he knew nothing. Four or five hours later the naval courier arrived and invited him quietly to open his dispatch, in which he learned the truth. The difficulty then was how to tell the King, who immediately sent for Barbezieux to reprimand him soundly. Such a reverse was a great embarrassment and the Court were completely bewildered. None the less, the King was soon able to compose himself, which was how I first observed that Courts are not for long downcast nor over-troubled by defeats.

Two days after the surrender the King went to Dinant and returned with the ladies to Versailles. I was expecting that Monseigneur would have seen the end of the campaign and had hoped to be in the detachment of musketeers left to guard him. It was therefore not without regret that I found myself on the road to Paris with the rest of my comrades. On one night of the journey the Court slept at Marienbourg with the musketeers under canvas surrounding them. It so happened that I had formed a friendship with the Comte de Coëtquen, serving in my troop. He was very pleasant, well-informed, high-spirited, and good-natured, which made him excellent company; but at the same time he suffered from melancholy, was more than usually idle, very rich through his mother, and quite fatherless. That night at Marienbourg it was his turn to give some of us supper. I went early to his tent, and finding him still lying on his bed I laughingly tipped him out of it and lay down there myself in the presence of some musketeers and a few officers. Coëtquen, in jest, seized his musket believing it to be unloaded and aimed it at me. To everyone's horror it went off. Luckily for me I was stretched out flat, for three bullets passed just three fingers' width above my head and, since the gun was pointed upwards, over the heads of our two governors who were strolling about outside. We had all the trouble in the world to set Coëtquen up again; he was not his old self for several days. I tell this tale as a lesson never to play with firearms.

To conclude with Coëtquen. The poor fellow did not long survive that incident. He left us shortly afterwards to join the King's regiment and before his departure described how his fortune had been told by a wise woman named du Perchoir, who plied that trade secretly in Paris, and had prophesied his imminent death by drowning. I scolded him for foolish and dangerous curiosity, because I have always been convinced that such persons know nothing and that this one must have been impressed by his strangely melancholy countenance, for he did look most sinister. A few days after leaving us he found a man in the same way of business at Amiens, who made a similar pronouncement. Proceeding with the King's regiment to join the rest of the army he stopped to water his horse in the River Scheldt and was drowned in full view of his comrades who were powerless to save him. It grieved me deeply, and for his family the loss was irreparable. He left two sisters, one of whom married the eldest son of M. de Montchevreuil; the other was a nun at the Calvaire.[1]

These tales of the musketeers have led me too far ahead. Before continuing the narrative I must retrace my steps so as to describe two royal marriages that were celebrated earlier in that year; the first, a most momentous occasion, was on 18 February; the second occurred a month later.

---

[1] The *Filles du Calvaire*. An order of Benedictine nuns founded at Poitiers (1616) by Antoinette d'Orléans and the Père Joseph, the *Eminence Grise* of Cardinal Richelieu.

CHAPTER II

1692

Marriage of the Duc de Chartres – First beginnings of the Abbé Dubois, later Cardinal and First Minister – Marriage of the Duc du Maine

THE KING, intent upon securing the state of his bastards,[1] whom he daily advanced in rank and honours, had already married two of them to Princes of the Blood. One, his sole remaining child by Mme de la Vallière, was the Princesse de Conti, now a childless widow; the second, his eldest daughter by Mme de Montespan, was the wife of Monsieur le Duc. For years past Mme de Maintenon[2] even more than the King had thought of nothing but their further advancement and both now wished to marry his youngest daughter to M. le Duc de Chartres. The latter was the King's sole and rightful nephew, far above Princes of the Blood by virtue of his rank and the court held by Monsieur his father. The marriage of the two aforesaid princes had provoked a public scandal. Of that the King was well aware, and he could easily imagine the effect of one even more glaringly improper. None the less he had turned it over in his mind for the past four years and had already made the first moves, which had been all the more difficult because Monsieur attached infinite importance to all that appertained to his rank, and Madame was of a nation that abhorred bastardy and misalliances and of a character that was little inclined to yield to persuasion.[3]

To overcome these many obstacles the King desired his old crony Monsieur le Grand[4] to enlist the services of his brother the Chevalier de Lorraine, who ruled Monsieur in everything. He had been compellingly handsome; Monsieur's taste was not for women; he made no attempt to disguise it; he had taken the Chevalier de Lorraine for his master and so

[1] Louis XIV had altogether thirteen illegitimate children. In 1692 there remained only three daughters and two sons. The dowager Princesse de Conti (by Mme de la Vallière), the Duc du Maine, Madame la Duchesse, the Comte de Toulouse and Mlle de Blois (by Mme de Montespan).

[2] Françoise d'Aubigné, Marquise de Maintenon (1635–1719). Married first the crippled poet Paul Scarron, then secretly Louis XIV (1684). She had been governess to his children by Mme de Montespan and loved them, Saint-Simon thought, most immoderately, especially so the Duc du Maine.

[3] She was one of the very few who dared to stand up to Louis XIV. Her letters to her aunt, the Electress of Hanover (mother of George I), give a devastating description of life at Versailles.

[4] Special name for the Grand Ecuyer de France, then Louis de Lorraine, Comte d'Armagnac. Equivalent of the Master of the Horse in the English royal household.

he remained throughout the rest of his life. The two brothers asked nothing better than to oblige the King in this delicate matter and, like sensible men, to reap some benefit for themselves. Their first attack was made in the summer of 1688. No more than a dozen Chevaliers of the Order[1] remained; everyone could see that promotions could not be delayed much longer. They therefore claimed that honour and with it precedence over the dukes. The King, who for that very reason had never yet given the Order to any Lorraine, had some qualms about doing so now; but the brothers insisted; they prevailed, and the Chevalier de Lorraine, having received his pay in advance, answered for Monsieur's consent to the marriage, and for finding the way to overrule Madame and M. le Duc de Chartres.

That young prince had been placed in the care of Saint-Laurent when he left the nursery. Saint-Laurent was a man of no account, an assistant to the head of the protocol in Monsieur's establishment, of humble appearance, but all in all the best man of his time to bring up a prince and form a great king. His low birth prevented their giving him a titular appointment, his exceptional merit made them leave him in sole charge; and, when custom demanded that the prince should have a governor, he was so in name only and Saint-Laurent continued in the same trust and with the same authority.

He was a friend of the Curé of Saint-Eustache, who himself was a man of much worth. That Curé had a valet named Dubois[2] who was previously valet to one of the legal advisers of Le Tellier, Archbishop of Rheims, who, seeing that he was clever, made him study, so that this Dubois became infinitely well versed in the humanities and even in history. But he still remained a valet, nothing more, and after the death of his first master entered the service of the Curé of Saint-Eustache. The latter, being pleased with him but unable himself to advance him, gave him to Saint-Laurent, hoping that he might better himself there. He satisfied Saint-Laurent who began to employ him in writing out the lessons of M. le Duc de Chartres. After that, wishing to make better use of him, he made him wear the *petit collet*[3] in order to clean him up somewhat, and thus brought him into the schoolroom to help in preparing the lessons, writing the essays, generally assisting and looking up words in the dictionary. I saw him often in those early days when I went to play with M. de Chartres. Later, when Saint-Laurent grew infirm, Dubois gave the lessons himself and did so extremely well; yet managed to be agreeable to the young prince.

Saint-Laurent, however, died very suddenly; Dubois continued

---

[1] The 'Order' always refers to the Order of the Saint-Esprit.
[2] Guillaume Dubois (1656–1723) made Cardinal and later First Minister of France when his former pupil became Regent. Detested by Saint-Simon.
[3] A 'dog-collar': the plain collar worn by candidates for ordination.

temporarily to give the lessons, and being now almost an abbé he succeeded in paying his court to the Chevalier de Lorraine and his friend the Marquis d'Effiat, Monsieur's first equerry, who also possessed great influence. To make Dubois tutor could scarcely be effected at one blow, but his protectors managed to obstruct other nominations, then used the prince's progress as an argument for preserving the *status quo*, and finally blasted.[1] him into office. Never have I seen a man more delighted, nor with better reason. Gratitude, and even more so the wish to keep his job, strengthened his attachment to his patrons, and it was therefore to him that the Chevalier applied in order to gain M. de Chartres's consent to his marriage.

Dubois gained the prince's confidence. It was not hard for him to persuade one so young and inexperienced to fear the anger of the King and Monsieur and to regard any alternative as heaven itself. Yet, despite all his efforts he could do no more than avoid a flat refusal. That, however, was enough. Dubois did not speak to M. de Chartres until the time was ripe; Monsieur was already won over, and the King when he received the word made haste to settle the matter. A day or two earlier Madame had got wind of it. With all her authority (which was not inconsiderable) she spoke to her son of the shame of such an alliance and extracted a promise that he would never consent. Thus M. de Chartres, weak with his tutor, weak with his mother, hating the one course and dreading the other, found himself in utter discomfiture.

Very early one afternoon as I was going along the upper corridor I saw M. de Chartres come out of the back door of his apartment looking monstrously harassed and unhappy, followed by a single officer of Monsieur's guard. As I was in his path I asked him where he was going so early and so fast; to which he replied shortly that the King had sent for him. I judged it unwise to accompany him, and so turning to my governor I simply said that I guessed it concerned his marriage and that we should soon have news. Certain rumours had reached me already and, since I was sure that there would be a scene, my curiosity made me vastly alert and attentive.

M. de Chartres found the King alone in his study with Monsieur, whom the prince had least expected to see there. The King greeted him affectionately, saying that he wished to provide him with an establishment, that the encircling war had put many eligible princesses out of reach, that no princess of the blood was of a suitable age, and that he could show his love no better than by offering him his own daughter, both of whose sisters were already married to princes of the blood. Such an alliance would make him more than a nephew, a son-in-law; but, none the less, eager though he might be for the match, he had no desire to force him but would leave him free to choose for himself. That statement, delivered with the awful majesty that came so naturally to the King, and addressed

---

[1] *Bombarder:* slang used in this sense by the Grande Mademoiselle in her memoirs.

to a terror-stricken princeling, totally unprepared for it, upset M. de
Chartres completely. He tried to dodge the question by laying the responsibility on Monsieur and Madame, and stammered out that the King was
master, but that his own inclinations depended on his parents' wishes.
'Well said!' exclaimed the King. 'But, if you consent, your father and
mother will not object.' Then, turning to Monsieur: 'Brother, is that not
so?' Monsieur agreed, as had previously been arranged between them,
and the King at once sent for Madame, saying that now only she remained
to be consulted.[1] Meanwhile he began a conversation with Monsieur,
both of them apparently unaware of M. de Chartres's embarrassment and
dejection.

Madame arrived. The King said at once that he did not suppose she
would object to an alliance which Monsieur desired and to which M. de
Chartres had consented, namely his marriage with Mlle de Blois. As for
himself, he confessed to being most anxious for it, and he shortly repeated the arguments used upon M. de Chartres, all this with a commanding air, yet as if never doubting that she would be otherwise than
enchanted, though he well knew to the contrary. Madame, who had
reckoned that her son would refuse on account of his promise (which he
had truly endeavoured to keep), was cornered and speechless. Shooting
two furious glances in the direction of Monsieur and M. de Chartres, she
replied that, since they were determined, there was no use in her saying
more and, dropping the briefest of curtseys, she returned to her rooms.
Her son at once followed her, but giving him no time to explain she drove
him away with a torrent of tears and abuse.

Shortly afterwards Monsieur went to her, and except that she did not
actually show him the door she spared him no more than her son, so that
he came away much abashed without having had the chance to utter a
word. By four in the afternoon all was over and that evening there was
appartement, as usually happened three times a week in winter. On the
other three nights there was a play, and on Sundays nothing.

What was called *appartement* was a reunion of the entire Court from
seven until ten in the evening, when the King sat down to table, in the
long suite of rooms that runs from the end of the great gallery[2] to the
landing before the tribune of the chapel. First there was a concert, then
tables were set for all kinds of card-games in the various rooms. One room
was for *lansquenet*, which Monseigneur and Monsieur always played, another for billiards; in a word, there was complete freedom to make up
parties as one pleased and to call for more tables if needed. Beyond the
billiards-room there was one for refreshments, and all were brightly lit.[3]

[1] No one seems to have consulted the bride, but she said: 'It does not matter whether he loves
me or not; the point is for him to marry me.' In the end the marriage did not turn out too badly.
[2] The *Salle des Glaces*.
[3] It was remarkable when Versailles was brightly lit. Ordinarily the corridors and outer rooms
were in darkness. Servants carrying torches lighted people on their way at night.

In the beginning the King used to attend and played for a while, but latterly he had ceased to come, although he liked everyone else to attend regularly, which they did, because they were eager to please him. His own evenings were spent with Mme de Maintenon, working in her room with the different ministers in succession.

On that particular night as soon as the concert was over, the King summoned from *appartement* Monseigneur and Monsieur, who were just sitting down to *lansquenet*; Madame, who scarcely gave a glance to her game of hombre; M. de Chartres, gloomily playing chequers, and Mlle de Blois, only just beginning to go into Society and that night most marvellously arrayed, although totally ignorant of the why and wherefore. She thought that she was summoned for a scolding and, being timid by nature and mortally afraid of the King, she trembled so violently that Mme de Maintenon took her on her knee and held her there, trying vainly to reassure her. With all this bustle of summoning the royalty, including Mlle de Blois, to Mme de Maintenon's rooms, rumours of a marriage spread through *appartement* at the same time that the King announced it to his family. The commotion lasted only for a few minutes. Then the same persons returned and the news was made public. I arrived at that precise moment, to find all the Court huddled together and bewilderment on every face. I soon learned the reason, but was not surprised, because of my encounter earlier that afternoon with M. de Chartres.

Meanwhile, in the gallery, Madame was walking up and down with Châteautiers,[1] her favourite and worthy of her trust. She was marching about handkerchief in hand, weeping unrestrainedly, speaking quite loudly, gesticulating, altogether presenting a remarkably good imitation of Ceres appealing to Jupiter after the abduction of her daughter Proserpine. Everyone left the stage clear for her out of respect, and passed her only in order to enter *appartement*. Monseigneur and Monsieur went back to their *lansquenet*. The former appeared much as usual, but no one ever looked more shame-faced than Monsieur, nor more embarrassed, and so he remained for several weeks to come. M. de Chartres seemed miserable and his intended acutely distressed and uncomfortable. Despite her youth and the splendour of the marriage she perceived and understood the entire background and dreaded the consequences. Indeed, the dismay was pretty general, except amongst a very few. As for the Lorraines, they triumphed. Sodomy and double adultery had served their turn by serving them well also. They rejoiced in their success, as having no shame left they had every reason to do.

The political happenings had made *appartement* appear superficially dull, but in fact it was most lively and interesting. To me it seemed shorter than usual, and ended with the King's supper at which I resolved to let nothing escape me. The King seemed no different, M. de Chartres

[1] Anne de Châteautiers. Died aged eighty in 1741.

sat near Madame who never so much as glanced at him nor at Monsieur. Her eyes were filled with tears, which fell from time to time, and she wiped them away, looking round at everyone as though to see how much they had been affected. The eyes of the prince, her son, were red also and neither of them ate much. I observed that the King offered Madame nearly all the dishes that were set before him, and that she refused them all most ungraciously, which did not in any way disturb his air of polite attention. It was much remarked also that after leaving the table, as the royal circle stood for a moment in the King's room, he made a most particular and very deep bow to Madame, during which she performed so neat and swift a pirouette that as he straightened himself all that he could see was her back receding towards the door.

Next day the entire Court called upon Monsieur, Madame and M. le Duc de Chartres, but no one uttered a word, merely bowed and moved silently on. Everyone then went to wait as usual in the gallery for the rising of the Council and the King to go to mass. Madame was there. Her son approached her as he did every day to kiss her hand, and Madame then dealt him such a resounding box on the ear that the smack could be heard several paces distant, which, happening in the presence of the entire Court, covered the poor prince with embarrassment and filled the vast number of spectators, myself included, with utter amazement. The huge dowry was announced that same day, and on the following the King went to return the visits of Monsieur and Madame. It was all vastly depressing; but after that no one spoke of anything but preparations for the wedding.

On Shrove Sunday the King gave a great State ball; that is to say one opening with a *branle*,[1] after which everyone was allowed to dance. I had paid a call on Madame that morning, and she had not been able to resist saying sourly that I seemed to look forward to the balls, which was natural at my age, but that she, being old, wished they were over. Mgr le Duc de Bourgogne danced for the first time at that ball, and led out Mademoiselle[2] in the *branle*. It was also the first royal ball at which I had danced, and my partner was Mlle Sourches, daughter of the Grand Provost; she danced beautifully. Everyone was magnificently dressed.

On Shrove Monday the entire royal party with the bride and bridegroom splendidly attired met shortly before noon in the King's study and from thence proceeded to the chapel. It was arranged as usual for the King's mass, except that two cushions were placed between his stool and the altar for the bridal couple, who thus had their backs to the King. Cardinal de Bouillon in full canonicals came from the sacristy at the same moment, married them, and said the mass. From the chapel they all went

---

[1] *Branle* or *bransle*—a processional dance.
[2] The Duc de Chartres's sister, Elizabeth-Charlotte d'Orléans, daughter of Monsieur and Madame.

straight to table. It was shaped like a horseshoe. The Princes and Princesses of the Blood sat to right and left in order of rank, with the King's two bastards at the ends, and after them, for the first time, the widowed Duchesse de Verneuil. Thus Henri IV's bastard M. de Verneuil rose to being a Prince of the Blood many years after his death, which is something that he certainly would never have expected. The Duc d'Uzès thought the whole thing so absurd that he marched in front of her shouting at the top of his voice: 'Room, room for Mme Charlotte Séguier!'[1] None of the duchesses paid their respects to her at that dinner, excepting only the Duchesse de Sully and the Duchesse du Lude, her daughter and daughter-in-law, which all the others thought so disgraceful that they dared not repeat it.

After dinner the King and Queen of England visited Versailles with their court. There was a gala-concert and great card-playing, with the King present nearly all the time, highly delighted and superbly dressed, wearing the blue ribbon outside his coat as he had done on the previous evening. The supper was arranged like the dinner, King James had his Queen on his right-hand and our King on his left, and all had their *cadenas*.[2] Afterwards the bridal pair were conducted to the apartments of the new Duchesse de Chartres. The Queen of England presented her with the nightdress, and the King of England gave the one for M. de Chartres, after at first refusing on the grounds that he was too unlucky. The blessing of the bed was performed by Cardinal de Bouillon, who kept them waiting a quarter of an hour, which caused people to say that such airs ill-became one who had just returned from exile, where he had been sent for refusing to give a nuptial blessing to Mme la Duchesse without an invitation to the royal banquet.

On Shrove Tuesday Mme de Chartres received in state. The King and Queen of England were there, also our King and the entire Court. The King's mass followed, and dinner as on the previous day. Mme de Verneuil had been sent back to Paris that morning. The general feeling was that she had already received more than her due. After dinner the King was closeted alone with the King and Queen of England;[3] and later there was another State ball, at which the new Duchesse de Chartres was led out by Mgr le Duc de Bourgogne. Everyone wore the same coat and danced with the same partner as before.

Ash Wednesday put an end to these sorry official revels and thenceforward the talk was all of those to come. M. du Maine was also set on marriage. The King at first put him off, saying bluntly that it was not for such as he to found a line, but, goaded by Mme de Maintenon who had

---

[1] Charlotte Séguier (1623–1704). Daughter of Pierre Séguier, Chancellor of France, of whom there is a famous portrait by Le Brun in the Louvre. Her second husband had been Henri de Bourbon, son of Henri IV by the Marquise de Verneuil.

[2] *Cadenas*. Their forks and spoons in a case.

[3] James II and his wife. It was a family party.

been his governess and still doted on him with a nurse's love, King Louis reluctantly consented to buttress him with the house of Condé, by marrying him to one of the daughters of M. le Prince, who was enchanted at the prospect. He saw the rank, consequence and alliances of the bastards daily increasing in splendour. This one, coming so soon after the marriage of his son, was no novelty; moreover, following so hard upon that of M. de Chartres, it would attach him twice as closely to the King[1]. As for Madame, she was even more enchanted. She had lived in terror lest the King, having had her son, might next require her daughter. The present proposal seemed, therefore, to offer salvation.

There were three girls to choose from. An extra inch in the height of the middle one gave her the advantage. All were excessively short.[2] The eldest daughter was beautiful, sensible, and high-spirited, but the fearful repression (to say no worse) endured by all who came under her father's domination completely broke her spirit. She learned to suffer patiently, with a quiet dignity that won her universal admiration, but she paid dearly for it. The effort did permanent injury to her health and she ever afterwards appeared listless and melancholy.

After approving M. le Prince's choice the King called upon Mme la Princesse in her apartments at Versailles to make the formal proposal, and as soon as Lent was over they were betrothed in his study. Immediately afterwards the entire Court drove out to Trianon, where there was *appartement* and a state supper for eighty of the ladies sitting at five tables with the King, Monseigneur, Monsieur, Madame and the new Duchesse de Chartres at their heads. On the following day, Wednesday, 19 March, the marriage was celebrated by Cardinal de Bouillon before the King's mass in the same way as the wedding of M. le Duc de Chartres. Dinner was the same, and supper also after *appartement*. The King of England handed M. du Maine his nightshirt. Mme de Montespan was not present and did not even sign the contract.[3] Next day the bride received the entire Court lying in bed.[4]

This marriage caused a quarrel between Mme la Princesse and her sister the Duchess of Hanover,[5] who wanted the Duc du Maine for one of her own daughters and felt that M. le Prince was cutting the ground

[1] M. le Prince's son M. le Duc was already married to one of the King's bastards; another was now to be M. le Prince's son-in-law, and a third was a bride of the King's nephew. Relationships in the King's family were becoming involved.

[2] Tiny even for that short Court; people called them 'the Royal Dolls'. The one chosen was Anne de Bourbon-Condé, called Mlle de Charolais. The youngest married the Duc de Vendôme, descendant of another royal bastard, in 1710.

[3] She had retired, highly respected, to the Convent of St. Joseph in Paris, and remained on affectionate terms with all her children except the Duc du Maine. 'All France called on her,' says Saint-Simon. 'It was regarded as a social obligation which the ladies of the Court impressed upon their daughters.'

[4] The custom was for ladies to receive lying in bed.

[5] Not Madame's aunt and correspondent the Electress Sophia but Mme la Princesse's younger sister Bénédicte of Bavaria, who had married the Duke of Brunswick-Zell in 1668.

from under her. She had been living a long time in France with her two daughters who were more than fully grown. They had no rank, never went to Court, saw very few people, and never Mme la Princesse except in private. Yet latterly they had taken to travelling with two coaches and a vast retinue of liveried servants, in a style quite incompatible with their position in Paris. One day that German duchess travelling in state met Mme de Bouillon[1] on the road; her servants rudely forced that lady's coach out of the way and most insolently made her pull up until they had passed. This happened shortly after the marriage of M. du Maine. Mme de Bouillon, mortally offended, then refused to speak to her. The Bouillon family were very numerous and at that time rich and powerful. Mme de Bouillon herself lived in considerable state. They all determined on revenge, and took steps accordingly. One evening, when they learned that the duchess was to go to the play, they went in a body with Mme de Bouillon and a great number of liveried footmen, who had orders to pick a quarrel with the duchess's servants. This they did with outstanding success. Her people were routed, her traces cut, and her coaches abominably maltreated. The German screamed in protest, complained to the King, applied to M. le Prince, but he was bored with her and did nothing. As for the King, he favoured the Bouillon brothers, and merely said that she had brought it upon herself. This so much incensed her that she there and then resolved to retire to Germany with her daughters, and did so a few months later, which turned out to be the making of them, for she married her elder girl to the Duke of Modena, who had recently resigned his Cardinal's hat in order to succeed to the dukedom.

[1] Marie Anne Mancini, Duchesse de Bouillon. Niece of Cardinal Mazarin.

CHAPTER III

1693

I Leave the Musketeers – Promotion of Seven new Marshals of France – The King goes to Flanders – Death of my Father – Battle of Neerwinden – Fortunes and Death of La Vauguyon – D'Aquin's dismissal, Fagon becomes the King's doctor – Origins of my friendship with the Duc de Beauvilliers

MY YEAR of service with the musketeers was now coming to a close, and my father asked the King his pleasure concerning me. When the decision was left to him, he chose the cavalry because he had sometimes held cavalry commands, and the King at once offered to give me without purchase-money a company in one of his own regiments. There was no vacancy at that time and so for the next four or five months I diligently continued my service with the musketeers. Then, towards the middle of April, I had the offer of a company just fallen vacant in the Royal-Roussillon, which had been badly mauled and was garrisoning Mons. Terrified lest I might miss the campaign I persuaded my father to accept. I thanked the King, who spoke very graciously to me. The company was brought to full strength in a fortnight. They were mostly greys as in the other royals, one of twelve companies of fifty troopers, making four squadrons in all.

I was at Versailles on Friday, 17 March, when the King made Choiseul, the Duc de Villeroy, the Marquis de Joyeuse, Tourville, the Duc de Noailles, the Marquis de Boufflers, and Catinat Marshals of France. The Comte de Tourville and Catinat did not receive the Order. M. de Boufflers was in Flanders[1] and Catinat on the Italian frontier; the rest were at the Court or in Paris. That same night I was at the King's dinner. He suddenly looked around the assembled company. 'Barbezieux,' said he, 'will learn of these promotions on his rambles.' No one said a word. The King was not pleased with his war minister's frequent jaunts to Paris, and not at all averse to showing how little he had influenced the promotions.

On 3 May the King announced that he was going to Flanders to command one of his armies with the new Maréchal de Boufflers, and under him Monseigneur and M. le Prince acting together as they had done at Namur. M. de Luxembourg was assigned to the other Flanders army with the Maréchaux de Villeroy and de Joyeuse serving under him. At the same time the Maréchal de Lorges was sent to the army in Germany; Catinat to Italy, and the new Maréchal de Noailles to Catalonia. Since an English

---

[1] The expression Flanders was used very loosely by Saint-Simon to cover all the area west of the Rhine between the Dutch Republic and the northern boundary of France.

invasion was feared Monsieur had command of the sea-coasts with the Maréchal d'Humières serving under him. M. le Duc de Chartres had the cavalry in M. de Luxembourg's army with M. le Duc and M. le Prince acting as lieutenants-general. M. du Maine was assigned to the Maréchal de Boufflers's army, and was also given the cavalry.

It was an innovation for marshals of France to obey superiors, but the drawbacks of equal commanders had sometimes proved disastrous. The King had therefore ordained that in the interests of his service the marshals should rank one below the other in order of seniority. This, in fact, made the subordinate marshals no higher than lieutenants-general. They received the same honours as their seniors, but took orders from them, acted only on their instructions, were rarely consulted, and never at all on secret matters relative to the campaign.

That same day, May 3rd, at exactly ten in the evening, I had the misfortune to lose my father. He was eighty-seven years old[1] and had never fully recovered from a serious illness contracted at Blaye two years earlier. For the last three weeks he had been suffering from gout. My mother had seen that he was sinking and had persuaded him to dispose of certain family matters, which, like a good father, he had attended to. She had also prevailed on him to resign his peerage in my favour. That day, as always, he had had friends to dine. When the evening came he had gone to bed quite free from pain or discomfort, then, whilst they were still talking, he had suddenly heaved three deep sighs one after the other. He was dead almost before they could call for help. There was no oil left in his lamp.

I learned the sad news on returning from the King's *coucher* (he was taking physic on the following day)[2] and that night I gave myself up to private grief. Early next morning I went to find Bontemps,[3] and afterwards to the Duc de Beauvilliers, who was in waiting, and whose father had been my father's friend. M. de Beauvilliers assured me of great good will on the part of the princes[4] and promised to petition the King for my father's governorships when he drew back his bed-curtain. They were instantly accorded. Bontemps, who also had been devoted to my father, quickly brought the news to me at the tribune where I was waiting. M. de Beauvilliers then came himself and bade me be in the great gallery at three o'clock, saying that he would have me summoned and would let me in through the studies as they removed the King's dinner.

By this time the crowd was beginning to leave. Monsieur at the head of the King's bed caught sight of me and called out loudly: 'Ah! Here is

---

[1] He was nearly 70 when our duke was born.

[2] The King spent the morning in bed on the day of his monthly purge.

[3] Alexandre Bontemps (1626–1701). The King's head valet and an old friend of Saint-Simon's father. He was an important personage, the King's confidant, superintendent of Versailles, secretary-general of Suisse et Grison and governor of Rennes.

[4] The King's three grandsons, the Ducs de Bourgogne, Anjou, and Berry, of whom Beauvilliers was governor.

M. le Duc de Saint-Simon!' I approached and expressed my gratitude by a very low bow. The King questioned me closely as to what had happened, saying many kind things of my father and myself, for he knew well how to sweeten his favours. He mentioned the Sacraments which my father had been unable to receive. I replied that only a short while back he had made a retreat of several days at Saint-Lazare, where he used to go to confess and say his prayers, and added something about the godliness of his life. The conversation lasted some considerable time and ended with the King exhorting me to continue in virtue and good conduct, and promising to protect me.

When my father was taken ill at Blaye, many persons had asked the King for that governorship, and he had rounded on them in a way unusual to him, saying: 'Has he not a son?' As a matter of fact he had resolved to grant no more reversions, but had always given my father to understand that his governorships would eventually be mine. M. le Prince had cast his eye on Senlis, and had asked for it after my uncle's death;[1] but the King gave it to my father and I inherited it at the same time as Blaye.

My uncle had commanded the Navarre regiment; he was a lieutenant-colonel and was acclaimed for his good looks at the promotion to the Order in 1633. He had died in 1690, on 25 January, and his wife followed him in April 1695. He was very tall, extremely good-looking, exceptionally well-built, full of commonsense, prudent, brave and upright. My father respected him deeply and closely followed his advice when he was in favour. The Marquise de Saint-Simon,[2] his wife, was imperious, grasping and ill-disposed. She contrived to transfer the greater part of my uncle's possessions to the Duc d'Uzès, to leave my father and myself to settle most of his debts, and to let the rest remain unpaid. She had set her heart on my marrying Mlle d'Uzès.[3] Having said this much about my uncle it is right and proper for me to enlarge a little on my father.

High birth and riches do not always go together. Our branch of the family was ruined by the wars, and my ancestors were left with little wealth or glory to repay them for their services. After serving in every campaign of his time my grandfather was forced to retire to his estates whence lack of fortune obliged him to send his elder sons as pages to the late King, a service that included many of the greatest names.

The King was passionately fond of hunting in open country, without the multitudes of huntsmen, hounds, relays, and all the other complications added by his son the present King; above all, without rides cut through the forests. My father had observed the King's impatience at the delay caused by changing horses, and conceived the idea of bringing the fresh horse nose to tail with the one on which the King sat. An active man

[1] Charles de Rouvroy, Marquis de Saint-Simon.
[2] The Marquise was the daughter of the Duc d'Uzès.
[3] Catherine Louise de Crussol. She died aged 20 in 1694.

could thus swing himself from one to the other without dismounting, and the change was made in a moment. This pleased the King exceedingly. He asked for my father whenever he needed a fresh horse, made inquiries about him, and gradually grew fond of him. When Baradet, the first equerry, became intolerably arrogant the King dismissed him and promoted my father to fill his place. Later, after the death of Blainville, he made him one of his first gentlemen.

My father thus became a favourite with no support other than the King's patronage, and he sought none other, not even that of the ministers nor of Cardinal Richelieu himself, which was one of his chief merits in Louis XIII's eyes. He told me that, before raising him in rank, which he wished to do, the King made secret inquiries concerning his birth and character, to discover whether his ancestry was sound enough to support a rise in fortune. These were the very words he used when he told my father about it later. He liked men of quality and endeavoured to know and advance them; which is how the saying originated concerning the three great squares and their statues in Paris: Henri IV among his people on the Pont Neuf, Louis XIII among the gentry on the Place Royale, and Louis XIV among the tax-collectors on the Place des Victoires.

My father was also master of the hunts of Saint-Germain and Versailles, and for a time grand-master of the wolfhounds. When he was made a duke and peer he sold his post as first gentleman, and with the money bought from his elder sister the estates of Saint-Simon which were her inheritance, and had them registered as his peerage.

He not only followed the King in all his wars, but several times commanded the cavalry and was commander-in-chief of all the arrière-bans[1] of the kingdom, comprising five thousand men of gentle birth, and persuaded them to waive their prerogative and serve beyond the borders of France. His valour and conduct won him a high reputation at the war and the close friendship of the famous Duc de Weimar.[2] I can say without fear of contradiction that no one envied him his favour, for he was modest and wholly unself-seeking, the best and most noble-hearted man that ever went to Court, where he made the fortunes of many, aided the unsuccessful and rendered an infinity of kind services.

After paying the last sad honours to my father I went to join my regiment at Mons. The brigade, consisting of my regiment and those of the Ducs de la Feuillade and de Quadt,[3] who was acting as brigade commander, adjoined the infantry on the left of the front line. When the army was assembled, I went to pay my court to the generals and the princes.

---

[1] An arrière-ban was a feudal ruler's summons to all feudatories to defend their country.
[2] Bernard Duke of Saxe-Weimar (1604–1639).
[3] A German Protestant in the service of France to whom the King had given a regiment of German cavalry. Converted to Roman Catholicism in 1635. Died 1693 of wounds received at Neerwinden.

On 18 May the King set out with the ladies[1] and enjoyed a week or so of their company at Le Quesnoy. He then sent them forward to Namur, and on 2 June placed himself at the head of the Maréchal de Boufflers's army. On the 7 of June he took the enemy camp to Gembloux, fifteen kilometres from Namur, and by so doing shortened the gap between his left wing and M. de Luxembourg's right to only half a league, allowing free communication between them. The Prince of Orange encamped at the Abbaye de Parc[2] was left in such a position that he could neither take in supplies nor emerge without having both the King's armies at his throat. He swiftly dug himself in, bitterly repenting of having allowed himself to be cornered so soon. It has since been learned that he several times wrote to his friend the Prince de Vaudémont, saying that all was lost and only a miracle could save him. His forces were inferior to the smaller of the King's two armies, both of which were abundantly supplied with waggons, food and artillery, and were, as you may well imagine, complete masters of the campaign.

In a position so perfectly adapted for great enterprises and with four whole months campaigning to turn them to maximum advantage, the King suddenly declared to M. de Luxembourg on 8 June that he was returning to Versailles and sending Monseigneur to Germany with the Maréchal de Boufflers and a vast reinforcement. M. de Luxembourg's horror was unparalleled. He explained to the King how easy it would be to force the Prince of Orange's trenches; to defeat him completely with one or other of the two armies, and to follow up the victory, assisted by the earliness of the season and the absence of any immediate opposition. He stressed the present expectations, so great and so sure, and the further likelihood that, should the Emperor[3] transfer large reinforcements to Flanders, Germany also might fall prey to the Maréchal de Lorges. But the decision had been made. Luxembourg, in despair at seeing so glorious and profitable a campaign slip from his grasp, went down on both knees before the King, but could not move him. It was Mme de Maintenon's doing. She had tried vainly to prevent the King leaving her in the first place; she dreaded his absences. The victorious start to the campaign might have tempted him to stay and reap the glory. Her tears at their parting and her letters afterwards were stronger arguments to him than the most urgent considerations of State or glory.[4]

On the evening of that tragic day M. de Luxembourg, worn out with grief, returned to his headquarters and confided the news to the Maréchal de Villeroy, M. le Duc and M. le Prince de Conti, who could scarcely believe it and gave free vent to their lamentations. On the following day

---

[1] Twenty-seven of them altogether.
[2] Near Louvain.
[3] Leopold I (1640–1705), Holy Roman Emperor from 1658.
[4] Madame wrote: 'The King cannot say that his expedition bore no fruit, since Madame de Chartres, Madame la Duchesse, and the Prince de Condé's wife have all returned pregnant.'

9 June, no one else had heard anything. As chance would have it, I went alone to M. de Luxembourg's headquarters, as I often had occasion to do, to hear the news and receive the next day's orders. Much was my astonishment to find no one there; all had gone to the King's army. Sitting apart on my horse I was ruminating over this extraordinary situation, wondering whether to return or press on to the King, when I saw M. le Prince de Conti coming from the direction of our camp, followed only by a page and a groom with a led horse. 'What are you doing here?' he asked, as he joined me, and, laughing at my astonishment, he told me that he was off to take his leave of the King, advising me to go with him and do likewise. 'What do you mean, "*Take your leave*"?' said I. Thereupon, he ordered his page and groom to follow at a distance and suggested that I should tell mine to do the same. Then, in fits of laughter, he spoke of the King's withdrawal and, notwithstanding my youth, decorated the story a little because he trusted me. I listened with all my ears, but unutterable amazement allowed me to ask only a few questions. In the midst of this discussion we met the general staff returning. We joined them, and the two Marshals, Monsieur le Duc, M. le Prince de Conti and three generals at once went aside, dismounted, and spent a good half-hour in arguing and, I may add, cursing; after which they remounted their horses and went their separate ways.

When we reached the King's quarters, we found amazement depicted on every face, and indignation upon many. Dinner was served almost immediately. M. le Prince de Conti went up to take his leave and, as the King was coming down the steps into the supper-room, the Duc de La Trémoïlle told me to go up and do the same, which I did, half-way up the steps. The King stopped and did me the honour to wish me luck in the campaign. As soon as he had gone to dinner, I went to find the Prince de Conti; we remounted and rode back to camp, speaking only of the news, which became public that day. Next morning the King and Monseigneur left for Namur, the latter continuing into Germany, and the King, accompanied by the ladies, going back to Versailles, never again to return to the front.

The effect of this departure was beyond belief, even among the common soldiers, even among foreign nations. The generals could not keep silent amongst themselves and the junior officers talked too loud and with total lack of restraint. The enemy neither could nor would contain their joy and astonishment; but nothing coming from them was more slanderous than what was said in the armies of France, the towns and at the Court. Even the Courtiers, usually so glad to return to Versailles, made it a point of honour to feel ashamed, and it was learned afterwards that the Prince of Orange had written to Vaudémont that she who had never yet disappointed him had demanded the King's return, but this was so monstrous he had not dared to hope for it. A second note had followed to the effect that deliverance was now certain for him; that a miracle had saved his army and the Low Countries,[1] and had been the only possible means of salvation. Amid all these reports the King, with the ladies, arrived at Versailles on 25 June.

On 14 July, M. de Luxembourg, riding out to reconnoitre near the Abbaye d'Heylissem, where he was encamped, received news that Tilly[2] was preparing to advance with a cavalry corps of six thousand men to a position whence he could harass our supply lines. Our general immediately ordered forty-four squadrons from our right wing to mount that very night and rode with them and the Princes, but only engaged the enemy on the following morning, for they had been warned by a monk of Heylissem and were already mounted and gone. We found them on top of a ridge with ravines before them. Marsin,[3] the Chevalier du Rozel and Sanguinet (an officer of the bodyguard) attacked them at three points. Sanguinet, galloping too fast, was thrown and killed and the Duc de Montfort,[4] who was beside him with the detachment of light horse, was dangerously wounded with six sabre-cuts that split his skull, leaving him scarred for life. Thiange,[5] always eccentrically dressed, charged on his own initiative and was seriously wounded by our side, who mistook him for the enemy. Finally we managed to break their front and sent them flying at such speed that scarcely any prisoners were taken.

The Maréchal de Villeroy went forward to take Huy with a large detachment, covered by the rest of the army under M. de Luxembourg. All was over in three days, without any casualties, except one subaltern of engineers and a few soldiers. I saw the rather miserable-looking garrison of mixed troops come out; they marched past the Maréchal de Villeroy and were much harried by our officers who, by the terms of the capitulation, had the right to search for deserters.

In the meanwhile I went off to a neighbouring barn with some officers of the Royal-Roussillon, and one or two others of the same brigade, so as to snatch a bite in the shade. As we were finishing, Boissieux, a cornet of my company, appeared bringing in with him Le Fèvre, a captain, formerly a swineherd, who had risen by sheer merit from the ranks and could still neither read nor write, though he was old. He was one of our finest skirmishers and never made a sortie without either seeing the enemy or bringing back reliable information as to his whereabouts. We liked, respected and cared for him. Boissieux told us joyfully that we were going to engage the enemy; that they had reconnoitred the camp beyond the River Geete, and that there was certain to be a great battle. We left him to

[1] Saint-Simon was apt to refer to the Dutch Republic inaccurately as Holland or the Low Countries, and the translator has not altered his usage.

[2] Count Tilly; a general in the Spanish army. Died 1715.

[3] Ferdinand Comte de Marsin. Maréchal de France in 1703. Killed at Turin 1706.

[4] Honoré Charles d'Albert de Luynes, Duc de Montfort (1669–1704). Not to be confused with the other Montfort, Saint-Simon's colonel.

[5] Claude Philibert de Damas, Marquis de Thiange. He was a nephew of Mme de Montespan.

tackle such food as remained and, after these tidings, remounted our horses. A moment later I met Marsin who confirmed them. Then I rode to the mill of Waremme where our senior generals had gathered with M. le Duc and the Maréchal de Joyeuse, whilst M. de Luxembourg was advancing with M. de Chartres and M. le Prince de Conti. I climbed up into the mill and, after hearing all the latest news, rode back to rejoin the Royal-Roussillon.

During the battle M. le Duc de Chartres charged several times at the head of the gallant squadrons of the King's household, with a coolness and courage worthy of his high birth, and was once surrounded and nearly taken prisoner. The Marquis d'Arcy, his former tutor, rode beside him throughout the action, showing the presence of mind of an experienced commander yet with all the dash of youth. M. le Duc, who was given the chief credit for the guards' last attempt to take Neerwinden, was always between us and the enemy. Our cavalry, forming and redeploying in the plain, charged five different times and in the end, after strong resistance, pushed the enemy back to the River Geete, in which many were drowned.

M. le Prince de Conti, when at last he became master of the village of Neerwinden, had received a blow on the side and a sabre-cut on the head, which was saved by the steel lining of his hat. The battle was over by four or five o'clock in the afternoon, after an action lasting twelve hours, on one of the hottest days of all that hot summer.

Here I shall break off for a moment to say a word about myself. I was in the third squadron of the Royal-Roussillon, commanded by the finest captain of all the regiment, a very gallant gentleman from Picardy named Granvilliers, whom we all liked and admired. Du Puy, another captain, on the right of our squadron, urged me to take his place for the honour of it, but I refused. He was killed in one of our five charges.[1] I had two attendants with me; one my old tutor, a man of some merit; the other my mother's equerry. I also had five grooms with the led-horses and a footman. I rode three charges on an excellent crop-eared bobtail, a dark bay, without once dismounting since four o'clock that morning. Feeling it tire under me, I turned to ask for another and perceived that my attendants were gone. People shouted for my servants, who were keeping fairly close to the squadron, and my valet, a man named Bretonneau, who had been with me since my childhood, asked angrily whether I did not wish I was as well mounted as the two missing gentlemen, who had long since disappeared. I got onto a very good-looking grey,[2] on which I rode two more charges, and the only damage was a cut on the crupper of the bobtail and some gold trimming torn from my blue coat.[3]

---

[1] This was in the middle of the battle of Neerwinden itself.
[2] The name of his grey horse was 'Capitaine'. The bob-tail was 'Le Petit Coureur'.
[3] Blue was the colour of the Royal-Roussillon uniforms.

My old tutor had in fact followed me, but at the beginning of the first charge his horse took the bit between its teeth and broke it, and he would twice have been carried amongst the enemy had not d'Arcy saved him on the first occasion, and a lieutenant on the second. His horse was by that time wounded, so he took a trooper's, but he had little better luck after these mishaps, for he then lost his wig and hat. Someone lent him a huge Spanish hat with a thistle stuck in it,[1] which he forgot and so came under fire from our own side. However, he at last reached the waggons and waited there until the end of the battle to hear what had become of me. As for the other, he disappeared from the beginning and had no adventures. I found him again after everything was over, when I had forgathered with other officers of our regiment for a hurried meal, and he was impudent enough to come up and praise himself for having provided me with a fresh horse at a critical moment. This piece of effrontery took me so much by surprise and made me so angry that I could not say a word, and I never afterwards referred to the matter; but, having seen what stuff he was made of, I fought shy of him when I returned to the front.

At the halt on the previous evening my servants had very prudently set aside a leg of mutton and a bottle of wine, when they heard of the coming action. I had polished it off only that morning with some of our officers who likewise had had no supper, and we were all feeling pretty hungry when we perceived in the distance two pack-horses with my yellow saddle cloths and some horsemen wandering about in the plain. Someone went after them and found my steward and brought him to us along with his convoy, which pleased us mightily.

I had written a few lines to my mother with writing materials that the above-mentioned equerry had remembered to put in his pocket, and I sent a servant off with it immediately. But a thousand obstacles delayed him which gave my poor mother a very bad twenty-four hours.

After we had eaten I took some retired officers with me to see the battlefield and, most particularly, the enemy trenches. It was extraordinary that in the short time available, and mostly in the dark, they should have managed to extend them all the way between the two villages[2] of what we called the front line, bank them up to a height of four feet, with wide, deep ditches behind, and make them perfectly regular on the flanks, which were contrived with small redoubts here and there, the gates and openings being covered by demi-lunes. The villages themselves were surrounded by natural shields of strong hedges and ditches, customary in that region, which was even better fortified than the rest of the country. The vast numbers of corpses, not so much filling as overflowing the streets, especially in Neerwinden, clearly showed how fierce the resistance had been and how dearly that hard-won victory had cost us.

---

[1] The Allies wore green leaves in their hats to distinguish them from the French, who wore white paper cockades.   [2] Neerwinden and Dormael.

We lost Lieutenant-general Montchevreuil, governor of Arras, and Lieutenant-general d'Artois. Ligneris was also a casualty and Lord Lucan,[1] captain of the King of England's bodyguard. The Duc d'Uzès had both legs shot away; Montfort, our brigadier, was killed at the head of his carabiniers. Quadt, our own colonel, I had seen killed by a cannon ball. The Duc de La Feuillade took over command of the brigade and acquitted himself with distinction. He then vanished and we did not see him again for more than half an hour. What he had done was to go and dress himself up, for he returned to us powdered and decked out in a fine red coat, covered with silver lace, and all his equipment and his horse's harness polished and resplendent.

The enemy lost the Prince de Barbançon (who had defended Namur), Count von Solms, the Earl of Athlone,[2] and many other generals. The Duke of Ormonde and the son of the Earl of Athlone[3] were taken prisoner. Their losses were said to amount to twenty thousand men; you would not be far wrong if you reckoned ours at nearly half that number. We captured all their cannon, eight mortars, many artillery waggons, quantities of standards and regimental colours, and a few pairs of kettle-drums. Altogether the victory may be said to have been complete.

The Prince of Orange, seeing with surprise that the continual and rapid fire from his cannons had not at all shaken our cavalry, though they had withstood it without wavering for six hours, rode angrily to the batteries, rating the gunners for their bad marksmanship, but, when he had seen the result, he turned his horse, crying out: 'Ah! That impudent nation!' He fought until almost the end and only retired with the Elector of Bavaria when he had seen that there was nothing more to be hoped for. The King's army remained for a long time on the battlefield, and at nightfall marched to a camp set up near general headquarters at the village of Landen. Several brigadiers, including ours, were overtaken by the darkness and slept with their columns wherever they happened to be.

Early next morning I went to general headquarters on the outskirts of the village. I saluted M. de Luxembourg, with whom were the princes, the Maréchal de Villeroy and some of the generals. I followed them when they went to inspect part of the battlefield, and they even rode out beyond the Geete where some pontoons still remained. I lent them my telescope through which they were able to see six or seven enemy squadrons still in flight under cannon-fire. I had a long talk with M. le Prince de Conti, who showed me his bruises and appeared not indifferent to his glory. I was especially pleased with the success of M. le Duc de Chartres, who

---

[1] Patrick Sarsfield, titular Earl of Lucan. He defended Limerick against William III and, after its fall, entered the French service in 1691.

[2] Godard van Ginkel, 1st Earl of Athlone (1630–1703). Saint-Simon was mistaken in supposing him to have been killed at Neerwinden.

[3] Frederick Christian Ginkel, 2nd Earl of Athlone. Again Saint-Simon is mistaken: the future second Earl was not taken prisoner at Neerwinden but at the siege of Aire in 1710.

was, as I have said, on almost friendly terms with me, and whom I saw more often in the army.

The enemy had retired on Brussels, but M. de Luxembourg's one thought seemed to be to rest and revictual his troops. His new-won laurels did not shield him from criticism; he was blamed for the battle itself and for not reaping its benefits. They said it was wrong of him to risk attacking an army in such a strong position and so widely entrenched, especially when his troops, although slightly superior in numbers, were exhausted after a long march. He was accused, not without reason, of having several times been within an ace of defeat, and of having won thanks only to the steadfastness and courage of his French soldiers. As to the fruits of victory, it was said openly that he deliberately neglected them so as to prevent the end of a war that was making him great and indispensable. To the first charge he had an easy answer, for he had been ordered to give battle and had not imagined that the enemy could in one short night have fortified their position and dug so many strong trenches, which he first observed on the morning of the battle. As to the second, I know too little to hold any opinion. It is true that all was over between four and five o'clock, with the enemy partly retreating, partly in flight; but it is also true that our troops could not have done more after the long march and twelve hours of fighting. The horses, too, were exhausted, especially the draught-horses of the cannon and the waggons; we were also quite lacking in food and munitions.

After numerous camps for rest, food, and observation the army approached Charleroi. The Maréchal de Villeroy took some of the troops forward to lay the siege and opened the trench on the 15–16 September. M. de Luxembourg covered him with the remainder, in which we were included. We were close enough, however, to ride over to the siege, and for the two armies to be in constant communication without the need of escorts. The Prince of Orange gave us no trouble, for he soon left his army and went first to Breda, then to hunt at Het Loo, and finally to the Hague. Charleroi beat for the parley on Sunday morning 11 October. There were few casualties and no one of distinction.

Charleroi made an honourable surrender after a classic defence. The three princes departed, and the army went into winter quarters. As soon as that had happened, my one thought was to return home as speedily as possible, after visiting Tournai and its splendid fortress. I found the roads and stages in great disorder and, amongst other adventures, a deaf and dumb postillion overturned my coach in the mud one night not far from Le Quesnoy. I therefore sought refuge at the house of the Bishop of Noyon, an old friend and kinsman of my father, and a Clermont-Tonnerre,[1] noted for his vanity and the eccentricities occasioned by that weakness. His entire house from floor to ceiling was decorated with his arms; there

---

[1] François de Clermont-Tonnerre, Doctor of the Sorbonne. Elected to the Academy in 1694.

were peers' robes (minus the bishop's mitre) hung all over the panelling; there were the keys (his badge) everywhere, even upon the canopy of the private chapel; his coat of arms was placed like a picture over the fireplace, with every imaginable accessory, coronet, armour, cap, etc., together with the insignia of all his Court offices. In one of the rooms I observed an illuminated scroll, which I might have mistaken for an ecclesiastical document, had there not been two nuns at either end. On closer inspection it proved to be his pedigree with the saints male and female in his ancestry especially distinguished. There were two other genealogical tables, one of them entitled 'Descent of the Most Noble House of the Clermont-Tonnerres from the Emperors of the East', and the other, '. . . from the Emperors of the West'.[1] He proudly showed me these possessions at which I duly marvelled, even if for a very different reason; and I then proceeded to Paris, although not without a number of setbacks. I thought at one time that I might get no further than Pont-Sainte-Maxence, where every horse was reserved for M. de Luxembourg. I announced to the postmaster, however, that I was governor of the place (which was true) and that I should have him locked up if he refused me horses (which might have been difficult); but luckily he was simple enough to take fright and gave me them.

There was a change at the Court which dumbfounded everyone. D'Aquin,[2] the King's chief physician, had been first physician also to Mme de Montespan but lost nothing by her dismissal; on the other hand, Mme de Maintenon, who regarded any one from that particular quarter as more than suspect, had never accepted him. He was an accomplished courtier, but rich, miserly, and grasping, eagerly seizing every possible opportunity to promote his family—his brother, an ordinary doctor, less than nobody, and his son, still more insignificant, whom he was pushing by way of the Council and intendancies.[3] The King was already becoming weary of his continual demands, when he had the audacity to claim the archbishopric of Tours for his other son, a mere abbé. That was too much, and Mme de Maintenon had him broken for it.

She, who liked to control every avenue to the King, had foreseen that, as he aged and his health deteriorated, a skilled and tactful doctor might become all-powerful. She had been gunning for d'Aquin some considerable time and seized on this offence to have him dismissed and replaced by Fagon.[4] It happened on All Saints' Day, a Tuesday, when Pontchartrain, whose department included the Court and the *maison du*

---

[1] In 1698, under the pseudonym 'Cousin', he published a history of 'Many saints in the Families of the Comtes de Tonnerre', and dedicated it to himself.

[2] Antoine d'Aquin, son of an obscure doctor; made the Queen's physician 1667, Chief Physician to the King 1672.

[3] Intendants: public officials, usually administrators in the provinces.

[4] Guy Crescent Fagon (1638–1718). The modern view is that Saint-Simon thought far too highly of him.

Roi as well as the navy, worked with the King in her room. He received orders to visit d'Aquin before seven next morning and tell him to remove himself forthwith to Paris; to tell him also that the King would allow him a pension of six thousand livres, and another three thousand for his brother to retire at the same time, with an absolute prohibition on seeing or writing to the King. The King had never talked so much to d'Aquin as at his supper and *coucher* on the previous evening, and had never seemed more kindly disposed towards him. Thus the end came like a bolt from the blue, destroying him without hope of recovery. The Court was astounded, but perceived whence the blow came when, on All Souls' Day, just two hours after d'Aquin received the news, the King declared Fagon to be his chief physician. D'Aquin, who was not a bad sort of fellow, was generally pitied; people even called on him in the short interval before he left for Paris.

Fagon had one of the wittiest and best minds in all Europe. He was interested in every facet of his calling, a great botanist, a good chemist, an expert surgeon, an excellent doctor and practitioner. What is more he was highly-skilled; no better physician existed; he even had a fair understanding of mathematics. Wholly unself-seeking, an ardent friend, but an unforgiving enemy, he admired virtue, honour, courage, and scholarship, and endeavoured to support these qualities wherever he found them, descending upon their opposites as though they offended him personally. He could be dangerous because, although generally well-informed, he was easily biased and, having made up his mind, almost nothing could shift him; yet, once convinced, he was so in all sincerity and did everything possible to repair the harm caused by his prejudice. He was the implacable enemy of those whom he called 'quacks'; that is to say claimants to secret knowledge and dispensers of cures, and there he certainly did go too far. He loved his own faculty of Montpellier, and all that school of medicine, almost to worshipping it. According to him, the only way to cure was by the accepted methods of those faculties whose laws to him were sacred.[1] Withal, he was a polished courtier, who perfectly understood the King, Mme de Maintenon, the Court and Society. He had been doctor to the King's children ever since Mme de Maintenon first went to them as their governess, which was when their attachment had been formed. Later he was made doctor to the Children of France and was promoted from them to be chief physician. His favour and consequence grew enormous, but he never forgot his function nor his manners, remaining ever respectful, always in his rightful place.[2]

[1] 'Pious in Medicine' was Molière's term for it.
[2] Madame wrote to her aunt: 'You cannot imagine what Dr. Fagon looks like; thighs like birds' legs, a mouthful of teeth, the upper row black and rotten, and large thick lips that make his mouth jut out. He keeps his eyes half-closed and his complexion is a dark yellow. He has a long face and an expression as sly as his character. At the same time he seems really extremely clever and tactful.'

Another unexpected event excited less surprise than amazement at the insecurity of favour. On Sunday, 29 November, as he returned from mass, the King learned that La Vauguyon[1] had killed himself with two pistol shots in the throat, after ridding himself of his servants by sending them to mass. He was one of the least and poorest of the gentlemen of France, but extraordinarily handsome, albeit of a swarthy, Spanish type of countenance. He had great charm also, and possessed a beautiful voice, which he accompanied most skilfully on the lute and guitar. What is more, he knew how to converse with the ladies and generally made himself gay and pleasant company.

With such talents and others less obvious, but equally serviceable in love, he managed to endear himself to Mme de Beauvais, at that time the Queen Mother's[2] first lady and her closest confidante. She was doubly sought after for possessing the King's ear and for being supposed to have had his virginity. However that may be, I well remember seeing her at Mme la Dauphine's[3] toilette, old, rheumy, blind in one eye, and with the entire Court at her feet, because the King spoke privately to her whenever she came to Versailles and paid her marked attention.

La Vauguyon, I repeat, managed to attach himself to Mme de Beauvais, and thus became acquainted with all who came to her house, and were willing to receive the young coxcomb for her sake. She gradually insinuated him first into the Queen Mother's circle, then with the King, until at last, under her protection, he became a fully-fledged courtier. He showed ability, volunteered for the service, and was employed at some of the German courts, rising to be ambassador to Denmark and later to Spain. Everywhere he gave satisfaction. The King later gave him one of the three military places on his Council and, much to the disgust of the Court, made him a Chevalier of the Order in 1688. Twenty years earlier he had married Saint-Maigrin's ugly daughter,[4] a widow with an only son. So long as the embassies lasted he managed to make ends meet, but when the boy grew up his mother was obliged to establish him, and La Vauguyon found his circumstances greatly reduced. He had received more honours than his due but, despite frequent hints, had extracted very little in the way of cash.

His money worries finally sent him mad, although for some time this passed unnoticed. The first signs occurred at the house of Mme Pellot,[5] widow of the premier président of the Rouen Parlement, who was in the

---

[1] André de Bétoulat de la Petitière, Seigneur de Fromentin. He became Comte de La Vauguyon through his marriage to the Comtesse de Broutay.

[2] Anne of Austria (1601–1666). Married Louis XIII in 1615, daughter of Philip III of Spain.

[3] Marie Anne Christine Victoire of Bavaria. Monseigneur's wife, who had died in 1690. See genealogical table.

[4] In her youth she was maid of honour to Anne of Austria and had been a great beauty.

[5] Madeleine Colbert, a relative of the great Colbert. Her husband M. Claude Pellot was the son of an extremely rich Lyons silk merchant.

habit of giving small, exclusive supper-parties, with cards to follow. Only the best people were invited and La Vauguyon was always included. One night at *brelan* she raised the bidding, and, on La Vauguyon's declining to play, she teased him, saying that it comforted her to see that he was a coward at heart. La Vauguyon said nothing then, but, after the game was finished and the company gone, he bolted the door, rammed his hat down over his ears,[1] drove her back against the chimneypiece, and, grasping her head between his two fists, announced that he had a good mind to pound her to a jelly to teach her not to call him a coward. There was Mme Pellot, very frightened, dropping perpendicular bobs between his two fists, and paying him every imaginable compliment, whilst he continued raging and threatening. At last he left her more dead than alive, but she, good, kind woman that she was, said nothing until after his death and continued to receive him, whilst he returned to her house night after night, as though nothing had occurred.

Shortly afterwards he encountered M. de Courtenay at Fontainebleau in the dark passage that runs from the upper drawing-room to the terrace near the chapel, and drew his sword despite the latter's astonished protests and reminders that they were in the King's house. At the sound of fighting people rushed out to separate them and called some of the Swiss Guard who were always on duty there. La Vauguyon struggled out of their clutches, ran to the King's study, tore open the door, rushed past an usher, and flung himself at the King's feet, crying out that he came to offer him his head. The King, who had just returned from dinner, and to whom no one ever entered unannounced, did not at all relish such a surprise. He asked angrily what was the matter; to which La Vauguyon, still kneeling, replied that his honour had overcome his duty and that, when M. de Courtenay had insulted him, he had drawn his sword within the palace. The King had the greatest trouble in the world to get rid of him by promising to see into the matter. He then had both men arrested and confined to their rooms. Two royal coaches appeared (the kind without armorial bearings or monograms on the harness, such as Bontemps used for the King's private missions) and bore them separately to Paris and the Bastille, where they remained for seven or eight months. You may imagine the scandal! M. de Courtenay was a valiant, but most mild-tempered, gentleman, who never in all his life quarrelled with anyone. He declared that he had not done so with La Vauguyon, but the latter protested his innocence, and, since no one as yet suspected him of madness, no one knew what to believe. At last, since no further explanation was forthcoming, and they were thought to be sufficiently punished, they were released, and shortly afterwards reappeared at the Court.

As you may imagine such public brawls went alongside domestic

---

[1] In the seventeenth century when the French cavalry wore great feathered hats, the command was: 'Settle your hats, Gentlemen, we have the honour to charge!'

quarrels which he concealed as long as possible. At last things became so bad that his poor wife was forced to leave Paris for her country estate. She did not long remain there, however, for she died that same year. This final disaster destroyed him. By her death he lost all his income, for he had none of his own and received little from the King. He was sixty-four years old and childless. It became known later that during the last two years of his life he had carried pistols in his coach and had often threatened his coachman and postillions on the way to and from Versailles. Had it not been for the Baron de Beauvais helping him with money he would have been quite destitute, especially after his wife's death. Beauvais vainly appealed on his behalf many times and it does seem incredible that the King, having raised La Vauguyon to such heights and shown him so much favour, should have allowed him to die of hunger and go mad from worry.

At the end of the year the reversion of M. de Pontchartrain's secretary-ship of State went to his son M. de Maurepas,[1] a counsellor of appeals at the Palais de Justice, not yet twenty, and minus an eye from smallpox. He was the only son, the elder having died, to the eternal sorrow of his parents.

Speaking of this appointment, the enemy bombarded Saint-Malo at this same time, doing little worse than breaking all the windows in the town by the terrible noise of some infernal machine that burst with an explosion before coming within range. M. de Chaulnes and the Duc de Coislin, who was due to preside at the States-general, hurried to the spot with many naval officers and several of the nobility.

My mother, who had been deeply concerned about me during the campaign, was determined that I should not fight a second until after I was married. We therefore had much talk on that grave topic. Although still very young I found the idea not altogether displeasing, but I resolved to make my own choice. I had a great position to maintain and felt very much alone in a world where wealth and consequence were more highly considered than all the rest. As the son of the late King's favourite and a mother no longer young when she married, I was entirely without pro-tectors. Yet not for millions would I have made a misalliance; neither fashion[2] nor financial stress would ever have induced me to stoop so low.

The Duc de Beauvilliers[3] never forgot that our fathers had been friends, nor that he and my father were also on that footing, so far as difference of age and life allowed. He had always shown me so much kindness when I paid my court to the princes, whose governor he was, that it was to him I turned after my father's death. His goodness, sweetness of disposition, and courtesy had made me love him. He was then at the very height of

[1] Jérôme Phélypeaux (1674-1747), son of Pontchartrain (later the Chancellor). He became Comte de Maurepas, and later de Pontchartrain.

[2] The nobles, impoverished by the wars and unable to obtain lucrative employment from the King, had set a fashion for marrying rich bankers' daughters.

[3] He was so punctual that he was known as 'La pendule de la Cour' and always apologized to his coachman if he was a minute late. As a boy he had wished to enter the priesthood.

favour, a minister of State, though still young, head of the finance council, and held his father's post as a gentleman of the bedchamber. The Duchesse de Beauvilliers's[1] high reputation also weighed with me, as did the happiness of their marriage. The chief difficulty was money, of which I stood in great need to repair my sadly depleted fortune, for M. de Beauvilliers had two sons and eight daughters to establish. In the end, however, my inclination prevailed, and my mother approved my choice.

Having made up my mind I decided that it would best become me to go straight for what I wanted, without hinting or sending some third party as negotiator. My mother provided me with a detailed and exact statement of all my possessions and debts. This I took with me to Versailles, where I sent to beg M. de Beauvilliers to suggest a time when I might see him alone and at leisure. Louville was my messenger. He was the son of a gentleman of quality and his mother was equally well-bred; moreover his family had been much attached to my father, who often assisted them at the time of his favour. Louville had his own reasons for gratitude, having been appointed a *gentilhomme de la manche* to M. le Duc d'Anjou entirely on my father's recommendation to M. de Beauvilliers. What is more, he had great personal charm and a fertile imagination that made him excellent company; yet he also had an aptitude for serious affairs and was capable of giving wise counsel.

An appointment was made for eight in the evening in Mme de Beauvilliers's private sitting-room, where the duke came to me alone, unaccompanied by her. I addressed myself to him, explaining the purpose of my visit and the reason why I preferred to see him personally, rather than employ the usual go-between. Then, after telling him my whole mind, I gave him a true account of my circumstances, and begged him to see how he might ensure his daughter's happiness as my wife. I added that I made no stipulations; that I would not bargain, that the only favour I sought was his daughter's hand and a marriage contract drawn up as suited him best, which my mother and I would sign without examination.

The duke's eyes were riveted on me. He appeared touched by my frankness and trust, and, after explaining his family circumstances, asked for time in which to confer with Mme de Beauvilliers, so as to see what they could do. He then stated that of his eight daughters, the eldest was between fourteen and fifteen, the second more than somewhat deformed and wholly unmarriageable, the third between twelve and thirteen,[2] and the remainder still at school at the Benedictine convent at Montargis. He added that his eldest had always wished to be a nun, and was determined on that vocation when he last saw her. As to wealth, he had not much

---

[1] She was the daughter of Colbert. The Duchesses of Chevreuse and Mortemart were her sisters. With the Dukes of Beauvilliers and Chevreuse, and Mme de Maintenon they formed the devoutly pious group at the Court.

[2] All three of them became nuns at Montargis; the eldest was made perpetual prioress.

and did not know whether he could content me, but he promised to do his utmost. I replied that he must realize from the manner of my proposal that fortune was not the attraction for me, nor even his daughter, whom I had never seen; it was rather himself and Mme de Beauvilliers whom I loved and wished to marry. 'But,' said he, 'what if my daughter is set on being a nun?' 'Then,' I said, 'I shall ask you for your third.' To this he offered two objections, first her extreme youth, second the possibility that the elder sister might change her mind later and marry, when he would wish to give her an equal dowry and perhaps find himself in difficulties. To the first I offered the example of his sister-in-law,[1] who had been even younger when she married the late Duc de Mortemart. To the second I suggested his giving me his third daughter on the assumption that her sister would marry. If the latter took her final vows he might feel free to pay me the difference; if otherwise, I would rest content with the junior's portion and wish her sister happiness with a better match than myself.

The duke, raising his eyes to heaven and almost beside himself with emotion, protested that he was torn in half and needed all his strength not to give her to me there and then. He dwelt on my conduct towards him, and adjured me, whether or not we made the match, to regard him thenceforward as a father. He embraced me as though I were already his son, and we parted to meet again at an hour to be fixed by him next morning at the King's *lever*. There he whispered to me as he passed to go to Mgr le Duc de Bourgogne's study at three o'clock, when the young prince would be playing tennis and the room empty. Unfortunately the curious are everywhere, and I encountered two such on my way who plagued me with questions because they met me in a corridor where they thought I had no business to be at that hour. I put them off as best I could and at last arrived at the prince's study, where I found his governor, and a servant posted outside to prevent others from entering. We sat down face to face across the study table and he gave me my answer. It was loving, but a refusal based on his daughter's vocation, and the embarrassment regarding the dowry should she afterwards change her mind. He also mentioned his receiving no salary for his offices, and the unpleasantness of being the first minister to have no present from the King at his daughter's marriage, for, he said, he could expect none in the present state of the finances. Every imaginable expression of sorrow, regret and affection was uttered by him. I answered in similar fashion and we parted with an embrace, neither of us capable of further utterance. It had been agreed between us to keep the matter a dead secret, and that was why we had been obliged to conceal our meetings and vary the appointed place.[2] I

[1] Marie Anne Colbert, wife of Louis de Rochechouart. They were thirteen and fourteen years old when they were married in 1679.

[2] They could scarcely have been more secret had they been plotting to kill Mme de Maintenon.

accordingly told M. de Beauvilliers of my two encounters and he urged me to be even more careful. I therefore did not tell Louville of this second conversation, although he was aware of the first and had been one of the two people whom I had met.

Next day at the King's *lever* M. de Beauvilliers whispered that he believed that Louville, who was trustworthy and our mutual friend, might be willing to act as go-between if I cared to confide in him. Such a suggestion roused my hopes just as I was beginning to despair. I spoke to Louville, gave him full instructions, and begged him to do all possible to serve my strong wish for this marriage. He accordingly arranged another interview for the following day in the little drawing-room at the end of the gallery, next to the late Queen's apartments, where no one went since they were closed after the death of Madame la Dauphine. There I found M. de Beauvilliers and said to him, between fear and hope, that I had been so much affected by our previous conversation that I was obliged to cut it short, and exhaust the first transports of grief in solitude (which was true). Now that he allowed me to continue I should say that there seemed to be only two obstacles, the dowry and her vocation. Regarding the first, I begged him to look again at my circumstances and do as best suited him. As for the vocation, I painted a lively picture of vocations that are all too often misconceived, ending in bitter regrets when the young lady finds herself imprisoned body and soul.

M. de Beauvilliers appeared deeply moved. He said he was touched to the heart; that had he myself and even M. le Comte de Toulouse to choose from he would prefer me for his daughter, and that he would never be consoled for losing me. He then took the statement of my circumstances to confer once more with Mme de Beauvilliers, saying as he went: 'But, if it proves to be a vocation, I can do nothing. We must obey God's will blindly for He is our salvation. To please and serve Him faithfully is the only good end and should be our sole aim.'

These words, so pious, so unselfish, so noble, coming from one in such high employment, increased my respect and admiration for him, and, if possible, my desire for the marriage. I repeated all to Louville, and when I went to the music that evening I placed myself where I could gaze on M. de Beauvilliers, as he stood behind the princes. Coming away I whispered to him that I felt incapable of living happily with anyone other than his daughter, and left him without waiting for an answer. Louville thought I should do well to speak to Mme de Beauvilliers on account of the perfect unity that existed between them, and he told me to call on her at eight o'clock next evening, in secret, behind locked doors. Louville was with her when I arrived. After thanking me she repeated M. de Beauvilliers's objections, but I very clearly saw that the real obstacle with her was the vocation. I said that there appeared to be two vocations and that we must be sure which was the more sensible, lasting and less dangerous for her. The young lady wished to be a nun, which would be acting blindly. I, having surveyed all the other young ladies of quality, wished her to marry me. Her wishes were likely to change; mine were constant. To go against her would do her no harm, since it would place her in the natural way of life and in a family where she would find as much or more religion than even at Montargis. To disappoint me, on the other hand, meant condemning me to a whole lifetime of unhappiness.

The duchess seemed surprised by my vehemence and the intensity of my desire for the marriage. She said that could I but see her daughter's letters to M. de Fénelon I should be convinced of her vocation. She added that, although she had done her utmost to persuade her to return home for seven or eight months in order to see the world, without using force she could not have prevailed; that she was in truth answerable for her daughter's life and not for mine, but that my advocacy had moved her and that she would confer again with M. de Beauvilliers, for, she said, she hated to lose me, with other flattering words and much showing of affection. At that moment (how I cannot conceive, since the door was locked) the Duchesse de Sully entered and we were interrupted. I left her very sad, reflecting that such pious and unselfish parents would never set their own wishes before a daughter's vocation.

Two days later M. de Beauvilliers requested me to follow him at a discreet distance along the narrow dark passage from the tribune into the corridor of the new wing. There he returned the statement of my finances, saying that he could see that I was a great lord in possessions as well as in other ways and that I must not wait to marry. He repeated his regrets, saying that God alone had been preferred to me, just as He would have been preferred to the Dauphin himself, had that prince wished to marry her; that if his daughter should change her mind and I still be free, she should be mine and he would have his heart's desire; that without straining his resources he would gladly lend me the eighty thousand livres which was the amount of my debts; that he must advise me now to look for marriage elsewhere, promising to be the intermediary and to take all my affairs under his wing. Deeply grieved, I replied that only necessity prevented my waiting until his youngest was fully grown, for surely all of them would not be nuns, and the interview ended with declarations of undying affection, with offers to assist me in matters great and small, and a mutual determination to regard ourselves thenceforward as father and son, bound in indissoluble union. Perhaps I have expanded too much on the details of this affair, but I felt it necessary to explain the perfect trust that existed ever afterwards between M. de Beauvilliers and myself, which, considering the difference in our ages and his extraordinarily reserved nature, would not otherwise be comprehensible.

Now therefore I was obliged to seek another marriage. Quite by chance my mother had the offer of the eldest daughter of the Maréchal-duc de

Lorges,[1] with his post of captain of the bodyguard, but nothing came of it at that time, and I went to the Abbaye de La Trappe[2] to seek consolation for my abortive alliance with M. le Duc de Beauvilliers.

La Trappe is so renowned and its reformer so famous that I shall not spread myself in portraits or descriptions. Suffice it to say that the abbey lies five leagues from my own estate of La Ferté-Vidame or Arnauld, that being the special name which distinguishes it from all the other French Fertés, which retain that title as a sign that they were once fortresses (*firmitas*). Louis XIII persuaded my father to buy the estate because it lay only twenty leagues from Saint-Germain and Versailles. This was our only estate that had a residence, and my father went there each autumn. He had known M. de La Trappe in the world, indeed they had been friends, and after the latter's retirement the bond between them grew even stronger. My father visited him several times a year and sometimes took me with him. I was little more than a child at that time, but M. de La Trappe's charm taught me to love him, and his holiness held me spellbound. I always longed to be with him and every year I gratified that wish, sometimes twice or three times, sometimes for weeks together; I never tired of the noble, moving sights at the abbey, nor of marvelling at all I learned of the man who had raised it to the glory of God and for his own spiritual needs, as well as for those of many others. He observed these sentiments in the son of his old friend and came to love me as a father, whilst I regarded him with tender veneration as though I were indeed his son. Such an attachment, strange perhaps in one so young as I, gained me the confidence of this most noble and saintly man, and I trusted him in return. My one regret is that I did not profit more from his advice.

The year ended with the return of the Duc de Vendôme and his brother[3] from the army of the Maréchal de Catinat. It was very noticeable how warmly they were welcomed, in contrast to the cool reception of M. le Duc, despite his being the King's son-in-law. M. le Prince de Conti was greeted with extreme coldness and M. de Luxembourg as though everyone had not been talking of him since the campaign opened. The King allowed him an audience, and that a short one, only after he had been back a fortnight.

---

[1] Marie Gabrielle de Lorges (1676–1743). They were married on 8 April, 1695. At first a marriage of convenience, it soon turned to one of love. Saint-Simon's affection and admiration for her is one of his most endearing characteristics.

[2] A Cistercian abbey in the Seèz diocese. The Abbot, M. de Rancé, was, until his death in 1700, Saint-Simon's spiritual director.

[3] Louis Joseph Duc de Vendôme (1654–1712) and his younger brother Philippe de Vendôme, the Grand Prieur (1655–1727). Their grandfather was a bastard of Henri IV.

CHAPTER IV

1694–1695

1694 – M. de Luxembourg's suit for precedence – Harlay, Premier Président –
My Letters of State – I exchange my Regiment and join the Rhine Army
under the Maréchal de Lorges – M. de Noyon, Academician, outrageously
mocked by the Abbé de Caumartin, who is disgraced – 1695 – Death of M. de
Luxembourg – The Maréchal de Villeroy succeeds him.

On my return from La Trappe, where I went only in secret so as to snatch
these journeys without arousing gossip about my extreme youth, I became involved in an affair that created a tremendous stir and had important consequences for me.

M. de Luxembourg, exulting in his victories and the universal acclaim,
believed that he was powerful enough to elevate himself from eighteenth
ducal peer in order of seniority to second, coming immediately after
M. d'Uzès.[1] Before I embark on the history of his dukedom and his suit
for precedence, a short pedigree will explain his position.

Let us begin with the hereditary Duchesse de Piney, daughter and sole
heiress of the second Duc de Piney. Her first marriage to Léon d'Albert
was arranged after her parents' death by the all-powerful Connétable de
Luynes.[2] She was widowed, aged twenty-two, after only ten years of married life and would seem to have had no very great opinion of her first
husband, nor of her two children by him. By that time the Connétable was
dead, and so no one could prevent her exercising to the full her power
over her children, nor from claiming a widow's right to remarry as she
pleased. Her choice fell upon a Clermont-Tonnerre, who by birth was
worthy of her, and the match may well have been dictated by love, since
by marrying him she lost both rank and titles as well as her noble name.
Immediately after the wedding, the couple went to the bride's magnificent
estate at Ligny, from which they hardly stirred during the remainder of
their lives.

[1] Rank was the supreme glory of the old French nobility. The ducal peers took seniority from
the date of the creation of their dukedoms, new dukes coming at the bottom of the list. Saint-
Simon was only 13th duke and peer, his father's elevation having been fairly recent.

M. de Luxembourg's suit was solely concerned with precedence, for he had been a duke and
peer since his marriage to the heiress to the Piney-Luxembourg dukedom in 1661. In 1694 he
ranked 18th, coming after seventeen earlier creations. He was trying to claim precedence as
from 1581, when his wife's great-grandfather was created first Duke of Piney. Had he won, he
would have taken precedence of all the seventeen dukes senior to him.

[2] Charles d'Albert de Luynes (1578–1621), favourite of Louis XIII and Constable of France.

42

François de Luxembourg
Created Duc de Piney 1577, elevated Peer of France (f)[1] 1581

Henri, 2nd Duc de Piney
Last male heir of the House of Luxembourg

1.
Léon d'Albert = Marguerite Ch. de Luxembourg = Ch. Henri de Clermont-
(Brother of   Duchesse de Piney   Tonnerre
the Connêtable
de Luynes)

2.

Madeleine Ch.
m. 1661   = François de Bouteville
(Became Duchesse de Piney   (Took the name of
on her marriage by the   Luxembourg after his
elimination of her half-   marriage. Created
brother and half-sister)   Duc et Pair de Piney,
                                                   with seniority from that
                                                   date (1661))

Henri Léon, Duc de Piney, imbecile,   Marie Charlotte, nun.
Ordained priest, d. 1697.   Later lady-in-waiting
Legally certified as a lunatic.   to the Queen and known
Pronounced sane and   as the Princesse de Tingry
immediately re-certified

It was to the new bridegroom's advantage to be rid of the children of his wife's first marriage. The son provided a pretext for himself by being an imbecile. They had him declared a lunatic and confined him at the Saint-Lazare, at Paris; then for fear lest anyone should marry him they had him ordained, and in that place and condition he spent the whole of his long life. The daughter had little sense, but was not absolutely foolish, so they made her a nun at the Abbaye-aux-Bois, near Paris. Later she used to say that they had forced her, but, since she was there for more than twenty years, part of the time as mistress of the novices, it does not seem that that was so. She was still exercising the latter function (in 1661) when M. le Prince extracted her, as I shall describe in due course.

M. de Luxembourg, the only son of that M. de Bouteville, so notorious for his duels, was born six months after his father's death. A noble name, courage, unbridled ambition, and great capabilities, accompanied by love of intrigue and dissolute living, enabled him to overcome the drawbacks of what was at first sight an astonishingly repulsive exterior. For, although no one could credit this who never met him, one did become accustomed to the sight of a hump that was medium big in front, but very thick and monstrously pointed behind, with all the usual accompaniments of such

[1] The title could descend in the female line.

deformities. Nobility and charm of manner transfigured him in his most ordinary gestures. When young Bouteville first entered Society, he attached himself to M. le Prince and followed him throughout the wars. His valour, vigour and immorality were exactly suited to that prince and many amorous adventures cemented their friendship. At the time of their return to France, Bouteville was thirty-three years old. He had won military renown, had become a general, and had earned his patron's gratitude by remaining loyal to the end, unlike most of his kind. They now began to look around for some reward that would make Bouteville's fortune and, at the same time, reflect lustre on M. le Prince. Between them they unearthed the hereditary Duchesse de Piney's daughter by her second marriage with M. de Clermont-Tonnerre. The girl was appallingly ugly, like a great vulgar fish-wife in a herring barrel, but by the elimination of the children of her mother's first marriage she would be immensely rich, and appeared to M. le Prince to offer an ingenious method of endowing Bouteville with a peerage.

They decided that first the nun must be doubly secured. She was prone to grumble at her vows and they feared lest her half-sister's marriage might provoke an embarrassing reappearance. M. le Prince therefore spoke to her through the convent grille, offering to procure a papal dispensation for her if she wished to re-enter the world, and the grant of a *tabouret*[1] to follow. She thereupon agreed to everything, promised never to forsake her vows, and signed what he asked. Nothing could have pleased them better than to have her thus recommitted, and the grace and favour *tabouret* added lustre to her sister's marriage. The Pope graciously accorded the dispensation, and the Court the *tabouret*, on the pretext that, as the child of the first marriage, she would eventually have inherited the duchy of Piney, had she not been a professed nun. They appointed her lady-in-waiting to the Queen, called her the Princesse de Tingry, and made her wear on her head-dress the badge of the Chapterhouse of Poussay in miniature, an emblem which she soon discarded.

As for the brother, they went through the farce of declaring him sane, extracting him from Saint-Lazare, and making him endow the new Mme de Bouteville in her marriage contract with all his estates, worldly possessions and the reversion of his title in return for a large sum of money paid by M. de Bouteville. That clause in the contract was of prime importance in the suit which now concerns us. Immediately after he had witnessed his sister's marriage they had him re-certified and returned to Saint-Lazare, from whence he never more emerged.

The wedding was celebrated on 17 March, 1661. M. de Bouteville then adopted the arms of Luxembourg on an inescutcheon with his own, and took to signing himself Montmorency-Luxembourg, as his children and grandchildren have done ever since. After this he at once began his suit for

[1] A stool without arms, on which duchesses sat in the presence of royalty.

rank as Duc de Piney, helped by M. le Prince, who obtained letters of a
new creation in his favour, into which the words 'so far as need may be'
were cleverly inserted, thus leaving him free to claim seniority from an
earlier elevation in 1581. With these letters he was admitted as a duke and
peer into the Parlement and at that time ranked last, below all other dukes
and peers.

The remainder of M. de Luxembourg's life is known to all. He was involved in the affair of La Voisin, the sorceress, who was accused of being
a poisoner and was burned on the Place de la Grève. He was then reproached for forgetting the rank for which he had worked so hard. He was
tried in the dock like a common malefactor and claimed none of his ducal
privileges. Thereafter he spent a long time in the Bastille, and left there
much of his honourable reputation. It was thought then that he had renounced his suit against his senior dukes. At that time there were still
ceremonies in which the dukes had a part; he never attended them and,
because his whole life was spent either at the war or in debauchery, he
remained forgotten until the promotions of 1688, when he claimed and
received the Order along with the other marshals of France, so as not to
prejudice his claim for precedence. Incidentally, that was when marshals
first took precedence over gentlemen of quality receiving the Order at
the same time, and M. de Luxembourg's action showed that he had by
no means renounced his claim.

When war broke out afresh (in 1693), this time between France and the
whole of Europe, the Maréchal de Luxembourg had good hopes of being
needed, of the chance to win glory, and thus the influence required
to gain his suit. And, indeed, so it happened, for after Maréchal
d'Humières's failure in the first campaign he was summoned to succeed
him. M. de Luxembourg assessed his campaigns solely by the number
of battles won, and thus, after the great victories of Leuze, a mere
cavalry duel, Fleurus, which gained us nothing, Steinkirk, where the
entire French army was within an ace of being trapped, betrayed by a
spy on the commander's own staff, and Neerwinden, which brought us
only Charleroi, he considered himself strong enough to press and win his
suit for precedence.

Intrigue, blandishments, sometimes downright servility served him
well. The fame of his victories and the glitter of his rank as commander
of the largest and nearest of the armies raised his prestige enormously.
The Court flocked around him, and Paris, dazzled by all his splendour
and captivated by his friendly and hearty manner, took him to its heart.
He was discovered by all to be a great man, whilst the rowdy young
adopted him as their example and excuse for their wild conduct and
debauches, for even at that age his behaviour was not much better than
theirs. He was popular in the army, a close friend of M. le Duc and M. le
Prince de Conti, a member of Monseigneur's intimate circle, and his

eldest son had recently married the daughter of the Duc de Chevreuse who, with his brother-in-law the Duc de Beauvilliers and their two duchesses, was in the highest favour and admitted to the King's most private conferences with Mme de Maintenon.

In the Parlement the plot was hatched already, for Premier Président Harlay[1] who led that august body by the nose believed that he could settle this great matter before the end of the season. He mistook the will for the deed. In honour of M. de Luxembourg's son's marriage his estate of Beaufort had been elevated to a dukedom registered in the name of Montmorency. Harlay managed to persuade the entire Parlement that by honouring the son King Louis was showing his approval of the father's claim for precedence, which shortly afterwards was pressed in earnest. The premier président's support gave great weight to this swindle, which was discovered too late for the remedy to take effect. That remedy was a letter from Pontchartrain, controller of finances, written on behalf of the King to inform the Parlement that the King took no sides and would remain perfectly neutral throughout the whole affair.

Harlay was the son of a former procureur-général and great grandson of the famous Achille d'Harlay, premier président of the Parlement, who succeeded his father-in-law the great Christophe de Thou. Coming from this long line of eminent judges, Harlay inherited all their gravity of manner and cynically exaggerated it, affecting modest impartiality belied by his actions and by his inordinate vanity which was very much apparent, although he did everything to conceal it. Above all, he publicly prided himself on his fairness and integrity; but the mask soon fell from that false face. He could be scrupulously fair in deciding between Peter and James, until he perceived some advantage to be gained. Then, at once, he was for sale. These memoirs will furnish sufficient examples of that, and, in the meanwhile, M. de Luxembourg's suit will reveal him as he really was.

Harlay was an expert on civil law and fully conversant with every branch of jurisprudence; he equalled the best in literature and was well-acquainted with history. Above all, he knew how to rule his colleagues with an authority that brooked no argument, such as no previous premier président had ever possessed. Sarcasm made him doubly formidable; his stinging reprimands to assemblies, advocates, or judges made one tremble at the thought of confronting him. Since the Court supported him in every way, he was their slave, and the very humble servant of those whose favour was assured. A skilled courtier and a remarkably clever politician, he used his high talents solely to further his desire for power and success, and to win for himself the reputation of a great man. Yet his honour was untrustworthy, his principles non-existent, his integrity a mere show, his humanity nil. In a word, he was a most consummate hypocrite, faithless, Godless, soulless, a cruel husband, brutal father, tyrant brother, friend

[1] Achille III de Harlay (1639-1712). Premier président of the Parlement since 1689.

only to himself, wicked by nature, delighting to insult, injure, and bring low, and never in all his life neglecting such an opportunity. Volumes might be filled with descriptions of him, yet still be lively reading, for he was a man of infinite wit, with a mind naturally inclined that way, and the prudence never to risk what might cause him to repent later.

To look at he was small, spare and active, with a wedge-shaped face, a great hooked nose, and fine, eloquent, piercing eyes, rarely glancing other than stealthily, but once fixed upon the face of a client or magistrate, enough to make him sink underground. He wore tightish coats, clerical neck-bands and similarly flat cuffs, with a deep brown, much bespeckled, short, bushy wig, and a high cap worn over all. In walking he stooped a little, with a falsely humble rather than a modest air, always hugging the walls in order ostentatiously to leave the way clear, and, at Versailles, quite unable to proceed without respectful, almost servile bows and scrapes to left and right.

The King and Mme de Maintenon had a soft spot for him, for it was he who, when consulted on the outrageous problem of legitimizing children without naming their mother, had offered the precedent of the Chevalier de Longueville,[1] by means of which the King's bastards were in fact rescued. In return for this service he was promised the Chancellorship of France, and given the confidence of the King, his children and their all-powerful governess, a trust which he did everything to conserve and successfully used to win himself privileges. He was also a kinsman and friend of the Maréchal de Villeroy, who had made him acquainted with the Maréchal de Luxembourg and now persuaded him to support the latter's suit. None of the dukes to be attacked was in favour except the Duc de La Rochefoucauld; a few of them, at most, were noticed by the King, the remainder merely well-regarded. Thus Harlay found no difficulty in deciding to act.

Racine, so famous for his plays and his commission to write the King's history, lent his admirable pen to polish M. de Luxembourg's statements, and redeemed their dryness with such flowery eloquence that they became delightful reading for ladies and courtiers. As a matter of fact, the ladies and young men and all the world of fashion and the Court were on his side. No one on ours was capable of winning them over, nor even of splitting their ranks, and when you consider the care that was taken to seduce the most important members of the Parlement by means of their friends, relations, mistresses, confessors and valets, you will realize that, headed by a president like Harlay, their party was by far the stronger.

You may well imagine that at my age,[2] without influence, kinsmen, or experience, except of the army, I had no acquaintance with the dukes

---

[1] Charles Louis d'Orléans, bastard son of the Duc de Longueville, Charles Paris, and the Maréchale de La Ferté. Killed during a siege of Philippsburg in 1692.
[2] Saint-Simon was eighteen.

whose seniority was questioned.[1] None the less, they thought it best to recruit everyone, for all men have friends and purses. M. de La Trémoïlle accordingly approached me at the King's *lever*, saying that his seniority and that of other dukes was challenged by the Maréchal de Luxembourg, who had revived an old suit in which my father had been on their side. He hoped, he said, that I should support them, even though the Maréchal was my commander, and he proceeded to pay me several highly delightful compliments. This was soon after my return from the war when I had heard nothing of the matter; but it did not take me long to form an opinion. I thanked M. de La Trémoïlle and the other dukes who thought highly of me, saying that in such good company I need not fear to go astray by following my father's lead, and assuring him that I should stand firm. He seemed much pleased, and that same day M. de La Rochefoucauld called on me and was very complimentary.

Thus recruited, I thought that I owed a duty to M. de Luxembourg, my commanding officer, who had treated me well, though he knew me only by name. I therefore visited him next day and asked his permission to side with the dukes over whom he claimed precedence. In all other matters, I said, I would obey him blindly, and even in this would not move without his consent, adding all the civilities due to his age and rank from one so young as myself. He heard me out with patience and courtesy, and said that I could not do better than follow my father's example, whereupon all the company assembled began to praise me. That duty done, my thoughts turned on how to promote the common cause without giving M. de Luxembourg unnecessary annoyance. Here I shall give a short summary of the legal proceedings, for to enter into full details of the laws, precedents, and prohibitions quoted on either side would fill volumes.

M. de Luxembourg claimed that peerages transmitted through the female dated back to infinity; that Mme de Tingry being under vows, although in the world, and her brother having passed his rank and estates to his half-sister, and being moreover a deacon and unmarriageable, that same half-sister, now M. de Luxembourg's wife, had also inherited the peerage, thus making her husband a duke and peer with seniority dating back to its creation; that the clause 'so long as need shall be' inserted into the letters patent granted him on his marriage denied the assumption of a new creation, the proof being that the King, when he had been pleased to issue the new letters patent in 1676, was not intending to elevate Piney to the peerage as from 1661, but only to transfer the inheritance to M. de Luxembourg. From the foregoing, M. de Luxembourg claimed that

---

[1] The seventeen dukes attacked were as follows, in order of seniority: d'Elbœuf, Rohan-Montbazon, Ventadour, Vendôme, La Trémoïlle, Sully, Chevreuse, Lesdiguières-Gondi (minor), Brissac, Chaulnes, Richelieu, Saint-Simon, La Rochefoucauld, La Force, Valentinois (Prince de Monaco), Rohan and Bouillon. Beauvilliers's peerage was too recent (1679).

beyond all doubt his seniority dated back to the original creation in 1581.

His opponents, on the contrary, claimed that elevations in the female line never continued indefinitely; that their validity terminated with the eldest daughter, in no circumstances passed beyond the second, and went to her only by the grace and favour of fresh letters continuing the peerage, with seniority from the date of such letters. The original peerage of Piney became extinct with the blood of the hereditary duchess's first husband, as was proved when she lost her rank and titles by re-marrying, whilst the peerage remained constant with the son of her first husband. As for the former's resignation and the handing over of his rights to his half-sister in her marriage contract, two considerations rendered this null and void, and a third made it impossible. Firstly, he was a certified lunatic both before and after the event, and only uncertified for the time required for him to sign, which was a mockery of justice. Secondly, the large sums given him by his half-sister's bridegroom and stated in her contract to be in return for the resignation made nonsense of the entire claim, for by two means only can one become a duke and peer, either by direct inheritance or by a new creation—buyers are specifically banned. Thirdly, the wishes of a lunatic, even supposing him to have been wrongly certified and to have received nothing in exchange, are wholly insufficient for the trans-ference of a peerage. Resignations are valid only for passing the succession to the next lineal heir, and then only with the King's permission, both conditions being unfulfilled in the present case. Finally, the clause 'so far as need may be', inserted into the letters of 1661, accorded M. de Luxem-bourg no rights whatsoever, since he later obtained fresh letters patent and accepted lower rank, and had he not done so he would never have become a peer.

Let me now say a word of his opponents. We must first eliminate MM. de Chevreuse and de Beauvilliers, for reasons which have appeared. M. d'Elbœuf merely swelled our numbers, taking no action, except that of remaining united. M. de Ventadour came sometimes to the sessions, did more or less what was asked of him, but, save for paying, his life was not of a kind to make him very effective. M. de Vendôme attended and spoke well, but, typically, would not brook any restraint. M. de Lesdiguières was an infant and his mother, a flighty creature, was wholly beneath the thumb of her cousin de Villeroy. It says much for her that she, being his guardian, added her son's name to the list of defendants. M. de Brissac, obscure, ruined, leading a rural life at Château Brissac, simply put his name with the rest. M. de Sully was steadfast, but seldom appeared. MM. de Chaulnes, de Richelieu, de La Rochefoucauld, and de La Tré-moïlle were those who bore the brunt, with good M. de La Force doing everything possible consistent with his dignity, and M. de Rohan the same. Both he and M. de Richelieu were, however, capricious and had dealings also with the other side. M. de Monaco was very keen, excepting with his purse, but though he cursed he paid; whereas it was perfectly hopeless trying to extract the necessary from the Duc de Rohan.

I attended every session of the Parlement; I studied the case and all that was happening. What I dared to say in court was well received; Riparfonds[1] and the two leading advocates made friends with me. The dukes seemed to like me; M. de La Rochefoucauld, despite his grimness and my name,[2] grew quite friendly; I became closely attached to M. de la Trémoïlle, and even gained a kind of influence over M. de Richelieu who was my father's intimate friend. We voted from our places; we did not interrupt one another; we never wasted a moment in compliments or gossip; no one became impatient at the length of the sessions, long though they were (not even M. de La Rochefoucauld, who always returned to Versailles for the King's *coucher*); every duke prided himself on punctuality and regular attendance.

When the trial began in earnest we presented our pleas all at the same time, two of us side by side in each coach. It was not long before we discovered Harlay's malevolence, for in this case, which should have been tried in open court by the assembly and the peers alone, we found that he was summoning small committees to meet and examine the suit privily at his house, where he could influence their findings. The reason was plain, he wished to have the judgment settled beforehand and over-rode every precedent in order to do so.

Whilst we let him do what we could not prevent, we were suddenly warned that M. de Luxembourg was issuing a fresh statement, a very few copies of which had been given secretly to such of the committee members as he most trusted. Since we were not shown this document it could not be used in court, but it was none the less hidden for fear that we should object to it, especially as M. de Luxembourg's lawyer was using it to influence the judges. It happened, however, that one of the committee men was shocked by a piece of trickery that might have lost us our suit. He lent the statement to the Duc de La Trémoïlle's secretary who copied it in one night and summoned us to an extraordinary meeting at Riparfonds's house on the following day, a Tuesday, so that we might hear it read. It was vital to concoct an answer there and then for the judgment was due to be delivered on the following Friday. We therefore decided to assemble on the Wednesday at Riparfonds's office and go thence in a body to demand an adjournment until Monday from Président Harlay.

We met as arranged at Riparfonds's house in the Rue de la Harpe, nine dukes including myself, and drove in procession in our coaches to the president's house at the time when he gave interviews after returning from the Palais.[3] We all drove into the courtyard, the porter opened the

---

[1] Etienne Gabriau de Riparfonds, the eminent lawyer in charge of the dukes' case.
[2] There had been an old quarrel on precedence between the families.
[3] Palais de Justice.

gates for us and said that he was within. The rumble of the coaches, however, must have made them peep through the window as we waited for all
to descend so as to mount the steps in a body, because a footman appeared
at the door and calmly announced that Harlay was not at home. Say what
we might, we could not induce him to tell us either where his master was or
when he would again be visible, and there remained nothing to do but
return to Riparfonds and deliberate. We each said what we thought of
this bare-faced attempt to silence us, this arrogant denial of justice in
sending us away, for it was very evident that the premier président had
been at home all the time.

At this point when we thought all was lost, one of the lawyers suddenly
inquired whether any one possessed Letters of State.[1] They gazed at each
other, but none of them owned such things, although he explained that
they were our last hope and described the procedure for their use. There
was general dismay; but, at that moment, I was able to say, smiling, that, if
that were all, our troubles were over, for as an officer I held such papers
and would willingly produce them, provided that they were served on
M. de Luxembourg alone. This brought me a round of applause from the
assembled dukes and lawyers, with praises, compliments, embraces, and
thanks, as though I was saving their very lives. M. de La Trémoïlle and
M. de La Rochefoucauld said out loud before the entire company that
they promised my letters should be used only against M. de Luxembourg.

Time pressed. I said that my mother had charge of them and that I
would fetch them from her. I went home and woke her, explaining somewhat briefly what was to do, but though she was sleepy, she tried to remonstrate with me because of my subordinate position with regard to M. de
Luxembourg. I interrupted her, however, saying that this was an affair of
honour, with the letters absolutely needed, promised, and urgently
awaited. Then, without stopping for permission, I took the key of her
cabinet and bolted with the letters. The dukes had been so much afraid
of my mother's refusing that M. de La Trémoïlle and M. de Richelieu
were sent after me to help in coaxing her, but I was already in possession
when they appeared. I conveyed to them my mother's apologies for she
was not yet visible. An unfortunate delay then occurred, giving her time to
change her mind, and she sent a message to us as we stood on the doorstep
to say that she forbade me to use my Letters of State against anyone as
powerful as M. de Luxembourg. Nevertheless I sent back the servant and
hurried into the coach after the two dukes, who were infinitely relieved to
see the Letters still in my hand.

I must explain the delay, for it really was a most unfortunate incident.

---

[1] Letters of State were given to ambassadors, army officers, and all who were obliged to be
absent on the King's service. They suspended all lawsuits whilst such persons were absent, and
could be renewed after six months if the absence continued.

M. de Richelieu happened to have had a *lavement* that morning, and had gone straight from the Place Royale to Riparfond's office without relieving himself, from thence to the premier président, then back to Riparfonds, had sat through our long discussion, and come after me, all in that condition. The moment he arrived at our house he asked in a great hurry to go to my closet, where he left an action of such colossal proportions that the bowl could scarcely contain it; and that was when my mother had the chance to think again.[1] To hazard all those displacements while holding a *lavement* required a faith which had to be seen to be believed.

I can hardly describe my delight at returning to the company, nor the applause and embraces with which they received me. The vexation had been great, and the lawyers had been as much distressed as we. Thus everyone competed to compliment and congratulate me, and I must admit to feeling much flattered. They decided that on the following day (which was the one before the judgment) I should go at ten in the evening with my secretary and solicitor, serve my letters on M. de Luxembourg, and notify his lawyer that I was on my way to Longnes eight leagues from Paris) to join my regiment. This was to offer some pretext for using the Letters of State. Later, however, I remembered that Monsieur was giving a grand ball for Monseigneur that night, at the Palais Royal, and that it opened with a *branle* for which I had promised to partner the Duchesse de La Ferté's daughter, who would never have forgiven me; and she was a great scold, without any regard for people's feelings. I therefore explained my difficulty to M. de La Trémoïlle, who promised to convince the other dukes that I could not draw such fury on myself. No one minded except M. de La Rochefoucauld, but I appeased him by leaving very early, and he undertook to explain my departure to the King.

When all was over my friends sent to fetch me from Longnes, where my exile had lasted only six days. I found everything in an uproar. M. de Luxembourg had lost all self-control, and the dukes opposing him were equally unrestrained. The Court and Paris had taken sides; friends were quarrelling; no one seemed able to stay calm or neutral. People shot questions at me regarding my Letters of State, but I had right and justice on my side, and a strong, well-organized party to support me, including some dukes whose favour with the King was greater than that of M. de Luxembourg. Moreover, I had taken certain steps to legalize my position, and I let this be known, since I realized that M. de Luxembourg and his friends might set upon me as the weakest of his enemies and the one who had dealt him the final blow. A few days later I noticed that he was not even returning my salutes. I drew everyone's attention to this and ceased bowing to him. At his age and situation he was the worst sufferer and presented a somewhat foolish appearance in the drawing-rooms of Versailles.

---

[1] M. de Richelieu was prone to find himself in such difficulties.

Our main object was now achieved, for above all we had been playing for time, and, by virtue of my Letters of State, the case was postponed until the following year.[1]

The regiment I had purchased[2] was quartered in the Paris region and thus assigned to Flanders, where I had no wish to be after all that had passed with M. de Luxembourg. On the advice of M. de Beauvilliers I wrote out my reasons for the King, but very briefly, and gave him my letter as he was going to his study after his *lever*, on the morning of a day's excursion to Compiègne and Chantilly to review his troops. I followed him to mass, and thence to his coach. He put one foot on the step, stepped back again and, turning to me, said: 'Monsieur, I have read your letter; I shall not forget.' And, indeed, very shortly afterwards I learned that I had been exchanged with the Chevalier de Sully, who was to go to Flanders in my place, and I to Germany in his. I was doubly pleased at having escaped from M. de Luxembourg, and at the King's treating me with so much kindness, more especially so when I learned that the Maréchal was greatly displeased.

I went therefore to Soissons to review my assembled regiment, having told the King beforehand, who spoke to me for a long time in his study, recommending me to be very strict, which is why I did more work in that review than I should have done without his advice. I had already called on the Maréchal de Lorges and the Maréchal de Joyeuse, and they had returned my visits. I was on good terms with the latter and admired M. de Lorges's integrity. In short I was as happy to be going to war with their army as I should have been wretched under the Maréchal de Luxembourg. We finally left for Strasbourg, where I was surprised by the magnificence of the city and the number and size of the fortifications.

Our German campaign passed off very quietly; we spent forty days encamped in great comfort at Gau Bockleheim in perfect weather, although perhaps rather on the cold side. It was during my free time at this camp that I began these memoirs in earnest, inspired thereto by my pleasure in reading those of the Maréchal Bassompierre, who first gave me the idea that I also should write down the events I might witness in my own times.

When we returned home we found that the Bishop of Noyon had been creating a diversion, all the more distressing for him because he was most dreadfully mocked by the whole of Society. You have already seen the kind of man he was. Even the King was amused by the vanity that made him take everything as a personal compliment; for, indeed, you might fill a book with stories of his conceit. It happened at this time that a place became vacant in the Academy and that the King desired it should be

---

[1] The case dragged on for nearly two years, and the Maréchal de Luxembourg, having so nearly won it, died in 1695, still only 18th duke.

[2] Saint-Simon had purchased for twenty-six thousand livres a newly-formed regiment of carabineers ('the cavalry-grenadiers') at the end of the previous campaign.

given to M. de Noyon, going so far as to let his wishes be known to the Academicians. Such a thing had never occurred before and M. de Noyon, who prided himself on his learning, was enchanted, not perceiving that the King merely looked for entertainment. You may well suppose that he gained every vote, without having to canvass for them. What is more, the King hinted to M. le Prince and all the best people that he would like them to attend the inauguration. Thus M. de Noyon became the King's first nominee to the Academy, without having dreamed of it, and the first for whose reception the King troubled to send invitations.

At that time the Director of the Academy was the Abbé de Caumartin[1] with the duty of replying to the bishop's inaugural speech. He well knew his vanity and his peculiarly florid style. He was young, brilliant, witty and, moreover, related to Pontchartrain, the Controller General of Finances. That kinship made him bold. Reckoning on Society's approval and the minister's support, he conceived the idea of diverting the public at M. de Noyon's expense. Accordingly he composed a long address based as closely as possible on the bishop's usual style, compacted of blatant self-praise and high-flown similes. The whole pompous rigmarole was one long satire, mocking and exposing M. de Noyon's vanity.

Fearing that he had exceeded all bounds of decorum, the Abbé for safety's sake took his work to M. de Noyon for correction, like a schoolboy to his master. He said that he wished to omit no just praise, nor say anything displeasing. The bishop, enchanted by such deference, read and re-read the speech. On the whole he was satisfied, but he could not refrain from improving here and there and adding a few more lines in self-praise. The Abbé was thankful enough to have his manuscript returned, but, when he saw the additions and corrections in M. de Noyon's own hand, he could scarcely credit his success, or the evidence of an approval that would save him in case of complaint.

The day of the reception came. The hall was overflowing with all the most eminent members of the Court and Society, for all had come to please the King as well as in search of amusement. M. de Noyon appeared, bowing right and left, followed by a numerous train and observing with visible pride the large and distinguished audience. Then, complacent as usual, he delivered himself of a speech so pompous, so flowery, that the company could scarcely contain themselves. The Abbé de Caumartin's reply, spoken modestly and slowly, only lightly stressing the more absurd and characteristic passages, would have aroused all his hearers, even had their malice not held them riveted, but as he continued his brilliance and wit surpassed all their expectations, although his daring plot had been known beforehand. The great outburst of applause when he finished completely intoxicated M. de Noyon, who had taken this praise as his due,

---

[1] Jean Lefèvre de Caumartin (1668-1733). Became Bishop of Vannes, later of Blois under the Regency.

and returned home hugely delighted with the Abbé, the audience, and the reception, and quite unaware of the true situation.

You may imagine the scandal, and what a figure of fun M. de Noyon presented as he discoursed in all the drawing-rooms of Paris on his successful speech, the Abbé Caumartin's reply, the general appreciation of him, and the King's pleasure. Unfortunately he took it into his head to crow to the Archbishop of Paris,[1] who disliked him intensely and had an ancient grudge to avenge. The incident had happened before the archbishop was made a duke, when the Court was still at Saint-Germain, where, unlike Versailles, there are no inner courtyards. M. de Noyon, entering in his coach, chanced to meet M. de Paris[2] walking. He had called him by name and the latter had approached supposing that he meant to get down and walk with him. No such thing! M. de Noyon leaned from the carriage, seized him by the arm and, chatting and complimenting in a most infuriating manner, had led him as on a leash to the foot of the great staircase. Still talking, he had gone upstairs, so totally unaware of giving any offence that M. de Paris dared not make a scene, though he remained none the less resentful.

You will thus realize what an admirable revenge that inauguration offered to M. de Paris. Yet he felt little satisfaction whilst M. de Noyon was so puffed up with pride. He therefore took advantage of the bishop's visit to undeceive him, hinting at what, as a fellow-churchman and well-wisher, he did not like to say frankly. He had to spend a considerable time skirting the subject before making himself understood by so vain a man, so far from imagining that anyone could mock him. M. de Noyon argued long before giving in, but eventually was forced to believe and consented, for the honour of the Academy, to take the advice of his friend the Père La Chaise. He rushed off immediately, confiding all and begging so piteously to know the truth that the good confessor scarcely knew whether to leave him a prey to ridicule or to risk injuring the Abbé de Caumartin. Finally he concluded that he must not deceive one who had trusted him, and with all possible gentleness told him the truth. The Bishop of Noyon's delight turned to violent rage, and in that state of mind he went straight to Versailles to lodge a bitter complaint against the Abbé de Caumartin.

The King had certainly hoped for a little mild entertainment, but he was a man who liked order and moderation in all things, and when he heard what had passed he was not amused. Moreover, he felt all the more annoyed because he had innocently caused a public scandal, and although M. de Noyon's follies diverted him, he felt some compassion. He therefore sent for Pontchartrain and ordered him to give his cousin a severe

[1] François Harlay de Champvallon (1625-1695).

[2] As a count and peer as well as a bishop M. de Noyon had the right to drive into the courtyard and up to the front door of royal residences; the archbishop, not being a peer, always had to get out and walk from the entrance-gates. Bishops were generally referred to as Monsieur (e.g. Monsieur de Noyon), but M. de Paris was also the public executioner.

reprimand with a *lettre de cachet*, commanding him to return to his abbey in Brittany, there to meditate until he had learned to make mocking speeches with better discretion. The first part of this order Pontchartrain immediately executed; the rest he postponed until the following day, when he pleaded the Abbé's youth, the huge temptation to mock the bishop's vanity, and the additions put into the speech by the bishop himself. This last excuse, offered humorously by so pleasant a minister, served to stop the *lettre de cachet*, but not the King's wrath. Pontchartrain, however, had expected no better and he contented himself with emphasizing the Abbé's great distress and his desire to ask M. de Noyon's forgiveness. He did indeed make the attempt, but was met by a flat refusal, for, after an outburst against the entire Caumartin family, the outraged bishop had retired to his diocese and remained there a very long time.

I must finish the story. Shortly after M. de Noyon returned to Paris, he fell desperately ill and received the last sacrament, but, before doing so, he sent for the Abbé de Caumartin, embraced him, put a fine diamond ring on his finger, and asked him to keep it with his love. After he had recovered he did everything possible to bring about a reconciliation with the King and continued to work to that end until his death. But Caumartin's prank had ruined him irretrievably and M. de Noyon gained nothing by his kindness except good in the sight of Heaven and the respect of Society.

M. de Luxembourg did not long survive his daughter's splendid marriage.[1] At the age of seventy-seven he had been living the life of a twenty-five-year-old and thought himself no older. He made up by extravagant spending for the amorous adventures no longer allowed him, and his private life with his son,[2] M. le Prince de Conti and Albergotti[3] consisted almost entirely in such low pleasures as private parties in the company of their whores. The whole burden of marches, orders, victualling, etc. in every campaign had devolved upon Puységur,[4] who even drafted his plans for him. But in his final calculations no one was ever more conscientious than M. de Luxembourg; no one more brilliant, prudent and far-sighted in the face of the enemy or in battle. He had daring and confidence, and at the same time a cool-headedness that allowed him to observe and foresee in the midst of the fiercest cannonade, in dangerously critical moments. That was when he was truly great.

---

[1] He had married his daughter to 'an old obscure bastard of the last of the Comtes de Soissons', and was thus connected with the royal family through Louis I de Bourbon, ancestor of the Condé and Soissons branches of the Bourbon family. Saint-Simon says of the couple, 'He was a stupid man who had never seen service and with no friends that anyone had ever heard of'. She was 'the very reverse of young, lovely, and amusing'.

[2] Charles François de Montmorency, later Duc de Luxembourg (1662–1726), also called the Prince de Tingry.

[3] (1654–1717). A Florentine general serving with the French army of Flanders.

[4] Jacques François de Chastenet, Marquis de Puységur (1655–1743).

At all other times he was idleness itself; no exercise, except where absolutely necessary; gambling; conversing with intimates; every night a
small supper party, nearly always with the same company, and, if they
happened to be near a town, an agreeable mingling of the sexes. At such
moments he was unapproachable. It was Puységur who had to give the
orders if anything urgent occurred. Such was the army life of that great
general, and it was the same in Paris, where the Court and Society occupied his days, and his pleasures the nights. In the end his constitution and
deformity defeated him. He fell ill at Versailles of double-pneumonia,
which Fagon viewed gravely from the first. All the most distinguished
people laid siege to his house; the Princes of the Blood never quitted it,
and Monsieur visited several times. After Fagon had given him up,
Caretti,[1] the Italian quack, who had had many successes, took up his
case and gave him some relief, but hope lasted only a few hours. The King
sent sometimes to inquire, but more out of courtesy than affection, for,
as I have said, he did not like him; but because of his glorious campaigns
the difficulty of replacing him became a tremendous anxiety.

When he grew worse, Père Bourdaloue,[2] the famous Jesuit, took complete charge. It then appeared urgent to reconcile him with the two
MM. de Vendôme, who, jealous of his friendship with M. le Prince de
Conti, had quarrelled with him and taken refuge in the army in Italy.
Roquelaure,[3] friend of all, and no one's confidant, succeeded in bringing
them to his bedside, where everything passed off well, with much good
will and few words. He then received the Sacraments, and testified to his
faith and steadfast trust in God. He died on the morning of 4 January,
1695, on the fifth day of his illness, mourned by many, although as an individual none had esteemed him precious and precious few had loved.

M. de Luxembourg on his deathbed saw none of the dukes whom he
had attacked; none of them would be disturbed for him. I myself did not
call nor send a single time to inquire, even although I was at Versailles,
and I must admit to feeling that I had been delivered of an enemy. People
maliciously tried to make me comment on his death, but I answered that
I had too much faith in the King's ability to find a replacement, and too
high an opinion of the other generals and armies to despair at the loss of a
marshal whom I personally had little reason to regret. I noticed that their
questioning soon dried up.

The Maréchal de Villeroy took his post as captain of the bodyguard,
and succeeded him in command of the Flanders army. This was what
everyone had expected. Villeroy was brought up with the King and was

---

[1] The Marchese (self-styled) del Caretto, known as 'Caretto the Healer'.
[2] Louis Bourdaloue (1632–1704). Noted for his severe sermons on morals. In earlier days he
once preached at Louis XIV in the chapel of Versailles, eliciting the indignant reproach, '*Mon
Père, vous m'avez fait mécontent de MOI-MÊME!*' Of Luxembourg he said that although he was
glad not to have lived like him, he hoped to die as well.
[3] Antoine Gaston, Duc de Roquelaure (1656–1738).

always on good terms with him, a trusted friend in private and with his mistresses. He and his father, the King's governor in times past, were the most servile and accomplished courtiers. Once or twice he had been out of favour, but the King's genuine liking, revived by cringing and compromise, always retrieved him.

CHAPTER V

1695

Death of the Princess of Orange – My Marriage – Marriage of my sister-in-law to the Duc de Lauzun – Death of my aunt the Marquise de Saint-Simon – Death of La Fontaine and Mignard – Illness of the Maréchal de Lorges – Vaudémont escapes from dire peril – The King breaks his cane on a valet – The Maréchal de Lorges has an apoplectic seizure

FROM the end of summer until the beginning of winter we made several attempts to negotiate a peace, on what grounds I do not know. It served only to swell our enemies' pride, and they desired it less in proportion to our eagerness, in which they perceived a marked contrast to our haughtiness at the end of all other wars. M. de Harlay,[1] State counsellor and the Chancellor's[2] nephew, an excessively thin and pale man, with good sense and but little else, went to Maestricht to sound the Dutch, who had the impudence to tell him that they supposed him to be a fair sample of the condition to which all Frenchmen were reduced. To this he answered pleasantly enough that if they would allow him to send for his wife they would gain a contrary impression; and, indeed, she was monstrously fat and with a very high colour.

Two events took place abroad following close upon one another. The first, at the end of January, was the death in London of the Princess of Orange. No notice was taken at the Court, for the King of England begged King Louis not to wear mourning, and MM. de Bouillon and de Duras were forbidden to do so as were other kinsmen of the Prince of Orange. People obeyed and said nothing, but such rancour was thought to be small-minded. There was some hope of a change in England, but not for long. It was soon observed that the prince seemed more widely accepted, more powerful, and better established than ever before. The princess had been deeply in love with him; was just as eager as he to seize the throne, and equally pleased to find herself queen in place of her father and his other children. She was sincerely mourned, and the Prince of Orange who had loved and trusted her, and always treated her with marked deference, was ill for several days after her death.

The other event was tragic indeed. By the terms of the English

---

[1] Not the Premier Président.

[2] In 1695 and until 1699 'The Chancellor' refers to Louis Boucherat (1616–1699), Chancellor of France.

revolution the Duke of Hanover,[1] being next in the protestant line, was due to ascend the throne after the Prince and Princess of Orange and the Princess of Denmark.[2] He was the eldest son of the Electress Sophia,[3] daughter of that Elector Palatine who lost his title and lands when he crowned himself King of Bohemia, and of a daughter[4] of James I of England. He had married his first cousin,[5] daughter of the Duke of Bruns-wick-Zell. She was extremely beautiful and for some years they lived to-gether happily, until the young and extraordinarily handsome Count von Königsmarck[6] arrived at their Court and eclipsed him. The Duke was jealous, had them spied upon, and made sure of what for the remainder of his life he regretted having known; but that came later. At that time fury seized him. He had the Count arrested and flung, that instant, into a fiery furnace. He then forthwith returned his wife to her father, who shut her up in one of his castles, closely guarded by her husband's henchmen. Soon afterwards he applied to the Consistory court to have his marriage annulled. Strangely enough it was so pronounced, which left him free to take a new wife, whereas the duchess remained bound to him and for-bidden to remarry. Their children, however, were declared legitimate; but the Duke of Hanover never altogether convinced himself of that.[7]

All that winter my mother had been busy trying to make a good match for me; she was distressed at having been unable to do so in the preceding year. I was an only son, with rank and establishments that made people think me highly eligible. There had even been some talk of Mlle d'Ar-magnac[8] amongst others, but it had all been very vague. For some time past the Duchess of Bracciano[9] had been living in Paris, separated from Rome and her husband. She lodged very near to us; was a friend of my mother, and saw her constantly. I fell quite under the spell of her charms and graces and was always at her house, for she gave me a kind welcome. Living with her were her two nieces, Mlle de Cosnac and Mlle de Royan, a Trémoïlle like herself. Both were orphans and heiresses. Mme de

---

[1] At that date, 1695, Ernest Augustus of Brunswick-Lüneburg (1629–1698) was Duke of Hanover. Saint-Simon here speaks of his son George Louis (1660–1727). Duke of Hanover 1698. George I of England 1714.

[2] Anne (1664–1714), younger daughter of James II by Anne Hyde. Married Prince George of Denmark 1683. Queen of England 1702.

[3] Electress of Hanover (1630–1714), to whom Madame wrote her letters.

[4] Elizabeth Stuart (1596–1662).

[5] Sophia Dorothea (1666–1726), married George Louis Duke and Elector of Hanover 1682.

[6] Count Philip von Königsmarck (1665–1694). The exact manner of his death is not certain, but he was somehow assassinated.

[7] It would appear from their letters that the duchess's affair with Königsmarck took place after the birth of George II.

[8] A Lorraine princess. One wonders whether Saint-Simon's views would have been the same had he married into that detested family.

[9] Marie Anne de La Trémoïlle (1642–1722). Married (1) the Prince de Chalais (widowed 1670), (2) Flavio Orsini, Duke of Bracciano, 1675. After his death in 1698 she called herself Princess Orsini (Fr. Princesse des Ursins, as she is called in the Memoirs).

Bracciano greatly desired to give me Mlle de Royan, and often mentioned establishments to us, hoping for some encouraging remarks on which to build. It would have been a rich and a great alliance, but I, being alone, needed a father-in-law and a family to protect me.

Phélypeaux, Pontchartrain's only son, had the reversion of his father's office. Smallpox had already removed one of his eyes, good fortune now totally blinded him so that not even a Trémoïlle heiress appeared to him beyond his range. He had been sniffing around this one for some time, and his father had been lavishing attentions on her aunt with the same end in view; but that lady, being clever, enjoyed his favours and secretly laughed at the reason for them. Pontchartrain had been an intimate friend of my father and much wished me to be the friend of his son, who made many advances. We saw one another constantly. He feared only me as a rival for the hand of Mlle Royan and tried his best to discover my opinion of her. I did not in the least mind his curiosity, still less his intentions, but I answered him in the vaguest terms.

My marriage was none the less fast approaching, for already in the preceding year the eldest daughter of the Maréchal de Lorges had been mentioned to us. The idea had been dismissed almost at once, but now both sides hoped for a renewal. The Maréchal, without wealth of his own, and whose first reward had been the bâton of a Maréchal de France, had married the daughter of Frémont, keeper of the King's jewels, who had amassed an immense fortune under Louvois and was considered to be the shrewdest banker of them all. Very soon after his marriage he was appointed captain of the bodyguard, a post left vacant by the death of the Maréchal de Rochefort. In the service he had earned a great reputation for honour, courage, and ability, and had successfully commanded the King's armies.

The disposition of the Maréchal de Lorges, so highly principled, frank and upright, was immensely pleasing to me; I had had opportunities of observing him closely during the campaign. The love and respect felt for him throughout the entire army, his high reputation at the Court, his noble birth and splendid style of living, the august alliances that offset the inferior marriage, which he, first of all his line, had been forced to contract, all made me most eager for the match. Moreover, his elder brother[1] was also highly esteemed and by some strange coincidence held similar rank, honours, and establishments. Most of all, the strong affection that bound together all that numerous family, and the Maréchal's good nature and sincerity, so rare, so real in him, was a great attraction. I hoped to find in them everything that I lacked to protect and promote my interests, and to enable me to live an agreeable life amidst noble kinsmen and a loving family.

In the irreproachable virtue of the Maréchal's wife, and the skill with

[1] The Maréchal-duc de Duras (1626-1704). They were nephews of Turenne.

which she had reconciled him with M. de Louvois and at the same time secured for him a dukedom, I found everything that I could wish for training a young wife whom I desired to live at the Court, where her mother was universally praised and respected. Elegant, wise, and full of dignity, she kept open house to the highest Society, never mixing, conducting herself with perfect modesty, yet ever conscious of the deference due to her husband's rank. By such behaviour she had caused her low birth to be forgotten by the Maréchal's family, the Court, and Society in general. It was by her character that she had won such general esteem. At the same time, all that she cared for was her husband, who gave her his absolute confidence, and lived with her and with her relatives on terms of mutual respect and affection that did him infinite credit.

They had an only son, a boy of twelve whom they loved to distraction, and five daughters. The two elder had spent their childhood at the Benedictine convent of Conflans, and for the past three years had lived with their grandmother Mme Frémont, whose house communicated with theirs. The eldest girl was seventeen, the second sixteen, and neither was allowed out of their grandmother's sight, for she was a woman of great good sense and perfect virtue, and in her youth had been very handsome; some traces of former beauty still remained to her. She was most devout, active in good works, and entirely devoted to the upbringing of her granddaughters; her husband, for many years past afflicted with paralysis and other ailments, had retained a clear mind and was capable of managing his own affairs. The Maréchale de Lorges lived amongst them all, busy with all manner of duties and charities, and they dearly loved and esteemed her.

Mme Frémont secretly preferred Mlle de Lorges, whereas the Maréchale doted on her sister Mlle de Quintin; indeed, had all depended on the mother's wishes, the eldest child would have been sent to a convent so as to further her sister's chances of a good match. Mlle de Quintin had dark hair and lovely eyes, whereas Mlle de Lorges was fair, with a perfect figure and complexion. Her expression was most pleasing; she was modest, yet noble in her bearing, and had, I thought, a graciousness that came from a naturally sweet and good disposition. When first I saw her I liked her infinitely the better of the two; there was no comparison for me; and I dared to hope that she would make my life's happiness, as she has done, solely and absolutely. Since she is my wife I shall say no more, except that she has proved far above all that was promised me, and beyond my fondest hopes.

My mother and I were given the necessary details by a certain Mme Damond, Mme Frémont's sister-in-law, a fine handsome woman, on excellent terms with them all and more used to the ways of good Society than is usual with people of such inferior birth. She negotiated the contract, and ably but honestly steered the affair to a successful conclusion. Finally, all the obstacles were surmounted for a consideration of four hundred thousand livres, cash down without concessions, and our living expenses for an indefinite period at the Court and with the army.

When all the arrangements were complete the Maréchal de Lorges spoke to the King on my behalf also, so as to avoid gossip. The King graciously said that he could not have done better, and went on to speak very kindly of me; which the Maréchal enjoyed telling me later.

Thus it came about that on the Thursday before Palm Sunday we signed the articles at the Hôtel de Lorges[1] and took the marriage-contract to the King. I had begun to visit every evening when suddenly the engagement was broken off over a misunderstanding which each side interpreted differently. Fortunately, however, just as deadlock was reached with everyone pulling in different directions, d'Auneuil, the Maréchal's brother and a maître des requêtes, came from the Provinces where he was on circuit and at his own expense removed the obstacle. I owe him that tribute as well as my eternal gratitude. God often employs the most unlikely instruments to carry out His will. The entire enterprise thus almost miscarried, but at last our marriage was celebrated at the Hôtel de Lorges on 8 April, a day which I count, with good reason, as the happiest day of my life. My mother behaved to me like a perfect mother. We arrived together at the Hôtel de Lorges at seven in the evening on the Thursday before Low Sunday. We signed the contract, and there was a great banquet for the nearest relatives on both sides. At midnight the Curé of Saint-Roch said mass and we were married in the private chapel. On the previous evening my mother had sent forty thousand livres' worth of jewels to Mlle de Lorges, and I a present of six hundred louis and the elegant trifles usual on such occasions.

We slept that night in the best bedroom of the Hôtel de Lorges. On the following day M. d'Auneuil, who lodged across the way, gave us a great dinner, after which the bride received visits in bed at the Hôtel de Lorges. All the best people called, from curiosity as well as civility, and one of the first to arrive was the Duchess of Bracciano and her two nieces. My mother was still in half-mourning with her apartments draped in grey and black, which was why we had chosen to receive company at the Hôtel de Lorges. We devoted one day to receiving visits and on the following went to Versailles. That same evening the King desired the bride to be presented to him in Mme de Maintenon's room, which my mother and hers accordingly did. On the way there the King had joked with me, and he spoke most graciously to them, paying them compliments and treating them with marked distinction. Thence they went to his supper, where the new duchess was given her *tabouret*. The King said as he sat down to table, 'Pray, Madame, be seated.' He looked up as his napkin was being unfolded and, seeing all the duchesses and princesses still standing, half-rose from his chair and addressing Mme de Saint-Simon said, 'Madame, I

[1] In the Rue Neuve-Saint-Augustin.

have already desired you to sit,' whereupon all those who had the privilege sat down, Mme de Saint-Simon between my mother and hers, who came after her in the order of precedence. Next day the entire Court visited her in bed in the apartments of the Duchesse d'Arpajon, which were more convenient being on the ground floor. The Maréchale de Lorges and I were present only for the visit of the royal family. On the day after we went to Saint-Germain and on to Paris, where I gave a great dinner at my house for all the wedding guests. Next day I gave a private supper for such as remained of my father's friends, whom I had informed of my marriage before the news was made public and whom I took great pains to cultivate as long as they lived.

It was not long before Mlle de Quintin also was married. M. de Lauzun[1] had seen her in her sister's bed with several other marriageable young ladies. She was fifteen and he sixty-three so that there was a terrible disparity between their ages, but his whole life until then had been a romance that, in his opinion, was not yet over, and he still had the ambitions and hopes of a young man. Since his return to the Court[2] and the enjoyment of his old privileges, he had done everything imaginable to regain the King's confidence, but without success. He believed that by marrying the daughter of an army commander he might act as go-between twixt him and the King, and, from discussing the affairs of the army of the Rhine, advance to succeeding his father-in-law as captain of the bodyguard, a post which he deeply regretted having lost.

With this in mind he had broached the subject to the Maréchale de Lorges, but she, knowing his reputation, cared too much for her daughter to entertain a marriage so unlikely to make her happy. M. de Lauzun became the more ardent, offered to take her without dowry, and had it suggested on those terms to Mme Frémont and the Maréchal, by whom it was discussed, agreed, and determined on for that all-important reason and much to her mother's dismay. She, however, at last gave her consent, seeing no other way of making her second daughter a duchess and the elder's equal, something on which she had set her heart. As for Mlle de Quintin, she feared even more having to accept Phélypeaux for a suitor and therefore joyfully took the Duc de Lauzun with his noble name, his rank, and his riches. In her inexperience she concluded that the difference in their ages meant, at most, two or three years of constraint, after which she might be free, wealthy, and a great lady. She would never otherwise have agreed, as she often admitted later.

That affair was arranged and concluded with the utmost secrecy. When the Maréchal de Lorges spoke to the King regarding it, the latter exclaimed, 'You are a rash man to take M. de Lauzun into your family. I

[1] The Lauzun of *La Grande Mademoiselle*. He died aged 91 in 1723.
[2] He had been imprisoned for nine years in the fortress of Pignerol because of his affair with Mlle de Montpensier (*La Grande Mademoiselle*), the King's cousin.

hope you may not regret it. Your private affairs are your business, but I only permit this marriage on condition that you never speak to him of mine.' On the day the news was made public M. de Lorges sent for me very early and explained his motives, the chief of them being that he had had nothing to pay and that M. de Lauzun was content to receive four hundred thousand livres after the death of M. Frémont. When we took the contract for the King's signature he teased M. de Lauzun and laughed most heartily, whereat Lauzun replied that he was only too glad to marry because for the first time since his return the King had joked with him. The wedding was celebrated so soon afterwards that there was no time to buy new coats. M. de Lauzun's presents to his bride were rich stuffs, jewels, and trifles, but no money. Only seven or eight persons were present at the wedding, which took place at midnight at the Hôtel de Lorges. The bridegroom insisted on undressing in private with his valets, and did not enter his wife's bedroom until everyone was gone, and she in bed with the curtains drawn.

No one approved of the match, nor could understand the father or the bridegroom, for the pretext of the dowry was not believed. Knowing M. de Lauzun's nature, it was generally assumed that there would be a rupture before long. Returning to Paris, we saw all the marriageable young ladies of quality driving on the Cours la Reine, and that sight somewhat comforted Mme la Maréchale de Lorges, as she passed by in her coach with the two daughters whom she had established so early in life.

A few days later, when the King was taking the air in his wheelchair in the Versailles gardens,[1] he questioned me closely regarding the ages and circumstances of M. de Lorges's children, going into details in a way that surprised me on the occupations and appearance of the daughters, asking whether they were liked, and whether none of them wished to take the vow. He then joked about the marriage of M. de Lauzun, and about mine; saying despite the gravity that never deserted him that he had heard from the Maréchal of my having acquitted myself well, but that he expected Mme de Lorges knew everything.

The celebrations were scarcely over before the Marquise de Saint-Simon died at the age of ninety-one. She was the widow of my father's elder brother, had inherited his wealth, and left us all her debts, because there were no children. A woman of spirit, proud, and resentful, she had never forgiven my father for marrying a second time, and did her best to estrange him from his brother. Our mourning was therefore free from grief. Her niece the Duchesse d'Uzès died at about the same time.

The deaths of two famous men caused more stir than those of these noble dames; de La Fontaine, who wrote the celebrated fables, yet was so boring in conversation, and Mignard, the illustrious painter. The latter

---

[1] The King had been using a wheelchair since his fistula-operation of 1686.

had an extraordinarily beautiful daughter whom he used for preference as his model. It is she whom we see in many of the splendid historical pictures in the great gallery and state drawing-rooms of Versailles, which paintings played no small part in turning all Europe against the King's person rather than against his kingdom.[1]

The troops being ready for service, the armies were assigned the same commanders as in the previous year, excepting in Flanders, where M. de Luxembourg was succeeded by the Maréchal de Villeroy, with M. le Duc de Chartres as general of cavalry, the two princes of the blood and M. du Maine, amongst others, as lieutenants-general, and the Comte de Toulouse serving at the head of his regiment.

Everyone now left for the frontiers. The army of the Rhine, in which I served under the command of the Maréchal de Lorges, made no delay in crossing that river, but scarcely had we confronted Prince Louis of Baden than, on 20 June, M. de Lorges fell grievously ill, encamped at Unter-Neisheim, with his right wing resting on Bruchsal,[2] and the enemy entrenched before Eppingen. Forage was very scarce since this was not to have been a permanent camp, and there was little to be found in the neighbourhood. The troops, usually so grasping, minded less for themselves than for their general. All the warrant-officers were told to ask urgently for a longer stay in camp; no army has ever shown more interest in the welfare of its commander, nor greater love for him personally. He was, in truth, in extremis, so much so that the doctors sent from Strasbourg despaired of him, whereupon I took it upon myself to prescribe English drops.[3] He was given a hundred and thirty in three doses. What they gave him in broth had no effect, the others, taken in Spanish wine, were completely successful. It is amazing that a spirituous remedy containing nothing purgative should have caused such strong motions in those he had already swallowed, for he had been taking the drops without result for the past twenty-four hours. The effect was gentle, but prodigious from the lower intestines, consciousness was regained, and there was a gradual outbreak of the purples. It was this eruption that saved him, but that was not the end of his illness.

In the meantime the army suffered cruelly. The Maréchal de Joyeuse, who had taken over the command, explained the situation to me and to M. de Lorges's nephews, saying that no matter what might ensue he would make no move without our consent. He treated us, like the great gentleman he was, with every possible care and consideration. When the troops learned that a decision had to be taken they proclaimed unanimously through the mouths of their officers that any amount of hardship

[1] 'I hear that he stinks alive, and his cankers will stink worse when he is dead, and so will his memory to all eternity.' Edward Verney (1685).

[2] On the River Saalbach, near Philippsburg.

[3] Black drops: opium, vinegar, and sugar in liquid form.

was preferable to endangering their general's life in the slightest degree, and they resisted all suggestions of moving camp.

Prince Louis of Baden sent trumpeters with offers of medicines and remedies of all kinds, a promise of complete safety for the maréchal, supplies of food and forage for himself and an escort should the army decide to leave him, with safe conduct if he wished to rejoin them later or went to any other place with his retinue. Prince Louis received the thanks which he deserved for his kind offers, but no one desired to take advantage of them.

M. de Lorges's health showed signs of recovery and the soldiers their joy, with bonfires everywhere, tables set up in all the tents, and those salvoes that can never be prevented. Never before nor since has a commander received such an universal testimony of affection. Meanwhile Mme la Maréchale de Lorges arrived first at Strasbourg, then at Landau, in one of M. de Barbezieux's chaises with his coachmen reinforcing hers so as to ensure all possible speed. The King sent La Cour, captain of the Maréchal's guard, with her, and questioned him for more than an hour at Marly regarding M. de Lorges's health, consulting Fagon personally, and appearing deeply distressed by this great mishap. At last it became possible to move the invalid to Philippsburg, where Mme la Maréchale de Lorges came to meet him from Landau; you may imagine their joy in being reunited. I had already gone ahead so as to be with her at Landau. The flower of the army escorted him to Philippsburg, together with most of the generals. On the day after, M. le Maréchal de Lorges was able to travel to Landau between sheets in a coach, followed by all those distinguished persons who had gone with him to Philippsburg. He established himself at the governor's residence, whilst I put up with Verpel, the engineer, in a very fine house close by. Next day everyone left to rejoin the army.

In Flanders interesting events had taken place. The Prince of Orange after many false marches to disguise his real intentions had suddenly turned on Namur and invested it during the early days of July. He was promptly joined by the Elector of Hanover with a large reinforcement, leaving the remainder of the Allied armies under the command of M. de Vaudémont. Such a move had been expected by the Maréchal de Boufflers, who had accordingly seen to it that the fortress was abundantly supplied. In fact, the whole enterprise had at first seemed foolhardy to our Court, from whence I received letters to the effect that everyone rejoiced at an enterprise so sure to ruin their army and without any chance of success. I myself thought differently, for I was persuaded that a man so able as the Prince of Orange would never lay an important siege without knowing well how to disengage, so far as human prudence could ensure.

Meanwhile, the Maréchal de Villeroy was pressing M. de Vaudémont as closely as could be, and the latter, by far the weaker, was making every endeavour to escape him. Both commanders believed that the outcome of the campaign was in their hands. Vaudémont was convinced that success or failure at Namur depended upon the security of his army; Villeroy that victory would seal the fate of the Low Countries, bring peace with glory, and all the personal triumphs that would be its accompaniment. Making the most careful preparations imaginable, he seized three occupied castles on the River Mandel, containing five hundred enemy troops, and thus managed to come so close to M. de Vaudémont on the night of 13 July that there seemed no possibility of the latter escaping him on the following day. He then sent a courier to the King.

At dawn on the 14th everything was ready. M. le Duc commanded on the right, M. du Maine on the left, M. le Prince de Conti had the infantry, M. le Duc de Chartres the cavalry. It was for the left wing to engage first because it was nearest the enemy. Vaudémont, taken unawares, had not dared to retreat during the night with the enemy so close, and so far superior in numbers and quality, for all his best troops were at the siege. None the less, having no cover of any kind, he could not risk standing his ground and the only thing that remained for him was to march by day, taking all precautions against an attack, with the hope of reaching the wooded country that lay a good three leagues ahead of him.

At the first ray of light the Maréchal de Villeroy gave orders for M. du Maine to attack and open the battle. His intention was to bring up all his forces in support, but for that he needed time and relied on the left wing to hold the enemy and delay his march. When nothing resulted from his orders he grew impatient and sent again five or six times to M. du Maine. He, however, first wished to reconnoitre, then to confess, and then to reorganize his wing, although the men had been in battle order for some hours past and were eager to fight. Amidst all these delays Vaudémont was marching away with all the speed that prudence allowed. The generals of the left fumed with rage. Montrevel, the senior lieutenant-general, could not contain himself and remonstrated with M. du Maine, reminding him of the Maréchal de Villeroy's repeated orders, the certainty of victory, the effect upon his reputation and the fate of Namur, the glorious results of a success there, and the impossibility for the enemy to defend the Low Countries if the only army capable of protecting them were to be defeated. He seized the duke's hand, he wept; his arguments were neither denied nor refused, but all were useless. M. du Maine stammered and procrastinated, and hesitated for so long that the chance was missed and M. de Vaudémont was permitted to escape from the most perilous situation in which any army could have found itself. He would, indeed, have been utterly destroyed had we, who could see and number his every man, made the slightest effort to attack him.

The entire French army was in despair. No man attempted to control the patriotic, angry criticisms that rose to their minds. Even private soldiers and troopers expressed their feelings; both officers and men were even more outraged than amazed. The best that the Maréchal de Villeroy could do was to detach three dragoon regiments to fall upon Vaudémont's rear. They captured a flag or two and created some slight disturbance amongst the last of the rearguard.

No one felt more outraged than the Maréchal de Villeroy. Too good a courtier to try to shift the blame on to someone else's shoulders, he relied on the support of his entire army, on the soldiers' eye-witness accounts, and on the criticisms which they had not tried to suppress. He thus sent a junior officer to the King to report that contrary to all expectations Vaudémont's speed had saved him. He did not enter into details, but re-signed himself to take the consequences, whatever they might be.

At Versailles the King had been counting the hours throughout the day and night in his eagerness to hear news of a brilliant victory. He was therefore more than bewildered to behold a single gentleman appear with the despatches instead of some distinguished personage, and he was bitterly disappointed to learn how quiet the day had been. The Court, anxious for the fate of sons, husbands or brothers, was left in suspense, and friends of the Maréchal de Villeroy appeared much embarrassed. So general and short a despatch, that made little of a grave and crucial event, considerably vexed the King, but he decided to wait until a further ex-planation should be forthcoming. In the meantime he carefully studied all the gazettes from Holland. In the very first he read of a great battle on the left wing, with fulsome praise of M. du Maine, who was said to have received wounds that prevented his leading his troops to victory, and that thus M. de Vaudémont had been saved. It said also that M. du Maine had been borne off the field on a shutter. The King was annoyed by this colossal irony, but he was still more vexed when a later edition retracted that account, stating that M. du Maine now appeared to have been unscratched. All this, combined with the absolute silence that had reigned since the battle, and the Maréchal de Villeroy's terse despatch giving no excuses, made him nervous and exceedingly suspicious.

A highly fashionable bath-attendant of Paris, named Vienne, had been in the King's service since the period of his amorous adventures.[1] He had gained a reputation by prescribing various drugs reputed to give oppor-tunities of greater satisfaction, and by this road had risen to be one of the four head valets. He was a very decent sort of fellow but a peasant, coarse and plain-spoken to a degree, and for that very reason and because he was truthful the King had got into the habit of asking him the things that others would not tell him, always provided that the matter lay within his compass. All this led to a Marly excursion where the King questioned La

---

[1] François Quentin, a much sought-after ladies' hairdresser. 'Il rendait des services d'un ordre tout particulier à Louis XIV, comme le dit en termes décents Saint-Simon.' M. Gonzague Truc, Ed. Bibliothèque de La Pléiade.

Vienne. He showed embarrassment because, being taken by surprise, he had no time to dissemble. The King's suspicions were increased and the valet was ordered to speak. La Vienne could resist no longer; he told the King something that he would have preferred never to know, and that drove him nearly to despair. He had overcome so many obstacles and jealousies, had taken so much pleasure in giving M. du Maine a high command; all his mind had been turned to speeding his promotion above the heads of the princes of the blood. The Comte de Toulouse was already an admiral, with his future assured; and it was therefore on the Duc du Maine that all his care had been lavished. At this moment his hopes were blighted and his disappointment was more than he could endure. He felt the army's contempt for his most cherished son, and the gazettes taught him what was being said abroad. His chagrin was great indeed.

This was the one occasion on which Louis XIV, outwardly so equable, so perfectly controlled in his slightest gestures, succumbed to his impulses. As he rose from table at Marly, accompanied by the ladies and in the presence of the entire Court, he happened to see one of the dessert-foot-men[1] pocket a sweet biscuit. That instant, his royal dignity forgotten and cane in hand, for with his hat it had just been returned to him, he rushed on the man, who, like the rest of the company thrust aside by the King's sudden descent, had no idea what to expect, thrashed him, cursed him, and finally broke the cane across his shoulders. Truth to tell it was of bamboo and very brittle. Then, still holding one end of it and still abusing the servant, who by that time had fled, he crossed the little salon and the ante-room beyond into Mme de Maintenon's apartment and stayed there more than an hour, as he did often when at Marly. Returning to his apartments he perceived Père La Chaise among the courtiers and cried out to him, 'Father, I have just thrashed a rascal soundly and broken my cane on him; but I do not think God will be displeased by that,' and there and then he confessed to him that so-called crime. The company present were still frightened to death by what they had witnessed or learned about from bystanders, and their terrors were increased by this strange scene. Some of the more intimate raised a murmur against the offender, whilst the unhappy priest made approving noises through his closed teeth to prevent the King from becoming still angrier in a public place. You may imagine the gossip to which this gave rise, and the general disquiet, since no one knew the cause, although all were aware that so small a provocation could not be the whole matter. At last the truth emerged, as the word was spread that Vienne, at the King's express orders, had been responsible for this unique and most unseemly display.

---

[1] *Valet du serdeau:* his duty was to take dishes from a side-table and hand them to the serving gentlemen.

The sad result of this happening in Flanders was the fall of Namur on 4 August, after twenty-four days in open trenches.

We left the Maréchal de Joyeuse separated from Prince Louis of Baden by the River Rhine, and M. and Mme la Maréchale de Lorges at Landau, where I went to visit them after we had re-crossed. During the six weeks that we stayed there the entire army, encamped not far distant, came to see them. Now that his health was restored M. de Lorges was all eagerness to be at the head of his army, and Mme la Maréchale to return to Paris. It would be impossible to describe the joy with which he was received; all those who could obtain leave came two miles out to meet him. Despite his orders, salvoes of artillery and musketry were let off repeatedly, and all night long there were bonfires and feasting, with tables set up for every regiment. The Maréchal de Joyeuse had not succeeded in being popular, he was said to have taken too much booty, and to have reduced the cavalry and waggon-horses almost to starvation point in a rich countryside. That was the reason for the universal delight at the return of an adored and unself-seeking general.

Shortly after this the army divided for reasons of supplies. The marshals remained with one half in the region of Alsace, and Tallard took the rest, myself and my regiment included, towards Hunsrück. I did not stay there long, however, for I soon learned that the Maréchal de Lorges had suffered an apoplectic seizure, and I immediately went to be with him, accompanied by his nephews, the Comte de Roucy and the Chevalier de Roye, and an escort given us by Tallard. The attack might have been of little consequence had it been taken in time, but he would never admit to being ill, and no one could force him to take precautions. As a result, violent remedies were needed, which succeeded at great risk to his life. Meanwhile the Maréchale de Lorges was back at Strasbourg, having had no rest in Paris. We all went to see her and remained with them until they both left for Vichy. By now it was the season for winter-quarters and I returned to Paris.

CHAPTER VI

1696

The Abbé de Fénelon and Mme Guyon – Fénelon becomes Archbishop of Cambrai – Secret struggle between the Archbishop of Cambrai and the Bishop of Chartres – Mme Guyon sent to the Bastille – Death of Mme de Sévigné – Death of La Bruyère – Maréchal de Choiseul commands the Rhine army – M. de Lauzun removes his wife from her home – Conditions of the peace-treaty with Savoy – Household of the future Duchesse de Bourgogne – I join the Maréchal de Choiseul at Philippsburg – His civility to me – Birth of my daughter – I return to Paris – Filthy slander regarding my return – M. de La Trappe painted from memory

BEFORE telling what took place after my return from the army I must relate some events that happened at the Court during the campaign. M. de Bryas, Archbishop of Cambrai, had died, and the King had given that rich benefice to the Abbé de Fénelon,[1] his grandsons' tutor. Fénelon was a man of quality without fortune. Conscious of high ability and of an amiable and beguiling personality accompanied by graces and talents and great learning, he had correspondingly high ambitions. For years past he had knocked at every door in the hope that one would open to him, but the Jesuits, whom he first approached as distributors of the richest prizes, snubbed him, and he fell back on the Jansenists[2] for consolation, hoping by his brilliance and the reputation which he intended to make among them to compensate for any worldly blessings that might pass him by. Some time elapsed before he was accepted, but eventually he was admitted to the private suppers where, once or twice a week, the greatest of them foregathered at the house of the Duchesse de Brancas.

I do not know whether he proved too sophisticated for them, or if he hoped to do better elsewhere than with men who had naught to share save their wounds. However that may be, their attachment gradually cooled, and after circling Saint-Sulpice for a considerable time he managed to form another there. Those priests were emerging from their first

---

[1] François de Salignac de La Mothe-Fénelon (1651–1715), Archbishop of Cambrai 1695.

[2] Jansenism, the doctrine of Cornelius Jansen the Flemish theologian (1585–1638) based upon an interpretation of Saint Augustine. It tended to deny free-will and to a belief in predestination. The Jansenists' most bitter enemies were the Jesuits. Louis XIV, who had a Jesuit confessor, destroyed their famous abbey of Port-Royal in 1710, but they continued to exist in France until the middle of the eighteenth century. Racine was their pupil, and Pascal, who retired there in 1654, their illustrious defender.

status of mere seminarians of a Paris church and were gradually becoming known. Low birth, narrow-mindedness, and a complete lack of protectors led them to obey Rome and its maxims implicitly, to avoid all that smacked of Jansenism, and to defer to bishops in a way that made them vastly welcome in most dioceses. To prelates who feared the Court for reasons of doctrine and the Jesuits for their determination to rule or to ruin, Saint-Sulpice appeared to provide a comfortable environment.

None of their members could in any way compare with the Abbé de Fénelon; it was easy for him to shine in their company and to find patrons ready to support him in exchange for his later protection. His piety delighted them, his doctrine, based on theirs and discreetly purged of any impurities collected from older associations, his charm, sweetness, and persuasive eloquence made him very precious to that new community and gave him what he had long sought, a group of friends ready and able to advance him. In the meanwhile he cultivated them with the greatest care, not absolutely joining them, for their views were too narrow to suit him, and continuing to make friends and acquaintances elsewhere. His was a winning nature, eager to like and be liked by everyone, from men of power to labourers and lackeys, and his genius in that respect admirably suited his aims.

At that period, when still unknown, he heard tell of that Mme Guyon[1] who has since made so much stir in the world that she needs no description from me. He went to see her; their minds agreed; their visions merged. Whether they fully understood one another in the spiritual way and novel language that emerged from their intercourse I do not know, but they believed that they did, and a partnership was formed. Although better known than he, she was still obscure, and their association passed unobserved because no one was watching; even Saint-Sulpice remained in ignorance of it.

The Duc de Beauvilliers had quite unexpectedly, almost against his will, become governor of the King's grandsons. He was head of the royal finance council and possessed the King's respect and confidence absolutely, so much so, indeed, that despite his protests he was given complete control over all the tutors and sub-governors of Mgr le Duc de Bourgogne. Needing advice at this time in the selection of a tutor he applied to Saint-Sulpice, where he had confessed for some time past, and of which he greatly approved. When those priests boasted of Fénelon's piety, excellent disposition, and ability, the duke, who had already heard him highly praised, saw him, fell a victim to his charm, and engaged him. Fénelon did not take long to comprehend the prime importance of completely winning the man who had thus set his foot on the

---

[1] Jeanne Marie Bouvier de La Motte (1648–1717), married Jacques Guyon 1664. She started being a mystic after her widowhood in 1676. Fénelon was equally attracted by her mind and her Quietist teaching.

ladder of fame, and the Duc de Chevreuse also, his brother-in-law and second self, who, like him, was in highest favour with the King and Mme de Maintenon. To gain their confidence became his first concern, and he succeeded so well that before long he was master of their hearts and minds and their spiritual director as well.

Mme de Maintenon had made it a rule to dine out once, and sometimes twice in the week with the Ducs de Beauvilliers and de Chevreuse at one or other of their houses, making a party of five with the sister-duchesses their wives, and a handbell on the table so as to dispense with servants and free the conversation. These dinners were conclaves that kept the entire Court in a state of alarm, and after a time Fénelon was invited to join them. With Mme de Maintenon he was almost as successful as with the dukes, for his piety acted on her like a charm. The Court observed by what giant strides he was advancing, and soon the courtiers flocked about him. But a desire to remain independent so as to pursue his designs; above all, fear of vexing Mme de Maintenon, whose preferences were for modesty and seclusion, prompted him to retire behind a mask of humility and his position as tutor. This made him appear all the more perfect to the high-ranking personages whom he had enchanted and whose patronage was all-important to him.

At the same time he did not forget his dear Mme Guyon. Already he had puffed her to the dukes, and he did so now to Mme de Maintenon. He even produced her in person, but apparently much against her will for a moment only, presenting her as a woman given wholly to God, whose humility and love of meditation kept her strictly apart, and who above all else dreaded notoriety. That spirit greatly pleased Mme de Maintenon, the lady's modesty combined with subtle flattery won her over completely, and she asked to hear her on religion. Mme Guyon needed cajoling, but seemed finally to yield to the charms and virtues of Mme de Maintenon, who fell into the trap so artfully prepared for her. Such was the situation when the Abbé de Fénelon became Archbishop of Cambrai, winning himself still further admiration for having made no move towards that rich prize, and for resigning a good abbey given him on his appointment as tutor.[1] As a matter of fact he was very careful not to appear to seek Cambrai, for the least hint of personal ambition might have ruined all his ambitions. What is more, it was not Cambrai that he sought.

Little by little he had appropriated to himself some of the more important sheep in Mme Guyon's little flock, but led them always under the instruction of that she-prophet. Chief among these were the Duchesse de Mortemart, sister of the Duchesses of Chevreuse and Beauvilliers, Mme de Morstein the former's daughter, and, most important of all, the

---

[1] The newly promoted Archbishop of Rheims remarked, 'M. de Fénelon has acted well according to his lights. I, in keeping my benefices, have acted well according to mine.'

Duchesse de Béthune.[1] All these ladies lived in Paris and came only rarely to Versailles, except surreptitiously, for a few hours at a time when the King was absent at Marly. Mgr le Duc de Bourgogne was still too young for these excursions and consequently his governors remained with him at the Château. Mme Guyon also paid flying visits from Paris and gave religious instruction to these noble dames. The Comtesse de Guiche,[2] Mme de Noailles's eldest daughter, who spent her entire life at the Court, escaped whenever possible to gather up the manna. L'Echelles and du Puys, *gentilshommes de la manche* to Mgr le Duc de Bourgogne, came also, and everything took place in an atmosphere of mystery that added fresh zest to Mme Guyon's ministrations.

Cambrai was a shattering blow to the little flock. They had been watching whilst ruin seized the Archbishop of Paris, and it was Paris that they coveted for Fénelon not Cambrai, a country diocese whose archbishop must occasionally be in residence and thus beyond their reach. Paris would have set him over the rest of the clergy, made him a power to be reckoned with and in a position to dare all successfully for Mme Guyon and her teaching, which they still kept a dark secret. Thus what dazzled the world deeply disappointed them, and the Comtesse de Guiche's affliction was so great that she publicly wept. Meanwhile the new archbishop had been careful to pay his respects to the foremost among the prelates and they on their side had been flattered by his visits. Saint-Cyr,[3] that well-guarded, almost inaccessible spot was appointed for his consecration; M. de Meaux,[4] arbiter of Church doctrine and master of the episcopacy, officiated, the King's grandsons attended, Mme de Maintenon and her select little court were present, no other invitations were issued, and the doors were secured against intruders.

Harlay the disgraced Archbishop of Paris had at first ruled the Church with the King's implicit confidence. Latterly, however, Père de La Chaise had managed to deny him any part in the distribution of benefices. Thus he had been estranged from the King, and Mme de Maintenon he had irrevocably offended by opposing the publication of her marriage, of which he had been one of three witnesses. That last was what had brought him to ruin. His great reputation throughout the entire kingdom, by which he had won so high a place in the King's regard, went for nothing when other influences prevailed. His wide learning, his eloquence and power in

---

[1] Marie Fouquet, daughter of Nicolas Fouquet the one-time Surintendant des Finances. She married the Duc de Charost, later Duc de Béthune in 1657. She died in 1716, aged sixty-six.

[2] Marie Christine de Noailles (1672–1748), married the Comte de Guiche, later Antoine Duc de Gramont, in 1687.

[3] The school for the daughters of impoverished noblemen founded by Louis XIV and Mme de Maintenon in 1685. The latter encouraged the girls to act plays so as to give them the polish required when they appeared in Society. The greatest possible contrast to the traditional training admired by Fénelon, from which they were supposed to emerge 'from depths of cavernous darkness into the blinding light of day'.

[4] Bossuet (1627–1704), Bishop of Meaux.

the pulpit, his excellent judgment of underlings, his able conduct of affairs, his authority in the Church, were weighed in the balance and were found wanting against his private life, his amorous exploits, his fashionable and courtly air. All of the latter had been known when first he was made a bishop, yet it had not injured him. Since Mme de Maintenon, in hatred, first resolved on his destruction it had become criminal, and she used it to procure for him endless humiliations. The proud, sensitive, and scholarly mind that had made him so great a Churchman and so perfect a courtier and gentleman (albeit not always dignified) could not long endure his decline in favour and the accompanying disgrace. The clergy, prone to envy, and Society, no longer able to use him as a purveyor of abbeys and bishoprics, abandoned him. All his abundant graces withered. The only solace that remained to him was to shut himself away with his mistress the Duchesse de Lesdiguières, whom he saw every day, either at her house, or at Conflans.[1] He possessed there an exquisite garden, neatly kept, and as they walked along its paths alone together gardeners followed them at a distance to rake away the traces of their feet.

Melancholy overtook him, and gradually increased accompanied by attacks of epilepsy. He knew what that meant but forbade his servants ever to speak of it or to seek help should they find him in a fit. He was only too well obeyed. Towards the end he went to rest at Conflans, where the Duchesse de Lesdiguières, who did not spend the nights with him, visited him every day, and they were always quite alone. On 6 August his morning was as usual, but at dinner-time when his butler came to announce the meal he found him in his study toppled over on the sofa, dead. Père Gaillard spoke the oration at Notre-Dame. The subject matter was more than delicate, the end had been horrible, but that famous Jesuit made the best of a difficult task. Praising what was laudable he stopped short at morality and produced a masterpiece of oratorical piety.

The King was much relieved by this death and Mme de Maintenon even more so. M. de Reims[2] had his post of head of the Sorbonne, M. de Meaux that of Superior of the House of Navarre, and M. de Noyon received his blue ribbon.[3] His nomination to the cardinalate and his archbishopric required rather longer discussion. M. d'Orléans[4] had the former in the most agreeable way imaginable, since neither he nor any one else had time to consider it. M. de Paris had died at Conflans at midday on Saturday, 6 August; the King was informed late that evening. On the morning of Monday, 8 August, he went into his study as usual to give the orders for the day, marched straight up to the Bishop of Orléans, who

---

[1] The Château of Conflans-l'Archevêque.
[2] Charles Maurice le Tellier (1642–1710). He was Louvois's brother.
[3] Of the Order.
[4] Pierre de Coislin (1636–1706), bishop, later cardinal.

stepped aside thinking that he wished to pass; but not so, the King took him by the arm and led him without a word to the end of the study where Cardinals de Bouillon and Fürstenberg[1] were in conversation. There the King abruptly announced, 'Messieurs, you will thank me for giving you such a colleague as M. d'Orléans. He has my nomination to the cardinalate.' Whereupon the bishop, who had expected anything but that and had no notion where he was being led, flung himself down and embraced the King's knees. There was loud applause from the company assembled in the study, and later from the Court and the public in general. The archbishopric of Paris took not much longer to settle, for it served to reward the Duc de Noailles for giving up his command to the Duc de Vendôme, and as a token of his return to favour. It was conferred upon his brother the Bishop of Châlons[2], who devoted his entire life to pastoral visits, the conduct of his see, and good works of every kind. His pious mother, sometime lady-in-waiting to the queen-mother, lived with him in seclusion, under his spiritual direction, confessing to him every evening, wholly occupied with her salvation in the utmost privacy. That was the prelate on whom the King's choice fell. He for his part had foreseen and dreaded the promotion and had therefore swiftly added his name to those of the many bishops who admired the *Réflexions Morales* by Père Quesnel,[3] reckoning thereby to ensure his absolute rejection by the Jesuits. It so happened, however, that for the first time Père de La Chaise was not consulted, Mme de Maintenon having taken charge, also, perhaps, for the first time. She did not want the Archbishop of Paris to be a Jesuit appointment; she wished him to be her own man; and M. de Noailles appeared to her to fill that bill. In the end she was successful and M. de Noailles received the nomination much against his will and against the wishes of Père de La Chaise. This was a fearful snub to the Jesuits, and one for which they never forgave M. de Noailles. Yet so far was he from soliciting the appointment that he had taken steps to avoid it, and when it was offered could not bring himself to accept. Only the King's repeated commands persuaded him to take up what was to him a very heavy burden.

M. de Langres died at this time, the son and brother of the two MM. de Gordes, who were chevaliers of the Order and senior captains of the body-guard. Their father, who died in 1642, used often to stop Louis XIII's coach, saying, 'Sire, you would not have me burst; for pity's sake make them stop'; and he would get out and relieve himself.[4] The King laughed

---

[1] The Prince of Fürstenberg (1629–1704), Bishop of Metz, then of Strasbourg, cardinal 1686. He was also Abbot of Saint-Germain-des-Prés.

[2] Louis Antoine de Noailles, Archbishop of Paris, later cardinal (1651–1729), whom Saint-Simon regarded almost as a saint, in contrast to the rest of the Noailles family.

[3] Pasquier Quesnel (1634–1719). The famous Jansenist whose controversies with Cardinal de Noailles were the cause of the Bull *Unigenitus*.

[4] No one ever dared to beg Louis XIV to stop for a minute in any circumstances whatsoever.

and admired him for it, as my father, who many times saw it happen, used often to tell me.

During all this time the new Archbishop of Cambrai had been congratulating himself on his success with Mme de Maintenon, with whose powerful support his expectations were indeed great; but there was no security whilst his influence was not complete. Now Godet, Bishop of Chartres,[1] also held to her, and by much closer ties, since he was diocesan and sole director of Saint-Cyr and her own confessor as well. In morals, doctrine, piety and the conduct of his diocese he was beyond reproach. He paid only short occasional visits to Paris and even rarer ones to the Court, where he came and went in a flash; but he saw Mme de Maintenon long and often, usually at Saint-Cyr, and obtained all else that he required by letters. He was a formidable rival, yet, impregnable as he seemed, there was something about his appearance that gave Fénelon room for hope; for that prelate, mistaking his grubby emaciated countenance, believed him to be a typical Sulpician, low, vulgar, almost simple, and without friends save amongst the mediocre clergy.[2] In short, he took him to be unprotected, lacking talent or scholarship, brought to prominence only through the chance of Saint-Cyr happening to lie within his diocese. Being so persuaded, Fénelon never doubted but that he might easily be dislodged through the doctrines of Mme Guyon, whom Mme de Maintenon already so greatly relished. He well knew how much the latter enjoyed a novelty.

As a first step Fénelon persuaded her to admit Mme Guyon to Saint-Cyr, in order that she might be seen and savoured to better advantage than at the occasional short after-dinner sessions at the houses of the Dukes of Beauvilliers and Chevreuse. She made one or two preliminary visits, after which Mme de Maintenon, liking her more and more, insisted on her spending the night. Gradually the length of the visits increased, until by her own admission she began to seek for and gather disciples in the school. Before long she had formed there another little flock, whose maxims and spiritual language appeared very foreign to that establishment, and monstrous indeed to M. de Chartres. That bishop was not at all what M. de Cambrai supposed. He was, on the contrary, a scholar and a sound theologian, humane, purposeful; polished to a surprising degree for one who had never emerged from the fundamentals of his calling, all of which made him fit to associate with the Court and Society. The most brilliant of the courtiers might have found his thought hard to follow and have gained much from his sermons; but his talents in that direction lay hidden because he never used them without real necessity. His freedom from ambition, piety, and rare integrity kept him independent, and all

---

[1] Paul Godet des Marais (1647-1709). Bishop of Chartres 1690, Bishop of Blois 1697.

[2] An example of Saint-Simon's dislike of Saint-Sulpice. He thought the priests common and ill-bred and took every opportunity to have a dig at them.

his other needs were supplied by Mme de Maintenon within the limits of their attachment.

No sooner did M. de Chartres learn of Mme Guyon's unorthodox teaching than he arranged to have admitted into Saint-Cyr two sensible intelligent ladies of a type likely to impress Mme de Maintenon, selecting them for their devotion to himself, and instructing them very carefully. They appeared at first attracted, then bewitched by Mme Guyon, attaching themselves ever more closely to her for spiritual direction. She, who saw their ability and high position in the convent, plumed herself on having made useful conquests. She then endeavoured to dominate them, confiding in them as being most capable of receiving her doctrine and rendering it palatable to the rest of the house. At this point both she and M. de Cambrai, whom she kept fully informed, were triumphant, and the little flock exulted. M. de Chartres bided his time. He observed, reflected, scrutinized the affair from every angle, and, when the time was ripe, struck.

Mme de Maintenon was horror-stricken by what he told her, and still more so when confirmation came from the lips of those two ladies in their written reports. She began to question the school-girls, and learned that although some had received more teaching than others, all were tending towards the same end, and that both the end and the way to it were vastly shocking. Finding herself in difficulties she went for advice to Fénelon, but he, not knowing what she had discovered, appeared embarrassed, which increased her suspicions. Quite suddenly Mme Guyon was removed from Saint-Cyr, and no pains were spared to obliterate the last traces of her doctrine. That, however, was easier said than done, for many had fallen under her spell and were truly devoted to her and her teaching, a fact which M. de Chartres used to expose her poison and throw doubt on M. de Cambrai. A defeat so totally unexpected left the latter stunned but not broken. He met it with spirit and quotations from the Saints. He stood firm, and his friends supported him.

As for M. de Chartres, well satisfied with having secured his position with Mme de Maintenon, he had no desire to entangle himself further with a man as well protected as Fénelon. Mme de Maintenon on the other hand, deeply resenting having been led to the brink of a precipice, became more and more furious with both Mme Guyon and Fénelon. She then heard that the former was secretly holding sessions in Paris. This was forbidden under the threat of dire penalties, but the only result was to drive her underground, for she could not resist giving instruction nor gathering together her flock in small groups at various private houses. When that also was discovered she was sent out of Paris, but returned almost at once to lie hidden in a mean little house in the Faubourg Saint-Antoine. From thence she never emerged, but the excessive devotion of her disciples made her presence suspected. Inquiries were made among the neighbours, revealing mysterious rites that were performed at a certain door before it was opened. A maid-servant carrying bread and vegetables was so closely followed that the police contrived to enter upon her heels. Mme Guyon was discovered and immediately driven to the Bastille,[1] with orders to treat her well but prevent her from seeing or communicating with anyone.

This final disaster was shattering to M. de Cambrai and the little flock, who met ever more rarely. The consequences spilled over into the following year, but at this juncture it seems best to leave matters where they stand and return to the narrative.

At this time Mme de Sévigné, who was so pleasant and such excellent company, died at Grignan, at the house of that daughter whom she idolized without sufficient cause. I was a close friend of the young Marquis de Grignan, her grandson. She was a woman whose gracious, unaffected charm and sweetness of disposition put shy people at their ease in conversation. She was also kind, and vastly learned in a number of subjects, although she never willingly displayed her learning.[2]

Shortly afterwards the public lost a writer of genius renowned for his style and knowledge of humanity. I speak of La Bruyère, who died of apoplexy at Versailles, after excelling Theophrastes in his own manner, by portraying quite inimitably the men of our time in his *Caractères*. He was a very decent sort of man and excellent company, simple, not at all the pedant, and wholly sincere. I knew him well enough to regret both his death and the books which his age and health had led one to expect from him.

The armies were assigned as in the previous year, except that the Maréchal de Choiseul took M. le Maréchal de Lorges's place with the army of the Rhine. Before appointing him the King took him alone into his study and made him describe in detail the objects outside the window, thus testing his eyesight, which was very bad at close quarters though he could distinguish things well enough at a distance. This change in M. de Lorges's circumstances soon led to another in his family circle. M. de Lauzun, who had insisted on marrying his second daughter only because he hoped to be reconciled with the King, never forgave the maréchal for being deaf to his hints. He did not know of the King's formal ban on him at the time of his marriage, but even had he known he would have thought M. de Lorges vastly incompetent for not overcoming it. He was especially annoyed by the latter's two nephews, who came and went like sons of the house, and mortally afraid of the effect of their youth and good looks on

---

[1] It was not to the Bastille that she was taken but to the fortress of Vincennes, further from Paris and less comfortable. Her idea had been to form a spiritual society to serve 'The little Master' (Christ), under the protection of St. Michael. It was to have been called '*Les Michelets*' and headed by Fénelon.

[2] He does not mention her letters here, but he knew about them for he noted in the margin of his copy of Dangeau's Journal. 'Mme de Sévigné, so famous for her conversation and her eminent friends in the highest Society; also for the *Letters*.'

his pretty young wife, although she never went out without her mother, and neither he nor Society could find anything to censure in her conduct. None the less he was jealous, and there being nothing now to restrain him he gave full vent to his feelings with vague accusations, suspicions, scenes over nothing, notes uttering threats or warnings, and continual ill-humour. Finally, choosing a time when the Maréchal de Lorges was on duty at Marly, he ordered his wife to meet him at his house next the Church of the Assumption, in the Rue Saint-Honoré, saying that he would send a coach to fetch her at six o'clock, and that she was henceforth to live there with him. Although everything had been leading up to this event there were sobs and tears from both mother and daughter, whose letters to him proved worse than useless. She was obliged to obey. Two of his old friends the Duchesses de Foix and du Lude received her with a new staff of servants, and he sent even her maids home that very night, providing her with two other young women whose virtue he had proved, with orders never to lose sight of her. She was forbidden to communicate with her father and mother, or with any members of her family except Mme de Saint-Simon. After the first few days of shock and wretchedness her youth and high spirits prevailed, helping her to endure his continual jealousy that was not far short of madness. Public opinion was very severe on him, and most sympathetic towards his wife and her parents; but no one was surprised.

I had met the Maréchal de Choiseul before leaving for the army, and he had made me many most civil offers. He was an acquaintance of my father, and being most honourable and full of proper feeling, he strove to oblige all those who had been attached to M. le Maréchal de Lorges. I made a point of joining him early at Philippsburg, where he pressed me to lodge at his headquarters, but I asked permission to stay in camp with my regiment. From June, as it then was, until September the maréchal and the Prince of Baden did no more than subsist and observe one another, after which we re-crossed the Rhine at Philippsburg. In Italy more was happening. The King determined to do everything possible to bring peace to his kingdom, which sorely needed it, and thought he might best do so by separating his enemies. Savoy seemed to offer reasonable hope, and he therefore entered into a secret treaty with that nation. The conditions laid it down that our troops should relinquish every fortress taken from Savoy during the war, and that a marriage should take place between Mgr le Duc de Bourgogne and M. de Savoie's daughter,[1] as soon as she reached the age of twelve.

Whilst I was still at the war, the King was afflicted with an anthrax upon the neck. It was at first thought to be a simple boil, but later when a fever developed there was cause for alarm and they lanced it several times.

[1] Marie Adélaïde of Savoy (1685-1712), daughter of Victor Amadeus of Savoy and Anne Marie d'Orléans, daughter of Monsieur by his first wife Henrietta of England.

Despite the pain he made a point of appearing every day at the Court, and worked sitting up in bed almost as much as usual. All Europe eagerly watched the course of a malady that was not without danger. Since nothing had happened, nor seemed likely to happen in Flanders the King sent a courier ordering the princes to return as soon as the Prince of Orange left his army, which he did a few days later.

It was during the course of this illness that the peace with Savoy was publicly proclaimed. The King also named two hostages to be handed over until the territorial clauses were fulfilled, and made arrangements for the reception of the little princess.[1] Her household was by far the hardest problem, for the Court had long been without either a queen or dauphine, and all the ladies of suitable rank and favour were actively canvassing for posts, often to one another's detriment. Anonymous letters flew about like flies, libels and denouncements were everywhere. In the end everything was settled in secret between the King and Mme de Maintenon whilst she sat by his bed; for she never left him, except when he allowed himself to be viewed by the Court, but for most of the time they were alone together. Mme de Maintenon was resolved to keep the training of the little princess for herself, so as to bring her up according to her own theories, win her love, and teach her to amuse the King without becoming a danger to herself in future years. She hoped also to gain a hold over Mgr le Duc de Bourgogne, doubly important to her now that her attachment to the Dukes and Duchesses of Chevreuse and Beauvilliers was cooling rapidly. That, indeed, was the main reason why neither of those ladies was appointed lady-in-waiting, a post which either would have filled with dignity and tact. The fact was that Mme de Maintenon had made up her mind to surround the princess with persons devoted to herself or too stupid to be dangerous. The names were announced on 2 September; they included:

> Dangeau, gentleman-in-waiting[2]
> The Duchesse du Lude, lady-in-waiting
> Mme de Dangeau, first lady
> The Comtesse de Roucy, second lady
> Mme de Nogaret, third lady.[3]

Finding no more work to do in the army, which was preparing to go

---

[1] The eleven-year-old princess was not going among strangers. The King was her great-uncle, Monsieur her grandfather, the Duke of Chartres her uncle, and James II at Saint-Germain also her great-uncle.

[2] Philippe de Courcillon, Marquis de Dangeau (1638–1720), author of the famous *Journal*, published, annotated by Saint-Simon, 1854–1860. Of Mme de Maintenon Dangeau wrote, 'She was so worthy, doing, when she was in favour, so much good and preventing so much harm that one cannot speak too highly of her'. Saint-Simon noted: 'See that! Vulgar, filthy, stinking, lying in his throat!' It was after reading Dangeau's *Journal* Saint-Simon decided to revise and edit his own *Mémoires*.

[3] A great crony of Saint-Simon. It was through her that he obtained much of his information.

into winter quarters, I decided to return to Paris. October was already far advanced; Mme de Saint-Simon had lost her grandfather, M. Frémont, and had been safely delivered of my daughter on the 8 September.[1] The maréchal allowed me to go. He had treated me with every consideration, I had become attached to him, and latterly he had begun to confide in me, of which, at my age, I felt very proud.

When I returned to Paris I found that the Court were gone to Fontainebleau. I had arrived somewhat early and had no wish for the King to learn of this without seeing me, lest he should think my behaviour underhand. I therefore made all speed to appear at the Court, where I was made very welcome and the King, as always, spoke kindly to me; but he did say that I was home rather soon, although he saw no harm in that. Now it was in my mind to risk a short excursion, so I was in great haste to return to Paris after paying my duty to the King. As I left the *lever*, however, and was about to step into my coach, Louville made me go aside into the theatre, which was always open and empty in the morning. He wished to warn me of a rumour to the effect that when the King had said that he was glad to see me safely home but thought it a little early, I had replied that I preferred coming straight to him as to my beloved, unlike some officers I knew who lay low for a time in Paris with their mistresses. Hearing this the blood rushed to my head. I ran straight back to the King's room, where a great company was still assembled, and I let fly at that revolting lie, saying that I would give much to know who had invented it, for I would make him eat his words, with blows if need be. And I remained there all that day, searching for fresh people to whom to repeat my words.

My rage made quite a sensation. As a matter of fact, the Maréchal de Lorges had stopped me when I tried to answer the King, but in no case whatsoever would I have stooped to such meanness. He and some of the older nobles gave me a lecture for speaking so loud in the King's house, and I let them have their say because they told me nothing that I did not know already, and of two evils I preferred the lesser—a possible reprimand from the King, or a few days Bastille, and had avoided one far greater. The King, himself, had been unaware of my fury, or else had decided to ignore it, and the commotion I caused effectively quashed the rumour and made me the more respected. I then started on my short excursion, which I shall now proceed to describe.

For a long time past my love and veneration for M. de La Trappe[2] had filled me with the desire to have his likeness; something permanent to

[1] Charlotte de Saint-Simon (1696–1763). Sadly deformed, she grew up a quarrelsome invalid, wasting her father's money in endless lawsuits. Against Saint-Simon's will, her grandmother insisted on her marrying the Prince de Chimay. He said of her, 'Some young women are happier unmarried, living on the interest of what one would have given them as a dowry.' But the wedding took place in 1722 none the less.

[2] Armand de Rancé (1626–1700) founded the Trappist order. He reformed his abbey, from which all Cistercians are descended, in 1662, with an order based on perpetual prayer and exceptional austerities.

endure after his death, just as his works would perpetuate his wonderful mind and spirit. His modesty forbade my asking him to sit for a portrait, especially since some hasty sketches already existed that had been drawn in the choir, and medals had been struck from them. These were not good enough for me; but to make matters more difficult he was now so frail that he seldom left the infirmary and was never in a place suitable for portrait painting.

Rigaud[1] was at that time considered to be the best in Europe for catching likenesses and strong, durable painting; but it needed much persuasion to induce a man so overburdened with work to leave Paris even for a few days. I had also to convince him that he was capable of painting a portrait entirely from memory. As it happened, it was probably this challenge, which at first dismayed him, that finally made him accept, for when a man excels in an art he likes also to be the first in a particular manner. However that may be, Rigaud at length agreed to make the attempt and devote the necessary time to it. My money may also have attracted him.

As I have already remarked, I kept my visits to La Trappe very private on account of my youth, and thus I was much concerned to prevent gossip regarding Rigaud's absence. I accordingly made it a condition that he should work only for me and in secret, and that if he wished to make a copy he should keep it hidden until in after years I allowed him to exhibit it. On his side he stipulated for a thousand écus, cash down, all expenses paid, and for the journey to be done in a single day by post-chaise, returning in the same way. I did not bargain, but consented to everything. All this had been decided in the spring, and we had agreed to act immediately after my return from the army. I had at the same time made arrangements with M. Maisne the new Abbot of La Trappe, and M. de Saint-Louis, a retired cavalry officer well liked by the King, both of whom had lived for many years at the abbey and desired a likeness no less than I.

On my return from Fontainebleau I slept one night in Paris, so as to settle matters with Rigaud, who followed me two days later to La Trappe. I had already briefed my two accomplices, and immediately after my arrival at the abbey I told M. de La Trappe that an officer-friend of mine so passionately desired to see him that I entreated his indulgence (for by that time he was seeing scarcely anyone). I added that my friend had such a bad stammer that he did not ask for a conversation, but would be well content simply with looking. M. de La Trappe smiled graciously; thought it very odd for an officer to be concerned for such a trifle, but kindly promised to allow himself to be looked at. When Rigaud appeared early next day M. Maisne and I took him into a little parlour where M. de La

[1] Hyacinthe François Honoré Mathieu Pierre-le-Martyr André Jean Rigau y Ros, known as Rigaud (1659–1743). Painter of a great number of famous official portraits, including several of the King, the Duc de Bourgogne, Philip V of Spain, Bossuet, etc. He seems to have taken from Van Dyck's portrait of Charles I the royal stance, one leg advanced, so typical of his portraits of Louis XIV.

Trappe was accustomed to seeing me on his way from the infirmary. It was a plain little room, with white-washed walls, and windows on two sides, containing a few religious engravings, one or two cane chairs, and the writing-table at which M. de La Trappe had compiled his books. Nothing had been changed since his retirement. Rigaud pronounced the lighting perfect, and when the new abbot sat down in M. de La Trappe's usual corner he thought that perfect also for his convenience. We then led him into another room where he could neither be seen nor interrupted, and he retired to fetch his paints.

That same afternoon I presented him as my officer-friend to M. de La Trappe, and he sat with us for about three-quarters of an hour in the place we had selected, making his stammer an excuse for not speaking. He then hurried away to jot down on canvas the ideas which he had memorized. I remained some time longer with M. de La Trappe, more in an endeavour to divert his mind than for serious conversation; but he had noticed nothing odd, and merely pitied my friend for his impediment. Next day the same scene was re-enacted, although M. de La Trappe had begun to say that for a man unacquainted with him and without conversation my friend had looked long enough, and he only allowed his joining us because he was too kind to refuse me. I, too, thought that Rigaud had seen sufficient, and what I saw of the portrait confirmed me in that view, for it was very like and very well done, but he absolutely insisted on a further session which M. de La Trappe was loath to grant for he was becoming tired of him. By persistence rather than persuasion I managed to overcome this; he saying that it was an absurd waste of time to gaze at a man who was not worth seeing, met no one, and wished only to be private. He said at last that he yielded to my desire to please a friend whom he found totally incomprehensible, but it was for the last time. I therefore told Rigaud that he must manage as best he could for there would be no further sittings. He said, however, that half-an-hour would be enough, and he was better than his word.

When he had departed M. de La Trappe again expressed bewilderment at being stared at so long and so hard by a species of mute. I replied that my friend was deeply interested in him and had long wished to see him; once in his presence, he had been too much enthralled to avert his gaze. Then I changed the subject as quickly as possible, because the reason was not such as I had stated and the whole affair was indeed most unusual. In truth, I greatly feared lest the reality should dawn on him, which would have made it difficult if not impossible to proceed with the plan. As luck would have it he suspected nothing.

Rigaud worked all that day and the following without again seeing M. de La Trappe, and achieved as finished a masterpiece as though he had been allowed to paint directly from his model. The likeness was perfect, the sweetly serene expression, the sparkle in the eyes, always so hard to render, the intelligent, noble countenance, the inward peace of one who is master of his soul, all this was faithfully reproduced, even including the personal charm that had not deserted him, despite the ravages caused by penance, old age, and suffering. On the morning before Rigaud left I made him do a drawing of M. Maisne seated at M. de La Trappe's writing-table, for the pose and habit, and the writing-table itself. He then returned to Paris to transfer that precious head life-size on to canvas, with the body, table, and all the other details. Rigaud was moved to tears watching the noble spectacle of the choir at high mass on All Saints' Day; thus he did not have the heart to refuse the abbot when he begged for a full-size copy of my original. Indeed, the painter was so delighted with his success in so novel a style that he made other copies for himself and for the abbey, putting in the habit and all the accessories as they appeared in the picture itself.

Doing this took him a long time. He explained that the effort of recalling mental images had driven him nearly crazy when he tried to finish these copies, and for several months afterwards he was incapable of undertaking other portraits. Vanity prevented him from keeping his promise to me although I sent him three thousand écus on the day that he returned. He could not resist displaying his masterpiece before sending it to me three months later, and thus my secret became public property; but I consoled myself with the thought that I had preserved for ever this famous and well-loved face, and given to posterity the portrait of a noble and holy man. I did not dare tell M. de La Trappe of my rascally trick, but I wrote him a letter before leaving the abbey, confessing all and begging his forgiveness. He was, indeed, much vexed, but he could not bring himself to be angry with me. He replied that a Roman emperor once said that he loved treason but hated traitors, he himself was just the opposite, for he loved a traitor but deplored his treachery.

I gave two copies to the abbey and two smaller ones to M. Maisne and M. de Saint-Louis. M. de La Trappe for some years past had been unable to close his right hand, but when I received the original I noted that Rigaud had painted him sitting with a pen in that hand. I therefore made a note on the back of the canvas, so that there might be no mistake, and added that he had been painted from memory lest there should be any suspicion of his having posed for the portrait. I returned to Paris on the day before the King was due to arrive at Fontainebleau with the little princess,[1] and was at the coach-door when he stepped down. I hoped by so doing to conceal the fact that I had been away on my short excursion.

[1] The King was enchanted with the little girl. He sent a courier galloping to Mme de Maintenon with the message, 'She is the prettiest and most graceful little person I have ever seen; a perfect picture, with beautiful sparkling eyes, wonderful black eyelashes, a pink and white complexion, and the finest and thickest flaxen hair imaginable'. The Court assembled to meet them on the top of the horseshoe steps at Fontainebleau. She was so small that when the King led her in it seemed as though she was sticking out of his pocket.

CHAPTER VII

1697

Affair of the Archbishop of Cambrai continued – Dukes of Chevreuse and Beauvilliers in disgrace with Mme de Maintenon – M. de Cambrai banished to his Diocese for ever – Dismissal of the Italian Players – I rejoin the Army of the Maréchal de Choiseul – Peace signed at Ryswick – Remarkable Retirement of Mme de Maintenon's Brother – Marriage of Mgr le Duc de Bourgogne – A Black Nun at Moret, most mysterious

AT THE beginning of the year the Spanish priest Molinos,[1] supposedly head of the Quietists and reviver of their ancient heresies, died in Rome in the prison of the Inquisition, which reminds me that it is time to return to Fénelon. I left Mme Guyon in the fortress of Vincennes, having omitted much else concerning her because it may be found in the relevant documents. You must none the less know that before they arrested her she was for several months in the charge of Bossuet, Bishop of Meaux, either at his palace or at the convent of the Visitation there, where he was able thoroughly to examine her in doctrine, but could by no means persuade her to change her beliefs.[2] As you may imagine, she had carefully purged them, in fact or in appearance, of anything likely to offend, and had cleared herself of blame in connection with her journeyings in company with Père de La Combe.[3] In truth, had she not been most scrupulous in that respect she would never have overcome the moral rectitude of the Dukes of Chevreuse and Beauvilliers, their duchesses, the Archbishop of Cambrai, and the many other noble persons who formed the élite of her little flock.

She grew weary at last of being M. de Meaux's prisoner, pretended suddenly to see the light, and signed a recantation in terms which he directed. After which he, being of a kindly and unsuspicious nature, was deceived and procured her freedom. Mme Guyon's abuse of that liberty was what caused her exile from Paris, and, after her surreptitious return, her imprisonment at Vincennes. Such conduct from a supposed convert,

---

[1] Miguel de Molinos (1640–1696). Of great repute as a director of consciences at Rome. He wrote a famous spiritual treatise, *Guida Spirituale*, in which some perceived dangerous errors. He was cited before the Holy Office and imprisoned until his death. Quietism was the doctrine that perfection in this world consists in continual passive contemplation of the Deity.

[2] What he objected to was her leaning towards Quietism.

[3] François de La Combe, a Barnabite friar (1643–1715). He and Mme Guyon made several missionary journeys together unchaperoned.

combined with the negative result of the Issy tribunal[1] and Fénelon's sly ruse in confessing to M. de Meaux so as to stop his mouth, finally drove that prelate to expose Mme Guyon's doctrine in a book entitled *Instruction sur les Etats d'Oraison*. The publication of this work appeared vitally necessary to him, not only to relate the affair of Mme Guyon in simple language for all to understand, but also to explain the part played therein by M. de Cambrai. Since he was fully informed of the whole matter, as much by M. de Cambrai's conduct and evidence at Issy as by Mme Guyon's writings, the work did not take him long, and before printing it he showed Fénelon the manuscript. The latter at once saw the dangerous import of Bossuet's book and the urgent need to forestall it. It would not, in fact, have been surprising had he already had such a work in preparation, if not finished and revised; otherwise his speed would have seemed incredible, especially since what he produced was unintelligible to all but the most learned theologians, experts in mysticism of a peculiarly abstruse variety. His book was entitled *l'Explication des Maximes des Saints*. It was printed in two columns, one containing so-called holy and orthodox maxims, the other those which Fénelon regarded as being dangerous, suspect, or heretical. This was in order to demonstrate the abuse that might be made of honest mysticism. Being in a desperate hurry to publish before M. de Meaux, he had the printing done at express speed and, moreover, persuaded the Duc de Chevreuse to sit all day at the printing office, correcting the proofs as they came wet from the press. These dramatic measures succeeded so well that after a few days interval M. de Cambrai was able to present copies to the entire Court and the first edition was completely sold out.

If his readers were shocked to find that he quoted no authorities, they were infinitely more so by his ponderous style, dogmatic assertions, and the unfamiliar language that made the book as hard to read as a foreign tongue. Harder still was the subtle complication of ideas that left them gasping for breath in the rarefied atmosphere of ecclesiastical philosophy.[2] As I say, few apart from theologians could understand M. de Cambrai's book, and those who managed to do so were obliged to read it over and over again. Thus he had the mortification of receiving no praise and precious little in the way of thanks. Worse still, some erudite persons imagined that beneath the exotic language they could discern pure Quietism, refined, expanded, purged of lewdness, freed from coarseness, but none the less very evident, and combined with certain self-styled truths that appeared highly novel, vastly hard to credit, and impossible to put in practice. Here, as you may suppose, I do not offer a personal

---

[1] Took place 1694–5. Mme Guyon's case was examined by three eminent churchmen, including Bossuet himself. The verdict was that although her writings were censured as being Quietist, she herself was declared to be both virtuous and pious.

[2] The literary merits of Fénelon's book were not in general so severely judged.

opinion on matters far beyond me, but merely report what was said everywhere at that time, for people spoke of little else even when ladies were
present. Which reminds me that they resurrected a remark of Mme de
Sévigné at the time of the disputes over spiritual grace: 'Pray give my
religion a little substance, it is becoming so purified that it evaporates.'

Everyone, as I have said, was shocked, and the King and Mme de
Maintenon were greatly vexed, particularly with M. de Chevreuse for
correcting the proofs and with M. de Beauvilliers for having taken it
upon himself to offer the King a copy without Mme de Maintenon's
consent; for of course M. de Cambrai should have made the presentation
himself. It may well have been that Fénelon feared a public rebuff and
expected to fare better with M. de Beauvilliers acting as a go-between.
The only result, however, was to disgrace the dukes still more in Mme de
Maintenon's eyes, M. de Chevreuse by engaging in a task so far below
his station, and for a work of which she completely disapproved, M. de
Beauvilliers by acting independently and betraying her confidence. It was
that last which she could not forgive, and that was what finally decided
her to ruin them both.

Amidst all this traffic in manuscripts and doctrines, M. de Cambrai
resolved to seek mightier aid, for apart from the Jesuits, who were all on
his side, he had no allies in France. He therefore determined, contrary to
all our customs, to lay his case before the Pope, hoping in this way to
flatter the Vatican, always so insistent on delivering the first judgment.
Needless to say that he fully counted on the powerful support of the
Jesuits in Rome. At this moment, however, the Jesuits themselves were in
difficulties for the King had been warned that they were all for M. de
Cambrai, and, worse, that Pères de La Chaise and Valois, the princes'
confessors, both approved of his book, which sent him into such a passion
that he rated them soundly. Their superiors at once took fright, not only
for the royal confessionals, but for the safety of their whole Society. A
meeting of the four-vow pundits[1] was called, at which it was decided to
bow before the storm, but at the same time to hold fast to the plan for
Rome.

By this time it was Lent, and Père de La Rue[2] was the King's preacher.
To everyone's amazement, on the feast of the Assumption, instead of
pronouncing the blessing and coming down from the pulpit, after making
his three points, he asked the King's leave to sound a warning against
certain fanatics who, so he said, were seeking to discredit the well-trodden
paths of the established Church and replace them with novel and misleading byways. Then, taking for his theme devotion to the Blessed
Virgin and preaching with all the zeal of a Jesuit defending his Society

---

[1] Of the Jesuits. The fourth vow was of absolute obedience to the Pope in matters regarding
foreign missions and heretics.
[2] Charles de La Rue (1643-1725). One of the most famous preachers of that time.

against mortal attack, he drew parallels from life, in which no one could have mistaken the leading figures on either side of the controversy. His second sermon, lasting a full half-hour, contained some blunt speaking most unusual coming from the King's pulpit. M. de Beauvilliers, sitting just behind the princes, was obliged to listen to all of it, and submit to being stared at by the entire congregation. That same day, the famous preachers Bourdaloue and Gaillard made their churches ring with similar cries of alarm, and even the Jesuit preacher in the parish church of Versailles followed suit.

The facts of the matter were that Père Bourdaloue, as honest a man as ever preached, never relished what was then supposed to be Quietism. For whether the doctrine of Fénelon and Mme Guyon, in defence of which the *Maximes des Saints* had been written, was or was not Quietism, to what degree it was, or whether not at all, is something which I do not pretend to know. Rightly or wrongly, it was so considered to be, and so it was dubbed. Therefore, since there must be names in order to avoid confusion, that is the term which I shall use for it with the public.[1]

It was at this point that M. de Meaux's book appeared, two volumes *in-octavo*, which he presented to the King, his friends, and the principal personages at the Court and in Paris. Part dogma, part history, it dealt with all that had taken place from the very beginning between himself and the Archbishop of Paris and Bishop of Chartres on the one hand, and the Archbishop of Cambrai and Mme Guyon on the other. The book was well-written, concise and moderate, supported everywhere on the authority of the Scriptures, in most striking contrast to the obscurity and rigid pronouncements of the *Maximes des Saints*, which book it swiftly and completely annihilated. There was not a man or woman at the Court who did not enjoy reading Bossuet's work and plume himself on having been able to digest it. Indeed, it was for a long while the chief subject of conversation at Versailles and in Paris, and the author was publicly thanked by the King. At this same time M. de Paris and M. de Chartres both published works in the form of long pastoral letters addressed to their dioceses, that of M. de Chartres being judged by many connoisseurs to be especially excellent, sound, and learned. It was upon that rock that M. de Cambrai foundered.

The two important books, so different in style and content and so differently received, caused a great commotion. The King intervened, ordering M. de Cambrai to submit his work for scrutiny to the Archbishops of Rheims and Paris, and the Bishops of Meaux, Chartres, Toul, Soissons, and Amiens, in other words, to his worst enemies and the clergy who supported them. M. de Cambrai obeyed—he could scarcely do otherwise; but he expected no good from their examination. In the interval

---

[1] *Avec le publique: with, like,* or *to the public?* If we only knew which he intended we might have a clue as to whether he meant the *Memoirs* for publication.

the death took place of the Bishop of Metz, leaving vacant a blue ribbon and a post of counsellor of State for Church affairs. That death came at a very bad moment for M. de Cambrai, who had the humiliation of seeing the Order presented to M. de Paris, and the appointment to M. de Meaux. That, however, was not all, for Mme de Maintenon dismissed three of the principal ladies of Saint-Cyr, one of whom had long been her friend and confidante,[1] and she did not conceal the fact that their enthusiasm for Mme Guyon and her doctrine was the prime cause of their departure. All of this and the examination of his book made him decide to write submitting his case to the Pope, and he begged the King's leave to proceed to Rome. Permission was refused. M. de Meaux submitted his own book to the Pope, and Fénelon was obliged to endure the further humiliation of receiving only a formal acknowledgment from His Holiness, whilst seeing Bossuet triumphant with the answer that came to him. All three letters were afterwards published. M. de Cambrai's was beyond everything skilful, urbane, and courtly. Brilliant in style and language, he tactfully softened certain phrases in his book that might have been considered too strong for the honour of the episcopy and the maxims of the kingdom, and yet managed to make mince-meat of both beneath a semblance of modest humbleness. That in itself made a good impression, for people are generally prone to envy success and dislike oppression. Everyone was supposed to have been against him, and therefore the arrant flattery of his letter was forgiven him on grounds of necessity. For a time he caught a glimpse of returning favour. But not for long. His enemies became thoroughly alarmed and set to work on the King, who, without so much as seeing him, ordered him first to Paris, then back to his diocese; from which he never afterwards emerged.

With the order to M. de Cambrai the King sent another summoning Mgr le Duc de Bourgogne for a long session in his study, apparently in an attempt to detach him from a tutor whom he loved, and regretted with a bitterness which years of separation were powerless to dispel. Fénelon spent only two days in Paris and then departed to Cambrai. Before leaving, he wrote a letter to a friend[2] which also was soon afterwards published. It was a kind of manifesto couched in pseudo-pious language, as from one who had lost all hope and no longer sought to restrain himself. The lofty sarcasm was relieved by so much wit and, as a measure of precaution, by so much clever contrivance that the reading of it was a positive delight, although no one could have thought it praiseworthy. All of which goes to prove that when a man is ruined he cannot easily maintain a prudent, contemptuous silence.

[1] Mme de La Maisonfort. Mme de Maintenon was usually loyal to her old friends. Her behaviour at this point looks like panic lest the King suspect a political intrigue. Madame wrote, 'Mme Guyon, Fénelon and their friends are plotting great changes at the Court if the King should die. They mean to give all the higher offices to members of their faction.'

[2] Presumably to M. de Beauvilliers.

Before leaving the prelates I must not forget the death of the Duchesse de Noailles, mother of M. de Paris. She was a gifted woman, well liked by the King and the two queens,[1] most amiable, virtuous, and deeply religious throughout all her life. Her birth was low; it was riches that had made possible her marriage. Immediately after her widowhood she retired from the world and lived in seclusion with her son, as I have described. Her death was a sad loss to him. One of her sisters married M. de Tamponneau, president of the Chambre des Comptes. This Mme de Tamponneau was immensely wealthy, with a fine house, luxuriously appointed, and she had somehow the gift of attracting the best people to her drawing-room without providing cards for their diversion or any kind of refreshment. Princes of the blood, great nobles, high officials, generals, and fashionable ladies were always at her house, the young were banished, and not everyone was admitted. She herself seldom went out, but when she did she was treated everywhere like a queen. I mention this because I find it so remarkable.

The King very hurriedly dismissed the entire troop of the Italian players and refused to engage others.[2] So long as they had confined themselves to lewdness and an occasional blasphemy people had laughed at them; but when they performed a comedy entitled *The False Prude*, in which Mme de Maintenon was instantly recognizable, they were told to close their theatre forthwith (they had already given four performances in succession and were making a fortune) and leave France within the month. This caused a tremendous stir; yet though the players lost their employment through their impudence and folly she who had them banished gained nothing, on account of the licence that this comical episode allowed in speaking of her.

The assignments to the armies were the same as in the previous year but the princes did not serve. I joined the Maréchal de Choiseul at Landau towards the end of May, two days before the armies assembled. We then advanced to Heppenheim where forage was more plentiful and it was there that we celebrated the taking of Ath.[3] Thereafter we spent the remainder of the campaign first in one camp then in another, wherever supplies were best, until, in November, as we were encamped at Marxheim, we received news that the peace had been signed at Ryswick. In Flanders little had happened since the fall of Ath to the Maréchal de Catinat.[4] There had been nothing to do anywhere but observe and subsist. The negotiations had dragged on interminably, for much time was wasted in ceremony and the presentation of credentials. The Dutch who

[1] Anne of Austria the Queen-mother, and Maria Teresa of Spain (1638–1683), queen of Louis XIV.

[2] These players had existed in Paris since the reign of Charles IX, 1560–1574.

[3] Ath lies in Hainault between Mons and Oudenarde.

[4] Nicolas de Catinat (1637–1712). Maréchal de France. He was one of Louis XIV's best generals and a brilliant negotiator. The soldiers called him '*Le Père de la Pensée*'.

were longing for peace had become weary of the delays, and far more so
the Prince of Orange, who was losing his popularity in England and could
not extract all that he needed from the English Parliament. His chief
aims had been to force King Louis to recognize him as the King of England and, if possible, to have King James and his family driven out of
France.

I shall not embark on an account of the treaty. It will doubtless receive
the same treatment as those that preceded it. The chief actors and various
interested and learned spectators will write down their explanations of its
terms and significance.[1] The news of its signing was first brought to the
Court at Fontainebleau by an aide-de-camp of the Maréchal de Boufflers
on Sunday, 22 September. On the following morning two other couriers
appeared, one of them sent by the Elector of Bavaria to take the news on
to Spain, and four hours later, still another arrived from the Spanish
plenipotentiary, to carry home the news. M. de Bavière was so petty as
to write asking the King to delay the ambassador's courier so that his own
man might be first in Madrid. Absurdly enough there was no trouble in
keeping him at the Court, for he did not have a penny to pay for his food
or horses and in the end the King had to allow him journey-money.

The King and Queen of England were also at Fontainebleau, and to
them the recognition of the Prince of Orange came as a bitter blow; but
they comprehended the need for peace and well knew that that particular
clause was scarcely less distasteful to King Louis.[2] They therefore consoled themselves as best they might, and even managed to appear grateful
to the King for refusing to have them expelled from France, or even from
Saint-Germain, as had been most insistently demanded. The King was
so sympathetic to their feelings that he issued orders for none of the
couriers bringing news of a signature to be admitted when he was with
them, not even if three or four should arrive together, and he forbade the
musicians to sing any songs of rejoicing until after the English court had
left Fontainebleau.

I must now mention a somewhat trifling event that was none the less
most remarkable. Mme de Maintenon, at that prodigious, incredible
eminence to which she had so miraculously risen, was not without

[1] There followed an interlude of five years separating the first and last parts of the European
war. The second part, lasting for ten years, is known as the 'War of the Spanish Succession'.
By the terms of the Peace of Ryswick France restored all the conquests in the Low Countries
and on the Rhine which she had made since the Peace of Nijmegen, excepting Strasbourg.
Louis agreed also to recognize William as King of England, but refused to abandon James II.
He did however promise not to support any enemies of England 'without exception', which
covered both James and his son the Prince of Wales. William (which appears strange in modern
times) agreed to pay James's wife Mary of Modena a jointure of £50,000 every year.

[2] Mortifying indeed. Sometime earlier when William's fortunes were not so high King Louis
had offered to give him his eldest illegitimate daughter in marriage, believing that William
would snatch at the honour. William's reply that Princes of Orange married the daughters of
great kings, not their bastards, was a snub never to be forgotten.

personal troubles, and her brother with his heedless talk played no small part in them. He was known as the Comte d'Aubigné. He had never advanced further than captain of infantry, but from the way in which he spoke of his campaigns it might have appeared that he had been most shamefully used by not being made a Marshal of France. At other times he would say half in jest that he had taken his full bâton's worth in cash. There were the most appalling scenes with Mme de Maintenon for not having made him duke and peer and for other benefits which he said had passed him by, leaving him with nothing but the governorships of Cognac and Aigues-Mortes and some faint expectation of the Order. He was for ever chasing after whores at the Tuileries and everywhere else, and living with them for most of the time, amongst their families and suchlike, and spending a vast deal of money on them.

He was a complete spendthrift, a madman who should have been shut up, but withal infinitely diverting, and with such witty sallies and repartees that one could not hear enough of them. Moreover, he was a good fellow and a gentleman, quite free from the vanity in his sister's position that might have made him insolent. He was that in any case, and in the pleasantest way imaginable, for he delighted in telling us of her life with Scarron and at the Hôtel d'Albret,[1] using no restraint when he described her amorous adventures and contrasted them with her present piety and majesty, marvelling all the while at her colossal good fortune. Yet for all that he was so diverting he was often embarrassing, for he never knew where to stop and held forth not only among friends but in company, at table, on a bench at the Tuileries, and quite freely in the great gallery at Versailles, where he was just as funny as elsewhere, constantly making casual reference to the King as 'm'brother-in-law'. I have heard him speak many times in that way, particularly at my father's house, where he was wont to appear more often than he was welcome, and always stayed to dinner. I used sometimes to chuckle at my parents' extreme embarrassment, for they often did not know where to look.

A brother of that kind, so incapable of restraint and with the wit to strike withering blows, fearing neither ridicule nor punishment, was an intolerable burden on Mme de Maintenon. In a different way she was little better off with her sister-in-law, the daughter of an obscure doctor who had risen to be King's procurator of the city of Paris. Mme de Montespan had made the match for him in 1678, thinking to do him a kindness at the time when Mme de Maintenon was governess to her children. But she was, if possible, even more plebeian than her birth, albeit virtuous and modest (as she needed to be with such a husband), marvellously stupid, of commonplace appearance, and so totally devoid of any social sense that

[1] As will be remembered Mme de Maintenon's first husband was the crippled poet Paul Scarron. The Maréchal d'Albret was the friend who had originally introduced her to Mme de Montespan, and was thus indirectly responsible for her 'colossal luck'.

Mme de Maintenon found it equally embarrassing to receive her in company or refuse her admittance. There was nothing to be done with her,
and eventually Mme de Maintenon saw her only in private. The poor
creature never went into Society, but spent her time with a few vulgar
cronies in her quarter of Paris, making frequent, only too well-justified
complaints of her husband, which his sister, though she queened it over
everyone else, could do nothing about; for he would not listen to reason
and sometimes even manhandled her.

At last, her patience becoming exhausted, she applied to Saint-Sulpice
on the grounds of his being completely irresponsible and always in need
of money. Those priests eventually persuaded him to leave his debauchery, indiscretions, and domestic quarrels in exchange for a quiet
life, with his expenses paid each month and ample pocket-money. On
those conditions he retired into a community for gentlemen and near-
gentlemen, established under the belfry of Saint-Sulpice by a certain M.
Doyen. The inmates lived in a kind of perpetual retreat in the practice of
religion and under the direction of the Sulpiciens. Mme d'Aubigné, for
the sake of peace and quiet, but still more at the desire of Mme de Maintenon, was prevailed on to enter a convent, telling her old cronies in confidence that she thought it very hard lines after all that had happened
and that they might well have spared her that.

M. d'Aubigné left no one unaware that his sister lied when she boasted
of his conversion. He said that he was besieged by priests and that they
would be the death of him if he stayed long with M. Doyen. Indeed, he
was soon out again with the whores at the Tuileries and wherever else he
could find them. They retrieved him, however, and gave him one of the
dullest and dreariest priests at Saint-Sulpice to act as his keeper, following him about like his shadow and boring him to extinction. His name was
Madot.[1] Anyone with an ounce of spirit would have refused such futile
employment, but that Madot had nothing better to do; no wit to occupy
himself otherwise, and no capacity even for feeling bored. Aubigné continually insulted him, but he was paid to be that and fully earned his
salary by an assiduity of which no other would have been capable. The
Aubignés had an only daughter[2] to whom Mme de Maintenon gave a
home, taking her with her wherever she went, lodging her in her own
apartments, and bringing her up as though she were indeed her child.

I arrived in Paris with most of those who had been serving in Flanders
and Germany and went at once to Versailles where I found the Court
just returned from Fontainebleau.[3] Mme de Saint-Simon had remained
there most agreeably during the entire excursion, and the King gave me

[1] François Madot (1675–1753). Became Bishop of Belley and later of Châlon-sur-Saône. An
example of the contempt which Saint-Simon felt for all the priests of Saint-Sulpice.

[2] Françoise d'Aubigné, who later married the Comte d'Ayen, the Duc de Noailles's eldest son.

[3] The annual six-week visit to Fontainebleau whilst Versailles was being cleaned and the
'foul air' changed for fresh. The windows in the Salle des Glaces were kept permanently sealed.

a very kind welcome. I found that there had been a slight domestic upset which I shall none the less mention because it led to higher advancement and one loves to look back to beginnings. It will also serve to explain the budding court of the little princess, on whom all eyes were turned because already the King and Mme de Maintenon were vastly diverted by her. The Court saw her only twice a week at her dressing-table. Thus she was always with her own ladies, to whom the King added a few others so that she should not constantly see the same faces. It was an immense favour to be allowed that privilege, which many coveted and had been refused.

Mme de Saint-Simon's modest appearance and behaviour had greatly pleased the King at Fontainebleau. He had several times remarked on it, which gave the Comtesse de Roucy, Mme la Maréchale de Lorges's friend, the idea of proposing her for that entrée to the Duchesse du Lude, who, believing that the Maréchale de Lorges had been hinting, went to call on her. She discovered that such a thing had never entered my mother-in-law's head, and thereupon told her that many who had asked had been snubbed, urging her not to appear over-eager.

Now it happened that the Comtesse de Mailly, an intimate friend of Mme de Lorges's and mine, a friend and kinswoman of the whole Mailly family, and especially of her brother-in-law the Abbé de Mailly later Archbishop of Arles, had already mentioned Mme de Saint-Simon to Mme de Maintenon, entirely on her own initiative. Mme de Maintenon had said that she should long since have been admitted, because people like Mme de Saint-Simon were just what the princess needed, and she told Mme de Mailly to say so, as coming from her, to the Duchesse du Lude. This she did, but as luck would have it she met Mme du Lude as she was going upstairs after visiting Mme la Maréchale de Lorges. The duchess was vastly astonished, so many highly favoured persons having been refused, and more than a little annoyed, for she felt convinced that Mme de Lorges had known already and was deceiving her. See how at courts the most straightforward actions are mistaken for trickery! Mme de Saint-Simon received her summons on the following day and every day afterwards during the remainder of the visit to Fontainebleau, and quite often since, much to the envy of those ladies who had been refused and of their families.

The King continued to be delighted with the princess, who fully merited his affection by her extraordinary precociousness, her charm, intelligence, and response to his advances. He determined to lose no time after her twelfth birthday, which fell on 7 December, a Saturday, before celebrating the wedding. He let it be known that he would like the Court to be resplendent and himself ordered some fine clothes, although for years past he had dressed with the utmost simplicity. That was enough for everyone, excepting priests and lawyers, to disregard their purses, or even their rank. There was hot competition in splendour and originality, with scarcely enough gold and silver lace to go round and the merchants' booths emptied in a very few days; in a word, unbridled extravagance reigned throughout the Court and Paris, for crowds went to watch the great spectacle.[1] The thing was carried to such a pitch that the King regretted ever having made the suggestion, saying that he failed to understand how husbands could be so foolish as to ruin themselves for their wives' clothes, or, he might have added, for their own. But he had slackened the reins; there was no time to remedy matters, and I almost believe that he was glad of it, for he loved rich materials and ingenious craftsmanship, and greatly enjoyed seeing all the fine clothes, praising the most magnificent and the best contrived. He had made his little protest on principle, but was enchanted to find that no one had heeded him.

This was not the last time that he so acted. He passionately loved to see every kind of splendour at his Court, especially on State occasiors, and anyone who had listened to his protests would have found themselves sadly out of favour. Indeed, amidst so much folly there was no chance for prudence; many different costumes were needed, and Mme de Saint-Simon and I spent twenty thousand *livres* between us. There was a dearth of tailors and dressmakers to make up the fine garments. Mme la Duchesse took it into her head to send archers[2] to kidnap those working for the Duc de Rohan, but the King learned of it and was not pleased; he made her return them immediately. It is worth noting that the Duc de Rohan was a man whom he actively disliked and never scrupled to pretend otherwise. He did something else that was particularly chivalrous, and showed how much he wished everyone to be smart. He personally selected a design for some embroidery to give to the princess. The embroiderer said that he would put everything else on one side so as to finish it. The King would not allow that; he told him most explicitly to finish all that he had on hand, and only then work on his order, and he added that if it were not finished in time the princess would do without it.

It had been announced that the rejoicings should last until Christmas, but be restricted to two balls, one opera, and a display of fireworks, and there were no more balls during the rest of that winter. In order to save argument and quarrels the King reduced the ceremonial to the bare minimum, ruling that there should be no betrothal in his study but only in the chapel before the wedding, so as to avoid having royal train-bearers, for in the chapel her train would be carried as usual by the captain of her bodyguard. He also ruled that Mgr le Duc de Bourgogne alone should take her by the hand to lead her to and from the chapel, and that M. le

---

[1] Versailles was open to the public on State occasions; anyone could attend the King's parties and eat his refreshments, provided he had a sword and a dress coat, or, if a woman, a court-dress. You left your sword with the officer at the top of the stairs.

[2] *Hoquetons:* archers or yeomen. They wore smocks like workmen, and so, one supposes, would look as innocent as removal men, which in this case they were.

Prince alone of all the princes should sign the curé's book. That, we concluded, was for the sake of the bastards, who might have felt humiliated at not signing, whereas the princes might have objected to their doing so. Mme de Verneuil was invited to the wedding and was given the lowest seat at the State banquet, as had happened at the marriages of the Ducs de Chartres and du Maine; but she was sent back to Paris immediately after. The Duchesse d'Angoulême, widow of Charles IX's bastard, was not asked because she did not rank as a princess.

On the morning of Saturday, 7 December, the entire Court went early to the apartments of Mgr le Duc de Bourgogne and followed him to those of the princess. She was already dressed, attended by only a few of her ladies, most of whom were gone to the tribunes and stands erected for spectators in the chapel. The royal family had visited her earlier and were waiting in the King's study, where the bridal pair presented themselves shortly after noon. The King then led the way to the chapel. The procession and everything else was just as it had been for the marriage of the Duc de Chartres, except that Cardinal de Coislin officiated at the betrothal and everyone knelt between that service and the marriage.

It was on the whole rather a boring day. At seven in the evening the King and Queen of England arrived to supper; the queen was seated between the two kings. On leaving the table everyone went to put the bride to bed, men being rigidly excluded by order of the King. All the ladies remained, and the Queen of England gave her the nightgown, which was presented to her by the Duchesse du Lude. Mgr le Duc de Bourgogne undressed seated on a folding stool in the ante-room, attended by the King and all the princes. The King of England gave him the nightshirt, which was presented by the Duc de Beauvilliers.

As soon as Mme la Duchesse de Bourgogne was in bed Mgr le Duc de Bourgogne entered and climbed into bed on her right side in the presence of the King and the entire Court. The King and Queen of England then left, the King retired to his *coucher*, and everyone else left the room, except Monseigneur, the princess's ladies, the Duc de Beauvilliers who stayed beside his pupil, and the Duchesse du Lude who stood at the other side. Monseigneur remained chatting for a quarter of an hour, after which he told his son to get out of bed, ordering him to kiss the princess, despite the Duchesse du Lude's protests. It turned out that she had the right of it, for the King took it much amiss, saying that he would not have his grandson kiss so much as the tip of her little finger until it was time for them to live together as man and wife. Because of the cold Mgr le Duc de Bourgogne dressed again in the ante-room and then went to sleep in his own room as usual. That naughty little rogue the Duc de Berry thought his brother far too meek; he said that he never would have left her bed.

I must mention one other event, in order to show what confidence the King reposed in his valets. During that visit to Fontainebleau everyone

was greatly surprised when soon after her arrival the princess, for she
was not then married, was sent by Mme de Maintenon to a little un-
fashionable convent at Moret, where there was nothing to interest her
and no nuns of high rank. She returned there several times during the
visit, which gave rise to many rumours. Mme de Maintenon often used
to go there from Fontainebleau, and in the end people had become
accustomed to her doing so. Now there was in that convent a professed
nun who was black, identity unknown, and never introduced to anyone.
Bontemps, whom I have already mentioned, the head valet, and governor
of Versailles, had placed her there very young and had paid a dowry (how
much no one knew), and continued to pay her a large pension every year.
He saw to it that she had all the necessary and as amply as befits a nun,
and furnished her with all the comforts that she could desire. The late
queen often visited there and appeared much concerned for the welfare
of that convent, and Mme de Maintenon was the same. Neither of them
paid particular attention to the black nun, but they were not less civil to
her than to the others. They saw her not every time, but most often when
they visited, and carefully inquired after her health, conduct, and the
way in which her superior treated her. Monseigneur went once or twice
and the princes also when they were children; and all of them saw the
black nun and asked kindly after her. She was regarded with far more
respect than well known and distinguished members of that community,
and she showed herself somewhat vain of the attentions and mystery surrounding her. She lived according to the rule, but it was plain to see that
her vocation was not unaided. She was once heard to say when Monseigneur was hunting in the forest nearby, 'Oh! that must be my brother
hunting.' She is supposed to have been a daughter of the King and Queen,
hidden away because of the colour of her skin at a time when the Queen
was announced to have had a mishap. Many courtiers were certain of it;
but however that may have been, the whole affair remained a mystery.[1]

---

[1] No real mystery, despite the many rumours. The Duc de Luynes, writing in the reign of
Louis XV, says that she was the child of Moorish parents, attached to the Zoo at Versailles, and
that Mme de Maintenon had placed her in the convent out of charity.

CHAPTER VIII

1698

Marriage of M. de Levis – Duke of Saint Albans sent as Envoy – Lapse of Cardinal d'Estrées – Danger for the Dukes of Chevreuse and Beauvilliers – Saintly goodness of the Duc de Beauvilliers and the Archbishop of Paris – Comical incident regarding M. de Cambrai and M. de La Trappe – Charnacé's ruse – Birth of my elder son – Curé de Seurre burned at Dijon – The Camp of Compiègne – Origin of my friendship with Pontchartrain – Scandal and separation of Barbezieux and his wife

Two marriages diverted the Court at the beginning of this year; the first was that of Mlle de Chevreuse and the Marquis de Levis, who later succeeded his father as lieutenant-general of Bourbonnais, where their estates were situated. He was a well-built young man, very much the soldier and thoroughly debauched, without the faintest gloss of an education, but for all that a man of wit and honour and with a strong desire to better himself. His father, of excellent understanding, was totally unprincipled. He lived retired at his country home, and in obscurity when he came to Paris. His mother gambled everywhere unceasingly, was monstrously mean, and as bulky and ill-clad as a fish-wife. None of which was suited to the manners and dispositions of M. and Mme de Chevreuse. Paucity of dowry, and birth equal to any alliance were what decided them, with the added inducement of a post as palace-lady reserved for the bride.

When the time came to sign the contract, the terms of which were already agreed, negotiations were suddenly brought to a halt over the marquis's Christian name. His father and mother inquired of one another in vain; it appeared that he had none; which led them to doubt whether he had been baptized. No one knew. They then remembered that his wet-nurse was still alive and in Paris. It was she whom they consulted. She told them that when they were taking the new-born baby to Bourbonnais to show him to his grandfather the late Marquis de Levis they had spent a night at the house of M. Colbert, Bishop of Auxerre. He had been much disturbed at the thought of so young an infant travelling so far unbaptized, and after trying in vain to obtain the parents' consent to private baptism, he had roused the nurse and baby early next morning and had baptized him in the chapel, letting them afterwards continue their journey without saying anything about it. In Bourbonnais, the christening was put off time and again for a number of reasons and still had not taken place when the nurse left the family, which troubled her not at all since she knew him to have been baptized.

This incident is so remarkable that I include it both for its own sake and because it so well illustrates the kind of people who could be capable of such negligence. As a result, M. de Levis, in the space of a single day, was obliged to undergo the ceremonies of christening, first confession, and first communion, with marriage to follow at midnight, in Paris, at the Hôtel de Luynes.[1]

Two days afterwards the Comte d'Estrées[2] married Mlle d'Ayen. Mlle de Toisy,[3] a rich and childless old party, who kept company far above her station, a friend of Cardinal d'Estrées and much cosseted by Mme de Noailles, contributed a large part of the inconsiderable dowry; and the Cardinal himself, hoping great things from the rising favour of the Noailles, smoothed the rest of the way from his own purse. He married them and said midnight mass in the chapel at Versailles. Mme la Duchesse de Bourgogne and the highest Society were present in the tribunes, and crowds of guests below. The wedding was celebrated at M. de Noailles's. Next day the new Marquise de Levis and the new Comtesse d'Estrées were appointed palace-ladies.

King William of England was gratified beyond measure at being recognized at last by King Louis and secure upon his throne. But usurpers cannot live truly satisfied and at peace, and this one bitterly resented the continued presence of the rightful monarch and his family at Saint-Germain. It was too close to King Louis and to England for his comfort. He had made every effort at Ryswick to have them banished, but our King had been obdurate. William now resolved to stake everything on one throw, and, by showering the King with compliments and tokens of respect, to see whether he could not gain what he desired by sweetness alone.

With this end in view he sent the Duke of Saint Albans,[4] a knight of the Garter, to congratulate the King on the marriage of Mgr le Duc de Bourgogne. He could scarcely have chosen a greater man for a more trivial mission; indeed, it was a wonder that he did not refuse, for as the bastard of Charles II, James's elder brother, he would have had every excuse. He made efforts to obtain special privileges on that account but was firmly though politely treated as no better than any other envoy from England. The dukes of that country do not rank as dukes in France, and neither do French dukes so rank in England. It is true that King Louis

---

[1] Four out of a possible six—he was spared only Extreme Unction and Holy Orders.

[2] Later the Maréchal de Cœuvres, and after his father's death the Maréchal-duc d'Estrées. The bride's name was Lucie Félicité de Noailles.

[3] Jeanne Jappin, wife of François Chaillou de Toisy. She had been the mistress of the Bishop of Langres; hence her great wealth. Women of the upper-middle class were always referred to as Mademoiselle, even after marriage, whereas official royal mistresses were called Madame, even if single.

[4] Charles Beauclerk (1670–1726).

made the Duchess of Portsmouth and her son the Duke of Richmond a brevet duke and duchess,[1] and on the spur of the moment he gave a *tabouret* to his friend Charles II's mistress, the Duchess of Cleveland, but those were special cases, not affecting the general rule.

Whilst on the subject of foreigners I must briefly mention the visit in the early months of this year of the Duke of Parma's brother, incognito, but the King was none the less anxious to do him honour and allowed him to kiss Mme la Duchesse de Bourgogne. He stayed in France for most of the year. I remember that at Fontainebleau, where people were more apt to give one another banquets than elsewhere, Cardinal d'Estrées wished to give one for him. He invited in great numbers the most distinguished people at the Court, and he invited me, too, together with many others who were not of his immediate circle to do honour to this Prince of Parma. As it happened, however, we were obliged to have our feast without him. The Cardinal, in the preceding days as he went about his business, had asked his guests as and where he found them; he remembered all but the prince. On the date appointed he suddenly called him to mind. He asked his staff which of them had taken the invitation; he learned that no such order had been given. Then he sent a message in a hurry. But it turned out that the Prince of Parma was otherwise engaged and had been bidden elsewhere for some time past. We teased Cardinal d'Estrées monstrously for the extraordinary lapse. It was not by any means his only one.

In the meantime there had been a great resurgence of the affair of M. de Cambrai, and documents piled up on either side. Père de La Combe was sent to the Bastille and awful things were said to have been discovered concerning him. Mme de Maintenon unmasked, and went into perpetual conference with the Bishops of Paris, Meaux, and Chartres. The last had not forgiven Fénelon for trying to snatch her from Saint-Cyr, his own territory, and the first, so recently connected with her by marriage,[2] still had the charm of novelty which she could not resist. Her aim was still to introduce M. de Paris into the distribution of benefices, in order to obstruct Père de La Chaise, whom she disliked as much as she did his Society. Thus any cause likely to benefit the archbishop or his interests was espoused by her, and she was equally ready to discredit those in a position to outweigh him in the King's regard. The Dukes of Chevreuse and Beauvilliers and their wives were already closely bound to King Louis by old ties of trust and friendship, which had been the cause of their prosperous and seemingly impregnable position at the Court, but which had not shielded them from envy. Now was the opportunity to dislodge them. Mme de Maintenon, led on by M. de Chartres, and already

---

[1] Louise de Kéroualle (1649-1734), Charles II's mistress, and Charles Lennox (1672-1723), who went to live in France after his father's death.

[2] Archbishop de Noailles's nephew the Comte d'Ayen had recently married Mme de Maintenon's niece.

vexed with both dukes because of their independent attitudes regarding *Les Maximes des Saints*, which the one had corrected and the other presented to the King, consented to their destruction, and the Duc de Noailles, hoping to reap the spoils, continually encouraged her. He believed, indeed, that if the Duc de Beauvilliers were to be dismissed from his post of governor to the princes he would be forced to leave the Court and that his lesser offices would then also fall vacant.

Troubles, increasing and multiplying over the condemnation in Rome of M. de Cambrai's book, became their chief weapon.[1] Mme. de Maintenon informed the King that he was bound in conscience to protect the true faith and dismiss the upholders of false doctrine from his councils, and she added the names of many unimportant persons to those of the Dukes of Chevreuse and Beauvilliers. To leave the latter as governor of the princes would, she said, give undue bias at Rome and cause embarrassment to the Pope. King Louis would have to answer before God for leaving so great an obstacle in the path of justice. It was high time to dismiss him and show the Pope that he might proceed unhindered.

Young though I was, I knew enough to fear the worst. Mme de Maintenon was in a state of eruption; she had allowed some unconsidered words to escape her in private, and had fairly let fly to Mme la Duchesse de Bourgogne, even before the palace-ladies. The clouds were gathering. The courtiers perceived them, and for the first time envy dared to show its face. Mme de Roucy, avid for vengeance[2] and basely eager to toady to Mme de Maintenon, recorded every word of such incidents, always returning triumphantly with some tasty morsel which, very imprudently, she would confide to me, though she well knew me to be a friend of both dukes. So blind is hatred! I carefully garnered all this information; I compared it with what I learned from elsewhere; I discussed the matter with Louville who, at my request, more than once remonstrated with M. de Beauvilliers; but all in vain. The latter did not at all realize the immediacy of the danger; he saw only the bare outline, for no one had dared to tell him all the facts. I therefore determined to go myself to make him face the truth, hiding nothing of what I had discovered.

I accordingly went to see him and carried out my plan to the very letter, adding, with perfect truth, that the King's faith in him had been shaken. M. de Beauvilliers listened attentively and did not interrupt me. Then, after thanking me for my love and solicitude, he confessed that he and

---

[1] Fénelon's book *Les Maximes des Saints* was not finally condemned until 1699. Twenty-three of his so-called virtuous maxims were pronounced rash, dangerous, and erroneous, and those who read or possessed the book were subject to excommunication. Cardinal de Bouillon, defending him at Rome, became so abusive to the other cardinals on the consistory that the Pope exclaimed, '*E un porco ferito!*' (He is like a wounded boar!)

[2] Beauvilliers had given evidence against her in a lawsuit over an inheritance, and she was still furious with him although she had won her case.

M. de Chevreuse and their wives had for some time past noticed that a great change had come over Mme de Maintenon, the courtiers, and even the King himself. But when I urged him to be more neutral, at least in appearance, to comply a little, and to speak to the King, I found him absolutely immovable. He simply said that from all he could hear he did believe that he was in danger; but that he had never coveted office. God had given him the posts which he held, and he was ready to relinquish them all at His command.[1] He said also that the only satisfaction he received from them was the good that they enabled him to do; without that he would be thankful to have God only to account to for his actions, and nothing but prayers to occupy him in retirement. These feelings, he said, were not mere stubbornness; he did sincerely believe that he was right and preferred to wait calmly and submissively to know the will of God, taking particular heed to do nothing that might give him cause for remorse on his deathbed. He then tenderly embraced me, and I departed deeply moved by those Christian, noble, and uncommon sentiments. Never shall I forget his words. Were I to repeat them a hundred times I vow that I should say them in the very same order that he spoke them.

At this critical moment when the storm seemed just about to break there occurred a miracle, and, by God's will, M. de Paris became his judge. The King, spurred on as to principles by the prelates and pressed over details by Mme de Maintenon, who openly proposed the Duc de Noailles for all M. de Beauvilliers's offices, held to the latter by a mere thread of his old esteem and friendship. Yet even that was enough to make him loath to cause him pain. Torn in half, he resolved to take one of the three bishops into his confidence. That he did not choose M. de Chartres may have been because that prelate's attachment to Mme de Maintenon was so close as to make them think alike on every subject. With M. de Meaux there was not that drawback, and moreover he was accustomed to confide in him on matters of conscience, for Bossuet still retained the *entrées* and special privileges of the time when he had been Monseigneur's tutor. He had also on many occasions been the sole witness of the angry scenes that had finally parted the King and Mme de Montespan, indeed, he alone had known of them and had endured all their quarrels. Be that as it may, despite that ancient bond, something prevented the King from approaching him now and made him turn to the Archbishop of Paris, the very one who might most reasonably have been excluded, since his own brother stood to gain by the outcome. The King, however, was undeterred by such a consideration and made the consultation so full as actually to promise that should M. de Beauvilliers be dismissed all his posts would be given to the Duc de Noailles.

---

[1] Beauvilliers wrote to his spiritual director on 10 June, 1698, 'If I do not say immediately whether Mme Guyon is either mad or bad I shall be dismissed from the Court. I am entirely in your hands'.

If M. de Paris had so decided the ruin of one duke and the advancement of the other would have been the work of a moment. Yet if the
nobility of M. de Beauvilliers had astounded me, that of the Archbishop
was to appear more marvellous still, for surely it is easier to submit humbly
to destruction by the will of God than to preserve the protector of one's
enemy and by so doing destroy the chances of a much-loved brother. That,
none the less, was what M. de Paris unhesitatingly did, with the result
that it was decided to dismiss only a few subordinates whose departure
would serve to demonstrate the King's carefulness without causing so
great a shock as the ruin of the Duc de Beauvilliers.

Thus the duke was saved and the King was very glad of it. All Mme de
Maintenon's influence had been powerless to destroy old ties of habit and
regard, and so in a lesser degree it had been with M. de Chevreuse who
would have fallen alongside M. de Beauvilliers. Both were again firmly
entrenched, for the King, his conscience clear, once more breathed freely
and became impervious to all assaults upon them. The storm did, however, break over other heads, and M. de Beauvilliers was too closely involved to be able to help them. A great number of M. de Cambrai's friends
were disgraced and Mme Guyon was transferred from Vincennes to the
Bastille where, since she was given two serving maids to wait, or perhaps
to spy, on her, it was concluded that she would remain for life.[1] The
shock of that bore hard upon the Dukes of Chevreuse and Beauvilliers
and their wives. At Versailles, where they went little into Society, the
effect was scarcely noticeable, but on the following Thursday, the fourth
after the news broke, the King went to Marly and there they suffered
almost complete isolation. No one willingly approached them, and when
chance or occasion brought people into their neighbourhood they were
on thorns till they had removed themselves, and made off as soon as
possible. This was a new situation for the sister-duchesses and a bitter
pill for them to swallow; but equalling their husbands in virtue and good
breeding, they made advances to none, remained calm, and watched with
seeming indifference the tide of the Court as it swept past them. Those
few persons who came up to them they greeted as usual, appearing not
unduly delighted and above all not seeking for notice, yet all the while
carefully noting the bearing of each individual and the varying degrees of
their fear, prudence, or estrangement. Their husbands, just as much
courted and even more sought after than their wives, were left totally
neglected, but they remained equally unmoved. This continued for a
time, and then little by little people returned to them as they saw that the
King's favour was as great as ever.

In the midst of all this something happened that more than a little

---

[1] Mme de Maintenon, however, wrote to M. de Noailles that she regretted the need for such
severity, adding, 'our Court-Quietists are abandoning Mme Guyon almost as inopportunely as
they at first supported her'.

disturbed me. M. de Meaux had once been a friend of M. de La Trappe; he had been to see him, and they occasionally corresponded. At the beginning of the controversy he had sent him the various documents, including M. de Cambrai's first publications and a copy of *Les Maximes des Saints*, asking him to examine them all and tell him in confidence what he thought of them. M. de La Trappe read everything with great attention. As a scholar and a most learned divine, M. de Cambrai's book deeply shocked and surprised him, and the more deeply he delved into it the more horrified he became. When the time arrived to answer M. de Meaux he wrote as to a friend, in confidence, firmly believing that his letter would be seen by no one else. Thus he did not choose his words as he would have done for a public utterance, but said candidly after very little preamble that if M. de Cambrai were to be believed it would be better by far to burn the Gospels and reproach Jesus Christ for coming into the world to deceive us.[1] The dreadful import of those words so much alarmed M. de Meaux that he showed them to Mme de Maintenon, who, eager to crush M. de Cambrai beneath every available authority, absolutely insisted on their being published.

You may imagine the cry of triumph from one side and the anguished shrieks from the other. M. de Cambrai and his supporters could scarcely find pens or tongues enough to voice their loud complaint against M. de La Trappe, who from his safe retreat had dared to anathematize an archbishop and rudely question his authority on a matter still under examination by the Pope. M. de La Trappe, deeply disturbed by the impression created by his letter, and still more so by being brought into prominence when he least expected it, wrote a second time to M. de Meaux, reproaching him for revealing a private communication that should have been burned as soon as read. In very truth, had they only paused to consider, M. de Cambrai and his friends might with better cause have directed their wrath against M. de Meaux and Mme de Maintenon, instead of M. de La Trappe. But their anger with the two former had spent itself; they now turned all their fury against the latter and never forgave him.

It sometimes happens for the best-conducted people to idolize the object of their passion, for such is human nature. I was passionately devoted to M. de La Trappe; very deeply attached to M. de Beauvilliers, and excellent friends with M. de Chevreuse. The latter two spoke freely before me and thus it occasionally happened that they let slip bitter criticisms of M. de La Trappe which I should much have preferred not to hear. I remember, for instance, that after dining one evening with M. de Beauvilliers in his apartment at Fontainebleau he proposed that M. de Chevreuse, the Duc de Béthune, and I should drive with him round the canal. We had scarcely started before old Béthune began on the subject of M. de La Trappe, and before long all three were at it hammer

---

[1] He was appalled by the Jansenist doctrine of predestined Grace, and the denial of free will.

and tongs despite my gentle protests and lapses into silence. At last, unable to contain myself any longer, I stated bluntly that though I realized it was not for me at my age to tell older men to hold their tongues, one might at any age ask to be let out of a carriage. Then, after telling them that I loved them still the same and would not see them less often, which I assured them was sure proof of my attachment, I begged them once again to consider my feelings and stop the carriage. MM. de Chevreuse and de Beauvilliers smiled at me and said, 'As you please; we are in the right of it, but we will say no more,' and they hushed the Duc de Béthune when he tried to continue. I wanted to insist, but not disagreeably, on being set down so as to leave them in peace; but they would not hear of it, and they were so good as never afterwards to say a word against M. de La Trappe in my presence. Old Béthune was not so considerate, however, but I felt no compunction with him and answered in such a way that he was quickly silenced.

One more word on this subject because the incident was really most peculiar. The Duc de Charost, old Béthune's son, was a very close friend of mine and always in and out of our apartment. He had been one of the earliest members of Mme Guyon's little flock and, as such, had been protected by the Dukes of Chevreuse and Beauvilliers, although they never talked to him of other matters. He had become perfectly infatuated with M. de Cambrai and was therefore fanatically opposed to M. de La Trappe. In general we laughed and joked together, but every so often he went too far in disrespect of that person. I had warned him many times to leave M. de La Trappe alone; I said that he might say what he pleased of anyone else and I would mock with him; but M. de La Trappe was a sacred subject to me and I entreated him to spare my feelings and not to provoke sharp answers which I should be unable to suppress. Yet despite repeated warnings he embarked on that very subject at Marly, after dinner in Mme de Saint-Simon's room, when we were alone except for Mmes du Châtelet and de Nogaret. I tried at first to stop him, reminding him of what I had so often said, but he pressed on from one jibe to another accompanied by bitter jests which he made no effort to restrain. Finally, he blurted out that M. de La Trappe was a patriarch to me and that no one else counted for anything. 'True!' said I furiously. 'We both have our patriarchs, but the difference is that mine has never been on the wrong side of the law.' (This was a short time after M. de Cambrai's condemnation by Rome.)

At that retort Charost, who had been standing, began to reel, and stammered out some sort of an answer. His throat swelled; his eyes started from his head, and his tongue protruded from his mouth. Mme de Nogaret screamed, Mme du Châtelet leaped for his cravat to untie it, whilst Mme de Saint-Simon rushed for the water-jug, dashed a few drops over him and tried to make him swallow some more. In the midst of all this I, immobile, observed how sudden a change can be effected by a paroxysm of rage on an excess of infatuation. Even so I could not be displeased with my retort.

It took the time of three or four paters to restore him. His first words were that nothing was the matter, that he felt perfectly well, but was grateful to the ladies. I then apologized, but reminded him that he had been warned. He tried to answer me, but the ladies interrupted him and we spoke of other matters until he had pulled himself together sufficiently to depart. Not for a moment were we less happy together afterwards, not even later that same afternoon; but what greatly benefited me was that he never again erred on the subject of M. de La Trappe. The ladies scolded me after he had gone, and all three turned upon me for they could not get over their surprise and alarm at what they had just witnessed. At last we all agreed for Charost's sake and on principle to tell no one what had happened and, indeed, no one knows to this day.

The King had Charnacé[1] arrested in the provinces. He was already much vexed with his conduct in Anjou, where he had been banished to his estates, and had had him taken into custody and sent to Montauban under suspicion of serious crimes, especially that of making false money. He was a man of spirit, who had been one of the King's pages, an officer of the bodyguard, and in the best Society before he was sent to his country house, where he committed many foolish pranks, although the King continued to show him kindness. One joke in particular of his was so funny that no one could have helped laughing.

There was a long and most beautiful avenue of trees leading up to his house in Anjou in the midst of which stood the little house and garden of a peasant-landowner. It appeared to have been built on that spot before the trees were planted, and neither Charnacé nor his father before him had been able to persuade the owner to sell, no matter how good a bargain they offered. Such obstructiveness is typical of many of these peasants who love to vex those who are bound to them by expediency or even sheer necessity. Seeing that there was nothing more to be done, Charnacé put the entire matter on one side for some years and said no more about it. At last, however, weary of having the enjoyment of his beautiful avenue entirely spoiled by one small cottage, he devised a most artful stratagem.

The peasant, who was by trade a tailor when he could find such work, lived alone without wife or children. Charnacé sent for him, saying that he had received an urgent summons to appear at Court for a mission of some consequence. He was in haste to be gone, but needed a new uniform. They struck a bargain there and then, with Charnacé further stipulating that since he dared not trust the man's word to deliver on time he would pay extra to keep him in the house, feed him, bed him, and give him his money cash down before sending him home again. The tailor

[1] Jacques Philippe de Girard, Marquis de Charnacé (1640–1726).

gladly agreed and set about his work. While he was thus occupied Charnacé had a plan drawn up, correct to the very last detail, of the dimensions of the cottage and garden, with the sizes of the rooms, the exact placing of all the pots and pans, and the position of the furniture. He then had the house taken down and removed together with all its contents, and rebuilt it at a distance of four musket shots from the side of the avenue, exactly as it had been before, both inside and out, with all the furniture and utensils replaced in their former positions. He had the little garden replanted exactly the same and, whilst all this was being done, smoothed over and tidied the avenue where it had stood, so that no trace of it remained.

This work was completed before the uniform, and in the meantime Charnacé kept his man under surveillance to prevent him from discovering the secret. At last all was ready; Charnacé delayed him until it was pitch dark, then paid him his money and sent him away well content. Off went the tailor down the avenue, which soon appeared considerably longer than usual. After a time he moved aside to the trees, but found that there were none. Perceiving that he had gone beyond them he turned back, groping his way from one to another. He followed their line by guesswork for a sufficient distance, then crossed over. But still no house. He could not understand it. He spent the remainder of the night in this pursuit. Dawn came, and with it light enough to see a cottage, but none was there. Rubbing his eyes he looked around for other landmarks, thinking that his sight had failed. Finally he concluded that the devil had come and had flown away with his little home.

Then, after casting backwards and forwards and gazing about on all sides, he perceived some distance from the avenue a little house as like as two peas to his own. He could not believe that it was his but curiosity made him approach the spot where hitherto no house had been, and to make doubly sure he tried his key in the lock. It fitted; he went in, and found everything which he had left exactly as he had left it. At that point he was near fainting, sure that it had been some wizard's handiwork, but before long mocking laughter from the château and the village revealed the truth to him and made him furious. He tried to go to law; demanded justice of the intendant; and everywhere they mocked him. The King himself heard about it and laughed, and Charnacé had the freedom of his avenue. Had he done no worse, he might have kept his reputation and his personal liberty.

In the morning of 29 May Mme de Saint-Simon was safely delivered, and God was pleased to grant us a son.[1] He bore, as I had done, the title

---

[1] Jacques Louis de Rouvroy (1698–1746), later Marquis de Ruffec. An intensely dreary young man, he and his equally boring younger brother were called the 'bassets' at the Court. With their poor sister *plus contrefaite qu'un sarment* (more twisted than a vine), and their tiny father, the whole family must have looked deplorable, but so many others were deformed, for example the Ducs de Bourgogne, du Maine and de Luxembourg, that with high wigs, high heels, tight stays, and paniers, they may have passed in the crowd.

of Vidame de Chartres. I do not know why we should so cherish these peculiar titles, but it is the same with every nation, and even those who realize their uselessness continue with them. Indeed, such titles as comte or marquis have ceased to be respected because so many lowborn, even landless, persons have adopted them, thus making them of no significance. That is why many men of quality who are marquis or comtes are absurd enough—if they will forgive my saying so—to resent being referred to by their titles. None the less, these titles originated from the ennobling of certain lands by royal favour,[1] and earlier, but now no more, had functions attaching to them. As it happened, the ranks have survived far longer than the duties. Vidames, on the other hand, were merely the chief officers of certain bishops, holding land in feoff from them, not from the kings, and in olden times leading their vassals into battle when the nobles fought one another or when the king summoned the nation's armies against a foreign enemy. That was before our kings had established the militia, which has gradually destroyed the idea of feudal service, together with the need for vassals and all the powers and dignities of the nobles. There is thus no comparison between the title vidame, that which designated the vassal and chief officer of a bishop, and the titles granted in feoff by our kings. Yet, since the only known vidames were those of Laon, Amiens, Le Mans, and Chartres, and all were distinguished, the title still seems worth having. The vidamry of Chartres was always held by the owners of La Ferté Arnauld, which my father purchased at the especial request of Louis XIII, and he acquired at the same time the feoff of Chartres, which is the vidamry.[2] That is why he gave me that title which I afterwards passed on to my son.

At this time a decree of the Dijon Parlement condemning the curé of Seurre to be burned caused great consternation. He had been convicted of many abominations ensuing from the errors of Molinos, and was a very dear friend of Mme Guyon. This event occurred most inopportunely in view of M. de Cambrai's reply to the *États d'Oraison* of M. de Meaux, a book which, unlike the reply to it, received and continues to receive universal praise. A short time before this, M. de Paris paid a visit to the Dukes of Chevreuse and Beauvilliers who already knew of his noble conduct towards the latter, and of the benefits thus gained for both of them. They parted well content with one another, and ever after, through all the ramifications of that affair, the dukes drew a wide distinction between M. de Paris and the other two prelates.

---

[1] Strictly speaking, the lands and not the owners bore the titles. One could acquire a title by buying an ennobled estate, as Saint-Simon's father did the Vidamry of Chartres.

[2] It was in 1635 that Saint-Simon's father bought La Ferté. It was a huge estate and must have been very expensive; one wonders where he got the money. Saint-Simon loved it and spent eight months there when he temporarily retired from the Court in 1709. Nothing now remains of the house, but the vast park, with its 12 km.-long surrounding wall, was recently used by the Citroën factory for secret tests.

Although we were now entirely at peace, the King resolved to amaze Europe with a demonstration of his might which, so his enemies believed, had been exhausted in a long and widespread war. His chief purpose was perhaps to give himself and even more Mme de Maintenon the pleasure of a splendid display of arms under the nominal command of Mgr le Duc de Bourgogne. It was thus on the pretext of showing that prince an image of war and teaching him its first principles, so far as that could be done in peacetime, that he announced a camp at Compiègne to be commanded by the Maréchal de Boufflers, under Mgr le Duc de Bourgogne. The vast numbers of troops required for it were duly assigned and the generals chosen, whilst the King at the same time fixed the date on which he intended going to Compiègne and let it be understood that he would be pleased to have an extremely large Court.

After that people spoke only of Compiègne, where sixty thousand men assembled under canvas. In smartness it was the marriage of Mgr le Duc de Bourgogne all over again, for the King hinted that he expected all the troops to be very splendid and to compete against one another in that respect. This set up such rivalry between them that there was later good cause for repentance. Not only were all the troops superbly equipped—indeed it would have been hard to single out any particular unit for a prize—but their commanders added horses, harness, and all the magnificence of the Court to the warlike splendour of the men themselves, and junior officers ruined themselves buying uniforms grand enough for any State occasion.

The colonels, and even many captains, freely offered the most delicious and abundant refreshments. Six of the lieutenant-generals and fourteen brigadiers were especially generous, but the Maréchal de Boufflers astounded everyone by his liberality, the perfectly organized and most delicate refreshments offered in the greatest abundance, his admirable taste and supreme courtesy during the entire time of the camp, by day and night and at all hours, so that in very truth he showed the King himself an example of how to give royal entertainment. Monsieur le Prince did excellently also, but the Maréchal showed even him what real elegance, ingenuity, and perfect taste could achieve. No spectacle can ever have been more glorious nor, indeed, more awe-inspiring; yet amidst it all the perfect serenity of the Maréchal de Boufflers and his household in being host to all-comers remained totally unruffled. Nothing ever ran more smoothly or silently than this tremendous undertaking, no one ever was more modest and seemingly carefree than this great general, who had made all the arrangements and continued to supervise them whilst all the time he appeared concerned only with the movements of the army.

Innumerable tables constantly replenished, meals served on the instant as soon as people presented themselves, officers, courtiers, spectators, even mere passers-by were welcomed as honoured guests with eager courtesy by his vast staff of servants. All manner of hot and cold beverages were served, everything indeed that could possibly be imagined in a list of liquid refreshments. French wines and foreign, and the choicest liqueurs were offered to all, and so perfect were the arrangements that immense quantities of venison and game arrived continually from every side; and fish from the seas bordering on Normandy, Holland, England, Brittany, and even the Mediterranean, provided day after day the most costly and exotic viands, delivered in post-chaises at precisely calculated intervals by a prodigious number of couriers. Even the water, which many had feared would become exhausted or cloudy with so much demand made upon it, was brought from Sainte-Reine, the River Seine, and other famous sources. Impossible to think of anything that was not provided, for the poorest wayfarer as well as the most honoured and invited guest.

Wooden guest-houses were built, furnished like comfortable Paris mansions, all newly constructed in perfect taste, and there were also huge tents, sufficient in numbers to form a separate camp. Kitchens were set up and butteries, with an innumerable staff of servants for the uninterrupted service of the tables, pantries, and cellars, all of which made a scene of such perfect order, speed, and propriety that it excited universal delight and admiration.

This camp was the first occasion on which the ladies treated as outmoded decorum discomforts which one would not otherwise have dared suggest to them. So many were eager to join the excursion that the King relaxed the rules and let all who wished come to Compiègne. That, however, was not at all what they desired, for every lady aspired to be appointed and commanded, not merely permitted, to be of the party, and for that reason they used every imaginable trick to cram themselves into the royal carriages. In the past the King had invariably selected the ladies to follow after the Queen or Mme la Dauphine in the coaches of the royal princesses; but now the Princesses, by which name the King's bastards were known, had their own friends and made the King consent to their travelling also in royal coaches; and he saw no harm in that and let them go on that footing. For this particular journey anything served provided one got there. No ladies were in the King's coach except the Duchesse du Lude with the Princesses.[1] Monsieur and Madame remained at Saint-Cloud and in Paris. The gentlemen of the Court attended in great numbers and for the first time dukes were billeted in pairs. I shared a lodging with the Duc de Rohan in a fine house belonging to the Sieur de Chambaudon, where we and our servants were most comfortably housed.

The King wished to give a demonstration of everything that happens in war. Thus Compiègne was step by step besieged, each procedure being

---

[1] Presumably also the Duchesse de Bourgogne.

much shortened. There were lines, trenches, batteries, saps, etc. Crenan commanded the defence. Some old ramparts ran around the château on the side facing the open country; the top, raised to a level with the King's lodging, overlooked the entire plain, whilst at its foot and stretching out a little beyond was an ancient wall and a windmill. Saturday, 13 September, was the date appointed for the assault of the fortress. The King, followed by all the ladies, in the loveliest possible weather, went out on to the ramparts, where crowds of spectators had already assembled, together with numbers of distinguished foreigners. From that point one could see the whole plain and the dispositions of all the troops. I was in the semi-circle around the King, very close to him, not m ore than three paces distant, with no one in front of me. It was the most glorious sight, that great army, with the vast crowds of spectators on foot and on horseback, keeping at a respectful distance so as to be out of the way. The manœuvres of the attack and defence were plainly visible because, display being the only purpose, neither side concealed themselves. There was, however, another sight that struck me so forcibly that forty years hence I shall be able to describe it as though it were yesterday. This was the spectacle which the King, standing at the top of the ramparts, presented to his entire army and the huge masses of onlookers of all kinds and conditions in the plain below and on the ramparts themselves.

Mme de Maintenon sat there in her sedan-chair, facing the plain and the troops, with the three glass windows closed. On the left-hand shaft sat Mme la Duchesse de Bourgogne; behind her, forming a semi-circle, stood Mme la Duchesse, Mme la Princesse de Conti, and the other ladies, and behind them the men. By the right-hand window of the chair was the King, standing, with a semi-circle of the highest-ranking gentlemen behind him. His hat was off most of the time, and every now and then he bent to speak to Mme de Maintenon through the glass, explaining what was going on and the reasons for each manœuvre. Whenever he did so she was sufficiently polite to lower the window four or five inches, never so far as halfway, for I noticed particularly, and I must admit to having been far more taken up by this scene than by the movements of the troops. Occasionally she opened the window first to ask the King some question, but most often it was he who first leaned down to give her information, not waiting for her to address him; but sometimes when she paid no attention he rapped on the glass to make her open.[1] He did not speak to any one else, save to give orders, a few words and very seldom, and he sometimes answered Mme la Duchesse de Bourgogne, who tried hard to persuade him to speak to her. Mme de Maintenon pointed things out to her and communicated in sign language from time to time through the front window, but did not open that, and the young princess screamed

[1] The poor woman suffered acutely from draughts, which made no difference to Louis XIV. Winter and summer, he threw the windows wide open when he worked in her room.

back a few words in reply. I closely scrutinized the faces of the onlookers. They all had the same expression of ill-concealed apprehension and shamed astonishment, and those in the semi-circles behind her chair gazed at her with far more attention than at the army, and all were acutely embarrassed.[1] The King often laid his hat on the roof of the chair whilst he bent to talk, and the continual stooping must have made his back ache considerably. The time was five in the afternoon, and the weather was as fine as heart could desire.

Just before the surrender Mme de Maintenon must have asked permission to withdraw, for the King cried out, 'Porters for Madame!' and they came and carried her away. Less than a quarter of an hour later the King himself retired, followed by Mme la Duchesse de Bourgogne and most of the assembled company. Many bystanders eyed and nudged one another, murmuring very low as they passed, for people could not get over the spectacle that they had just witnessed. It was the same with those in the plain; even the soldiers asked about the sedan-chair, so that it became necessary to silence the officers and discreetly prevent the troops from asking questions. You may imagine the effect upon the foreigners and their remarks concerning it. All Europe heard of it, and the incident was as much talked of as the camp itself, for all its pomp and majesty.

The interval was so short between the King's return from Compiègne, on 24 September, and his departure for Fontainebleau, on 2 October, that I shall record here an incident which took place before the first of those excursions but was not finished until after the second. It may seem somewhat flat compared to all that went before and followed, but my own part in it was too great to allow me to pass it over, and in order to explain it properly I must remind you of my relationship with certain important personages. My situation with them did me so much credit that I cannot help feeling some embarrassment at mentioning it again, but apart from the fact that truth is vital, it had so great an influence on my life that I must not omit anything.

I spoke some time ago of the marriage of M. de Pontchartrain's only son with a sister of Mme de Saint-Simon's first cousin the Comte de Roucy. They had wanted her simply for the sake of the alliance, and to judge by the way they made use of it for all their relatives it greatly benefited them. There was no one whom they courted more assiduously than Mme de Saint-Simon, for they much wished her to become attached to their new daughter-in-law, who, with all the advantages of birth, was good, gentle, and intelligent, for all that she was a Roucy. She was also very sensible and had a lively fear of making errors, which gave her a

---

[1] The Duc de Noailles in his *Histoire de Mme de Maintenon* remarks that considering the general tone of the Court, Mme de Maintenon's appearance should not have caused so much surprise.

timidity very becoming to her years. Although she had been in compara-
tive liberty for so short a time, she had the grace and wit required to
make a charming, agreeable woman and, with experience, gained a knowledge of the world far above what one would have expected from a young
person raised in an abbey at Soissons, and thrown into the lap of a
family where for a time her every move was watched. She had, however,
the disposition to love and be loyal to all those to whom she owed affection. Similarity of character and tastes soon endeared her to Mme de
Saint-Simon, and a friendship sprang up between them which grew
closer as the years passed until, in the end, they were like sisters. M. and
Mme de Pontchartrain were enchanted.

Whether or not it was for that reason, but one day before the end of the
winter [1697] when I was visiting Pontchartrain in his study, as I sometimes did after the marriage although not usually at his private times, he
suddenly said that he had a favour to ask, which he set so much store by
that he hated to risk my refusal. I replied as was fitting to a minister holding one of the highest offices of State, but he insisted, in that warm, persuasive manner which he could turn when he so pleased to any subject,
that that was mere civility and not at all what he wished. He said that he
wanted plain-speaking, and hoped that I would grant what he most
earnestly desired. He then immediately continued, 'The privilege of your
friendship, so that I may rely on your goodwill, as you always may on
mine; for you are honest, and if you give me your word I shall know that
I can trust you.' Considering my youth, I was astounded[1] and relapsed into
saying something about the honour and the difference in our ages and
employments; but he interrupted, pressing me even harder, saying that
from his frankness I must see that he was in earnest and wanted a straight
answer. I shall omit many other delightful things he said, but I did at last
perceive that his intentions were serious and that we were about to enter
into a solemn compact.

I therefore spoke my mind, and after a word or two expressing gratitude, esteem, and friendly feeling, I told him that I had one friend
already who must always come first with me (naming M. de Beauvilliers
whom I knew he disliked), but that if he cared to have my friendship
under those conditions I would gladly give it him and be more than
proud to have his in return. He at once embraced me, saying that this was
candour indeed, and that he honoured me the more for it. We then gave
one another our solemn promises, which we fully kept, for we remained
close friends until his death, with ever-increasing confidence and intimacy. Immediately after leaving him I went to tell all to M. de Beauvilliers, who embraced me tenderly, assuring me that M. de Pontchartrain's
request did not surprise him in the least; still less so did my conduct towards himself. The strange thing was that Pontchartrain never mentioned

---

[1] He was twenty-two and Pontchartrain fifty-four.

the matter to his son and daughter-in-law and no more did I. Thus no one at the Court ever knew of this quite remarkable attachment between two men so entirely different in every other way.

Still another friendship most unusual for a young man of my age was that which I enjoyed with the Bishop of Chartres. He was my diocesan bishop at La Ferté and had often stayed at my house, at first in company with the Abbé de Bailly, an old friend of my father. Gradually, a mutual trust and friendship had grown up between us; but on account of his situation with Mme de Maintenon I never used his influence, save once on a very trivial matter, as I shall recount in due course. I none the less often saw him at his home and at my house at Paris, and we understood one another perfectly.

Towards the end of the year the King determined to put in hand three major works which should have been done long before this—the chapel at Versailles, the church of Les Invalides, and the altar of Notre-Dame of Paris. The last was in fulfilment of a vow of Louis XIII, taken too late to be put into effect, and for which he had made responsible his successor,[1] who then proceeded to forget it for the next fifty years.

M. de Barbezieux ended the year with a scandal which he might very well have avoided. He had recently married Mlle d'Alègre.[2] He treated her like a child, and in no way restrained his love-affairs or changed his accustomed way of life. M. d'Elbeuf pretended to be her lover so as to insult him. The young woman, much offended by her husband's conduct, listened to bad advice and made him jealous. He yielded to that passion; lost all sense of proportion, saw things as they were not, and did what none but he has ever done, namely, declared himself publicly a cuckold; tried to prove it; failed, and was believed by no one. You cannot imagine anyone so furious at being unable to make himself thought a cuckold. All that he discovered was the indiscretions, the thoughtless actions of an innocent but ill-advised young girl, endeavouring to bring back her husband by pretending to give tit for tat. But Barbezieux was too angry to see reason. He sent a courier summoning her father to return at once from his estates in Auvergne, couched in such language that d'Alègre, who was not the cleverest of men, believed that he was being sent for to receive promotion. He was thus very unpleasantly surprised when he learned the facts. Separation was the only course, the affair having become so desperate. Mme de Barbezieux was a prisoner in her husband's house and ill in bed. Her husband vowed that she was pretending and wanted to put her in a convent there and then; her father and mother wished to keep her with them. At last, after an appalling rumpus on a very slight pretext, the King was asked by both gentlemen to intervene

[1] Louis XIII's vow of 10 February, 1638, to dedicate his Kingdom to the Virgin Mary.
[2] Barbezieux the Minister for War had married her in the winter of 1696. He had been a widower for eighteen months. She died aged twenty-six in 1706.

and decreed that she was to return to her parents until fully recovered, and that they were then to take her to a convent in Auvergne. Regarding the dowry, Barbezieux repaid it in full, but demanded from d'Alègre all the necessary to bring up and support his two little daughters. People greatly pitied d'Alègre and still more so his daughter, and Barbezieux was strongly criticized. What was still worse, he ever afterwards did d'Alègre every conceivable bad turn, and used all his power and influence to that end.

CHAPTER IX

1699

Low cunning of the Lorraines, I put myself straight with the King – Prince Elector of Bavaria named inheritor of the Spanish throne and immediately dies – Death of Racine, his fatal aberration – Birth of my second son – Most remarkable journey to the Court by a blacksmith of Salon – Pontchartrain made Chancellor of France – Rise of Chamillart to be Controller-General of Finances – The King imposes silence on the Jesuits and Benedictines over a new edition of Saint Augustine

ON 6 JANUARY a dreadful scene took place in the apartments of Mme la Duchesse de Bourgogne at the audience given to Lord Jersey the English ambassador.[1] It would be beyond the scope of these memoirs were I to describe the origins, endeavours and successes of the House of Lorraine,[2] in their attempt to gain precedence in France. Suffice it to know that the Court order for *entrées*, royal marriages, christenings, and funerals, often gave rise to quarrels between the duchesses and these foreign princesses, and that our kings always left these matters undecided, believing that it benefited them to encourage perpetual bickering. This is not the moment to argue the rights and wrongs of such an opinion.

On ordinary occasions at the Court and in Society, at the *cercles*,[3] audiences, plays, etc., there was never any trouble and duchesses and princesses sat down wherever they happened to find room. Indeed, there had been no quarrels at all until, in the latter days of Mme la Dauphine de Bavière,[4] the Princesse d'Harcourt began to show contentiousness, and Mme d'Armagnac followed her lead.[5] The former had increasingly come under Mme de Maintenon's protection because Brancas, her father, had

---

[1] Edward Villiers, grand-nephew of the first Duke of Buckingham.

[2] It was said of the Lorraines that they paid their court to the King of France but that their hearts were with Austria. They were notorious double-dealers and spied for Prince Eugene. Saint-Simon was not alone in suspecting them. There was a running fight for precedence between the younger members of that family and the French dukes in general.

[3] *Le cercle*, the semi-circle of folding stools on each side of a royal princess's armchair at receptions, etc.

[4] Monseigneur's late wife Marie Anne Christine of Bavaria. Saint-Simon was fifteen when she died in 1690.

[5] The Princesse d'Harcourt was the wife of the Prince d'Harcourt. Her father, the Comte de Brancas, died in 1681. Mme d'Armagnac's husband was Prince Camille de Lorraine-d'Armagnac.

been an exceptionally good friend. In truth, it would have required some such very strong reason for Mme de Maintenon to have befriended so thoroughly undeserving a person; but like all commoners, who have no knowledge beyond what they learn by chance, she was dazzled by that spurious title of princess, believing that nothing distinguished it from the genuine article.

The heads of the House of Lorraine were very much alive to this partiality of hers, and therefore it was with the full support of M. le Grand and the Chevalier de Lorraine that their sister-in-law and the Princesse d'Harcourt proceeded to take action at the moment when Mme la Duchesse de Bourgogne was beginning to hold a court. Hitherto they had been unwilling to risk anything in the King's presence that had not been tried elsewhere successfully, or that he had not been given time to assimilate, but on the very day after the marriage of the little princess they attacked with unprecedented insolence at the first *cercle* over which she presided. By that time the princesses had long ceased to sit below the duchesses, and they were already claiming the right-hand-side, which they often secured by vigilance and concerted action. They had now to deal with a highly nervous lady-in-waiting who desired only popularity, greatly feared Mme de Maintenon, and was thus prepared to submit to anything. As for Mme la Duchesse de Bourgogne, she was altogether too young to know what was proper or to impose her will.

Such then was the situation when the Lorraines resolved to bid for further promotion and felt strong enough to obtain it. By chance or design the first audience of Lord Jersey with Mme la Duchesse de Bourgogne, on 6 January, provided the occasion. The ladies arrived early on the scene from various directions before the doors were thrown open. The most punctual of the duchesses were nearest the threshold and entered first. The Princesse d'Harcourt and the other Lorraines followed. The Duchesse de Rohan took the highest stool on the right. A moment later, when all the duchesses were seated and the late-comers, titled and untitled, were still arriving, for the ladies attended in great numbers, the Princesse d'Harcourt crept up behind her and told her to move across to the left side. Much amazed, the Duchesse de Rohan replied that she was perfectly comfortable where she was. Thereupon the princess, a tall, powerful woman, without more ado placed her two arms at the duchess's waist, twisted her round by force, and sat herself down in her place. Mme de Rohan, completely flabbergasted, half-convinced that she was dreaming, merely curtsied to Mme la Duchesse de Bourgogne and went over to the other side, still only dimly realizing what had happened to her. The rest of the ladies, however, were most monstrously shocked and alarmed. The Duchesse du Lude dared not say a word, still less so Mme la Duchesse de Bourgogne who, young as she was, did understand the rudeness and lack of respect.

Mme d'Armagnac and her daughter and stepdaughter, in their determination to sit on the right-hand side at the audience, which was about to
take place in the room adjoining the princess's bedroom where they then
were, had taken seats near the communicating door on the left side of the
bed, although by so doing they were below the duchesses. Remarking that
the room was becoming too crowded they now entered the audience-
chamber and took *tabourets* on the right-hand side of the *cercle*, which had
already been prepared. When Mme la Duchesse de Bourgogne had finished
dressing everyone went into the other room. Mme de Saint-Simon was
six weeks or two months gone with child; she had arrived late and had sat
down on one of the furthest stools on the left-hand side so as to be very
near the audience-chamber when everyone rose. The business of moving
from one room to another always took a long time; she began to feel faint
and in no condition to remain on her feet. She therefore went into the
other room and sat down for a moment on the first available *tabouret*, on
the right of the *cercle* because that was nearest. It so happened that she
had settled two places above Mme d'Armagnac, but whereas the latter
faced the centre of the room, Mme de Saint-Simon had her face to the
wall, and they were thus almost back to back. Mme d'Armagnac saw that
she felt unwell and offered her some Queen of Hungary water,[1] but when
the seats began to be filled she declared that since she had arrived first she
could not believe that Mme de Saint-Simon intentionally sat above her.
My wife, who had sat down only for the time being, made no reply but
at once crossed the room and re-seated herself even before the ladies
were arranged in order of rank, and she asked another duchess to sit in
front of her to screen her until everyone else had passed.

I soon learned of what had happened at Mme la Duchesse de
Bourgogne's *toilette*, and also that the princess was feeling very much
inclined to speak to the King and Mme de Maintenon. It appeared to me
to be highly important not only not to swallow the insult, but to endeavour to obtain advantage from it, and we some of us therefore went
into conference. After that the Maréchal de Boufflers went to tell M. de
Noailles, and I to M. de La Rochefoucauld, as soon as he returned from
the King's shoot. The general opinion among us was that M. de Rohan
should appeal to the King on the following morning, alone, because King
Louis feared and disliked anything smacking of a concerted action.[2]

Whilst I was at the King's supper Mme de Saint-Simon sent for me to
come to her at once in the courtyard, where she was waiting in her coach.
I went. She said she had just heard from Mme de Noailles, who had met
her coming straight from the Duchesse du Lude as she was leaving

---

[1] Oil of rosemary distilled in alcohol; to dab on her forehead like eau-de-cologne. It was also
kept in bottles in the rooms to sprinkle here and there if the smells became a little too strong.
Rosemary was thought to be a defence against the Plague.

[2] Louis XIV never could forget the *Fronde*, the rebellion of the nobles in 1648, when he was a
boy of ten years old. It affected all his dealings with them.

M. de Duras's apartment next door, that the three Lorraine brothers had been at the King's shoot and had kept entirely to themselves the whole time; had seemed to be arguing about something; and that finally, after a lengthy discussion, M. le Grand had left the other two and approached the King, had spoken to him for some time, and had been overheard by M. de Noailles complaining that Mme de Saint-Simon had tried to take Mme d'Armagnac's place at the audience that morning so as to sit above her. What the King answered had been inaudible and exceedingly short. After that M. le Grand had rejoined his brothers.

Mme de Saint-Simon was horrified at the spiteful twist given to that most innocent and natural occurrence, and at the additional lie. She had been to tell Mme de Noailles, whose advice was that I should speak to the King that very evening, since it appeared that the Lorraines, hard put to it to defend the Princesse d'Harcourt's attack on Mme de Rohan, had seized on the incident with Mme de Saint-Simon in order to be the first to complain and claim tit-for-tat. That is a perfect example of the artfulness of these gentry, with their public falsehood against the evidence of an entire audience. The baseness of such a trick, although so ill-contrived, made me extremely angry. I went to consult M. de La Rochefoucauld, who was quite sure that I should speak to the King myself that evening at his *coucher*. 'I know him well,' he said, 'speak boldly but respectfully, and only of what concerns yourself. Let M. de Rohan have his say to-morrow; that is his business. Believe me,' he continued, 'men like you should speak for themselves; your frankness and modesty will please the King far better than the words of any other.' I began to argue with him for I wished to see whether the advice came from his heart or only from his head, and I therefore suggested going quickly to the Maréchal de Lorges and asking him to intervene. 'No, no, a thousand times no!' said the duke, 'that would not do at all. Speak for yourself. If I can manage to put in a word later at the *petit coucher* I will do so.' Hearing him say that finally determined me.

I took up my position beside the fireplace in the salon[1] at the time of the King's *coucher*, and when he appeared I simply waited until he entered his room to undress. After he had bidden good night to the company, and had withdrawn to the fireplace to give the orders whilst those without the entrées retired, I went up to him and he immediately bent down to hear me, gazing fixedly at me all the while. I said that I had just learned of M. le Grand's complaint concerning Mme de Saint-Simon; that nothing in the world was more dear to me than his esteem and approval, and that I begged permission to tell him the facts. I then at once related all that had happened, as I have done here, forgetting none of the circumstances. Then I stopped, remembering M. de La Rochefoucauld's warning, without a word of the Lorraines or M. le Grand, and

[1] The Salon of the *Œil de Bœuf*.

I felt afterwards that simply by telling him the plain unvarnished truth I had given an absolute denial. He did not once interrupt me from the moment I first opened my mouth. When I had quite finished he said, 'That is good, sir,' looking very gracious and well-pleased; 'no harm in that,' smiling and nodding at me as I retired. After a few backward steps I moved smartly forward again and once more assured him that every word I had spoken was true, and he answered me as before.

My talk with the King had been so long and the hour so unorthodox that it had aroused everyone's curiosity, although most suspected that it concerned the events of that morning. I spoke to the Maréchal de Boufflers after he had taken the orders, and then called on the Duc de Rohan, because I had promised him that I would. They had both heard something but pressed me to tell them all, which I gladly did, especially to the latter so as to encourage him. Early next morning M. de Rohan established himself by the door of the study just before the King's return from mass, and stepped forward as he approached. The King signed to him to enter and led him to the window, whereupon the door was closed and they were left alone.

I considered that I had played my part and therefore remained watching beside the chimney-piece of the salon, separated from them by the length of the King's bedroom. After close on a quarter of an hour M. de Rohan emerged looking exceedingly happy; the Duc de Noailles went straight in and out to take the orders, and they both came to me beside the fireplace. Then we all went into the King's bedroom and gathered round the fire, and the Duc de Rohan repeated his conversation to us without forgetting a single word. He said that he had appealed for justice on account of the Princesse d'Harcourt's insult to his wife; spread himself over the aggressions of the Lorraines and the impossibility of avoiding quarrels; stressed the want of respect for Mme la Duchesse de Bourgogne, and fully explained the affair of Mme de Saint-Simon and Mme d'Armagnac, with the Lorraines' wicked endeavour to extricate themselves by a false accusation. In short, he had spoken with vehemence, good sense, and dignity. The King had replied that he already knew of the matter through Mme la Duchesse de Bourgogne, the Duchesse du Lude, from myself on the previous evening, and from the Maréchal de Lorges that morning. We had all said the same, and he believed us. He praised the Duchesse de Rohan for her respect and self-control, and said that he thought the Princesse d'Harcourt had been monstrously impertinent. He also said severe things concerning the Lorraines, and twice vowed that he would take pleasure in bringing them to order. I heard later through my friends the palace-ladies that Mme de Saint-Simon had been marvellously well served by Mme la Duchesse de Bourgogne, and that a somewhat lively scene had taken place between the King and Mme de Maintenon, who only with the greatest difficulty obtained permission for the Princesse d'Harcourt to go to Marly next day, as usual. As for Mme d'Armagnac, her daughter and daughter-in-law, all three of them were firmly excluded. So ended that alarming episode and we were at last able to have some peace.

For the past five or six months, the King of Spain,[1] having finally lost hope of begetting children and suffering from a life-long infirmity that visibly worsened, had been endeavouring to establish the succession of his vast kingdom.[2] He was exasperated beyond measure by the innumerable proposals that it should be divided after his death. He therefore made a will, bequeathing the succession of all his crowns and realms entire to the Electoral Prince of Bavaria, aged seven years, who was, through his mother, the undoubted heir to the Spanish throne, having regard to the renunciation of our King at the time of his marriage and in the peace-treaty of the Pyrenees. As soon as this will had been signed Cardinal Portocarrero informed the Marquis de Beuvron secretly of the contents, and the latter dispatched the news to the King. Neither then nor after it became public did King Louis show the least trace of resentment. Nor did the Emperor say anything. His fervent hope was to add this vast inheritance to his other dominions; but his council at Vienna had methods of their own. It was not long since he had used them to rid himself of the late Queen of Spain, Monsieur's daughter, who was childless and with too much influence over her husband to please him. Thus when the Electoral Prince died very suddenly in the early days of February no one doubted that the cause lay with the council at Vienna. This deed revived all the Emperor's hopes and plunged Europe into all the anxieties of planning the measures to be taken on this great question of the Spanish succession, which everyone rightly believed to be imminent.

Some time after this [21 April] we lost the famous Racine, so celebrated for his magnificent plays. No man's wit was ever more soundly based nor more delightfully expressed; he did not act the poet, but was in every way decent, modest, and, towards the end, a perfect gentleman. He was friends with the highest-ranking members of the Court as well as with men of letters. It is for them to write of him, they will do so better than I. He wrote two plays, *Esther* and *Athalie*,[3] for the entertainment of the King and Mme de Maintenon and the education of the young ladies of Saint-Cyr. They are dramatic masterpieces of extraordinary difficulty, firstly because there is no love in them, and secondly because, being Biblical tragedies, the exact historical truth had to be preserved, out of respect

---

[1] Charles II (1661-1700), King of Spain from 1665.

[2] His monarchy covered Spain, the two Sicilies, Milan and other parts of Italy, the Spanish Netherlands, Sardinia, and a very large part of the Americas.

[3] Mme de Maintenon thoroughly approved of play-acting for the girls at her school, but she had considered *Andromaque* a little too strong for them in the love-passages, and had asked Racine to be more careful in future. Hence *Esther*.

for Holy Writ. The Comtesse d'Ayen and Mme de Caylus[1] out-acted all the rest when they were given before the King and a very small and exclusive audience in Mme de Maintenon's apartment. The Court was allowed to go several times to see them at Saint-Cyr, but only by invitation.

Racine, conjointly with his friend Despréaux,[2] was charged to write the biography of the King. That work, the plays above-mentioned, and his friends, gained him some special favours,[3] and it sometimes happened that when the King had no ministers working with him in Mme de Maintenon's room, for example on Fridays or when bad weather, especially in winter, made their sessions seem very long, they would send for Racine to amuse them. Alas for Racine! He was subject to sad aberrations. On one such evening when he was sitting between the King and Mme de Maintenon in the latter's room, the conversation turned to the Paris theatres. They exhausted the Opera and started on the Playhouse. The King inquired about the plays and actors and then asked Racine why, by all accounts, the Playhouse had fallen so low compared with what it had been in the old days. Racine produced several reasons, and finally remarked that in his view, for want of good new plays and writers, the actors had been reviving bad old ones, especially Scarron's worthless comedies that bored everyone to tears. Thereupon his widow turned scarlet, not so much for the honour of the much-maligned cripple, as at the mere mention of his name before his successor. The King was not amused. Sudden silence restored the wretched Racine to his senses and to the knowledge of the abyss into which his straying wits had cast him. He was, in fact, the most embarrassed of the three, not daring to raise his eyes or open his lips again. Silence reigned for many minutes, so severe, so deep had been the wound. It ended finally by the King dismissing him, saying that he desired to work, and Racine left them, still quite bemused, making his way to his friend Cavoye's apartment, there to confess his blunder. It was indeed a terrible lapse, but he could do nothing to repair it, and never afterwards did the King or Mme de Maintenon either speak to him or glance in his direction. This afflicted him so deeply that he fell into a decline and died less than two years after the event.[4] He none the

---

[1] A niece and a first cousin of Mme de Maintenon. Mme de Caylus's *Souvenirs* of the Court of Louis XIV and the Saint-Cyr school are famous and extremely entertaining.

[2] Nicolas Boileau-Despréaux (1636–1711) the poet and friend of Molière and Racine. In 1677 he and Racine were jointly appointed historiographers royal and accompanied Louis XIV on several campaigns. Mme de Sévigné thought it a bad choice since both the poets were civilians and ignorant of war. She says that Louis once rebuked Racine for not going a little out of his way to watch a battle from the front line. Racine replied that that was just what he had intended to do, but that his new uniform was not delivered in time.

[3] Such as the *entrée* for the King's *petit lever*, a lodging in the Château de Versailles, and the post of King's reader.

[4] Probably untrue. Saint-Simon may have attributed to Racine a lapse of Boileau's which did not at all impair the latter's health. At one time there was a slight coolness towards Racine because of his tendency to Jansenism, but he died of an abscess on the liver and was buried at Port-Royal with the King's consent.

less put those years to good use for his salvation. He asked to be buried at Port-Royal-des-Champs,[1] with whose illustrious inmates he had in his youth formed an attachment which his poet's life had scarcely interrupted, although they cannot have approved of that. The Chevalier de Coislin was also buried there beside his famous uncle M. de Pontchâteau.[2] You cannot imagine how much these two burials vexed the King.

On 12 August Mme de Saint-Simon was most happily delivered, and God was pleased to grant us a second son, who bore the title of Marquis de Ruffec, from a fine estate in Anjou which my mother had bought from hers.

A most remarkable event caused a great amount of speculation. There arrived in hot haste at Versailles a master-farrier from the little town of Salon, in Provence. He applied to Brissac, major of the bodyguard, to take him straight to the King to speak with him in private. No rebuffs put him off. He was so persistent that they finally informed the King, who sent word to say that he did not speak to all-comers. The farrier none the less insisted, vowing that he had things so secret, so personal to impart that would the King but see him he would realize that the mission was indeed for him alone and of vital importance. He then asked to see a minister. Thereupon the King ordered him to be taken to Barbezieux with instructions that he should be heard. What was really astonishing was that this farrier, just arrived at Versailles and never before having left his work or his province, refused to speak to Barbezieux on the score that only a minister of State would serve and that Barbezieux was not so highly placed. The King then suggested M. de Pomponne,[3] and the man spoke to him without further ado. The rest of his story will make short reading.

Returning to his home one night he had found himself by the trunk of a tree not far from Salon, enveloped in a brilliant light. A woman clothed all in white, but robed and crowned like a queen,[4] very fair and shiningly beautiful, called him by name, bidding him listen carefully. She was, she said, the queen who had been the wife of the King, and she told him to go to Versailles and repeat her words to the King himself, adding that God would protect him on his journey, and that when the King heard a secret which only he knew, he would believe the truth of all the rest. If the farrier were not allowed to see the King he was to ask for a minister of State, but on no account to speak to any other, and certain matters were for the King's ear alone. She ordered him to set out immediately, and to

---

[1] Port-Royal-des-Champs, the famous Jansenist monastery in the valley of the Chevreuse (now in the District of Paris). Louis XIV feared and persecuted Port-Royal as a nest of possible republicanism and a centre of revolt against the established Church.

[2] Sébastien Joseph du Cambout, the so-called Abbot of Pontchâteau (1634–1690). He was so humble that he asked to be employed as a gardener when he retired to Port-Royal.

[3] Simon Arnauld, Marquis de Pomponne (1618–1699) who was responsible for Provence.

[4] Queen Maria Teresa, who had been dead for sixteen years.

execute his task with boldness and despatch, or else death would be his punishment. The farrier promised all and immediately the queen vanished leaving him in total darkness. He lay down there by the foot of the tree, scarcely knowing whether he was asleep or awake, and then returned home sure that it had been an hallucination.

Two days afterwards he passed the same spot, again saw the vision, and received the same instructions with threats of punishment if he did not obey. He was further told to go at once to the intendant of the province, who would give him money for his journey. By this time the farrier was convinced, but, balancing between the fear of disobeying and that of taking action, he could not decide what to do for the best, and so did nothing and remained silent. He spent a week in that condition, and then for the third time saw the vision, whose threats were now so fearful that his only thought was to be gone. Two days later he arrived at Aix and appeared before the intendant of the province, who unhesitatingly urged him to make the journey and gave him money for the public coach. Nothing more was ever learned.

He had three two-hour-long interviews with M. de Pomponne, who reported to the King in private and was ordered to describe them at greater length to a council consisting of the Duc de Beauvilliers, Pontchartrain, and Torcy,[1] at a time when Monseigneur was elsewhere. It was an immensely long session; perhaps other matters were discussed later. However that may be, the King decided to grant the farrier an interview. He did not disguise himself, but saw him quite openly in one of the outer offices, and had him introduced by the small staircase that leads to the *Cour de Marbre*, the one which he used when he went hunting or walking. He saw him a second time a few days afterwards, and on each occasion spent an hour with him, making sure that no one was within earshot. On the day after the first interview, as the King was walking down that same staircase to go hunting, M. de Duras,[2] who was in such favour that he could say more or less what he pleased, began to speak contemptuously of the farrier with the vulgar phrase that if he were sane the King was a commoner. The King at once stopped; turned round, something he almost never did when walking, and replied, 'Then I must be a commoner, for I have had a long talk with him and he spoke vastly good sense.' These last words he uttered in a tone of such unusual gravity that it reduced his companions to silence and made them open their eyes and ears very wide indeed.

After the second interview the King divulged that the farrier had told him of an event occurring more than twenty years earlier, and known

---

[1] Jean Baptiste Colbert, Marquis de Torcy (1665–1746), minister for foreign affairs and 'the posts', which meant that he could open letters, etc.

[2] The Marquis de Duras (1625–1704), nephew of Turenne and brother-in-law of the Maréchal de Lorges.

only to himself, for he had told no one. It was, he said, concerned with a ghost which he had seen in the forest of Saint-Germain, and which he was very sure he had mentioned to no one. He spoke several times in praise of the man, reimbursed him for all his expenses, paid him a gratuity, and paid for his journey home. The King also instructed the governor of his province to watch over him, and without changing his circumstances to see that he lacked for nothing all the rest of his life.

The most remarkable thing of all was that none of the ministers would ever speak of him. Their closest friends tried over and over again to drag something from them and were never successful, for they always evaded them with jests and laughter, skating over the surface, and never once allowing it to be penetrated. This was what happened to me with MM. de Beauvilliers and de Pontchartrain, and I know for a fact that no one else succeeded any better with them, nor with MM. de Pomponne and Torcy. As for the farrier, he proved equally uncommunicative. He was a simple fellow about fifty years of age. Those who had the care of him did all that was possible to make him speak, but he merely answered, 'I am forbidden to speak,' and would not be persuaded by any means. He returned to his trade and lived exactly as before, or at least so the clergy of his province informed me, including the Archbishop of Arles, whose country house is at Salon, where is also the birthplace and tomb of the famous Nostradamus.[1] Nothing more was ever discovered, and in the end the investigators tried to convince themselves that this simple country-man had been the victim of a very bold practical joke.

Nevertheless, there was at that time living at Marseilles a certain Mme Arnoul whose life-story was a romance in itself. Old, poor, ugly as sin, and a widow, she had inspired violent passions, had dominated the most important men in the places where she had lived; had succeeded in the most singular circumstances in marrying that M. Arnoul[2] who was governor of the port of Marseilles, and, by her scheming, had made herself so much loved and redoubted that most people thought her a witch. She had been Mme de Maintenon's dear friend in the days of Scarron and had ever since corresponded with her secretly. These two statements are true. A third, which I most definitely cannot vouch for, is that both the vision and the farrier's message were contrived by her with no other object than to oblige the King to proclaim Mme de Maintenon queen.

---

[1] Who journeyed from Salon to Paris in 1556, saw Catherine de' Medici and foretold the death of Henri II. Not so surprising that this farrier was taken seriously.

[2] Pierre Arnoul (1651–1719). His wife, that redoubtable female, had already married the elder son of her previous marriage to the widow of Pierre Arnoul's father. By these two marriages she made her husband stepfather and stepson of her elder son, and stepfather and step-brother of the younger. She herself became the daughter-in-law of her own elder son and sister-in-law of the younger, all without incest or a dispensation. She is said to have arranged her own funeral and to have died on the day that she predicted.

The farrier never mentioned her nor had he seen her, but no other solution has ever been forthcoming.

M. Boucherat, chancellor and keeper of the seals,[1] died in Paris on the afternoon of Wednesday, 2 September; and at eight in the evening his sons-in-law, MM. d'Harlay and de Fourcy, returned the seals to the King, who left for Fontainebleau on the following day, taking them with him. M. de Pontchartrain, the premier président,[2] and MM. Courtin, Daguesseau, Pomereu, and La Reynie were the most fancied to succeed him. There was no one else of sufficient calibre. It did not take long for the King to choose M. de Pontchartrain; he was inclined that way by habit, and Mme de Maintenon confirmed a partiality that had been very steady even in times of storm and stress.

Pontchartrain had been controller-general of finances since 1689. He had taken office with the utmost reluctance and had made many efforts to resign; but neither Louvois, who recognized his great ability, nor Mme de Maintenon would hear of any change. Of all the King's ministers the controller-general was the most important to her, for she needed his support on behalf of her numerous charities, and, still more useful, he could bring to or divert from the King's notice such persons and matters as she thought desirable. Pontchartrain was the minister with whom he was most accustomed to working, and had gained enormous influence, for there was no man more gently persuasive.

He was a very short man, thin, but well proportioned for his small size, whose face sparkled with animation and intelligence and more than fulfilled its promise. There never was a man so quick of understanding, so cheerful and pleasant in conversation, so swift and confident in action, so sure in his judgment of other men, or so clever in outwitting them. Predominant amongst all these good qualities, his simple wisdom and cheerful good sense made him delightful to have dealings with, in trifling as well as in greater matters. His integrity was remarkable, apparent in everything that he did, and, underlying the lightheartedness that remained with him until the end, was much piety, kindness and, let me add, decency, both before and after he undertook the finances, and even during the period of his administration so far as he was able. At the same time he confessed that this was why he had found the finances so disagreeable, and he said as much very bitterly to those who reproached him. Thus he had often tried to resign them and it had only been by artfulness that his wife had persuaded him to stay, asking him to defer his decision for a couple of days, then for four, then perhaps for a week. I have heard him say many times that his idea of bliss was to end his days as an honorary counsellor at the Parlement, living in a house in the cloisters of Notre-Dame.

[1] Louis Boucherat (1616–1699), Chancellor of France 1685.
[2] Harlay.

Mme de Pontchartrain, a woman of great good sense, prudence, and wisdom, had nothing common about her except her face. She was very liberal, loved present-giving, and was most skilled in the arts of devising and organizing parties of pleasure that were lavish and splendid in the highest degree, yet most admirably ordered and without waste. Surprising to say no one knew the Court and Society better than she, and, like her husband, she possessed infinite tact and charm of mind. Her advice and deportment were of the greatest use to him, and he was wise enough to profit by them; their union at all times was very close. Religion was her sure foundation, continually increasing, and leading her to spend much time in prayers and pious reading. Yet she was always gay and admirable company, for they both excelled in conversation that went far beyond mere tittle-tattle. Both were eminently capable of friendship, and he of helping, and hindering too if he saw cause. What they gave to the poor was unbelievable; Mme de Pontchartrain, especially, kept her eyes and purse ever open for their needs, always searching for those ashamed of admitting to poverty, such as distressed gentlefolk or young women without protection, whom she rescued from danger and anxiety by finding marriages or employment for them, or by giving them a pension, and all with the utmost secrecy. Better parents never existed than this couple, nor people more truly courteous—respectful I might almost say, for they knew their places and those of others amidst all the confusion of favour, power, and office.

They managed for a long time to remain on good terms with Mme de Maintenon, but gradually a coolness sprang up between her and Pontchartrain, whom she could not manage as easily as she would have wished. Mme de Pontchartrain, whom she liked at all times, tried hard to persuade him to be more pliable, and for her sake Mme de Maintenon forgave an obstinacy which she would have tolerated in no one else. At last, however, her irritation became so intense that she was delighted to be rid of him honourably by way of the chancellorship.

As I have already mentioned Boucherat died on the evening before the King went to Fontainebleau. No one had believed him capable of outlasting the day. When the King left the council that morning he had said to Pontchartrain, who was the last to go, 'How would you like to be Chancellor of France?' 'Sire,' replied Pontchartrain, 'I have so often asked you to take me from the finances and to make me an ordinary minister or secretary, you may judge of my pleasure at leaving them for the highest office of all.' 'Very well,' said the King, 'say nothing of this, but if the chancellor should die, and he may well be dead already, you shall be chancellor and your son a secretary of State.' Pontchartrain embraced the King's knees; seized the opportunity to beg leave to keep his old apartment at Versailles, and retired happier than he had been in all his life—not so much at the chancellorship, although I have heard that he was delighted by that, but at having finally quitted the finances, which every day became more of a burden to him.

The suspense lasted from that Wednesday until the following Saturday when Pontchartrain was due to come to Fontainebleau. That same evening, on his way to Mme de Maintenon's room, the King told the Maréchal de Villeroy to send Pontchartrain to him the moment he arrived, which he did. He went there first of all, and emerged Chancellor of France. Everyone else was at the play, but when an officer of the bodyguard came to tell M. de Villeroy that the King had asked for the seals in Mme de Maintenon's room and that M. de Pontchartrain had been seen taking them away, no one was much surprised, and all thoughts turned to the question of the new controller-general of finances. We did not have long to wait.

After supper that same evening the King informed Monseigneur and Monsieur in his study that he had dispatched one of Mme de Maintenon's servants with a note written in his own hand to Chamillart, telling him that he had the office of controller-general. The news was made public at his *coucher*, and thence spread to the entire Court.

Chamillart[1] was a big man with a rolling gait, whose frank, open countenance expressed nothing but goodness and kindness and more than fulfilled that promise. His father, governor of Caen for ten years, had died in 1675, and a year later his son became a counsellor of the Parlement. He was sensible, industrious, not well-educated, but fond of good company, altogether an excellent fellow and very much the gentleman. Gambling he loved, but chiefly for the pleasure of it, and he played all card games well. It was that talent that had raised him somewhat above the level of the men of the law;[2] but the real reason for his swift advancement was his skill at billiards, a game which the King greatly enjoyed and for many years played every evening in winter with M. de Vendôme and M. le Grand, and either the Maréchal de Villeroy or the Duc de Gramont to make a fourth. Hearing that Chamillart was an expert player they tried him out in Paris, and then praised him to the King with such good effect that he was summoned to Versailles. He arrived—and the King discovered that their praise had not been exaggerated. M. de Vendôme and M. le Grand then took him under their wing until he had become a fixture

---

[1] Michel Chamillart (1652–1721). One of Saint-Simon's dearest friends and like Pontchartrain old enough to be his father. He was not remarkably able but his unaffected frankness must have been a welcome relief amongst fawning courtiers. Years later, when he was also secretary for war and hideously over-worked, his arrogance made him intolerable.

[2] *Hors de sa robe.* The magistrates and law-officers at the Palais du Parlement wore dark gowns like the clergy, in contrast to the scarlet robes of the nobility. Theoretically the *gens de robe* (men of the long robe) were despised because they sold their services to the State for money. The riches and power of the clergy came to them for the glory of God, whose servants they were. It was the privilege of the *noblesse de l'épée* (men of the sword) to offer their lives *freely* in the defence of their country; their wealth was the land of France. That is the origin of their snobbery and their disdain for the *noblesse de robe*.

at the King's billiard-table, where he outplayed them all. His conduct all the time was so modest and becoming that he pleased both the King and the courtiers, who, contrary to their usual custom, protected him instead of sneering at the newcomer from Paris. Gradually the King came to appreciate him more and more, and praised him so heartily to Mme de Maintenon that she, too, desired to meet him. She also learned to like him and invited him, perhaps in order to please the King, to call on her from time to time. In the end she developed quite as great a partiality for him.

Despite his constant excursions to Versailles, where at that time he had no lodging, Chamillart appeared punctually each morning at the Palais du Parlement and worked there with an industry that greatly pleased his colleagues, who gave him credit for not putting on airs, as so many do after receiving favours. He gradually collected useful friendships, and before long the King had him made a *maître des requêtes*,[1] so as to give him more leisure and fit him for further advancement. After that he had a lodging at the Château of Versailles, a rare privilege, almost unique for a man of his condition. That happened in 1686. Three years later he was appointed governor of Rouen. He implored the King, with whom he was already on familiar terms, not to banish him, but the King replied that he was sending him to Rouen for exactly the opposite reason, since its nearness would allow him to return for visits of six weeks or more. Then the King invited him to Marly, and kept him at his own table for *brelan* and other games. At such times, when the stakes were too high, he shared with a partner, but he was also extraordinarily lucky.

After three years in that governorship the post of intendant of finances happened to fall vacant and the King gave it him. He remained there for the next ten years, always on the same excellent terms with the King, even though by that time billiards was out of fashion. He meanwhile cherished Mme de Maintenon, with the result that she entrusted him with the revenues and temporal business of Saint-Cyr, which brought him into close association with her and won him the friendship of M. de Chevreuse, whose estates bordered on Versailles and who now and again exchanged parcels of land with Saint-Cyr. With so much in his favour and the assistance of Mme de Maintenon the choice of Chamillart for controller-general was never for a moment in doubt, and the King openly congratulated himself on so wise a selection.

In office Chamillart behaved with a courtesy and patience hitherto unknown. He never appeared put out by futile suggestions or the most outrageous and repeated demands. In all this he was assisted by his calm, even temper, but he was by no means a stupid man. The way in which he refused a request showed his dislike of being obliged to do so, and his pleasure in granting a favour enhanced the value of it. He was, indeed,

[1] A judge of appeal.

naturally disposed to be obliging, and it pained him to have to disappoint people even by a little. The intendants of finances were devoted to him, for his manner towards them dispelled any resentment they might have felt at finding a junior placed over them. The courtiers all liked him because he assisted them in many ways and was civil and approachable, whilst the King constantly showed him marks of an affection that was almost friendship and daily increased. His wife and he were first cousins. She was worthy and infinitely courteous, and knew nothing except how to play cards—not for enjoyment, but because she could think of nothing better to do, nor even what next to say once she had inquired about health. Court-life proved incapable of educating her for, truth to tell, she was the most virtuous and the stupidest woman alive, and of no use whatsoever to her husband.

I cannot leave the subject of Chamillart without mentioning an action for which alone he deserves to be remembered. It happened at the time when he was only a counsellor at the Parlement, but played billiards three times a week with the King, returning each night to Paris. His working-day was thus much curtailed, but, as I have already said, this did not prevent him from attending regularly at the Palais du Parlement. One day, just after he had finished a case, the loser came to him crying out for justice. Chamillart listened with characteristic patience whilst the man swore to having offered in evidence a certain document that must surely have won his suit. He failed completely to understand how he had come to lose it. Chamillart, not having seen the papers, swore that it had not been submitted. The litigant swore that it had. Chamillart, still protesting, then re-opened the brief that was still lying upon his table, the judgment barely having been signed. He discovered the document. There was the wretched man in despair, and Chamillart trying to read and begging him for silence. At last, after examining it for some time, Chamillart exclaimed, 'You are perfectly right! I had not observed this paper. I cannot imagine how it escaped my notice. It would have won you your case. You were claiming damages of twenty thousand francs and by my negligence you are out of pocket. Come back tomorrow and you shall be repaid.' The man was so dumbfounded that Chamillart had to repeat his words. He returned a couple of days later, and Chamillart, who had raised part of the money on his possessions and borrowed the remainder, counted out twenty thousand francs into the victim's palm, asking him only to keep the matter secret.

This incident taught him the incompatibility of briefs, lawsuits, and the playing of billiards three nights in every week. Thenceforth he still attended regularly at the Palais and was no less industrious; but he ceased to act in lawsuits and sent back the briefs he had already accepted, asking the president to place them elsewhere. You may think that a noble action for a lawyer, especially for one as poor as he was in those early days.

The year ended with the King stopping a quarrel between the Jesuits, who started the rumpus, and the Benedictines. The latter had recently produced a fine edition of Saint Augustine, whose teaching is not that of the Jesuits. In order to have it suppressed these gentlemen employed their usual subterfuge; the work, so they said, was pure Jansenism. They attacked. The Benedictines replied. Both sides grew violent. Having run dry of proofs and arguments, but not of slanders and assertions, the Jesuits had still not managed either to harm or suppress the book. Angry as they were, credit must be given them for breaking off hostilities when they saw that they had failed, on receipt of the King's direct order neither to write nor give utterance on that subject in any manner whatsoever. It was Pontchartrain[1] who wrote both letters. Soon afterwards the Jesuits had the chagrin of seeing that same edition solemnly approved by Rome.

CHAPTER X

1700

The King ceases to pay for alterations to the courtiers' lodgings – Court Balls – Death of M. de La Trappe – Testament of the King of Spain in favour of M. le Duc d'Anjou – The Duc d'Anjou becomes King of Spain

THE YEAR began with an economy. The King announced that he would no longer pay for the changes made by courtiers in their lodgings,[1] which had cost him more than sixty thousand livres since Fontainebleau. Mme de Mailly was thought to be the cause, for she had changed hers annually in the past three or four years. The new arrangement was better in that one could get alterations made as one wished without first obtaining the King's consent; on the other hand one had to pay for everything.

From Candlemas to Lent there was a continual succession of balls and entertainments at the Court. The King gave several at Versailles and Marly, with wonderfully ingenious masquerades and tableaux, a form of diversion that vastly pleased him under the guise of amusing Mme la Duchesse de Bourgogne. There were concerts and private theatricals at Mme de Maintenon's; Monseigneur gave balls, and the most distinguished persons took pride in offering entertainment to Mme la Duchesse de Bourgogne. Monsieur le Prince, though his rooms were few and small, contrived to astonish the Court with the most elegant party in the world, a full-evening-dress ball, masks, tableaux, booths with foreign merchandise, and a supper most exquisitely staged. No one at the Court was refused admittance to any part of it, and there was no crowding nor any other inconvenience.

One evening when there was no ball Mme de Pontchartrain gave one at the Chancellery, and it turned out to be the gayest of them all. The Chancellor received Monseigneur, the three princes, and Mme la Duchesse de Bourgogne at the front entrance at ten o'clock and then immediately went off to sleep at the Château. There were different rooms provided for a full-evening-dress ball, masks, a splendid supper, and booths for the merchants of various countries, China, Japan, etc., offering

---

[1] The lodging given to a courtier was one huge, high room with a door on to a corridor and windows overlooking one of the little courts. Each courtier subdivided with entresols and partitions to make a warren of tiny rooms according to his needs. Servants slept in cupboards under the hen-roost staircases to the entresol rooms. There would be a privy, but few had kitchens. The Saint-Simons were greatly favoured when they were given a lodging and the King built one for them in the yard in 1710.

vast quantities of objects of beauty and virtue, all chosen with exquisite taste. No money was taken; all were presents offered to Mme la Duchesse de Bourgogne and the other ladies. There was also a concert in her honour, a play, and tableaux. Never was anything better conceived, more sumptuous, nor more perfectly organized, and Mme de Pontchartrain in the midst of it all was as gay, civil, and unruffled as though she had no responsibilities.

Everyone enjoyed themselves immensely, and we did not reach home until eight in the morning. Mme de Saint-Simon, who was always in Mme la Duchesse de Bourgogne's retinue (a great favour), and I never saw the light of day in the last three weeks before Lent. Certain dancers were not allowed to leave the ball-room before the princess, and once at Marly when I tried to escape early she sent orders for me to be confined within its doors. The same thing occurred to others also. I was truly thankful when Ash Wednesday came, and for a couple of days after felt quite stunned. As for Mme de Saint-Simon, she was worn out by Shrove Tuesday and did not manage to stay the full course. The King amused himself also in Mme de Maintenon's room with some selected ladies, playing *brelan*, *petite prime*, and *reversis*[1] on the days when he had no ministers or little work to do, and those diversions continued well into Lent.

On 23 September the King went to Fontainebleau. The King and Queen of England arrived on the 28th[2] and stayed until 12 October, receiving all manner of civilities from the King and the entire Court just as in past years. M. de Beauvilliers, whose wretched state of health had sent him to Bourbon, returned on 4 October somewhat recovered.

Whilst we were at Fontainebleau I suffered the terrible affliction of the death of M. de La Trappe. One evening at the King's *coucher* M. de Troyes[3] showed me a letter announcing that he was *in extremis*, which amazed me since I had heard nothing from La Trappe for the past ten or twelve days, at which time his health was as usual. My first impulse was to rush off there immediately, but my friends made me reconsider that hasty action. Instead, I sent to Paris for an excellent physician named Andry whom I had once taken with me to Plombières. He started at once, but M. de La Trappe was already dead when he arrived. These memoirs are too mundane for comments on a death so noble, so precious in the sight of God. Suffice it for me to say that the eulogies were all the greater because the King publicly praised him; asked to see the accounts of his death, and more than once spoke of it to his grandsons for their

[1] *Brelan* and *petite prime* were card games; *reversis* was played with counters painted red on one side and black the other. A red counter between two blacks was turned to show the black side, and the object was to get all the counters turned to show one colour or the other.

[2] According to Dangeau, each of the visits of James II and his wife cost the King twenty thousand écus (very approx.: £2,500).

[3] The Bishop of Troyes, François Bouthillier de Chavigny.

edification. Every part of Europe seemed to feel a bitter loss; the Church mourned for him, and even Society paid its tribute. That day, so joyous for him, so tragic for his friends, was 26 October, between noon and half past, in the arms of his bishop and in the presence of the whole community, at an age of nearly seventy-seven years, forty of which were spent in deepest penitence.

I cannot conclude without mentioning a most touching and honourable mark of his affection for me. As he lay upon the ground on straw and ashes, in the way of all Trappist monks when they die, he deigned to remember me, and charged the abbot to tell me that just as he did not doubt my true affection he was very sure that I knew his tende r love for me. There I must end; all else would be out of place.[1]

The King of Spain was growing steadily weaker, having several times in the past twelve months been on the verge of death. The succession had therefore become an urgent matter that caused acute concern throughout the whole of Europe. King William, whose influence had vastly increased since the formation of the Grand Alliance which had ended with the Peace of Ryswick, now undertook to settle the question, when it should arise, in such a way as to avoid a war. He loved neither France nor the King, and indeed had good cause to hate both. Moreover, he dreaded an extension of their power, having just witnessed in a ten years' war with all Europe ranged against them how formidable that power still was, even after those other wars, which, in King Louis's reign, had been a long procession of victories. Despite the late Queen's renunciations[2] he could not believe that Louis XIV would allow this great inheritance altogether to pass him by, and he therefore devised a partition which the latter might be disposed to accept in exchange for a guarantee of peace, even although France's power would not thereby be much increased. This plan he submitted first to King Louis, who, tired of war and at an age when peace becomes desirable, accepted with few stipulations. This done, he applied to the Emperor; but there not all his skill and authority availed.

The Emperor demanded the entire succession, standing firm on the renunciations, vowing that he would never submit to see the House of Austria driven from Italy, as it would have been had King William's plan to give the Spanish fortresses of the Tuscan coast to France been carried into effect. Under pressure from France, England, and Holland he grew obdurate, swearing that it was against all nature and custom to partition these realms before the death of King Charles of Spain, the head of his House and his close relation. These objections and, more especially, the spirit that engendered them he soon made known to the Spanish king,

---

[1] Saint-Simon bequeathed to the Maréchale de Montmorency, 'as a mark of true affection, the wooden cross edged with metal with which the holy Abbot-reformer of La Trappe was blessed, and which I have worn constantly since his death.'

[2] Maria Teresa, daughter of Philip IV of Spain, renounced all right to the Spanish throne for herself and her descendants when she married Louis XIV in 1660.

urging him forthwith to sign a will in favour of his kinsman the Austrian archduke.

King Charles thereupon raised as much commotion as though the project had been to skin him alive. But, with his body growing every day more feeble, his conscience took an ever stronger grip as he began to see the things of this world by the light of that awful torch which is lit for the dying. Finally, drifting, irresolute, torn apart, unable to support that state yet incapable of decision, he conceived the idea of consulting the Pope as an infallible oracle, writing him an immensely long epistle, casting all his cares on that paternal figure, and promising to abide by his advice.

The answer came without delay. The Pope wrote that, in a state of health very similar to that of His Most Catholic Majesty, he was conscious of soon having to account to the Universal Shepherd for the flock entrusted to his care. He had thus the strongest possible motive for giving advice that could not afterwards be held against him. His conclusion therefore was that the interests of the House of Austria were as nothing to his immortal soul, seeing clearly, as he did, that the sole and legitimate heirs of the Spanish monarchy were the children of the Dauphin of France and their descendants, and that Austria had no rights therein whatsoever. The plain duty of the King of Spain, he said, was to ensure that the totality of his succession passed into the hands of one of the Children of France. The King's letter and the reply of Innocent XII were kept a profound secret; nothing was known about them until after Philip V's arrival in Spain.

Although King Charles was by this time *in extremis*, he had strength enough to see his previous will burned in his presence and to sign another in favour of the Duc d'Anjou. His condition was made public a few days later, and a few days after that he expired. The will was then opened and the news sent to the King by courier.[1] It arrived as he was about to go shooting. The shoot was cancelled, and he went to dine as usual *au petit couvert*, displaying no kind of emotion, merely announcing the King of Spain's death, saying that he would drape,[2] and adding that there would be no more *appartements*, plays, or other entertainments at the Court for the rest of that winter. When he returned to his study he ordered his ministers to be at three o'clock in Mme de Maintenon's room. The meeting lasted until seven in the evening, after which he continued to work with Torcy and Barbezieux together, Mme de Maintenon being present the entire time. Next day he held the usual council of State in the morning, and when he returned from shooting he held another similar to that of the previous day in Mme de Maintenon's room, in her presence,

---

[1] For a fuller account of this episode see *Saint-Simon at Versailles*.
[2] Draping the coaches and harness with black, and black hangings in the rooms.

7

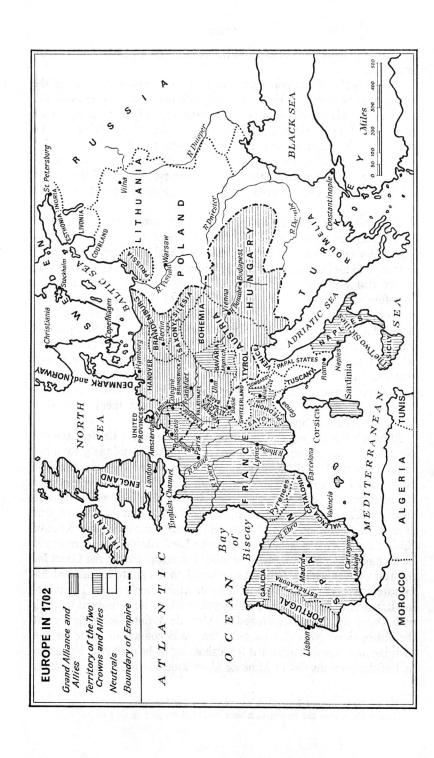

EUROPE IN 1702

Grand Alliance and Allies

Territory of the Two Crowns and Allies

Neutrals

Boundary of Empire

from six o'clock until ten. Although the Court were well accustomed to the privileges accorded her, it was new to see her taking part openly in the affairs of the nation, and people were astounded when two State councils were summoned to meet in her room for the most important deliberations of the King's reign, or, indeed, of any previous reign.

The King did not immediately declare his intentions, for he said that all things considered it would be best to wait another twenty-four hours, so as to hear more from Spain and know whether the Spaniards were of the same mind as their late king. He dismissed his ministers and ended his day, as I have already described, with Mme de Maintenon, Torcy, and Barbezieux. At last, on Wednesday, 10 November, he publicly made the announcement. The Spanish ambassador having in the meanwhile received news of the Spanish people's eagerness to welcome the Duc d'Anjou there seemed no more room for doubt. On Monday, 15 November, the King left for Fontainebleau, taking with him in his coach only Mgr le Duc de Bourgogne, Mme la Duchesse de Bourgogne, Mme la Princesse de Conti, and the Duchesse du Lude. He ate a morsel in his coach, and arrived at Versailles towards four o'clock. The Court was very large, for curiosity had prompted vast numbers to assemble even before the King's return.

On the following day, Tuesday, 16 November, immediately after his *lever*, the King summoned the Spanish ambassador to his study, where M. le Duc d'Anjou had already arrived by the back way. The King, presenting him, said that the ambassador might greet him as his sovereign, whereupon he immediately fell upon his knees in the Spanish fashion and made a somewhat lengthy address in that language, to which the King replied that as his grandson did not yet understand it, it would be for him to answer. Then, against all custom, the double doors of the study were opened wide, and he commanded all present, almost a crowd, to enter. Gazing majestically over that great assembly, he announced, 'Messieurs, behold the King of Spain. His birth has called him to that throne, also the will of the late king. The whole Spanish nation desires to have him and asks me to let him go. It is the will of Heaven, and I gladly obey.' Then, turning to his grandson, 'Be a good Spaniard; that is your first duty now; but never forget that you were born a Frenchman, and foster the unity between our two nations. That is the way to make them happy and to preserve the peace of Europe.' Once more pointing with his finger towards the ambassador, he said, 'If he is guided by me you will be soon a great noble; he cannot do better at present than follow your advice.'[1]

When the commotion had somewhat subsided the two other Grandsons of France stepped forward and all three tenderly embraced many times,

---

[1] Voltaire says that at this moment Louis XIV exclaimed, 'There are no longer any Pyrenees!'

their eyes wet with tears.[1] The King then went to mass as usual, and the King of Spain walked beside him at his right-hand. In the tribune, the entire royal family, that is to say down to and including the grandsons of France but no further, took their places in order of rank on the King's foot-rug, and because there were no *prie-dieux* all leaned on the carpeted balustrade, but the King was the only one to have a hassock; the rest kneeled upon the ledge, hassockless. The King took his hassock and offered it to the King of Spain, and when he would not accept it it was put on one side and both heard mass without a hassock. After that two hassocks were always provided when they went to mass, which was often. Thus for the remainder of his stay in France the new king was treated in every way as a reigning monarch by the King and all the Court.

At last on Saturday, 4 December, he left France. Early in the morning before any entrée he went to the King and remained with him a long time, afterwards going to Monseigneur for a long time also. They then heard mass all together in the tribune, with a great crowd of courtiers below. On leaving they went at once to the King's coach, Mme la Duchesse de Bourgogne sat at the back between the two Kings, Monseigneur in front between his sons, Monsieur by one door and Madame by the other,[2] with a larger and more resplendent escort of lifeguards and cavalry than usual. The entire road as far as Sceaux was lined with carriages and vast numbers of spectators, and when they arrived there shortly after noon they found the town full of ladies and courtiers, guarded by two companies of musketeers. As soon as they alighted the King traversed the whole length of the lower rooms, entering the last of them alone with the King of Spain and leaving the rest of the company assembled in the salon. A quarter of an hour later he summoned Monseigneur, and soon afterwards the Spanish ambassador to bid his royal master farewell. Then Mgr and Mme la Duchesse de Bourgogne entered together with Monsieur and Madame and M. le Duc de Berry, and, after a short interval, the princes and princesses of the blood. The double doors were thrown open so that we could see them all weeping bitterly. The King presented the princes to the King of Spain, saying, 'Behold the princes of my blood and yours! Our two nations must now regard themselves as one. Our interests must be the same. It is my hope that these princes will be as closely attached to you as they are to me; you cannot have better nor more faithful friends.' All this took up more than an hour and a half, and at length the time came to part. The King escorted the King of Spain back through all the rooms, embraced him many times, holding him long clasped in his arms. It was a most moving sight.

The King then retired to compose himself, which took some consider-

---

[1] Anjou was a grave and gentle young man and acted as peacemaker in the family quarrels. His brothers were genuinely fond of him and sorry to see him go.

[2] In seventeenth-century coaches the occupants sat in rows facing the horses, as in a bus.

able time. Monseigneur got into his carriage and returned to Meudon,[1] the King of Spain entered his coach with his brothers and the Duc de Noailles and went to sleep the night at Chartres. King Louis drove out in a light carriage with Mme la Duchesse de Bourgogne, Monsieur and Madame; after which they all returned to Versailles. Some officers of his household accompanied King Philip on his journey to Spain, Desgranges as his master of ceremonies, secretaries, equerries, and La Roche as head valet, together with various servants, and a few others in the nature of doctors and dentists.

M. de Beauvilliers, who was almost dead from taking too much quinine for a persistent fever accompanied by most distressing diarrhœa, took his wife with him on the journey, and Mmes de Cheverny and de Rasilly to keep her company. The King absolutely insisted that he should start and endeavour to go the whole way.

Let them go, and let us marvel at the ways of Providence that disposes of man's intentions and the fate of nations. What would Ferdinand and Isabella have thought, or Charles V and Philip II, who so often attempted to invade France and were accused of aspiring to world-monarchy? Or Philip IV, himself, with all his precautions at the time of the King's marriage and the Peace of the Pyrenees? What would he have said at seeing a son of France become King of Spain by the will and testament of the last of his line and the unanimous wish of the Spanish people, without French plots or intrigue, indeed, quite unbeknown to our King and his ministers, who felt nothing but anxiety in deciding and sorrow in the acceptance? What deep, what grave reflections do such thoughts provoke! But they would be out of place in these Memoirs. Let us return to the narrative, for I could not earlier interrupt this sequence of fascinating events.

---

[1] Monseigneur's country house.

CHAPTER XI

1701

[*The War of the Spanish Succession had, in part, an accidental origin. Both Louis XIV and his detested kinsman William III wished to avoid a fresh war over the fate of the Spanish monarchy. To avoid war, the two rulers made an attempt to secure the succession of the last—and childless—Spanish Habsburg king, Charles II, to a Bavarian prince. The other claimants were to be bought off with pieces of the immense Spanish dominions. They were immense; all of Spain; half of Italy (the Duchy of Milan and the Kingdom of the Two Sicilies); Sardinia; most of modern Belgium; nearly all the settled parts of North and South America, including the treasure-houses of Mexico and Peru; the Philippines and some smaller naval and military outposts. Any thought of partition of the great inheritance was abhorrent to patriotic Spaniards and, on his deathbed, Charles II was induced to leave everything to the second grandson of Louis XIV, Philip Duc d'Anjou. If the Duc d'Anjou did not accept, the inheritance was to go, intact, to the Archduke Charles, the second son of the Holy Roman Emperor Leopold, head of the junior line of the Habsburgs. Louis XIV had to take the gamble of breaking his agreement with William III or run the risk of seeing the whole prize go to the family of his chief continental rival, the Emperor. He chose to risk war. (The same danger of being outflanked on the South by a presumably hostile power, in this case Prussia, led Napoleon III to declare war in 1870.) To add to the anger of William III, Louis XIV, overcome by family and perhaps religious feeling, responded to the pleas of the dying James II and recognized his only son, 'the Old Pretender', as King of England. This was sufficient to get English support for the policy of William III. Thus the 'War of the Spanish Succession' began. The Duc d'Anjou, now Philip V of Spain, was accepted everywhere in the Spanish dominions and the Allies agreed to support the claims of the Archduke Charles. A riding accident killed William III and gave Louis XIV a much more formidable opponent, John Churchill, Duke of Marlborough.*]

Preparations for war in Italy – Death of Barbezieux – Chamillart Secretary of State – Death of Bontemps – French troops disarm Dutch garrisons in the Netherlands – Chocolate for the Jesuits – Mlle Rose a most eccentric pietist – Helvétius at Saint-Aignan – King James sent to Bourbon – Philip V enters Madrid – Monseigneur stricken with indigestion – M. de Chartres refused permission to serve – Death of Monsieur – Interesting visit of Mme de Maintenon to Madame – Adventure of the Abbess of La Joye – Indisposition of Mme la Duchesse de Bourgogne – Oddness of Mme de Sainte-Hérem – the Princesse des Ursins appointed duenna to the new Queen of Spain – Marriage of Philip V – Death of James II – Fagon cut for a stone

WHILST all these events were happening in Spain the Emperor had been using every means to increase his armies. He poured his soldiers into the Tyrol, and in Rome took strong measures to prevent the Pope from formally investing the new King of Spain with the crown of Naples and Sicily. In that he did succeed, but on the other hand, the Pope accepted King Philip's nominations to benefices in that kingdom as though he were fully recognized, and announced in both places that although for various reasons formal investiture was postponed, he now regarded the prince as the sole and rightful King of Spain, Naples, and Sicily. Thus it had become necessary to prepare for active war in Italy, and Tessé was despatched to Monsieur de Savoie, who liked him personally because he had negotiated the Peace of Ryswick and the marriage of Mme la Duchesse de Bourgogne. We should urgently need the assistance of Monsieur de Savoie for transport and supplies; it was essential therefore to make sure of him and also of the Duke of Mantua, with whom Tessé was likewise on excellent terms. The latter had accordingly been sent to Italy laden with instructions, and, whilst Torcy laboured on the political problems, Barbezieux faced a tremendous task in organizing the troops, supplies, and other requirements for waging war.

In the midst of all this work Barbezieux had the immense chagrin of seeing Chamillart quite unexpectedly appointed minister of State. It was a bitter humiliation for one whose father and grandfather had for the past sixty years played a major role in the government of France. Chamillart, having held office for barely two years, was to him a new man, scarcely beyond the state of being kept standing in Barbezieux's ante-room as he had stood in that of Barbezieux's father before him. His sudden promotion to be an equal appeared altogether abominable to the war minister, a personal affront all the less bearable because he dared not complain.

Chamillart himself, who had never expected such early promotion to the council, did all that a modest and well-intentioned man could do in the way of propitiation. But it was not Chamillart with whom Barbezieux was incensed; it was the promotion itself, which his proud, headstrong nature could not endure. No sooner did Tessé leave him than he gave himself up to dissolute living. He had built a house named L'Etang, set in some fields between Versailles and Vaucresson, at the end of the park of Saint-Cloud. It was the most depressing place imaginable but within easy reach of the Court. He had spent millions on it. There he retired to drown his sorrows in feasting and drinking with his boon companions, and in other more private pleasures; but his resentment still remained and that, combined with more dissipation than his health could stand, brought him to his death. He returned to Versailles with a sore throat and a high fever that in a man of his sanguine temper required frequent bleedings, which his debauched life rendered most dangerous. His illness appeared fatal from the first; it lasted only five days, giving him barely time to make a will and confess when his uncle the Archbishop of Rheims had finally convinced him of his parlous condition, which he had been disputing even with Fagon. He died in the prime of life with steadfastness, his family around him, and his door continually besieged by the entire Court. It happened at the beginning of a Marly, on Twelfth-night. His life ended before he was thirty-three, in the very room where his father had died.

He had trained the King to postpone working with him when he was drunk or had a party that he did not wish to miss. He used to send word that he had a fever. The King bore with him because his work was useful and efficient, and because he liked to believe that he could form his ministers and do everything himself; but he never cared for him and soon perceived what lay behind those absences and pretended fevers. Madame de Maintenon protected him for personal reasons; he stood in awe of her and was made to continue in that state. All in all, he had the makings of a great statesman, but was appallingly dangerous. It is even questionable whether his death was any loss to the State because of his inordinate ambition. To the Court and Society he was no loss, for much advantage came to them from the death of one whose great abilities would have made him tyrannous as his power increased.

Immediately after his death the King was informed at Marly, to which he had gone two hours earlier from Versailles in such certain expectation of the event that he had directed La Vrillière to affix the seals everywhere.[1] Fagon, who had condemned Barbezieux from the start, disliked him as much as he had disliked his father, and was slightly suspected of having purposely bled him too much. Be that as it may, he had let slip some pleased remarks on the unlikelihood of his return when he left the sick-room for the last time. None the less, some private persons and ladies of fashion stood to lose by his death, and there were mournful faces in the salons of Marly; yet when all were at table and the Twelfth-night cake was cut the King showed a joviality which he seemed to wish imitated. Not content with calling aloud, 'The Queen drinks!'[2] he beat upon his plate with his spoon and fork as though in a tavern, and made others follow suit. There ensued a terrible din that lasted at intervals throughout the entire supper, with the one-time mourners making more noise than any and giving vent to even longer bursts of laughter, and Barbezieux's dearest friends making most noise of all. On the following day the King did not appear. The courtiers had two days in which to speculate on the vacancy. I gave myself full marks for guessing right.

Chamillart was spending his Twelfth-night at his house at Montfermeil,

---

[1] When anyone of importance died the police fixed seals on all the doors and windows until a thorough search had been made of house or lodging and all documents and letters removed or scrutinized.

[2] James II and his queen may have been at Marly.

and it was from thence that the King summoned him by one of Mme de Maintenon's footmen, bidding him appear at his *lever* on the following morning, at the end of which he was called into the study and given Barbezieux's office. Chamillart, being prudent, asked to resign from the finances, rightly estimating that there was no comparison between that perilous work and the war department, and when the King refused to hear of his quitting he pointed out the impossibility for one man to fill two posts that had kept both Colbert and Louvois fully occupied. It was, however, precisely because of the quarrels between those two ministers that the King had determined to unite their departments, and he was thus deaf to all Chamillart's protests.

Chamillart was a good man and true, with clean hands and excellent intentions, civil, patient, obliging, a firm friend and a poor enemy, loving his country but most of all the King, and on very good terms both with him and with Mme de Maintenon. His understanding was limited. Like most men of poor spirit and little learning, he was stubborn, cocksure, greeting with a pitying smile those who differed from him in argument, and quite unable to grasp their points of view. His judgment in men and affairs was faulty, for he was greatly influenced by those whom for various reasons he admired, or had made his close friends without much cause. His capabilities were nil, yet he thought that he knew everything, a state of mind all the more pitiable because it had come to him with office, more from stupidity than arrogance, certainly not from vanity, for he was wholly devoid of that. What is strange is that it was his very incapacity that had aroused the King's affection. He admitted his ignorance at every step, and it became the King's pleasure to teach and guide him, being as proud of Chamillart's successes as though they were his own and excusing all his errors. Society and the Court likewise made excuses for him, charmed by his approachability, his obvious delight in granting favours, his distress at ever having to refuse, and his endless patience. His memory was so good for people and affairs, despite the thousands that passed through his hands, that individuals were constantly touched to find that their cases were familiar to him even after a lapse of several months. He wrote exceeedingly well also, in a lucid, readable style most pleasing to the King and Mme de Maintenon, who never ceased to praise and encourage him, praising themselves at the same time for laying on those feeble shoulders two burdens, either of which might well have broken the strongest back.

Bontemps, chief of the four head-valets of the King's bed-chamber and governor of Versailles and Marly, where he was responsible for the administration of the buildings, hunts, and many other expenses, died at this time. Of all the indoor servants he was the one longest and best trusted by the King in all his intimate personal affairs. A tall, well-built man, he had latterly become monstrously stout and heavy, and was nearly

80 years of age when he died of apoplexy on 17 January. He was most secret, most faithful, and entirely devoted to the King. It will explain all to say that it was he who arranged the nocturnal mass in the King's study, at which Père de La Chaise officiated in the winter of 1683–1684, when the King married Mme de Maintenon in the presence of Harlay, Archbishop of Paris, Montchevreuil, and Louvois.

In that direction one may truly say, like master, like man, for Bontemps was a widower and had living with him at Versailles a certain Mlle de La Roche, mother of the La Roche who went with the King of Spain as his head valet, and kept his place for twenty-five years until his death. Mlle de La Roche did not appear in public and scarcely ever at his house, from which she never emerged, but she ruled him absolutely without seeming to do so. Everyone knew that she was his Maintenon and that he had married her; but why he never announced the fact was a complete mystery. Bontemps was rough and brusque in manner, yet respectful and always in his place, which was at his home or in the King's private apartments, where he entered at all hours and always by the back offices. His only skill lay in serving his master, and he was wholly intent on that, without ever departing from his sphere. Over and beyond the intimate functions of his two employments, all the secret orders and messages, the private audiences, the sealed letters to and from the King, in fact all the mysteries passed through his hands. That might well have ruined the character of one known to have been influential for the past fifty years, and with the Court at his feet. Yet he never forgot his place, far less so, indeed, than the young blue footmen under his orders.[1] He harmed no one and always used his influence for good. Great numbers of people, some of them highly placed, owed their fortunes to him, and he was modest almost to the point of breaking with them if they so much as mentioned it. He loved procuring favours solely for the pleasure of it, and it may truly be said of him that he was throughout his life a father to the poor, a refuge for the disgraced and afflicted, and the kindest fellow imaginable. Thus, although his credit was much diminished through age and infirmity, his death was publicly mourned at the Court, in Paris, and in the provinces. Everyone felt it as a personal loss, and the tributes paid to his memory were both innumerable and extraordinary. In him I lost a true friend, who never ceased to respect and be grateful to my late father.

Blouin, another head-valet, succeeded Bontemps to the governorships of Versailles and Marly, in the same way that Bontemps had gained them after the death of Blouin's father. He also had charge of the secret correspondence and private audiences. He was a man of some intelligence, jovial, but exceedingly withdrawn, choosing his friends from the best at the

---

[1] The blue-uniformed footmen attending on the King and the Court at Versailles.

Court, keeping a table of exquisite viands for a small company of high-ranking young coxcombs, or those who made up in other ways for lack of titles. Cold, proud, self-sufficient, easily made insolent, he was not notably malicious, but none the less one whom it did not pay to cross. He was very much of a personality, whom the great and the ministers redoubted and flattered, for when he chose, which was rarely, he could assist his friends, but never others; at all times he was a danger, taking aversions without cause and being then capable of infinite harm.

Several items of good news now arrived close after one another, beginning with M. de Savoie's promise, couched in the required terms, to allow our troops to pass freely into Italy. Thereafter came a victory in Holland that seemed almost miraculous, like a transformation scene at the Opera. Briort, our ambassador there, had fallen ill and our affairs were in the greatest disorder. The States-General, in league with England, were doing everything possible to disarm our suspicions until their plans for war were fully matured. They demanded conference after conference,[1] procrastinating with all the greater confidence because Briort was in no state to attend to business. King William, meanwhile, was urging the King to comply with their desires but, however much he may have longed for peace, King Louis could not close his eyes to the Emperor's openly hostile actions, nor to the bad faith of his one-time allies.

The Dutch had twenty-two battalions in the fortresses of the Spanish Netherlands, serving under Spanish commanders, who each had also a small number of Spanish troops. A plan was drawn up to be rid of these Dutch. The King approved it, and the Maréchal de Boufflers was sent to Brussels to confer with the Elector of Bavaria, who acted as Governor-general of the Spanish Netherlands. These plans were so brilliant, so secret, and so perfectly executed that on the morning of Sunday, 6 February, French troops entered all the Spanish fortresses at the same moment, unopposed. The gates were thrown open for them, and the Dutch, taken completely by surprise, were disarmed without a shot being fired. The Spanish governors then informed the Dutch soldiers that they had nothing to fear; the King of Spain, they said, simply preferred to use French troops, and they would remain under arrest until orders for them were received from France. These orders when they arrived were far from what was expected and very far from prudent. The King, in his sincere desire for peace, had convinced himself that by returning their soldiers with their arms and all manner of courtesies, he would reassure the Dutch people (for there had been a loud outcry) and make them anxious to keep the peace. He was wrong.

He gave back to the Netherlands twenty-two excellent battalions, well-armed and equipped. Had he decided to keep them the Dutch might have

[1] To negotiate the recognition of Philip V.

been rendered incapable of war, to the great discomfiture of England, the Emperor, and all that Grand Alliance that was now forming against the Kings of France and Spain. The King's orders to free the Dutch troops arrived on Friday 11th, just six days after the capture of the fortresses. The States-General, who had been expecting something very different, acknowledged the gesture with expressions of delighted gratitude that concealed very effectively their warlike intentions.

This success in Holland was crowned by the arrival of a Spanish fleet with more than sixty millions' worth of gold and silver, and twelve millions in merchandise, not to mention smuggled goods and the sailors' parcels.[1] I shall take this opportunity to tell of a cargo, this time from the Netherlands, that arrived in Spain after the new king's entry into Madrid. When some of the ships were being unloaded eight vast packing-cases were discovered, labelled *Chocolates for the Very Reverend the Father-general of the Society of Jesus*. They were so heavy that they seemed likely to break the backs of the carriers, who promptly demanded double pay on account of the weight. The extraordinary difficulty which they still seemed to encounter with these comestibles aroused so much comment that when the crates arrived in the warehouses of Cadiz the officers opened one of them. It appeared to contain nothing but thick bars of chocolate packed one upon another, but when one of the bars was lifted out the weight of it was phenomenal. They tried another with the same result and then tried to break it but without success. As they redoubled their efforts, however, one bar burst open and they discovered that the crates were entirely filled with gold bars covered with a finger-thick layer of chocolate. Madrid was notified, and there was much mirth despite the holy character of the aforesaid Society. The Jesuits were also informed, but to no purpose, for those cunning politicians preferred to lose their precious chocolate rather than admit to ownership. Protesting that they knew nothing of the matter, they stuck so firmly to their word that in the end the King of Spain received the gold, no small amount, as you may well imagine, with eight huge crates filled with big, thick, solid bars. The chocolate that covered them went to the men who discovered the trick.

Shortly after this Cardinal de Noailles banished from his diocese that notorious pietist Mlle Rose,[2] who was a perfect enigma with her trances and visions, her most extraordinary conduct, and her aptitude for directing her directors. She was an old woman of Gascony, or rather from Languedoc, too well-endowed with the gift of speech, square-shouldered, of medium height, monstrously thin, yellow, and hideous, but with a bright and piercing glance which she could make tender when she chose.

---

[1] *Pacotilles:* small bundles of merchandise which sailors were allowed to bring home duty-free.
[2] Sister Rose de Sainte-Croix. Her name was Catherine d'Almerac.

She was eloquent, learned, and looked impressively like a prophetess, sleeping seldom and on bare boards, eating next to nothing, dressing very poorly, and allowing herself to be seen only in private. There was always something of a mystery surrounding her, for she appeared quite genuine and made some astounding and permanent conversions. She also made many remarkable pronouncements, some concerning secrets of the past, others of the future, which came to pass as she had foretold, and she healed the sick without remedies. There were wise and pious persons to whom she became attached, who believed in her throughout their lives and had nothing to gain by pretending to do so. One such was the famous M. Duguet, noted as much for his writings as for his saintly life.[1]

Mlle Rose spent many years in her native province, tending the sick poor and making converts by her piety. Then for one reason or another she came to Paris, with no particular doctrine, but strongly opposed to Mme Guyon and tending very much towards the Jansenists. It was there that she encountered the Comte du Charmel and later M. Duguet, both of whom fell under her spell as completely as M. de Cambrai had once fallen to Mme Guyon. After she had been living for some time in semi-retirement M. Duguet and M. du Charmel, not to mention herself, conceived a great desire that she should be seen by M. de La Trappe so as to record the impression on that great man of her strange personality and in the hope of raising her supposed reputation for saintliness. All three of them left Paris without warning and descended upon La Trappe, where no one had heard a word of their intentions.

M. du Charmel put up at the ordinary guest-house and the other two with M. de Saint-Louis, whom I have already mentioned, and who leased the Abbey House beyond the wall. He was quite unable to refuse them lodging or avoid asking them to dine at his table. As chance would have it I also was staying at La Trappe during their visit and so had several opportunities of meeting both Mlle Rose and M. Duguet, which was no small favour for they kept themselves private. I must confess that I thought her more eccentric than anything else, but M. Duguet wholly captivated me. We walked together every day in the garden of the Abbey House, conversing not only on religious matters, wherein he excelled, but on anything and everything. A flower, a blade of grass, a bush, art, the professions, dress, all gave him occasions to talk and instruct, and he spoke so naturally and eloquently, and so lucidly that one was fascinated by the charm of his conversation and at the same time astounded by his scholarship. The respect and veneration which he felt for Mlle Rose and his pleasure and admiration at her remarks never failed to surprise me. M. de Saint-Louis, on the other hand, could not endure her and said so

---

[1] Jacques Joseph Duguet (1648–1733). Author of *L'Institution d'un Prince*; commissioned by the Duke of Sardinia. A man of vast learning, and a student of theology. He was also a militant Jansenist. Later he confessed that he had been carried away by the piety of Sister Rose.

frankly to M. du Charmel. He did not conceal his feelings even from M. Duguet, which distressed both of them more than a little.

They were far more distressed by the gentle determination with which M. de La Trappe refused to see her during the whole of their six-week visit; and, moreover, that he should have based that refusal less on ill-health than on total ignorance of her extraordinary methods. Neither his mission nor his character, he said, fitted him to make examinations of that nature; and his state of being dead to the world in a life of penitence did not allow him to be distracted by fruitless inquiries. Far better to suspend judgment and pray for her than dissipate his strength on matters altogether beyond his scope. Thus they left as they had come, much mortified at having failed in the object of their journey.

For some time afterwards Mlle Rose lived at Paris more or less in concealment among the converts of her neighbourhood. When these increased in numbers she appeared more often in public and finally became renowned as a directress. Cardinal de Noailles then had her examined, and I think that M. de Meaux also saw her. Be that as it may, she was banished from the diocese. She had meanwhile converted a fine-looking young man, whose father, a gentleman of quality, was once major of the garrison at Blaye and very wealthy. This young fellow left the King's service, followed her in exile to Annecy and never afterwards left her. His name was Gondé. Nothing more was ever heard of her although she lived to a great age.

The pretext for Mlle Rose's visit to La Trappe was to see a convert that she had made near Toulouse, an exceedingly handsome curé who had then been living in not too holy a fashion. He was the brother of a certain M. Parazar, a counsellor of the Toulouse Parlement. She had persuaded him to leave his parish and enter La Trappe, but she must have had a hard struggle over that, for he always swore that she made him a monk in spite of himself. None the less he was a good one, so good indeed that when Monsieur de Savoie applied to La Trappe for a brother to reform the Abbey of Tamiers this one was sent and he became the abbot. He was so successful there that Monsieur de Savoie, who was at times subject to bouts of piety, made several retreats at Tamiers and gave him his full confidence.

M. de Beauvilliers's illness, a loosening of the bowels that had afflicted him for some years past, was now worsened by fever. He had had considerable difficulty in reaching his home at Saint-Aignan, near Loches, and lay there *in extremis*. I learned after his departure that Fagon had given him up and had sent him to Bourbon as a counsel of despair and to be rid of the sight of him. When this news reached me from Saint-Aignan I hastened to the Duc de Chevreuse, urging him to throw caution to the winds and send Helvétius[1] there immediately, and I was overjoyed

---

[1] Adrien Helvétius (1661–1727). Monsieur's doctor, father of the famous encyclopaedist.

to hear that he had already decided to do so and was leaving with him on the following day.

Helvétius was a tall Dutchman whom the doctors had rejected on the grounds that he had taken no degree. He was also the pet abomination of Fagon who, because his influence with the King was paramount, aspired to rule the entire medical profession, as well as all those unfortunate enough to need its services. Helvétius was what they termed a *quack* in their language, supposedly deserving nothing but contempt and persecution, and liable to bring down Fagon's wrath and ill-will on all who employed him. Yet he had lived for many years in Paris and had cured many who were condemned by the doctors, more especially the poor to whom he was immensely charitable. At a certain time each day he attended as many as chose to present themselves at his house, giving them remedies and often food as well. He was notably successful in the cure of intractable dysentery; indeed, it is to him we owe the use and different preparations of ipecacuanha for treating diseases of that nature, and the knowledge of how to diagnose others for which that remedy is unsuitable. That is how he won his reputation and, what is more, he was an upright man and sincere in his beliefs. He was also excellent for smallpox and other poisonous complaints, but in other respects only mediocre.

M. de Chevreuse informed the King of his intention to call in Helvétius and the King gave his approval. The extraordinary thing was that Fagon himself appeared glad of it. On another occasion he might have flown into a rage, but he was so sure of M. de Beauvilliers dying at Saint-Aignan that he was well-pleased to let him do so in Helvétius's care. Thank God the contrary occurred! Helvétius did indeed find him *in extremis*, but he set him on the road to complete recovery in less than a week and he was able to return to the Court. He arrived at Versailles very early in the morning of 8 March; you may imagine with what joy I ran to embrace him. As I was returning from his apartment and about to cross the King's ante-room, I saw a crowd gathered round one side of the fireplace and stopped to know the cause. The throng parted, and I saw Fagon lying all unbuttoned, with his mouth open, giving every appearance of a dying man. It was a fit of epilepsy. He suffered from them sometimes, which was why he lived immured in his apartment and paid such short visits to the few courtiers whom he still attended—no one was ever permitted to see him in his room.

As soon as I had satisfied my curiosity I continued on my way to the Maréchal de Lorges's apartment, entering his drawing-room with such a rapturous smile that the visitors, always present there in great numbers, asked me what I had been doing to make me look so happy. 'What have I been doing?' said I, 'I have come from embracing a sound man whom his doctor condemned, and I have just seen that same doctor at death's door.' I was indeed overjoyed for M. de Beauvilliers and sincerely angry with Fagon on his account. When they asked me to explain further I told them all, and everyone at once began to discuss Fagon's health, for he was an immensely important figure at the Court and greatly feared, even by the ministers and the King's valets. All the time that this was going on M. and Mme de Lorges were making signs to me to hold my tongue, and they afterwards reproached me for my foolhardiness; but it never seemed to reach Fagon's ears, and I remained on excellent terms with him.

Shortly after this time King James fell seriously ill and was paralysed down the whole of one side of his body, although his wits were not fuddled. The King, and following his example the entire Court, paid him visits of courtesy. Fagon then sent him to Bourbon accompanied by his queen, and the King provided everything for them with the greatest munificence. He sent d'Urfé with them to act as his representative and to ensure that they received the same honours as himself, even although they had desired there to be no ceremony.

On 19 February the new King of Spain finally reached Madrid, having been welcomed everywhere on his journey with huge crowds and public acclamations, and in the towns with public holidays, bull-fights, vast numbers of ladies, and all the local nobility. When he arrived the crowds were so dense that they counted sixty persons crushed to death. Outside the city and along all the streets through which he passed, the way was lined with coaches, filled with ladies in their finest attire, and Buen Retiro,[1] where he spent the night, was overflowing with courtiers and members of the nobility. The Junta[2] and many grandees greeted him at the door of his coach, and Cardinal Portocarrero tried to kneel to kiss his hand; but that King Philip would not allow, raising and embracing him and treating him in every respect as a father. To be brief, the members of every council, all the men of eminence, a vast company of ladies and gentlemen were presented to him, and the entire household of the late King Charles. The streets were decorated, and in the Spanish fashion lined with benches displaying beautiful paintings and a mass of silver ornaments, with here and there a splendid triumphal arch. Impossible to conceive of more sincere and wide-spread demonstrations of rejoicing.[3]

The King of Spain was well-made, in the very flower of youth, fair-haired like his grandmother[4] and the late king. By nature he was grave, silent, and reserved, and thus admirably suited for life in Spain. He was moreover meticulously polite to all, and already knew the differences of rank of all those who had been presented to him, having had time to study

---

[1] The King's country house at the gates of Madrid.

[2] The Spanish privy council: the word means a meeting.

[3] Saint-Simon thoroughly approved of Spain and the status of Spanish grandees. In moments of despair at the way France was governed he sometimes thought of becoming a Spaniard; but time brought disillusionment.

[4] Maria Teresa.

them during his long journey with Harcourt.[1] He quite removed his hat or slightly raised it to everyone, which so much offended a few of the Spaniards that they complained to Harcourt, who answered that in all essentials the king would comply with the custom of Spain, but that they must allow him his French courtesy. You would hardly believe how much that little courtesy won the people's hearts.[2] Knowing no one, he allowed himself to be guided by Harcourt and those Spaniards who had done most to implement the late king's testament. Thus most of his time was spent with Cardinal Portocarrero, the Duke of Medina-Sidonia, and the Count of Benevento,[3] whose offices brought them constantly into his presence. The rest were complete strangers to him, not excepting Harcourt, and he was therefore very glad to escape into the company of the few Frenchmen who had followed him, although, apart from Louville who had been his *gentilhomme de la manche* since he was seven, he knew none of them well. Louville more than any other became his friend and confidant, for M. de Beauvilliers had strongly recommended him as being full of resource and sagacity, devoted to him in every way, and thoroughly deserving of trust. He was that and more also, for he was a gay and lively companion, alleviating with his witty sayings and repartees the king's graveness and formality, and proving a great comfort to him in a strange land.

Louville was M. de Beauvilliers's close friend, and being also a friend of Torcy, master of the posts, he was able to write personal letters, sure that both they and his private codes would be safe from scrutiny.[4] Knowing the king intimately, as he did, he was able to ease matters for Harcourt and Portocarrero, and he greatly assisted many other grandees and nobles, with the result that everyone liked him exceedingly. Very soon afterwards, when Harcourt fell seriously and lengthily ill, the whole burden fell upon Louville, who thereafter ruled both Spain and the king. He saw and copied all the letters to our Court, and public business of every kind passed through his hands. Shortly after his arrival King Philip took to wearing Spanish dress with the *gollila*[5] and made certain changes at his court; for instance, he reduced the number of his serving-gentlemen from thirty to six and cancelled the appointments of those not yet fully trained. He retained the Count of Benevento as High Steward, who became so devoted that he wept every time the king looked at him. Towards the end of April the King of Spain's betrothal was announced to

[1] Henri de Beuvron, Duc d'Harcourt, not to be confused with the before mentioned Lorraine Harcourts. He was the French ambassador and met King Philip at the frontier.

[2] A lesson not lost. Queen Victoria brought up King Edward VII on Saint-Simon's memoirs, and he also studied and practised these nicely graded hat-raisings.

[3] They were the chamberlains.

[4] One source of Saint-Simon's information about Spain.

[5] A stiffly starched linen shelf jutting below the chin and obliging the wearer to keep his head up. It was acutely uncomfortable.

Monsieur de Savoie's younger daughter, the sister of Mme la Duchesse de Bourgogne, who was overjoyed to think that her father thus stood to become father-in-law of the two most powerful monarchs in Europe.

Meanwhile, King William of England, who seized every occasion to reform the Grand Alliance and direct it against France, was finding it hard to raise the necessary funds. Endeavouring to throw dust in our King's eyes by offering false hopes of peace which every fact belied, he persuaded his obedient servants the Dutch to recognize Philip V as the rightful King of Spain and later did so himself. Thus at that time the prince was accepted as king by the whole of Europe, excepting only the Emperor. Now although King Louis was gratified by a gesture so clearly pacific he did not cease to make great preparation for war, and since he also controlled Spain, the Spaniards themselves lost no time in making ready.

Let us now leave Spain and take up once more the narrative in France at the point where it was interrupted.

On the evening of Saturday, 19 March, when the King was undressing as usual in his closet, loud cries for Fagon and Félix[1] were heard coming from the bedroom full of courtiers, and a great hubbub. Monseigneur had suddenly been stricken. He had spent the day at Meudon; had eaten only a light luncheon there, and had stuffed himself with fish at the King's supper. Like the King and the two queens, his mother and grandmother, he was a vast eater. He did not reappear after supper but went straight down to his apartments, where, as was also his custom, he had gone immediately to his closet. No sooner did he sit down to undress than he lost consciousness. His valets were distracted; some of the courtiers attending his *coucher* rushed to the King's room in search of Fagon and Félix, exciting the commotion which I have described. The King rose that instant all unbuttoned and went down to Monseigneur by the steep little dark staircase leading from the end of his ante-chamber into what was known as the 'staircase-cupboard',[2] a windowless closet at the side of the small court, with a door into the *ruelle* beside Monseigneur's bed[3] and another into the first state-room overlooking the garden. This 'cupboard' had a bed in an alcove where Monseigneur often slept in winter-time; but as it was so very small he always dressed and undressed in his bedroom. Mme la Duchesse de Bourgogne, who had also gone to her apartments, came running at the same time as the King, and in a moment Monseigneur's vast apartment was packed with spectators.

They found him half-naked, being walked, or rather dragged, up and down his room by the servants. He did not know the King when he spoke

---

[1] First surgeon to the King.

[2] *Le Caveau.* An earlier and more luxurious version of the young Mitfords' *Hons' Cupboard*, where family secrets could be aired. The dark little staircase was the *Petit Escalier du Roi*, which Louis XV found so handy when he visited the *Parc aux Cerfs*.

[3] *La Ruelle*, the space between the bed and the wall, where visitors sat to gossip.

to him, nor anyone else, and resisted Félix, who in that critical moment bled him notwithstanding and was successful. When his senses returned, he asked for his confessor, but the King had already summoned the curé. They administered several emetics, which took no effect for some considerable time. Two hours later, however, there was a prodigious eruption both above and below. At half-past two the danger seemed to be over, and the King, who had shed tears, retired to bed leaving orders that he was to be called in case of accident. At five o'clock all was peace again; the doctors left him to rest, and sent everyone from his room. People had been arriving at Meudon all through the night from Paris. He escaped with nothing worse than a week confined to his room, where the King visited him twice daily. When he was better he played cards all day long or watched others play. Had the calamity occurred a quarter of an hour later the first valet, who slept in his room, would have found him dead in his bed.

Monseigneur was popular in Paris, probably because he went often to the Opera. The fish-wives of Les Halles[1] decided to put themselves in the picture and sent a deputation of four to inquire after his health. He had them admitted; one of them put her arms round his neck and kissed him on both cheeks, the rest kissed his hand. They were received with honours; Bontemps took them on a tour of the apartments and gave them dinner; Monseigneur gave them money, and the King also sent a present. This made them very proud, and they had a grand *Te Deum* sung at Saint-Eustache followed by a banquet.

Meanwhile the armies were assembling, for Flanders under the command of the Maréchal de Boufflers, for Germany under the Maréchal de Villeroy. Mgr le Duc de Bourgogne was to have commanded the latter, but Monsieur's resentment when M. de Chartres was not allowed to serve caused there to be a cancellation. The King had originally consented, banking on the false assumption that Monsieur would be put out at his son being given no command and would forbid him to accept lesser rank. He had therefore made M. de Chartres's service dependent on Monsieur giving his consent. But for once Monsieur and his son were in agreement, for they reckoned that if M. de Chartres were content with a subordinate post in the present campaign, his age would compel the King to give him an army in the following year. The King, who for exactly the same reason was determined that he should not go, had, dare I say so, been caught napping. But trapped he was not; he merely showed signs of frayed temper by an irritable refusal to hear anything more on the subject. That was a mistake, for M. de Chartres proceeded to embark on youthful escapades that proved far more embarrassing to King Louis. With other young blades of a similar age he was planning to escape to Spain, or even to England, but Monsieur, knowing his son and knowing that none of

[1] Visits of the fish-wives at times of royal illness became a tradition.

these crazy schemes would be put into action, said nothing and was glad of the King's discomfiture.

At last the King spoke out, and when Monsieur appeared not to mind chided him for having no authority over his son. Thereupon Monsieur flew into a rage, more from policy than real anger, and turning upon the King asked to be informed how he should deal with a grown-up son who was given nothing better to do than kick his heels in the great gallery and forecourt of Versailles, a married man yet quite destitute, and seeing his brothers-in-law[1] loaded with appointments, households, governorships, and other dignities, for no cause or motive, and totally against all precedent. His son, he added, was in a worse plight than any gentleman of France of comparable age who could serve with the armies and earn promotion and rank; that idleness was the mother of evil; that it was hard for him to see his only son falling into dissolute habits with bad companions and indulging in hare-brained schemes, and that it was beyond endurance to be asked to reproach a high-spirited youth unjustly thwarted, and be unable to blame the one who had brought him to that pass. No one could have been more astounded than the King to hear such plain talk. Never before had Monsieur let fly at him in anything approaching that tone, and it was all the more upsetting because, although the logic was unanswerable, the King had no intention of giving way. Despite the suddenness of the onslaught he mastered himself sufficiently to reply in a brotherly rather than a kingly tone. He said that parental love excused all, embraced Monsieur, and did everything possible to restore him to good humour. The whole of that heated argument was carried on by Monsieur in angry tones and by the King rather more softly, but when they finally parted the former was still furious, and the latter much vexed, although he was anxious not to make a stranger of his brother and still more so that their quarrel should not be noticed.

Monsieur then returned to Saint-Cloud, but was never afterwards on his old affectionate terms with the King. To adopt a stiff attitude went quite against the grain of his weak character and lifelong habit of submission. What is more, he was truly devoted to the King and had been used to treating him in private with brotherly freedom and to receiving the like, together with all manner of kindnesses and tokens of love—and of respect too, always provided that there was no danger of giving him any importance. When either he or Madame suffered the smallest ill the King had been accustomed to visit them immediately and to continue in so doing if the malady endured. Six weeks earlier, however, Madame had had a double tertian fever and had done nothing about it because, after her German fashion, she took no account of remedies or doctors.[2] The

---

[1] The Duc du Maine and the Comte de Toulouse.

[2] She suffered from tertian ague. She had some reason for distrusting the French doctors with their repertory of bleedings, emetics, and purgings that ended so often in untimely death.

King, who was secretly vexed with her, as will shortly appear, for reasons quite apart from the affair of M. de Chartres, did not call on her although asked by Monsieur to do so. Monsieur, ignorant as to the real cause, had taken this as a public affront and, being inordinately proud, had been mortally offended.

Other ills of the spirit also beset him. His confessor Père du Trévou, a gentleman of good family from Brittany, had, though a Jesuit, been keeping him on as tight a rein as possible. He had cut him off from disgraceful pleasures in penance for his past life, and from other pleasures also which Monsieur himself considered permissible. He often told him plainly that he would not be damned for him, saying that he would be thankful for a change of confessor if Monsieur thought him too strict. To this he had appended that Monsieur had best beware, for he was old, worn out by debauchery, short in the neck, fat, and to all appearance likely to die of apoplexy at any moment. Those were awful words for the ears of the most voluptuous and life-loving of princes, accustomed to complete idleness and by nature incapable of any kind of reflection, serious reading, or self-examination. He feared the devil; he remembered that his late confessor had not wished to die in that employ and that before his death he had spoken in similar terms. They had made sufficient impression on Monsieur to make him a little examine his conscience and live in a manner that passed as austere in him. He prayed a great deal by fits and starts, obeyed his confessor, rendered account for the rule imposed by the latter regarding his spending on gambling and amusements, and on other pursuits as well, endured patiently his many homilies, and meditated on them. He grew sad, down-hearted, and chattered less (that is to say not more than three or four gossips rolled into one), and before long everyone had noticed the change. It was not to be wondered at that such heart-ache and the suffering he endured regarding the King should have been too much for so weak a man, and one so recently turned to self-restraint, and enduring repentance. Its effect was to cause a total revolution in that over-fed body, for he was a vast eater, not only at his meals but all day long.

On Wednesday, 8 June, Monsieur came from Saint-Cloud to dine with the King at Marly, and as usual entered the study after the council of State had left. He found the King angry because M. de Chartres, unable to attack him directly, had been upsetting his daughter.[1] The fact was that M. de Chartres had fallen desperately in love with Mlle de Séry, Madame's maid of honour, and was pursuing that affair in a tactless and high-handed manner. Taking that as his theme the King coldly reprimanded Monsieur for his son's conduct. Monsieur, in the state he then was, needed no such excuse to lose his temper, and before long they were at it hammer and tongs. An usher, hearing the din, went in to tell the King

[1] The Duchesse de Chartres.

that he could be heard distinctly from the drawing-room and then immediately retired. This made them lower their voices but did not stop the quarrel; and finally Monsieur flew into a rage, telling the King plainly that when M. de Chartres was married he had been promised the earth and had so far extracted no more than a governorship. He added that those people were right who had warned him that he would reap nothing from such an alliance but shame and contempt, with no advantages whatsoever. The King, more furious every moment, replied that the war necessitated economies and that since Monsieur was so unhelpful his pension should suffer before the King so much as touched his own purse.

At that point dinner was announced and they left the room to go to table. Monsieur was scarlet in the face, his eyes bright with anger, which made some of the ladies observe that he appeared in great need of bleeding. Dinner was as usual, with Monsieur eating prodigiously as he invariably did at his two meals, not to mention his copious draughts of chocolate every morning and all that he ate at other times in the way of fruit, sugar-biscuits, and the titbits in his pockets and in the drawers of the tables and cabinets. When they rose the King walked out alone, and Monsieur returned at once to Saint-Cloud.

That evening after supper the King was in his study with Monseigneur and the Princesses when an attaché arrived from Saint-Cloud with a message from M. de Chartres. He was admitted, and told the King that Monsieur had been seized with exhaustion at supper, but felt better after being bled and had been given an emetic. It appeared that, supping as usual with the ladies, he was in the act of pouring a glass of wine for Mme de Bouillon as the entrées were served, when he had suddenly stammered and pointed with his finger. He used occasionally to speak in Spanish, so that some of the ladies asked what he meant, whilst others cried out in alarm. It was all over in a moment, and he fell into the arms of M. de Chartres in a fit of apoplexy. They carried him to his bedroom, shook him, walked him up and down, bled him copiously, and administered a powerful emetic without arousing more than the faintest sign of life.

The King, who ordinarily rushed to Monsieur's aid on the smallest provocation, went instead to Mme de Maintenon and had her wakened. After a quarter of an hour closeted with her he returned to his room at midnight, ordered the carriages to be made ready, and sent the Marquis de Gesvres to Saint-Cloud with instructions to return and rouse him if Monsieur grew worse. He then went to bed. I believe that because of their quarrel he half-suspected a plot to relieve the tension, and had consulted Mme de Maintenon because he preferred to fail in what was proper rather than be tricked.

After the King had retired to bed one of Monsieur's pages came to say that he was better and had sent to M. le Prince de Conti for some Schaffhausen water, which is excellent for apoplexy. An hour and a half later, however, an officer arrived from M. de Chartres. He roused the King, reporting that the emetic had had no effect and that Monsieur was *in extremis*. Hearing this the King rose and left for Saint-Cloud immediately. Impossible to describe the tumult and disorder of that night at Marly, or the horrible scenes in the pleasure-palace of Saint-Cloud. Everyone at Marly rushed thither helter-skelter, seizing any carriage that came to hand, without asking leave or any regard for manners. Monseigneur went with Madame la Duchesse in a state of alarm because he, too, had been having bad attacks of indigestion. It was all his equerry could do to half-drag, half-carry him trembling to his coach. Shortly before three in the morning the King arrived to find that Monsieur had not regained his senses for a single moment. There had been a glimmer of life when Père du Trévou had begun to say mass, but it did not last. In the most solemn scenes there are often comic incidents. At that precise moment Père du Trévou turned round and shouted into Monsieur's ear, 'Monsieur, don't you know your own confessor? Don't you remember dear old Père du Trévou?', which had made those least affected laugh in a somewhat disgraceful fashion.

The King seemed much moved. He was generally prone to weep and therefore burst into tears. Indeed, he had no cause not to love Monsieur, and even though they had been on bad terms for the past couple of months these sad moments must have reminded him of their old affection. He may have blamed himself for precipitating Monsieur's death by that morning's quarrel; he may also have felt some disquiet, since Monsieur was the younger by two years and had appeared quite as healthy as himself, if not more so. He remained at Saint-Cloud long enough to hear mass at eight o'clock, then, since Monsieur was past human aid, Mme de Maintenon and Mme la Duchesse de Bourgogne persuaded him to wait no longer and they all returned together to Marly. As he was leaving he said some kind words to M. de Chartres, both of them in tears; whereupon the young prince clasped his knees, crying, 'Alas! Sire, what will become of me? I have lost Monsieur and I know you do not love me.' The King, surprised and deeply affected, embraced him, speaking very lovingly.

The crowd gradually melted away, leaving Monsieur dying on the day-bed in his study, exposed to the view of all the lackeys and under-servants, most of whom from love or self-interest appeared deeply distressed. The upper servants and those whose situations were gone rent the air with their cries, while the women ran hither and thither with their hair unbound, shrieking and wild as bacchantes. Meanwhile Madame, who had never possessed much affection or regard for her husband but keenly felt the loss of her position, stayed in her own apartments crying out at the top of her voice, 'No convent for me! Do not speak to me of a convent! I will not go to one!' She was not out of her mind, but remembered that by the terms of her marriage contract she would have to choose between a nunnery and retirement at the Château de Montargis. It may be that she saw better hope of escape from the one than from the other, or else, knowing how much cause she had to fear the King, although even then she did not know all, she may possibly have dreaded a convent. However that may be, as soon as Monsieur was dead she entered her coach with her ladies and drove to Versailles followed by M. and Mme la Duchesse de Chartres and their entire households.

Next morning, a Friday, M. de Chartres went to the King, who was still in bed and who spoke to him very kindly, bidding him thenceforth consider him as his father and promising to protect his honour and interests and to forget all the past small vexations. He said further that he hoped M. de Chartres would forget them also, and that these promises of affection would persuade him to return the King's offered love. You may well imagine that M. de Chartres answered in a proper spirit.

After such awful scenes, such tears, such demonstrations of tenderness, no one believed that the remaining three days of that Marly could be otherwise than miserable. Yet when the ladies went to Mme de Maintenon's room at midday on the morning after Monsieur's death, they found the King already there with Mme la Duchesse de Bourgogne and heard them singing opera-prologues from the ante-room. After a little while, however, he perceived her sitting looking very wretched in a corner of the room. He appeared surprised, asked Mme de Maintenon what had upset her, and tried to distract her by joining in games with her and some of the ladies.[1] Nor was that all. When they came from dinner, that is to say shortly after two o'clock, just twenty-six hours since Monsieur's death, Mgr le Duc de Bourgogne invited the Duc de Montfort to play a hand of *brelan*. '*Brelan!*' cried Montfort amazed. 'You must have forgotten; Monsieur is not yet cold!' 'Indeed I know it,' said the prince, 'but the King will not suffer anyone to be dull at Marly. He has ordered me to set everyone playing and to show the example myself.' They then sat down to play cards, and before long the entire drawing-room was full of gaming-tables.

On Saturday, 11 June, the Court returned to Versailles, where the King immediately visited Madame and M. and Mme de Chartres, each in their apartments. Madame, who was deeply disturbed by her situation with the King at this crucial period, had begged the Duchesse de Ventadour[2] to see Mme de Maintenon on her behalf. This the duchess had done. That lady had replied civilly enough, but said only that she would call on Madame after dinner and would like Mme de Ventadour to be present. This was on Sunday, the day after the return from Marly. After the first courtesies everyone left, except the Duchesse de Ventadour. Madame

---

[1] She may have been sad at losing a kind grandfather.
[2] Madame's lady-in-waiting and later governess of Louis XV.

then invited Mme de Maintenon to be seated, and her need must have been great indeed to induce her to do that. She then spoke of the King's unkindness during her illness, and Mme de Maintenon listened politely, afterwards replying that the King had commanded her to say that their common affliction obliterated all other feelings in his heart, provided only that he had more reason to be content with her in future, not only on the subject of M. de Chartres, but in other matters of even graver importance, which he had not wished to mention during her illness, although they were the real cause of his displeasure. Hearing this, Madame, who believed herself secure, began to protest that except concerning her son she had never said or done the smallest thing capable of vexing him, and she managed to infiltrate all manner of complaints and self-justifications. Whilst she was continuing in this way, Mme de Maintenon drew a letter out of her pocket and showed it to her, asking if she recognized the hand. It was one of Madame's private letters to her aunt the Duchess of Hanover, to whom she had written all the gossip of the Court, afterwards stating in so many words that no one knew what to think of the King's relationship to Mme de Maintenon, whether it was marriage or whoring, and then proceeding to discuss external and internal politics, holding forth at length on the poverty of France, and saying that it would never be relieved. That letter had been opened by the Post Office, as most letters were and still are opened, and having been found altogether too strong for the usual extract to suffice, the original had been sent to the King. You may well imagine that seeing that sight and hearing that reading Madame expected death within the hour. There she was crying, with Mme de Maintenon gently persuading her of the enormity of every paragraph, especially since it was intended for a foreign country. Mme de Ventadour set herself to make conversation so as to give Madame time to breathe and recover sufficiently to think of something to say. The best plan seemed to be to admit all she could not deny, with apologies, prayers, and promises for the future.

Mme de Maintenon coldly triumphed over her whilst she wept, explained, and wrung her hands. What a terrible humiliation for that proud and haughty German! At last Mme de Maintenon let herself be mollified, as she had fully intended, after enjoying her revenge. They embraced, they promised a fresh start and a new friendship. Mme de Ventadour wept for joy, and the seal on their reconciliation was the King's promise not to say another word. In the end everything becomes known at courts, and if I have somewhat spread myself on this anecdote, it is because I knew it at the time and found it so fascinating.

After long months spent in testing and taking observations in all parts of Europe, war finally broke out when Imperial troops in Italy fired upon some twenty of our soldiers as they crossed the Adige below Vicenza in order to bring a boat to our side of the river. One Spaniard was killed and most of the remainder taken prisoner, for despite repeated demands the Austrians refused to return them, saying that an agreement must first be signed. The King thereupon despatched several generals to Italy, including Tallard, who had been making a small fortune out of commissions on some minor appointments which the King had charged him to sell. One such was the governorship of the province of Foix, which he disposed of to Ségur, a gentleman of quality from that district and a great gallant, although he had lost a leg in the battle of Marsaglia.[1]

In his youth he had been amazingly handsome, and was still gay, charming, and gallant. In those early days he had been captain of the Black Musketeers, quartered at Nemours when the King was at Fontainebleau. He played the lute enchantingly. Nemours bored him. He made acquaintance with the Abbess of the convent of La Joye,[2] not far distant, and wooed her so effectively through her ears and eyes that he left her with child. In the ninth month of her pregnancy the lady-abbess found herself in trouble and her nuns began to think her seriously indisposed. She had made her arrangements for too far ahead, or else was mistaken in her reckoning. Be that as it may, she left her abbey, ostensibly to take the waters, but, as always happens, the start was delayed until evening and she got no further that night than Fontainebleau, where she stayed to rest at a low tavern, overflowing with customers because the Court was in residence. That rest was a disaster for her. The pains began during the night, and the child was born. The entire inn was awakened by her cries, so that before long she was attended by far more in the way of doctors and midwives than she wished. In a word, she drank her bitter cup to the very dregs, and before morning the news was out.

The Duc de Saint-Aignan[3] heard the tale from his servants as they were dressing him, and he thought it so comical that he saved it to tell the King at his *lever*, for in those days he enjoyed a joke, and he laughed heartily at the idea of the lady-abbess fleeing to hide her shame and then laying her egg in a public tavern in the very centre of the Court and only four leagues from her abbey, although that part was not known until later. On his return the duke found anguished faces and observed some of his servants making signs to others not to speak. He demanded to know the reason, and at last one footman bolder than the rest revealed that the abbess of his merry tale was none other than his own daughter, who had been making desperate appeals for rescue during the interval.

Who then was put out of countenance? No one more completely than the Duc de Saint-Aignan, who had regaled the King and the entire Court and was now made a laughing-stock. He did what best he might to maintain his dignity and removed his abbess, bag and baggage; but the scandal

---

[1] In the north of Italy.
[2] In the diocese of Sens.
[3] The pious Duc de Beauvilliers's father.

had been so public that she was obliged to resign, and lived more than forty years after buried in another convent. That is why I never encountered Ségur at the house of M. de Beauvilliers, even although the latter was particularly civil to him when they met elsewhere; but, indeed, so he was to all.

Mme la Duchesse de Bourgogne was by this time in full possession of the King's heart and that of Mme de Maintenon, whom she called 'aunt'. She caressed them, made them laugh, submitted to them, tried continually to please them, and treated them with a familiarity which they found enchanting. She now developed a fever, brought on by imprudently bathing in the river after eating an immense quantity of fruit. The Court was about to return to Marly. The King, whose fondness ceased with frustration, would neither postpone the excursion nor leave her at Versailles. The fever increased to such a degree that she appeared to be dying. She twice made her last confession, having had two dangerous relapses in the course of a week. The King, Mme de Maintenon, and Mgr le Duc de Bourgogne never left her bedroom. When at last she showed signs of recovery, thanks to emetics, bleedings, and other remedies, the King determined to leave on the appointed day, and it was all that the doctors and Mme de Maintenon could do to induce him to delay another week; at the end of which time they were obliged to go. For a long time afterwards Mme la Duchesse de Bourgogne was so weak that she retired to bed each afternoon, whilst the ladies of her household and others specially favoured played cards to amuse her. After a time more were admitted, and then any who could afford the high stakes, but never any men, excepting the *grandes entrées* who accompanied the King on his morning and afternoon visits on his way to and from hunting.

It was about this time that old Saint-Hérem died at his house in Auvergne. He was over eighty, and for a period had been master of the wolf-hounds. Everyone liked him, so much so, indeed, that in 1688 M. de La Rochefoucauld had remonstrated with the King for not giving him the Order. He was by birth a Montmorin, but the King was none the less convinced that he was of low origin. Courtin, the privy counsellor, was his brother-in-law (they had married two sisters), and the King had them confused in his mind. The King was set right in this matter of Saint-Hérem's birth, but he never did give him the Order, although others received it afterwards.[1] His wife was the oddest creature imaginable. She once succeeded in boiling her own leg in the middle of the River Seine, near Fontainebleau. The water had proved too cold for her liking when she was bathing, and she had had large quantities heated on the bank and poured around and over her, with the result that she was severely scalded

---

[1] François Gaspard de Montmorin, Marquis de Saint-Hérem (1621–1701). One of Saint-Simon's grievances was that Louis XIV never troubled to learn the rank and breeding of his nobles, and if corrected for a mistake persisted in his former opinions.

and remained housebound for a week. In thunderstorms she had a habit of going down on all fours under her day-bed, and obliging her servants to lie piled on top of her, so that the thunder might lose its effect before it reached her. She ruined both herself and her husband with her follies, for they had once been wealthy, and what she spent in having the Gospels read over her would not be believed. The King gave them a pension, for their finances were in a shocking state. Their son[1] had the reversion of Fontainebleau; he was a very gallant gentleman and my friend. Speaking of Fontainebleau, it was in this year that they doubled the size of the Galerie de Diane, making a splendid suite of rooms, and a number of smaller rooms on the floor above.

Whilst all this was happening King Philip of Spain sent an ambassador extraordinary to Turin to sign his marriage-contract and empower the Prince de Carignan, that famous, wise, and able mute, to wed the Princesse de Savoie in his name. This ambassador was a man of infinite charm and tact, at home in any court. Surnamed Homodeï, he was a brother of the cardinal of that name and bore the title Marquis of Almonacid until his marriage with the eldest daughter of the Marquis of Castel-Rodrigo. He was further entrusted with the task of escorting the new queen to Spain and was appointed her master of horse, whilst Count San-Estevan-del-Puerto was placed in control of her household.

Nothing could have bettered those two nominations, but a still more important position remained unfilled, that of the duenna, who would be responsible for the training and upbringing of the young queen.[2] A French lady would not have done, Spaniards were untrustworthy and might have made her unhappy, a compromise was sought, and the only solution proved to be the Princesse des Ursins. She was French by birth, had lived in Spain, had spent the greater part of her life in Rome and Italy, and was a widow without children. She was a Trémoïlle by birth, and her husband, head of the Orsini family and a grandee of Spain, had been recognized as the first layman of Rome, with other high distinctions. Mme des Ursins was not left wealthy by her husband, but she had paid long enough visits to France to be well known at our Court and to have friends there; what is more, she was sincerely attached to both Duchesses de Savoie.[3]

In age and health she was eminently suitable, also in appearance.[4] She was rather taller than the average, a brunette, with eloquent blue eyes that expressed all that she desired, a perfect figure, fine shoulders, and a

[1] He was Charles Louis de Montmorin.

[2] The duenna fulfilled the functions of a governess at the French Court. Always a grandee of Spain, she was usually a widow and of the highest rank. She lived in the palace and never left the side of her charge, presenting persons of quality at audiences, ordering her pupil's dresses, controlling personal expenses, and following her everywhere.

[3] The wife and mother of the Duke of Savoy.

[4] She was sixty. Here follows Saint-Simon's perfect woman.

face that was charming without being strictly beautiful. She had a noble air, with something almost regal in her bearing, and always, in everything that she did, an unaffected grace which I have never seen equalled in mind or body, for she was witty in every way imaginable. She could flatter, caress, persuade, or moderate; she loved to please for pleasing's sake, and her charm was impossible to withstand when she wished to have her way or win one over. Withal, and despite her high-bred air, she was attractive rather than awe-inspiring; wholly delightful in conversation, never at a loss, and always amusing, because of the many countries and peoples that she had seen and known, and because of her gentle way of speaking and agreeable voice. She read widely and reflected on her reading. With a vast acquaintance among the best society and long practice in entertaining she was exquisitely polite to all, but discriminating according to age and rank. Above all, she was most particular to make advances to no one without dignity and propriety.

At the same time she loved intrigue, for she was highly ambitious, on a noble scale far beyond her sex, and, indeed, beyond what is usual even with men, and she had a masculine longing for fame and power. Her mind was infinitely subtle without giving that appearance; her head was always full of schemes, for she knew her world better than most and perfectly understood how to lead and govern it. Coquetry and impulsiveness were her great and over-powering weaknesses; she persisted in them well into old age, which made her apt to wear dresses unsuitably young and to live at all ages far beyond her strength. At heart she was arrogant and proud, seeking to gain her ends without too much care for the means, but acting, so far as was possible, under a cloak of kindliness. Her nature on the whole was kind and obliging, but she would accept nothing by halves and expected her friends to stand for her against the world. On her side, she was ardent and true in friendship; neither time nor distance could cool her affection, but conversely, she could be a bitter and an unrelenting foe, ready to pursue her hate to the very gates of Hell.

To sum up, no one could equal her in grace, intelligence, and charm; and the unaffected eloquence, which was so attractive in all that she said, allowed her to utter whatever she pleased in the exact manner that she intended, with never a word or a gesture that was not as she wished. Most secretive about herself, most safe for her friends, delightfully gay yet never unladylike, always perfectly decorous in public, and even in private where there was less need, with an even temper that allowed her to be mistress of herself at all times. Such was that famous woman who for so long ruled the Spanish court and the entire kingdom. Her reign and her disgrace have caused so much stir in the world that I think it right to enlarge upon her character in order that you may have a picture on which to form your judgment.

A woman with her ambitions was naturally eager for an appointment so much to her taste, but she had the wisdom to perceive that she was approached for lack of others with suitable qualifications, and that once offered the post could not be refused. She therefore hesitated long enough to increase the desire for her, not enough to vex or appear ungracious, but quite sufficient to make them thank her for accepting. Savoy had wished for her quite as ardently as France, but although she had been in close correspondence with the two duchesses she now avoided Turin. The etiquette had always prevented her from seeing them otherwise than *incognito*, and although that had been easily managed on her earlier journeys it was impossible in the present circumstances. She therefore settled everything with them by letter and travelled direct from Rome to Genoa, and from Genoa to Villefranche, where she awaited the arrival of the new little queen.

The marriage was performed at Turin, by proxy and with very little pomp, on 11 September, and on the 13th the queen left Savoy, arriving at Nice a week later in order to embark in the Spanish galley that was to take her to Barcelona. She was brought to Nice in a French ship, but the sea tired her so much that she begged to be allowed to continue her journey on land through Provence and Languedoc. Her intelligence and grace, her courteous and becoming manner in the few short speeches which she was obliged to make, and her interest in everything were astonishing in so young a princess and raised the Princesse des Ursins' highest hopes.

Louville was at the Roussillon frontier to pay his duty and give her the king's presents, and the king went to meet her at Figueras, two days journey from Barcelona. Her new Spanish household had been sent to join her ahead of Louville, and all her Piedmontese staff had already left. She appeared to mind that parting more than Mme la Duchesse de Bourgogne in similar circumstances and she had shed many tears, feeling, no doubt, utterly lost amid so many strange faces. The only one whom she at all knew was the Princesse des Ursins, and even with her there had been little time to form a friendship in the short journey from the seaside. When they finally arrived at Figueras the king was so eager to see her that he rode out on horseback and returned beside the door of her coach. It was then that Mme des Ursins proved a great support to them both in the embarrassment of their first meeting, even though she was quite unknown to the king and still almost a stranger to the little queen.

There followed a second marriage ceremony by the diocesan, without great pomp, and soon afterwards they sat down to a supper served by Mme des Ursins and the Spanish ladies. It had been agreed that the first courses were to be cooked in the French way and the second after the Spanish fashion. That arrangement, however, displeased the serving-ladies and some of the gentlemen also, and they conspired to upset it. Indeed, they behaved scandalously. On one pretext or another, the weight or heat of the dishes, or the clumsiness of the servants offering them, they contrived to overturn all the French dishes before they reached the table, whilst the Spanish ones they served without mishap. The affected concern on the ladies' faces was too obvious to miss, but the king and queen wisely paid no heed, and Mme des Ursins, though greatly vexed, did not say a word.

After a long and most uncomfortable meal the king and queen retired, and it was then that the latter's pent-up feelings exploded. She began to cry for the return of her Piedmontese; child that she was, she felt helpless against such insolence and when bedtime came flatly refused to go, saying that she wished to return home. Everything possible was done to dissuade her, but to everyone's astonishment and dismay her mind was made up and she proved quite determined. The king, all this time, was undressed and waiting for her. Finally the Princesse des Ursins, having exhausted her powers of persuasion and argument, was obliged to go and explain what had happened. He was disappointed, but even more he was sorry for her. Until that time he had been wholly continent,[1] which had made it all the easier for him to like her, and he was thus more than willing to believe that her obstinacy would not endure beyond that night. They did not meet until the following day, and then only after both were dressed. Luckily it is not the custom of Spain to allow witnesses, not even close relatives, at the bedding of a bridal pair, and therefore what might have been a nasty scandal remained secret between the young couple, Mme des Ursins, one or two maids of honour, some valets, and Louville.

Louville and Mme des Ursins then sat down to discuss how to alter the mind of a child who could speak so resolutely. The night was spent in exhortations and in promises regarding the events at supper. In the end the queen consented to remain queen. Next day the Duke of Medina-Sidonia and Count San-Estevan were consulted and it was agreed that the king should refuse to sleep with her that night, so as to mortify her and set her down a little. This was accordingly done. They did not see each other for an entire day, and by evening the little queen was miserable. Her pride and her childish vanity had been wounded; it may be also that she had begun to like the king. The palace-ladies and the few gentlemen who had abetted them were severely reprimanded, and so were any relatives who happened to be present. There were excuses, apologies, alarms, and promises for the future. Quiet and decorum reigned once more. The third day was peaceful, and the third night vastly agreeable for the young couple. On the fourth day, all being set to rights, they returned to Barcelona, where feasting and revelry were their only thought.

The King of England's stay at Bourbon did him little good and he was thereafter obliged to live the life of an invalid. After the middle of August he began to fail and about the 8 September he had a paralytic seizure

[1] It was not until after his marriage that Philip V's extravagantly amorous nature revealed itself.

combined with other ills, which made them despair of his life. King
Louis, Mme de Maintenon, and all the royal family visited him continually; he received the Last Sacraments with a piety that bore witness
to his virtuous life, and his death was expected every moment.

At that juncture the King made a gesture more typical of the chivalry of
Louis XIII and François I than of his usual prudence. He left Marly,
where he had been staying, on Tuesday, 13 September; went to Saint-
Germain, where the King of England's weakness was such that he could
scarcely open his eyes, and announced that he had come in person to
assure him that he might die happy regarding the future of the Prince of
Wales,[1] whom he proposed to recognize forthwith as King of England,
Scotland, and Ireland. The few Englishmen present threw themselves at
his feet, but King James himself gave no sign of life. Immediately afterwards the King went to the Queen of England and gave her a similar
promise, and the Prince of Wales was summoned and informed also. You
may imagine the grateful thanks of both mother and son. Soon after he
returned to Marly the King announced these decisions to the entire
Court, amidst general acclamations.

The gesture was indeed magnanimous, but second thoughts,[2] although
less widely publicized, were not long in coming, for no action of the
King's could have done more to falsify his position or belie the promise
solemnly given at the Peace of Ryswick to accept William of Orange as the
English king—a promise that had so far been faithfully kept. The announcement touched King William at his most tender spot and all England with him, not to mention the Dutch. It demonstrated how little
trust could be put in the treaty and made it easy for them to muster all
the princes of the former alliance to break openly with France, independently of the House of Austria.

As for the Prince of Wales, recognition was of no service to him, for it
re-awakened the former jealousy and suspicion of his enemies in England
and attached them still more firmly to King William and the Protestant
succession. They became even more vigilant and ruthless in their dealings
with the English Catholics, and with those suspected of favouring the
Stuart cause. King Louis had expressed his personal hopes by that recognition, but there was no more likelihood of his bringing the Prince of
Wales to the throne than there had been of his restoring King James by
force of arms, at a time when he had also to protect his grandson on the
Spanish throne. In the short time that remained to him the King of England showed that he was moved by the King's gesture; but he made King
Louis promise that there should be no public ceremonies after his death,

---

[1] James Francis Edward Stuart, the Old Pretender (1688–1766).

[2] Louis XIV was subject to rash impulses and second thoughts. Saint-Simon tells us that in
1685 he allowed two cardinals to have folding-stools for the services of the Order. On second
thoughts he had them back in their pews like everyone else except the royal family. Saint-Simon
says that 'They silently swallowed the affront'. On this occasion there was no going back.

which occurred at three o'clock, in the afternoon of 16 September, in this same year, 1701.

Towards the end of King James's illness M. le Prince de Conti stayed at Saint-Germain and never once left the Queen of England's side, for they were first cousins through their mothers,[1] whose mother had been Cardinal Mazarin's sister. The Nuncio Gualterio stayed there also and, anticipating the Pope's instructions, acknowledged and saluted the Prince of Wales as the King of England. On the evening after the king's death the queen went to the Convent of the Filles de Sainte-Marie de Chaillot. On the following day, at seven in the evening, the King of England's body, with a very small escort and only a few coaches containing the most eminent Englishmen of Saint-Germain, was taken to the house of the English Benedictines in the Rue Saint-Jacques, where it was placed in the chapel, like that of any private individual, until such time, very far distant, as it might possibly be conveyed to England. King James was so well known to the world, first as Duke of York and later as King of England, that I need not say much of him here. He was greatly to be admired for his valour and virtue; even more so for his noble acceptance of adversity; and most of all for his conspicuous piety.

The English ambassador Lord Manchester did not return to Saint-Germain after the recognition, but left France without leave-taking a few days after the King went to Fontainebleau. King William received the news at his house at Het Loo, in Holland. He did no more than announce the bare facts, but he flushed scarlet and pulled his hat down over his eyes, for he could not control his emotions. Then he immediately sent orders to London to dismiss Poussin, who was King Louis's chargé d'affaires in the absence of a French ambassador, and to return him at once to France. That bombshell was so swiftly followed by the signature of a Grand Offensive and Defensive Alliance against both France and Spain, by the Emperor, the Empire, England and Holland, that the King had no other choice than to increase the size of his armies.

At the very end of that Fontainebleau Louville returned from Barcelona. The pretext was to report to the King of all that had happened at the Spanish court and especially of the marriage of their most Catholic Majesties; the true reason was to obtain the King's permission for King Philip to sail to Naples and place himself at the head of both armies in Italy.[2] Louville had several lengthy audiences with the King alone in his study, sometimes with Mme de Maintenon also present; and I, too, managed to see him alone and to satisfy my curiosity. I had offered to drive him to Paris on the day of the King's departure, but I jestingly made it a condition that he should first drive with me tête-à-tête around the canal. The King of Spain had charged him expressly to make that

---

[1] The Duchess of Modena and the Princesse de Conti.
[2] The French and Spanish armies.

8

excursion, but there had been no time for it in the five or six days of his visit. Accordingly, on the morning of Monday, 14 November, he drove alone with me before our departure. On our return we picked up Mme de Saint-Simon and the Archbishop of Arles (later Cardinal Mailly) and made the journey to Paris in one stage without changing horses. I was overjoyed to have had that opportunity for I was able to talk to him comfortably and intimately, and I asked him so many more questions on the way to Paris that he arrived quite hoarse and speechless.

Fagon, the King's first physician, was cut for a stone by Maréchal the famous Paris surgeon whom he preferred to all those at the Court. Asthmatic, hunch-backed, emaciated, in very poor health and subject to epilepsy, Fagon was what they called a bad subject, but he none the less recovered thanks to his self-control and the skill of Maréchal, who removed from him a stone of vast proportions. It was an operation that shortly afterwards brought Maréchal to be the King's surgeon.[1] King Louis showed intense anxiety regarding Fagon's condition, for where his own health was concerned he trusted him absolutely, and he made him a present of an hundred thousand francs. You saw the kind of man that Fagon was on page 33 at the beginning of these Memoirs.

So ended that year, and with it all the King's happiness.

---

[1] After Félix's death in 1703.

PART II

LIFE AT THE COURT

CHAPTER XII

1702

[*The War of the Spanish Succession had opened already with the brilliant campaign in Italy of Prince Eugene, the Austrian commander. Opposing him, the French and Spanish armies were commanded by the Duc de Vendôme and the Maréchal de Villeroy, whom the Allies captured towards the end of the campaign.*

For the campaign of 1702 Louis XIV decided to direct his strongest army against the Dutch Republic with the Marshals Boufflers and Tallard in command, in consultation with the Duc de Bourgogne. The death of William of Orange occurred on 8 March, and after much deliberation the Dutch appointed the Earl of Marlborough, as commander-in-chief of the combined Dutch and English armies. In November, when the campaign ended (much to the relief of the French), Marlborough had captured the fortresses of Kaiserswerth, Venloo, Roermond, Stevenswerth, Maestricht, and Liège, and the navigable rivers of the Rhine and the Meuse were in the control of the Allies. The Duke of Berwick, a general in the French service, although Marlborough's nephew, wrote, 'We in the camp of the Mehaigne heard the news (of the cease-fire) with great content, for in the mood to let everything slide in which we found ourselves, the operations of the enemy would not have met with any resistance from our side.' The armies went into winter-quarters during the first week of November.]

Court Balls and plays in Mme de Maintenon's room – Death and adventures of the Abbè de Watteville – The King of Spain's journey to Italy – Schemes of the Duc d'Harcourt – He delays the general promotion – I quit the service – I am received at the Parlement – Changes in Madame's household – Mme de Clérambault – Medal of Louis XIII – Death of William III – Marriage of Chamillart's brother – The Campaign in Flanders – Period of my closest friendship with M. le Duc d'Orléans – Abortive advances to me of M. and Mme du Maine – Death of the Duc de Coislin: his character and eccentricity – Death of my father-in-law the Maréchal de Lorges – Characters of the Prince and Princesse d'Harcourt – Death of the Duchesse de Gesvres – Capture and release of Marlborough – Orry sent back to Spain – Origins of my great friendship with Chamillart

THE YEAR began with balls at Versailles, many of them masked. Mme du Maine held several in her bedroom, keeping her bed the entire time because she was pregnant, which gave a most peculiar effect. Some were also given at Marly, but those were not masquerades. Mme la Duchesse de Bourgogne enjoyed all of them enormously. The King, in strict privacy but often, and always in Mme de Maintenon's apartment, saw pious plays, such as *Absalon* and *Athalie*,[1] performed by Mme la Duchesse de Bourgogne, M. le Duc d'Orléans,[2] and the young Comte de Noailles, to name some of the principals, wearing most magnificent actors' costumes. Old Baron,[3] an excellent professional actor, instructed and acted with them, also one or two of M. de Noailles's servants. There was room for only forty spectators. Monseigneur and the two princes, Mme la Princesse de Conti, Mme du Maine, and the palace-ladies were admitted, but only two or three of the most favoured courtiers, and not always so many. Madame attended wearing her deepest mourning, for the King, knowing her love of the theatre, had invited her especially, saying that as his close relative her mourning need not debar her from what took place in his presence in such extreme privacy. What was more to the point, Mme de Maintenon wished to show her that the past was forgotten.

The death at this time of the Abbé de Watteville[4] caused little stir, but the enormity of his life deserves mentioning. He was one of the Franche-Comté Wattevilles, became a Carthusian monk early in life, and after taking his vows was ordained a priest. He was a man of spirit, independent, impulsive, most ill-suited for the yoke which he had chosen to bear. At last, continual abstinence having become too much for him, he resolved to escape. He succeeded in obtaining lay clothes, money, pistols, and a horse, but not in altogether disarming suspicion. His prior at any rate felt uneasy, for he opened his cell with the pass key. There he found Watteville in plain clothes on a ladder, just about to jump over the wall. Picture the prior about to call the alarm, and Watteville in the calmest possible manner shooting him dead with his pistol and vanishing.

Two or three days later, having avoided towns and villages as much as possible, Watteville discovered a wretched, lonely little inn in the depths of the country in which he might safely dine. He dismounted and asked what there was to eat. 'A leg of mutton and a capon,' replied the landlord. 'Splendid!' said our ex-monk. 'Put them both on the spit.' The landlord tried to object, saying that both would be too much for any man alone, and that it was all they had in the house. Watteville grew angry. He swore that a man should have as much as he wanted, provided he could pay for it and had sufficient appetite; whereupon the landlord dared say no more and both joints were soon spitted.

Whilst the meat was thus cooking another horseman appeared, and he, too, asked what was for dinner. When he learned that there was nothing beyond what was roasting and that all was reserved for one diner, he seemed vastly surprised. He suggested that he should pay for and eat his share of it, and was quite astounded when the landlord doubted whether

[1] *Absalon* by Duché de Vancy (1668–1704). *Athalie* by Racine.
[2] M. de Chartres had succeeded Monsieur as the Duc d'Orléans.
[3] The famous comedian. His real name was Michel Boy. D. 1729.
[4] Jean de Watteville (1613–1702). Abbot of Baume-les-Moines, near Lons-le-Saunier.

the gentleman who had ordered would consent. The stranger then went upstairs to Watteville, addressing him courteously and asking his permission to pay and eat. Watteville refused. There ensued an argument. Tempers were lost. To be brief, our monk treated the other as he had the prior by shooting him dead. He then went calmly downstairs to the terrified innkeeper; had both the leg and the capon placed before him, ate them to the bones, and fled the country.

Being at a loss where to hide, he chose Turkey where, to cut a long tale short, he had himself circumcised, went over to Islam, and enlisted in the Turkish militia. His conversion was regarded with favour; his valour and spirit won him distinction; he was made a pasha, and became the confidential agent of the Turks in Morea, where they were at war with the Venetians. He captured fortresses, and made himself so useful that he soon felt strong enough to better his situation, for he could not be completely at home in Turkey. By some means or other he managed to gain an interview with the commander of the Venetian forces and struck a bargain with him, promising verbally to deliver over to him several Turkish forts and their secret plans in exchange for the Pope's absolution for all his crimes (murder and apostasy included), given in proper form; full protection from the Carthusians, or from being placed in any other monastery; plenary restitution to secular life, with the same rights as those who had never left it, and permission to practise in the priesthood and to claim any benefices whatsoever. The Venetians found him too valuable an ally to spare efforts on his behalf. The Pope decided that the Church's best interests lay in supporting Christianity against the Turks and readily granted all that the pasha had asked.

When Watteville was assured that all these provisos had been properly executed by the generalissimo of the Venetian army, he took steps to make good his side of the bargain. He then escaped to their army and was brought to Italy in one of their ships. He went to Rome, was graciously received by the Pope and, thus wholly reassured, returned to his home in Franche-Comté and proceeded to divert himself by plaguing the Carthusians. His remarkable exploits brought him into notice in the first conquest of Franche-Comté.[1] He was judged to be a man of action and intrigue. He dealt directly with the Queen-mother, then with the ministers, who found him useful during the re-conquest of that province. He did, indeed, make himself useful, but not for nothing; for he had stipulated in advance for the Archbishopric of Besançon, and did, in fact, receive that nomination after the re-conquest. The Pope, however, could not bring himself to sign the documents, citing in protest the murders, the apostasy, the circumcision. The King agreed with the Pope, and the Abbé de Watteville was forced to be content with the Abbey of Baume

---

[1] Franche-Comté, capital Besançon, was part of the Holy Roman Empire from 1382–1678. It became French by the Peace of Nijmegen.

(the second best in Franche-Comté), another good abbey in Picardy, and many other rewards. Thereafter he lived mostly at his abbey at Baume, sometimes on his estates, occasionally at Besançon, more rarely in Paris and at the Court, where he was always treated with respect.

Everywhere he kept good stables, good hounds, open house, a lavish table, and good company. He used no restraint with the country girls, and in every way lived not only like a great noble, much feared and respected, but like one of the old régime, tyrannizing over his lands and abbeys, often over those of his neighbours, and being especially dictatorial at his home. Intendants shrugged their shoulders, but by express orders from the Court left him alone, not crossing him in any way, not even regarding his taxes, which he paid more or less as he chose, nor in his quarrels, which were sometimes bloody. With such a reputation and in so strong a position he delighted to visit the Carthusians from time to time, in order to crow over them for having quitted their order. He lived thus until near on ninety, continuing in licentiousness yet still respected. His brother's grandson long afterwards married a half-sister of M. de Maurepas.[1]

At this time the burning question was the decision whether or not the King of Spain should join his army in Italy, and since such questions are rarely decided on their merits the intrigues surrounding this one well deserve mentioning. It was Louville who first thought of the journey to Italy. He had consulted M. de Beauvilliers and Torcy, and having made sure of their approval had given the idea to King Philip before returning to France. Louville was intelligent, sensible, and eager, but he was also stubborn, and once imbued with an idea nothing could divert, still less stop him. This eagerness, coupled with an abundance of ideas, made him apt to commit indiscretions, as he now did in reporting to the King on the affairs of Spain and King Philip's desire to go to Italy. When, for instance, he was asked to describe that king's marriage, he told all of what had happened at supper, the scene with the Spanish ladies, the tears and childish petulance of the little queen in declaring that she would not sleep with the king, in fact, all as I have recounted it. Yet Louville was obliged to make some report, and he could hardly have concealed so public a scandal, especially since Mme des Ursins was bound to have mentioned it in her letters to Mme de Maintenon. That lady, moreover, knew much of what he had said in private to the King, and that he was close friends with her pet abominations the Duc de Beauvilliers, Torcy, and the Duc de Chevreuse, to whom he had confided very much that was beyond the knowledge of the ambassador, the Duc d'Harcourt, who had been at death's door since the King of Spain's arrival, far removed from business and the gossip of the Court.

---

[1] Jean Frédéric Phélypeaux, Comte de Maurepas (1701–1781). Son of Jérôme de Pontchartrain and grandson of the Chancellor.

Louville's blunder antagonized Mme la Duchesse de Bourgogne, who allowed herself to be persuaded by Harcourt's friends that he was unkind to her sister the young queen. Many of her ladies joined in the chorus abusing him, either because they disliked his friend the Duc de Beau-villiers, or wished to please Mme de Maintenon. You will recollect how much that lady detested the Dukes of Chevreuse and Beauvilliers, more especially since she had been on the very verge of ruining them and had been forced to see them and their wives return to even higher favour. You will also recall her attachment to M. d'Harcourt, how much she had bene-fited him, and the impure though strong reasons for her affection.[1] Har-court, that most skilled of courtiers, now hoped to extract even more from her; and thus a request which he made for leave of absence from Spain and his swift return to France were prompted more by ambition than by any need to preserve his health. His reception at the Court confirmed his most sanguine hopes, for Mme de Maintenon took him under her wing and procured for him frequent private audiences with the King. At that moment the affairs of Spain were of first importance, which made it easy for Harcourt to pass from thence to giving advice on other matters, and the King heard him for the sake of his staunch ally.

Now out of the four ministers comprising the council of State Mme de Maintenon could be sure only of one, Chamillart, whose avowed protec-tress she was. Beauvilliers and Torcy were in disgrace with her, and Pontchartrain was not much better liked. She had rid herself of the latter, as you have seen, by way of the Chancellery, but the fact that he no longer had occasion to thwart her did not at all mollify her, indeed, rather the contrary, for Pontchartrain would not placate her, and his obvious dislike of Chamillart fomented her ill-will. She therefore resolved to insinuate Harcourt into the Council, and it was for that reason that she desired the King to grow accustomed to him during the private interviews that daily became more like consultations. She had put him on good terms with M. du Maine and the most important valets, whilst he, by well-calculated deference and tact, had won over M. de La Rochefoucauld and those few whose duties brought them closest to the King. The giant stride which he appeared likely to take, such as no man of quality had ever been able to achieve, had smoothed his path in all these attachments. It became an honour to have his acquaintance; at courts no more is needed to find friends everywhere.

Such then was the situation at Versailles of M. d'Harcourt, and at Madrid his prospects were no less rosy, for King Philip had come to like him immensely on the journey from Saint-Jean-de-Luz and in the short time before he fell ill. Indeed, just before his return to France the king had confided to him his desire to go to Italy and had asked him to urge

---

[1] An allusion to the 'better than good' terms on which his father was supposed to have been with her in the old days.

the matter with King Louis, adding a pressing invitation to return sword in hand and attend him in the campaign. Such favour, such brilliant prospects, passed all bounds, not of Harcourt's ambition which was limitless, but of what one man could achieve; for no two aims could have been more conflicting than to enter the council of State in France, and at the same time be the King of Spain's counsellor with the army in Italy, where the commanders were MM. de Villeroy and de Vaudémont,[1] men of the highest reputation and influence. Thus he found himself in a dilemma, all the more complicated because he wished to keep Spain in reserve lest the obstacles to his entering the council should prove too strong to overcome. He could not appear to go against the King of Spain's wishes for fear of losing his esteem, but, on the other hand, he was so near his heart's desire that he had at all costs to avoid being summoned back to Spain. By some means or other he had to delay King Philip's journey and do so in a manner that would arouse no suspicion. This was no easy task, since he had to deal with Louville, who believed the king's excursion to be vitally important and was strongly supported by Beau-villiers, Torcy, and the Chancellor.

In the meanwhile King Louis, powerfully influenced by Mme de Maintenon, had almost convinced himself that Harcourt and not Lou-ville was the man with the best knowledge of Spain and the Spaniards. Thus he was more than somewhat perplexed how to decide in the matter of the journey, and he eventually took a step that was entirely without precedent at the Court. He commanded his ministers, that is to say, the Duc de Beauvilliers, Torcy, and Chamillart, to meet at the Chancellor's house, and ordered the Duc d'Harcourt to be present also, so as to debate with them the pros and cons of the matter and afterwards report to him personally. Never before had such a meeting of ministers taken place without the King. Never before had an outsider been summoned to join their deliberations. Most astonishing of all, this outsider was a peer, whose rank should quite certainly have excluded him. This immense favour caused Harcourt to be regarded with extreme respect, as one who had broken a spell, and must be on the very brink of entering the council. Louville, with Mme de Maintenon against him, was not considered of sufficient importance to join their deliberations; Beauvilliers and Torcy knew and agreed with his views, but there was no question of inviting him.

The arguments in favour of the King of Spain's excursion were to avoid giving the bad impression of a young and healthy prince lingering at home when the whole of Europe was arming to dethrone him or pre-serve his crown; the danger to his reputation, and the need to break the tradition of idleness and cowardice in the last three Spanish kings,

---

[1] The same Vaudémont as the one mentioned earlier. He changed sides after the Peace of Ryswick.

who had never quitted the districts around Madrid in times of war. Against his journey it was advanced that his person might be endangered and, even more vital, that funds did not suffice for far more important projects, let alone an enormously costly royal progress and campaign.

The report when it reached the King taught him nothing that he did not know already. His own inclinations, based on personal experience, were in favour of the journey; Mme de Maintenon and Chamillart had made him hesitate. He may also have had another matter on his mind, a large-scale promotion of generals and the creation of several new marshals. What is certain, at any rate, is that he had written down four names in his own hand—Rosen, Huxelles, Tallard, and Harcourt, intending to limit himself to those four. Being very intimate just then with Harcourt he spoke of this promotion, and even hinted something about marshals. Harcourt, in a perfect frenzy lest he be one of them and sent abroad on duty at the very moment when, so he believed, he was about to join the council, managed to dissuade the King from making any at all; but quite inexplicably for so clever a man, he boasted of this to the Marquis d'Huxelles, himself, out loud, in a corner of the great gallery, perhaps in response to some question regarding the promotions. However that may be, Huxelles, outraged and astounded, turned his back furiously on Harcourt, exclaiming, 'Damn you! If you'd not been a duke you'd never have done it!' Meanwhile Harcourt, looking in the very pink of good health, began to complain of colic, pains in the night, insomnia, and every other invisible disease, so as to give himself an excuse for refusing to serve abroad, and still continued with the support of Mme de Maintenon to have frequent interviews with the King during which he invariably opposed the ministers' advice. Most of these conversations turned on Spain or the conduct of the war, and the King usually repeated Harcourt's arguments to Chamillart.

At this point Chamillart's good friends the Dukes of Beauvilliers and Chevreuse made him reflect on the danger to himself should Harcourt enter the council, for they pointed out that once the latter had achieved his heart's desire he would never rest until he had taken the first place, and that it would be hard, to say the least of it, to oppose one who shared the favour and patronage of Mme de Maintenon. Chamillart then set himself to try by every means to have Harcourt made a marshal and quickly sent abroad. It was whilst the King still hesitated that, so they say, an unforeseen event made him decide not to create any marshals at all. 'They say,' I repeat, because although I believe the story to be true I am not absolutely sure of it. This at any rate is what is supposed to have occurred. Mme la Duchesse de Bourgogne, with her pretty, charming little ways, and her delight in keeping the King and Mme de Maintenon amused at all times, was privileged to take all kinds of liberties. One evening, when she was rummaging amongst the King's papers on the little table in Mme de Maintenon's room she came on the note with the names of the four new marshals. As she read it, her eyes filled with tears, and she cried out to the King not to forget her dear Tessé, who, she said, would die of grief if he were forgotten. She always made a point of seeming fond of Tessé, because he had negotiated the peace with Savoy and her marriage and because she knew that by doing so she pleased the King. This time, however, he was vexed with her for reading the list and, whether because he had already decided to make no marshals or was determined on not advancing Tessé, he said angrily that she need not distress herself for no one would be promoted.[1]

In the meantime the King of Spain was sending ever more urgent letters about his journey. Time was passing. A decision had to be reached. Chamillart, having quietly detached himself from Harcourt, now withdrew his opposition, consent was granted, and Louville was commanded to go and inform King Philip. Harcourt then realized that Spain was lost to him, for although he had disguised his manœuvres as much as possible, he knew that Louville would tell the king what he had done to thwart his wishes. All his efforts were now aimed at entering the council. I do not know whether his vanity again betrayed him, or whether he hoped to overcome his opponents by bluff. Be that as it may, he had the audacity to make jokes regarding the ministers' dread of having him as a colleague, vowing that they stayed awake all night, whilst he slept the clock round. Half of that may have been true, but it can scarcely be believed that his own sleep was serene. His talks with the King went on as before, until one day, by his inordinate conceit, he finished them, and with them all his hopes. He had always taken the standpoint of being directly opposed to the ministers' advice, and had begun to speak contemptuously of their arguments, pointing out flaws and suggesting alternatives. One day when the King was defending his ministers' views and Harcourt hotly attacking them, the latter let slip a remark to the effect that such men were blatantly stupid. That sentence put an end to interviews of every kind and slammed the half-open door of the council-chamber in his face. The King was jealous of his ministers' reputations and in no mind to belittle them. What is more, he had begun to realize that by admitting Harcourt he would be obliged to endure the same eternal quarrels and bickering which he had suffered in the time of Louvois and Colbert.

Harcourt vainly tried to retrieve himself. In vain did Mme de Maintenon endeavour to reconcile him with the King and find pretexts for audiences. All was useless. The King had made up his mind; there were no more talks with Harcourt, although in other ways he was well enough treated, even shown favour. Harcourt did indeed suffer greatly. He had warded off the marshal's bâton with all imaginable care, and in so doing

---

[1] It is possible that Saint-Simon never knew that she regularly gave state secrets away to her father, even when France and Savoy were at war again in the following year.

had both lost the King of Spain's friendship and failed to prevent his journey. He had also failed to achieve his great ambition, in which for so long he had seemed near to success. Mme de Maintenon, who had her own reasons for feeling disappointed, comforted him as best she could with hopes of a future when he might try again.[1]

When the promotion of generals was finally put into execution it proved to be very sweeping, comprising seventeen lieutenants-general, fifty brigadiers, forty-one colonels of infantry, and thirty-eight of cavalry. But before recounting the action which that promotion led me to take, I must first describe how during that winter I was received into the Parlement.

In dealing with his bastards the King always gave immediate effect to the honours which he granted them, without waiting for the usual warrants, letters patent, notifications, or decrees to be published. Yet, for many years past, he had made it a rule that peers might not be received into the Parlement without his consent. That he never refused, but he had lately begun to withhold permission if the peer were not yet twenty-five years old, thus gradually instituting a custom which might later become the general rule. I was aware of this and accordingly deferred my own reception until a year after my twenty-fifth birthday, on the plea of forgetfulness.

My first action was to call on President Harlay, who was overwhelmingly polite. I was then obliged to call on the princes of the blood and finally on the bastards.[2] M. du Maine, when I visited him, asked me to repeat the date, then with a delight that appeared restrained only by modesty and good manners, he exclaimed, 'I shall be most careful not to forget. Such an honour! So gratifying that you desire my presence! You may be sure of me,' and so saying he escorted me as far as the gardens, for this was at a Marly, and I was of the house-party. The Comte de Toulouse and M. de Vendôme replied less effusively but no less pleasantly, and were as polite as M. du Maine. Cardinal de Noailles had never once attended at the Parlement since he received the Roman crimson because his hat did not entitle him to a seat higher than that of his rank as count and peer. I elected to visit him at one of his public audiences. 'You are aware,' said he, 'that I no longer have a seat?' 'On the contrary,' I replied, 'I know that you have a most splendid place, and I beg you to take it at my reception.' He then smiled, and I smiled also, for we perfectly understood one another.[3] Later he personally escorted me to the top of his staircase,

---

[1] The Duc d'Harcourt did try again in 1705, 1708, and 1709, and failed on each occasion, probably because Torcy, and the Dukes of Beauvilliers and Chevreuse, whom he had deeply offended, stood firm against him.

[2] The bastards had to have courtesy calls paid on them because although not peers they sat, like princes of the blood, above dukes in the Parlement.

[3] Saint-Simon meant that they both understood that a French archbishop-peer was worth any number of Roman cardinals.

both doors open wide,[1] and we walked together side by side, I on his right hand. M. de Luxembourg was the only one not to hear from me on that occasion. I had never forgiven him those abominable warrants,[2] but he was not my friend and I did him no wrong.

Dongeois[3] was at that time acting as registrar of the Parlement. He was a man whose ability and constant attendance had made him very knowledgeable in the customs of that body. I knew him well, and therefore went to consult him about the correct procedure. Yet despite the honesty and kindness of his intentions the good man laid three traps for me, but luckily I was on the watch and fell into none of them. He said that out of respect for the Parlement I should make my first appearance there in a plain black coat unadorned with gold lace; that out of respect for the princes of the blood, whose short mantles were worn longer than their coats, I should not allow mine to come below the level of my jacket, and that out of respect for the premier président I should call to thank him on the morning after my reception, still wearing parliamentary dress. He did not bluntly make these suggestions but tactfully hinted at them. I made no issue of it, but I did the exact opposite, and having been alerted I took care to warn all those who were received after me, and they defended themselves likewise. It is by such ruses that many humiliations have come upon the dukes, one after another, in a constant stream that almost passes belief.[4]

The reforming of the army after the Peace of Ryswick was on a very large scale but very haphazard. The quality of the various regiments, especially of the cavalry, and the merits of their commanding officers were ignored by Barbezieux, who was young and impulsive, and to whom the King gave a free hand. I myself had no acquaintance with him; my regiment was re-formed, and as it was very good parts of it were allocated to the Royals and the rest incorporated in the Duras regiment. My company was added to that of Barbezieux's brother-in-law the Comte d'Uzès, of whom he took particular care. It was small consolation to hear that others were being treated in the same way, and I was deeply disappointed. The colonels of regiments re-formed like mine were placed at the bottom

---

[1] A privilege of dukes and peers.

[2] This M. de Luxembourg was the son of the Maréchal. The lawsuit for seniority had been reopened after the Maréchal's death in 1696, and to Saint-Simon's rage the Luxembourgs won it. Their rank was confirmed by warrant to date from 1662, and the claim to date the peerage from the first elevation, 1581, was not disallowed, merely adjourned. When the verdict was given, the Dukes of La Rochefoucauld and Estrées had to seize Saint-Simon round the waist to prevent him from hurling himself from the gallery, shrieking, 'Impostor! Scoundrel!'

[3] Nicolas Dongeois, a nephew of Boileau.

[4] Saint-Simon's snobbishness was in part at least concern for the welfare of France. He saw a vile plot to reduce the nobility, whose interests, he believed, were also those of the peasants and of the entire country, in favour of bastards, tax farmers and professionals, with purely mercenary ambitions. Of course King Louis distrusted dukes because of the *Fronde*, and Saint-Simon, whose dukedom was not won on the battlefield, was particularly jealous for his rank—facts that may have coloured their different points of view.

of the list in their new regiments, and I was ordered to serve under Saint-Mauris, a gentleman of Franche-Comté and a complete stranger to me, although his brother was a lieutenant-general and well regarded. Shortly after this, the petty discipline that runs alongside active service demanded two months' service from officers at the tail of new regiments. That seemed monstrous to me. I went, of course, but I had been indisposed for some time past, and having been recommended the waters of Plombières I asked for leave of absence and for the next three years spent there the two months when I should have been exiled to a strange regiment, with no troops to command and no work to do. The King did not seem to mind. I often went to Marly; he spoke to me sometimes, a very good sign that was much remarked upon; in a word he treated me kindly, indeed better than most of my age and rank.

From time to time officers junior to myself were promoted; but they were veterans who had earned regiments by long and distinguished service, and I could understand the reason. Talk of a general promotion did not excite me, for birth and rank counted for nothing. I was too junior to be made a brigadier; my entire ambition was to command a regiment and fight at its head in the coming war, thus avoiding the humiliation of having to serve as a supernumerary aide-de-camp to Saint-Mauris. The King had distinguished me after the Neerwinden campaign by giving me a regiment; and I had brought it up to strength, and, dare I say so, commanded it with care and honour in four successive campaigns until the war ended.

The promotion was announced; everyone was astonished at the numbers, for there had never been so large a list. I eagerly scanned the names of new cavalry brigadiers, hoping to find my own, and was mortified to see five junior to me mentioned. My pride was most deeply hurt but I kept silent for fear of saying something rash in my vexation. The Maréchal de Lorges was most indignant and his brother-in-law[1] not less so, and they both insisted that I ought to quit the service. I myself felt so angry that I was much inclined to do so; but my youth, the war beginning, the thought of renouncing my ambitions in my chosen career, the boredom of being idle, the tedious summers when conversation would all turn on war and partings, the advancement that could be earned by distinguished conduct, were all powerful deterrents, and I spent two months in mental agony, resigning every morning and every night reversing my decision.

At last, driven to extremes and harried by the two marshals, I resolved to take advice from men on whom I could rely, and to choose them from different walks of life. I finally decided upon the Maréchal de Choiseul, M. de Beauvilliers, the Chancellor, and M. de La Rochefoucauld. They knew how I was placed and were indignant on my behalf and, moreover, the three last were courtiers. This was most desirable,

---

[1] The Maréchal de Duras.

for what I wished to discover was what the best people would think, particularly the solid men about the King. Above all I sought for advice that would not leave me a prey to indecision, rash impulses, or afterthoughts. Their verdict, given unanimously and most firmly, was that I should leave the service. They all agreed that it would be both a shame and most unsuitable for a man of my rank who had served with honour at the head of a good regiment to return to fight without regiment, troops, or even a company to command. They added that no duke and peer, especially not one with an establishment, wife and children, should consent to be left a mere soldier of fortune, whilst others of lesser degree received employment and commands in a large-scale promotion.

I did not take them as my judges in order to ponder their advice. My course was clear; but though I knew they were right I still hesitated, and three months passed in a torment of doubt before I could bring myself to act. When I finally did so, I followed the advice of those same arbiters. I was very careful to display no hurt feelings, for I wished to leave public and especially military opinion to judge of my having been passed over. The King's anger was inevitable; my friends warned me of it, and I was fully prepared. Need I say how much I dreaded it? He invariably took offence when officers left the service, calling it desertion, especially where the nobility were concerned. What really nettled him, however, was that a man should leave him with a grudge, and anyone who did so felt his displeasure long afterwards, if not for ever. Yet my friends drew no comparison between the disadvantage of resigning, which, at my age, would soon cease to affect me, and the disgrace of continuing to serve under such humiliating conditions. At the same time they insisted on my taking all possible precautions.

I accordingly wrote a short letter to the King, in which without complaining, or any sign of discontent, or mention of regiments or promotion, I stated my distress at being obliged to leave his service for reasons of health. I added that my consolation would be to attend on him assiduously, with the honour of seeing and paying my court to him all the time. My advisers approved my letter and on Tuesday in Holy Week I presented it myself, at the door of his study, as he returned from mass. I went thence to Chamillart, with whom I had little acquaintance at that time. He was leaving to go to the council, but I told him my story by word of mouth, showing no sign of discontent, and immediately set out for Paris. I had already put many of my friends, both men and women, on the alert, to report anything, no matter how trivial, that the King might say on the subject of my letter. I stayed away for a week; returning on Easter Tuesday, I learned that the Chancellor had found the King in the act of reading it, and that he had exclaimed angrily, 'Here is another deserter!' and had thereupon read my letter aloud word for word. On that same evening I attended on him for the first time since he had heard from me.

After that, for three consecutive years I received no sign of favour from him, and he never missed the smallest opportunity (for want of greater ones) to make me feel how deeply I had offended. He never spoke to or looked at me except by accident. He never mentioned my letter or the circumstances of my leaving his service. I was no longer invited to Marly, and after the first few visits I no longer gave him the satisfaction of refusing me.[1] I must end this sorry tale. Fourteen or fifteen months later he paid a visit to Trianon and supped with the Princesses. The custom on those occasions was for him to make a list, a very short one, of the ladies whom he wished invited. This particular visit was from a Wednesday to a Saturday, and Mme de Saint-Simon and I were doing what we usually did when he went to Marly, that is to say, dining at L'Etang with the Chamillarts on our way to sleep in Paris. We were just sitting down to table when Mme de Saint-Simon received a message to say that she was on the King's supper-list for that evening. We were astounded and returned at once to Versailles. She then discovered that she was to be the only lady of her age at the King's table; the rest were Mme de Chevreuse, Mme de Beauvilliers, the Comtesse de Gramont,[2] three or four chaperones, the palace ladies, and no others. She was invited again on the Friday, and thereafter the King always nominated her on his rare excursions to Trianon. I soon learned the reason for this favour and it struck me as absurd. He never invited her to Marly, because husbands had the right to go there with their wives. His intention was to show me that his disfavour was towards me alone and did not extend to my wife.

We none the less persevered in waiting on him as usual, but we never sought for invitations to Marly. We lived a pleasant enough life among our friends, and Mme de Saint-Simon continued to enjoy all the pleasures to which the King and Mme la Duchesse de Bourgogne summoned her, even although she could not share them with me. I have dealt with this matter at length because it throws light upon the King's nature.

Soon after this, Madame with the King's approval made some changes in her household. It was all settled one evening when he called on her after mass. She pensioned and sent away her maids of honour and their superintendent, and took instead, but with no official standing, the Maréchale de Clérambault and the Comtesse de Beuvron.[3] They had been her dear friends for a long time, but Monsieur had disliked them

[1] No one was nominated for Marly, the procedure was to step forward and say to the King, 'Marly, Sire?', and risk a refusal.
[2] An Englishwoman, Elizabeth Hamilton (1641–1708) who married Louis XIV's favourite Philibert Comte de Gramont, whose tempestuous love-affairs caused him to be exiled in 1662. He joined the gay court of Charles II in England, and was there almost forced into marriage with her. At 80 he wrote, or inspired his brother-in-law Count Anthony Hamilton to write, the famous Memoirs of his amorous intrigues, which were first published in 1713.
[3] Mme de Clérambault was one of Saint-Simon's main sources of information regarding the royal family's doings; the Bishop of Troyes was her uncle. Mme de Beuvron had been a great friend of Mme de Sévigné.

and she had had to wait for them until after his death. Madame gave them each a salary, and the King gave them lodgings at Versailles. They attended her wherever she went and were included in the Marly excursions without having to ask for an invitation.

Mme de Clérambault was the daughter of Secretary of State Chavigny,[1] and a relation of the Pontchartrains, whom she often visited at their country house. I used to meet her there most frequently, as well as in their apartment at Versailles. She was a remarkable old lady who, when she was off duty and in the mood, could be excellent and most amusing company, full of character and spontaneously witty, seemingly without effort of any kind. At other times she would go for days on end without uttering a syllable. She had been at death's door with consumption in her girlhood, and had recovered by stoutly refusing to speak a single word for an entire year. Being by nature cold, quiet, and even-tempered, the habit had grown on her, yet you cannot imagine anyone with more spirit, or a neater turn of phrase when she so pleased. Although she came so late to court-life, she found it completely absorbing, and she developed such skill in listening to and comprehending all that happened that her tales, when she deigned to tell them, were fascinating in the highest degree. Yet she took care to expand only with a few, and then only in strictest privacy.

She adored gambling, although in other ways she was excessively stingy; she loved private and confidential gossip, and cared for nothing else in the world. I well remember how at Pontchartrain on the loveliest afternoon imaginable she stopped short on the bridge that leads into the garden on her way back from mass. Then, turning slowly round to face the company, 'There!' said she, 'that is enough walk for today. Tut-Tut! let us hear no more about it but go at once to the tables.' After that tiny outing she took up the cards, pausing only for her two meals and thinking monstrously ill of those who left her still at it at two o'clock on the following morning. She ate next to nothing and drank very little, sometimes only a glass of water. If she had had her way, her meals would have been brought to her on a tray at the tables. She was learned, especially in history and the sciences, but never allowed that to be seen. She always wore a mask[2] in her coach and chair and whilst walking in the gallery. It was an old-fashioned custom of which she could not break herself, not even when driving with Madame in her coach. She used to say that fresh air brought her skin out in pimples and, as a matter of fact, she kept her good complexion all her life, which lasted more than eighty-four years.

All in all, she was greatly feared and respected. She claimed to be able to see into the future by computation and divining in the dust, which is

---

[1] Léon Bouthillier, Comte de Chavigny (1617–1652). Supposed to have been Richelieu's illegitimate son. He was the arch-enemy of Saint-Simon's father.

[2] These masks were made of black velvet and called a *touret*. You held the handle of it in your mouth, which may have encouraged the Maréchale's silence.

what endeared her to Madame who relished such arts immensely;[1] none the less, she took care not to parade her gifts. To put the final touch on the portrait of an eccentric who ranked almost as a personage at the Court, she had a sister, a nun of Saint-Antoine, in Paris, who possessed, so they said, even greater wit and learning. That nun was the only person for whom the maréchale felt any affection, she often went to visit her from Versailles and although inordinately mean overwhelmed her with offerings. When she fell ill, the maréchale called continually to inquire, but once assured that the poor woman would not recover, 'Alack!' she said, 'My poor sister! Tell me no more.' The sister died, and never afterwards did she mention her to anyone. As for her two sons, she cared nothing for them, but she could scarcely have done otherwise although they had great influence over her. When they died she showed not the smallest sign of grief, not even immediately afterwards.

It was about this time that the eulogists first perceived that the peak of prosperity had passed for the King and that in future they would have nothing to praise beyond his endurance. The vast numbers of medals that had been struck for every possible occasion, however trivial, were therefore to be collected, engraved, and made to form a numismatic history of his reign. The Abbés Tallement, Tourreil, and Dacier, three learned members of the French Academy, were commissioned to accompany these engravings in a huge tome, magnificently produced by the printing office of the Louvre.[2] There was also to be an introduction, and since the history was to begin with the death of Louis XIII his medal was necessarily included as a frontispiece, accompanied by a description of the monarch himself. Some acquaintance of the three gentlemen had recollected my very proper gratitude to King Louis[3] and believed that it might inspire me beyond my usual capabilities to write that part of the introduction and the description beneath his medal. They requested me to do so. My heart betrayed my head, and without stopping to consider my lack of skill I consented, on the understanding that they would keep my name secret and so spare me the ridicule of Society.

I accordingly set to work, keeping a strict watch on my pen lest the son be overshadowed by the father in a work designed for the former's glorification. When all was finished (it took me no more than a morning for I had no room to expand), I submitted my piece to the editors. I then suffered the usual fate of authors. My essay was praised and seemed in no

---

[1] She had predicted that she would die before Madame. On the day of Louis XV's coronation (1722) Madame felt poorly and thought it might be dangerous to attend. She consulted the maréchale. 'Go, Madame,' said the latter. 'You are perfectly safe, I feel in good health.' But she died quite suddenly and Madame almost immediately followed her.

[2] L'Imprimerie du Louvre: the royal printing office set up by Cardinal Richelieu in one of the ground-floor galleries of the Louvre.

[3] Saint-Simon inherited his father's passionate devotion to the memory of Louis XIII, who had made him a duke and peer.

way excessive. I congratulated myself, greatly pleased to have devoted three hours, no more was needed, to my just gratitude. When the proofs were read, however, the editors took fright, for some truths unvarnished shine so bright that they dim all that art can contrive by magnification or belittlement. The life of Louis XIII furnished many such. I had been content to state the bare facts, but they had none the less stolen glory from the descriptions that followed, or so it seemed to those who embellished them. They therefore set themselves to prune and falsify, minimizing wherever possible, so as to prevent their hero from being dwarfed by unwelcome comparisons. At last they perceived that it was not I whom they needed to correct but the facts themselves, whose lustre only complete suppression could diminish. Their task was indeed a vain one, for although some truths could be eliminated not all could be, and all in their eyes were calculated to belittle their hero. That problem, exaggerated by an over-riding desire to flatter, made them decide to display the medal of Louis XIII plain, as a frontispiece, with no mention or description of that prince, save for two lines stating that his death had allowed his son to ascend the throne.

Meditation on such flagrant injustice might lead one altogether too far. I did not suffer by it; for I remained, as promised, protected by obscurity. Meanwhile the labours of Chamillart were becoming increasingly burdensome. There were vast sums to be raised for the needs of the armies. Vendôme from Italy, encouraged by M. du Maine under the direction of Mme de Maintenon, sent courier after courier extolling his own vigilance and projects, and purposely exaggerating small skirmishes brought about by the close proximity of the enemy's lines; the Comte d'Estrées,[1] spending a week in Paris after his return from Naples to Toulon, received the King's orders to embark the King of Spain at Barcelona and escort him to Naples, returning forthwith to Toulon, where the Comte de Toulouse would be waiting to take ship for his first appointment as admiral. This announcement necessarily caused great disappointment to M. le Duc d'Orléans and the two princes of the blood.[2] The Maréchal de Boufflers was at the same time given command of the Flanders army under Mgr le Duc de Bourgogne.

King William of England was wholly occupied in calling all Europe to arms against France and Spain. He was in Holland, making the final adjustments to that vast enterprise which he had set in motion as soon as he learned the terms of the King of Spain's will. He was staying at his hunting-box at Het Loo,[3] at the very height of this gigantic task, when he

[1] Vice-Admiral, later the Maréchal-duc d'Estrées (1660–1737).
[2] The Prince de Conti and M. le Duc, neither of whom would Louis XIV consider for an independent command. The King preferred to use men whom he could make and unmake, bastards, or men whose rank he had personally created, not those whose royal blood or inherited rank made them in any way independent. Moreover he was wildly jealous of Conti's popularity.
[3] Near Arnhem.

received the news of the death of his father-in-law King James and of our King's recognition of the Prince of Wales as rightful King of England. Such an action gave him the excuse to break out in all directions and to move without concealment. He assumed the royal purple for mourning, draped his coaches, and hastened by every means, whilst still in Holland, to cement that formidable league which was now named the Grand Alliance. He then returned to England to arouse the nation and extract the necessary monies from the Parliament.

Grown old before his time by excessive labours in the affairs of State that were his life-long, all-absorbing passion, and to which he brought such consummate skill, such masterly genius, King William had come to possess supreme authority in Holland, the English throne, the trust, nay the absolute dictatorship of all Europe, save only France. He now met with a breakdown in his health and strength. His mental powers were not affected, nor did he relax at all the innumerable tasks of his cabinet; but he began to experience a difficulty in breathing greatly increased by the asthma which he had suffered for many years past. He understood what was happening; his powerful mind would not allow him to be duped, and he accordingly caused the greatest doctors of Europe to be consulted on his behalf under assumed names. Fagon was one of those so consulted, ostensibly for a priest, and he, acting in good faith, dismissed the case advising the patient to prepare for imminent death. The disease continued its progress and William again asked Fagon's advice, this time without concealment. When the latter recognized in him the case of the priest he did not change his opinion, but gave it rather more consideration, prescribing with much sound reasoning such remedies as he judged most likely to relieve, although they could not effect a cure.

At last the time came when King William must have realized that the greatest like the least must die, and have known the vanity of what the world calls fame. He still rode on horseback and felt better for the exercise, but, being very thin and weak and having no longer strength to grip, he had a fall and the shock hastened his end.[1] When dying, religion occupied his mind as little as throughout his life. He made the necessary arrangements, talked to his ministers and friends with surprising calm, and a presence of mind that deserted him only in the final moments notwithstanding that during his latter days he had been afflicted with vomiting and diarrhoea. Being solely concerned with the affairs of this world, he saw his end approach without misgiving. He had the satisfaction of leaving his Grand Alliance so firmly based that he had no fear of its disuniting after his death, and with good hope that victory would ensue from

---

[1] It had happened on 8 March. William was riding his favourite 'Sorrel' in the park at Hampton Court, when the horse stumbled over a mole hill and the King was thrown, breaking a collar bone. The mole was 'the little gentleman in black velvet' who became so famous in Jacobite toasts.

the terrible blows which he had planned to strike against France. Such thoughts may have brought him consolation in dying, for him they took the place of spiritual comfort, but it was a trifling and empty consolation that left him to face the Eternal Verities alone. In the last two days of his life he was kept alive with strong drink and spirits. His final nourishment was a cup of chocolate. He died on the morning of Sunday, 19 March, at ten o'clock in the morning. His sister-in-law Princess Anne, the wife of Prince George of Denmark,[1] was at once proclaimed queen. A few days later she appointed her husband Lord High Admiral and Generalissimo, recalled her maternal uncle the Earl of Rochester, and Sunderland, notorious for his ability and treachery,[2] and admitted them both to her council. She also sent Lord Marlborough, later to become so famous, to Holland to execute her predecessor's plans.

Our King did not learn of this death until the following Saturday when La Vrillière[3] received a courier from Calais, a boat having managed to slip through the blockade on our ports. The King told no one except Monseigneur and Mme de Maintenon, to whom he sent a message at Saint-Cyr.[4] On the following day, when confirmation arrived from all quarters, he no longer kept it secret, although he made little comment and appeared totally indifferent. Remembering the disgraceful rejoicings in Paris during the last war, when King William was believed to have been killed at the Battle of the Boyne,[5] he ordered that such scenes should not be repeated. He also proclaimed publicly that he would not wear mourning, and he forbade the Duc de Bouillon, the Maréchaux de Duras and de Lorges, and all other relatives of King William to do so. Such an order was unprecedented. The bulk of the English nation mourned for King William, and so did most of the inhabitants of the United Provinces; but a few good republicans sighed with relief at having once more regained their freedom. The Grand Alliance was very deeply shaken by this loss, but it was so well and strongly founded that William's spirit continued to inspire it. Heinsius,[6] his confidential agent, whom he had raised up to be Grand Pensionary, kept his memory green, and urged on the leaders of the Dutch Republic, their generals and allies, to such effect that it appeared almost as if King William had not died.

[1] Prince George of Denmark had been naturalized English in 1689.

[2] He was president of James II's privy council and deserted him for William.

[3] Louis II Phélypeaux, Marquis de La Vrillière, a commoner. He had succeeded to his father's secretaryship of State through the influence of Mme de Maintenon, who married him to Mlle de Mailly for whom it was a dreadful mésalliance.

[4] She spent most of her day there, returning to Versailles only in the afternoon in time for the King's visit.

[5] A French expeditionary force had been sent to help James II in Ireland in 1690, and was there defeated by William in a famous victory.

[6] Antonius Heinsius (1641–1720). One of Louis XIV's most bitter enemies in the War of the Spanish Succession. He had been a personal friend of William.

I would not recount anything so trivial as the marriage of Chamillart's brother,[1] did it not mark the beginning of something supremely ludicrous which Society, often proud for the wrong reasons, always cringing before favour and influence, calmly accepted ever afterwards. Chamillart had two brothers who, one might almost say, excelled one another in futility. The elder was that Bishop of Dol whom he later had appointed to Senlis, and who finally had to be given Condom[2] and forbidden ever to emerge from that diocese, although a better man never breathed. The other was as evil as his stupidity would allow; moreover, favour and advancement had completely turned his head, so that when he somehow succeeded in becoming a sea-captain, he forthwith styled himself the Chevalier de Chamillart. His eldest brother, who even then was on bad terms with Pontchartrain, took him out of the navy, promoted him to colonel in one step, and married him to the only daughter of Guyet, the *maître des requêtes*—vastly wealthy and handsome. Her father he made an intendant of finance, although he had no more competence for that post than his daughter's bridegroom had for commanding a regiment. It has long been the practice for youngest sons to take the title of Chevalier; but married men cannot be so styled, and this one now proceeded to call himself Comte de Chamillart, for nowadays anyone and everyone may assume the *de*. Chamillart's brother was, however, the very first instance of a man marquisifying or countifying a bourgeois surname,[3] and at the same time Chamillart's son-in-law took to calling himself Marquis de Dreux. There he made an error, for had he taken the title of Count he might have attached himself to the royal family of the Comtes de Dreux; but no doubt he later had cause to be thankful for his modesty in that respect. People mocked him in secret, but publicly no one dared to omit these titles or the *de*, or even query them, even when they were still no more than captains. Very many citizens have since followed their example, which is now accepted for the brothers of presidents in provincial parlements. It has apparently become an appanage, like the title of Duc d'Orléans for the King's brother. The Paris judges, who are not to be compared with them, did not imitate them for some considerable time; after which a few of them fell for that juicy morsel.

Let us now return to Spain. When Louville arrived in Barcelona with the King's consent to King Philip's journey, he found the Catalonian parliament no longer in session and the king overjoyed that nothing now prevented his departure. The Comte d'Estrées welcomed him on board his flagship with all imaginable honours and the little fleet flew the Spanish

---

[1] Jérôme Comte de Chamillart.
[2] In Guyenne. He was promoted to that see with the object of keeping him as far from Versailles as possible.
[3] Originally it was the *land* not the owner that bore the title. Thus a man was duke or marquis or count of some especial part of the country.

ensign during the voyage. As soon as he had safely embarked the queen also left Barcelona attended by the Princesse des Ursins. They spent the night at the famous convent of Our Lady of Montserrat, on the way to Saragossa, where she presided over the provincial parliament of Aragon.

It was Easter Sunday when the King of Spain landed at Pozzuoli, near Naples. After remaining there a short time to receive the papal legate, he hurriedly continued on his way to Milan and placed himself at the head of the armies. Having now recorded King Philip's journey, let me add that after obtaining nearly all the money that she asked from the parliament of Aragon, the queen went from Saragossa to Madrid, where for form's sake she took the chair at sessions of the Junta, although Cardinal Portocarrero was acting as regent. There was an affectionate meeting of the cardinal and his old friend Mme des Ursins, who, on the pretext of training the queen in State affairs, had already begun to meddle in them herself. Nothing, at this time, could have exceeded the little queen's good sense, graciousness, and amiability throughout the entire journey and on her arrival at Madrid. This was partly her nature, but it also reflected great credit on the Princesse des Ursins for the pains she had taken in instructing her. She had given no less thought to winning the queen's heart, and there she had succeeded beyond her fondest hopes. I have now said enough of these great personages for them to have become familiar; we shall now return to France with the Comte d'Estrées. M. le Comte de Toulouse joined him at Toulon with a very large personal staff. At the same time, the heir to the throne left for Flanders with only Moreau, his head valet, to attend, provide for him, and introduce his visitors. This appeared so monstrously improper to M. de La Rochefoucauld that being on terms of friendship with the King he could not resist mentioning it at his *lever*, but the King replied nothing. He was by far less concerned with the dignity of his grandson than with the fact of his having to pass through Cambrai,[1] which it would have been too pointed to avoid. He issued strict orders that Mgr le Duc de Bourgogne was not to sleep there nor even stay for a meal, and to prevent his having any private conversation with the archbishop he forbade him to leave his coach. Saumery[2] was instructed to keep watch to see that these commands were obeyed, and he did so argus-eyed, with an air of authority that shocked everyone present.

---

[1] Where the disgraced Fénelon was archbishop.

[2] Saint-Simon's view of the Marquis de Saumery conflicts with that of the Duc de Bourgogne, who wrote to Fénelon, 'I cannot wait to express my joy at the thought of seeing you again with the King's permission. He has made it a condition, however, that I do not speak to you in private; but I shall obey that order and still converse with you as I please because I shall have Saumery with me. He will make a third in our first conversation after a five years' separation. His name will be enough for you; you know even better than I how secret he is, and more than that, he is your very good friend.'

When Mgr le Duc le Bourgogne arrived Fénelon was waiting for him at the posting-house. He walked up to the door of the coach, and Saumery who had previously alighted to give him the King's orders stood at his elbow the entire time. The young prince touched the hearts of the crowd by the transports of joy that, despite his reserved nature, overcame him when he saw his old tutor. He embraced him many times, long enough to whisper in his ear in defiance of Saumery's unwelcome presence. They stayed only long enough to change horses, but did not hurry in so doing. They then embraced once more and parted, having spoken of nothing except their healths, the state of the roads, and the journey. The place had been too public and the spectators too much interested for their conversation not to have been fully recorded; but since the King was obeyed to the very letter he could not well object to what might have taken place during their embraces, nor to the loving, longing glances exchanged between the prince and the archbishop. The Court, however, took notice, and so did the army; veneration for Fénelon, which despite his disgrace had increased in his diocese and spread even to Flanders, now permeated the army and those who reflected on a life to come began to prefer the road through Cambrai to any other means of reaching the front. Mgr le Duc de Bourgogne stayed for seven or eight days at Brussels, where every Spanish subject of any eminence came hastily to pay his court. He then placed himself at the head of the army.

The campaign in Flanders was unfortunate. The Elector of Brandenburg and the Landgrave of Hesse[1] besieged and captured Kaiserswerth in the early stages. Blainville did marvels in the defence; there were many attacks. England and Holland formally declared war upon France and Spain. Their united armies were commanded by the Earl of Athlone for the States-General and Lord Marlborough for the English. The latter was Mylord Churchill, King James's favourite and raised by him from the status of a very poor gentleman and brother of his mistress (who was Berwick's mother)[2]. King James made him an earl and gave him a company of his life guards. He also gave him command of the army at the time of the Prince of Orange's invasion, and Marlborough would have surrendered it to that prince had not Lord Feversham, brother of the Maréchaux de Duras and de Lorges, prevented him. Marlborough's wife had been the life-long friend of Princess Anne and was her lady-in-waiting when she ascended the throne. Queen Anne confirmed her in that appointment and at the same time sent her husband to Holland as ambassador and commander of the army. Soon afterwards she made him a duke and a knight of the Garter. There will be all too many occasions to

---

[1] Commander of the Imperial army.
[2] Arabella Churchill; her son the Duke of Berwick, fighting on the French side, was thus Marlborough's nephew, and the natural son of James II.

speak of him in the future, for it was by our disasters that he made his glorious reputation.

The Maréchal de Boufflers was accused of having missed an excellent opportunity of defeating him at the beginning of that campaign. The chance did not come again. We subsisted in enemy country. We hoped to bring them to battle near Nijmegen, where, so they say, we might have had the advantage over them, for there seemed nothing, or very little to prevent us. The cannonade lasted throughout the day. We captured a few wagons and some stores, and killed a few of their officers, but little by little they withdrew to the shelter of Nijmegen and slipped away from us on the other side. Kaiserswerth, Venloo, Roermond, the citadel of Liège, and some smaller fortresses were their spoils of that first campaign and the tokens of their future victories.

Mgr le Duc de Bourgogne acquitted himself admirably, showing great keenness and courage, but being still under tutelage he could only allow himself to be advised and remain cheerful under fire. When the army was no longer in a position to attack the enemy the King recalled him to Versailles, and M. du Maine, who had been with him, followed shortly afterwards. The latter had had several opportunities of showing ability as a lieutenant-general, and M. de Boufflers dared to hope; but he continued to behave in character. The King suffered a disappointment that brought back unhappy memories of an earlier campaign; but he realized at last that laurels would not come easily to that well-loved son, and regretfully decided never again to expose him to hazards which he so little relished.

I should not pause to record anything so trivial as what follows were it not a most important episode in my life, and of some interest in showing how small beginnings may have great consequences. Mme la Duchesse d'Orléans, taking advantage of the greater freedom and importance that had been hers since the death of Monsieur, had a fancy to hold a separate court at Saint-Cloud. The King gave his consent, on condition that she kept the company select, not mixed, save perhaps for remnants of Monsieur's household whom she could not well exclude. The idea had been under consideration for some time past, and amongst other Court ladies she had especially invited Mme de Saint-Simon, who had promised to attend. When the time came, however, it so happened that we had arranged to go for six weeks to La Ferté, for Mme la Duchesse d'Orléans was not able to fix her dates until the King's Marlys had been announced. As soon as these were discovered, the princess made Mme de Saint-Simon give her solemn word to return to her on the very day that she went to Saint-Cloud. And so it happened. The Duchesse de Villeroy wrote on the princess's behalf, and my wife returned immediately. The company was most exclusive; the pleasures and diversions never flagged; M. le Duc and Mme la Duchesse d'Orléans did the honours of that lovely house most graciously; the luxury and freedom made the visit delightful, and for the first time Saint-Cloud could be enjoyed without vexation.[1]

At the beginning of these Memoirs I described how M. le Duc d'Orléans and I had been boys together and close friends when he was still M. le Duc de Chartres. Our intimacy had lasted until he was fully grown, and even throughout the campaign of 1693, when he had commanded the cavalry in M. de Luxembourg's army. But when his ambitions were thwarted he took a pride in licentiousness, following the bad examples of M. le Duc and the Prince de Conti. The rakes of Paris gained a hold over him. Resentment at being forced into an unsuitable marriage drove him to seek consolation elsewhere. Disappointment at being refused the command of an army and the governorships and other offices which he had been promised finally led him into dissolute living, which he carried to extremes in order to show contempt for his wife and the King's displeasure. Such a life, so vastly different from mine, had driven us apart. I had seen him only on rare occasions—visits of courtesy lasting a few moments—during the past seven or eight years. We did not even frequent the same houses. When we did happen to meet he always gave me a welcoming smile, but my life suited him as little as his did me, and eventually our separation had become complete.

The death of his father, although it brought him closer to the King and Madame, did not alter his way of life. He conducted himself rather better towards her and was somewhat more respectful to the King, but his debauchery had become a habit. It was the fashion for young men of his age, and he relished the contrast to what he regarded as the boredom of respectability. Thus the people whom he most admired were those who went to the furthest extremity in licentiousness. The very slight change in his position at the Court brought none in his excesses, nor in those private pleasures in Paris, which he continually indulged in. It is not yet time to give a portrait of this prince, whom you will see playing a prominent part on the world's stage, and in varying situations.

It so happened that Mme Fontaine-Martel was at Saint-Cloud on that occasion. She had been one of the ladies of Monsieur's court and had moved all her life in the highest society. Her husband was Mme la Duchesse d'Orléans's master of the horse and, by virtue of his office (though he was so gouty that no one ever saw him), she spent her life at the Court and was included in all the excursions, sometimes even to Marly. She used often to sup with the Maréchal de Lorges, who kept open house twice a day and a most excellent table. By dint of meeting her often we had become friends,[2] and she sometimes inquired why I no

---

[1] Monsieur, as before mentioned, 'did not care for women'. Many respectable people were shocked by the effeminate, but decorative company he gathered round him at Saint-Cloud.

[2] Mme Martel must have been a charmer: Voltaire wrote:

'*Martel, l'Automne de vos jours*
Vaut mieux que le printemps d'une autre'.

longer saw M. le Duc d'Orléans, saying that it was a thousand pities since, despite the difference in our lives, we were well suited in many ways. I laughed, and let her have her say; but one day at Saint-Cloud she attacked M. le Duc d'Orléans on the subject in the presence of Mme de Saint-Simon. They both said many amiable things of me, and the duke ended by remarking that he wished I did not think him too great a rake to be seen in his company. They reverted to the subject continually during the rest of the house-party, even wishing that it were not too late to send for me, and, in M. le Duc d'Orléans's words, vowing to overcome my scruples when they next saw me at Versailles.

Mme de Saint-Simon was then asked to write to me. I answered as my duty required. She returned to La Ferté and informed me that the matter had gone too far for me not to comply. I thought at first that it was no more than a whim on the part of Mme Fontaine-Martel and M. le Duc d'Orléans's courtesy, and that no more would happen, for I was convinced that we no longer had anything in common. I accordingly decided to remain adamant, or at the very most to pay a formal call. I was mistaken. That call when I finally paid it (for I continued to delay despite M. le Duc d'Orléans's continual reminders to the ladies) was received with intense pleasure. Whether our old friendship was suddenly reborn, or whether he was glad of someone with whom to be intimate at Versailles, where he was usually bored, he gave me such a welcome that I almost thought myself back in the old days at the Palais Royal. He asked me to visit him often; he pressed me to come; he appeared, dare I say it, to be proud of my return, and did all in his power to bind me fast. My own affection for him revived as a result of his many advances, and there soon began a second friendship that lasted for the rest of his life, save for occasional lapses brought about by intrigue after he had become Regent. This close attachment exposed me to many dangers, and for some time made me a person of importance. I think I may truly say that it proved no less profitable to the prince than to his humble servant, and, indeed, had M. le Duc d'Orléans so pleased he might have drawn from it even greater benefits.

I must here recount one other trifling episode because its outcome was in total contrast to the above and much thwarted my hopes of advancement. M. de Lauzun was still greatly distressed by his loss of favour with the King and continually sought some approach that might reinstate him. With that end in view he revived an old acquaintance with M. du Maine, hoping through him to influence Mme de Maintenon to move the King on his behalf. He therefore proceeded to insinuate his young wife into Mme du Maine's circle, encouraging her to gamble for high stakes (which she enjoyed) and thus become a necessity at their tables. Mme du Maine soon came to rely on her company at Sceaux, where M. du Maine, always eager to attract the highest Society, used her as a bait to catch Mme de Saint-Simon. It was a way of being agreeable and Mme de Saint-Simon allowed herself to be persuaded, but not regularly by any means. I have reason to believe that M. and Mme du Maine had formed a design to win me as well. In myself I meant nothing to them, and they well knew how much I despised their rank. They had nothing to fear from me at that time, but from policy and uncertainty of the future they sought goodwill everywhere, and where I was concerned they wished to remove a thorn that might harm them in days to come. Thus they began to praise me to my wife and her sister, hoping with much earnestness to have the pleasure of seeing me at Sceaux, and finally suggesting to one and the other that they should persuade me to accompany them. Much surprised by this unlooked for approach from persons with whom I had had no dealings, I suspected a motive and that, in itself, made me pause to consider. I could not accustom myself to their unparalleled rank; I felt in my heart a great longing to see it removed from them, which, in turn, made me desire to contribute to that end one day. This urge was so strong that I knew I should have no power to resist. How then could I consort, yet not be friends, with people who made me such apparently disinterested advances; who had the power to mend my situation with the King, and who seemed so eager to win me with kindness? How could I accept their friendship and its proofs and still harbour my resentment? Honour, honesty, would never countenance such double dealing. Useless to examine my heart and reflect upon my present unhappy situation. To me no favours were enough to make me consent to the perpetuating of such rank, or renounce the hope of working for its removal. Thus resolved, I stayed firmly at the stage of exchanging compliments, unmoved by their messages and the reproaches of Mme du Maine, to whom I had hitherto scarcely spoken and who now held me long in conversation in the King's room.

At length they tired of pursuing me. They were most deeply offended, but they did not allow it to show and redoubled in civility towards Mme de Saint-Simon. I have always believed that from that time onwards M. du Maine made up his mind to injure me, and that he set Mme de Maintenon against me, for she never knew me, yet not until after the death of the King did I discover how absolutely she hated me.[1] It was Chamillart who then told me, adding that she was against him when he finally managed to restore me to Marly and other favours. I had long suspected that she did not like me, but as long as the King lived I did not know to what extent. Chamillart did not wish to disturb me, still less to unloose my all too eager mouth, for already at that time I was too free regarding those whom I thought I ought not to like, and was far too little checked by thoughts of their rank and influence.

[1] It was not unnatural. She had loved M. du Maine from the time when he was her little pupil, and could scarcely be expected not to detest his avowed enemy.

To complete this account of my situation with M. du Maine. Some considerable time later Mme la Duchesse de Bourgogne kept Mme de Lauzun at Marly after the other guests had left, and when she should have returned with Mme du Maine, who had driven her down. Although she tried to excuse herself for that reason, Mme la Duchesse de Bourgogne insisted, telling her to inform Mme du Maine that she would drive her back herself. Mme du Maine was so foolish as to let fly at the Duchesse de Lauzun next day, and in such a manner that she left her drawing-room vowing never to return. M. du Maine called to apologize; Monsieur le Prince to make excuses; they both set to coaxing M. de Lauzun; he was all but placated; his wife, however, was adamant. I was enchanted to find so good a pretext for Mme de Saint-Simon to absent herself from a house where the company was becoming more than mixed, and wherein we certainly had nothing to gain, and from that time onwards she saw Mme du Maine only on state occasions, despite the fact that they did everything possible to lure her back. I think that that episode confirmed their ill-will towards me, if anything further were needed. After that Mme la Duchesse de Bourgogne always took Mme de Lauzun with her to Marly, a great favour which Mme du Maine took much amiss. At last, after some years, M. du Maine and M. de Lauzun grew tired of the quarrel and arranged that Mme du Maine should apologize to Mme de Lauzun at Madame la Princesse's apartment at Versailles; that the apology should be graciously accepted, and that two days later Mme de Lauzun should call on Mme du Maine. That was done, and well done. M. du Maine was present beside his wife when Mme de Lauzun called, so as to avoid unnecessary embarrassment and enliven the conversation. Mme de Lauzun made that one visit suffice, and saw her thenceforth only on great occasions; Mme de Saint-Simon therefore did the same. This long account may now appear vastly superfluous, but will in due course be seen as most important.

Shortly after this came the death of the Duc de Coislin, a great affliction to his brother the Cardinal, and a sad loss for all men of good will. He was very short and insignificant in appearance, but the soul of honour and virtue, and a brave man into the bargain. He was also witty and possessed a fund of vivid and truthful anecdotes from which one could gain an immense amount that was interesting. His politeness was so excessive as to be devastatingly absurd, but it never caused him a loss of dignity. He had been a lieutenant-general of some distinction, and later a general commanding cavalry, but he sold that commission and quitted the service, thereby mortally offending M. de Louvois. With so many fine qualities that made him respected by all and genuinely esteemed by the King, he was such an odd character that I cannot resist some anecdotes. A Rhenish count, captured in one of the Duc de Coislin's battles, surrendered to him personally. The duke wished him to sleep on his bed,

consisting of a single narrow mattress; they argued about it so long and
so politely that in the end both of them slept on the floor, one on either
side. After the duke's return to Paris the count came to call on him, having
been granted leave on parole. Endless civilities on the way to the door.
At last the count, exasperated beyond endurance, dashed from the room
and locked the door from the outside. The duke, undefeated, leapt from
the window, which was only a few feet above ground-level, and was at
the coach door before the count emerged believing that the devil had lent
him wings. Unhappily the duke's thumb was dislocated in the descent.
Félix called to set it. He called again in course of time and found it cured.
On the way to the door, picture M. de Coislin trying to hold it open for
Félix, and Félix mortally embarrassed trying to prevent him. A tug-of-
war ensued with both men straining at the handle until, suddenly the
duke let go and fell to wringing his hands. It was his thumb, re-dislocated,
and Félix had to do his work all over again. You may well believe that
there was much merriment when the King was told.

One might never end the tales of his infuriating politeness. We met
him one day, Mme de Saint-Simon and I, when we were returning from
Fontainebleau, standing in the road at Ponthierry with his son Monsieur
de Metz, his carriage having broken down. We sent to beg them to
travel with us. Messages flew backwards and forwards until I was obliged
to step down into the road myself, despite the mud, and implore them to
enter our coach. Monsieur de Metz, himself, became enraged by all the
compliments and finally overbore him. When at last he had consented and
his foot was on the step, he began to make conditions, protesting that he
could not think of displacing 'my young ladies'. I replied that they were
two housemaids, perfectly capable of waiting until his coach was repaired.
It was of no use, we had to promise to let one remain with us. When we
reached his coach the two girls alighted and during the courtesies, which
were not short, I told our groom to shut the door as soon as I was back
inside, and ordered the coachman to drive on. This manœuvre might have
succeeded had not M. de Coislin, protesting that he would jump out if we
did not stop for one of the girls, suited the action to the word so promptly
that if I had not clutched the band of his breeches he would have fallen
out. There he was with his face pressed against the outer panel of the
door, shouting that he wanted to get out and struggling to be free. We
had the greatest difficulty in recovering him, protesting all the while that
he would have jumped had I not intervened. The girl was finally picked up
but to make matters worse she had collected an immense amount of filth
on the road which she brought with her, and Monsieur de Metz and I
were nearly squashed in a coach intended only for four.

It would be absurd to record here the death of Petit if the circumstances were not so strange. He was very old and for a long time past had
been Monseigneur's doctor. He was an intelligent man, well-informed,

upright, and experienced, yet he died without ever being willing to admit that the blood circulates. This seems so extraordinary to me that I feel it is worth mentioning. The other strange circumstance is that his post was given to Boudin,[1] of whom it is not yet time to speak, but there will be all too much to say of him later, for most important reasons.

The King went to Fontainebleau on 19 September and there received the news that the Maréchal de Villeroy had been freed.[2] Very soon after the Emperor had been informed of the agreement for an exchange of prisoners he sent to give him his freedom, and gallantly refused to accept the ransom, which had been settled at fifty thousand pounds. Villeroy's freedom cost France very dear, but it pleased the King. One somewhat shocking novelty at Fontainebleau was the sight of Madame in public at the play in the second year of her mourning for Monsieur. She made some objections at first, but the King said that what happened in his residence should not be compared with what was suitable in public places.

At the time of the battle of Friedlingen[3] I suffered one of the most bitter afflictions of my entire life, when I lost my father-in-law the Maréchal de Lorges. Although otherwise in perfect health, he was attacked by a stone, with symptoms which he at first mistook, or deliberately ignored, wishfully hoping that nothing might prove to be amiss. For the last six months of his life he remained confined to his house where, such was the general affection in which he was held, there seemed to be a perpetual court attending on him, rather than the faithful company of his friends. When the disease had reached a point where it could no longer be denied, his family were deceived by the reputation of a certain Brother Jacques, and chose him rather than the ordinary surgeons to perform the operation. This man was neither monk nor hermit, but affected a strange-looking grey hood, and had invented a new method of making the cut to one side. This had the advantage of being quicker and of avoiding the distressing results of such operations when performed in the normal way. In France there are fashions in everything; Brother Jacques was all the

[1] Jean Boudin, the King's apothecary. A pupil of Fagon, he was a strong supporter of the bleeding, purging, emetic school that killed so many of the royal family.

[2] Villeroy's incompetence had allowed him to be captured by Prince Eugene at the siege of Cremona. His soldiers sang gleefully:

'Let Frenchmen thank Bellona
For luck without a parallel
For we have kept Cremona
And also lost our general'.

It was by the intercession of James II's widow, Mary of Modena, whose brother the Duke of Modena was a great friend of the Emperor, that he was sent home without ransom.

[3] Villars's victory over the Imperial army, 14 October, 1702. Saint-Simon, who disliked Villars personally and was therefore singularly blind to his merits as a general, says that the French cavalry put the enemy to flight and charged up a steep hill in pursuit. Villars at the bottom lost sight of them and believed that he had lost the battle. He sat weeping under a tree until another general returned shouting that the battle was won. Whereupon Villars charged after his cavalry crying, 'Victory, Victory!' and taking all the credit to himself.

rage and everyone praised him. They had his operations followed for three months, during which out of twenty patients only very few died. M. le Maréchal de Lorges meanwhile retired from the world and prepared himself for the ordeal with fortitude and truly Christian resignation. The preferences of his family and his own desire to secure for his son the reversion of his captaincy in the bodyguard meant far more to him than any personal inclinations.

The operation was performed on Thursday, 19 October, at eight o'clock in the morning. He said his prayers on the previous evening. Brother Jacques refused all advice and assistance, excepting from Milet, a surgeon-major of M. de Lorges's company, of whom he was very fond. They discovered first a small stone, then a number of large polyps, and beneath these one enormous stone. Any surgeon knowing more than just how to handle the knife would have removed the smaller stone and let that be all for the time being. He would then have used ointments to soften and dissolve the fleshy growths, and only after that have tried to take away the large stone. Brother Jacques lost his head; he was in truth no better than a good barber-surgeon; he tore out the polyps, but the operation had already lasted more than three-quarters of an hour and had become so agonizing that he dared not proceed further, and left the great stone untouched. M. le Maréchal bore it all with unflinching calm and courage.

Soon after it was over, his wife, the only member of his family whom he was allowed to see, went to him. He held out his hand to her, saying, 'Here I am as they wished me to be,' and when she answered cheerfully, he added, 'God's will be done.' His entire family and many of his friends had forgathered at his house in great anxiety at his dreadful ordeal. Suddenly the Duc de Gramont, whom Maréchal had cut a short time before, burst into the room prophesying the horrible complications that would set in one after another, and beseeching them to send for Maréchal and the qualified surgeons. Brother Jacques would not hear of that, and Mme de Lorges, fearing his anger, refused to send for anyone. His prophecies proved only too accurate and before long Brother Jacques himself was crying for help. It was given him on the instant, but by then it was too late.

M. le Maréchal de Lorges died on Saturday, 22 October, at four in the morning with the Abbé Anselme, the famous preacher and director, constantly at his side. The scene at the house was heartbreaking, for no man was ever more deeply and universally regretted. In addition to my own sincere grief I had that of Mme de Saint-Simon to support, and I many times feared to lose her. Nothing could compare with her love for her father, nor with his for her, and moreover they were identical in heart and mind. Me he loved as though I had been his own son, and I loved and revered him as the best of fathers with the fondest and most entire trust and confidence.

The Prince d'Harcourt[1] was at last permitted to return and make his bow to the King after an absence of seventeen years. He had been in the service of Venice, had distinguished himself in Morea, and returned to France only after the peace with Turkey had been signed. He was a tall, well-built man, with a ranting, strutting deportment that made him look for all the world like a country-actor. He was a great liar, a libertine in mind and body, wildly extravagant, a notorious swindler, indulging in secret debauchery that had kept him in a state of penury throughout his life. After his return to France he hovered without being able to settle anywhere, and quite incapable of living with his wife, in which he was not far wrong, or of adapting himself to the Court or to life in Paris. He finally established himself at Lyons, with his wine, his harlot-mistresses and company to match them, and a pack of hounds and card tables to pay his costs at the expense of such greenhorns, fools, and rich merchants' sons as he could lure into his net. He then grew bored and returned to Paris. The King, who despised him, at first refused to receive him, and only after two months of the Lorraines making excuses and apologies for his conduct was he allowed to make his bow. His wife, who was included in all the excursions, was a favourite of Mme de Maintenon for the powerful but impure reason that I have already described,[2] but she failed to get him to Marly, where husbands went by right and without special permission if their wives were invited. She stopped going there herself, hoping that Mme de Maintenon would obtain that favour for her; but she was mistaken, Mme de Maintenon had thought it her duty to protect her, but was tired of her demands and gladly suffered her absence; whereupon she took fright and went to Marly alone; but the King held firm and never once admitted the Prince d'Harcourt. That somewhat barred his way at the Court, but he did not return to the country, until he settled for good in Lorraine.

The Princesse d'Harcourt was the kind of person who warrants a description in order that you may better understand a Court that cheerfully accepted such a person. She had at one time been gay and handsome, but though still far from old her airs and graces had turned to brambles,[3] and at the time of which I speak she was a gross, vulgar, bustling creature, with a skin the colour of putty, thick blubber-lips, and hair like tow, perpetually falling down like all the rest of her soiled and filthy attire. She was for ever scheming, demanding, making mischief, quarrelling, cringing low as the grass or riding high on a rainbow, according to her company. A blonde fury! Worse, a harpy! for she possessed the same manifest wickedness, evil temper, and treachery, and was miserly and

---

[1] Alphonse Henri de Lorraine, Prince d'Harcourt.

[2] He had been '*plus que bien*' with her.

[3] *Gratte-cul*, a gross word to describe old women. '*Chaque rose se change en gratte-cul.*' When the rose-petals fall nothing is left but a hard and scratchy pod.

grasping as well. Worst of all, she was a glutton, and so eager to relieve herself that she drove her hostesses to desperation, for although she never denied herself the use of the convenience on leaving table, she sometimes allowed herself no time to reach it at leisure, leaving a dreadful trail behind her that made the servants of M. du Maine and M. le Grand wish her to the devil. As for her, she was never in the least embarrassed, but lifted her skirts and went her way, saying on her return that she had felt a little faint. She made money at every possible opportunity, and laboured as hard to gain a hundred francs as a hundred thousand. The tax-commissioners were not easily rid of her, and she cheated her tradesmen and merchants to the best of her ability. At cards her impudence in cheating was quite extraordinary, for she did so openly, and, when challenged, jeered and pocketed the money. Yet since that had always been her custom, people regarded her merely as a vulgar woman with whom it was unsafe to gamble—and this at Marly, playing *lansquenet* in the presence of Mgr and Mme la Duchesse de Bourgogne. People avoided her at other games as much as possible, and whilst stealing all she could she never missed saying that anything she won unfairly would be given to charity, because, she explained, 'at cards one is always liable to make mistakes'. She said this because she was professedly religious and relied on that method to quieten her conscience. For the same reason she went to all the church services and took communion regularly, even after gambling until four in the morning.

Once when she was at Fontainebleau she called on the Maréchale de Villeroy between vespers and benediction. That lady naughtily suggested a game of cards in order to see whether she would miss church. The princess hesitated, saying that Mme de Maintenon was sure to be at the chapel. Mme de Villeroy coaxed her, exclaiming that even she could not notice all who were absent, and they sat down to play. But Mme de Maintenon, who rarely paid calls, suddenly took it into her head to enter as she passed the door of the maréchale's apartment at the foot of her staircase. The door was flung open and she was announced. It had the effect of a bombshell on the Princesse d'Harcourt. 'I'm ruined!' she exclaimed, for she was never one for restraint. 'God save us! she will see me gambling when I ought to be in church!' and she dropped her cards and fell down in a swoon. The maréchale was convulsed with laughter, and Mme de Maintenon, entering by slow degrees, found them in that condition with five or six onlookers. Mme de Villeroy, who had a ready wit, explained that the honour of her visit had thrown them into some confusion, indicating the disordered appearance of the Princesse d'Harcourt; at which Mme de Maintenon with a majestically benign smile turned to the casualty saying, 'Do you intend going to benediction in that state, Madame?' Hearing this the princess emerged from her swoon in a furious temper, exclaiming that certain people liked to play tricks of that kind, especially

Mme de Villeroy, who plainly expected Mme de Maintenon's visit and had coaxed her to gamble in order to make her miss prayers. 'Coaxed!' cried the maréchale. 'There is no other way of amusing you. You hesitated a second, but your inclinations decided the matter.' 'There, Madame,' she continued, turning to Mme de Maintenon, 'that is my only crime,' and all of them began to laugh. That joke kept the Court amused for several days, for the princess was hated, feared, and despised by everyone.

Mgr and Mme la Duchesse de Bourgogne were always playing tricks on her.[1] One night they made twenty Swiss guardsmen enter her bedroom beating their kettle-drums. Another time, when it was snowing at Marly, they waited until she was in bed and asleep; then they and their suite gathered up snow from the terrace in front of the upper rooms, and softly entering her room with the master-key, they suddenly drew back her curtains and pelted her with snowballs. The dreadful old creature woke up with a bound, all crumpled, furious, and gasping for breath, with snow in her ears, her hair unfastened, screaming her head off, and wriggling like an eel to find some means of escape. The scene kept them amused for more than half-an-hour, until the nymph was a-wash in her bed, with water everywhere and a flood on the floor. They might well have caused her death. Next day she sulked, as she often did when too much baited, for she not unreasonably considered that one who bore the name of Lorraine should not let herself be made a laughing-stock.

The death of the Duchesse de Gesvres also occurred at this time. She was separated from her husband who was the scourge of her entire family and had wasted millions of her money. She was a du Val by birth, the only daughter of Fontenay-Mareuil, who was the French ambassador at Rome at the time of the Duc de Guise's Neapolitan adventure.[2] She was a tall, gaunt, witch-like person, who stalked like those giant birds called Numidian cranes. She used occasionally to appear at the Court, and for all her oddity and the starved look to which her husband had reduced her, she did not lack virtue, spirit, or dignity. I remember one summer when the King took a fancy to spending the evenings at Trianon. He allowed the entire Court both male and female to follow him there, and there was a great collation for the Princesses his daughters and their friends, and for other ladies also when they pleased. On one such evening the Duchesse de Gesvres took it into her head to go to Trianon for the supper. Her advanced age and strange appearance provoked the Princesses to mock her in whispers with their favourites. When she perceived this she unhesitatingly told them what she thought of them, so short and sharp that

---

[1] They were 20 and 17 years old.

[2] In 1647 the Duc de Guise had assisted the Neapolitans to revolt against Spain, hoping by so doing to secure for himself the crown of Naples.

they were reduced to silence and lowered their eyes. But that was not all. When supper was over she again expressed herself with so much frankness, yet so comically that panic seized them and they apologized, crying out for mercy. Mme de Gesvres then condescended to spare them, but she warned them that it was only on condition that they mended their manners, and they never afterwards dared to look her in the face. Nothing was ever more lovely than those evenings at Trianon. All the flowers were changed every day in the flowerbeds, and I have seen the King and the Court driven indoors by the scent of the tuberoses. They perfumed the very air, but were so potent that although the garden was vast, descending in terraces to a branch of the canal, one could not stay long outside. Let us now return to more serious matters.

The King returned from Fontainebleau on 26 October, spending one night *en route* at Villeroy, where he appeared to feel as much at home as in any of the royal residences,[1] and where he talked long and affectionately to the Maréchal. Arriving at Versailles, he learned that the fortress of Liège had been captured by storm; that La Chartreuse, which we all believed to be strongly fortified, had fallen soon after, and that his Flanders army, weakened by detachments sent to the Rhine, had retreated within its lines and was in no condition to continue the campaign.

Lord Marlborough after dispersing his army went down the Meuse by barge[2] with a deputy of the States-General attached to the combined armies. On their way down the river a group of partisans from Gelderland suddenly appeared on the bank and forced them to land at gunpoint. It was nearly a glorious capture, but the foolish fellows satisfied themselves with inspecting the deputy's pass and let Marlborough go free, mistaking him for a groom.

On Monday, 4 December, at the end of the *conseil de dépêches*[3] of which Mgr le Duc de Bourgogne was a member, the King told him that in future he would attend the finance council and even the council of State; that for a time he would listen and learn without voting, but that later he would be glad for him to play his full part. The prince was taken completely by surprise, especially since Monseigneur was very much older when he had been admitted, and he was much gratified by the honour.

---

[1] According to Saint-Simon the King felt uncomfortable in any house except his own, and strongly disliked visiting.

[2] The best way of reaching The Hague. Marlborough was accompanied by three Dutch representatives, servants, his cook, and twenty-five soldiers to guard them. A mounted escort was supposed to guard them, but the Guelders marshes forced them to leave the river where a French trap had been set to catch generals leaving the front by water. An Irish deserter from the Dutch army made the capture, dragging their barge ashore by the tow-rope. Did the Irishman let them go from sheer stupidity? One reporter said, 'The lieutenant did not sin through ignorance,' another, 'Lord Marlborough did not exercise his usual economy.' You may imagine the excitement at Versailles, and the disappointment when it was learned that only Marlborough's cook had been kept a prisoner.

[3] The least important of the councils, as it were a news conference.

Mme de Maintenon had acted in this for love of Mme la Duchesse de Bourgogne, and M. le Duc de Beauvilliers's report of the young prince's steadiness and maturity had carried great weight. Mme la Duchesse de Bourgogne was in transports of joy, and M. de Beauvilliers was much pleased.

Speaking of councils, there was a notable change in the order for the State council of Spain. Hitherto the State councillors, who correspond with our ministers, had sat in the king's presence, whereas the secretary for foreign affairs always stood at the end of the table, or, if he preferred, knelt on a cushion. I do not know whether our secretaries of State, although they had always remained standing, objected to doing so in the face of seated ministers,[1] or whether our King made the ruling of his own accord in consideration of the services which Ubilla, the Spanish secretary, had rendered him at the time of the late king's will. Be that as it may, it was on King Louis's recommendation that the King of Spain, when he arrived at Madrid, made Ubilla sit at the end of the table. This innovation caused a scandal, as does every novelty in a country that abhors them; it passed, however, and Ubilla received a Castilian title and was called the Marquis of Rivas; but such titles mean little or nothing.

Orry was sent back to Spain at the same time.[2] He was hard of hearing but extremely shrewd, had sprung from the gutter, and had followed many different employments to gain his livelihood and advancement. He began life as a tax-gatherer, and was then the Duchess of Portsmouth's agent; but she detected him in some knavery and dismissed him. Thereafter he returned to his first calling, managed to secure sundry commissions from high financiers, gave them satisfaction, and was finally passed on to Chamillart. When it became desirable to know the precise state of the Spanish finances and how they were administered, but not in such a way as to alarm those in charge, Orry was proposed and later appointed, and he had recently returned to make his report. Mme des Ursins who had had the opportunity to meddle in the affairs of State during the queen's regency, on the excuse of training her young charge, was becoming enamoured with the idea of controlling them altogether. Orry had courted her; she had appreciated his outlook, finding him very willing to fawn on her and to work under her auspices. He provided her with a most useful channel by which to stick her nose into the finances. They had formed a mistress-valet attachment, and he brought her strong recommendation when he came to France. Chamillart, delighted that his candidate had met with such hearty approval, used all his influence to

---

[1] On special folding armchairs, called *perroquets*, carried round after them for fear of their being reduced to the armless *ployants* provided at Versailles.

[2] Jean Orry, banker (1652–1719). Philip V finally appointed him to administer the Spanish finances. Saint-Simon cultivated him despite his gutter-origins and his dishonesty. These counted for little compared with his capacity for giving information.

support him, and saw that he was given commissions of a kind to en-
hance his prestige when he returned to Spain. We shall find Orry rapidly
becoming a man of very great importance.

The year ended with the marriage of my brother-in-law[1] to Chamillart's third daughter. The affair had been the talk of the town since the
summer, so much so indeed that I thought it best to ask the Maréchale
de Lorges how I should reply to questions. When she assured me that
there was no truth whatever in the rumour, I considered it right and
proper to give her my views very plainly of a match so undesirable for
rank and family connections, and very little better in the way of wealth.
I then suggested to her the daughter of the Duc d'Harcourt,[2] who was far
more suitable by birth and her father's brilliant position, but when that
idea was not welcomed I said no more. At that point M. de Lauzun intervened. He had inevitably been drawn into the family circle during M. de
Lorges's operation, and had surprised us all by taking the maréchale into
his home in the first days of our common sorrow. He now hoped to reap
some benefit. He reckoned to earn Chamillart's goodwill by pressing for
the marriage, and then to use him in effecting his reconciliation with the
King. Lauzun had little difficulty in convincing the Maréchale, who was
already determined on the match, or in persuading my brother-in-law
himself, who readily believed that it would lead to his advancement.

Thus everything was signed and sealed without Mme de Saint-Simon
and myself hearing anything beyond rumours. I did speak once again to
Mme de Lorges describing my feelings, but when I found that all was
finally settled, I thought it would be best to call and congratulate Chamillart. I was all the more ready to do so because Mme de Noailles had
warned me not to parade my discontent. The Chamillarts, she said,
already knew my sentiments, which would have no effect on the match. I
therefore paid my call. I was then quite unacquainted with Chamillart,
except as one knows the ministers in office, indeed I had hardly ever
spoken to him other than in the way of business; but he left a group of
bankers with whom he had been working to come to me and converse.
It had originally been my intention to limit myself to congratulations, but
he straightway began to tell me all the details of the wedding,[3] and confided to me his difficulties with the Maréchale de Lorges, who had made
endless trouble over the settlement. He was in fact so friendly that I, who
was longing to confide, could not resist being equally frank. He told me
that the pension of twenty thousand livres, which the bridegroom had
received from the King at his father's death, was granted expressly for

---

[1] The Duc de Quintin, who shortly after his marriage adopted his father's title Duc de
Lorges. Saint-Simon was devoted to his wife and called her '*ma grande biche*' (my big sweet-
heart).

[2] The ambassador to Spain, before mentioned.

[3] Chamillart became perhaps Saint-Simon's best and most enjoyed friend. He could be gay
and natural with him as he could never be with Beauvilliers and Pontchartrain.

this marriage, and he showed me a letter from the Maréchale that made me blush for shame. I believe that such a trustful conversation (begun in that spirit by Chamillart) must be quite unparalleled between men so slightly acquainted and of such different ages and employments.[1]

On Wednesday, 13 December, we accordingly all forgathered at L'Etang, Chamillart's country house, where the Bishop of Senlis wedded my brother-in-law to his niece, with a dowry of no more than an hundred thousand écus and board and lodging paid everywhere, which allowed me the continued use of the late Maréchal de Lorges's apartment in the Château de Versailles. There was a large and lavish banquet, and nothing could have exceeded the delight of M. de Lauzun, the joy of Chamillart and his family, or the courtesy extended by them all to Mme de Saint-Simon and myself. I was surprised, as I have said, by the frankness of his first talk with me; I was now quite dumbfounded by the manner in which he asked me for my friendship. There was much more than ordinary politeness in his words, and when I realized that he was in dead earnest, I felt so overcome that he noticed it. I replied to him in the exact words which I had used in a similar situation with the Chancellor. I told him of my intimacy with Pontchartrain, of my friendship for his son, and of Mme de Saint-Simon's great affection for his wife (they were first cousins but closer than many sisters), and I concluded by saying that if he would have my friendship under those conditions I would give it joyfully. Touched by my honesty, he said that I had made him more than ever anxious to win my affection. We then made each other solemn promises which we kept faithfully and lovingly until his death.

Chamillart had quarrelled violently with Pontchartrain and his son, and they with him. There were no limits to their enmity, and that being so I thought it prudent to go immediately after leaving L'Etang to tell the Chancellor of all that had passed. He heard me as kindly as M. de Beau-villiers had done on a similar occasion, and so did his wife and daughter-in-law. His son also was as pleasant as his nature would allow. The families of both Chamillart and Pontchartrain were considerate of my feelings and forbore to speak of one another in my presence when other people were about. When we were alone they were not so careful for they believed that they could trust me, and in that they were not mistaken.

That was how I became as close a friend of Chamillart as I already was of the Dukes of Beauvilliers and Chevreuse and of the Chancellor and his son (so far as that last was possible). I thus became initiated into many important affairs and gained at the Court a reputation for seriousness far beyond that of other young men of my age. Chamillart soon gave me proof of his affection by trying to reconcile me with the King, and although he did not succeed I was none the less grateful.

[1] Chamillart was 50, Saint-Simon 27.

One day not long afterwards, when I was talking to his wife, she became even more confidential than usual, saying how glad she was that I liked them better than I had expected, and when I pretended not to understand, she added that they had long known of my absolute disapproval of the match, but were curious to hear the reason. In my astonishment I turned sharply to look her in the face, admitted that what she said was true, and continued that since she had asked me I would speak frankly. All the same, I thought it might be unwise to tell all, and therefore simply said that I believed that one should not undertake something bigger than oneself in marriage, and particularly not ministers, who were liable to be obstinate and unreasonable. If one did so, I said, one was in danger of being over-ridden by the very friends to whom one looked for help and advancement. Equal marriages, on the other hand, pledged both sides to contribute in equal proportions and gave surer hope of success. I then smoothed matters by saying that had I known them better I should have urged the marriage instead of disapproving of it. My readiness to be frank with so little coaxing greatly pleased her; but indeed she and her husband had been very generous to treat me as they did and to make all the advances. The conversation on that day set the seal upon our close friendship and intimacy.

The marriage was as onerous as I had predicted to the Maréchale. Hard as iron for them,[1] it was pure gold for me. Not in wealth, indeed, for Mme de Saint-Simon and I both abominated the idea of what was called 'doing business' at the Court (a pursuit by which many well-bred persons continually enriched themselves), but in the joy of Chamillart's friendship and the services which he enabled me to render to my friends. I also began to receive, and that very soon, the satisfaction of my curiosity in many matters of interest concerning the Court and State, for I was fully posted with information every day regarding everything. With Mme Chamillart I did not talk of such things, but I expanded with her husband and he with me, and I repeated everything to Mme de Saint-Simon, for it was right to keep her informed.[2] Suffice it to say that the marriage, while it lasted, went very ill between husband and wife, and that my brother-in-law ruined himself by quitting the service very soon afterwards. Not even the offer of promotion to brigadier long before his time would serve to restrain him. Mme de Saint-Simon and I became the repository for all Chamillart's misery in that direction, and for all the squalid secrets of their domestic unhappiness. Mme la Maréchale de Lorges failed to win the Chamillarts' affection or esteem, and at last had the good sense to go into retirement, which might be counted as a good deed to her in the next

---

[1] As Chamillart became more and more overwhelmed by the work of his two departments, Finances and War, he grew difficult, stubborn, and overbearing.

[2] In 1706 Saint-Simon wrote that his best friends advised him always to tell his wife everything. 'I never found advice more prudent, wise, and useful than hers. She saved me from many disasters both great and small; I took advantage of her counsel on every point.'

world and was certainly only less admirable in this. To do her justice, I must add that towards the end of her life she did retire absolutely, living in fasting and penitence, full of good works, and the examination of her conscience. It was very many years before I could make up my mind to be reconciled with her.

Let me say once more that I should never have embarked on this squalid and uninteresting occurrence, had I not thought it needful to describe the origin and cause of my intimacy with Chamillart. Thanks to his friendship I was able to know and to act in a manner far beyond my years or apparent situation, whilst at the same time I was kept as fully informed by the opposing camp, I mean by the Chancellor and his son, and by M. de Beauvilliers also, who was on bad terms with them but a friend of Chamillart. The latter's daughters,[1] with whom I was also very friendly, kept me posted with a thousand titbits of feminine gossip, which was often of far greater significance than they realized, opening my eyes to an infinity of powerful intrigues and supplementing what I learned from my friends amongst the palace-ladies, and from the Duchesse de Villeroy, to whom and to her mother-in-law the Maréchale I was very deeply attached. I was on good terms with the Duc de Villeroy[2] also and constantly in their company; but I could never become accustomed to the high and mighty airs of the maréchal. He used to sniff loudly in all directions, sounding for all the world like a pneumatic pump; and I said as much to his wife and to his son and daughter-in-law, who laughed about it but could never bring me to order.

---

[1] Chamillart's daughters were the Marquise de Dreux, the Duchesse de La Feuillade, and now the Duchesse de Quintin-Lorges.
[2] The Maréchal's eldest son.

CHAPTER XIII

1703

[The situation in Europe and in the war was completely changed.

In the Cévennes *a French army was fully occupied in quelling a revolt of the Huguenot peasants, who, armed and helped by the Protestant powers, and fighting heroically for religious freedom, were proving as hard to suppress as their counterparts in the Maquis of World War II.*
France lost Savoy *when the Duchesse de Bourgogne's father Victor Amadeus II changed sides for the second time. He was outraged at his treatment by the Duc de Vendôme the French commander, and impressed by Prince Eugene's victorious Italian campaign, as well as by Marlborough's successes in the Low Countries. He listened to the voice of prudence.*
France gained Bavaria *when the Elector Maximilian II suddenly defected from the Allies; joined Louis XIV; and declared war on the Emperor at the head of a strong and well-equipped army.*
In the Low Countries and on the Rhine *the French were driven by Marlborough from fortress after fortress; but their army was not brought to battle and was thus not defeated by the end of the year as Marlborough had hoped.*
Portugal declared war against France and Spain. *The Allies recognized the Austrian Archduke Charles as Charles III of Spain. He went to Portugal with a large force of English troops to begin an invasion of Spain and dethrone Philip V.*
In Hungary *a rebellion of the peasants was engaging nearly all the attention of the Emperor and Prince Eugene. The fighting was violent in the suburbs of Vienna and the Emperor and his government made constant appeals to England and the Dutch Republic for troops and money. The hostile Bavarian army on his frontier put him in great danger.*

The commanders.
In the Cévennes, *Montrevel.*
In Piedmont, *Vendôme.*
In the Low Countries and on the Rhine, *Boufflers, Tallard, and Villeroy opposing Marlborough, Captain-general of the combined Anglo-Dutch army.*
In Portugal, *Berwick and the Archduke Charles.*
In Hungary, *Prince Eugene, fighting the rebels.]*

Marlborough is made a duke – Assignment of commands – Fanatics, Montrevel is sent into Languedoc – Maréchal becomes the King's first surgeon – Brief disgrace of the Comtesse de Gramont – Birth of the Duc de Chartres – Mgr le Duc de Bourgogne captures Brisach – Portugal joins the Allies –

Treachery of the Duke of Savoy – Changes in Spain – Schemes of the Princesse des Ursins – The Archduke Charles declared Charles III of Spain by the Allies – A new Junta in Spain – Eccentricity of the late Duke of Alba, father of the new Spanish ambassador

THE FIRST day of the new year, 1703, was that on which the King made an announcement at the chapter of the Order regarding the unparalleled honour which he was conferring on Cardinal Portocarrero. The King nominated him for the first vacancy among cardinals of the Order, and since all four places were filled gave him leave to wear the Order in the meantime. He sent him a diamond cross and more than fifty thousand écus, by which gift he was extraordinarily gratified. About this time Marlborough was made a Duke in England with a pension of five thousand pounds sterling, a truly prodigious sum.

The dispositions were soon made for the armies; nothing needed to be altered in Italy for the Duc de Vendôme remained there. The Maréchal de Villeroy, who had spent most of the winter in Brussels, had command of the Flanders army with the Maréchal de Boufflers. Tallard was given an army on the Moselle, and the Maréchal de Villars, who had stayed at Strasbourg, the army for Germany. The latter sent back for his wife, to whom he was a loving and a jealous husband in about equal proportions, and gave her a duenna in the shape of one of his sisters, who never took her eye off her anywhere for a number of years, and thought even that a better life than starving with her husband Vaugüé on their country estate, to which she never returned. There was great mockery and the precautions were not always successful.

A person of similar sex but far more notorious gained her liberty at this time. The friends of Mme Guyon, ever loyal and devoted to her, were beholden to the never-ending kindness and compassion of Cardinal de Noailles, who had her released from the Bastille after several years solitary confinement and gained permission for her to retire into Touraine. That was not her final appearance, but she never again lost her freedom. Thus the Cardinal merited the gratitude (to say the least) of all her little flock.

Montrevel, one of the new Marshals of France, was sent into Languedoc where the Protestants were causing some anxiety. Their numbers and the severity of Bâville the intendant had roused them to revolt. Many of them had taken up arms and were doing cruel execution among the curés and other priests. Foreign Protestants were secretly fanning and stoking the fires that threatened to burst into a dreadful conflagration. Broglie, who commanded the local troops, although in fact he merely carried out the orders of Bâville, his brother-in-law, stayed on for a while under the new marshal. Reinforcements were sent, together with a certain Julien[1] who

---

[1] Jacques de Julien, a Dutchman who had become a Catholic in 1693.

had been enticed out of the service of Savoy. He had done great damage in the previous war, was a brave adventurer, and knew the country.

Montrevel did not find the Fanatics as easy to defeat as he had expected. They were given that name because each large group of the rebellious Protestants included an alleged prophet or prophetess, supposedly God-inspired, who abetted the ringleaders to incite their trusting and obedient followers to the utmost ferocity.[1] For very many years Languedoc had been suffering under the tyranny of Bâville the intendant, who in his resolve to be all-powerful had secured military command of the entire province for his brother-in-law. He was a shrewd and intelligent man, well-informed, energetic, industrious, but sly, utterly ruthless, and well aware how to put his friends under so great an obligation that they became his slaves. Above all, he had a lust for power, crushing all opposition, ready to stick at nothing in order to gain his ends. He vastly increased the revenue from his province by his invention of a capitation tax and that had brought him into prominence. The ministers feared his ability and ambition; did their utmost to keep him away from the Court, and as an inducement to remain where he was gave him a free hand, which he unscrupulously misused. Whether he and Broglie wished to display their military genius I do not know, but they so harried the un- or ill-converted[2] that in the end they rebelled against him, and it was later learned that both Geneva and the Duke of Savoy were secretly furnishing them with arms and money, the former with preachers also, and the latter with skilled military tacticians. Indeed it had been something of a mystery that the rebels were time after time stripped of all they possessed and still continued to subsist and fight. It was fortunate for us that fanaticism seized these people, driving them to sacrilege, murder, and the torturing of monks and priests. Had they refrained from maltreatment except according to the rules of war and claimed only freedom of conscience and relief from oppression, many Catholics moved by fear or pity, or hoping for a lessening of taxation, might have come out into the open and carried the majority with them. Whole cantons were of their persuasion, and much the greater part of some towns, such as Nîmes, Uzès, etc., and very many gentlemen of good birth and position in the district took them secretly into their houses and warned them of danger. The rebels could safely

---

[1] They were also known as the *Camisards* because they wore over their clothes a white shirt, which could quickly be removed.

[2] As Louis XIV aged he became ever more firmly convinced of his Divine Right. It upset him profoundly that some people should refuse to be of the King's religion. He said that Protestantism concealed 'the bad effects of liberty'. Thus he encouraged Protestants to recant, offering propaganda, bribes (12/6 per convert), threats, and sterner measures. In 1680 he had sent his dragoons to torture, whip, rape and convert, with the result that there were thirty thousand converts in Poitou alone. He thought of himself as an *apostle*, but Saint-Simon remarked that his methods differed somewhat from those of the original twelve. Mme de Maintenon was not convinced that the conversions would last, and disapproved of torture.

turn to them for help, for these gentlemen were for the most part themselves receiving support and orders from Geneva or Turin. The Cévennes
and the wild mountains and deserts of the surrounding country provided
wonderful hiding places for this kind of people, and it was from there
that they made their raids.

Broglie wanted to play the general, but he was treated and behaved in
every way like an intendant, and was without troops, artillery, provisions,
or stores of any kind. Thus Montrevel was obliged to apply for all these
things, and whilst he waited for them to arrive the Fanatics continued to
ravage the province, with very slight losses inflicted on them by Julien.
Broglie was then recalled, being totally incompetent, but he had the
audacity to say that he had been promised the Order. Three or four
lieutenants-general were then sent to join Montrevel with twenty battalions and some artillery which he found very little use for. They hanged
some of the ringleaders whom they had captured in ambushes and small
skirmishes; all were of the very dregs, and their party was neither intimi-
dated nor discouraged.

So many troubles at home and abroad did not stop the King from enjoying his Court balls at Marly.

At about this time Félix the King's chief surgeon died, leaving a son
who showed no wish at all to attempt the same profession. Fagon, whom
the King and Mme de Maintenon trusted implicitly in matters of health,
gave the post to Maréchal, head-surgeon of the Charité hospital at Paris,
a man of the highest reputation and ability, who had cut him for a stone
with the greatest possible success. Apart from skill in his profession
Maréchal had little learning but he had a great deal of sense and a knowledge of human nature. He was the soul of honour, upright, and truthful,
and he hated those who were otherwise. He was also a good man and a
kind one, capable of loyal and devoted service, and very ready to speak out
and to tell the King some home-truths, once he had become established,
which happens very soon in relationships of that kind. You will discover
later that I have good reasons for enlarging on the character of this man
who, in the King's private service, managed to remain kind and respectful
despite his favour, and despite a certain innate vulgarity. I, and my
father before me, had lived all our lives in the neighbourhood of La
Charité and Maréchal was our family doctor. He had loved us all, and
continued to do so even after his promotion.

I well remember his telling Mme de Saint-Simon and myself of an
adventure that deserves to be remembered. It happened less than a year
after his appointment, when he was already in high favour and intimate
with the King, yet seeing, as he always had done, the sick of all kinds who
needed his help at Versailles and in the neighbourhood. One of the surgeons of Port-Royal-des-Champs asked him to visit a nun whose leg required amputation. Maréchal agreed to go on the following day, but as he

left the King's *lever* next morning he was asked to undertake another operation. He declined on the excuse of his previous engagement at Port-Royal. Hearing that name, one of the faculty took him aside, asking whether he was aware of what he risked in going there. Maréchal, who was completely ignorant of the scandal attaching to Port-Royal, was amazed and became still more so when told that he was courting dismissal. He could not believe that the King would object to his supervising the removal of a nun's leg; but to settle the matter he promised to tell the King before going. He accordingly appeared at the return from mass and because that was not his usual time the King looked surprised and asked what he wanted. Maréchal told him quite simply what had happened and of his great astonishment, whereat the King stiffened as he always did when something displeased him, and remained silent and thoughtful for the space of two or three *paternosters*. At last he said, 'You may go, on condition that you give yourself plenty of time, and ask to be shown the entire convent. Observe the nuns closely in the choir and wherever else they take you. Make them talk, ask questions, and come back this evening and tell me everything.'

Maréchal, more surprised than ever, went to Port-Royal and did all that was required of him. The King meanwhile waited impatiently, asking for him several times, and when he returned keeping him for more than an hour asking questions and listening to his answers. Maréchal had nothing but praise for the convent; he said that the first words addressed to him were to ask after the King's health, that nowhere was he more fervently prayed for, as he could bear witness, having attended their offices in the choir. He was filled with admiration at their charity, patience, and penitence, and vowed that he had never visited a convent where the saintliness and piety had impressed him more. At the end of this account the King gave a deep sigh and said that evidently they were saints and had been too much persecuted; that too little allowance was made for their ignorance and zealousness, and that people went much too far in criticizing them. This was his honest and sensible reaction to the plain account of an unbiased person speaking freely of what he had observed. But the King was already committed to the views of their enemies, whose influence was paramount with him. This fleeting glimpse of the truth was soon obliterated. He had wholly forgotten it when some years later Père Tellier persuaded him to destroy Port-Royal down to the very stones of the foundations, and to plough over the ground on which it had stood.

Félix had enjoyed the life-time gift of a little house in the Versailles park, at the end of the canal where all the fountains finish. He had made it extraordinarily pretty. The King now gave it to the Comtesse de Gramont. The Comte de Gramont's scandalous memoirs tell how she was Hamilton by birth and how he came to marry her in England. She had been beautiful and well-proportioned and still preserved traces of her good looks and noble breeding. No one was ever wittier than she, nor, despite her haughtiness, pleasanter or more polite. She embellished these qualities, became one of the queen's ladies, spent her life among the best people of the Court, and was always on excellent terms with the King, who delighted in her wit and came to enjoy her free and easy manner in the houses of his mistresses. She was a woman with a past, but had somehow managed to remain respectable and, being well provided with teeth and claws, made herself redoubtable at the Court, even with the ministers, whose goodwill she took little pains to cultivate. Mme de Maintenon feared but could not remove her, for the King was too much diverted in her company. She on her side sensed Mme de Maintenon's dislike and jealousy; she had seen her rise from the gutter to out-top the tallest cedars, but had never brought herself to toady to her.

Mme de Gramont was born of Catholic parents and was sent very young to be educated at Port-Royal. There had remained in her a grain of good seed that recalled her to the practice of her religion even before old age, the world, and her mirror need have caused her to mend her ways. Because of that religious feeling and her early training, her love for those who had taught her, and whom she had never ceased to revere, was stronger than her prudence; and this seemed to provide Mme de Maintenon with the best hope of ruining her with the King. Mme de Maintenon failed none the less, much to her chagrin, for the Comtesse delivered herself with so much grace and wit that the King's rebukes ended in nothing and their intimacy was rather increased than otherwise, even to the point when she could risk an occasional sidelong glance in Mme de Maintenon's direction, and a jest not untinged with malice.

One day, emboldened by success, the Comtesse de Gramont resolved to make a retreat at Port-Royal for the whole of the week of Corpus Christi. Her absence was remarked; the King was bored, and Mme de Maintenon seized on every opportunity to mention where she had gone. On her return the King expressed himself very plainly to her husband, ordering him to repeat his words to the Comtesse, and thus when she came to apologize her excuses were ill-received. She was sent forthwith back to Paris, and the Court went to Marly without her. Towards the end of that excursion she wrote the King a letter, sending it through M. de Gramont; but her friends could not persuade her to write to Mme de Maintenon, nor to send even the shortest message to her. Her letter received no answer. It seemed to have failed; but a few days later when the Court had returned, the King sent word by her husband that she might come. She was shown up to his study by the backstairs, and although she remained quite explicitly firm regarding Port-Royal, she consented to refrain from such thoughtless actions (which is how the King referred to her retreat) and promised to oblige him in that respect. She never called on Mme de Maintenon, whom she continued to see only in the King's presence, as had been her custom, but with him she seemed on better terms than ever.

All this, however, had happened during the previous year. The gift of Félix's little house, which she renamed *Pontallier*, was much remarked upon as a sign of her favour. It soon became the rage to go there, and Mme la Duchesse de Bourgogne and the Princesses visited her very often. Not everyone was welcomed who wished to be invited, and Mme de Maintenon's anger, which she dared not display, kept away only a few of her most ardent admirers and even them not entirely, especially after Mme la Duchesse de Bourgogne had set the example. As for the King, he sometimes liked to display his independence, and indulged his partiality for the Comtesse de Gramont all the more readily for that. At the Court her behaviour was always the same, neither up nor down.

In consolation for that small vexation Mme de Maintenon was delivered from a much greater one—namely her brother, who died at Vichy, still under the vigilant eye of Madot, that priest of Saint-Sulpice, who was shortly afterwards rewarded with a wealthy bishopric. I find that I have nothing further to say regarding M. d'Aubigné. I have already said enough. The King, who detested any signs of mourning, refused to allow Mme de Maintenon to drape her apartment as was then the custom for a brother or a sister, and would not even consent to her women-servants wearing black. She herself was permitted only the very palest mourning, and that for an exceedingly short time. Nothing fell vacant at his death beyond a collar of the Order and the governorship of Berry, which the Comte d'Ayen, her niece's husband, inherited.

On Saturday, 4 August, when the King was at Marly, Mme la Duchesse d'Orléans gave birth to a son at Versailles.[1] M. le Duc d'Orléans went to ask the King's permission for him to bear the title of Duc de Chartres; to which the King replied, 'Is that truly all you desire?' M. le Duc d'Orléans said that members of his household had been urging him to ask for more, but that in such difficult times he thought it would be indiscreet. 'I shall anticipate your request,' said the King, 'and give your son the pension of a senior prince of the blood, fifty thousand francs.' That brought M. le Duc d'Orléans's income up to one million and fifty thousand francs altogether; viz., six hundred and fifty thousand livres of his pension, a hundred thousand livres interest on the dowry of Mme la Duchesse d'Orléans, one hundred and fifty thousand livres of her pension, and fifty thousand of that of M. le Duc de Chartres, aged two days, not counting all Madame's pensions.

Mgr le Duc de Bourgogne, after various minor engagements with the enemy, crossed the Rhine. The Maréchal de Vauban joined him shortly afterwards and on 15 August Brisach was invested. The fortress held out until 6 September and then surrendered with three thousand and five

[1] Louis, later Duc d'Orléans.

hundred men remaining from the original garrison of four thousand. They marched out through the breach with all the honours of war and were escorted to Rheinfels. The defence had been only half-hearted.

Mgr le Duc de Bourgogne conducted himself throughout with honourable distinction, appearing constantly in the trenches where he behaved with quiet, unassuming courage. Marsin, now lieutenant-general, who had been attached to him during the whole of the campaign, often remonstrated with him, but to no effect. His liberality and concern for the wounded, his friendliness, and his proper appreciation of rank and merit in others won all hearts in the army. He was most unwilling to leave, and did so only at the King's repeated command to return to the Court at Fontainebleau, where he arrived on 22 September.

Portugal defected from us at this time, or rather, we deserted Portugal, for we could not fulfil our promise to send a naval force to protect them from the English. They therefore signed a treaty, which was doubly necessary since by themselves they clearly could not deny the enemy the use of their ports. The only way in which the Allies could invade Spain was through Portugal, for the Archduke could land nowhere else, and for that reason alone it would have been infinitely desirable to prevent him and save another costly and dangerous war at a time when we had many armies to maintain on other fronts. For the Allies on the other hand it was of great advantage to create a diversion, and they thus wasted no time in coercing the King of Portugal into signing a treaty, which more than once appeared likely to cost King Philip his throne.

At almost the same moment the Duke of Savoy's treachery was unmasked. Phélypeaux, our ambassador, a more than usually clear-sighted man, had for some time past been issuing warnings, but no one had listened. The treaties, the two royal marriages,[1] the typical blindness and optimism of Vendôme had all seemed reassuring, Mme de Maintenon could not bring herself to think evil of the father of Mme la Duchesse de Bourgogne, Chamillart was convinced by Vendôme and quite carried away by his assurances, and the King viewed everything through their eyes. At last, when it was too late, his eyes were opened. But before telling of the desperate remedy to which we were driven after so long refusing to accept the truth, I must describe the entire change that had come over Spain and return to where I left off.

You will recollect that the Princesse des Ursins had been appointed duenna at the time of the Queen of Spain's marriage, and her behaviour during the queen's nominal regency while the king was absent in Italy. You will therefore be aware that she aspired to govern. Her method was to instil into the young queen a passionate interest in the affairs of State and a longing to play an active part in them. Then, by working on the king's amorous nature and the charms of his wife, to bring about a

[1] Those of the Duchesse de Bourgogne and the Queen of Spain.

triumvirate in government, leaving ceremony to the king and putting the authority into the queen's hands, that is to say into her own. For so vast an enterprise it was vitally necessary to obtain King Louis's approval, for at the beginning at least he ruled the Spanish court no less absolutely than his own, and in this she was wholly successful.

Mme des Ursins conceived this stupendous plot from the moment when she first saw the King and Queen of Spain together. She had won the love and trust of the latter during that first journey from Provence to Barcelona, and was greatly assisted therein by the dismissal of the Piedmontese household and the disgraceful conduct of the Spanish ladies at the wedding-feast. That had made the little queen feel destitute of all other protection so that she gave herself up completely to Mme des Ursins. Her early training and education had been just as good as that of Mme la Duchess de Bourgogne, she was highly intelligent, and for all her immaturity showed herself to be willing, sensible, and firm of purpose. She likewise displayed a patient and enduring courage that was greatly enhanced by her grace and gentleness. The love and devotion of the Spanish people for King Philip, which more than once saved his throne, was largely due to his queen, whom they all still remember with affection and sorrow—all of them, I say, lords, noble ladies, soldiers, and the rabble alike. A young person of such high quality, led by a woman of the calibre of the Princesse des Ursins, was likely to go far, and did so. On the long journeys from Barcelona to Saragossa and from Saragossa to Madrid there was ample time for affection to grow and for some tactful instruction as well, and the provincial parliament of Aragon, which the queen attended for form's sake, served also as an apprenticeship for the duenna, since Spanish etiquette did not permit the queen ever to be unchaperoned in the presence of men.

As I have said, the queen gave her all the trustful love of which a young girl is capable, and never found her otherwise than charming, gentle, amusing, and protective. Mme des Ursins made her most assiduous in attending meetings of the Junta, in order to attend them herself, and with great cunning used the ministers' love of their queen to persuade Cardinal Portocarrero, Archbishop Arias, and Ubilla (whom I shall henceforth refer to as Rivas) to discuss with her the questions of the day before they were raised at the Junta. You may well believe that Mme des Ursins did not fail to curry favour with the French Court meanwhile. She wrote by every post, in letters directed to Mme de Maintenon, detailed accounts of everything concerning the queen, displaying her to the very best advantage; and these letters Mme de Maintenon always passed on to the King. At the same time she was very careful to write also to the King of Spain in Italy, and she trained the queen to write to him and to her sister Mme la Duchesse de Bourgogne. While praising the queen the Princesse des Ursins mentioned affairs of State in the most natural way imaginable since she was a witness of all that took place, then gradually began to comment on them, thus persuading the two monarchs to regard her as a person who, because of her duty to accompany the queen, was thoroughly well-informed, but at the same time neither meddlesome nor ambitious.

Having fully established her authority in Spain, provided that France would support her, she slowly and deliberately coaxed Mme de Maintenon into believing that were she to be given power in State affairs she would use it in blind obedience to that lady's wishes. By that means, she delicately suggested, Mme de Maintenon would rule in Spain even more thoroughly than she did in France, for she would merely issue orders, with no need for finesse. It was Mme de Maintenon's passion to know, meddle with, and control everything, and she listened to the voice of the siren. To govern Spain unhindered by ministers seemed to her perfection and she eagerly accepted, not seeing that in fact Mme des Ursins would rule since nothing would be known save through her and no opinions voiced that were not hers. Thus it was that a close intimacy arose between these two redoubtable women, leading to the almost dictatorial power wielded by Mme des Ursins. Yet such was the latter's cunning and King Louis's weakness that he actually preferred to rule his grandson in this devious way through the queen, rather than direct him openly through the proper channels.

Having successfully taken that giant stride and concluded a secret compact with Mme de Maintenon, the Princesse des Ursins' next move was to snare the King of Spain in the same net. Philip V was naturally inclined to be ruled, and a deliberately repressive training had fixed his character. As Duc d'Anjou he had been the younger brother of a spirited and quick-tempered prince, subject to violent rages and headstrong in the extreme (I say this all the more readily because, as you will see, virtue triumphed in the end). Until recent events he had been regarded as a perpetual subject of France, and therefore a possible danger to his brother unless made completely subservient. Thus they damped his energies and broke his spirit until, by working on a passive and naturally gentle nature, they had made him incapable of thinking or acting for himself, and willing in everything to be guided by others. Extreme piety had been instilled into him, and that too had kept him obedient, since he was given no practice in logic. Thus, despite natural good sense and the ability to think clearly if somewhat slowly, Philip V was perfectly disposed to be governed. But beside these characteristics so favourable to the plans of Mme des Ursins, still another had lately appeared that was totally unlooked for, arising as it did from a struggle between morality and an amorous nature. The prince was now found to possess such a nature, so strongly and abundantly that it inconvenienced him to an almost dangerous degree during his absence in Italy. Everything about

him swelled prodigiously, and the cause of the inflammation, finding no
outlet through organs equally strong, and as yet unaccustomed to yielding
to the calls of nature, flowed back into his blood, resulting in considerable
attacks of the vapours. It was this, in fact, that had speeded his return,
for he could find no relief until he had rejoined the queen. You may judge
from the above how much he was in love with her, and how easy it was
for her to rule him in public affairs, especially under the tutelage of her
clever, ambitious companion.

King Philip soon learned to share his wife's love and respect for Mme
des Ursins and tried by every means to please her. Before long the meetings of the Junta had become a mockery, since all business was done by
the king in private, most often in the presence of the queen and the princess. In any case, he took no decisions until he had discussed the matter
with them, and this practice was not even questioned by our Court. Cardinals d'Estrées and Portocarrero complained bitterly and our ministers
supported them, but all in vain: Mme de Maintenon refused to listen,
and the King thought that he was being subtle in giving more and more
power to the Spanish queen.

The old friendship between the Princesse des Ursins and the two cardinals, on which our Court had chiefly relied, was thus destroyed by her
ambitions and the opportunities which she found for acting alone. Once
sure of ruling the King of Spain through his queen, she did not hesitate
to display her power, and her conduct towards them resulted in endless
bickering and reconciliations, for although not strong enough to be rid of
them entirely, she resolved to drive them beyond endurance by paying
no more heed to them than necessity required. Her first endeavour was to
divide them and destroy them one at a time; but before long they
realized her intentions and united against her. The open quarrels that
ensued provoked a public scandal. Meantime, Harcourt, who was still
hoping to be made a minister and still in Mme de Maintenon's confidence,
decided to become involved in the affair since he had now no other excuse
for private interviews. He accordingly struck up a friendship by correspondence with Mme des Ursins, who was glad of his advice regarding
the Spanish court, where she was still relatively a newcomer. His conversations with the King were renewed, which they never would have been
had the affairs of Spain been conducted through the ambassador and
ministers in the usual way.

Thus there was hindrance to our ambassador, hindrance to our ministers, and to those of Spain as well, complete mystery surrounding our
intentions and those who executed them, and absolute frustration for
the Estrées family who saw themselves supplanted by the Princesse des
Ursins. And all this time private discussions were taking place between
Mme de Maintenon and the King, mostly in the presence of the Duc
d'Harcourt, who readily sacrificed his friendship with Portocarrero and

all the benefits he had derived therefrom in order to keep Mme des Ursins secretly informed on matters of importance.

As for Louville, who had been King Philip's confidant and guide, he now found himself cast aside. The gaiety and high spirits that had so cheered the king, his vigilance, and the trust reposed in him by our ministers had all seemed dangerous to Mme des Ursins. She had set the queen against him before ever he returned, and Harcourt ruined him with Mme de Maintenon by representing him as being devoted to the Duc de Beauvilliers whom she could not abide. When Louville returned to Spain he found his lodging gone (for after the queen's arrival men were excluded from the palace) and without a lodging his meetings with the king were rare, for the latter spent his time either in the queen's apartments or in those of the Princesse des Ursins which were adjacent. All the business of the kingdom was disposed of there, out of the sight of the ministers of either court. Orry, who now administered the finances, made a fourth in those deliberations, and the results were communicated to the Junta on the following day, or even later on many occasions.

Thus the Princesse des Ursins and Orry between them ruled Spain, with no one to gainsay them, for they used Rivas like a mere secretary, waiting only for the moment when they could be quit of him altogether, as they were quit of all those who had been most concerned with executing the will of Charles II. The few Frenchmen who had followed King Philip to Madrid were now recalled to France, with the exception of two or three who had endeared themselves in time to Mme des Ursins. The Junta became useless for any purpose of the two cardinals, and to make it doubly so and to fatigue those elderly gentlemen, she arranged for it to meet at ten o'clock at night. After they ceased to attend it became a waste of time since only Rivas remained. Yet the wide scope of the latter's appointments continued to cause her anxiety, and she conceived the idea of removing both him and his offices so as to avoid the need for a successor. She accordingly arranged to disassociate him from all his posts, comprising every government department except those of finance and commerce, which were administered unofficially by Orry. You may well imagine that little remained to poor Rivas after being denuded of so many responsibilities. That however was only a prelude, for soon afterwards he was dismissed altogether. He survived the loss of offices and fortune in an obscurity that ended only with his death twenty-five years later, but during that time he had the satisfaction of seeing very many changes and the downfall of his enemy.

On Wednesday, 19 September, the King slept at Sceaux[1] and went on next day to Fontainebleau. On 3 October the English court paid a visit, returning to Saint-Germain on the 16th. News was received that the

[1] The Duc du Maine's country house.

Emperor had declared the Archduke[1] King of Spain and made no secret of the fact that he was sending him at once to invade Spain through Portugal. It was learned at the same time that a victory had been won over the Imperial army at Hochstaedt,[2] with great slaughter; four thousand Austrians left dead on the field, and as many more taken prisoner, together with great numbers of standards, ensigns, and drums, thirty-three pieces of cannon, boats and pontoon bridges, and all their baggage. We lost less than a thousand men; in fact it was a triumph for the Elector and Villars. A courier, sent twenty-four hours later by the Maréchal de Villars to report in detail, gave assurances that the defeated army could not be reformed in this campaign, and said that the Elector was preparing to march against Prince Louis of Baden, who was lying before Augsburg with twenty thousand men. At the end of October the Archduke arrived in Holland and was recognized as Charles III by the Dutch Republic, England, Portugal, Brandenburg, Savoy, Hanover, and most of the other European powers. The Pope, however, whom the Emperor informed by letter, sent the envelope back unopened when he learned what it contained.

The war was drawing very close to Spain, and King Philip made Tserclaes[3] return from Flanders to command his troops, with other general-officers to serve under him. The King received him most graciously when he passed through France, and decided to send a French army as well under the Duke of Berwick, with Puységur as second-in-command, in sole charge of the infantry, cavalry and dragoons. Puységur was a gentleman of Soissons, no more, but his family was of ancient and noble origin, and he was of a kind to make a distinguished career as a soldier, or even a statesman. He had risen in the King's regiment of Infantry to the rank of lieutenant-colonel, which is where the King had first learned to appreciate his ability and extraordinary keenness, coupled with a modesty and candour that remained with him all through his life in every rank and employment. Under no consideration would he tell the King other than the plain truth, for which King Louis much esteemed him, often having private interviews with him, some of them in the presence of Mme de Maintenon. He was not afraid to oppose the Maréchal de Villeroy and M. de Vendome[4] despite all their favour, or to produce arguments to show that he was right. We shall soon see Puységur moving in higher spheres, for the King made him resign his colonelcy to make

[1] The Archduke Charles (1685–1740), the Emperor Leopold I's second son, who was later proclaimed Charles III of Spain by the Allies, although never recognised as such in Spain. He became Charles VI, Holy Roman Emperor (1711).

[2] Hochstaedt in Bavaria. One of several French victories over the Imperial armies in 1703. At Blindheim (Blenheim) near Hochstaedt Marlborough and Prince Eugene crushingly edfeated the French army in the following year.

[3] Albert Octavius von Tserclaes, Count Tilly (1646–1715), a grand-nephew of the famous Austrian general Tilly.

[4] Vendôme hated him because he openly criticized his personal conduct and idleness in command.

better use of him with greater responsibilities. In the end he rose to be a Marshal of France with everyone's approval, and received the Order as well. Puységur combined great honesty with a readiness to do others justice in his reports; his heart and mind were ruled solely by love for his country, often at the risk of his own advancement. He could stand firm and needed many times to do so, and he never weakened; but none the less he never forgot his place.

Twenty battalions, seven regiments of cavalry and two of dragoons marched to Spain, and many generals were ordered to go there also; in the meantime Villadarias the commandant in Andalusia caused considerable disturbance among the Portuguese in Algarve by invading them with six thousand men before the Allies had shown any signs of fulfilling their promises. Mme des Ursins, at this point somewhat embarrassed by the retirement of the two cardinals and the dismissal of all the former ministers, proceeded to cover her tracks by a piece of absolute sharp practice. She quickly formed a new Junta, composed of Don Manuel Arias, governor of the council of Castile, whom she detained on the king's authority just as he was leaving for his archbishopric of Seville, the Marquis of Mancera, and the Abbé d'Estrées as French Ambassador. She kept them in session as long as seemed necessary to lull the storm, and meanwhile took care to see that they dealt with nothing important. She employed them with trifles suitable for any sub-committee, whilst the serious work was done in the queen's apartments, or in her own, with Orry making a fourth with the king. The decisions arrived at between them were communicated to Rivas or to the secretaries of State for war or foreign affairs, and put into execution forthwith if speed were necessary. Arias was the only one of sufficient consequence or ability to trouble her; as for the abbé, having rid herself of his uncle, she welcomed him. He was well-proportioned, urbane, not remarkably intelligent, eaten up with vanity, almost fatuous on the subject of himself, his talents, the glory and high employment of his family, and his own diplomatic missions, and although honourable and possessed of a great desire to do well he made many blunders and was often ridiculed. His way of life had barred him from the episcopacy; regard for his family, especially for his uncle the cardinal, had caused that slur to be concealed by employing him abroad. To listen to him one might have thought his posts had been of immense importance, but in fact there had been little, often nothing for him to do. He was not rich and kept a sharp eye on his money. He had been our ambassador to Portugal but had carefully avoided that country, and Cardinal d'Estrées, who never resisted a joke even on the subject of his family, used to say that he had made his exit from Portugal without making his entrance. Mancera, the third of the councillors, was so ancient that the Princesse des Ursins felt perfectly at ease with him. You shall soon see how she managed to rid herself even of this shadow of a Junta.

The Duke of Alba, the new Spanish ambassador, arrived in Paris with his wife the Duchess, and his only son who was still a child. He was the ninth duke. His father,[1] who died in 1701, had married the paternal aunt of the Dukes of Arcos and Banos, that is to say one of the Ponce de Leon family. He was a widower, a knight of the Golden Fleece, had held many high offices, and finally became a counsellor of State. He was a man of vast intelligence and some learning, but was sadly eccentric. When Philip V arrived in Spain he expressed great pleasure, giving vent to many bitter and diverting jibes against the Austrian royal family, including several noblemen who were generally thought to be his friends. Louville was sent to pay a call on him at Madrid. He discovered him in a somewhat filthy state, on his right side between two sheets, where he had been for months past without changing his position or allowing them to make his bed. He said he had no strength to get up; yet his health was excellent. The fact was that he was in despair because his mistress had grown tired of him and had left him. He had sent out parties to search for her throughout the whole of Spain, and, such is piety in countries of the Inquisition, had had masses and prayers said in the churches for her return. Finally he had taken this vow to remain in bed without shifting off his right side until she was recaptured. That piece of folly he confessed to Louville as though it were a matter of some gravity and perfectly reasonable. Many visitors called to see him, some of them of the highest birth, for he was good company. With that vow to hamper him he was unable to play any part at the death of Charles II or at the accession of Philip V, whom he never saw despite his protestations of loyalty. He carried on in this absurd fashion until the day he died, never leaving his bed nor turning off his right side. This was such extraordinary behaviour, and so clearly proved that I thought it worth mentioning of a man who in all other ways was sensible and intelligent.

His only son, Don Antonio Martinez de Toledo, the ambassador to whom he always referred as Martin, as is becoming the fashion in Spain, was not prepossessing to look at, but was both intelligent and learned, very prudent, wise, and dignified, filling his post in these tragic times with courage and good judgment, greatly to the satisfaction of his court and ours, by whom he was truly esteemed and treated with marked respect. His wife was exceedingly lively and even more hideous than himself; she caused a little merriment at first, but in the end Society became accustomed to her. Both were intensely pious, he very sound in doctrine, she more after the Spanish fashion; they kept great state in France. The Duke of Alba made his bow privately to the King in his study as soon as he arrived. His wife was also presented in the study after the King's supper, by the Duchesse du Lude, who was especially nominated for that

---

[1] Antonio, 8th Duke of Alba. He was so old that they nicknamed him the 'Eternal Father'.

duty. The King remained standing and talked with her for some considerable time. The Duchesse du Lude then escorted her through the
gallery to Mme la Duchesse de Bourgogne's apartments, to which the
latter had returned immediately after supper so as to be ready to receive
her. Everything was more brightly lit than usual. Mme la Duchesse de
Bourgogne greeted her standing and kissed her both coming and going;
the King only kissed her on arrival. Afterwards the Duchess of Alba
called on Madame and on Mme la Duchesse d'Orléans, but without the
Duchesse du Lude. Everyone was pleased to give them that unusually
cordial welcome, for the Duc d'Harcourt had made known their affection
for France, demonstrated on more than one occasion.

The King and the Emperor faced war within as well as without their
frontiers. The Malcontents of Hungary, in terrifying numbers, supported
by many of the lords and nobles, had captured some of the mountain
towns of Hungary and part of the mines. Many castles had been surrendered to them, where they had seized a number of cannons. Parties of
them had come down on to the plain and were appearing in arms in the
neighbourhood of Pressburg. Armed bands were setting fire to villages of
which the flames were visible from Vienna, and the Emperor himself was
nearly taken by surprise at a hunting-lodge where he was dining. That had
alarmed him sufficiently to make him send to Pressburg for the crown of
Hungary and have it taken to Vienna for safe-keeping.

Meanwhile the Fanatics in Languedoc and the Cévennes were engaging a large body of our troops, who from time to time hacked to pieces
a small group, but did little damage to the main forces. Some Dutchmen
were captured bringing them arms and money as well as splendid promises
of help. Geneva also kept them secretly as well supplied as possible, and
furnished them with preachers.

The year ended with another dispute in which I played an even more
prominent role. On certain church festivals when the King went to high
mass and vespers a lady of the Court always handed round a collecting bag
for the poor. The Queen, or when there was no longer a queen the
Dauphine, nominated ladies for each occasion, and in the interval between the two Dauphines Mme de Maintenon took on herself the task of
selection. So long as there were maids of honour one of them was always
chosen, but when these posts were abolished a young lady of the Court
was nominated, as I have described above. The Lorraines, whose high
rank was gained solely by their exploits at the time of the *Ligue*, and who
had since cunningly improved their position by constant vigilance and
intrigue, were always ready to snatch an opportunity. They were copied
by others who had managed to extract similar rank from the King.[1] These
slyly began to avoid the task of handing round the bag, so as to make it

[1] Saint-Simon is referring to the so-called 'foreign princes' and in particular to the Duc de
Rohan, who, so he thought, did not qualify in any way for a princely title.

their right and privilege to abstain and thus, as by their marriages, to insinuate themselves on a level with princesses of the blood. It was a long time before anyone observed or even suspected what they were at, but at last the Duchesse de Noailles, her daughter the Duchesse de Guiche, and the Maréchale de Boufflers discovered what was afoot. Others began to see and to talk of it, and they spoke to me also. Mme de Saint-Simon happened to be at the King's vespers one day in full court-dress. It was the feast of the Conception when there had been no high mass, and Mme la Duchesse de Bourgogne had forgotten to name a lady; she therefore threw the bag to my wife, who handed it round when the time came. At that moment we none of us had any idea that the Lorraine princesses would use that as an excuse to abstain when it was their turn.

After I was warned, I determined that all the other duchesses should be equally crafty until the chance came to make things even. The Duchesse de Noailles spoke to the Duchesse du Lude, but being faint-hearted she merely shrugged her shoulders, and there was always some new, ignorant, or timid duchess willing to collect from time to time. At last the Duchesse du Lude was fairly tormented by the Duchesse de Noailles into speaking to Mme la Duchesse de Bourgogne, who determined to see just how far the Lorraines intended to go. Accordingly, at the next festival, she named Mme de Montbazon. That lady was young, pretty, often present at the Court, and in every way fitted to give a lead to others, but she happened to be in Paris, where it was fashionable to go before the Christmas festivals. She sent excuses, pretending to be ill although in fact in perfect health, spent half a day in bed, and afterwards went about as usual. After that nothing more was needed to reveal a plot. Neither the Duchesse du Lude nor even Mme la Duchesse de Bourgogne herself dared to pursue the matter further though the latter was much annoyed, with the result that from that time onwards no duchess had either the will or the courage to take round the bag. The other ladies of suitable rank soon perceived what was happening. They saw that the duty of the collection was being left entirely to them and they, too, began to shirk it, so that after a time it fell into all sorts of hands and was sometimes omitted altogether.

The matter was pushed so far that eventually the King grew angry and was on the point of making Mme la Duchesse de Bourgogne herself collect. That I heard from the palace-ladies, who wished to prevent us from going to Paris, and attempted to frighten me by saying that the King had not forgiven me for leaving the service and that the storm would break on my head. It was certainly true that I still was not going to Marly and was in the same situation with him as I described earlier. They then flattered me by suggesting that this might prove to be my opportunity. I therefore agreed to remain on condition that my wife was not asked to collect, but since no such assurance could be given me we went to Paris. The next to refuse was the Maréchale de Cœuvres, on the plea that she was a grandee of Spain, and the Duchesse de Noailles sent her daughter as a substitute. On still another of the festivals Chamillart's two daughters, both duchesses,[1] were nominated, and both refused although they were not able to leave Versailles. It was then that the rocket went up.

The King had been greatly exasperated by the intrigues, and ordered Monsieur le Grand, to make his daughter collect in church on New Year's Day, 1704. Early next day I was warned by the Comtesse de Roucy, who had been told by Mme la Duchesse de Bourgogne who was present at the time, that the King had gone to Mme de Maintenon looking very grave, exclaiming that he was extremely vexed with the dukes because they showed less willingness than the princes; that none of the duchesses would collect, but that Monsieur le Grand had consented for his daughter as soon as asked. He had added that the behaviour of two or three of the dukes he would never forget. Mme la Duchesse de Bourgogne would not name them out loud, but she whispered to Mme de Dangeau and a moment later asked her to advise me to be careful. We heard this at the Chancellor's house, he having been a third party to the conversation, and neither of us had any doubt that I was one of the dukes mentioned. I then explained what had happened and asked the Chancellor for his advice, which was to do nothing until I had learned more.

Very early next day I went to see Chamillart. He told me that at Mme de Maintenon's apartment on the previous evening, even before he had had time to open his portfolio, the King had asked him angrily what he thought of those dukes who were less compliant than the princes, and had hastily added that Mlle d'Armagnac[2] agreed to take round the bag. Chamillart replied that such matters never reached his department and that he had first heard of the affair on the previous evening. He said that he knew the dukes were unhappy because the King blamed them for not divining his wishes, and that the princes were delighted at receiving credit for something which the dukes would gladly have done had the King spoken to them as frankly as he did to Monsieur le Grand.

The King had muttered something to himself, and then continued that it was very strange, but that since I had left his service I thought of nothing but rank and privilege and picked quarrels with everyone; that I was the chief instigator of all this fuss, and that he had a good mind to send me away so far that I should be unable to annoy him for a very long time. Chamillart said that I concerned myself with such matters because I was abler and more intelligent than most, and that since the King had given me my rank and precedence he should not be displeased at seeing me protect them. Then, smiling a little, he had added soothingly

---

[1] The Duchesse de La Feuillade, and the Duchesse de Lorges.
[2] M. le Grand's daughter, whom Saint-Simon might have married.

that the King could of course send anyone wherever he pleased, but that
it seemed a great deal of trouble when a single word would have the same
effect. The King was not, however, mollified. He merely said that what
had most of all annoyed him was the refusal of Chamillart's own daughters
(especially the younger), through their husbands and apparently at my
suggestion. To this Chamillart had replied that one of his sons-in-law
was absent and the other had merely made his wife conform. The King
had still continued to grumble until at last they settled down to work.
Chamillart strongly advised me to speak to him at the earliest possible
opportunity, so as to explain the dukes' point of view regarding the
collections, and then to say something in my own defence. After I left
him I went to consult the Chancellor. He too advised me to see the King
without delay. He said that to wait would merely increase his annoyance,
and that in talking to him I must take care not to appear angry. He bade
me be hopeful regarding the outcome, ask for an audience in the study,
and if the King should stop and wish to hear me then and there, to say
that I could see he did not wish to give me an audience at that time, that
I hoped it might be for another, and instantly retire. It was indeed no
small matter for me, so young and out of favour, to go and engage the
King in private conversation.[1]

I usually did nothing without the advice of the Duc de Beauvilliers.
Mme de Saint-Simon, however, did not wish me to consult him, for she
was sure that he would tell me to write, which would be less tactful and
less effective than speaking; besides which, letters were never answered.
She thought also that Beauvilliers's advice might be embarrassing if it
was contrary to that of the two ministers. I agreed with her, and went to
wait for the King to pass on his way from dinner to his study, to which I
asked leave to follow him. Without answering he made a sign for me to
enter and walked over to one of the window-recesses.

Just as I was about to speak I saw Fagon and other members of his
household cross the room, so I waited until they had gone and I was left
alone with the King. I then told him that I had heard he was vexed with
me because of the affair of the collection; that I was deeply anxious to
please him and could endure no delay in begging him to hear my side.
At this he looked very severe and said nothing. 'Sire,' I continued, 'it is
indeed true that after the princesses refused to hand round the bag I
avoided that duty for Mme de Saint-Simon, in the hope that all the
duchesses would abstain, and some of them I actually prevented, thinking
that Your Majesty would approve.' 'But,' interrupted the King angrily,
'refusing the Duchesse de Bourgogne shows a lack of respect. It is refusing
Us!' I answered that the manner in which the ladies had been named gave

---

[1] Anyone might whisper a request into the King's wig as he walked to or from the chapel.
The almost invariable answer being, 'We shall see!' That was an 'interview'. To speak in the
study was an 'audience', and a very solemn occasion.

us the impression that Mme la Duchess de Bourgogne had no hand in the nominations and that the Duchesse du Lude, or more frequently the first gentlewoman-in-waiting, chose whomsoever she pleased. 'Monsieur,' interrupted the King once more in the same angry tone, 'you have been speechifying, have you not?' 'No, Sire.' 'What?' are you saying that you have not talked? . . .' He ran on in this furious manner until I, also, developed enough courage to interrupt in a voice louder than his own. 'No, Sire,' I said again, 'I have already explained, and had I said anything else I should have told Your Majesty, just as I have frankly admitted avoiding for my wife and preventing the other duchesses. I have always believed, and with good cause, that since Your Majesty expressed no wishes in this matter you were either ignorant of what was happening, or knowing did not care. Let me most earnestly entreat you to believe that had any of the dukes, more especially myself, any reason to think that you desired it in the very least, all the duchesses would have been eager to take round the bag, and Mme de Saint-Simon with them, on all the festivals. If that did not show my desire to please you I would gladly have handed the bag myself like any country churchwarden.

'How, Sire,' I continued, 'could Your Majesty imagine that we should think any duty beneath us that was performed in your gracious presence, more especially one which duchesses and princesses do every day in the Paris churches as a matter of course? The truth is, Sire, that the princes are so quick to snatch special privileges that we have to be on the watch, particularly in this matter of refusing to collect.' 'But they did not refuse,' said the King, albeit somewhat mollified, 'they were never asked.' 'Indeed, Sire,' said I stoutly, 'they did refuse, not the Lorraines, but others' (by whom I meant Mme de Montbazon). 'The Duchesse du Lude may have informed you of that, or if not she should have done so, for that was what decided us to act. We know that Your Majesty is plagued with arguments and rulings, and we hoped that our evading the collection would have sufficed to prevent the princes from taking advantage. As I have already said, Sire, we believed that Your Majesty neither knew nor cared since you made no sign.' 'Oh! very well, Monsieur,' said the King quietly, 'the matter will not arise again because I have already told Monsieur le Grand that I wish his daughter to collect on New Year's Day, and I am glad for her to set the example, for I care much for her father.'

Looking straight at the King I then entreated him, for my own sake and for that of the other dukes, to believe that he had no more obedient subjects than ourselves, for we knew that all our dignities came from him and that our lives were enriched by his bounty. He was our King, our universal benefactor, the absolute master of our rank and privileges; it was for him alone to raise or lower them, to treat them as his own, in the hollow of his hand. Then, most graciously, with an air wholly kind and gentle, he said several times that that was a very proper way of thinking and speaking, and that he was well pleased with me. I seized the opportunity to tell him how much it grieved me that no matter how hard I tried to please him some people never failed to do me disservices, which I confessed I could not forgive. I added that I could not help but suspect Monsieur le Grand, for he had not forgiven me since the affair with the Princesse d'Harcourt.[1] 'But,' I said, 'Your Majesty saw then that I was speaking the truth, whereas Monsieur le Grand was not. I think Your Majesty will remember, so I shall not trouble you by repeating.'

The King said that he did remember perfectly, and I think that he would have heard me patiently had I chosen to repeat the story, for his manner was both kind and considerate, but I did not think it wise to detain him any longer. I therefore concluded by imploring him to be so gracious as to tell me if ever he heard ill spoken of me, for he would see that so great a favour would swiftly be followed either by a justification, or a confession and a plea for forgiveness. When I had finished speaking he was silent a little while, as though wishing to see whether I had more to say. He then left me with a slight, but most markedly gracious bow, saying that now all was explained and that he was satisfied. I retired bowing very low, feeling mightily relieved and at the same time most thankful that I had managed to put the whole matter before him about the dukes, the princes, and especially about M. le Grand. The fact that the King had remembered the affair of the Princesse d'Harcourt, and his silence over M. le Grand, convinced me that I owed to the last named the trouble which I once again had circumvented.

As I left the King's study looking greatly pleased, I encountered Monsieur le Duc and some other gentlemen waiting to attend the King's *botter*.[2] They stared at me as they passed, for they were surprised by the length of my audience, which had lasted a full half-hour. It was exceedingly rare for private persons to be granted any audience at all, and none lasted more than half that time. I went straight back to my apartment and relieved Mme de Saint-Simon of her anxiety.

---

[1] A quarrel over precedence between the Princesse d'Harcourt and the Duchesse de Rohan in which Mme de Saint-Simon had innocently been involved.
[2] The ceremony of putting on the King's boots.

CHAPTER XIV

1704

[*At the end of the campaign of 1703 the French had gained control of the Moselle and, by the capture of Landau, of the Upper Rhine. They could now march freely into Germany and on to Austria (because Bavaria was now on their side). The Emperor was attacked from within by the Hungarian Malcontents, and a strong Franco-Bavarian army on the frontier was preparing to press on even to Vienna. The Holy Roman Empire seemed about to disintegrate. In the spring of 1704 it looked as though the Grand Alliance, reduced to England and the Dutch Republic alone, would collapse altogether.*

In those circumstances the Allies decided that as soon as the campaign opened Marlborough should march the British army and as many troops as the Dutch could spare six hundred miles across Germany to the Danube, there link up with the Imperial army, and rescue the Emperor by attacking the French and Bavarians.

This plan was so bold and kept so secret that the French marshals in the Low Countries and Germany were completely foxed. They expected Marlborough to campaign along the Moselle, or in Alsace, or march to besiege Frankfurt, or attempt to recapture Landau. They therefore waited for the King's orders, meaning to intercept Marlborough as soon as he turned along one or other of the rivers leading to those objectives. But the British army marched steadily eastwards away from them, and by the time that they realized Marlborough's intentions it was too late to stop him.

On 1 July Marlborough met the Margrave of Baden (commander-in-chief of the Imperial army) and Prince Eugene (second-in-command) near Ulm on the Danube. They decided that the two former should join forces and attack the French and Bavarians, whilst Prince Eugene marched to the Rhine to prevent Villeroy and Tallard from coming to the help of the Bavarian Elector.

On 13 August the Battle of Blenheim was fought. The French and Bavarians suffered a catastrophic, murderous defeat, from which the France of Louis XIV never recovered.

The commanders
>   On the Danube. *The Elector of Bavaria and Marsin opposing the Margrave Prince Louis of Baden and Marlborough.*
>   On the Rhine. *Villeroy and Tallard opposing, at the end of the campaign, Prince Eugene.*
>   In Italy. *Vendôme.*
>   In Portugal. *Berwick and Puységur.*]

The Comte d'Ayen becomes Duc de Noailles – Death of Bossuet – The Archduke reaches Lisbon via England – Negligence and crimes of Orry – Disgrace of the Princesse des Ursins – The Duc de Gramont ambassador to Spain, his

character and disgraceful marriage – He attracts the King's anger by display-
ing too much subtlety – Princesse des Ursins banished to Toulouse – The Duke
of Mantua in Paris incognito – Deceit of M. de Vendôme – Movement of the
armies – Birth of the Duc de Bretagne – Battle of Blenheim – After the
Battle – Naval victory off Malaga – Return of Orry – Pedigree, assassination
and character of Vervins, the strangeness of his latter days – Alarming inter-
lude in the dazzling career of the Duchesse de Bourgogne – Tessé en route
for Spain visits Mme des Ursins – Return of the Comte de Toulouse — The Duc
d'Orléans's untimely jest – Death of Mme d'Aiguillon – Berwick commands in
Languedoc

AT THE beginning of the year, the Maréchal-duc de Noailles at last
obtained Mme de Maintenon's consent to transferring his dukedom to his
son the Comte d'Ayen, who took the title Duc de Noailles, whilst his
father continued to be styled Maréchal de Noailles. Mme de Maintenon
had firmly refused to allow her niece to be seated when she married;
and had obliged her to earn her *tabouret* by a few years delay. She had
these bashful moments, strong whiffs of the sewers from which she
sprang, but they were not more than skin deep.

The Church and Society at this time lost two prelates who shone most
brilliantly in either sphere. Bossuet, Bishop of Meaux, was one, the other
was the famous Cardinal von Fürstenberg. Both are too well known for
me to have anything to say of men so greatly and diversely celebrated.
The first will ever be lamented and was so universally at his death, for his
noble works even in his extreme old age put to shame many learned and
industrious bishops and scholars in the prime of their lives. The other,
after having troubled and influenced all Europe for so long, had been
for some considerable time nothing but a useless encumbrance. Chamillart
obtained the post of first almoner to Mme la Duchesse de Bourgogne
for that imbecile brother of his who was Bishop of Senlis, and Bissy,
Bishop of Toul, was finally persuaded to accept Meaux. A diocese close
to Paris seemed to him most likely to advance his ambitions, and he had
great hopes of Meaux, which was within range of the Court and would
thus give him opportunities to use his wits, as he soon demonstrated.

The Archduke after a long wait in Holland and Southern Germany
whilst preparations were being made for his voyage to Spain, had encountered terrible gales that twice drove him to shelter in England, where
on the first occasion he visited Queen Anne and her ministers. He had
arrived in Portugal with very little support and found that everything
necessary was lacking there. That great impediment, and the loyalty of
the Spaniards to their king, were not what he had been led to expect, for
the Constable of Castile had assured him that all Spain was in revolt.
Since nothing stirred, apart from a few individuals either when the Archduke arrived or later, the Constable was entirely discredited.

I have deferred until now the following event and some others, because they will be more understandable and agreeable if read altogether rather than separately, and especially since the last of them occurred not later than the end of May. You will remember the Princesse des Ursins' brilliant situation in Spain and the firm support which she had won at Versailles, depriving the King's ministers of all knowledge and part in Spanish affairs, and dealing directly with Mme de Maintenon and the King. Only Harcourt was in their confidence. M. de Beauvilliers, who could see no hope of redress, was driven to ask the King to excuse him from having anything to do with Spain. The Chancellor had heard nothing of that country for months past, and, as for Chamillart, he was far too much burdened by the work of the finance and war departments to have noticed that anything was amiss. Had it not been for his intimacy with the Dukes of Chevreuse and Beauvilliers he might not have been unwelcome to the two ladies, but he had no leisure for other matters, and they pretended out of consideration for him to say nothing of Spain beyond very brief requests for troops and funds, etc., which were within the natural scope of his departments.

In Spain, the princess and Orry governed alone. They alone distributed offices and favours and decided everything, with d'Aubigny[1] often making a third, and the queen present when she felt so disposed but always agreeing with them. King Philip allowed his days to be governed by the queen. If he wished to change anything in his usual time-table for hunting, *mail*,[2] or other sports, he sent Vazet his French barber, who was devoted to Mme des Ursins, to ask her permission, and was guided by the answer she returned. He thus fell into a habit of submission,[3] and every evening went to the queen's, or more often to Mme des Ursins' apartments, to learn what they had settled that day, and to give them the agenda for next day's meeting of the council for their consideration. On the following morning he informed the council of their rulings; not that the members were permitted to vote on them, they met only for form's sake and to hear from Rivas the edicts which he had written down at the king's dictation. As for the French ambassador, the Abbé d'Estrées, he dared not question anything; if he wished to make some observation he made it privately to Mme des Ursins and Orry, who barely listened to him and proceeded as before. The princess's power was thus absolute, and her only concern was to remove from her path anyone who appeared likely to wish to obstruct, or demand even a tiny share of her authority.

---

[1] Jean Bouteroue d'Aubigny. Handsome and humorous, says Saint-Simon, very broad bodily and in his wit, he had been for many years the princess's so-called equerry.

[2] The game of *pall-mall*, an old game resembling croquet. It was played in an alley, hence the name of the London street.

[3] Louville said of him, '*C'est un roi qui ne règne pas et ne règnera jamais.*' He was always the tool of someone, his wife, Mme des Ursins, his grandfather, or his confessors.

The arrival of the Archduke in Portugal at this time required that
Berwick and Puységur should be with the French army on the frontier.
Puységur was the first to leave. The King had given him the sole responsibility for the administration of the troops, magazines, and supplies,
that is to say for all the ordering, inspection, and distribution, and, having
done so, was confident that every measure had been taken to ensure a
successful war in Spain. From the Pyrenees as far as Madrid Puységur
found everything in perfect readiness for the supply of the French troops,
and he returned glowing reports. At Madrid he worked with Orry, who
showed him on paper that all the warehouses on the road to the Portuguese frontier and along the frontier itself were filled and ready, with more
than sufficient provisions for the army and all the monies necessary for the
campaign. Puységur, with his honest, truthful nature, and having seen for
himself that all was in perfect order between the Pyrenees and Madrid,
did not for a moment imagine that Orry might have neglected the frontier,
especially not since there was a chance of winning the war outright before
the Archduke received support from the Allies. Still less did he suspect
that Orry, the minister responsible, had had the effrontery to show him
documentary evidence of plans none of which had been put into effect.
Thus, feeling perfectly confident, Puységur wrote again to the King
highly praising Orry, and therefore by implication Mme des Ursins, for
wise and prudent administration.

Puységur then left Madrid for the Portuguese frontier to make an
inspection and final adjustments, so that when the French army and its
commander arrived the troops might immediately go into action. What
was his horror when he found that on the road from Madrid to the frontier
nothing was prepared to victual an army on the march, and that along the
frontier itself there was nothing at all of what Orry had shown him on
paper. Puységur could hardly bring himself to believe the criminal negligence evident on every side. He went personally to inspect the storehouses which Orry's maps had marked as being overflowing with provisions. All were empty, not even cleaned. You may imagine his disgust
at having been so cheated. He reported at once to the King, admitting his
fault, if such it could be called, in having believed Orry and his papers,
and immediately set himself to do, not what was originally planned, for
that was now out of the question, but at least the best possible so as to
allow the army to subsist whilst fighting a campaign.

Orry's behaviour, his downright insolence in deceiving a man who
would immediately discover the truth, seems utterly incomprehensible.
One can understand a rogue cheating, but not of having the audacity to
deceive regarding facts so soon to be unmasked; and yet that was exactly
what Orry, with the assistance of the Princesse des Ursins, did, trusting
in the spell which together they had cast over Versailles. Such was their
blindness, moreover, that at this critical moment when they should

have been terrified at the probable effects of their misconduct, Mme des Ursins committed her crowning folly.

She had so securely pinioned the wretched Abbé d'Estrées (who believed, I know not why, that his entire future depended on his holding his sorry post in Spain), that he had consented to the incredible proposal that he—the French ambassador—should write to the King only after first consulting her, and show her his letters before sending them. Such bondage would have hindered a man in any situation; it was sheer folly for an ambassador, destructive alike to his own interests and to those of his employer; at last it became so intolerable even to the Abbé d'Estrées that he began to cheat her of an occasional despatch. His cunning, however, was no match for her vigilance; she soon received word of it from the post-office and took steps to be informed at the first opportunity. She was so notified and acted with all speed. She sent for the ambassador's private letter to the King, opened it, and as she suspected, found little to like in the contents. What most enraged her was that in describing the meetings of the committee composed of herself, Orry, and d'Aubigny, the abbé had grossly exaggerated d'Aubigny's influence, adding that he was constantly at her elbow and that no one doubted but that they were secretly wed. This put her into such a fury that she wrote in the margin in her own hand the words, 'His wife, never!' and showed the despatch in that condition to the King and Queen of Spain and to many of the courtiers, thus creating an alarming disturbance. To crown that piece of folly, she proceeded to forward the abbé's letter to King Louis, with the note written on the margin, bitterly complaining of him for having the insolence to send a despatch without first consulting her, and for the abominable suggestion regarding the marriage. Meanwhile the Abbé d'Estrées was complaining equally bitterly of her violation of the posts and the disrespect shown by opening and making public a private letter addressed to the King of France by his ambassador.

At this point the Queen of Spain, urged on by the princess, made such an appalling scene with the abbé that his continuance in Spain as ambassador became an impossibility. As for King Philip, he took little part in the quarrel, but that little was on the side of Mme des Ursins. Perhaps the sound judgment and sense of fitness that were his fundamentally, though he kept them repressed beneath frigid inertia, showed him the enormity of her action, perhaps he was incapable of decisive action on anyone's behalf. Be that as it may, he did not act.

It so happened that Puységur's despatch from the frontiers of Portugal reached the King shortly before the Princesse des Ursins's letter. It put King Louis most violently against Orry, and against the princess herself, for they were considered to have acted together, and she had written supporting his lies in every possible way. Our ministers, who had abandoned Spain only out of desperation, took advantage of the King's visible anger

to attack the whole government of Spain in the hope of retrieving something of their proper functions. Harcourt, meanwhile, used every endeavour to support Mme de Maintenon in defending Orry. He realized
full well that his future depended on the success of Mme des Ursins, and
that if she were to fall the ministers would not tolerate any further interference by him. The outcome was in the balance when that fatal letter
and the forwarded despatch arrived from the princess, together with her
bitter complaints of the Abbé d'Estrées, addressed both to the King and
the ministers. The scandal was too great and had been too public for
King Louis to avoid discussing it with the latter. Puységur's accusations
against Orry and the best means of restoring the situation had in some
degree already been considered. Mme des Ursins' letter, arriving at that
precise moment, seemed to provide convincing proof against both of them.
From that instant they were doomed. Mme de Maintenon was helpless;
it would too clearly have shown her bias had she tried to excuse a want of
respect so blatant and so deeply resented. No argument of Harcourt's
could remove that obstacle.

A decision was reached to send the princess immediately back to Rome
and to recall Orry; but it was feared that they might flatly refuse to leave
and that King Philip would be unable to resist the queen's tears. After
what had happened there was no telling what they might do next, and
thus the final agreement was to proceed with extreme caution so as to
ensure that the shot when fired did not miss the target. The King sent the
princess a severe reprimand for a piece of unexampled audacity in thus
flouting the respect due to His Majesty and the private nature of his
correspondence with an ambassador. At the same time a courier was sent
to the Abbé d'Estrées with a copy of the reprimand and a word to say that
his complaint was justified—nothing more. Whereat he, who had expected
at least her instant dismissal, despaired at seeing her relatively untouched
and himself left a victim to her insults and those of the queen and applied
for his recall. He was taken at his word, which seemed a fresh triumph
for the Princesse des Ursins, leaving her mistress of the field. Whilst she
was thus being lulled into a false security, Cardinal d'Estrées, as much to
annoy her as from any love for his nephew, seized the opportunity to
secure for the latter some mark of the King's approval, since he had been
recalled for no fault of his own in the midst of a public scandal. A bishopric? He was still youngish and good-looking, he had had love-affairs,
moreover he was on the list of the abbés whom the King had vowed never
to make bishops. Abbeys? Not sufficiently dazzling for their purpose. In
the end they all agreed upon the Order of the Holy Ghost, as a sign displayed continually upon his person of the King's satisfaction, and a very
great honour among the clergy because of the few places allotted to
them. The King encountered a certain difficulty since all these places
were already filled, but he finally announced that he would reserve for the

Abbé d'Estrées the first ecclesiastical blue ribbon that should fall vacant. He did not have long to wait, for the death of Cardinal von Fürstenberg soon left a vacancy. The King received the news as he was dressing and immediately sent Blouin to Cardinal d'Estrées informing him that he proposed to give him the Abbey of Saint-Germain-des-Prés, lest modesty should prevent his asking for it. Such notable favours to uncle and nephew, following so close upon one another, immensely gratified them both, but the cardinal, who was normally high-minded and unworldly, did not scruple to say that his greatest pleasure was in the annoyance to Mme des Ursins. In truth, it did give her much food for thought.

In Portugal the campaign opened despite the lapses of Orry, and the King of Spain was all eagerness to join the army. Mme des Ursins, who preferred to keep him in view, used all her influence and that of the queen to prevent his departure or persuade him to take the queen with him. But King Louis, quietly putting his plans into operation, had already written to his grandson, saying that after going all the way to Lombardy to fight his enemies, it would be shameful if he did not lead his army in the Spanish peninsula, especially since the Archduke, his chief antagonist, was there in person. He held King Philip firmly to that idea and at the same time flatly opposed his desire to take the queen, on the grounds of expense and the distraction from his main purpose. Accordingly, in the middle of March the King of Spain left the queen in Madrid and placed himself at the head of his army, accompanied by the Abbé d'Estrées until such time as a new ambassador had been appointed. This was the point which the King had wished to reach before dealing with the Princesse des Ursins, for the queen had such an extraordinary ascendancy over her husband and such an infatuation with that lady, that he had no hope of avoiding disgraceful scenes unless husband and wife were separated.

No sooner was that accomplished than the King wrote to King Philip again, this time demanding the permanent exile of Mme des Ursins; and he wrote in a way calculated to convince him of the absolute need, and to stiffen him against all objections. He sent a letter at the same time to the queen, even firmer in tone, enclosing an order for the Princesse des Ursins to leave Madrid and Spain forthwith and to retire into Italy. That sudden blow reduced the queen to despair, but not so the lady at whom it had been aimed. She realized at once what had occurred and the emptiness of her short-lived triumph; but she also realized that although at present there might be no reprieve all was not lost, and she left nothing undone to prepare the ground for an eventual return. To begin with she induced the queen to ask only for a few days respite, but she used them to place in the post of duenna an easily removable substitute, the Duchess of Montellano, who was the best of women, but stupid, nervous, eager to please, as I myself later discovered.[1] She also selected one of the queen's ladies, with whom she devised a plan to receive information and relay instructions, and she taught the queen how to act towards either court, so as to bring about her own return and preserve her reputation. In a word, she quietly made her arrangements on the pretext of needing time to prepare for her long and unlooked for journey, and calmly allowed commands and couriers to accumulate one upon another until she felt ready to depart.

She left about a fortnight after first receiving marching-orders, but moved only to Alcala, a small town seven leagues distant from Madrid (about as far as Paris is from Fontainebleau). The queen went with her two leagues upon her journey, saying and doing everything possible to convince her of her everlasting affection. Mme des Ursins had taken care to explain to her that their separation, no matter for how short a time, would mark the end of her own influence also and the beginning of her unhappiness. Thus the queen wept for herself as much as for her friend. They say that the princess more than once slipped quietly back to Madrid; but after stubbornly remaining for five weeks in Alcala, with a coolness highly commendable in the circumstances for she was inwardly seething with indignation and misery, she made her way to Bayonne by very easy stages, and the longest, most frequent halts that she dared to risk.

In the meantime the Abbé d'Estrées's successor was appointed, and to everyone's amazement it was the Duc de Gramont,[2] who had name, rank, and appearance to recommend him, and nothing else whatsoever. His wit and the great reputation of the Maréchal his father had won him a share in the pleasures of the King's youth and had placed them ever afterwards on terms of intimacy. He had been forced into marriage with the Maréchal de Castelnau's daughter, having gone somewhat too far with her in gallantry,[3] and at that time had a low reputation for valour, and very little better for cards, business, or the administration of his governorships of Bayonne, Béarn, etc., where the authorities kept careful watch on his accounting. His private life was not much more edifying, and avarice was the worst of his faults. After the revels of the King's early youth and the period of gambling that succeeded them, the long years of gravity ended all excuse for daily private conversations. He therefore tried to salvage some thread of intimacy through the King's love of flattery by proposing to write a royal biography, and indeed the King was gratified to have found so noble an historian, and granted him many audiences to hear the first part of the manuscript. The Duc de Gramont made capital out of that, but his quill was not rightly cut for so heroic an enterprise,

[1] She was duenna to the Duc d'Orléans's fourth daughter when she married the Prince of the Asturias in 1721. Saint-Simon went to Spain as ambassador-extraordinary to arrange their marriage.

[2] Not to be confused with the Comte de Gramont of the famous Memoirs.

[3] The wedding was in 1668. Their daughter became the Maréchale de Boufflers.

which he undertook merely to curry favour, and he did not proceed very far.

When his son's marriage connected him with the Noailles and he had become the father-in-law of the Maréchal de Boufflers, he grew still more determined to make something of himself. He canvassed for every vacant embassy, including that of Holland, but in truth he was as ill-suited for an ambassador as for an historian. None the less, by sheer persistence he won Spain, at a moment when few but he would have cared to face Mme des Ursins. He was notorious in Society, especially for having disgraced his family by a second marriage with an ancient person named La Cour, a one-time housemaid in the employ of Mme de Livry.[1] Many years earlier des Ormes, comptroller of the King's household, who gambled all day long in that salon, had seen her, liked her, and taken her publicly for his mistress; thus the Duc de Gramont, a friend of des Ormes and constantly supping with them both, must have been aware of a relationship that continued for a number of years, in fact, until des Ormes' death. However that may be, when des Ormes died Gramont took her and finally married her, though by that time she was old, ugly, and blind in one eye. Such gossip regarding a private individual would be of little interest, were it not for the outcry made by the duke's family and for what followed.

The marriage was secret, until the Duc de Gramont took it into his head to use it to pay his court to the King by imitation, the sincerest form of flattery, at the same time directing an even higher compliment to Mme de Maintenon by having it publicly announced. He used the grubby chins of Saint-Sulpice[2] and the canting, hypocritical little beards who have the cure of souls at Versailles[3] to hold up for admiration this wonderful deed of piety and morals, and to offer it as an example in their sermons. You may imagine the effect on King Louis and Mme de Maintenon. The moment of the duke's announcement was the eve of his departure to Spain, and the pretext the desire to be accompanied by his gracious duchess. That crowned his incredible folly and produced results totally different from what he had expected. Mme de Maintenon was not amused by the implied comparison, and the King flew into such a rage that the Duc de Gramont dared not face an audience with him. He was flatly forbidden to let his wife assume any of the privileges or marks of her rank in any place whatsoever, or in any circumstances to bring her to Court, or, most especially, ever to let her set foot on Spanish soil. But no matter how angry the King and Mme de Maintenon may have felt, they could not take Spain from him, for that would have been too obvious. Their resentment lingered none the less. No one else but the Duc de

[1] Marie Antoinette de Beauvilliers, sister of the pious duke, and married to the Marquis de Livry, the King's high steward.

[2] *Barbes sales*; typical of Saint-Simon's loathing for the clergy of Saint-Sulpice.

[3] *Barbichets*; his contemptuous name for the Missioners of Saint-Lazare, whose priests wore chin-beards in imitation of their founder St. Vincent de Paul.

Gramont could ever have imagined gaining favour by that odious comparison; and as a final blow he was expressly ordered not to see the Princesse des Ursins when he passed her on his journey.

That lady, on the road to Bayonne, was hoping against hope to be allowed to come to Versailles to plead her cause. Her expectations cannot have been great at that moment, but she kept up her courage as she had done in Madrid. She knew that at Courts even the worst storms blow over in time, provided that friends are staunch and one remains undismayed. Thus Mme des Ursins, her coach-wheels turning ever so slowly, never ceased to entreat for permission to come to Court. Not that she dared to hope for so much, only that by dint of prayers and protests she might for the time being escape Italy and find refuge in France. That once achieved she felt that she would soon extricate herself entirely. Were she banished to Italy, Harcourt would be cut off from all those personal details from which he made his living, and Mme de Maintenon have no means of directly managing affairs in Spain. Both of them had begun to feel her loss and when the first explosion had subsided they took courage. The King had been obeyed; he had had his vengeance and had crowned it by the award of the Order to the Abbé d'Estrées and the Abbey of Saint-Germain to his uncle. That was humiliation enough for a dictatress of the Princesse des Ursins' mettle. After such condign punishment was there not room for mercy? Moreover, might it not be as well to bear gently on the Queen of Spain in matters unrelated to government or influence.[1] Such at least were the arguments used by Mme de Maintenon. The scheme was limited to the avoidance of Italy, for the King was determined on eventual banishment and needed careful handling. This was no time to arouse suspicion. They therefore settled on Toulouse as her place of residence, and with immense difficulty extracted permission for that as a purely temporary grace. With the mighty influence of Mme de Maintenon thus working on her side; with Harcourt, so well-informed and so clever, as her spy, and with the Queen of England,[2] another friend, to strike the blows which Mme de Maintenon dared not deliver for fear of showing her hand, it seemed impossible for the princess to remain long encaged at Toulouse.

In the end the Duc de Gramont received permission to visit her on his way to Spain, and that was the first sign of weakening. The reason given was the need to prepare him for his coming task, but the real cause was the desire to give way to the queen in trifles and thus make it possible to deal with her. He gained nothing from the interview, however, for he was so crestfallen and frightened when he left the Court after announcing

---

[1] The queen cried bitterly when they said good-bye and gave her her portrait encircled in diamonds.

[2] Mary of Modena, James II's wife, was Italian by birth. Saint-Simon says that she and Mme des Ursins had always been friends.

his marriage that he could neither endear himself to that redoubtable woman in a private conversation, nor explain his stiff, unfriendly attitude to those who had been hurt and angered by it at the Spanish court. Let us now proceed, leaving Mme des Ursins at Toulouse, although at Bayonne she had again received orders to go to Italy, and the Duc de Gramont on his way to Spain.

Orry at this time was commanded to return to Versailles to account for his barefaced lying and the maladministration that had delivered the Archduke and prevented the conquest of Portugal by the French and Spanish armies. The progress made by our troops despite the almost complete lack of all necessities showed how easy that conquest might have been, had even half of the supplies promised to Puységur by that impudent scoundrel been forthcoming.

In the early part of May the Comte de Toulouse, preceded by the Maréchal de Cœuvres, left for Brest where they embarked together on the same ship.

The Duke of Mantua who was inconvenienced by his duchy becoming a theatre of war, and who had surrendered it willingly to King Louis, thus rendering him great service in the Italian war, decided to pay a visit to France, where he felt sure of finding a warm welcome. He made a detour through Charleville, which also belonged to him, and arrived in Paris with a large suite just two days before Whitsun. He stayed at the Luxembourg, which was especially and magnificently furnished for him with furniture belonging to the Crown; his ordinary servants were put up in the Rue Tournon, where the ambassadors extraordinary are lodged, and he was provided, morning, noon, and night, with seven meal-tables at the King's expense and served by his officers. There were other tables also for his great retinue. He travelled *incognito* under the name of the Marquis de San Salvador, but that could not strictly be adhered to for a prince who by giving up his capital had presented us with the keys of Italy. On the day after Whitsunday he drove to Versailles with draped coaches displaying his cipher alone, and was admitted into the great courtyard, where none are allowed to drive save those who possess the honours of the Louvre.[1] He was taken to the apartments of M. le Comte de Toulouse and offered refreshments of every kind. Thence he went up by the little staircase to the King's offices and was received, the King standing still, not taking even one step towards him. The Duke spoke first, and for some considerable time; the King then answered, heaping courtesies upon him, and afterwards pointed out to him Monseigneur, the two princes, M. le Duc d'Orléans, Monsieur le Duc and M. le Prince de Conti, and then M. du Maine, announcing their names as he did so. No one else was

[1] *Les Honneurs du Louvre—droit de cousin, droit de carosse, de chaise, de livrée.* Called 'cousin' by the King and the right to bring your coach or chair and your liveried servants into the great courtyard of the Louvre.

present except the *entrées*. The Duke of Mantua asked permission to present his suite. That done, the King, followed by all who were in the study, went straight into the great gallery and escorted him to Mme la Duchesse de Bourgogne who happened to be unwell and was therefore in bed. There were several ladies in full dress attending her, and the King presented the Duke of Mantua in the *ruelle* beside her bed. They stayed with her a quarter of an hour, after which the King took the duke the entire length of the gallery and showed it to him, and the two salons also, returning with him to his study, where after a brief conversation, the King all the time vastly gracious, the duke took his leave and returned to Paris.

A week later he paid another visit to Versailles, saw the gardens, and was again received by the King, going up by the little staircase, and only Torcy present. A few days afterwards Monseigneur gave a great dinner for him at Meudon, which was unusually lively, for the duke was excellent company. Monseigneur then showed him the house and took him for a long drive through the gardens in a light carriage. Another day he visited the stables and kennels of Versailles, the menagerie, and Trianon. He returned once more, slept in the Comte de Toulouse's apartment, was shown all the King's horses, and went for a ride in the park of Marly. On all these occasions the King saw him, always with Torcy present.

M. de Vendôme and his brother[1] kept the King supplied every week (and sometimes more often), by couriers from both their armies, with promises and hopes of enterprises guaranteed to take place in two days' time and all ending in smoke. Conduct so clearly harmful to their reputations was as difficult to understand as that of the King in supporting this mockery and continuing to be satisfied with them. That reaction so typical and yet so strange, repeated as it was in every campaign, may perhaps serve as one more proof of the all-too-powerful influence exerted on him by that kind of birth,[2] of his protection for that reason alone of M. du Maine, and of all that you have seen and will see him do for bastards as such. From time to time some small clash appeared to justify their fine talk, concerning, as it did, very broken country where two great armies faced one another as on a chess-board. In mid-May, M. de Vendôme attempted to drive a few Imperial troops out of Trino.[3] He arrived on the scene too late, as usual, and the birds had flown. He attacked the rear-guard, but found it so powerfully protected by infantry covering the retreat that despite his superiority he had a hard task to dispose of them. He claimed four hundred killed and many prisoners. Could one but count the numbers which Vendôme claimed to have killed or captured in each campaign, not to mention waggons, they would probably have amounted

---

[1] Philippe de Vendôme, a most dissolute character. He was the Grand Prieur de France, the highest national rank conferred by the Order of the Knights of Malta.

[2] Their grandfather was a bastard of Henri IV.

[3] On the Po, near Ferrara.

to more than the entire enemy army. It is exactly the same with certain gamblers who complain of their losses the whole year round, one or two actually swearing that they lose a million when in actual fact it is never more than fifty thousand francs. Licentiousness, debauchery, and a familiar manner with soldiers and warrant-officers made Vendôme popular with the greater portion of his army; the other part, discouraged by his idleness and arrogance, most of all by the brazen audacity of his assertions, feared his power and influence too much to contradict the excessive praise that had made him a hero for nothing, and the King, who loved everything calculated to bolster himself in that opinion, thus became the chief instrument of his own flagrant deception.

The armies of Flanders and Germany had been in suspension ever since the opening of the campaign. The Emperor, close pressed by the Hungarian Malcontents, with that part of his empire in absolute revolt, Vienna thrown into confusion by raids and looting not only in the suburbs but within the city, his menagerie burned, and his life in danger when he rode into the country, turned all his thoughts to Bavaria. Most of all he feared lest the Prince Elector at the head of his own and a French army should drive him back against the Malcontents, leaving him no means of escape. This danger appeared no less great to the Emperor's allies, and it caused them to decide to march all their forces into the very heart of the Empire. That was what had made the early part of the campaign in Flanders so aimless, for the Allies took enormous care to keep their true intentions secret, so as to steal a march upon the Maréchal de Villeroy and reach the Rhine as much before him as possible. The Maréchal de Tallard,[1] who had crossed that river earlier in the season, was meanwhile moving towards the mountain passes; he met with no opposition, and spent the whole of the 18 May with the Elector of Bavaria. The Duke of Marlborough marched on towards Coblenz, leaving both marshals uncertain whether he intended to attack on the Moselle or merely wished to draw off the bulk of our forces in that direction. Soon, however, he gathered speed, reached the Rhine, crossed it at Coblenz on 26 and 27 May, and marched steadily on. Villeroy had by now reached Arlon, but still suspecting a ruse he believed that it was the Englishman's intention to embark his infantry and return them by river to Flanders far more quickly than he himself could arrive there, in order to attack along the coast. Acting on that assumption, he left part of his infantry near the Meuse, in a position where they would have time to join the Marquis de Bedmar,[2] whilst he, himself, with the remainder and his cavalry

---

[1] One of the most distinguished figures at the court of Louis XIV. Soldier, diplomat, and writer, he had deep misgivings when he received orders to go to the rescue of Bavaria, believing that neither the policy nor the force given him was strong enough to overcome Marlborough, Prince Eugene, and the Margrave of Baden.

[2] The Marquis de Bedmar (1652–1723). A Spaniard commanding the Spanish troops in the Low Countries.

proceeded to follow Marlborough. The Elector and Prince Louis of Baden[1] were keeping very close to one another. As soon as Tallard received this news from the Court and the Maréchal de Villeroy he left the Elector and recrossed the Rhine with his army. He reached Landau, and Villeroy crossed the Moselle between Trèves and Thionville. Bedmar stayed in Flanders commanding the French and Spanish troops remaining there. M. d'Overkerque commanded the opposing Dutch army.

Marlborough, however, crossed the Main between Frankfurt and Mainz, continued steadily on by the mountain road between Heidelberg and Darmstadt and so crossed the Neckar. At this point Villeroy and Tallard met to confer; after which Tallard led his army back across the Rhine by the Strasbourg bridge on 1 July. By that time Marlborough was at Ulm, and Prince Eugene, having left Vienna, had taken his army there also. They held a conference at that place[2] with the Prince of Baden, with their three armies encamped around them. Villeroy followed Tallard over the Rhine and entered the valley of the Quinche, in order to be in communication with him and able if necessary to join him with advanced detachments.

Both marshals had wasted a precious fortnight in the Palatinate with reviews and field-days, waiting for orders to come from Versailles. Villeroy, who had long been accustomed to patronizing Tallard, his cousin and admirer, in no way altered his attitude when the latter was given an independent command. Tallard, who was now his equal, if only in that respect, considered his arrogance misplaced and did his utmost to shake off the yoke which Villeroy so unjustifiably imposed on him, which caused some rather absurd situations but did not affect the army in general. At length Tallard, the wiser of the two, reflected that their equality would cease when they returned to the Court, and that consideration restored order to some extent. The time so lost by them was the beginning of all the misfortunes which the King suffered in Germany. Tallard ought to have advanced and the Maréchal de Villeroy remained guarding the passes. In the end that was what they did, but by then it was too late. Here I must pause, lest these sorry events in Germany should make me lose track of what was happening elsewhere, and retrace my steps a little before returning to the Danube.

I should have mentioned earlier the birth of the eldest son of Mgr le Duc de Bourgogne, born at Versailles at five in the afternoon of Wednesday, 25 June.[3] It was an immense joy for the King; the Court and Paris went almost wild in their demonstrations of rejoicing and loyalty. The

---

[1] The Margrave (1655–1707). Before he changed over to the Allies he had commanded the Spanish army in Flanders.

[2] The first meeting between Marlborough and Prince Eugene and the beginning of that marvellous comradeship in arms.

[3] The first Duc de Bretagne, who died less than a year later.

King gave a fête at Marly and sent the most exquisite, as well as the most magnificent presents to Mme la Duchesse de Bourgogne, who had by then left her bed. In spite of the war and his great cause for resentment against M. de Savoie, the King wrote to give him the news, but he sent the letter to M. de Vendôme to be forwarded. There was every opportunity to repent of so much rejoicing, since it lasted less than a year, and of so much money ill-spent in revelry at that particular moment, considering the straits we were in.

As I have already said, the Grand Alliance had at that time every reason to fear total disaster for the Emperor and to go with all their might to his defence. What hopes might not have been fulfilled had the armies of Marsin and Tallard, combined with that of the Elector, achieved even the least of the successes open to such strong forces united in the heart of Germany, and with the army of the Maréchal de Villeroy to guard their rear! But you shall see what bad generalship and ill-luck can do or, to be more truthful, Providence, that mocks men's hopes and in an instant can deliver or cast down the greatest of kings.

Tallard reached Ulm on 28 July, stayed there for two days resting his army, brought it to Augsburg on 2 August, and joined the Elector and the Maréchal de Marsin on the 4th. From that moment, the Elector, full of confidence at finding himself at the head of three complete and flourishing armies, burned to use them to win a battle that would place the Emperor at his mercy between the victorious Malcontents and a triumphant Franco-Bavarian army. This bright hope was the Elector's undoing. He did not pause to weigh the uncertainties of battle against the firm assurance of success if he did nothing. He was surrounded on three sides by rich and unspoiled country, of which he was master; before him the land had been ravaged by enemy armies crossing and encircling it in their marches and consuming all fodder and foodstuffs. Behind the enemy the country was equally devastated, and from thence it was no great distance to the ruination caused by the Malcontents' raids. Country so ravaged could not have furnished a week's sustenance for the vast forces of the Allies, and had the Elector been content to do nothing but observe they would have been forced to retreat for lack of food, leaving the field to him. Not to have made that decision was the first error and the vital one. Marsin and Tallard, however, since their arrival in Bavaria, had thought only of making themselves agreeable to the Elector, and they thus did nothing to check his eager longing to give battle. It became their sole aim, and all the easier for them to attain because a battle was what the Allies themselves most desired, and their only hope of salvation.

Thus the Elector marched with supreme confidence in the direction of the enemy, arriving in the morning of 12 August on Hochstaedt plain, a place of good omen to him because of the battle which he had won there in the previous year.[1] His order of battle was highly irregular. The armies were not combined. The Elector's, commanded by Arco, occupied the centre; Tallard's formed the right wing, and Marsin's the left, with no interval between them greater than that between the centre and wings of one single army. The Elector commanded over all; but Tallard directed operations, and since he could not see further than ten paces before him, he fell into grievous errors which no one could rectify. A few hours after the Elector's arrival on the plain he received news to the effect that the enemy, that is to say Marlborough and Prince Eugene who had combined their armies, were coming to confront him. It was timed to perfection. Our generals had the entire day in which to choose their battle-ground and make their dispositions. They could scarcely have done worse at either. A widish and not too marshy stream ran parallel to the front of our three armies; a spring forming a long and broad patch of bog almost separated the two lines of the Maréchal de Tallard's army—a terrible position for a general who was free to choose his ground in a vast plain, and one that later became disastrous. On his extreme right but slightly to the rear was the large village of Blenheim, into which with unexampled lack of foresight he crammed twenty-six battalions of his army under the Marquis de Clérambault, with Brigadier-general Blanzac supported by five regiments of dragoons within its enclosures, and a brigade of cavalry behind them. An entire army to defend that village and protect his right, and his main strength depleted by that amount!

The plan of the earlier battle of Hochstaedt, won on that same ground, would have been a good plan to follow. No one, it appears, thought of that. There were two possible courses open to them, either to take up a position along the stream running parallel to the front of the armies, so as to deny its passage to the enemy, or to attack them in the disorder of their crossing. Either plan was good; the second the better; neither was adopted. They chose a third alternative, to leave a wide space between our troops and the stream and to allow the enemy to cross it at leisure, so as to topple them into it backwards, as someone later remarked. With such dispositions it is hard to believe that our generals were not smitten with blindness. The Danube flowed so near to Blenheim that it made a far better support for our right than that village, which it was quite unnecessary to defend.

At dawn on 13 August the enemy arrived upon the plain; they immediately took up a position along the stream, and were observed as the day was breaking. They must have been vastly surprised to discover our armies deploying in battle order at so great a distance. They took full advantage of the stretch of open ground which we had left free for them, and formed their lines at leisure without encountering the least opposition

---

[1] Although Saint-Simon speaks throughout of the 2nd Battle of Hochstaedt I have preferred to call it the Battle of Blenheim for the sake of clarity.

from us. That is exactly the truth, although posterity may find it hard to believe. It was nearly eight o'clock before all these dispositions were completed and during all that time our armies watched them unmoved. Prince Eugene and his army took the right wing and the Duke of Marlborough the left. Thus he faced Tallard's army, and Prince Eugene that of Marsin.

At last the armies came to grips, and at first Prince Eugene could gain no advantage over Marsin, who, indeed, repulsed him, and might have been able to follow that up had it not been for the misfortunes of our right. There the first charge was unsuccessful, the *gendarmerie*[1] faltered, bringing great confusion to the cavalry adjoining them, although many regiments did marvels. But two errors were responsible for the loss of that ill-fated army; the second line, separated from the first by the aforementioned patch of bog, was in no position to give proper support, and the long distance which had to be covered in order to reach the head of the spring and go round it made a rally impossible. The squadrons of both lines were thus unable to pass through the gaps, those of the second line could not maintain the impetus of the charge, nor those of the first rally behind them. As for the infantry, the absence of the twenty-six battalions in Blenheim left a great gap, not in spacing, because the remainder were brought together, but in breadth of front and in strength. The English, soon perceiving the advantage which this lack of infantry offered them, and the disorder of the cavalry on our right, profited by it with all the ease of troops manœuvring on a wide expanse of firm ground. They charged and charged again; in short, they routed the whole of our right wing after that first charge so weakly supported, despite all the efforts and valour of our generals and the steadiness of several regiments. The Elector's army, quite unprotected, and attacked in the flank by those same English, next began to waver, notwithstanding prodigies of valour on the part of the Elector and the immense courage of his Bavarian officers. But they, at least, resisted strongly. The picture at that moment was of Tallard's army beaten and routed in the greatest confusion imaginable, the Elector's army, still fighting gamely but quite unable to withstand attacks from the front and rear simultaneously, and already beginning to retreat, and Marsin's wing charging and gaining ground upon Prince Eugene, who more than once thought the result in doubt.

Meanwhile the troops in Blenheim village, which were being heavily attacked, not only defended themselves lustily but twice repulsed the enemy and pursued them far out into the plain. Tallard, seeing his army in flight, pressed on to Blenheim in order to withdraw the troops there and put them to better use elsewhere. This task was made all the more difficult because he had given them express orders on no account to leave the village, not even a single man, no matter what might happen. As he

---

[1] The famous regiments of the *Maison du Roi*, the Household troops.

was galloping full tilt in that direction with Silly and one of his staff, un-
escorted, he was recognized and surrounded and all three of them were
captured.

During all this confusion Blanzac was in Blenheim, wondering where
Clérambault his commanding officer could be, for he had been missing
the past two hours. The answer was that flying for his life he had been
drowned in the Danube. He had attempted to swim his horse over the
river, accompanied by a mounted groom, and supposedly with the intention of afterwards becoming a hermit. The servant crossed safely; he
was drowned. Blanzac was thus left alone in command, and in great difficulties on account of the general confusion, which he could both see and
hear, and because he received no fresh orders from the Maréchal de
Tallard. It so happened that Valsemé, a brigadier-general of the *gendarmerie* separated from his troops, came riding by at that moment so close
to the village that Blanzac, perceiving him, called out asking him to find
Tallard and obtain instructions. This Valsemé did his best to do, but he
also was taken prisoner and Blanzac was thus left without orders or any
superior officer. I am here merely repeating Blanzac's own justification
for his subsequent actions, which was later very ill-received by both the
King and the public in general. No one could gainsay him, however, because only those who were in Blenheim knew the truth and all his officers
made the same excuse. The highest ranking among them began at this
point to discover that the powder was running short; that the ammunition
carts were quietly disappearing without asking leave from anyone, and
that some of the soldiers were frightened and beginning to spread alarm.
They then saw Denonville, a captured officer, riding towards the village
with an Englishman waving a white handkerchief, asking for a parley.
But Denonville, at that time an exceedingly handsome and somewhat
spoiled young man, instead of speaking privately to Blanzac and the other
senior officers, proceeded to harangue the troops guarding the village,
advising them to give themselves up and preserve their lives for the King's
service. Blanzac, seeing the bad effect which he was having on the soldiers,
silenced him with the harshness that his conduct deserved, ordered him to
go, and began himself to address the troops in a different spirit. The harm
was done, however, and only the Navarre regiment raised a cheer for
him; the rest remained glum and silent. Here I must again mention that
I only repeat Blanzac's words.

Shortly after Denonville's return to the enemy lines an English milord[1]
appeared from the same direction, asking to speak on parole with the
commanding officer. He was taken to Blanzac, whom he informed that
the Duke of Marlborough wished him to say that he was present in person
with forty battalions and sixty pieces of cannon, in a position to send for
whatever reinforcements he might need; that he was about to surround

[1] He was George Hamilton, first Earl of Orkney.

Blenheim; that Tallard's army was in flight and what remained of the Elector's in full retreat; that Tallard himself and many other generals were captured; that Blanzac had no hope of deliverance, and that he would be well advised to surrender unconditionally, rather than needlessly cause the death of many good and brave soldiers on either side, since in the end he needs must be overwhelmed. Blanzac wished at first to send him packing, but the Englishman urged him to accompany him on parole for two hundred yards outside the village so as to see the situation for himself. This Blanzac did, taking with him d'Hautefeuille, colonel-general of dragoons. Great was their horror when they saw with their own eyes the Elector's retreat and the preparations for the attack on Blenheim, and could no longer doubt the truth of what the English lord had told them. They re-entered Blenheim. Blanzac called together his officers, told them of the surrender proposed and of what he and d'Haute-feuille had just seen. They all understood the terrible shock that their surrender would be to their country, but the horror of their situation appeared even greater to them and all agreed to accept the enemy's terms, arranging as best they could to preserve for the King's service by ransom or exchange the twenty-six battalions and twelve squadrons under their command. That disgraceful capitulation was then hastily put down on paper and signed by Blanzac and his generals and corps commanders, with the one exception, I believe, of the colonel of the Navarres. It was then put into force.

In the meanwhile Marsin had continued not only to hold but to repulse and gain an advantage over Prince Eugene. When, however, he learned of the rout of Tallard's army, together with a large portion of the Elector's that had been carried away in their flight, his only thought was to make the best use of his own army's completeness by retreating and gathering together the stragglers, a manœuvre which he executed without opposition. Marlborough was astounded at his marvellous good fortune; Prince Eugene could not comprehend it, and Prince Louis of Baden who had been laying siege to Ingolstadt refused to believe it and was indignant at having had no part in their victory. The Elector was the only one on our side to keep his head, and he proposed the only sound plan in the circumstances. He suggested that they should remain in Bavaria, taking advantage of excellent communications and abundant supplies of every kind. The others realized too late the mistake they made in not listening to his advice. His country, alone and undefended save by a very few troops, held out against the Imperial army throughout the entire winter; but it was not our fate to halve our losses. The Elector could not gain a hearing, for the determination of every other commander was to retire upon Villeroy's army and unite with him as soon as possible.

The enemy offered no hindrance to that project. Indeed, they were enchanted to see our armies bent upon a retreat which, after such a victory, they would have had the greatest difficulty in forcing upon us. The union of our armies was very different from earlier conjunctions. It took place on 25 August at Donauschingen, to which place the Maréchal de Villeroy had advanced. Marsin gathered up not more than two thousand and five hundred foot-soldiers and as many cavalry (eighteen hundred of them dismounted)[1] from the remains of Tallard's army, which had lost thirty-seven battalions altogether, namely the twenty-six in Blenheim and eleven others, either dead or dispersed. The *gendarmerie* in particular, and generally speaking all the cavalry, were accused of having done very badly. They had fired their carbines and pistols instead of charging sword in hand like the enemy, although it was our usual custom to draw swords; thus the cavalry on both sides changed their practice and ours was the loser by it. At last, at the end of August, our armies arrived beneath the fortress of Kehl at the end of the Strasbourg bridge, and Prince Eugene, returned to the lines of Stollhofen,[2] made it appear as though he intended to cross the Rhine.

The Duke of Marlborough, who had done everything with his army, kept the Maréchal de Tallard and the highest-ranking officers and sent them to Hanau, until he was ready to take them to England to adorn his triumph. Half of the remainder he handed over to Prince Eugene. It made a considerable difference to them, for that prince treated them very harshly, whereas Marlborough treated all, even the humblest, with the utmost care, consideration, and politeness, and with a modesty even more noteworthy, perhaps, than his victory. He took trouble to see that this good usage continued until they crossed over into England, and the rank and file, by his express orders, received all the kindness and comforts possible.

The King received the bitter news on 21 August, by a courier from the Maréchal de Villeroy. The Austrian troops left in the Stollhofen lines by Prince Eugene sent a trumpeter with letters from many of our captive officers who were given permission to write to their families. By that courier the King learned that a battle had taken place on the 13th, lasting from eight o'clock in the morning until dusk; that the Maréchal de Tallard's entire army was either dead or taken prisoner; that no one knew Tallard's own whereabouts, nor whether the Elector and Marsin had taken part in the action. There were letters from Blanzac, d'Hautefeuille and Denonville, but these gave no explanation and appeared distracted. Racked with anxiety, the King opened all the private letters, but he learned nothing from them, and remained for six days in the dreadful situation of knowing that all was lost in Bavaria, and yet unaware of what

---

[1] The French horses had been suffering from a disease, probably glanders, even before the battle.

[2] The Allies' fortified lines at Stollhofen, on the Rhine, approximately twenty miles below Strasbourg.

had happened. The few people who had written sent nothing but personal news, or at the most news of friends, for everyone feared that their letters might be opened and were thus in no hurry to pass on the bad news, or comment on events and individuals. Marsin was wholly engrossed with his retreat and wrote only to Villeroy, and then only on that subject. The Elector, indignant at the losses he had sustained and the neglect of his advice to remain in Bavaria, was content to send the King a couple of lines as he crossed the Rhine, bearing his respects and an assurance of loyalty to their common cause. Thus nothing was known for certain, and such scraps of information as did arrive served only to increase our fears for the general situation and the fate of friends.

The shameful surrender at Blenheim was one of the first things to leak out in a sentence or two of the letters from Blanzac, Denonville, and d'Hautefeuille. Some other officers let fly against the *gendarmerie* and certain generals, but no details were given. Amongst others the Comte de Roucy came in for some abuse; he and Blanzac were nephews of the Maréchal de Lorges and their boyhood had been spent in his house with his own children. Their wives, whom I knew very well, sought for me everywhere, imploring me to go to Chamillart at once and persuade him to speak to the King on their behalf. This I did, with the result that he saved them from any serious consequences. The King made every effort to obtain news for himself. He ordered all the letters that arrived to be brought to him for examination; but nothing came, or nothing of interest. Everything that anyone knew was tacked together, but even so no one could make head or tail of what had happened, and neither the King nor anyone else could imagine how an entire army, for such it was, placed in and around a village, could have been induced to sign a surrender. It was enough to make one's head reel. Little by little the details began to filter through in the letters, and on 20 August Silly arrived at L'Etang, having been granted leave on parole by the Duke of Marlborough to give the King Tallard's account of the disaster, on condition that he returned immediately. Chamillart took him straight to Meudon, where for a very long time before his dinner the King was closeted with them both.

We were not accustomed to defeat, and this one for sufficient reasons had been totally unexpected. It appeared, moreover, to have been the result of a series of monstrous errors, faulty plans, and panics, any one of which, had it been averted, might have changed the outcome. Irresistibly one is reminded, on a smaller scale, of the miraculous victories and fearful disasters which God dealt out to his chosen people, according to whether they remained faithful or forsook his worship. You may readily imagine the dismay in France, where every noble family, not to mention the rest, had some member dead, wounded, or missing; the difficulties of Chamillart when he sought to re-form an army entirely destroyed, dead, or imprisoned, and the agony of the King, who so lately had the Emperor's fate

within his grasp and now saw himself reduced to defending his own kingdom from the banks of the Rhine. What followed showed no less clearly
the heavy hand of the Lord. We lost our reason, we trembled in Alsace.
Our bitter scorn for the Maréchal de Villeroy was submerged in the royal
favour. You shall see that Tallard was magnificently rewarded and Marsin
left unnoticed. He appeared to deserve nothing since he had not failed, for
the King did not at all blame him for not standing firm in Bavaria. All his
anger fell upon certain regiments that were disbanded and upon a few
individuals, the innocent as well as the guilty, whose entire punishment
consisted in receiving no further employment with the armies. Denonville was the only officer to be dismissed with ignominy and to lose his
regiment. He was so finally ruined that after his release he did not reappear. I am not saying that his shameful speech before Blenheim deserved no punishment, but it was no eloquence of his that made the
troops drop their arms and surrender, it was the words of the Englishman
who spoke afterwards. Yet Denonville was the only man in that army (for
such it was) who was punished for surrendering it to the English without
a shot being fired, and the colonel who alone refused to sign the surrender received no reward whatsoever. The public on the other hand did not
mince their words on the subject of the marshals, generals, and individuals whom they held responsible, nor on officers who had been censured in the letters. This created a scandal vastly embarrassing for their
families. It was a long time before their nearest relatives dared to show
their faces in public, and some of them were not away long enough for
their comfort.

Amidst this general woe the revels and rejoicings over the birth of the
Duc de Bretagne continued unabated. The city of Paris gave a fête with a
display of fireworks on the river, which Monseigneur, the princes, and
Mme la Duchesse de Bourgogne watched from the windows of the
Louvre, with a large number of ladies and gentlemen from the Court.
There was lavish spending on eating and drinking, but that, however,
aroused more annoyance by its untimeliness than admiration for its bra-
vado. Shortly after this the King gave a fête with illuminations at Marly,
to which the court of Saint-Germain was invited, all to do honour to
Mme la Duchesse de Bourgogne. The King thanked the mayor of Paris
for the river-fireworks, saying that Monseigneur and Mme la Duchesse
de Bourgogne had thought them very splendid.

The King did not long remain in the shadow of the defeat of Blenheim,
for he received a small consolation of little benefit to the State, but very
much after his own heart. The Comte de Toulouse, who was in every
way the opposite of his brother the Duc du Maine, had spent his first
campaign as an admiral wandering impatiently about the Mediterranean,
not daring to come to grips with the enemy, who were too strong for
his fleet. For this season he had obtained enough to put him on level

terms with Admiral Rooke,[1] who had been wintering at Lisbon waiting for reinforcements from Holland and England. M. de Toulouse's dearest wish was to encounter Admiral Rooke's fleet and attack it. He had the King's permission to do so, and on 24 September he caught up with the Englishman near Malaga and fought him from ten o'clock in the morning until eight at night. There had not for many years been a naval battle so fierce and protracted. The enemy had the advantage of the wind throughout, and when night came it favoured their retreat. None the less, the success was all on the side of M. de Toulouse, whose ship fought Admiral Rooke's flagship for a long time and dismasted her. He could thus boast that he had won a victory, and when the wind changed he chased Rooke all the following day as the latter made for the shelter of the Barbary coast. The enemy lost six thousand men; the ship of the Dutch vice-admiral was blown up; several others were sunk, and a few dismasted. We lost neither ships nor masts, but the victory cost us dear in the lives of high-ranking and distinguished officers, besides those of fifteen hundred soldiers and sailors killed or wounded.[2]

The Comte de Toulouse acquired much honour by that campaign, and finally came to anchor off Malaga, where Villadarias[3] visited him on board his flagship, and obtained everything that he required for besieging Gibraltar on the fullest possible scale. Three thousand men were landed with fifty great cannon, and, generally speaking, all the equipment for a siege. Ten warships and six frigates were also sent to assist him.[4] As soon as these matters were duly dispatched, M. de Toulouse and his fleet returned to Toulon.

It was about this time that Orry arrived at the Court. The King would not see him and was on the point of having him tried and hanged, as he richly deserved; but Mme de Maintenon quietly averted that punishment because it would have told too strongly against Mme des Ursins. Aubigny, the princess's equerry, had remained at Madrid to act as a kind of confidential agent for his mistress. He was given a pension of a thousand ducats, despite the low state of the Spanish finances, and a house in Madrid at the King of Spain's expense. The queen never ceased to implore that the Princesse des Ursins might be allowed a hearing at Versailles and then permitted to return to her, and when this was refused she

[1] Admiral Sir George Rooke (1650–1709). Knighted for distinguished service at the battle of Cape La Hogue.
[2] The historian Charles Bourel de La Roncière wrote of the battle that 'the vanquished in default of the laurels gathered the fruits of victory'. The English lost more men killed than at Blenheim but the French losses were even greater.
[3] The Marquis of Villadarias, governor of the coast of Andalusia.
[4] The consequences of the Allies' capture of Gibraltar earlier in the campaign were far-reaching. When Louis XIV realized that it could not be retaken by sea he withdrew 50,000 men from all parts of Spain for a land siege. The land defences of Spain were thus so fatally weakened that it lay open to invasion. Berwick had strongly disapproved of this manœuvre, which was one reason for his recall.

turned violently against the Duke of Berwick, whom she believed to have been the cause of Orry's disgrace, notwithstanding that Puységur had complained of him much earlier. Her repeated demands for Berwick's recall grew so passionate that this was finally granted her so as not to drive her frantic, and the amiable, popular Tessé, whose health was good or bad as his personal interests demanded, was appointed to succeed him. Harcourt and Mme de Maintenon knew perfectly well what they were doing when they procured for him that nomination, which was of infinitely less benefit to the army than to their schemes for governing Spain.

During September there was a most dreadful murder. The Comte de Grandpré, Chevalier of the Order 1661, and elder brother of the Maréchal de Joyeuse, Chevalier 1668, who died childless, left children by his two marriages. His second wife was the daughter and sister respectively of two Marquis de Vervins, each of whom was the King's high steward. Of these two the son died young in 1663. He was a son-in-law of the Maréchal Fabert, and consequently a brother-in-law of the Marquis de Beuvron and also of Caylus, father of that Caylus who emigrated to Spain, of the husband of Mme de Caylus who was Mme de Maintenon's first cousin, and of the Abbé de Caylus who was recently made Bishop of Auxerre. This Vervins married the Maréchal Fabert's eldest daughter and died leaving her great with the Vervins of whom I am now speaking. After her husband's death she re-married in Flanders with the Comte de Mérode.[1]

Vervins had endless lawsuits with his first cousins, the children of his father's sister and the Comte de Grandpré, by whom he was greatly harassed during the whole of his life. At last he seemed about to win them all, but one of these cousins, who owned various priories and called himself the Abbé de Grandpré, had him assassinated just in front of the Sisterhood of Mme de Miramion, as he was driving along the Quai de la Tournelle. He received several sword-thrusts, and his coachman also when he tried to defend him. When an action was brought the abbé fled abroad and never returned, and shortly afterwards, being found guilty, he was sentenced to death on the wheel. Vervins had lived under threats from him for a considerable time. Vervins himself was a big, very handsome man, with a passably agreeable face, a little wit, some culture, and a great gift for stealing women. He was also eccentric, extremely idle, intimately connected with the love-affairs and diversions of Monsieur le Duc, and a great man in High Society. He left the King's service young, paid frequent long visits to his house in Picardy, yet was always warmly welcomed on his return to the Court. At last, saying nothing to anyone, he retired to an estate in Picardy without cause for complaint or unhappiness, or any money troubles whatsoever, for he was rich, well-established, and had

---

[1] A short example of the kind of pedigree attached to nearly every character in the Memoirs.

never married. What is more, he had no religious intentions, he had no mind for them; no sickness, he had always been in the best of health, and no building ambitions, he employed no builders. Still less was he moved by a love of hunting, for that pleasure he never indulged in. He spent several years at his home, writing to no one and, which seems absolutely incomprehensible, without stirring from his bed, except to have it made.[1] There he dined and supped alone; dealt with such trifling business matters as still concerned him; received the few people whom he could not refuse, and from the time he opened his eyes in the morning until he closed them at night, did needlework embroidery in his bed, with sometimes a little reading. He continued in that extraordinary life until the day of his death. I think it right to record this because it is really so very singular.

The King went to Fontainebleau on 12 September after spending the day at Sceaux. The Court of Saint-Germain arrived on the 23rd and stayed until 6 October. Soon after his arrival the King learned that the Allied armies had crossed the Rhine by the bridge at Philippsburg, and somewhat later that Prince Louis of Baden had laid siege to Landau. In the meanwhile, Prince Eugene and the Duke of Marlborough commanding their army of observation had advanced to the River Lauter. Amidst these adversities Villars had almost succeeded in dispersing the Fanatics; most of their leaders were either dead or conciliated and gone from the country; five or six of those who remained were allowed to retire to Geneva. It was reckoned that only about an hundred now remained in the Cévennes highlands and that there was no longer any reason for troops in Languedoc.

An affair then took place which it might be wisest to suppress, but is most fascinating to recount for one who observed as keenly as I. What induces me to proceed is the fact that the main outlines were known at the time, and that the histories of royal persons of all centuries and nations swarm with such amorous adventures. Well, shall I continue? We had an adorable princess, whose gracious charm and kindness had so completely captured the hearts of the King, Mme de Maintenon, and Mgr le Duc de Bourgogne that even their extreme vexation with her father the Duke of Savoy could not lessen their delight in her. The King kept no secrets from her, worked in her presence with his ministers, and was careful for her sake not to speak against her father when she was within hearing. When they were alone she would jump on to his knee kissing and hugging him, and with pretty teasing ways rummage through his papers, opening and reading his letters[2] (sometimes against his will)

---

[1] Saint-Simon's other recumbent figure, the Duke of Alba, would not even get up for that. How did Saint-Simon with his passion for truth know all this for sure?

[2] The King once exclaimed, '*La coquine, elle nous a trahi!*' (The little wretch has betrayed us), but he forgave her. It is possible that Saint-Simon did not know that she acted as her father's spy.

and treating Mme de Maintenon much the same. Yet she never made mischief for anyone, indeed she was kind to all and softened the blows whenever she could do so. She was considerate of the King's servants, even the humblest, gentle with her own household, and lived on terms of easy intimacy with all her ladies, young and old. She was the life and light of the Court; every one adored and lived to please her. When she was not there everything seemed flat and dull; her presence enlivened all the pleasures. Her extraordinary favour made her of immense importance and her sweet ways won all hearts. In that dazzling situation her own heart was not insensible to love.

Nangis, whom we know today as a vastly boring Maréchal de France, was at that time a model of perfection—a pleasant enough countenance, though nothing remarkable, a good figure, but not out of the ordinary; he was trained for love and intrigue by his grandmother the Maréchale de Rochefort and Mme de Blanzac[1] his mother, past-mistresses in those arts. They introduced him very young into the highest Society, of which they were central figures. His only talent was for pleasing the ladies, conversing in their private languages,[2] and winning the trust of the most desirable by a discretion beyond his years and no longer practised in this century. He was the height of fashion. He had been given a regiment when still a mere lad, had shown keenness, industry, and brilliant courage at the war, which the ladies magnified and which at his age was sufficient. He much frequented the court of Mgr le Duc de Bourgogne, who was about his age, and was vastly well treated there. That prince, who passionately loved his wife, was physically no match for Nangis;[3] but the princess responded so perfectly to his advances that to his dying day he never suspected that her glance had strayed to another. Stray it did, however, and to Nangis, and before long her partiality increased. Nangis was not unresponsive, but he feared an explosion; moreover he was not heart-free. Mme de La Vrillière, not strictly beautiful, but as pretty as Cupid and possessed of all his charm, had captured him. She was the daughter of Mme de Mailly, Mme la Duchesse de Bourgogne's lady-in-waiting, and was always at that court. Jealousy soon brought enlightenment; but far from yielding gracefully to the princess she made it a point of honour to keep her conquest, outdo her rival, and carry him off as her prey. The struggle was hideously embarrassing for Nangis. He dreaded his mistress's temper, which to him seemed nearer an eruption than in fact it was. He loved her truly, but had

---

[1] Her first husband, whom she married at the age of 12, was the Marquis de Blanzac (d. 1690). Her second was the Comte de Blanzac, father of the Blanzac who surrendered at Blenheim.
[2] See Molière's *Les Femmes Savantes*. Ladies of fashion studied the 'aristocratic' origins of words and spoke a language that excluded those which were of peasant origin and therefore 'vulgar'. There was also a specially refined love-language.
[3] The Duc de Bourgogne had a hump. One shoulder was so much higher than the other that he could not stand straight and walked with a limp. In the official portraits his hair is carefully arranged to conceal the malformation as much as possible.

everything to fear from an outburst and believed himself already lost. On the other hand, reluctance would ruin him just as surely with so powerful a princess, who would one day be all-powerful, and who was certainly not of the kind to yield to, or even endure a rival. His perplexity, for those in the know, provided endless entertainment.

At that period I was constantly in and out of Mme de Blanzac's house in Paris, and the Maréchale de Rochefort's at Versailles. I was intimately friendly with many of the palace-ladies, who saw all and hid nothing from me. I was the firm and trusted friend of the Duchesse de Villeroy, and of the Maréchale as well; so much so, indeed, that although they had quarrelled incessantly I managed to reconcile them and they lived together in loving intimacy until death parted them. Everything that went on at the princess's court was known to the Duchesse de Villeroy through Madame d'O and the Maréchale de Cœuvres, who doted on her; they were her confidantes and something more as well. My sister-in-law the Duchesse de Lorges was not less well-informed, and every evening she told me all that she had seen and heard during the day. Thus from day to day I was amply and precisely instructed. Apart from the fact that I was hugely diverted, there might have been serious consequences, and ambition demanded that I should be fully posted. Eventually, what was at first kept a close secret came to the eager ears of the entire court; but whether from love of an adored princess or from fear all kept silence, observed everything, gossiped among themselves, and preserved the secret that had not been entrusted even to them. That feat, however, was not accomplished without a certain rancour sometimes insolently displayed on the part of Mme de La Vrillière, and distress, accompanied by slight chilliness from the princess towards her, which for a long time provided a truly remarkable spectacle.

Now whether Nangis was too faithful to his first love and required rousing, or whether it happened by chance, a rival appeared on the scene. This was Maulévrier (a son of Colbert's brother, the one who died of grief at not being made a marshal at the same time as Villeroy) who was married to one of the Maréchal de Tessé's daughters. Maulévrier was certainly no beauty, in fact there was something very common about his whole appearance; he was not of the right stuff for gallantry. He kept his wits about him; had a fertile imagination in secret love-affairs, and unbounded ambition so little unrestrained by good principles that it came very close to madness. His wife was pretty, silly, and beneath the appearance of an innocent virgin spiteful to the last degree. On account of being Tessé's daughter she enjoyed the privileges of driving in the royal carriages, sitting at the Court, Marly, and joining in all the pleasures at the court of Mme la Duchesse de Bourgogne, who, as I have mentioned, prided herself on showing gratitude to Tessé for negotiating her marriage, a sentiment of which the King thoroughly approved. Maulévrier was one of the first to discover and profit from Nangis's predicament. He obtained the *entrées* to Mme la Duchesse de Bourgogne through his father-in-law, appeared continually before her, and finally, fired by Nangis's example, dared to sigh. When she seemed not to hear them he risked a letter. Some said that he tricked Mme Quentin,[1] Tessé's intimate, into believing that they came from him; that she passed them on as of no consequence, and that he received answers also under cover of Tessé's name. I shall suppress what other things were believed. Be that as it may, nothing of all this escaped observation, and all was silently observed. On the pretext of affection for Mme de Maulévrier the princess went several times to call on her during the Marly excursions to condole on the coming absence of her husband,[2] and on one or two occasions Mme de Maintenon went also. The Court wondered laughing whether the tears were for him or for Nangis; but the latter was roused to such a state of jealousy that he caused Mme de La Vrillière a perfect paroxysm of anguish and her temper to rise to boiling point.

That tocsin reached Maulévrier's ears; but what does any man care when love or ambition drives him mad? He feigned the chest malady, took to a diet of milk, pretended to lose his voice, and so far controlled himself that no intelligible words passed his lips for more than a year. Thus he avoided the campaign and remained at the Court. He was fool enough, however, to confide this plan (and others as well) to his friend the Duc de Lorges, who instantly confided it to me. His idea was that by thus putting himself under the necessity of whispering to everyone, he might be able to whisper also to Mme la Duchesse de Bourgogne before the entire Court, without impropriety or suspicion that he said anything secret. He contrived in that way to say whatever he pleased to her every day, and chose his moments so carefully that they were not overheard; moreover, amidst ordinary remarks to which she replied out loud he interlarded others, that evoked short responses heard by no one but himself. People became so used to this manœuvre that they ceased to notice, except to pity him for his distressing impediment. There did arrive a time, however, when those closest to Mme la Duchesse de Bourgogne knew better than to gather round her when Maulévrier approached, and that state of affairs continued for more than a year. He reproached her frequently, but in love reproaches seldom succeed. He was tormented by Mme de La Vrillière's ill-humour; he thought it revealed that Nangis was happy and he wished him not to be. At last rage and jealousy drove him to the point of sheer folly.

One day after Mme la Duchesse de Bourgogne's mass he presented himself at the tribune. As she left he offered his hand to lead her away, choosing a day when he knew that Dangeau, her gentleman, would be

---

[1] She was the Duchesse de Bourgogne's head-housemaid.
[2] At the war.

absent. Her equerries, who were all subordinate to Tessé his father-in-
law, were accustomed to allowing him that privilege on account of his
vanished voice and drew back respectfully so as not to overhear. The
ladies followed as usual at some considerable distance, and thus through
all the crowded state rooms from the chapel to Mme la Duchesse de
Bourgogne's apartments he enjoyed the convenience of a tête-à-tête, and
not for the first time. On this particular day, however, he roundly abused
Nangis to the princess, called him every name under the sun, threatened
to tell all to the King, Mme de Maintenon, and her husband, almost
crushed her fingers in a frenzy of passion, and so escorted her to her door.
When she entered, trembling, almost fainting, she made straight for her
privy and summoned Mme de Nogaret,[1] whom she used to call 'Nanny',
and turned to whenever she needed comfort. To her she described what
had happened, saying that she had felt ready to drop, and did not know
how she had survived or ever reached her apartments. She had never
appeared so much upset by anything. Mme de Nogaret in absolute
secrecy and with well-placed confidence told the whole story to Mme de
Saint-Simon and myself that same evening. Meantime, she advised the
princess to be as careful as with a dangerous lunatic, a man quite incapable of self-control, and above all to avoid being compromised. To make
matters worse he began after that to threaten, making all manner of
attacks on Nangis, as though he had been insulted and wished for satisfaction. And although he never explained why, the reason was plain
enough. You may imagine the terror in which Mme la Duchesse de
Bourgogne lived; the fears and comments of Mme de La Vrillière, and
the effect it all had upon Nangis. He was firm enough not to panic or
quarrel, indeed, the very idea of quarrelling in such a cause made his
blood run cold. He saw his whole future at the mercy of a raving lunatic,
and accordingly resolved to avoid Maulévrier as much as possible, to
appear very rarely at the Court, and to remain silent.

Mme la Duchesse de Bourgogne's agonies endured for six long weeks
without her actually experiencing anything more serious than her monstrous apprehensions. I never discovered what finally happened, nor who
it was that informed Tessé, but someone did so, and he acted with marvellous discretion in persuading his son-in-law to follow him to Spain
with the promise of astronomical rewards. He spoke also to Fagon, who
from the vantage points of his own fireside and the King's study had seen
and known everything. Fagon was a man of great sagacity; kind-hearted,
and well able to take a hint. He pronounced it as his professional opinion
that since Maulévrier had tried in vain every known remedy for a weak
chest and a lost voice, nothing remained for him but to seek a warmer
climate. The coming winter, said Fagon, would certainly kill him if he
remained in France. This story was given out to the Court and also to the

[1] Saint-Simon's crony.

King, whom Fagon could convince of anything regarding medicine, where he feared no opposition even from Mme de Maintenon. Both took him at his word and no suspicions were aroused. Tessé then acted with all speed to remove his son-in-law from the Court and the kingdom, not only to put an end to his folly and the terror it was causing, but to avoid awkward questions about so ill a man being fit to travel.

It was at the beginning of October that Tessé finally left Fontainebleau for Spain accompanied by Maulévrier, but he was too clever to go there direct. His aim was to make a fortune and he well knew that in Spain fortunes came from the hands of the Princesse des Ursins. What is more, he knew our Court and was not unaware that Mme de Maintenon was her friend. He considered therefore that it might not displease that lady if he mentioned that the success of his mission to Spain largely depended on the goodwill of the king and queen; that although he did not know the facts regarding Mme des Ursins he knew, like everyone else, that she was very dear to their Catholic Majesties, and that a visit to her *en route* might seem an attention very gratifying to them both. With that argument he persuaded Mme de Maintenon to gain permission for him to pass through Toulouse on the sole pretext of becoming better armed for the King's service. His suggestion was indeed very pleasing to Mme de Maintenon for it gave her an opportunity to send letters privately containing much information that Mme des Ursins needed to know.

There occurred at the beginning of November a deplorable incident from which the State still feels the ill-effects. Pontchartrain,[1] secretary for the navy, was the scourge of that department and of all those who came under his dominion. He was a man of parts, industrious, and capable, but tactless in every possible way, surly, over-meticulous, ready to play the schoolmaster to all, supremely treacherous, loving to harm purely for the sake of it. He was jealous of everyone, even of his own father, who bitterly complained of him to his friends; a cruel tyrant to his wife[2] who, though spirited, was sweetness, gentleness, and virtue personified and the idol of the entire Court; a bully to his mother; in a word, a monster, only tolerated by the King for his horrifying revelations regarding his department in Paris,[3] which he controlled with a malice that put d'Argenson[4] in the shade. All admirals were thorns in his side, but an admiral who was also the King's bastard was a positive torture. There was nothing in the world he would not have done to harm M. le Comte de Toulouse and frustrate his plans; no obstacle that he did not place in his path, no means unused to render his fleet unserviceable. He disputed all his honours and privileges, above all his authority, which he sometimes succeeded in

---

[1] Not Saint-Simon's friend the Chancellor, but his mortal enemy Count One-Eye (Comte Borgne), Jérôme Phélypeaux, Comte de Maurepas.
[2] The Comte de Roucy's sister and Mme de Saint-Simon's first cousin and great friend.
[3] He was also Secretary for the Royal Households.
[4] The Marquis d'Argenson, the chief of police.

reducing even when by its very nature it should not have been questioned. To act in this way towards a son of the King's loins was a far more hazardous proceeding than to attack a Son of France; but Pontchartrain contrived to use the King's vanity and confound the natural father with the monarch, persuading him that the matter concerned a King and his admiral, no more. Thus affection was banished from the mind of a sovereign who always infinitely preferred sovereignty to any other relationship. Acting behind this mask the secretary for the navy was all-powerful, able to obstruct M. le Comte de Toulouse with hindrances calculated to make him fail and enough delays to drive him to despair, without the possibility of an appeal. His conduct became a public scandal at sea and in the ports where the fleet weighed anchor, for he was abhorred in the navy, whereas the count was adored for his courtesy, liberality, and keen sense of justice. The Maréchal de Cœuvres, M. d'O, and the other officers of high rank and standing had received no better treatment and they finally resolved to urge on M. le Comte de Toulouse a course of action on which he was already decided, namely to ruin Pontchartrain by demonstrating the ill-effects of his obstruction, revealing him to have behaved with premeditated malice or even worse in an attempt to gain the King's favour. Only a man of Pontchartrain's reckless character would have put himself in so supremely dangerous a situation, which his father, mother, and wife had foreseen and fruitlessly tried to avert. His blindness continued until the actual moment of the count's arrival, though all his family had received warning of the coming storm, and Pontchartrain, himself, should have suspected something from the greetings of the returning officers.

When, however, the day came for M. de Toulouse's private audience to report on his campaign and at the same time on Pontchartrain's conduct, Mme de Pontchartrain, fighting back her shyness, went to him in Mme la Duchesse de Bourgogne's apartment and almost forced him to speak to her alone in another room. There she burst into tears, confessed her husband's crimes, described her fate were he to be punished as he deserved, and so disarmed the count that he promised to forget the past, provided he were given no cause to remember it. He said later that he could not resist Mme de Pontchartrain's wretchedness, and that no matter how firm his determination his weapons would have fallen from his grasp at the thought of that poor woman in the hands of an infuriated cyclops[1] with no other employment than to torment her.

That was how Pontchartrain gained his reprieve, but the State suffered dearly for it. Fear of being in the power of an admiral who was also the King's son made him resolve to destroy the navy itself so as to render it

---

[1] 'Smallpox removed one eye, but success totally blinded him . . . His glass eye was permanently weeping, which gave him a false, surly, scowling appearance, frightening at first sight, but not half so alarming as it should have been.'

unfit to take that admiral to sea, and to that object he set his entire mind. He succeeded only too well, for the Comte de Toulouse never again saw either ports or ships, and thereafter only very inferior squadrons put out to sea, and that as seldom as possible. Pontchartrain actually had the temerity to boast of that in my hearing.

Denonville pleaded so hard that finally the King consented to his coming to Versailles to justify his conduct, and the Duke of Marlborough immediately granted him several months' leave of absence.[1] The duke had lately returned to Holland after visiting the Electors of Brandenburg and Hanover, the Landgrave of Hesse, and several other German princes. He then sent for Tallard and the other high-ranking prisoners and took them to England to adorn his triumph.

To everyone's surprise and disgust Tallard was made governor of Franche-Comté, but as M. le Duc d'Orléans humorously remarked, one could not refuse a hand-out to a man who was ruined. As he said this quite spontaneously and out loud the jest spread like wildfire, but the King was gravely displeased. A few days later he gave a forty thousand livres pension to the little Comte de La Marche, the infant son of the Prince de Conti. It seemed a prodigious sum, as indeed it was in those days. Today it is like a drop in the ocean compared with what those princes have extracted since the King's death.

The Duchesse d'Aiguillon died in Paris on 18 October. She was the unmarried sister of the Duc de Richelieu and one of the oddest people imaginable, as well as the most spirited. All her life she had been a mixture of pride and simplicity, the fine lady and the nun. She managed her affairs so badly, although later she repaired them, that for a time she could not afford to keep a carriage. She might have asked others to take her when she wished to drive out or have hired a chair, but no, she preferred independence in one of those wheeled conveyances called *vinaigrettes*[2] that ply for hire at the street corners, with a man pulling in front and a boy to push at the back. In such a vehicle she called on Monsieur at the Palais Royal and bade the man enter by the gates. The guards barred his way, and no matter what he said they would not admit him. Mme d'Aiguillon heard all in silence. Then, as they trundled her away, she quietly bade the man stop at the first draper's in the Rue Saint-Honoré, where she had a red cover fitted to her *vinaigrette*, there and then

---

[1] Marlborough enjoyed being kind when the service did not suffer thereby. At this time he wrote to Godolphin about 'a letter from a young woman of quality that is in love with the Comte de Lyons (also a prisoner). He is at Lichfield. I am assured that it is a very virtuous love, and that when they can get their parents' consent they are to be married. As I do from my heart wish that nobody were unhappy, I own to you that this letter has made me wish him in France, so that if he might have leave for four months, without prejudice to Her Majesty's service, I should be glad of it.'

[2] *Vinaigrettes* were also the name for the small ornamental boxes containing a piece of flannel soaked in vinegar, to revive ladies suffering from tight stays. In this case the vinegar may have been a deodorant.

outside his shop-door, and was immediately wheeled back to the Palais-Royal. The guards when they saw the scarlet cover on a vehicle of that description were much astonished and inquired the reason for it. Then Mme d'Aiguillon gave her name and with immense dignity ordered the man to pull her in, at which the sentries let them pass. By this time all the occupants of the Palais Royal were watching, and Monsieur himself came to a window with his entire court to see her arrive in her magnificent wheelbarrow. After that Mme d'Aiguillon took such an affection for it that she left the cover on and used it constantly, so draped, until the day arrived when she was able once more to keep a carriage. She took, and many times discarded, the white veil of the Filles du Saint-Sacrement, in the Rue Cassette; gave them great sums of money, and behaved in every way as though she were their superior, but she never brought herself to take the vows; she had been wearing their veil for many years when she died in that convent at the age of seventy. She was very wealthy at that time and had remained unmarried.

At the end of the year Villars, having more or less quietened the Fanatics, was ordered to return to Paris, and the Duke of Berwick was sent into Languedoc to replace him. They were unwilling to leave Berwick without some high command after his distinguished service in Spain and the sudden manner of his recall.

CHAPTER XV

1705

The Abbé d'Estrées receives the Order – Villars extracts a Dukedom –The Princesse des Ursins in Paris – Death of the Duc de Bretagne – Villars's good campaign – Wit and Malevolence of Lauzun – The Princesse des Ursins triumphant – Courtenvaux's terrible reprimand from the King – Raising a Militia – Widely different views of our ministers regarding a peace-treaty – Death of the Duc de Beauvilliers's two sons – Piety of their parents – Roquelaure attempts to justify his negligence – Anecdote about the Abbé, later Cardinal, de Polignac

ON THE first day of the new year the Abbé d'Estrées was received into the Order of the Holy Ghost, wearing a rochet and purple hood like the bishops. Harcourt held the baton during the ceremony because, at the changing of the guard, the captain of the old guard carries the baton until after the King's mass and hands it to his relief at the door of the chapel. While the oath was being administered the King happened to turn round and was shocked to see Harcourt wearing his tunic among all the robed knights of the Order. That incongruity had never struck him before and never did again, but at that time he was horrified and his first impulse was to give Harcourt the Order there and then. On second thoughts, as he later remarked, he reflected that he would have to give it to the other captains also, and he spent the remainder of the ceremony trying to decide whom to knight and whom not to knight. Finally he fixed on the Marshals of France because by dubbing them all no one would have anything to complain about, and by limiting himself to those few none need feel excluded on personal grounds. There was much to confute that fallacious argument. Marshals of France, as such, had no right to the Order and many of them never received it. That rank, or rather that purely military office of the Crown, for such it is, is given for military merit without reference to birth, and it was for men of birth that the Order was instituted. Even at that time the rule was the same, for of the nine marshals without the Order several were not born to wear it, and a few others, though men of rank, were not of the right quality. But to be brief, the King improvised, and acted accordingly. On leaving the Chapel he had the word given to the knights to go at once to his study instead of remaining drawn up in two lines in his bedroom. He wished, he said, to hold a chapter. He did hold one immediately after his return and nominated the entire body of the Marshals of France at one blow, which caused M. de Lauzun to say that the King, like all good generals, took his decisions in the field.

It is now time for us to come to the Maréchal de Villars, the most abundantly and consistently fortunate of all the millions of men born during the reign of Louis XIV. He was commonly supposed to have been the son of the town-clerk of Condrieu; but his father none the less had a regiment, probably of militia, and won his suit for nobility in 1635. Everyone knows how that kind of research into heredity is done. The investigators are not of noble rank; for the most part they abominate and seek only to debase it. They scamp their work, their secretaries clear the ground for them, and many nobles are made for money. Hence the saying that they make more than they unmake. Be that as it may, through his grandmother who was a Louvet, which is the family name of the Cauvissons (not that that cuts much ice), Villars was allowed to claim kinship with the ancient family of Villars, lords of Dombes, who were equal in rank with those of Dauphiné, with whom they inter-married, owning great estates and a dukedom.

That is a strange preamble to what now follows. The King and Chamillart were greatly perturbed by Blenheim and its disastrous consequences. It was the first defeat which he had suffered, and the reverse reduced him from attacking Bohemia and Austria to the defence of Alsace, which was considered exceedingly difficult after the loss of Landau, not to mention that of the Elector's country, Bavaria, left a prey to the Emperor's vengeance. Tallard was a prisoner; Marsin appeared too inexperienced, and unfit to be trusted with so great a task; Villeroy, such as he was, was destined for Flanders with the Elector. Boufflers was out of the running and so were all the other marshals. As for the princes of the blood, the King would have none of them at the head of his armies. There remained only Villars, for Harcourt had taken precautions to see that no one wanted him away from the Court, especially not Mme de Maintenon, who could not do without him in the critical time through which they both were passing. Villars also had her protection and for the same reason (his father's friendship in her Scarron days) and consequently Chamillart, too, approved of him. He had been making claims for a dukedom since he left Bavaria, and his exploits and lootings in Languedoc had made him still more audacious. He attributed the settlement there entirely to his own labours, giving none of the credit to Montrevel, and had been inundating the King, Mme de Maintenon, and Chamillart with letters on the subject of the mistakes at Blenheim and afterwards, telling them what he would have done, grieving that he had not been with the armies; in a word, bragging with his usual effrontery, which served him rather better than usual on this occasion, because he was dealing with anxious people, greatly perplexed how to choose a general for the weighty task on the Rhine and Moselle, and ever ready to be flattered and believe promises.

Mme de Maintenon went into action. She understood the urgency and the dilemma; she forgave Villars for his lootings and his insolence to the Elector on the grounds of inexperience, and pushed him forwards; whilst he, seeing that his letters were relished, allowed them to perceive his disappointment at his ducal claim being ignored. When they had finally got it into the King's head that Villars was his only choice, it was easy to demonstrate that it would never do to have him upset and offended, and at that point the lady and the minister succeeded in producing a dukedom for him on arrival. He was accordingly sent a courier with orders to finish as quickly as possible in Languedoc, and to return with all speed to the Court. He arrived at Versailles on 15 January, and made his bow to the King when the latter returned from a drive to Marly. As the King stepped down from his coach he told him to go upstairs and that he would speak to him. When he was dressed and had gone to Mme de Maintenon's room he had Villars summoned and said as soon as he caught sight of him, 'I have no time to talk to you now; but I shall make you a duke.' That monosyllable was worth more to Villars than any number of audiences, for in truth it was his whole aim. He withdrew in perfect transports of delight; but the favour he had received caused enormous astonishment, to say no more, and the entire Court against its usual custom made no effort to conceal its horror. All the dukes and the aspirants to that rank were similarly afflicted, the former to have been given an equal of that low kind, and the latter to be obliged to give him precedence. The murmurs were for once stronger than prudence, congratulations were cold and short, and the new duke, searching for them hither and thither, and sometimes anticipating them without much satisfaction, displayed with evident ill-breeding profound respect for some and extreme disdain for others.

The siege of Gibraltar was proceeding as well as could be expected. Six English vessels made their appearance on 24 December, escorting seven frigates purposing to enter with supplies for the besieged. They were attacked and four were captured, but the other three could not be prevented from taking in reinforcements of a thousand men, as well as food and munitions. The King of Spain detached four thousand troops to support the besieging army.

Marlborough was greeted in England with public rejoicing and extraordinary honours. The House of Commons sent a deputation; he was harangued by the Speaker, and also by the Lord Keeper when he took his seat in the House of Lords. They would not let Tallard go to London, nor anywhere near that city, where he had for so long been our ambassador. He and the other important prisoners were sent to Nottingham, a long way from London and a very long way from the sea. The rest were dispersed to other towns. All were given their liberty in the places where they were imprisoned, with freedom to walk out into the country but not to stay the night away, and unobtrusively they were very closely watched.

We left Tessé and Maulévrier bearing, designedly, many important letters for the Princesse des Ursins, and others also from Mme la Duchesse de Bourgogne to the Queen of Spain. You may judge that their journey was not unsuccessful from the fact that Tessé was made a grandee on the very day of his arrival at Madrid. Mme des Ursins, indeed, regarded their visit as the first sign of approaching deliverance, and themselves as people of some eminence who might prove useful to her with both courts. Maulévrier did everything to encourage her in that view (he had good reasons for deceiving her), and she was suitably impressed. She was too well informed not to have learned of the many visits paid by Mme de Maintenon and Mme la Duchesse de Bourgogne to his wife, and when his version of the story was supported by Tessé's she felt that no price was too great for so bold a schemer with inner knowledge of the Court. Thus she placed entire confidence in both of them, and assured them, even before they arrived in Madrid, that the King and Queen of Spain trusted them equally well. As for those sovereigns, she ruled them and their affairs from Toulouse even more despotically and with less competition than Cardinal Mazarin had ever governed the Queen-mother.

When, therefore, Tessé and Maulévrier finally arrived in Madrid, bearing still more letters, they were greeted with open arms. At their very first interview there was an outpouring of emotion, especially from the queen, who placed in them her best hopes for the return of her dear princess without whom she could not endure her life. At that point Tessé was obliged to leave for a conference with Berwick on the Portuguese frontier, but Maulévrier for reasons of health remained in Madrid and took his father-in-law's place in all the discussions. The queen agreed in everything with the princess and Mme de Maintenon, and Maulévrier took full advantage of the fact that he was the only Frenchman in whom she could confide. She greatly enjoyed their interviews and gave him the *entrée*, which allowed him to visit her with the king at all hours. With advisers like Tessé, Mme la Duchesse de Bourgogne, and the Princesse des Ursins to guide him he pushed such privileges a very long way. As a secondary issue the queen wanted the recall of the Duc de Gramont our ambassador, guilty of the, to her, unpardonable crime of opposing the princess's return. She saw to it therefore that all affairs, even the most pressing, miscarried under his direction, and worse, as part of a deep-laid plot, she persuaded the king to disregard his grandfather's wishes and reject all the ambassador's advice. The aim was first to exhaust King Louis's patience and then convince him that only the presence of Mme des Ursins, honourably treated and given full authority, could ensure obedience and restore the former happy relationship.

When the ground had been well prepared and our King somewhat appeased by the princess's banishment and Tessé's letters, they judged that the time was ripe for action. Harcourt, who still maintained his privilege of conferring with the King on Spanish affairs, gently enlightened him as to the utter dependence of King Philip on his queen and of her violent feeling against King Louis, whom she had determined to oppose in every way, even against her own interests. His information, he said, was that her temper was ungovernable, but that she might have some provocation in view of the continued harsh treatment of one whom she loved and had defended with all her might. All that was needed to mollify her was a very small favour of no importance to affairs of State, namely permission for Mme des Ursins to plead her case at Versailles and then be allowed to live where she pleased, with the exception of Spain and the Court of France. At length the King consented to be appeased, and truly had the queen's anger and resentment been allowed to grow unchecked there might well have been disastrous consequences, for after the defeats of Blenheim and Gibraltar and the revolt in Catalonia, unity between the two crowns was more than ever necessary.

Louis XIV, whom the truth never reached within the barrier by which he surrounded himself, was the only man in the two kingdoms who did not understand that Mme des Ursins's coming to Versailles guaranteed her return to Spain with even greater authority than before. He was saddened by continual rejections and worried by the confusion they had caused, but his final capitulation took his ministers completely by surprise. No sooner, however, was the great word pronounced than a courier was sent speeding to Toulouse, bidding the Princesse des Ursins come to Paris and Versailles as soon as she cared to make the journey. Her joy exceeded her wildest hopes, yet at the prospect of returning to Spain her poise was no more disturbed than by the bombshell that had descended on her in Madrid. She remained mistress of herself, and turned her mind to drawing every possible benefit from her present situation. Thus she kept up an appearance of being still out of favour, hopeful, yet very humble, and she instructed her friends to adopt the same tone, for she feared above all things to revive the King's anger and suspicion of her. With immense self-control she made her arrangements, appearing in no great haste to leave Toulouse, but going soon enough to show eagerness and profit to the full by that long-awaited favour.

Meanwhile at the Court the excitement was intense and only the friends of Mme des Ursins preserved their equanimity. Everyone knew that her appearance heralded important changes and people prepared to greet her as a rising sun likely to transform the face of the earth. Some who had never been heard to speak her name now called her their dear friend and congratulated one another on her return. Others, friendly with her enemies, did not scruple to profess delight, uttering fulsome praises in the hope that they might be repeated. She finally arrived in Paris on 4 January. The Spanish ambassador and his duchess drove with an escort to meet her at a great distance from the city, took her back to sleep at his house, and gave a fête in her honour. Many other distinguished people drove to meet her also, and the Noailles went further than any. She had good cause to be satisfied with her triumphant return, but wisely decided to remove from the ambassador's residence, thinking it best to remain unattached.

The King was at Marly at that time, and Mme de Saint-Simon and I were of the party, as was often the case after Chamillart had restored me to favour. In the absence of the Court the house where Mme des Ursins lodged in Paris was besieged at all hours by a prodigious crowd, although she kept her door closed, on the plea of needing rest, and never went out. It was curiosity, ambition, prudence, and fashion that drew the crowds, and not more than a quarter were admitted, but the ministers none the less took fright and when Torcy himself received a royal command to visit her he was completely overwhelmed. He made no attempt to escape, however, merely obeyed like one who accepts defeat; but throughout the entire interview he remained visibly embarrassed and she cold and unbending. It was at that moment that the Princesse des Ursins changed her tone. Where previously she had been humble and supplicating she now clamoured for justice, accusing those who had misled the King into treating her harshly, and made a spectacle of her in both kingdoms.

The King returned to Versailles on Saturday, 10 January, and Mme des Ursins arrived there on the same day, putting up in the town at Alègre's[1] house. I visited her immediately, not having been able to go to her before on account of nightly balls at Marly. My mother, however, had seen her several times in Paris, where Mme de Saint-Simon and I had already sent to tell her of our joy and longing to be with her. As a matter of fact, I had never ceased in correspondence with her and had received many marks of her affection. She gave me a warm greeting, but I was a little disappointed because Harcourt soon afterwards arrived and I thought it more tactful to leave them. She delayed me for some small commission, promising to see me again before long when we should have more leisure to converse. On the following day, just a week after her return, she dined alone, put on court-dress, waited on the King, and was alone with him in his study for two and a half hours. She then called on Mme la Duchesse de Bourgogne, and was closeted alone with her also for a longish period. Next day she saw Mme de Maintenon in private on a most intimate footing. She returned on the Tuesday when there was a very long conversation between the three of them. One month later a colonel of the Spanish army arrived, sent by the King and Queen of Spain for the sole purpose of thanking King Louis for having received her. Her next move was to announce that she proposed to stay until the end of April. She had gone a long way to be able thus to decide the length of her visit; but truly no one

¹ Yves Marquis d'Alègre (1653–1733). He was a lieutenant-general and a very capable officer.

doubted her eventual return to Spain, even though permission was not yet given.

I called on her again two days after my first visit. She was as kind as ever, but reproached me a little for having been more friendly before her troubles. That, however, was all forgotten in our conversation, for she spoke very frankly and seemed to wish to trust me. She made many affectionate gestures towards Mme de Saint-Simon also. Let us leave her now to her triumph and turn for a while to other matters.

We lost Mgr le Duc de Bretagne[1] very suddenly. Mgr, and especially Mme la Duchesse de Bourgogne were deeply afflicted and the King displayed much pious feeling and resignation. Immediately afterwards, that is to say on 24 April, he went to Marly, making a selection to go with him, in other words, without people having to ask. Mme de Saint-Simon and I went. A long attack of gout seized the King and kept him there for more than six weeks, and after that seizure the King's *coucher* was no longer public but became a time reserved for those with the *entrées*. There was no ceremonial beyond that of the body of the infant prince being taken in a royal coach, not draped, with an escort of guards and pages bearing torches. In the same coach Cardinal de Coislin sat with the heart on a pillow on his knees. M. le Duc representing the princes of the blood sat beside him, M. de Tresmes, representing the dukes (not as first gentleman), and Mme de Ventadour, the governess, sat in front. Neither the King, Monseigneur, nor Mgr and Mme la Duchesse de Bourgogne wore mourning. M. le Duc de Berry and the entire Court wore it as for a brother. After Saint-Denis the heart was brought back to the Val-de-Grâce.[2] Paris and the public were deeply moved by this loss.

[*An explanation may be needed here of Marlborough's rage at being cheated of a battle and, in the following anecdote, the point of Lauzun's malicious play with his snuff-box.*

At this period an entire campaign could be won or lost in a single battle. A general who felt strong enough to win would stake everything on trying to bring one about. This was not always easy, for cavalry needed a wide expanse of flat open country to charge and manœuvre and there are comparatively few such plains in western Europe. Timing was of immense importance; in Marlborough's day a quarter to a third of an army consisted of horse-soldiers requiring forage in vast quantities. Once assembled in battle array they had to fight or disperse, otherwise they would starve. Thus Marlborough, having come to face Villars on suitable ground at Sierck, believed that with the Margrave's reinforcement he could win another Blenheim. When the Margrave arrived a week later than expected, the chance had gone.

---

[1] The Duc de Bourgogne's eldest son, born 25 June, 1704. Madame wrote to her niece, 'The poor little Duc de Bretagne died last Monday. I am firmly convinced that the doctors dispatched the poor little prince to the other world with their bleedings and emetics. But no one ever listens to me.'

[2] The famous church of the convent in the Rue Saint-Jacques built, 1645–1665, by Anne of Austria.

Later, when Villeroy was within range of Marlborough and on suitable terrain in the Low Countries, he was the stronger, thanks to Villars's reinforcement. Why did he not attack? The anxious Court at Versailles concluded that there must be some unforeseen obstruction on the ground. Infantry, even more than cavalry, needed smooth, firm country to fight over. Everything for them depended on marching close together in perfect formation, firing in unison, behind the hedge of their bayonets. Quite small obstacles, a little ditch, a bank, a low hedge, a stream with marshy, or even firm, banks (cf. Blenheim) was extremely dangerous and required careful planning to negotiate, for the slightest disorder of the ranks left them helpless before a cavalry charge. Therein lay Lauzun's malice.]

Villars campaigned that season in a manner worthy of the greatest generals. It had been the enemy's intention to cross the Saar, fall upon Alsace from the north-east, and penetrate as far into France as their luck would carry them. Marlborough mustered an army of more than eighty thousand men near Trèves, whilst Villars took up his position at Sierck and stood firm, not daring to attack although greatly superior in numbers. Prince Louis of Baden[1] approached from that side and rode on ahead to confer with Marlborough, whereupon the Maréchal de Villeroy sent d'Alègre to reinforce Villars with twenty squadrons and fifteen battalions, which Villars awaited with perfect equanimity because his position was very strong indeed. As it turned out he had no need of them, for Marlborough, unable to attack him alone with any hope of success or subsist facing him in a district where forage was scanty, was obliged to retire on Trèves. Villars then sent word to d'Alègre to halt at whatever place the courier intercepted him because he no longer needed reinforcements. Marlborough's fury was so great at being foiled by Villars's excellent dispositions that he sent a note by a trumpeter saying that he would have attacked on 10 July as originally intended had Prince Louis not arrived six days late and with orders not to fight, of which he bitterly complained.[2] Villars, thus relieved of anxiety for himself, sent a very large detachment led by four lieutenants-general to the Maréchal de Villeroy, whom the enemy by their movements seemed about to attack. Having given them that to think about he marched into Alsace with the remainder of his army, took Wissembourg, drove the Imperial troops from their lines on the Lauter, captured several small castles and five hundred prisoners, and spread his army over the country which they had been occupying. Thus by his strong position at Sierck he forced Marlborough to alter his entire plan of campaign, and skilfully took advantage of Prince Louis's absence to overthrow the lines of Lauterburg, which had formed a barrier from

[1] Saint-Simon speaks of him as Prince of Baden, but he was in fact Landgrave of Hesse and Margrave of Baden, and is usually referred to as 'The Margrave'.
[2] 'Tell Marshal Villars that I am in despair because the Margrave has broken his word, and that I can hold only him responsible for the breaking up of all our plans.' He added according to another report, 'Be assured that my contempt of him does not equal my respect for you.'

the mountains to the Rhine, hemming us into our territory of Alsace. On 17 June the enemy suddenly abandoned Trèves and arrived below Maestricht.

I cannot leave the subject of Flanders without giving an amusing example of M. de Lauzun's malice. You will remember that when he married my sister-in-law his sole aim was to become once more on intimate terms with the King by finding a fresh pretext to discuss Germany, since the Maréchal de Lorges at that time commanded there. When that plan miscarried[1] he pretended to be indisposed so as to obtain permission to drink the waters of Aix-la-Chapelle. No one in their right minds believed him; only fools, of which there were many, spoke of a mysterious illness. A mystery there certainly was, but not what they thought. To be sure, he never intended to drink the waters; what he hoped was to meet distinguished foreigners, extract information, and gain favour by reporting to the King, thus making an excuse for a private audience, with an order, perhaps, to return and gather more. He was unsuccessful. Every foreigner of importance was otherwise occupied in time of war; the only one he met was Hompesch,[2] a lieutenant-general of the Dutch army who later rose to high rank, but was not then what Lauzun required, though for want of better he talked continually of him after his return.

Lauzun did not stay long and returned by way of the Maréchal de Villeroy's army. The latter, fearing his malicious tongue, gave him all the honours due to one who had commanded the King's army in Ireland.[3] He kept him entertained for three days, allowed him to inspect the troops, and gave him an escort of staff-officers to show him the front line. At that moment the opposing armies were drawn up facing, and very close to one another with no obstacles to separate them. Thus everyone expected a battle, more especially as it was known to be the King's wish, which was why Lauzun had particularly desired to inspect that army. The officers accompanying him took him within sight of the enemy's advance guards; then, becoming wearied by his questions and advice, they deliberately exposed him to pistol-fire at the risk of his being taken prisoner, a folly for which they might have paid dearly since they would certainly have been captured along with him. Now Lauzun was an exceedingly brave man; moreover he possessed that cool courage that calmly assesses the degree of danger and acts as quietly as though sitting in a room. Therefore, since he had no responsibilities and nothing to do but observe, he amused himself at their expense by multiplying his advices and questions and pausing in places of real danger when he perceived that the accompanying gentry longed to remove him elsewhere; for indeed they

---

[1] Because of the Maréchal de Lorges's death.

[2] Count Hompesch, a Prussian. He served under Marlborough at Blenheim.

[3] In 1689, when Louis XIV sent a small army to invade Ireland in an attempt to put James II back on the throne.

soon realized their folly in trying to mock a man who would always go one better.

When he returned to Versailles people crowded round him to hear news from the armies. He affected his usual air of being backward, down on his luck, rusty, incapable of seeing an inch beyond his nose. Next day he called on Monseigneur who cared little for him but disliked the Maréchal de Villeroy even more. He was asked innumerable questions regarding the dispositions of the opposing armies and the reason why they were not joined in battle. M. de Lauzun hummed and hawed, admitted that he had indeed ridden between the armies and very near the enemy's advance-guards, but continually returned to the magnificence of our troops, their eagerness to fight, and their cheeriness at being so close to the enemy. At last Monseigneur cornered him, which was just what he wished. 'Very good, Sire,' said he, 'since you press me; I examined every inch of the ground to right and left as well as in between the armies. Truly, there were no streams or gullies, and I saw no sunken roads, nor slopes either up or down, but I must admit to there being some obstacles which I did very clearly perceive.' 'But what could they have been,' said Monseigneur, 'since you say there was nothing in between the armies?' Lauzun kept him in suspense, continually repeating his list of non-existing obstacles. At last, when everyone was quite exhausted, he drew out his snuff-box; 'You see, Sire,' he said, 'there was something that might badly have entangled their feet. Heather bushes of a sort, not very stiff or prickly ones, and indeed not particularly close-growing, that I must say, but high heather, high as, oh!, how shall I describe it?' (looking everywhere for a comparison) 'Ah! as high, I vow, as this snuff-box.' There were peals of laughter from Monseigneur and the entire company, and M. de Lauzun turned on his heel and left them. He had had what he wanted. The tale spread to Versailles and thence to Paris, and it reached the King's ears that very evening. That was Lauzun's way of thanking the Maréchal de Villeroy for the honours paid to him, and his consolation for not finding what he had sought at Aix-la-Chapelle.[1]

The Princesse des Ursins, successful beyond her fondest hopes, continued to control the affairs of Spain from Paris. Rivas, secretary of the Junta and famous for drawing up the testament of Charles II, was finally dismissed, and the Duc de Gramont was fast driven to despair by State business that invariably miscarried when he handled it. At last, weary of the King of Spain's perpetual snubs, he requested an audience of the queen, hoping to do better with her. He obtained one and explained at length many important and urgent matters concerning the siege of Gibraltar,

---

[1] There is a certain similarity between Lauzun and Saint-Simon. Both were ambitious, clever men, eager for responsibility, and eating their hearts out in unemployment. But Lauzun's part in the nobles' revolt put him out of the running, and Saint-Simon was too much the artist to be a good administrator. Enforced idleness turned both men sour.

to which she listened quietly enough. When he had finished, however, she gave a sour smile, asking whether he did not consider it unbecoming for a woman to interfere in State matters, and turned her back on him. This was too much and he asked for his recall, which admirably suited Mme des Ursins. She had been unwilling to demand it herself, but apart from the fact that she did not forget old injuries, it was important for her to have the ambassador on her side. The new ambassador was Amelot,[1] a man of honour, amiable, polite, and firm enough, but above all wise and modest, who had held posts in Portugal, Venice, and Switzerland and had been liked and had done well in all of them. Mme des Ursins had very long interviews with him.

The King returned to Marly, where there were several balls. You will readily believe that Mme des Ursins was included in the party. She was lodged on the *Perspective*.[2] Nothing could have exceeded the radiance of her air, or the attentions lavished on her by the King, who treated her like a foreign queen making her first visit to the Court. All his courtesies she received in a truly regal manner, a mixture of graciousness and respect that was long out-moded, somewhat reminiscent of the court manner in the Queen-mother's day. Whenever she appeared the King seemed to put his entire mind to the business of her entertainment, pointing out this and that, and consulting her every wish with a gallant, almost flattering air that never for an instant flagged. Her frequent private talks with him and Mme de Maintenon, lasting for one hour, and often for two, and those which she had alone with that lady during the morning, made the Court regard her as a kind of goddess. It was fascinating to watch the nobly-born, the powerful and the favourites fawning upon her. Her very glances were remarked, and if she dropped a casual word to high-ranking ladies as she passed their faces were wreathed with smiles of gratification. I saw her every morning. She always rose very early, and dressed and had her hair arranged at that time so that she was never seen at her dressing-table. I used to arrive before her important visitors, and we talked together as freely as in the old days. She told me many details concerning State affairs, and the views of the King, and especially of Mme de Maintenon, on many people. We used often to laugh at the way in which highly respected people toadied to her, and the sneers they attracted if she happened not to notice them; also the meanness of those who, having done their best to harm her at first, were now boasting of life-long friendships.

I was flattered to have the confidence of this goddess. It was much noticed and made me suddenly respected. Not only had several distinguished persons found me alone with her in the morning, as the notes

---

[1] Michel Jean Amelot, Marquis de Gournay (1655-1724). He was a most successful ambassador; later he fell into disfavour on suspicion of Jansenism, but the Spaniards requested his reappointment, and he went back to Spain.

[2] The *Perspective* at Marly was the avenue of pavilions for the use of very important guests.

which they rained upon her frequently mentioned, but very often they had been unable to converse with her at all. What is more, she often called me to her in the drawing-room, or I was seen to whisper something in her ear with an air of intimacy that was much envied but not often copied. She never saw Mme de Saint-Simon without going to her, praising her, and drawing her into the circle surrounding herself. Sometimes she would take her to a mirror and arrange some detail in her dress or her hair, just as she might have done to her own daughter in private. At other times she would draw her apart and talk to her for some considerable time in an undertone, always with a few whispered exchanges and others aloud that were not comprehensible. People inquired with surprise not unmixed with envy the reason for this obvious affection,[1] but what they found particularly annoying was that when leaving Mme de Maintenon's room, after being closeted with her and the King, Mme des Ursins invariably went straight to Mme de Saint-Simon in the first anteroom, where she had the right to wait along with other ladies especially privileged, and began to speak in a soft voice. That made everyone open their eyes and brought my wife many compliments.

Something more substantial was that, as we learned from trustworthy sources far removed from Mme des Ursins, she repeatedly praised my wife to the King and Mme de Maintenon, and did her all manner of services, none of them solicited, with the most perfect tact imaginable; also that she more than once told them that no lady at the Court was more discreet, dignified and sensible, more fit in every way, although so young, to be made a palace-lady forthwith, and later succeed the Duchesse du Lude as first lady-in-waiting to Mme la Duchesse de Bourgogne. I am sure that although like everyone else at the Court the King and Mme de Maintenon already had a very high opinion of her, those words of the Princesse des Ursins made a lasting impression. Indeed, the future proved them to have been of far greater consequence than suited our comfort.[2] Mme des Ursins did not forget me in her praise; but when a woman praises a woman it has more effect. Her kind way of treating us, and her good offices lasted until, after many postponements, she finally left for Spain in the middle of July.

The favours that she received were stupendous: a pension of twenty thousand livres from the King, and thirty thousand livres for the expenses of her journey; her brother, blind M. de Noirmoutiers, granted a brevet dukedom, and her second brother the Abbé de La Trémoïlle advanced to the cardinalcy by the nominations of both France and Spain. Well satisfied and loaded with honours such as no other subject had ever

---

[1] She was an old friend of his mother, and her influence on Saint-Simon as a boy was one of the most important in his life.

[2] When in 1710 Mme de Saint-Simon was obliged to become the Duchesse de Berry's lady-in-waiting.

received, she left, as I have said, in mid-July and spent a month upon the road. You may imagine her reception in Spain, where the king and queen drove more than a day's journey from Madrid to meet her. And that was the woman whom the King had been so determined to destroy that, according to Maréchal, he boasted to Fagon and Blouin of his skill in parting her from the King and Queen of Spain so as to be quite certain of not missing his aim.

On 22 September the King left for Fontainebleau, spending a day and a night at Sceaux on the way. The King of England arrived on 1 October and returned to Saint-Germain on the 12th. His mother had been distressingly incommoded by a pain in her breast from which the worst was feared, although that did not come to pass, and she was not able to go to Fontainebleau that year.

Soon after the King's arrival a terrible thing happened to Courtenvaux. He was the eldest son of M. de Louvois, who procured for him the reversion of his office,[1] and then removed it when he was found to be incapable. To make up to him for that disappointment M. de Louvois purchased for him the captaincy of the Hundred Swiss, which is without question the highest and most lucrative post in the King's household after the great offices of State.

Courtenvaux was a very small man, obscurely profligate, with a voice that squeaked. He had served badly and seldom with the armies, and was despised and neglected by his family and the Court, where he was on no one's visiting list. He was miserly and boring, and though his manners were modest and respectful he was apt to fly into furious rages when the mood took him. In short, he was a monstrously stupid fellow and was everywhere treated as such. One met him nowhere, not even in the houses of his sister and sister-in-law, the Duchesse de Villeroy and the Maréchale de Cœuvres. The King at this time was becoming more and more avid for information regarding everything that went on, and was even more interested in gossip than people imagined, although he was well known to be vastly inquisitive. He now ordered Blouin the governor of Versailles to enlist extra members of the Swiss Guard, apart from those who ordinarily guarded the gates of the parks and gardens, the doors of the gallery and State apartments at Versailles, and the drawing-rooms at Marly and Trianon. The newcomers were to wear the King's uniform but to be answerable only to Blouin. They were given secret orders to prowl around morning, noon, and night on all the staircases and in the corridors, passages and privies, and when the weather was fine into the courtyards and gardens. They were told to conceal themselves, watch, follow, and take notes of people's entrances and exits, whom they visited, who accompanied them, overhearing as much of their conversation as

[1] The War Department.

possible, remembering how long each person had remained in any place, and then, returning, to make a report. These functions, in which some officers and a number of the valets also joined, were most ardently performed at Versailles, Marly, Trianon, Fontainebleau, or wherever else the King happened to be. Courtenvaux was infuriated by the importation of the new Swiss, for they were not subject to his authority and subtracted from his own hundred some of the promotions and rewards which he would otherwise have had to sell. Indeed he became so angry that he constantly vexed and harassed them in their duties.

Between the great hall of the Swiss Guard at Fontainebleau and the guardroom of the King's bodyguard there is a narrow passage that connects the staircase with the rooms which Mme de Maintenon then occupied. At one end is a square room containing the outer door to her suite and leading straight into the guardroom. It also contains a second door that gives on to the balcony surrounding the oval courtyard, and communicating with the staircases at many different points. The square room is thus a kind of public passage, used by everyone in the palace when they do not go out-of-doors by the courtyards, and it provides an excellent place from which to mark people's comings and goings. Until this particular year, many of the bodyguard and some of the Swiss Guard had usually slept there, and when the King passed on his way to or from Mme de Maintenon they had stood to arms together. Indeed, to all appearances the square room was an extension of the two guardrooms. When the King suddenly decided to let Blouin's Swiss sleep there instead of the Hundred Swiss Courtenvaux was maddened. Without asking the Captain of the bodyguard, who would have told him that his men had been displaced at the same time, he allowed himself to believe that the change was a further attack on his Swiss by Blouin's contingent. He then flew into such a passion that he spared them neither threats nor insults; but they put up with his abuse because they were under orders and too wise to take offence.

The King did not learn of the trouble until he rose from supper that evening. He walked straight on into the large oval-shaped study followed by his family and the Princesses' ladies who, at Fontainebleau, formed a semi-circle around him in that room because there are no other drawing-rooms. He then had Courtenvaux summoned. As soon as the latter appeared at the study door he shouted at him across the full length of the room in a terrible, angry voice, so novel in him, so entirely without precedent, that not only Courtenvaux but all the Princesses and ladies, and everyone else assembled in that room shook with fright. One could hear him shouting far away in the bedrooms. Threats of dismissal in terms most harsh, most unusual coming from his mouth, rained upon Courtenvaux, who stood there almost fainting with terror and ready to sink through the floor, without the time or the power to defend himself. The reprimand ended with the King violently ordering him to 'Get Out!', which Courtenvaux had scarcely strength left to do, let alone drag himself off to his quarters. Little though his family cared for him, they were much alarmed for themselves, and each of his relatives sought the aid of some powerful protector. Mme la Duchesse de Bourgogne, who was deeply fond of the Duchesse de Villeroy and the Maréchale de Cœuvres, did her best by speaking to Mme de Maintenon and even to the King himself, who was eventually mollified, after giving warning that he would dismiss Courtenvaux at once if there were any more of his nonsense.

The real reason for that appalling scene was that Courtenvaux by drawing attention to the new system had revealed its motive, which thereafter became evident to the entire Court. The King preferred his spying activities to be most carefully concealed and had intended that no one should notice the change or feel at all suspicious. He was therefore utterly infuriated by a disturbance that had warned and forearmed everyone. Although Courtenvaux was already out of favour, despised, quite without the least acquaintance, he was now more frowned upon than ever, and so remained for the rest of his life. Without his family's help he would most certainly have been banished there and then and his salary confiscated.

The King left Fontainebleau on 26 October and returned by way of Villeroy and Sceaux, where he spent the night. The losses in Flanders and Italy, greater in the hospitals than in the field, caused a decision to increase every company by five and to raise a militia of twenty-five thousand. This brought great poverty and distress to country districts. The King was duped into believing that men were ready and glad to enlist by being shown hand-picked samples of four or five as he passed on the road to Marly, and was primed with stories of their valour and good cheer. I more than once heard them tell him these tales, and I heard him repeat them afterwards with evident self-satisfaction. Yet from personal observation of my own estates and hearing what was said there I knew that this levy was driving people to desperation, even to the point of mutilating themselves to avoid enlistment. There was much weeping and many loud cries that they were being taken to their deaths, and indeed that was mainly true, for most were sent to Italy, and none ever returned from there. Everyone at the Court knew the truth of the matter. They looked another way when the King was told lying tales and believed them, and they later whispered to one another their real thoughts of such abominable flattery. I often saw Callières[1] at this period; he had become friendly with me, and I learned much from him. Blenheim, Gibraltar, Barcelona,[2]

---

[1] François de Callières (1645–1717). His son married the Duc de Chevreuse's daughter. He had been sent as plenipotentiary to the Dutch Republic. Saint-Simon much admired his honesty and ability.

[2] Barcelona fell to the Allies on 4 October.

Tessé's unsuccessful campaign, the revolt in Catalonia and the neighbouring districts, the sad failures in Italy, the exhaustion of Spain, and that of France, which was becoming ever more apparent by the lack of men and money, the incompetence of our generals whom the arts of flattery protected from blame, all these gave me food for reflection. I came to the conclusion that the time had come to end the war, rather than run the risk of even greater disasters, and it seemed to me that this might be done by giving up to the Archduke the possessions that were hard for us to hold, and settling for a partition similar to the one proposed by England and generally accepted until the testament of Charles II. This would allow Philip V to remain a great king, giving him the whole of Italy, except for Tuscany, Venice, Genoa, the Papal States, Naples and Sicily. The King would hold Lorraine and some other regions, and the Dukes of Savoy, Lorraine, Parma, and Modena be placed elsewhere. I made this plan in my head, without writing it down, and I spoke of it to Callières more to learn what he thought of it than with any idea that he would consider it good and practical politics. I was therefore surprised to find that he approved of it. He urged me to put it down on paper, and offer it as a proposal to the three ministers whom I knew best. I hesitated for several days. Finally, encouraged by Callières, I promised to speak to those three gentlemen, but could not bring myself to write anything down. M. de Beauvilliers, to whom I first spoke, thought it a most excellent plan and eminently sensible; M. de Chevreuse thought the same. They were anxious for me to speak to the other two. The contrast in their replies might not be so striking if modesty prevented my recording what they said; it was entirely characteristic of them both. The Chancellor, after listening with great attention, said that he felt like kissing my feet and that it must be put into effect. Chamillart said gravely that the King would not surrender a single windmill of the Spanish inheritance. After that I understood what illusions we harboured and how much the future was to be feared.

At this time I shared with deep sorrow the terrible grief and anguish of M. and Mme de Beauvilliers. They had two sons sixteen and seventeen years old;[1] both well proportioned, both extraordinarily promising. The elder had just received a regiment without previous experience, and the younger was to have had one also. The younger died of smallpox at Versailles, on 25 November; the same sickness took the other also; he died of it on 2 December. The parents, grief-stricken by the first death, went at once to make their sacrifice at mass, and both of them took Communion. At the second death they displayed the same faith, the same courage, the same piety. Their anguish was none the less extreme, a gnawing sorrow that remained with them for the rest of their lives. There was no outward

---

[1] Saint-Simon forgot. The Comte de Saint-Aignan was 16 and the Marquis de Beauvilliers 13 years old.

change; M. de Beauvilliers fulfilled his normal functions, but at home he gave himself up to grief and for several days saw no one outside the circle of his immediate family and most intimate friends. No sermon that I ever heard was half so moving as the sorrow and resignation of them both, their terrible suffering in no way lessening their submission and trust in God. Continuing silent, gentle, outwardly serene, but abstracted, they ever and again uttered some words of hope that sanctified their tears.

When the first shock had worn off I quietly changed the subject when M. de Beauvilliers spoke to me of his children. This he observed, saying that he knew that I believed I was acting for the best in trying to divert his thoughts. He felt grateful, he said, but there were so few to whom he could speak openly that he begged me to let him continue when he felt the need to talk. He added that it gave him comfort and that he only did so when hard-pressed. I obeyed him, and very often when we were alone he would speak of his sons, and I could see that it did him good. His son-in-law was not of a kind to console him; he persisted in making his wife remain in Paris, and all the other daughters of M. de Beauvilliers were nuns.[1]

The armies of Flanders and Italy dispersed; Marsin, and shortly afterwards Villars, returned. The Maréchal de Villeroy was the last to arrive, choosing to make an entrance during matins on Christmas Day. The King's welcome was such as to make him very glad to have it observed by so many, and he was even more delighted at the commotion he had caused. He spent the rest of divine service ogling the ladies, acknowledging the greetings of high-ranking persons and the low bows of others, beating time, meanwhile, to the music in the most elegant fashion imaginable and with a precision that obviously pleased him.

Roquelaure was granted a short audience of the King soon after his return, to give him an opportunity to excuse himself for his negligence in not guarding the Brabant lines, his flight, and all the resulting confusion. He had been persuaded by the King, in exchange for a brevet-dukedom, to wed Mlle de Laval, one of Mme la Dauphine's ladies with whom King Louis was much in love. No one could ever forget Roquelaure's remark, delivered out loud in public at the birth of his eldest child, 'Ah! Mademoiselle, you are very welcome; I did not expect you quite so soon'; and indeed she did come to them very early. He was a jester by profession who, amidst much that was vulgar, occasionally produced something witty, as will be seen from the above. The King never ceased to be fond and considerate of Mme de Roquelaure, who was better fitted than anyone I know to make her way at a court. He could not endure to let her be made wretched by her husband's disgrace, and you will learn in due course how he was quietly promoted to a higher command.[2] The marriage brought not

---

[1] The eighth Beauvilliers girl had just taken the veil.

[2] 'All France was scandalized when Roquelaure was sent to replace Berwick as commander-in-chief in Languedoc' in the following year.

one penny to a family already deeply in debt, but her charm and the King's affection made her wealth most secure. In the reign of Louis XIV happy beauty was the best possible dowry.

Before I leave this year I must recount an anecdote that had repercussions later, as you will discover in due course. The Abbé de Polignac was at last back in circulation after his exploits in Poland and the banishment that succeeded them.[1] He was a big, well-proportioned man, with a handsome, intelligent face, and a particularly charming manner. He possessed a store of knowledge and a most pleasing delivery; his sermons were manly, quietly eloquent, vastly moving; he chose his words skilfully and turned a neat and original phrase, with the result that he seemed quite unaffected and extraordinarily persuasive. There was nothing he liked more than to bring abstruse subjects within the comprehension of ordinary folk, for he had a working knowledge of every art, craft, and industry, and could tell diverting stories regarding them. On his own subject, the Church and the ministry, he was far less knowledgeable. He liked to please everyone, the valets and serving-maids as well as their masters and mistresses, and he always aimed to touch their hearts and minds and eyes. It was easy to think oneself witty and clever in his company, for he tuned his conversation to his hearers, and his flattering manner made people like him personally and admire his talents. Yet underneath he was devoured by ambition, without love or gratitude or thoughts for any except himself. False, dissolute, caring little by what means he achieved his ends, without respect for either God or man, he managed to conceal his true nature with a tact that duped most people. Moreover he was amorous, but from coquetry, ambition and opportunity rather than from lust. But if his heart was false and his soul in none too good order, his judgment was nil, his plans misguided, and the righteousness in him non-existent; which was why every negotiation aborted in his hands.

Apart from all these natural advantages he was the possessor of noble birth without the wealth to correspond with it; thus he was protected from envy and attracted kindness and goodwill. The most agreeable ladies of the Court, the most respected dowagers, the most eminent among the gentlemen, the people of fashion of either sex were firmly on his side. From the beginning he had aimed at a cardinalcy; twice he had begun to work for a degree, twice abandoned the idea. Desks, seminaries, study for the episcopy, stank in his nostrils; he could never bring himself to

---

[1] He was ambassador to Poland when the King of Poland died in 1696. Polignac managed to convince Louis XIV that the Prince de Conti would be elected as the new king if he were allowed to stand. Louis sent money to Poland, gave the Order to all distinguished Poles in France, and dispatched the unwilling Prince with yet more money provided by the famous banker Samuel Bernard. Augustus II, Elector of Saxony, obtained the vote, however, and the abbé was exiled to his abbey in Normandy, with an absolute ban on his coming anywhere near the Court or Paris.

endure them. What he preferred was something more showy, more comprehensive, more in the nature of affairs of State or secret intrigue. He was continually surrounded by the best society after his return; even the King surrendered to his charm and included him in every Marly.

None the less he allowed one piece of abject flattery to escape him which was so empty, so obvious, that it was never forgotten. He was in the King's following in the gardens at Marly when it came on to rain. The King said something civil to him about his cassock being a poor protection. 'Sire,' he replied, 'that makes no difference; the rain is not wet at Marly.' Everyone laughed openly, and the tale was long held against him.

Agreeably placed as he now was he began to envy Nangis, who was a permanency, and the situation in which he had once seen Maulévrier. He sought to share their happiness[1] and used the same approaches. Mme d'O and the Maréchale de Cœuvres became his friends; he endeavoured to obtain a hearing, and was heard. Before long he was braving the dangers of the Swiss on fine nights in the Marly gardens. Nangis looked wretched; Maulévrier, though out of reach at the time, flew into a violent rage when he returned. The abbé shared also their good fortune, for everything was observed, everyone whispered, yet strict silence was preserved. It was not enough, however, for Polignac to triumph over his age; he wanted something more substantial. His learning in the arts and sciences, and his experience of State affairs prompted him to seek entrance to the study of Mgr le Duc de Bourgogne, which seemed full of promise if once he could gain admittance. As a start he needed to capture those who held the key, and the Duc de Beauvilliers first of all, because although the young prince's education was finished he still retained his entire confidence. Beauvilliers's ministry and his pupil took up his entire time; he was neither learned nor particularly well-read; the abbé knew none of his friends, and could not approach him directly, but the Duc de Chevreuse seemed less occupied (I shall soon have cause to explain why he only *seemed* so). Chevreuse, I say, seemed more accessible. He could be lured by books and mathematics, and once lured would fall an easy prey; that was how the abbé captured him. His attention caught in the few moments when he appeared in public at Versailles, he was first tempted by the bait of some problem or fascinating and difficult question, then easily held in conversation for long spells in the gallery, after which the door of his apartment was left slightly ajar for the Abbé de Polignac, although it rarely opened to others. Before long M. de Chevreuse was charmed. There were times when M. de Beauvilliers put in an appearance, and then the abbé was discreet, reserved, about to leave. Gradually they began to detain him when they had leisure. Chevreuse praised him to his brother-in-law. The abbé took advantage of every good occasion. The two dukes were one in heart and mind; please one and you pleased the

[1] With the Duchesse de Bourgogne.

other. He had been received by the Duc de Chevreuse, before long the Duc de Beauvilliers entertained him. The two of them were completely absorbed, not to say overwhelmed, by their duties and although they spent their days at the Court where their offices and favour made them persons of note, they lived like hermits, voluntarily ignorant of all that happened around them. Being charmed by the Abbé de Polignac and knowing nothing more about him, they decided that it would be a good action to put him into touch with Mgr le Duc de Bourgogne, himself so delightfully learned, so well able to profit and be entertained by Polignac's conversation. To think and to act were one and the same with them; and there was the abbé in the seventh heaven. We shall see how far he advanced with the young prince; but it is not yet time to speak of that, rather must we retrace somewhat our steps.

I had watched all Polignac's manœuvres with Chevreuse. Alas! charity did not keep me as firmly muzzled as it did the two dukes. One evening at Marly I went to have a talk with the Duc de Beauvilliers, as I did nearly every day. His confidence in me went far beyond my years, and I was at liberty, even accustomed, to say anything to him, even about himself. I told him therefore what I had noticed for some time past regarding the Abbé de Polignac and the Duc de Chevreuse. I added that no two men at the Court were less suited to one another, and that except for Torcy all the abbé's friends were anathema to them; that M. de Chevreuse was being duped, for he was merely a bridge to bring Polignac to M. de Beauvilliers himself, so as to gain admittance to Mgr le Duc de Bourgogne's study. I was too late. M. de Beauvilliers was already fallen a victim; but as yet he had had no direct dealings with the abbé and thus had not considered bringing him and the prince together. 'Well!' said he, 'where is all this leading, and what do you conclude?' 'What I conclude,' I replied, 'is that neither of you know anything about the Abbé de Polignac. You will both be duped by him; you will introduce him to Mgr le Duc de Bourgogne, and that is all he wants.' 'What harm is there in that?' he exclaimed, interrupting me. 'And if his conversation can be of any profit to Mgr le Duc de Bourgogne, how can we do better than bring them together?' 'As you will,' I said. 'Interrupt me; go your own way; but I tell you that I know him, and that of all men at the Court you two are least suited to him and most likely to obstruct him. Once established in Mgr le Duc de Bourgogne's study he will charm him like a serpent and have you both dismissed, though you may think yourselves quite secure in the prince's affections. After that he will rise upon your ruins.' At that word M. de Beauvilliers's expression changed entirely; he appeared greatly provoked and exclaimed that he would listen no more; that I passed all bounds; that I had too low an opinion of mankind; that what I foretold was neither possible nor at all what the abbé intended, and that rather than argue he begged me to be silent. By that time I, too, was angry. 'Monsieur,' said I, 'I'll say no more, but one day you will find out that I am right. That is my last word.' I then changed the subject, and he followed suit resuming his accustomed manner with me. Here we must break away for the moment and prepare to meet the fearful upheavals of the year which we are about to enter.

CHAPTER XVI

1706

Death of Bellegarde, his remarkable life-story – I am selected for the Roman embassy – Tragic fate of Maulévrier – Disposition of the armies – Mme de Roquelaure consoled – Battle of Calcinato – The siege of Turin decided – Battle of Ramillies – The King over-indulgent with the Maréchal de Villeroy – M. le Duc d'Orléans receives the command in Italy – Death of the Abbé Testu – My private relations with M. le Duc d'Orléans – Mlle de Séry becomes Mme d'Argenton – M. le Duc d'Orléans at Turin – Battle of Turin – Confusion of the retreat – Death of Marsin – Escapade of Mmes de Nancré and d'Argenton – Return of M. le Duc d'Orléans – Le Feuillade recalled and disgraced – Mme de La Chaise at Marly – Brawl between M. de La Roche-foucauld and the Duc de Tresmes – Ridiculous behaviour of Mme de Maintenon

I DO NOT know whether it was the misfortunes of the past year or the great things planned for the new that persuaded the King to embark on winter pleasures, in order to encourage his people and show the enemy how little he cared for their successes. However that may be, everyone was greatly surprised when in the early days of January he announced that there would be balls at Marly on every excursion until Lent, and nominated the ladies and gentlemen who were to dance. He said also that he would be glad if impromptu balls were given at Versailles for Mme la Duchesse de Bourgogne. Thus many such were given, and at Marly there were masquerades from time to time. On one occasion the King insisted on the gravest and most elderly persons attending the ball in masks, men and women alike, and to prevent there being any exceptions he went himself and remained for the entire evening with a muslin cloak over his coat; but that thin disguise was not permitted for others, who all had to be properly masked and dominoed. M. and Mme de Beauvilliers were most completely so. Mentioning them in such a connection would have been description enough to those who knew the Court. It vastly diverted me to see them and laugh with them discreetly. The court of Saint-Germain came to every ball and the King made many dance who were long past the age for it, including the Duc de Villeroy, M. de Monaco and several others. As for the Comte de Brionne and the Chevalier de Sully,[1] their dancing was so perfect that age did not count for them.

---

[1] He became the Duc de Sully in 1712 and was a patron of Voltaire. His wife was Mme Guyon's daughter.

At about this time old Bellegarde, who had a long and distinguished record of service, died at the age of 80. He was a general and a commander of the Order of Saint-Louis. In his day he had had an extremely good figure and was a great gallant. He was for many years the lover of the wife of one of the chief magistrates of the Parlement, who suspected as much, to say the least of it, but had his own reasons for not objecting—they said that he was impotent. One fine day the wife, who was amorous by nature, brought to her husband's study a little boy in a peasant's smock. 'Eh! wife,' said he, 'who may this child be?' 'This is your son,' said she firmly, 'I come to present him to you; is he not handsome?' 'What do you mean, son?' he exclaimed. 'You know perfectly well that we have no children.' 'I know perfectly well that I have had this one, and that he is yours also,' she retorted. The poor fellow, seeing her so determined, scratched his head, but did not hesitate long. 'Very well, wife, no scandal! I shall put up with this one, but you must promise to make me no others.' She did so promise, and she kept her word, but Bellegarde still continued to haunt their house. The little boy thus became one of the family. His mother loved him well, his father not at all, but he was prudent. Neither of them ever called him other than Ibrahim,[1] and they accustomed their friends to that nickname. I was an eye-witness to all this when I was a boy, for the magistrate was one of my father's intimate circle and I often saw Ibrahim; but I did not know his history until later. When he grew up he wished to be a soldier like his real father and the other did not object. He was killed in Italy; I shall not say where nor in what rank, for he left a son, a very decent kind of man, who recovered from the Parlement the magistracy which his supposed grandfather had been holding at the time of his death. I could not resist telling this extraordinary tale; all the persons concerned were so well known to me.

For the past five years Cardinal de Janson had been in charge of the King's affairs at Rome. He had filled the post worthily and more as a good Frenchman than a cardinal, which had not at all pleased the Pope or his court. Indeed he had been on bad terms with the former, and the latter, which expects obedience from everyone, had positively ill-treated him. He had been seriously indisposed for some time and had been asking to be recalled. This was finally granted, and there being no cardinal to replace him, the Abbé de La Trémoïlle,[2] for want of any other, was made chargé d'affaires at his departure. That made it necessary to consider sending an ambassador with all speed to Rome, where there had not been one since the Duc de Chaulnes's sudden visit for the election of the new Pope,[3] after the death of Innocent XI.

Gualterio the nuncio first mentioned the embassy to me. He was all for

[1] Ibrahim is the name of the hero of a famous novel by Madeleine de Scudéry.
[2] The Princesse des Ursins' dissipated brother.
[3] Alexander VIII, 1689–1691.

France and it mattered much to him to be sure of the friendship of the
French ambassador. Being only thirty at that time, the idea of my becoming an ambassador appeared quite fantastic, in view of the King's dislike
of young men, especially in affairs of State. Callières spoke to me later; I
answered him in the same vein, pointing out the difficulty of having any
success in Rome without being ruined in the process, and adding that,
situated as I was, such an embassy might prejudice my further employment. On Tuesday, 11 March, just a week after the nuncio had spoken,
he entered my room at one o'clock in the afternoon, his arms outstretched
and beaming with delight. Then, hugging and kissing me, he begged me
to bolt the door and that of my ante-room as well, lest anyone should see
his footmen. After which he informed me that he was in the seventh
heaven because I was to be appointed ambassador to Rome. I made him
repeat this twice, for I could not believe my ears, and I told him that
his wish must be father to his thought for the whole idea was impossible.
He joyfully swore me to secrecy, saying that Torcy had just told him in
confidence that the decision had been taken at that morning's council,
but that the King had forbidden him to announce it until after the next
meeting. I could not have been more astounded if one of the portraits
on the walls had opened its mouth and spoken. Gualterio urged me with
all his might to accept; then, it being time for him to go to dinner, he left
me and I went at once to tell Mme de Saint-Simon, who was as much
amazed as myself. We sent to ask Callières and Louville[1] to come to us
immediately, and the four of us held a conference there and then. They
all agreed that I ought not to refuse. I went thence to find Chamillart and
reproached him heatedly for not giving me some warning. He smiled at my
wrath, saying that the King had insisted on secrecy; as for the rest, he
most strongly advised me to accept. He was just setting out for L'Etang
and we for Marly, where he promised to see us on the following day. I
went on the same mission to the Chancellor, who laughed at me and gave
me the same advice as Chamillart; I could extract nothing from him
whatsoever regarding the council. He then left for Pontchartrain, saying
that he would see us on his return. M. de Beauvilliers had gone to Vaucresson after the meeting; I managed to see him for a moment when he
came to Marly for the council; but he made the same excuse as the others
when I sought to extract information. My trouble was to decide on my
reply before the proposal was put to me, and I dreaded that Torcy might
appear at any moment. I must admit to feeling flattered at being chosen at
my age for such an important post, especially since I had not even considered it and had not been recommended by anyone. At that time I had
not even the smallest acquaintance with Torcy; M. de Beauvilliers was
far too cautious to have proposed me without first discovering whether I
could afford it; the Chancellor had not been present, and Chamillart

[1] Now returned permanently from Spain.

would never have acted without my consent; moreover, he was on none too good terms with Torcy and would not have risked interfering with his department by suggesting a name to the King.

Years later, after the King's death, I asked Torcy, who had become my close friend, how it was that I came to be chosen for Rome. He protested that he had known nothing until the day of the council, save that someone was to be appointed and that the King did not want to create a new dukedom. When he had begun to read the dispatches the King had interrupted saying that the time had come to appoint an envoy, that he wished to have a duke, and that they had only to read down the list until a suitable name occurred. He then took up a small almanac and began to read out the names. My seniority soon brought him to mine, whereat he paused, saying, 'How about this one? He is young, but capable, etc.' Monseigneur, who would have preferred d'Antin,[1] said nothing, but Mgr le Duc de Bourgogne supported me, and so did the Chancellor and M. de Beauvilliers. Torcy praised their judgment but suggested continuing down the list. Chamillart remarked that they would find no one better. The King thereupon closed the almanac, saying that there seemed little point in going further and that he would decide on me; but that they were to say nothing for the time being. After that there was no more discussion, and Torcy went on with the dispatches. That was what I was told more than ten years later by a truthful man who had no possible reason for concealment.

Beauvilliers and Chamillart each separately examined my debts and revenue, and the expenses and emoluments of an embassy. Mme de Saint-Simon brought them our account books for the former and discussed the situation with them; the rest they arrived at by guesswork. Both men thought that I should accept. The duke decided that I could afford the post without being ruined, and said further that if I refused, especially after having left the service, the King would never forgive me, but would regard me thenceforward as an idler by preference and would make me feel his displeasure on every possible occasion. All of which would harm my interests both present and future far more than failure in an embassy. In the end they convinced me, and I accepted. That is to say I resolved to accept, and with great pleasure as I am bound to admit. Mme de Saint-Simon, wiser and more cautious than I, and sad at the thought of leaving her family, gave her consent also, but less gladly. Here I cannot deny myself the pleasure of repeating what those three ministers, each separately and of his own accord, said to me of that young woman of 27 (as she then was), whom none the less they had long known at the Court and in family matters, for they had been our advisers at every step of our married lives. They all three counselled me most earnestly to keep nothing from her in all the affairs of my embassy, to have her seated at

[1] Son of the Marquis and Marquise de Montespan, married the Maintenon's niece.

the end of my table when I read or wrote my dispatches, and to consult her judgment in everything. I have rarely listened so gladly to advice, and I hold it equally meritorious in her that she both deserved their praises and lived afterwards as though she were ignorant of them, for she did hear them from my own lips, and later from theirs also. As it happened I had no chance of following their counsel at Rome, for I never went there, but I had practised it at home long before they spoke, and for the rest of our lives I continued to tell her all. I cannot resist adding that I never found a wiser, shrewder, nor more useful counsellor, and I readily admit that she steered me clear of many difficulties both small and great. I relied on her help in everything without reserve. The support which she gave me was invaluable both in my personal conduct and in public affairs, wherein the part I played was not insignificant during the last years of the King's reign and throughout the Regency. She was a most dear and rare contrast to those spoilt and useless wives whom ambassadors are cautioned to leave behind and to tell nothing; and an even greater one, perhaps, to those women who are domineering and self-important, for she was the very pattern of exquisite sensibility, correct in every way, yet always very quiet and gentle. Far from being self-assertive, she seemed wholly unconscious of herself, and always, throughout her entire life, was uniformly modest, virtuous, and amiable.

Despite the King's injunction my nomination gradually became known. Yet Torcy still said nothing, and I scarcely knew what to tell my friends as I was put off from one council-meeting to another. We returned to Versailles; we went again to Marly; people were no longer guarded, and M. de Monaco, son of an earlier ambassador, offered at one of the balls to lend me what remained in Rome of his father's furniture and carriages. All the time that we were dancing Mme de Saint-Simon and I could hear people exclaiming, 'Look! there is the ambassador,' or 'the ambassadress'. The situation became so embarrassing at last that I implored Torcy through Callières to bring the affair to an end in one way or another. He himself felt the improprieties of the position and the awkwardness for me, but he dared not press the King. The real cause of the delay was that some hope had arisen of persuading the Pope to make the Abbé de La Trémoïlle a cardinal and generally of hastening the nominations for the nineteen vacant hats, a matter that was setting all Rome in a fever and could not long be delayed. Yet delayed it was, which was why my own nomination became known before the proper time.

To conclude this long-drawn-out tale of my Roman embassy, matters remained in that uncertain state until the middle of April, when I at last learned my fate. We were at Marly at that time, lodged in the same pavilion as Chamillart, whom I begged to come to my apartment after the council and tell me privately what my fate would be. He accordingly visited me in Mme de Saint-Simon's room where we were waiting

impatiently. 'You will be much relieved,' said he, 'and I very sorry, for the
King has decided after all not to send an ambassador to Rome. The Pope
has relented concerning the Abbé de La Trémoïlle, and the new cardinal
will take charge of the King's affairs with no ambassador.' Mme de Saint-
Simon was indeed delighted; it almost seemed as though she foresaw the
dreadful disrepute into which the King's affairs would fall, the resulting
financial embarrassments, and all the troubles that we should have had
to endure had we gone to Rome. I had had ample leisure in which to reflect during the interval and easily consoled myself for missing a most
gratifying appointment. D'Antin and Dangeau had both been furious
at my preferment, for they had each hoped for a dukedom and had been
left firmly discouraged. Being unable to find any more effectual means of
barring the promotion of a young man over their heads, and knowing how
wary the King was of brains and education, they again and again praised
me to him on those counts, applauding him for his choice of me, which
had become public because of the delay. M. and Mme du Maine had
never forgiven me for refusing to haunt Sceaux, despite all their advances,
which I have already described. I had never concealed my feelings regarding the bastards' usurpations of rank; to see me singled out for promotion alarmed and angered them, and I can attribute only to M. du
Maine, who by nature was fearful and evilly-disposed, Mme de Maintenon's extraordinary aversion for me, which until that time I had never
suspected. Chamillart admitted as much to me after the King's death,
and said moreover that he had more than one set-to with her on that
account, and that she had been the main obstacle in the way of recon-
ciling me with the King after I left the service. When pressed, she had
never been able to produce any particular crimes against herself or her
dear ones, but had spoken vaguely of my being arrogant, rebellious,
opinionated; he had never been able to persuade her otherwise, nor even
to mollify her. This reputation for brains and reading, capabilities and
industry, was only too easily passed on to the King through the same
channels, M. du Maine with poisoned praise, Mme de Maintenon by
more direct methods. So successful were they in setting the King on his
guard, that they led him on to think me dangerous, so as to confirm him
in his antipathy, and very soon afterwards I observed a change in his
manner, a general decline that could end only in mortal illness, in other
words, disgrace. I eventually recovered, but the time has not yet come
for that. The same impression of me was given to poor Monseigneur,
who meekly accepted all that d'Antin and the Lorraines chose to tell him.
Such then was my unhappy situation at the Court, and it was not long
before I perceived it.

Maulévrier returned from Spain at this time and went at once to Marly,
where both his wife and we were of the party. He had much to report
of the Princesse des Ursins and the Spanish court, and was therefore

admitted to Mme de Maintenon's room for tête-à-tête conversations, some
of them lasting more than three hours, which in between whiles he carefully nourished with notes and memoranda. Mme de Maintenon, who was
avid for information about Spain and took to new acquaintances with
extraordinary zest, saw to it that the King also listened to his news. This
sudden rise to a pinnacle of favour after facing imminent ruin completely
turned Maulévrier's head; he began to despise the ministers and to ignore
the warnings sent him by Tessé. The State affairs which he had handled
in Spain, and his private audiences with the Spanish queen, provided him
with an excuse for being alone with Mgr and Mme la Duchesse de Bourgogne, each separately, occasions when she indulged him and he claimed
all from her. Her fondness for Nangis and the Abbé de Polignac also
infuriated him. He had the temerity to demand a sacrifice; he did not
obtain one. His wife, her vanity wounded, made advances to Nangis,
who responded to them in order to mask his real attachment,[1] and when
Maulévrier perceived this it was more than he could bear. He knew his
wife's nature well enough to dread her spite. These violently conflicting
motions of his heart finally drove him out of his senses.

One day when he happened to be at home and there was some small
matter to be set right the Maréchale de Cœuvres tried to see him. He
bolted himself into his room and from the further side of the door reproached her to the point of vile abuse for the whole of one hour, whilst
she waited patiently in the hope of seeing him. Thereafter he visited the
Court rarely and stayed mostly in Paris. He took to going out at unusual
hours, taking cabs[2] at a distance from his house and having himself driven
to the back of the *Chartreuse*[3] and other isolated places. There he would
walk alone, whistling. Sometimes a grey footman[4] would emerge from a
dark corner to hand him a letter, sometimes one was thrown to him from
an upper window; once he stopped by a milestone to pick up a box that
was found later to be full of papers. I learned of these mysterious doings
at that very time from those whom he was rash enough to take into his
confidence. He wrote letters both to Mme de Maintenon and to Mme la
Duchesse de Bourgogne, but to the latter almost invariably through the
medium of her maid Mme Quentin. I myself knew several persons, including M. de Lorges, to whom he showed the covers of letters and read
some of them aloud, especially one from Mme Quentin seeking to pacify
him concerning Mme la Duchesse de Bourgogne, and containing a message from the latter couched in the clearest and strongest terms to the effect
that he might always count on her.

---

[1] To the Duchesse de Bourgogne.
[2] Cabs had plied for hire by the hour in the streets of Paris as early as 1650.
[3] The famous Carthusian Monastery in the Rue de Vaugirard, in the present XVIe
arrondissement.
[4] A *grison*, one of the grey-liveried footmen used for carrying the royal family's secret
messages.

He paid a final visit to Versailles to see her privately, and made a terrible scene. He dined that same evening with Torcy, with whom he remained on outwardly friendly terms, and was mad enough to describe his rage and all that had passed to the Abbé de Caumartin, the intimate friend of Tessé and the rest, who later repeated it word for word to me. He thence returned to Paris, where, rent asunder by the pangs of a pretended love now become a reality, and reeling with jealousy and ambition, his mind became so much disturbed that doctors were summoned and he thenceforward saw only indispensable persons at moments when he was least confused. All kinds of hallucinations passed through his head; sometimes he babbled wildly of Spain, at others of Mme la Duchesse de Bourgogne and of Nangis, whom he wished to murder or have assassinated. Occasionally, filled with remorse for his treatment of Mgr le Duc de Bourgogne, whose friendship he had so ill-repaid, he uttered thoughts so dreadful that none dared to stay with him. Often he was gentle, remote from the world, haunted by memories of his early training for the Church, and at such moments a confessor was needed to assure him of God's mercy. Most often he believed himself to be mortally sick and about to die.

Meanwhile Society and even some of his near relations imagined that he was still play-acting, and to put an end to that they told him that the world thought him a lunatic and that he had better show himself and stop his nonsense. That was the final blow. He realized that it meant the collapse of those ambitions that had been his consuming passion, and he fell into deep melancholy. His wife, a few devoted friends, and his servants watched over him with extraordinary vigilance, but he managed to elude them all at about eight o'clock on Good Friday morning. Entering a passage that ran behind his apartment, he opened a window and threw himself into the courtyard below. His head was broken on the cobblestones. Such was the end of that ambitious man, whose wild and dangerous passions drove him out of his mind and deprived him of his life, the tragic victim of his own hand.

Mme la Duchesse de Bourgogne learned of the event that same evening when she was with the King at Tenebrae, in the presence of the entire Court. She appeared unmoved; but in private her tears flowed unchecked. They might well have been tears of compassion but were not so charitably interpreted. It was noted that Mme Quentin went next day to the poor wretch's house in Paris, although it was Holy Saturday, and that she had called there already on several occasions. The pretext given was to condole with Mme de Maulévrier, but no one believed that story; there were supposed to be other more urgent reasons for the excursion. His widow, despite her grief, kept a cool head, and no one doubted but that she had possessed herself of all his papers before taking refuge in a convent for the first year of her bereavement. Mme la Duchesse de Bourgogne wrote her a letter which she displayed with pride, and several of that princess's ladies visited her, but she received them coldly, and to Mme de La Vallière she was so rude that they quarrelled, although they had been close friends.

At Marly, after Easter, we found Mme de Maintenon looking depressed, uncertain, cross, and quite unlike her usual self with Mme la Duchesse de Bourgogne. They were closeted together alone and for long periods, from which the princess emerged in tears. Everyone was certain that what all had known long since was now discovered by Mme de Maintenon. Indeed, some suspected Maulévrier of having revenged himself by sending her certain letters. Meanwhile Mgr le Duc de Bourgogne was beginning to become anxious over his wife's melancholy and her redrimmed eyes, and he more than once seemed on the verge of learning more than would have benefited him. Love, however, is wilfully blind, and he accepted readily enough the excuses offered. The flood of reproaches ceased, or at least grew less, and the princess consented to appear cheerful. We could not help wondering how much the King had discovered. I made so bold as to discuss the matter fully with the Duc de Beauvilliers. He had been aware of what was going on and had suffered deeply for Mgr le Duc de Bourgogne; indeed he had been in daily terror lest he discover an affair of the kind that nearly always comes to light eventually. M. de Beauvilliers had had no esteem for Maulévrier, and although as a true Christian he deplored his sad end he was vastly relieved by his death. Tessé, in Spain, was no less thankful to be rid of his troublesome son-in-law, and did not sufficiently disguise his feelings.

Let us finish once and for all with this delicate matter. The Abbé de Polignac, Maulévrier's other rival, was urged by Torcy to leave the country forthwith,[1] but although all eyes were now fixed upon him he could not bring himself to do so. At last, however, he was compelled to go. It was remarked that Mme la Duchesse de Bourgogne wished him a prosperous journey in a manner very different from her usual, and few believed in the headache that kept her all day long extended upon a couch in Mme de Maintenon's room, with the windows tightly closed and a flood of tears when evening came. This was the first occasion on which the public did not spare her. Madame, walking in Versailles gardens a few days later, found two verses, as rude as they were apposite, scrawled upon a balustrade and some pedestals, and she was neither discreet nor benevolent enough to hold her tongue. But Mme la Duchesse de Bourgogne was much beloved and the verses had little influence because everyone united in suppressing them.

The King disposed of his armies in much the same way as in previous years. M. de Vendôme for Italy, Tessé for Catalonia, Berwick on the

---

[1] Torcy, shortly before this, thinking that his flirtation with the Duchesse de Bourgogne was becoming dangerously public, had persuaded the King to make him auditor of the Rota, with honourable exile to Rome.

Portuguese frontier, the Maréchal de Villars in Alsace, Marsin on the Moselle, and the Maréchal de Villeroy in Flanders, all with generals serving under them. At the same time he recollected the tears in Mme de Roquelaure's lovely eyes and to the disgust of the entire French nation sent her husband to take over Berwick's command in Languedoc. The Comte de Toulouse and the Maréchal de Cœuvres left for Toulon with the intention of making all preparations to give naval assistance at the relief of Barcelona. The major importance of that expedition allowed them to expect that Pontchartrain would not behave as he had done in the previous year. Experience taught them, however, that perseverance in his chosen course suited his interests much better even than a victory at Barcelona.

The plans for the forthcoming campaigns were worthy of the years of the King's prosperity, those happy years when men and money abounded and our ministers' word was law in Europe because of their outstanding statesmanship. The King wished to open with two pitched battles,[1] one of them in Flanders, the other in Italy; to prevent the Imperial army from massing on the Upper Rhine, drive the enemy from their lines, and later lay siege to Barcelona and Turin. The exhaustion of Spain and the near-exhaustion of France ill-suited such grandiose designs. Chamillart, worn out by the double responsibility of the departments once ruled by Colbert and Louvois, bore little resemblance to either of those great statesmen, and our generals were equally unlike M. le Prince and M. de Turenne[2] or those vanished heroes their pupils. Our commanders were courtiers, spoiled and favoured soldiers created in the King's study, for the King believed that as with his ministers he presented them with ability along with their letters patent. In his early days Louvois had been exasperated at having to reckon with generals who were great men; he took good care to make no others of that quality. He preferred weak men who hid their incapacity under his protection, and he therefore held merit and talent at arm's length. What is more he persuaded the King to believe that he could direct campaigns from his study, which was flattery with a purpose, for by so doing Louvois himself commanded in the King's name to the great detriment of the service. Thus the generals whom Louvois made were kept in leading-strings, with neither the will nor the freedom to seize a lucky chance, for by the time that a courier had reached Versailles and returned with permission the opportunity was lost. Thus hampered, directed, fearful and unsure, they continually waited for orders and received no encouragement from their staff-officers who were promoted by seniority, without previous responsibility of training. The love

---

[1] This was most unusual, for campaigns were normally aimed at the capture of fortresses and lines of communication, so as to force the enemy to retreat at the end of the summer for want of winter quarters or the means to transport supplies.

[2] Louis II de Bourbon, '*Le Grande Conde*' (1621–1686) and the great Turenne (1611–1675), Maréchal de France 1643.

of rich living so permeated the armies that men wished to live there as luxuriously as in Paris, which prevented generals from learning to know their officers and place reliance on those with judgment and ability. No longer were there councils of war in which men learned by listening to others and voicing their own opinions, and thought it shameful to say one thing and act differently. No longer did the young give heed to the old, and the old speak from their experience, giving reasons and conclusions. Today, since they cannot speak of what they do not know, the only talk among officers is of gaming, horses, and women. The generals now see them only in crowds; in private they spend their entire time writing and despatching couriers, all immensely costly, and mostly quite useless. In the evenings they are closeted with three or four administrative officers who seldom know their work.

On 11 March M. de Vendôme[1] had a vastly long audience of the King in his study at Versailles, and took formal leave before returning to Italy. He had managed by degrees to climb back into favour. The King gave him no more precise instructions than to seek out the enemy and bring him at once to battle, which M. de Vendôme promised to do, but you shall see how he kept his word. He then left for Antibes and there embarked in one of the royal galleys that carried him to Genoa, from whence he joined his army. He found everything in admirable order, but quickly spread it abroad that his forces were so much weakened and disordered that nothing could be done with them. Not even the absence of Prince Eugene availed to hurry him, still less the King's order to act swiftly. He painstakingly mustered fifty-eight battalions and six thousand horses at his headquarters, at Castiglione delle Stiviere,[2] and at dawn on 19 April marched to Montechiaro, where the enemy had been wintering in a fortified camp, which they abandoned at his approach. They retired upon Calcinato, where Vendôme, following close upon their heels, found them drawn up for battle at the top of a hill. He suddenly and fiercely attacked them, and since the odds were very unequal, for they numbered not more than ten to eleven thousand, he made short work of beating and routing them, killing three thousand and capturing twenty flags, ten pieces of cannon, and eight thousand prisoners, including a colonel. Our soldiers made good use of twelve hundred new coats which they found in Calcinato; they found nothing else. The enemy threw away six thousand rifles, all of which were recovered by Vendôme, offering an écu a piece for them. We suffered few losses, for the affair had been more like a rout than a battle. Vendôme marched again on the 22nd to complete his victory; but

---

[1] For the Duc de Vendôme's character and filthy personal habits see *Saint-Simon at Versailles*. Mme de Maintenon wrote to Mme des Ursins in 1708: 'M. de Beauvilliers says that one does not command armies from a chaise-percée; yet that is his (Vendôme's) habitual seat.'

[2] S.W. of Lake Garda, where another great battle was fought in 1796, when Napoleon and Augereau defeated the Austrians.

the enemy retreated on the evening before he reached them and concealed their whereabouts so successfully that he could not engage even their hindmost rearguard. Prince Eugene, arriving on the day following the battle, had restored the situation so swiftly that we reaped none of the fruits of victory. None the less, the greatest possible hopes were aroused and M. de Vendôme was lauded to the skies,[1] even though, far from making further attacks, he was compelled to remain on the defensive for the rest of the time that he stayed in Italy.

Before leaving Italy I must say a word of Turin. The vast preparations made during the previous year for a siege that did not take place greatly speeded the arrangements for this year. The King's justifiable anger with M. de Savoie; the victory at Calcinato, so recent, so grossly inflated; the hopes of further victories in Italy, and a very keen desire to plunder and ravage M. de Savoie's possessions, all made him especially eager for that undertaking. Chamillart, who was wiser than people believed, realized all the dangers of the situation and had grave doubts of La Feuillade, his young and inexperienced son-in-law, who was destined for the command. He therefore resolved to re-examine the plan of action with the Maréchal de Vauban in the King's presence, and since Vauban had at one time mistakenly been lent to M. de Savoie for the very purpose of strengthening Turin's defences, it seemed only reasonable to Chamillart to make him the overall commander. It is hardly believable that despite the King's long experience of Vauban's ability, and well-founded trust in him, he should there and then, in his presence and that of the embarrassed Chamillart, have confirmed La Feuillade in the command.[2] Crack troops, hand-picked officers, abundant supplies, powerful artillery, chests full of money were freely despatched to him. His wishes and their fulfilment were almost simultaneous; in a word, he was treated in a manner fitting the well-beloved son-in-law of an all-powerful minister of war and finance, whose fondest hopes for the continued support and prosperity his family rested in him. You may well imagine that nothing was left undone to ensure his success.

La Feuillade duly established himself before Turin on 13 May, and set about to build his lines and bridges. The man appointed as his chief engineer was Tardif, whose sole experience hitherto had been the organization of small sieges in Bavaria. Thus responsibility for this mighty task was placed squarely upon the shoulders of two complete novices, who for that reason alone were also completely stubborn. Let us now leave them to settle down, and return to Flanders.

The King was never more urgent than in impressing upon the Maréchal

---

[1] The results of the battle may have been disappointing, but Vendôme had at least won the victory which the King had asked for. Strange how Saint-Simon's loathing of royal bastards and their descendants made him blind to any great qualities in them!

[2] Louis XIV may have thought that his being a commoner would present difficulties. Vauban himself was of that opinion.

de Villeroy his desire that the campaign should open with a pitched battle. He had begun to feel the burden of the war and longed for it to end; but he wished to impose a peace, not accept one, and he demanded great things of his generals and troops. The successes in Italy and on the Rhine[1] appeared to him comparable with his victories in earlier campaigns, and he loved Villeroy so well that he desired the final glory to be his. Thus, in the interval between the latter's return to Flanders in mid-April and the mustering of his army, the King had incessantly goaded him to be swift in obeying his express commands. Villeroy's proud, impatient spirit was nettled by these repeated admonitions. He began to imagine that the King doubted his courage, and resolved to stake all at once in an effort to vindicate himself. Yet although the King greatly wished for a battle in Flanders he also wished to be sure of winning it, and thus as soon as the Rhenish lines were destroyed and Fort Louis relieved he sent Marsin orders to leave part of his army with Villars and march with eighteen battalions and forty squadrons to join the Maréchal de Villeroy in Flanders. At the same time he instructed the latter to take no action until that reinforcement had arrived. Four couriers following one upon the other repeated this command, and Villeroy received all of them, as his replies proved. None the less, stung by the King's continual exhortations to fight, he decided to force the issue without waiting for Marsin's support. I wish especially to stress that fact because it caused the fatal rift between Villeroy and Chamillart, who showed me the original letters sent by the King himself to the maréchal at the start of the campaign, and the replies; also some other letters that were sent before the action began. That quarrel, however, does not yet concern us.

Villeroy, as I have said, was determined to give battle despite his orders to wait for Marsin. Although Marlborough had crossed the sea earlier that year his troops were not fully mustered, and thus Villeroy outnumbered him, a fact that gave him confidence. He had no doubts of a victory, and did not want to divide the glory with anyone; not with Marsin and his reinforcement, nor even with the Elector himself, notwithstanding that the latter was in supreme command. In fact, he had left that prince in Brussels entirely ignorant of his intentions. On 21 May, Villeroy advanced towards the spot where, in the previous year, Roquelaure had allowed our lines to be over-run. When he learned that Marlborough was also on the march and approaching he halted, and on the morning of the 23rd, Whitsunday, made his dispositions on ground where the late M. de Luxembourg had made it an inflexible rule never to be exposed to battle. Villeroy knew this; it was his tragedy and that of France that he forgot. Before taking up his position he reported by courier to Versailles, where-

---

[1] Villars and Marsin on the Upper Rhine had retaken Hagenau and Duremburg and nearly all the territory on the left bank which the Allies had captured after Blenheim in the previous year.

upon M. le Duc d'Orléans prophesied to all who cared to listen that if he persisted in accepting battle at that place he would certainly be defeated.[1] M. de Luxembourg, he said, had always firmly refused to commit his troops on that terrain, and had given his reasons on the spot, which M. le Duc d'Orléans then proceeded to explain most clearly. Events proved him only too good a prophet.

Villeroy nevertheless placed the *Maison du Roi* and two cavalry brigades in between the villages of Taviers and Ramillies. Taviers covered the flank of the *Maison du Roi*. Its situation was on a slope near the River Mehaigne, with marshes behind. In the village itself he posted the Comte de La Motte with six battalions of the Elector's troops and three regiments of dragoons. In the village of Ramillies he established twenty-four pieces of cannon, supported by twenty battalions, later reinforced by an even greater number of infantry. With the rest he occupied the ground extending towards the village of Autréglise, kept the right wing of his second line in its customary order, and brought the left wing into position before an extremely awkward marsh that stretched out beyond that wing, which was more or less in line with the right wing. Just as he was completing these dispositions, the Elector, who had received barely sufficient warning, arrived at full gallop from Brussels. He had good cause for complaint and perhaps also for censure when he saw what was happening; but there was no time for recriminations and little enough to finish what was in hand, to which task he lent himself with great good will, leaving the rest aside for a more suitable time.

It was two o'clock in the afternoon when the enemy appeared on the field of battle in excellent order and came first under the fire of our cannon in Ramillies. It obliged their troops to halt until the arrival of their artillery that very promptly returned our fire. That cannonade lasted a full hour, after which they marched upon Taviers, taking two of their guns with them. There they encountered rather less in the way of opposition than on their right and captured the village. It was at that precise moment that their cavalry went into action. They had seen in time that the swamp protecting our left would prevent the right wing of an opposing army from coming to grips with it, and had quietly passed the whole of the cavalry of their right wing behind their centre, forming it up line upon line behind the cavalry on their left.[2] Thus their whole force of cavalry now faced our right wing ready for action, whereas half of ours remained uselessly before the marsh, incapable of doing anything. They had

---

[1] The ground at Ramillies was thought to be dangerous to defend because it was a hollow and thus the communication lines from side to side were excessively lengthy.

[2] Villeroy was wrong; Marlborough knew that the marsh was impassable for *both sides*, yet he began by ordering his cavalry to advance across it, leading their horses, whilst the French waited to destroy them. At the perfect moment he brought them back and moved them quietly behind his centre to the other side. When that manœuvre was complete he exclaimed, 'Now I have five horses to their two.'

watched the enemy melt away before their eyes; yet although they might have imitated the manœuvre they did not budge. Gession, who commanded the left wing as the senior lieutenant-general, had been gravely disquieted, but no more. He had been ordered to remain where he was, and although he had sent an aide-de-camp for further instructions none had been forthcoming.

Guiscard, the senior lieutenant-general on our right, set that wing in motion in response to the enemy's manœuvre. The *Maison du Roi* charged magnificently, their red squadrons driving straight through the lines of the opposing cavalry and breaking their ranks, whilst their right swept the foremost line quite away. By that charge they gained more than five hundred yards and at once turned to charge again and successfully an enemy squadron that was attempting to take them in the rear. Then they rallied, and after making a half-turn to the right charged another six squadrons. At this point, however, a fourth line of cavalry confronted them and they were at the same time attacked once more in the rear. This disaster occurred to them sooner than to those on their right, who could give them no help. A like catastrophe had already taken place on their left. The enemy, line upon line, continually opened their ranks to let our squadrons pass through, and then closed them again to attack both in front and behind. The village of Taviers no longer protected them, for as I have said the enemy had captured it and were using our own cannon there against us. Ramillies was too far away to save them. Thus our troops were compelled to recross as best they might a narrow swamp, dangerous in the middle, and none would have succeeded had not a company of infantry stationed themselves on their own initiative at the verge and screened with their fire those who managed to cross over.

The disorder and unequal odds of that final charge caused many casualties and much bitter grumbling. Such of the *Maison du Roi* as had been able to remain together rallied and continued to fight behind the village of Ramillies. The cannon-fire was tremendous. Our troops penetrated into the centre of the enemy but were promptly thrown back by vastly superior numbers, and in the ensuing confusion the enemy captured the village itself and all the guns which we had placed therein. The Duc de Guiche, who commanded the guards, resisted for four hours and did marvels, but the second line of cavalry of our right (mostly Bavarians and Walloons) flatly refused to obey their orders to support the front line. In brief, our left wing remained useless, its face pressed up against the marsh with no enemy to oppose it, and it did not move from that position. Our right wing was broken, our centre crumpled, and our infantry, almost the whole of which had been committed, driven back. The Elector had been everywhere at once, displaying great courage. The Maréchal de Villeroy had galloped distractedly about, totally incapable of parrying the succession of blows that rained upon him. He had shown valour; nothing more; but no one had ever doubted that in him or that he possessed many other excellent qualities. At last nothing remained to be done except retreat. The army began its march in good order, but when night fell the darkness brought confusion and the road to Judoigne[1] became blocked with baggage wagons, lighter vehicles, and such of our cannon as we had managed to recover. All of these were taken by the enemy. Louvain was reached at length, but the army was not considered to be in safety until the Wilworde canal had been crossed, although they were not close on our heels. Brussels became the first-fruit of their victory. Antwerp, Malines, and Louvain followed soon after by taking an oath of fealty to the Archduke, and that was only the beginning of the return of the entire Spanish Netherlands to the House of Austria.

That battle, which had such swift and important consequences, cost us less than four thousand men, but a great dispersal of troops, almost all of whom returned to join their units in a remarkably short space of time. M. de Soubise lost one of his younger sons serving with the gendarmes; Gouffier, d'Aubigné colonel of dragoons, Bernières staff-major of the regiment of guards and a major-general, Lord Clare brigadier-general,[2] and Brigadier-general Bar of the cavalry, a man of singular merit and one of my close friends, were killed. Many others were wounded, and many important persons were taken prisoner. Marlborough treated them all with infinite politeness and allowed several of them to return immediately for three months' leave on parole.[3]

The King did not learn of this defeat until Wednesday, 26 May, when he was roused. Everyone was amazed at the obtuseness of the Maréchal de Villeroy, who sent a letter to Dangeau[4] by the same courier, praising the courage of his son, mentioning that his wound was a sabre-cut on the head and not serious, and giving no more information of any kind. I was then at Versailles. Never did I witness so much anxiety and dismay. What made matters infinitely worse was that knowing only the broad outlines of the affair people were left without news for six whole days; even the post failed to arrive. The days seemed like years as we waited in ignorance of the details and outcome of the battle, filled with anxiety for the fate of friends and relatives. The King was reduced to asking for news from the courtiers, and no one could give him any. At length, finding the suspense intolerable, he decided to send Chamillart to Flanders so as to be sure of some news through him and a report on the condition of the

---

[1] Forty-five kilometres from Brussels.

[2] Charles O'Brien, Viscount Clare. An Irishman in the service of France and the Old Pretender.

[3] Louis XIV was so much moved by Marlborough's treatment of prisoners that he allowed Vaubonne, a partisan captured in Italy fighting on the side of the Allies and a very gallant Frenchman, to return to his home at Orange for three months' leave at Marlborough's special request. The King had been much vexed by Vaubonne's inflammatory speeches and did not at all relish granting him leave, but he said he did so for Marlborough's sake.

[4] Dangeau was at that time the Lord Chamberlain.

army. Chamillart accordingly stepped into a post-chaise at five o'clock in the evening of Sunday, 30 May, saying that he was going to L'Etang, where I had been dining with his wife and daughters, and drove straight to Lille. It was another profound shock for the Court when the man in charge of the finance and war departments, responsible for giving all the innumerable and vitally important orders, at that critical moment suddenly vanished. His sudden appearance no less astonished the army when he arrived at the headquarters at Courtrai, where the Maréchal de Villeroy called on him. After that interview a noticeable formality appeared in their relationship with one another. On the following day Chamillart visited the Elector, who received him like a prince fallen on bad times and conscious of his distresses. He returned to Versailles at eight o'clock of the evening of Friday, 4 June; went straight to the King in Mme de Maintenon's room, and remained there until supper giving them an account of his journey.

We learned at last that after several forced marches the army had reached Ghent, and that the Elector had wished to stand there in order to defend the passage of the Scheldt. Villeroy, however, was so utterly shattered by his failure that he most violently opposed that plan, and Ghent was accordingly abandoned with all the surrounding country. The army then retired to Menin and the campaign ended. Thus, with the exception of Namur, Mons, and a very few other fortresses, the entire Spanish Netherlands was lost and part of French Flanders also, and all of this happened with such incredible rapidity that the enemy were as much astounded as we. The dismay became more general with the return of many who had been believed lost; but what was lost irretrievably, and thus lost all that followed, was the head of the Maréchal de Villeroy. Nothing had availed to steady him; no one could calm him; he would neither look nor listen, but imagined enemies, dangers, and defeats in all directions at once, and found security nowhere.

Overwhelmed by the tragic failure of a plan for which he had been solely responsible, stricken with remorse for having refused to wait for Marsin despite repeated orders, he became totally distracted. He would hear no advice, but remained as stubborn after as before the event, and because of his high rank and favour with the King, grew to be a danger to the State, bringing France very close to disaster. The King, himself, maintained an appearance of calm but he felt the defeat deeply and in all its aspects. He took personally all the criticisms levelled at his body-guard and complained about them with some bitterness, for he was sensitive where their reputation was concerned, and perhaps also for his own safety. The soldier-courtiers, however, gave good accounts of them, which deceived no one but the King. Not that there was any reason for abusing them, but testimonials in such circumstances carry little credence. None the less, King Louis seized upon them joyfully, and sent messages to his guards through their guardrooms to the effect that all was now clear to him and that he was much pleased. Yet no matter what may have happened during that ill-planned battle, the previous reputation of the guards was so great and their valour later so magnificent that their very name is an inspiration to the rest of the army and a source of envy and fear to their enemies.

The responsibility for this sad reverse was directly that of the Maréchal de Villeroy. His alone had been the plan, which he had communicated to no one, not even to his commander-in-chief the Elector, and at last the King was persuaded that the time had come when favour must be tempered by misfortune. A general in the Emperor's service would have been executed for such a lapse; it was typical of King Louis to be more indulgent even than before. He pitied Villeroy and defended him; he wrote letters to him in his own hand advising, even requesting him as a friend, to send in his resignation, adding that he wished him to make it clear that he resigned of his own volition, and that he would be glad to welcome him at his Court. To anyone ignorant of the facts all this might sound unbelievable, but Chamillart showed me the letters, each one more pressing than the last, in a vain attempt to break down the maréchal's resistance. The effect upon Villeroy of the first of these letters was a sense of the King's extraordinary kindness; but in the end that kindness was his undoing, for he came to believe that he would keep his command if he stood firm. He accordingly replied with many flowery embellishments that since he felt in no way to blame, was neither sick nor wounded, had indeed been unfortunate but had not failed, he could not disgrace himself by seeming to confess that he was unfit to command an army of the King. The King was vexed but not yet indignant. He wrote a third time and then a fourth, always in the same loving strain, but still evoked the same kind of answer. At last he lost patience and gave up all hope of bringing him to reason.

Whilst this amiable correspondence was proceeding the King had also written to M. de Vendôme, proposing that he should return to take over the command of the Flanders army. Vendôme seemed destined to repair the misfortunes of the Maréchal de Villeroy, or at least to be appointed with that intention, for he had been sent to the Italian army after Cremona for that same reason. For all his boasting, he was now beginning to feel the unlikelihood of success at Turin, or even of maintaining the campaign in Italy at all, for Prince Eugene, with the reinforcements that had joined him after the Battle of Calcinato, had entirely changed the outlook in that theatre of the war. He therefore regarded the proposal as something of a deliverance; it flattered his vanity to be regarded as a saviour, and since Flanders was considered already lost his mind was easy regarding his new responsibilities. What he could neither salvage nor repair would be attributed to Villeroy's mistakes, and what little he could achieve would be hailed as miraculous. This plan was being shaped in strictest secrecy, but it brought the need for still another change, the appointment of a successor to M. de Vendôme. Chamillart, who suffered intensely because of the overwhelming disasters that had occurred during his ministry, believed that a prince of the blood might do much to raise the morale of a French army. He desired also to conciliate the princes by displaying his willingness to do in the public interest what his predecessors had feared even to contemplate.[1] He accordingly suggested the Prince de Conti for Flanders, but when the King refused even to consider that proposal, he mentioned M. le Duc d'Orléans as being suitable for Italy, since his rank and seniority would give the other princes no cause for complaint. Until that time the King had stood firm against giving the command of his armies to his blood relations, partly so as to avoid having to raise them in rank, but especially on account of M. du Maine, who he sadly realized was not fit for war. Now, however, because of necessity and the awful gravity of the situation he allowed himself to be persuaded by his favourite minister, who had prudently obtained Mme de Maintenon's support.

Thus on Tuesday, 22 June, at Marly, the King called back M. le Duc d'Orléans after bidding good night to those who came to his study each evening and was closeted with him for a full quarter of an hour. Meanwhile, in the salon, I was vastly entertained as the rumour spread of this new departure. We were not long without news. M. le Duc d'Orléans left the King's study, passed through the drawing-rooms on his way to visit Madame,[2] returned a moment later, and announced that he was appointed to command the army of Italy. That same evening at his *coucher*, to which only those who had the *grandes* and *secondes entrées* were admitted since his attack of gout, the King, although still much offended with him, was good enough to say that the Maréchal de Villeroy had pressed so hard for his recall that he could no longer be denied. That was the last plank thrown to a drowning man in memory of a long friendship. Villeroy had the folly to reject it, and that was what brought him to disgrace. Orders were sent bidding him return forthwith, but later the King amended his letter, commanding him to await M. de Vendôme's arrival in Flanders, where the enemy had very promptly seized possession of Ostend and Nieuport. After that the Maréchal de Villeroy was sent to Dunkirk to command all that part of maritime Flanders.

Although it is not yet time to describe the character of M. le Duc d'Orléans, I cannot refrain from saying something of the terms on which I stood with him after our reconciliation, which I have mentioned elsewhere. His friendship and confidence in me were very great, and I was

---

[1] Because of memories of the *Fronde*.
[2] Madame wrote that her son 'appeared three fingers taller' on being given his first command.

most sincerely attached to him. I saw him alone in his *entresol* almost every afternoon at Versailles. He always reproached me if I did not come often enough and allowed me to speak with absolute freedom. No subjects were barred; he discussed everything with me and liked me to conceal nothing that concerned him. It was only at Versailles and Marly that I saw him, in other words at the Court. I never visited him in Paris; for one thing I seldom went there, and then only for one night, or very occasionally for two, when I had duties or business. His pleasures, his companions, and the life he led in the city did not attract me and from the beginning I had compacted with him to have no dealings with his staff at the Palais Royal, or with his friends and mistresses. Nor did I desire to have any greater intimacy with Mme la Duchesse d'Orléans, whom I saw only on state occasions, and I took good care to meddle with nothing that went on in their houses. I had always believed that to act otherwise would be extremely vexatious and lead to mischief-making; thus I would hear no gossip concerning them.

On the evening when he was appointed to command in Italy I followed him from the salon to his own rooms, where we had a long conversation. He told me that orders had gone to Villars to join the Italian army as second-in-command; that Vendôme would not leave until his arrival, and that the King had extracted his promise to do nothing without that marshal's consent, and nothing contrary to his wishes. He said that he minded that restriction very little compared with his having achieved his life-long wish without even having to ask for it. At that point I thought I could render no better service to him, Chamillart, or the State than by showing him quite clearly how much he owed to Chamillart for his appointment, making him understand that no matter how great the disparity in rank, a minister would always have the mastery, and if he so pleased could infuriate the greatest of princes. I said that honour, gratitude, and his reputation past and in the future, all demanded that harmony and complete frankness should exist between them, more especially to exclude the scoundrels who for personal advantage would try to sow discord and distrust. He listened gladly to my advice, explained his instructions at considerable length, and commanded me to write to him often and freely.

He had for some time past been in love with Mlle de Séry, young, well-born, but poor; a pretty, lively, impulsive girl with a roguish look that gave as good as it promised. Her cousin Mme de Ventadour had found her a post as one of Madame's ladies, and while she was attached to that household she became pregnant and bore M. le Duc d'Orléans a son.[1] That brought her dismissal, but the prince grew more and more devoted

---

[1] Jean Philippe, Chevalier d'Orléans (1702–1748), who became the *grand prieur* of France 1719.

12*

to her, and although she was overbearing and let him know it, he only loved her the more. Many things at the Palais Royal were governed by her wishes; she even acquired a small group of courtiers and made many friends, and Mme de Ventadour, despite her pose of repentance and morality, continued to be her friend and made no attempt to conceal her attachment. Mlle de Séry appeared to have good advisers, for she chose this moment when M. le Duc d'Orléans was radiantly happy to persuade him to legitimize their son, and not content with that, declared that it would not be becoming for her as a mother, publicly acclaimed, to be addressed as Mademoiselle. There was no precedent for calling her otherwise, since Madame is a privilege reserved for unmarried Daughters of France and daughters of duchesses in their own right. That, however, in no way deterred the mistress or her lover. He proceeded to give her the lands and estate of Argenton and took advantage of the King's favour to extract with much difficulty letters patent and permission for her to be Madame and Comtesse d'Argenton. Such a thing was unheard of. Difficulties were expected over the registration by the Parlement, but M. le Duc d'Orléans, though on the eve of departure and hard pressed with state affairs, went personally to see the premier président and the procureur-général, and the registration was effected. His appointment to the command in Italy had been received with acclamations at the Court and in Paris. This news somewhat quelled the pleasure and caused a good deal of complaint, but a man in love thinks only of pleasing his mistress and gladly sacrifices all for her sake.

Everything concerning that affair was set, sealed and delivered without a word of it passing between us. I was vexed about the act itself, and vexed that he had spoiled the brilliance of his departure by so public and improper a breach of morals. But that was all. I remained true to the decision which I had taken when we were first reconciled, namely, never to refer to his household or his mistresses. He knew full well that I disapproved of what he had done for this one, and was extremely careful to keep his mouth shut.

The Abbé Testu[1] died at this time, a most remarkable character who had mixed all his life with the best Society of Paris and the Court and was himself excellently good company. In the past he had been a permanency at the Hôtel d'Albret and intimately attached to Mme de Montespan, whom he saw when he pleased at the time of her highest favour. He was equally attached to the then Mme Scarron, and visited her in her obscurity bringing up the children of the King and Mme de Montespan. He continued to see her as often as he chose even after her incredible good fortune. They wrote to one another frequently throughout his life and, with her, he had real influence. He was also on terms of friendship with

---

[1] Jacques Testu, a member of the French Academy and a very great friend of Mme de Sévigné.

her intimate circle, more especially with M. de Richelieu and his wife, and with Mme d'Heudicourt and Mme de Montchevreuil. Many people of distinction in various walks of life were his friends, but he deferred to none of them, not even to Mme de Maintenon. Not every one could have his friendship. He was one of the first men known to suffer from what they call the vapours[1] and was much incommoded by them, as well as by a spasmodic tic that at every moment disunited his entire countenance. He liked to make himself prominent everywhere; people mocked him for it, but they let him be. He was a very good friend and obliging, and by stealth brought great happiness to many and promotion and even wealth to some. Withal he was a simple-hearted and a good man, upright and without personal ambition; but he was also hot-tempered, highly dangerous, unforgiving, even to the point of pursuing with rancour those who offended him. Tall, thin, fair complexioned, at the age of 80 he had taken to making his servants empty a ewer of iced water drop by drop on to his bald head, not allowing one spot to touch the floor. That habit had increased in later years. His death was a loss to his friends and to Society also. Altogether he was very highly esteemed and much sought after until the day of his death.

It was not long before we learned of the changes in the Italian command under M. le Duc d'Orléans. Villars would have none of it. It had not at all suited him to take orders from M. de Vendôme and a young prince he may have thought equally unpalatable. Riches and the highest honours were his already; he did not hesitate, but said quite flatly that the King might remove from him the command of the Rhine army and employ him or not as he so pleased, but to go to Italy he could not endure and he prayed the King to release him. Any other man than the fortunate Villars might have been disgraced; from him everything was acceptable. His courier returned to him with orders to remain at the head of his army, and another was sent to Marsin to go at once to Italy by the Swiss road in his stead. The King meanwhile extracted the same promise from M. le Duc d'Orléans regarding Marsin as he had required for Vendôme.[2]

The ladies[3] of Savoy had quitted Turin in good time and had retired to Coni, M. de Savoie having treated with scant courtesy the King's offer of a safe-conduct to any other place of their choice. He himself left at the end of June, taking with him his entire court, his baggage, and three thousand of his cavalry, which left only five hundred and twenty hussars

---

[1] Vapours: From the *Dictionnaire de l'Académie* 1694. 'Vapours in the human body—exhalations that are said to rise from the stomach or bowel towards the brain . . . An illness whose ordinary effect is to render melancholy, sometimes even lacrimose, and which constricts the heart and fogs the mind.' In other words, flatulence.

[2] To do nothing without prior consultation or without his consent.

[3] The two duchesses, the mother and grandmother of the Duchesse de Bourgogne and the Queen of Spain.

for the defence. He then began to travel the length and breadth of his dukedom, hoping that La Feuillade might follow him; which hope was fulfilled, for the latter immediately handed over the direction of the siege to his subordinates and set off in pursuit, leaving behind no more than forty battalions who became exceedingly weary and made little progress.

La Feuillade's rash excursion exhausted his entire force of cavalry, tired out his infantry marching hither and thither across country, and over-burdened those who still continued with the siege. It was mad of him to lose precious time chasing a will-o'-the-wisp at the expense of the main objective, the capture of Turin. Speed there was of the essence, for every hour counted in view of the likely approach of Prince Eugene.[1] Courier after courier was despatched stressing the urgency of the siege, but all in vain. Time wasted could not be recovered, and at length Chamillart was compelled to inform his son-in-law of the bad impression that his wild goose chase after M. de Savoie was creating at the Court.[2] No one on the spot had the courage to remonstrate with him.

When M. le Duc d'Orléans arrived he was dissatisfied with all that he saw, being convinced that the attacks were directed at the wrong points (in this his opinion coincided with that of Vauban); that the siege-works were faulty, and that the whole operation was monstrously delayed. He was civil to La Feuillade, but seeing no reason why victory should be sacrificed to his whims he made many changes. No sooner had he departed than La Feuillade reversed his orders and continued as before, listening to no one's advice from start to finish. His arrogance with his officers, even with his generals, his foolish belief that he could rule by personal valour alone, assisted by the fact of his being the son-in-law of the all-powerful war minister, made him generally disliked and put his staff into so evil an humour that they did their bare duty without regard for the final objective. They would neither remedy mistakes nor seek to improve matters, acting thus from resentment and fear of being told to mind their own business. With such a commander, who had started badly, lacked sufficient forces (more had been impossible to provide), and was ill-served by his staff, the wherewithal to capture Turin was wanting. From time to time the news of some outwork being taken was sent post-haste by courier to Versailles and hopes were renewed, but our trenches proceeded so slowly that La Feuillade himself complained of them in his letters.

On 17 July M. le Duc d'Orléans joined M. de Vendôme on the Mincio and conferred with him, not so much as the prince wished, but as much as he was able. That so-called hero had committed irreparable mistakes, for

---

[1] Vendôme had written to the King, 'Once Turin is taken all the difficulties of the war here will be smoothed away.'

[2] They were saying that La Feuillade's only interest was in the personal glory of capturing a reigning prince. Chamillart had written, 'Your honour is at stake.'

Prince Eugene had crossed the Po almost before his eyes, and no one knew what had become of our twelve battalions posted on the further bank near the place where he crossed. Vendôme wished these errors to remain concealed; on the other hand he looked forward to Marsin's arrival for the pleasure of giving orders to a Maréchal de France and flourishing the royal warrant with his authority. He therefore shunned conferences whenever possible, and cut them short when they proved unavoidable. What he did not escape, however, was the clear gaze of the young prince as he endeavoured to learn the task that was shortly to be his. M. le Duc d'Orléans contrived to lay bare, face to face with him, all the failings which he had long suspected from a distance, and many other errors as well, of which he did not conceal his true opinion, albeit with courtesy. M. de Vendôme was unable to defend himself or to make excuses.

Marsin at last arrived and Vendôme made haste to depart. M. le Duc d'Orléans at once attempted a minor engagement under the command of General Médavy,[1] which, had it succeeded, would have checked Prince Eugene's advance, but the plan failed when the town of Goito[2] made a cowardly surrender at the very moment when Marsin was approaching to relieve it. M. le Duc d'Orléans then travelled post-haste to rejoin M. de Vendôme at Mantua in order to confer with him and agree upon future plans, as had been arranged. The reason for his journey was to suggest the dismantling of a pontoon bridge which M. de Vendôme had caused to be assembled near Cremona. It was true that as yet only a very small number of enemy troops had managed to cross the Po; but despite M. de Vendôme's obstinate assurances to the contrary they had made light of every obstacle in crossing the other rivers in their march towards Piedmont. In vain did M. le Duc d'Orléans argue that they would cross the Po with equal ease. M. de Vendôme refused to listen. They were still at it hammer and tongs when news arrived that a small section was already across; whereupon M. de Vendôme exclaimed that five or six ruffians meant nothing. Then, whilst he was still pooh-poohing, a succession of dispatches were received stating that their entire army had crossed. Vendôme, who had just announced that they would never dare to make the attempt,[3] quite unblushingly remarked, 'Well! They are over, I can do nothing; they will have many other obstacles to overcome before they get to Piedmont,' and turning to M. le Duc d'Orléans, 'Any orders, Sir? There is nothing more for me here; I am off tomorrow.' And so he was, leaving M. le Duc d'Orléans to bear the entire burden of his errors.

Thus abandoned by Vendôme, but even worse left under the tutelage

---

[1] Lieutenant-general, later Maréchal, the Comte de Médavy (1655–1725). He had been holding his ground in Italy, too strong for the Austrians to risk attacking him.

[2] Near Mantua.

[3] Vendôme had written to Versailles on 10 July, 'You may be quite sure that Prince Eugene will be unable to disturb the siege of Turin.'

of the Maréchal de Marsin,[1] M. le Duc d'Orléans gathered together the fragments of his scattered army and, after some days spent in observing the enemy's movements, set up his headquarters between Alessandria and Valenza so as to prevent their crossing the River Tanaro or force them to give battle. That crossing was the only one by which they could enter Piedmont; if they did not attempt it they must abandon the relief of Turin; but such an attempt would mean a fight on terms so disadvantageous to them that all the evidence seemed to prove their defeat inevitable. But when M. le Duc d'Orléans proposed that plan to the Maréchal de Marsin the latter would by no means consent. What his reasons were no one could divine, for he gave no reasons. He seemed completely under the influence of La Feuillade, and La Feuillade's one thought was for reinforcement by M. le Duc d'Orléans's army. Marsin's desire may have been to support in every way the son-in-law of an all-powerful war-minister and so to please him. What neither of them perceived was that everything depended on preventing a relief, even the personal reputation of La Feuillade himself.

Having been refused the maréchal's consent, M. le Duc d'Orléans's only course was to give way and to bring his army to join the besiegers. He arrived before Turin on the evening of 28 August. La Feuillade was now under two superior officers, which should have made him more docile, but he had gained so complete an ascendancy over Marsin that the real authority was still with him, to the great misfortune of France. The aim of all was the capture of Turin, but the means of so doing and the plans of action caused innumerable disputes. M. le Duc d'Orléans was incensed to learn that La Feuillade had cancelled the changes he had ordered on his first visit of inspection. It now seemed to him that no progress had been made; that everything was at a standstill; worse still, that no one had any idea what next to do. La Feuillade himself had become so bad-tempered because of his want of success, and had acquired so much ill-will from all his officers, generals included, that none of them took the smallest interest in the siege. M. le Duc d'Orléans inspected the outposts and siege-works, visited the lines, and saw the gap through which Prince Eugene might be expected to essay a relief. Everything seemed to him unsatisfactory, the trenches were badly constructed, far too long, and extremely ill-guarded, and all the time news continued to arrive of the advance of the Imperial army determined to effect a rescue of the city.

---

[1] Marsin was suffering from a morbid depression. He gave his confessor a tragic letter for Chamillart on the day before the Battle of Turin. 'As this letter will not reach you until after my death I beg you to preserve my secret. Ever since I received the King's command to go to Italy I have not been able to clear my mind of the conviction that I shall not survive this campaign, and death, in the workings of God's pity, thrusts itself upon me day and night. Since I have been in this country nothing has relieved my presentiments except my trust in God. P.S. At this very moment the enemy are across the Po.'

At that point M. le Duc d'Orléans was in favour of suspending the siege-operations and marching against the enemy; but once again he met with opposition. The dispute grew so heated that Marsin finally agreed to hold a council of war with all the generals. He was in no doubt of the issue, nor of the voting for that matter, for he was generally supposed to possess a secret document,[1] and La Feuillade, as Chamillart's son-in-law, controlled all their destinies. In the event they voted servilely and in unison, with the result that the remedy made the harm incurable. M. le Duc d'Orléans solemnly warned them of the disasters that must inevitably follow, and then declared that having no authority he could not rightly be expected to bear responsibility for a national disgrace. Immediately afterwards he called for his post-chaise and prepared to leave the army. Marsin, La Feuillade, and the generals did their utmost to dissuade him, and eventually he was prevailed on to stay, but only on condition of having no part in the command, issuing no orders, and formally giving up all his authority to Marsin and La Feuillade.

La Feuillade's stubborn and tragic refusal to march was founded solely on the wishful hope that Prince Eugene might fear to attack his lines, and that if he retired Turin would fall, not thanks to the army of M. le Duc d'Orléans but to the siege-operations which he himself had directed. Thus the glory would be all his own. There lay the true reason, supported by much false logic and all the ardour of hot-headed youth, that overruled Marsin's judgment and brought about the ruin of France. Such was the deplorable state of affairs during the last three days of that calamitous siege. The Duc d'Orléans meanwhile, having stripped himself of authority, remained mostly in his quarters, sometimes walking, but for the most part writing a strongly worded report to the King of Marsin's conduct, a document which he showed to Marsin, asking him to despatch it by his next courier, since being no longer part of the army he did not wish to send one himself.

On the night of the 6–7 September, however, which was the day of the Battle of Turin, M. le Duc d'Orléans was woken by a partisan with news that Prince Eugene was approaching. In spite of his determination not to interfere, he arose and went to Marsin, who was peacefully asleep in bed, showed him the message, and suggested marching that instant to meet the enemy in order to take them by surprise as they negotiated a difficult stream which they would be bound to cross. That plan was certainly the right one in those circumstances. Saint-Nectaire,[2] long since made a chevalier of the Order and a soldier of great experience, appeared at the same moment in Marsin's tent to confirm the news and uphold the prince's advice. But it was written in the Book of Eternity that France

---

[1] Voltaire and other historians say that after the fighting had begun Marsin could at any time have produced a secret warrant to take over the sole command.

[2] He was the Marquis de Senneterre, ambassador to England in the reign of George I.

would be stabbed in the heart that very day. The maréchal refused to budge. He insisted that the news was false, that Prince Eugene could by no means be so near, and that M. le Duc d'Orléans would do well to return quietly to his bed. Whereupon that prince, more indignant even than before, returned to his quarters quite resolved to leave everything to those blind, deaf leaders who would neither see nor hear. Soon after his departure news came from all sides of Prince Eugene's approach; but he firmly refused to interfere.

One or two of the generals then came to him and almost forced him to mount his horse; and he rode listlessly at a slow trot along the front of the encampment. The events of the past few days were by now common knowledge to the soldiers, many of whom had served with him at Leuze, Steinkerk, and Neerwinden. His rank and reputation for firmness and good sense (of which old campaigners are excellent judges) had set them grumbling because he was no longer in command, and one of the Pied-montese called him by name asking if he was refusing them his sword. Those words did more to move him than anything that the generals had said. Answering that so proper a request could not be refused, he then and there cast aside his most justifiable anger and turned his whole mind to the problem of saving Marsin and La Feuillade despite themselves. By that time, however, there was no possibility of leaving the lines and making new dispositions, even had they so desired, for the enemy were already within view and steadily approaching. Marsin, more dead than alive at finding his hopes disproved, was deep-sunk in reflections that were no longer of any consequence. He was like a condemned man, quite incapable of giving coherent orders.

The gaps in the lines were very wide, and M. le Duc d'Orléans sent for forty-six battalions stationed on the heights of Capucino under the command of Albergotti,[1] and quite useless there so far as the siege and Prince Eugene's advance were concerned. But La Feuillade, more greatly feared and better obeyed than the prince, forbade Albergotti to move, despite M. le Duc d'Orleans's repeated orders. The latter then sent for them again; but again La Feuillade forbade them to march, and they did not do so. Meanwhile, in some measure to fill the gaps, the Duc d'Orléans mixed squadrons of cavalry with the battalions, thus strengthening the foremost rank at the expense of the second, for he still hoped to be joined by Albergotti's forty-six battalions. He also sent to other distant troops, urging them to hurry across a small bridge and join him in guarding the lines; but La Feuillade, still impelled by a fiend, went personally to the bridge as soon as he learned of that order and prevented their crossing. So widespread was the mutiny that when M. de Duc d'Orléans himself ordered an officer commanding a squadron of the Anjou regiment to

---

[1] Count Francesco Albergotti, a Florentine in the service of France and Spain. Saint-Simon thought him dangerous and a favourite of Vendôme.

march the latter flatly refused to obey. Thereupon the duke slashed him across the face and had him reported to the King.

The attack which began at ten o'clock in the morning was pressed with incredible ferocity. Prince Eugene fought in the ranks and was among the first to break through in the gaps caused by our want of troops. Marsin was wounded in the middle of the battle, with a thrust that pierced the lower part of his abdomen and broke his spine. He was taken prisoner at the same moment and borne off to a distant blockhouse. La Feuillade rode distractedly hither and thither, tearing at his hair, quite unable to give orders of any kind. The Duc d'Orléans gave them all, but was monstrously ill-obeyed. He did marvels none the less, always appearing where the fighting was hottest, cool and composed, seeing all, noting all, present wherever there was most need for remedy, heartening both officers and men by his example. He was twice wounded, once slightly upon the hip, then more seriously and painfully upon the wrist; he remained unmoved, however, and seeing that the entire front was about to crumble, he called the officers by name, cheered on the men, and himself led a charge of the mixed squadrons and battalions. At last, overcome by pain and loss of blood, he was obliged to leave the field, but he scarcely gave them time to attend to his wounds before returning to the thick of the battle. Unhappily the terrain, the battle order, and the want of discipline all conspired to throw our troops into confusion. Le Guerchoys with his marine brigade three times repulsed the enemy with great slaughter, spiked their guns, and three times restored the line, until at last, weakened by his losses in officers and men, he appealed to his supporting brigade to advance to his help against fresh troops coming against him. That brigade and its commander, whose name is best forgotten, flatly refused to move. That was the last moment when there was any kind of battle order; what followed was confusion, chaos, flight, rout, and defeat. To make it all the more horrible, the generals in every branch of the service with very few exceptions thought only of their baggage and the booty they had acquired by plunder, and by adding to the disorder instead of resisting it, made themselves worse than useless.

When M. le Duc d'Orléans finally realized that the shameful day was lost, he turned his attention to leaving as little as possible upon the field. Withdrawing his light artillery, ammunition waggons and the troops in the most forward trenches, he gathered around him such of the generals as he could muster, and explained to them briefly but clearly that the best line of retreat lay through Italy, where the French were still masters. They might then hope to confine the enemy to the districts around Turin; prevent their return through Italy, and leave them to starve in a devastated country from which there was no escape. A proposal of that nature, however, was vastly shocking to those mean-spirited officers, who hoped to salvage from the wreck of their campaign a swift return to France with all the wealth that they had accumulated during their time in Italy. Even La Feuillade, who had the best of reasons for being submissive, tried to oppose the prince, until the latter, quite out of patience with his impertinence, told him to be silent and let the rest speak. The remainder with one exception refused to support him. Their minds were still affected by the day's disorder, and M. le Duc d'Orléans was weak from loss of blood. He ended the discussion by saying that neither the time nor the place warranted longer argument; that he was tired of being so often proved right and yet so little trusted, and that since he now had authority he ordered them without more ado to march to the bridge and into Italy. He had no more strength left; mind and body were equally exhausted, and after marching with them for some time he flung himself into his postchaise.

He thus accompanied the retreat. As they crossed the bridge over the Po he could hear behind him the generals grumbling at the decision to go to Italy instead of to the France that tugged so hard at their heartstrings. The complaints from one officer became so loud that the Duc d'Orléans, rightly indignant, thrust his head out of the window and taunted him with the name of his mistress, saying that for all the use he had been he had better have remained with her. That sally quietened them all, but it was written that folly and hesitation should continue to undermine our army and bring salvation to the Allies. As they were debouching from the bridge on the Italian side, an officer galloped to the head of the column to inform M. le Duc d'Orléans that the enemy were in possession of the passes ahead. Cross-questioned, he said that the forts were strongly defended, that he had seen the standards of the White Cross regiment, and was almost sure of having recognized M. de Savoie himself. Notwithstanding these assurances, the prince who knew that part of Italy very well distrusted the report and proposed to continue on the march, sending scouts forward to reconnoitre. To this, however, the generals would not agree; the road to the Alps was safe and they directed the army by that route with all that they still possessed in the way of supply and ammunition wagons. Thus after half a day's further march M. le Duc d'Orléans discovered that he had neither food nor ammunition, and that with the greater part of the army headed towards France the road to Italy was no longer in question. Rage and despair at the continued mutiny, not to say treachery, combined with the pain from his wounds to make him sink back into a corner of his chaise and bid them go where they pleased and consult him no more.

Such is the true history of the catastrophe in Italy. It has since been learned that the officer's report was quite contrary to the facts, and that there were no enemy troops of any kind to oppose our retreat into Italy, nor even the smallest obstruction. What is more, a success which Médavy reported two days later would have made M. le Duc d'Orléans absolute master of Italy, with Prince Eugene cornered helplessly between his forces and the part of Savoy that was in our possession. That news, which reached M. le Duc d'Orléans at Oulx, in the Alps, where he had set up his headquarters, being unable to go further on account of his wounds, was his crowning misery.

To return to Marsin. When they bore him off to that distant block-house he asked only once whether M. le Duc d'Orléans still lived. He then made them send for a priest; dictated a personal letter, placed in an envelope addressed to M. le Duc d'Orléans the latter's report to the King which he had been asked to forward; spoke thereafter only of God, and expired during the night. He was an exceedingly short man, a great talker, an even greater toady, or rather a lackey, wholly concerned with his own advantage although not dishonest, pious after the Flemish man-ner, more obsequious than polite, utterly engrossed in cultivating those who could help or injure him, futile, quite lacking in depth, judgment, or ability. He was unmarried when he died and not by any means old.

Whilst these events were taking place I had been spending a month at La Ferté and had been receiving there the news from Italy, for M. le Duc d'Orléans had kept me regularly posted, writing by his own hand when he did not wish others to know the matter. I was thus fully aware of the disasters impending and already feeling vastly apprehensive when a gentleman from Rouen, going to his brother's house nearby, stopped to speak to Mme de Saint-Simon and me as we were walking with company in our park. He told us of the defeat at Turin and the truth regarding M. le Duc d'Orléans, the Maréchal de Marsin and the rest, just as the King received it by courier three days later, and I four days later in letters from the Court and Paris. We never discovered how the bad news had travelled with such extraordinary, nay incredible speed, for the gentleman would not tell us, only affirming the truth of what he said; and as he died very shortly after we never saw him again. I was so deeply dis-turbed that the disaster should have happened under M. le Duc d'Or-léans's command, although he was in no way to blame for it, that I con-tracted a fever and went straight to Paris without stopping at Versailles, where I had no wish to fall into the hands of the faculty. Nancré,[1] bearing the detailed despatches, arrived almost at the same time as myself, and although I had no acquaintance with him I sent to beg him to visit me, since I was indisposed and could not go to him. He came at once, for he had received orders to see me. We were closeted alone together two good hours. He informed me that the King exonerated his nephew entirely, and urged me to write exactly as I felt without reservation. No need for that, the public and even the jealous courtiers crowned him with laurels even in defeat, and praised him all the more because fortune had frowned on

---

[1] The Marquis de Nancré, one of the Duc d'Orléans's cronies and much attached to his mis-tress Mme d'Argenton. The Duchess disliked him intensely.

him. That fact is as memorable as it is unique, and I can remember no other example of such unanimous acclaim in so complete a disaster. All the blame fell on Marsin, and, despite Chamillart's endeavours, on La Feuillade.

After Nancré's return to M. le Duc d'Orléans, who was extremely ill from the effects of his wounds, the new Mme d'Argenton and Mme de Nancré (widowed stepmother and close friend of the aforesaid Nancré) set off together for Lyons, each in a separate postchaise and with the utmost secrecy. Thence they proceeded to Grenoble and lay concealed at an inn. M. le Duc d'Orléans had not yet arrived at Grenoble on his way home; but he learned on the road of their escapade and was very angry, sending them word that they were to return immediately for he would on no account see them. But they had not travelled all the way from Paris to Grenoble to be sent away unseen, and they waited for him. In the end it was more than he could endure to know his mistress so close at hand and remain unforgiving, and accordingly, at seven or eight in the evening when the day's work was done, he bolted his door, settled comfortably in his room, and had the females sent up to dine with him and one or two cronies by a back staircase. That state of affairs continued for four or five days, at the end of which time he sent them back and continued on his journey home.

That ridiculous episode created a public scandal. People were genuinely grieved by the slur on his private reputation, and those who were jealous of him, especially Monsieur le Duc and Mme la Duchesse, made a rumpus, only too happy for the excuse to break the silence. I, as you will remember, had firmly resolved never to speak to him of his mistresses; but he had written to me, as soon as his wounded wrist permitted, with such candour that I could not keep silent when everyone else was crying out against him. He received my letter with one from Chamillart, written on behalf of the King who tactfully did not wish to write himself, advising him to send back the two women and warning him of the bad impression created by their journey. Neither letter reached him until after their departure, and that was his only reply. He arrived at Versailles on Monday, 8 November towards the end of the King's dinner, which he was eating in bed, as always on the days when he took physic. No one ever received a warmer welcome. He then went to Monseigneur at Meudon and afterwards returned to sup in private with the King. That same day, as soon as he was done with the royalty, I visited him. He took me into his study and it was there that he thanked me with real emotion for my candour in writing to him of the escapade, vowing that he had at first been truly angry, but that the temptation of knowing them so close had been too much for him. 'But, Sir,' I interrupted, 'you do now see the folly of it?' 'Indeed, indeed,' said he, 'but none of us is perfect.' When we were alone with the doors closed we went deeply into many matters, and I acquainted him with the situation at the Court as it concerned himself, with other things which I could not mention in my letters even though I had used a cipher. He then talked of Italy and painted a shocking picture of the generals of his army, as I have described them, only worse, and of all the other misfortunes (to use no stronger word) that had caused the great defeat at Turin.

He said also that he believed La Feuillade would be broken, judging by what the King had said. M. le Duc d'Orléans had striven to palliate his offences, enormous though these had been, but the King had rebuked him for making the attempt, speaking in a harsh, bitter tone which he had used for no one else. The prince added that at present La Feuillade was in Dauphiné, hoping against hope that he might be allowed to retain his command there, but that from the way the King had spoken his recall seemed certain. During our many subsequent conversations he thoroughly informed me of all that had happened, and the returning generals and other officers told me still more. It was not long before all idea of renewing the campaign in Italy was abandoned. The very most that could now be achieved was a defensive war in the direction of the Alps and the strengthening of the Spanish army with the remnants of our troops in Italy, in an effort to regain some vestige of superiority.

Shortly after this, La Feuillade received his orders to return; but that prospect seeming very dreadful to him he had the folly to try to get the order countermanded, stayed where he was, and sent courier after courier to Chamillart, until the King lost all patience with him and Chamillart was covered with confusion. A final courier prevailed on him to return, but he waited several days in Paris before summoning enough courage to show his face at Versailles. His father-in-law at last managed to extract permission to bring him to Mme de Maintenon's apartment so as to avoid a public audience, and produced him there on Monday, 13 December when he came to work with the King. As soon as the King perceived them on the threshold, he rose, went to the door, and without giving either of them time to utter exclaimed to La Feuillade with a more than ominous expression, 'We are most unfortunate, Sirrah, both of us!' He then immediately turned on his heel, leaving La Feuillade still standing in the doorway, for he had been given no chance to enter, and withdrew at once without daring to reply. The King never spoke to him again. It was very long before he allowed Monseigneur even to take him to Meudon, or suffered him to be at Marly for his wife's sake. People observed that the King ever afterwards averted his glance if it turned on him. So fell that Phaeton. La Feuillade realized that his situation was hopeless; he sold his horses and announced in a semi-public fashion that having commanded armies he could not serve as a mere lieutenant-general. Yet being so disgraced, there was nothing so vile and ignoble that he did not use it in his efforts to climb back into favour. He took to complaining of his lot, and making excuses to people who were totally uninterested, and thus, after being feared and envied, he made himself despised and unpitied. I think that there never was a man more wrongheaded, nor more fundamentally dishonest down to the very marrow of his bones. Let us now return to what happened at home during the Italian calamity, which followed close after those of Barcelona[1] and Flanders.

The King displayed a great willingness to oblige Père de La Chaise, by granting him a signal favour. That priest who was of gentle birth wished to be regarded as noble. His brother, the Archbishop of Lyons's equerry, then master of his hunt, had become captain of the King's *gardes de la porte* through the confessor's influence, and his son had had the post after his death. He had married a Gué-Bagnols, of a wealthy Parisian legal family. Père de La Chaise minded bitterly that he could not obtain permission for her to go to Marly, but the King, despite his partiality, could not bring himself to allow the niece to eat at Mme la Duchesse de Bourgogne's table or use her coaches. It so happened that year that the King wished to spend Saint Hubert's Day at Marly; that Mme la Duchesse de Bourgogne being pregnant could not join the excursion—which on that account was from Wednesday to Saturday only—and that Madame had such a bad cold that she, too, was prevented from going. The King perceived that this was a chance unlikely to occur again, and he promptly seized it. He nominated Mme de La Chaise for Marly, but in the circumstances she did not secure the right to eat or use the coaches, and that privilege she never subsequently obtained. Not everyone, however, observed that fine point although all knew that she had been to Marly. Père de La Chaise was enchanted.

That same Marly produced a most ridiculous squabble. It was raining, but not enough to prevent the King from going to watch the planting in his gardens. His hat became wet through; another was needed. The Duc d'Aumont was on annual leave; the Duc de Tresmes acted as his deputy. The King's dresser[2] produced the fresh hat; de Tresmes handed it to the King. M. de La Rochefoucauld was present. It all happened in a moment. Although the Duc de Tresmes was his friend he went perfectly mad; his rights were infringed, his honour involved, all was lost. There was the greatest difficulty in separating them. Their rank forgotten, they accused one another of all manner of encroachments, no one dared to interrupt them, and all for the sake of a hat everything was in an uproar. Dare

---

[1] Barcelona had been captured by the Allies in the previous year. In early March a Franco-Spanish army under Philip V and Tessé had laid siege to it; but on 11 May they were forced to withdraw. Saint-Simon said that the French gunners were slow and ill-trained, and continually changed the position of the cannon. This was because they received a special bonus (*un droit pécuniaire*) every time a cannon was moved.

[2] One of the twelve *portmanteaux du roi*. The duties were 'to place in His hands His hat, gloves, cane, handkerchief, hunting-horn, tennis-balls, etc., put on or remove His coat, change His handkerchief or cravat, hold the royal sword when the King does not wear His spurs....'

one say it? For all the world like a brawl among servants. During that same Marly Mgr le Duc de Bourgogne ceased going to the concerts although he greatly enjoyed the music. He also sold the jewels which he had inherited from the late Mme la Dauphine, a very great quantity, and gave the money to the poor. For some time past he had not been attending the plays.[1]

I should have grave doubts about soiling this paper with the tale of the operation for a fistula which Maréchal performed on Courcillon,[2] Dangeau's only son, at his house in the town of Versailles, were it not for the supremely ridiculous circumstances that attended it. Courcillon was a young man of brilliant courage who had commanded one of the late Cardinal von Fürstenberg's regiments, a highly lucrative post. He had excellent brains, some culture even, but his mind was wholly bent on pranks, practical jokes, mischief-making, and impiety, combined with most obscene debauches, of which this operation was generally assumed to be a result. His mother was an intimate friend of Mme de Maintenon, and they two were the only people at the Court or in Paris who were ignorant of his way of life. His mother, who doted on him, was deeply distressed and could scarcely bear to leave him, even for a moment. Mme de Maintenon began soon to share her concern and took to sitting every day at Courcillon's bedside until it was time for the King to visit her. She often went to him early in the morning and stayed to eat her dinner. Mme d'Heudicourt,[3] whom I have mentioned before, was occasionally allowed to come and entertain them, and almost no one else was admitted. Courcillon listened to their pious talk, gave vent to such reflections as his condition forced on him, and spoke of religion. They marvelled at him and spread it abroad that he was a saint. Mme d'Heudicourt and the few others who heard these moral sentiments, and were acquainted with that pietist, who now and then slyly showed them the tip of his tongue, could scarcely stifle their laughter or resist whispering the tale to their friends. Courcillon, though fully aware of the honour of having Mme de Maintenon as his daily nurse, was rapidly dying of boredom, for he could see his cronies only in the evening when she and his mother had left him. He lamented to them bitterly in the most furious yet comical fashion imaginable, burlesquing his own pious reflections and the ladies' credulity, with the result that his illness, while it lasted, provided a spectacle that diverted the entire Court and made a mockery of Mme de Maintenon. No

---

[1] He was becoming almost fanatically religious.

[2] A godson of Cardinal von Fürstenberg. His leg was amputated at the Battle of Malplaquet in 1709. The severance was very high and he was in extreme danger; but when he saw his father in tears at his bedside he implored him to go away; he said that the old man pulled such funny faces that it was killing him with laughter.

[3] Bonne de Pons, Marquise d'Heudicourt (1644–1709), Mme de Maintenon's favourite crony. 'She never in her life said a good word for anyone unless accompanied by a few most devastating *buts*.'

one dared to undeceive her, so that she continued to have an affectionate and admiring respect for Courcillon's virtues and to quote him as an example. The King also gained that impression, although Courcillon took no pains after his recovery to cultivate his useful reputation, and in no way deviated from his accustomed behaviour. Mme de Maintenon noticed nothing; not even his subsequent neglect altered her sentiments towards him. In truth, apart from her superb tact in dealing with the King, she was the very queen of simpletons.

CHAPTER XVII

1707

Economies in New Year Gifts – The Elector of Cologne is made a bishop – Birth of the second Duc de Bretagne – Death of the Comte de Gramont – Union of Scotland with England – Court Balls – Assignment of commands – Exhaustion of Chamillart – Tax on Baptisms and Marriages – Death of du Chesne – Vauban and the King's Tithe – Battle of Almanza – Origin of M. le Duc d'Orléans's friendship and respect for Berwick – Opportunity sadly missed in Spain – Médavy's alternative plans for Italy, both good, both rejected – Return of Vaudémont – His nieces, their characters and conduct – Horrible discovery of Mme la Duchesse de Bourgogne – The King sleeps at Petit-Bourg – I take the waters at Forges

THE CRITICAL state of the finances, which had been greatly aggravated by the expenses of the war and all our losses in men and territory, had obliged the King for the past two or three years first to reduce and then to dock completely the New Year presents which he was in the habit of giving to the Sons and Daughters of France. They had amounted to a very great sum, for the royal treasury had regularly supplied him with thirty-five thousand gold louis, no matter what their value, to give to his relations on New Year's Day. In this year, 1707, he limited himself to twenty-five thousand. The blow fell hardest upon Mme de Montespan,[1] to whom the King had given twelve thousand gold louis annually ever since her final retirement from the Court. The Marquis d'O had been responsible for taking three thousand to her every three months, and he was now instructed to tell her that the King could give her no more than eight thousand. Mme de Montespan expressed no dismay whatsoever; she replied that she minded only for the poor, to whom, indeed, she had given most lavishly.

The Elector of Cologne,[2] who had never been ordained, now resolved to take Holy Orders. The Archbishop of Cambrai met him at Lille and in five consecutive days endowed him with the four lowest,[3] made him subdeacon, deacon, ordained him priest, and finally consecrated him bishop. He greatly enjoyed his priestly functions in the years that followed, especially saying mass and playing the pontiff.

---

[1] She died in this same year, 1707.
[2] Joseph Clement of Bavaria. He had been banished from his estates by the Emperor.
[3] The *lower orders*: porter, exorcist, reader, and acolyte.

Mme la Duchesse de Bourgogne, on Saturday, 8 January, was safely
and very speedily delivered of a Duc de Bretagne, a little before eight
o'clock in the morning. There was great rejoicing, but the King, having
already lost one, forbade all the extravagances of the previous birthday,
which had cost enormous sums. He wrote to the Duke of Savoy to inform him of the new arrival, despite the war and all his dissatisfaction,
and he received a reply thanking and congratulating him.

At the end of January the Comte de Gramont[1] died in Paris, where he
scarcely ever went. He was more than 86 years old and until he was 85,
and even after, had enjoyed perfect health in body and mind. He was the
uncle of the Maréchal de Gramont, whose mother was a sister of that
Maréchal de Roquelaure who was beheaded for duelling. He had begun
in the service of Monsieur le Prince, had followed him to Flanders, then
went to England,[2] and there married a Miss Hamilton,[3] with whom he
had been carrying on a somewhat public love-affair until her scandalized
brothers compelled him to marry her. He was a most notable wit; one of
those mocking spirits excelling in quips, who neatly and accurately held
up to ridicule people's faults, weakness, and absurdities, branding them
irredeemably and for ever with two flicks of his evil tongue. He gloried
in doing so in public, face to face with his prey, and for preference within
the King's hearing. Neither merit, rank, favour, nor office availed to protect any man or woman from him, however great their birth. In this way
he slyly kept the King informed of many mischievous matters and was
thus allowed to say what he pleased of everyone, even of the ministers. He was like a mad dog, attacking everyone in his path, and his
notorious reputation for cowardice shielded him from the usual consequences. But beyond all this, he was a most blatant swindler, and a
barefaced cheat at cards, playing for the highest stakes, grasping with
both hands yet always a pauper, for although he extracted vast sums
from the King's bounty he never appeared able to improve his circumstances.

The King gave him free gratis the governorship of La Rochelle at the
death of M. de Navailles, but he sold it for a vast sum to Gacé, who became Maréchal de Matignon. He also had the *premières entrées* and never
stirred from the Court. He could not stoop low enough when he needed
the services of someone whom he had injured, but turned on them
viciously as soon as he received what he wanted. Faithless, and wholly
without personal honour in matters of every description, he willingly told
innumerable droll stories against himself, glorying in his own baseness.
Indeed, he recorded it for posterity in his Memoirs, which may be read
by anyone, although his worst enemy would not have dared to publish

---

[1] The Gramont of the Hamilton Memoirs.
[2] Having been expelled from the Court for his extravagant love-affairs.
[3] Elizabeth Hamilton (1641–1708).

them. In short, he behaved as he pleased restraining himself in nothing, and never a day passed but he vilified someone.

When he was 85 and mortally ill his wife tried to speak to him of God; but the complete oblivion in which he had lived all his life made him regard the mysteries with utter incredulity, and when she had finished he said, 'But, Madame, is what you say really true?' When he heard her recite the Paternoster he said, 'I think that is a beautiful prayer, who wrote it?'[1] In fact he had not the smallest inkling of any religion whatsoever. You might fill volumes with his sallies and repartees but they would be quite meaningless unless you took into consideration the effrontery, the wit, and often the vicious cruelty of his gibes. With such vices and no redeeming virtues he trampled down the Court and kept it in a state of terror. Thus his death relieved the courtiers of a pest whom the King had esteemed and favoured throughout his entire life. In 1688 he was even made a chevalier of the Order.

At about this time the English succeeded in consummating that great union which they had for so many years desired and which the Prince of Orange had failed to bring about. I refer to what they called the Union of Scotland and England and what the Scots more accurately described as reducing their country to the status of a province.[2] Scottish independence was valid so long as they possessed their own parliament, but at the beginning of this year, by intrigue, bribery, and perseverance, the Scottish parliament was persuaded to let itself be annulled and to join thenceforward in a single parliament to sit in England for both kingdoms. It was to be represented in the House of Lords by twelve[3] Scottish peers elected by the peers of their kingdom, who assembled in Edinburgh for that one election, under the presidency of a Scottish peer appointed by the sovereign, in this case, Queen Anne. That number, so vastly inferior to the English peers, was in no position to counter any proposals of the London parliament. The Scots were tempted by the influence which they hoped to exert in purely English matters, and the measure was finally passed on condition that the combined parliaments should thereafter be known as the Parliament of Great Britain. Thus the Scots no longer needed to feel anxious regarding their commerce or any other part of their government, of which the English became absolute masters. It passes understanding how so proud a nation, hating the English, well acquainted with them through past sufferings, and, moreover, so jealous of their own freedom and independence, should have submitted to bow their necks beneath such a yoke.

[1] He is also credited with having said, 'That Lord's Prayer is indeed very fine, Comtesse; but you must admit that the "Hail Mary!" is somewhat frivolous.'

[2] The union was of vital personal interest to France because it dealt a mortal blow to hopes of a Jacobite restoration.

[3] Saint-Simon was mistaken; there were sixteen, not twelve peers.

There were balls at Marly throughout the winter. The King gave none at Versailles; but Mme la Duchesse de Bourgogne went to several given by Madame la Duchesse, the Maréchale de Noailles, and others, most of them masked. She went also to Mme du Maine who had taken more and more to performing plays with her household and some retired actors. The entire Court went to see them, but were at a loss to understand the pleasure they got from the fatigue of dressing up, learning by heart and declaiming long speeches, and making a public spectacle of themselves upon a stage. M. du Maine, who dared not oppose her for fear of her brain turning completely, as he tartly remarked to Madame la Princesse in Mme de Saint-Simon's hearing, stood by one of the doors and received the company. Apart from the folly of them such entertainments were not cheap.

In the meantime the King had appointed the commanders and generals of his armies. The Maréchal de Tessé was nominated at the beginning of February to the command in Italy. The Maréchal de Villars was assigned to the army of the Rhine, and M. de Vendôme to Flanders under the Elector of Bavaria. Berwick remained in Spain. M. le Duc d'Orléans, who wished to forget his disagreeable experience in Italy and saw no prospect of an army being recalled from there, applied to go to Spain also. He could not have served under the Elector of Bavaria, and it was not desirable to mortify the latter by giving him a superior. Thus there remained only Spain, to the discomfiture of the Duke of Berwick, because after what had happened with the Maréchal de Marsin the prince was given the supreme authority. It was a great joy to him to have command of an army, and this time not in name only, but also in reality. He began therefore to make preparations. The King asked him whom he intended to take with him; M. le Duc d'Orléans mentioned Fontpertuis amongst others. 'Fontpertuis!' said the King much vexed. 'The son of that madwoman, that Jansenist, who followed M. Arnauld everywhere? I cannot allow that.' 'Upon my word! Sire,' said M. le Duc d'Orléans, 'I do not know what his mother was; but her son, a Jansenist! He does not believe in God.' 'Is that so,' the King replied, 'are you quite sure? In that case there is no harm at all; you may certainly take him.' M. le Duc d'Orléans, bursting with laughter, repeated the remark to me that same afternoon. And to think that the King had been misled to the point of seeing no difference between a Jansenist and an atheist, and indeed, of the two, to preferring the latter![1] M. le Duc d'Orléans thought this so funny that he could not keep it to himself, but repeated the story in fits of laughter to the Court and in Paris. Even free-thinkers marvelled at the extremes to which the Jesuits and Saint-Sulpice were prepared to go. The extraordinary thing

---

[1] The Duc d'Harcourt once said, 'Jansenist is the name one gives a man when one wishes to ruin him at Court.' The King is said to have thought Marly and Port-Royal 'incompatibles'. It is noteworthy that the adjective républicain was only used for Port-Royal.

was that the King did not appear in the least vexed with M. le Duc d'Orléans and never in any way reproached him, and Fontpertuis was attached
to him in both his Spanish campaigns. He was much debauched, and a
great tennis player, a man of wit and an intimate friend of those who
formed M. le Duc d'Orléans's circle in Paris; all of which made him very
attractive to that prince.

Chamillart, crushed under the double burden of the ministries of war
and finance, had time neither to eat nor sleep. Whole armies destroyed
by defeats in almost every campaign, frontiers suddenly and alarmingly
narrowed by the folly of luckless commanders, were exhausting the
nation's resources in men and money. The minister, at his wits' end to
find fresh replenishments of both and still provide for current needs, had
more than once declared his inability to hold two appointments which in
happier days had kept both Colbert and Louvois fully occupied. The
King, however, remembered the quarrels that had so wearied him at that
time and could not bring himself to transfer the finances to another.
Chamillart was thus compelled to make a virtue of necessity. At last his
health failed. He began to suffer from the vapours, from loss of consciousness, from giddy fits; everything pointed to his exhaustion; he could
digest nothing; he grew thinner visibly. Yet the wheels had to be kept
turning, and in his departments he was the only man capable of making
them turn. He wrote a most pathetic letter to the King begging to be discharged. He concealed from him nothing of the chaos in his affairs, nor
of his inability to mend matters, lacking time and strength. He reminded
him of the many other occasions when he had sent him short reports revealing the true situation. He impressed him with the hundreds of urgent
problems that came crowding upon him, each demanding long and con-
centrated attention, for which, even had his health permitted, the multi-
plicity of his other essential tasks left him not an hour to spare. He ended
by saying that it would be a poor return for the King's trust and kindness if he did not say in all honesty that were he not replaced all would
be lost. He always wrote to the King leaving wide margins, and the King
made notes alongside in his own hand and so replied to his letters.
Chamillart showed me this one after it was returned to him, and I saw
with vast amazement the following end to a short note in the King's
handwriting, 'Well then! We shall perish together.'[1] Chamillart was both
touched and grieved, but that did not restore his strength. He began to
miss meetings of the councils, especially of the *conseil des dépêches*,
whenever he could avoid them; when he could not, the King allowed him
to speak first instead of waiting his turn, and then let him go. The reason
was that he could no longer stand, and that at the *conseil des dépêches* all
the secretaries of State, ministers included, had to remain standing the

---

[1] The King scribbled in the margin of another of Chamillart's letters, 'We are both to be
pitied in these stormy times; but we must do our best and not let ourselves be discouraged.'

entire time. Only princes, that is to say Monseigneur and Mgr le Duc de Bourgogne, the Chancellor, and dukes, for instance M. de Beauvilliers, were seated.

The need to raise money had become so great that all manner of different means were employed to levy new taxes, on each of which the tax-farmers made unrestricted profits, for the parlements had not for a long time past been in any condition to remonstrate. For example, a tax was now set on baptisms and marriages, regardless of religion and the sacraments, and totally without consideration for the most essential and frequent practices of civilized society. The tax was most onerous and very deeply resented. It promptly produced the utmost confusion. The poor and many others of low degree took to baptizing their children in their homes instead of carrying them to church, and to marrying by mutual consent before witnesses, if they could find no priest willing to unite them privately without the formalities. There were thus no certificates of baptism, no certainty of its having been performed, and no legal status for the children of such marriages. The tax-farmers made searching inquiries to prevent practices so prejudicial to the interests of the State; that is to say, they multiplied the penalties and questionings in order to collect the money. The general protests and murmurs turned in some places to sedition. At Cahors things went so far that the two battalions stationed there could scarcely prevent the peasants from seizing the town, and the troops intended for Spain had to be sent, thus delaying their departure and that of M. le Duc d'Orléans. In Périgord the peasants rose *en masse*, plundering the town-halls, taking possession of one country town and one or two châteaux, and compelling some of the gentry to be their leaders.[1] They were not incited by the new converts, but loudly proclaimed that they would pay their property and capitation taxes, the tithe to their priests, and the dues to their landlords, but that they could pay no more, nor endure to hear of other taxes and suchlike vexations. In the end the authorities were obliged to allow the tax on baptisms and marriages to lapse, much to the disgust of the tax-gatherers, thousands of whom had enriched themselves by using oppressive methods.

Du Chesne, a most excellent physician, good and charitable and a man of honour, who succeeded Fagon in the service of the Sons of France when the former rose to be the King's physician, died at Versailles aged 91. He never married[2] nor amassed any great fortune. I mention him particularly because he retained perfect health in mind and body until the end of his life by eating a salad every evening at his supper and drinking nothing but the wine of Champagne. That was the diet he prescribed.

---

[1] The small gentry suffered nearly as much as the peasants from the disproportionate weight of the taxation falling on them. The burning of the archives in town-halls and châteaux in various places heralded the destruction of the entire system during the Revolution.

[2] He did in fact marry and became the father of sixteen children.

He was neither a glutton nor a drunkard and, unlike most doctors, he was not a blustering charlatan.

Vauban, surnamed Le Prestre, was a gentleman of Burgundy, no more, but perhaps the most honourable and upright man of his day. What is more, although he had the reputation for being more skilled and learned in the art of siege-warfare than any other engineer, he was the simplest, truest, and most modest of men. He was medium tall, somewhat stocky in build, very soldierly in his bearing, but with a loutish, not to say coarse and brutal appearance that totally belied his character, for there never was a man better natured, gentler, nor more obliging. He was courteous without servility, almost miserly with the lives of his soldiers, and possessed the kind of valour that bears every burden and lets others enjoy the credit. When, in 1703, the King informed him of his intention to make him a Maréchal de France, Vauban begged him first to reflect that that honour was never intended for men of his condition who could not command the King's armies.[1] It might be embarrassing, he said, if the marshal in command at a siege were found to be his junior in rank. This generous objection, supported with such manifestly unselfish arguments, only increased the King's desire to advance him. At that time Vauban had already laid fifty-three sieges, twenty of them in the King's presence, and thus King Louis could feel that after a fashion he was making a marshal of himself and gilding his own laurels. Vauban received the rank with a modesty equal to his previous unselfishness, and one and all acclaimed a most signal honour to which no other man of his condition was ever raised before or since. Such was he when he was elevated to be a Maréchal de France. You shall now see how he was brought broken-hearted to his grave for the very qualities that had earned him his laurels, and that, in any country but France, would have won for him honours of every other kind.

A patriot in the true sense,[2] he had always been moved by the sufferings of the peasants under the disproportionate burden of taxation.[3] His professional experience had taught him the need for government spending and the little likelihood that the King would consent to retrench in his pleasures or his pomps. He therefore despaired of there being any alleviation of their ever-increasing afflictions. With such considerations in mind he never made a journey (and he continually crossed and recrossed the country from end to end) without making precise records of the values and yield of the land, the trades and industries in the various provinces and towns, the nature of the taxes, and the methods of collection. Not only that, he sent secret agents travelling throughout the entire kingdom so as

[1] He was not of noble rank, but apart from that, as an engineer, he had had no experience of commanding troops in battle.

[2] Saint-Simon is supposed to have invented the word patriot.

[3] The peasants and the very poor paid the full amount of the taxes. Nobles, landowners, clergy, and the officials of all kinds had dispensations and reliefs on various pretexts.

to compare their assessments with his own. He devoted at least twenty
years to that research and spent on it large sums from his own purse. In the
process he gradually became convinced that the only sure source of
wealth was the land, and accordingly began to evolve an entirely new
system of taxation. When his work was already far advanced there
appeared several booklets under the authorship of Boisguilbert, the military governor of Rouen, who had been working on the same idea for
some years. Vauban read these with interest and resolved to support the
author by revising and correcting his work for him and adding some final
touches of his own. The two men were in complete agreement in principle, but not in every detail; for example, Boisguilbert was chiefly
anxious to remove the most onerous of the taxes and above all the huge
charges levied by the collectors, which sums did not enter the King's
coffers but impoverished the peasants solely for the enrichment of the tax-
farmers and their agents, who made vast fortunes in that way, even as
they do today.

Vauban, on the other hand, attacked the system itself. He proposed
abolishing levies of every kind and substituting in their place a single tax,
divided into two parts, the first part to be on the ownership of land rated
at one-tenth of its yield; the second, at a somewhat lower rate, on commerce and industry, which he thought should be encouraged, and certainly
not hindered. This single tax he wished to call the King's tithe. At the
same time he suggested certain just and simple rules for its collection,
based on the value of each parcel of land and the number of the local
population (so far as that could be estimated with any accuracy). Vauban's
book when it finally appeared was everywhere acclaimed, and those best
able to understand his calculations expressed admiration for its soundness
and clarity. But the plan had one incurable defect. It produced more
wealth for the King than he had received by the older methods; it relieved
the peasants from ruin and oppression, and left them the richer by all
that did not go to him; but at the same time it destroyed an army of
financiers, agents, and petty officials of many different kinds, obliging
them to live by their own labours and not at the public expense, and sap-
ping the very foundations of those vast fortunes which we have seen
amassed with such incredible rapidity.

That in itself was enough to condemn the book; but Vauban's real
offence was that his plan attacked the authority of the controller-general
himself, his influence, wealth, and immense power, together with an army
of intendants, secretaries, agents, and underlings, leaving them incapable of favouring or harming anyone. It is scarcely to be wondered at that
with the interests of so many powerful individuals involved there should
have arisen a conspiracy to defeat a new system, however beneficial to the
State, the King, and the people. Moreover the whole of the legal profession rose up in revolt, for it is the magistrates who administer taxation by

means of their agents in every department of government. No doubt it was family loyalty that roused the Dukes of Chevreuse and Beauvilliers to protest, for they were the sons-in-law of M. Colbert, whose motives and methods were far removed from those advocated by Vauban. They were further misled by Desmaretz's[1] clever, specious arguments, and Chamillart, so kind-hearted, so anxious for the public good, also fell beneath his spell. As for the Chancellor, remembering a time when he, too, had controlled the finances, he flew into a rage. In short, only those who were without influence or private interests supported Vauban, and by those I mean the Church and the nobility, for the people themselves, who stood to gain so much, never realized how close they had come to a deliverance which only good citizens lamented.[2]

Thus it came as no surprise when the King, sheltered and prejudiced as he was, gave the maréchal a frigid reception on accepting his book; you may well imagine that the ministers were no better pleased when they received their copies. From that moment onwards Vauban's past services, his military genius, his virtues, and the King's regard counted as nothing, and thenceforward he was viewed as being no better than a lunatic lover of the peasantry, a scoundrel bent on undermining the power of the ministers and consequently the authority of the King himself. King Louis said as much to his face, and he did not mince his words. Those words were echoed by all that part of the nation who had thought themselves attacked and wished to be revenged, and the unhappy Vauban, who was loved by all right-thinking Frenchmen, did not long survive the loss of his master's favour. He died in solitude a few months later, wasted by grief and in a distress of mind to which King Louis appeared wholly insensible, even to the point of seeming unmoved by the death of one who had been a distinguished and most useful servant.[3] Vauban's fame, however, had spread throughout Europe, even the enemy revered his name, and in France itself he was sincerely mourned by all who were neither tax-farmers nor their agents.

To do Chamillart justice, despite his disapproval of Vauban, he was willing to give his system a trial, but most unfortunately he chose for that purpose a district near Chartres in the intendancy of Orléans, where Bouville, who married Desmaretz's sister, was in charge. She had friends who owned estates in that neighbourhood and had procured tax-relief for their farmers, which was enough to wreck the whole experiment,

---

[1] Nicolas Desmaretz (1648–1721), nephew of Colbert, who had him made an intendant of finances. He was disgraced, then retrieved by Chamillart, and at this time was director-general of financies under Chamillart.

[2] Mathieu Marais, an eminent lawyer of that time, wrote, 'M. de Vauban would have done better to spend his entire life in strengthening fortresses, even if he had been forced to include Saint-Denis and Vaugirard, instead of inventing that tithe, from which they removed all that was good and left only what was oppressive.'

[3] Dangeau, on the other hand, wrote, 'The King was much upset and said, "I have lost a man wholly devoted to me and to the State." '

depending as it did on fair and accurate assessments. Thus all Chamillart's good intentions turned sour and gave fresh ammunition to the enemies of the new system.

Vauban's entire work was accordingly condemned; but the proposal for a King's tithe was not forgotten, and some years later it was levied, not as a new and comprehensive tax, according to Vauban's plan, but on all kinds of possessions, over and above the existing taxes. It has been renewed whenever there has been a war, and even in peace-time the King always retains it on all appointments, salaries, and pensions.[1] That is why in France one must beware of even the wisest and most salutary intentions, and why all the nation's sources of wealth are running dry. Yet who could have warned the Maréchal de Vauban that his great efforts to relieve all the inhabitants of France would serve only to add to their burden a new and supplementary tax, more permanent, harsher, and more costly than all the rest put together? Such a terrible lesson is enough to discourage the wisest proposals in the field of taxation and finance.

The army commanders left to take up their various commands. M. le Duc d'Orléans stopped at Bayonne on his way to Spain in order to visit Charles II's widowed queen, who offered him an armchair, which he could never have claimed as a right and took good care to refuse on this occasion.[2] The King approved his doing so, and no one in Spain wished to complain. As a result, however, the authorities became determined to do him no less honour than at Bayonne, and the King of Spain sent his first major-domo with the royal coaches and horses to meet him at Burgos, and arranged for him to be treated everywhere like an infante of Spain. At the court he received similar treatment from the king and queen, the princes, the grandees, and Society in general, without the least difficulty arising either there or in France.

Speaking of courts and Society, high-living had now become so customary in the armies that officers had all the luxuries that were formerly scarcely known even in permanent headquarters. *Haltes chaudes*[3] on the march were things of the past, and the meals taken to the trenches during sieges were not only abundant and of several courses, but the ices and desserts looked like ballroom-suppers with a profusion of liqueurs of every kind. Such expense was ruinous to the officers, who vied with one another in extravagance and were obliged to quadruple the number of their servants and the wagons so misused, thus often leaving the army itself in a state of hunger. It was a long time before there was any complaint, even from those who were being ruined by these expenses, and still no one had the courage to economize. Finally, during the spring of

---

[1] This practice ceased in 1718, giving place to far higher dues.

[2] The situation was an awkward one. Orléans was only the nephew not the son of Louis XIV; all manner of jealousies and suspicions might have arisen if he had accepted the dues of higher rank.

[3] 'Hot Halts', when the troops stayed long enough to cook a meal.

which I am speaking, the King made an order forbidding lieutenants-general to have more than forty coach-horses, colonels more than thirty, and brigadiers more than twenty-five. That ruling went the way of many others on the same subject. No country in Europe issues wiser laws and better rulings that are obeyed for shorter periods. No one enforces authority, and thus it often happens that within twelve months people have ceased to comply, and by the second year the rule itself is forgotten.

You already know that the need to send troops to quell the revolt at Cahors had delayed M. le Duc d'Orléans's departure for Spain. That delay cost him dear. The Duke of Berwick, outnumbered in infantry and about to be attacked in mountain country, thought it wisest to retreat into the plain where he could use his cavalry in support. Asfeld,[1] who had commanded on that frontier throughout the winter, managed to find sufficient supplies for the troops despite great difficulties, but by the spring everything in the surrounding country had already been taken for the army, and Berwick was obliged to go to the mountains for provisions. The enemy, who had assembled very early in the year, made forced marches in the hope of catching him there at a disadvantage. Their army was commanded by a Portuguese, the Marquis of Minas, in combination with Ruvigny, now Lord Galway, who commanded the English troops.[2]

Made over-confident by Berwick's withdrawal, they pursued him closely and were drawn out on to the plains at the frontier of Valencia, where Berwick would gladly have fought them. He knew, however, that M. le Duc d'Orléans, who had stopped at Madrid barely long enough to salute the king and queen, was making all haste to join him, and being subordinate to that prince in fact as well as in rank he had no wish to offend him by cheating him of a victory. He therefore played for time, despite the most daring attempts to draw him out. The attacks increased in number until, mistaking his inactivity for weakness, the enemy sought him out in force at his camp. Asfeld was the first to have warning of the coming attack. He sent word to the Duke of Berwick with whom he was on excellent terms, and took it upon himself to make his dispositions without waiting for orders. Berwick made his own with equal dispatch; rode at full gallop to inspect what Asfeld had done; gave his approval, and turned his whole mind to the coming battle. At the start we had some success, but before long the right wing began to crumble under furious cannon-fire. Berwick arrived on the spot, restored the situation, and after that the field was ours. The battle lasted less than three hours and our victory was general and complete; it had begun at three o'clock on the afternoon of 25 April. The routed enemy were pursued until dark, losing

---

[1] The Chevalier d'Asfeld. Later Maréchal de France, died 1743.
[2] Curious that in this battle the English, commanded by a Frenchman, should have been beaten by a French army led by an Englishman.

all their cannon and supply wagons and a very great number of men. Our own losses were extremely light, the only notable ones being Puysieux's only son, a brigadier of the infantry and a man of high promise, and Polasstron, colonel of the Crown regiment. When all was over, Count Dohna[1] who had retreated with five battalions into the mountains, and could find neither food nor water there, nor any means of exit, sent word to the Duke of Berwick offering to surrender with all his troops. We captured in all eight thousand prisoners, including two lieutenants-general and eight hundred other officers, also a vast quantity of flags and standards. Thirteen battalions altogether.

It was Cilly of the dragoons who brought the good news to L'Etang, where Chamillart was giving a great supper-picnic for which Mme la Duchesse de Bourgogne had come from Marly, and I also was present. I was hugely astonished to see Cilly but guessed at once that there had been a victory in Spain and promptly asked him for news of M. le Duc d'Orléans. It was a great disappointment to learn that he had not taken part. Chamillart whispered the news into Mme la Duchesse de Bourgogne's ear and into mine also, and went immediately with Cilly to inform the King. Madame hurried away to confer with Mme de Maintenon, much distressed at learning that her son had joined his army too late, and one of the musicians, hoping for the worst, rushed to tell Mme la Princesse de Conti who there and then gave him a handsome gold watch which she happened to be wearing.[2] At Marly everyone surrounded Mme de Maintenon's door, for the King in his joy went straight to tell her the glad news.

Cilly had left Spain on 26 April, the day after the victory of Almanza, and had made the journey direct without going to Madrid. M. le Duc d'Orléans that same day joined up with the army, as it marched towards Valencia through fertile country, never moving out of range of our storehouses. Berwick rode out a very long way to meet him with a great escort, feeling most apprehensive of his reception and of M. le Duc d'Orléans's anger at finding his task already done. After the disaster of Turin this was a further grievous blow to his pride, although of a different kind. His dearest hopes had been blighted, and even the people seemed to have conspired against him.[3] His honest admiration and generous acknowledgement that Berwick had done everything possible to delay the battle put the latter's mind at rest, but none the less the prince could not avoid showing his disappointment, for he had tried by every means to hasten his arrival, even to cutting his stay in Madrid to the bare minimum required for saluting the king and queen.

M. le Duc d'Orléans was truly convinced beyond all doubt that

---

[1] One of Marlborough's veterans.
[2] She was a jealous rival of her half-sister the Duchess of Orléans; she and her set still hoped that the Prince de Conti might succeed to the duke's command if he failed.
[3] The Cahors revolt had caused him to miss the battle.

Berwick could not have remained passive when the enemy attacked his camp, and once that point had been settled there was no cause for a quarrel. Indeed, that first battle laid the foundations of mutual friendship and esteem. Not that they by any means always agreed, for the Duc d'Orléans was apt to be venturesome and sometimes took risks, being persuaded that excessive caution often destroys a chance of glory or achievement. Berwick, on the other hand, although valiant of heart was timid in other ways; he was too much addicted to precautionary measures and reserves, and rarely felt satisfied that he had enough of either. That did not make for agreement, but the prince was commander-in-chief, and Berwick was so scrupulous in his loyalty that, once having vainly used every argument in his power against a proposal, he turned his whole mind to making a success of it, not resentfully, but eagerly and willingly, even down to suggesting novel expedients to counter unforeseen difficulties; making the plan his own, for all the world as though he had been its originator. That is how M. le Duc d'Orléans spoke of him to me on more than one occasion. It is a rare quality to find in a man who has won a considerable victory and is moreover stubborn by nature and fond of having his own way. But as M. le Duc d'Orléans often said, Berwick was good-natured, loyal, and honest; ever anxious to make a success of the business in hand, easy to live with, vigilant, industrious, and ready to take infinite pains whenever necessary. M. le Duc d'Orléans also said that although they were very often at variance, Berwick was the man with whom he most liked to make a campaign. That to my mind speaks volumes for both of them.

I had a private cipher which the prince had given me on leaving, and which we coded and decoded ourselves. We never used it unless we sent our letters by courier. I now wrote urging him to reap all the fruits of this great victory[1] by leaving Berwick in Aragon with a small army and taking the remainder to join the Marquis de La Floride on the Portuguese frontier. The enemy had neither troops nor stores there and the King of Portugal was in no condition to resist. It was the one sure way to end the Spanish war in two campaigns. You may imagine the advantage that would have given us, and the glory for M. le Duc d'Orléans had he been able to achieve it. Unfortunately it proved to be impossible. M. le Duc d'Orléans wrote to me that the plan itself was a good and a sound one, and perfectly practical for an army of non-eaters and non-drinkers; but that on all the long road through the Spanish provinces there were neither storehouses nor provisions of any kind, nor regular stopping-places, nor any means of obtaining supplies; that if the army had managed to subsist in Aragon it was with the utmost difficulty, and that the great heat already beginning and soon to become intolerable added one more drawback

---

[1] In France as well as in Spain great things were expected to follow.

to the design. He continued by saying that he intended to work very hard to prepare against these obstacles for the following year, and to spend the rest of the campaign with that object in mind. In the opinion of everyone on the spot he performed miracles in successfully laying siege to Lerida, defeating isolated portions of the enemy army on several occasions, and capturing many small fortresses.

The King advanced Cilly to lieutenant-general before sending him back to Spain, and gave his permission for Berwick to accept the grandeeship offered him by the King of Spain, of the first class, and with the reversion to whomsoever of his sons he might select. Feeling that even that was not enough, King Philip also made him a knight of the Golden Fleece.

Meanwhile, in Italy, it had been planned early in the winter to remain on the defensive. Médavy, with the troops left him by M. le Duc d'Orléans on his march to Turin during the previous campaign, had managed to hold Mantua and a number of other small fortresses; but since no further troops were forthcoming he could attempt nothing else. There were only two courses to pursue, and Médavy proposed both, with a promise of success for the first which he personally favoured. This was to hold out in Lombardy, keeping a firm grasp on such possessions as we could defend, more especially Mantua, provision them well, fatigue the enemy by sorties and the necessity for laying sieges, and so prevent them from planning to attack us at home relieved of any opposition in Italy. The other project was to take his small army through Italy to Naples, which still remained a Spanish possession but could not long do so unless reinforced. That would at least have saved Naples and Sicily for Spain, and not have lost everything by complete inaction. But it was written that the storm-clouds gathering over us should become ever darker, and that our gross errors of the past campaign in Italy should be crowned by its total abandonment.

Vaudémont[1] was instructed to negotiate in combination with Médavy for the safe return of our troops and their supplies and a road of retreat through Savoy, in exchange for the surrender of all our Italian possessions. You may imagine whether he had any difficulty in concluding a treaty so humiliating to France, so glorious and beneficial to her enemies. At the end of April, Vaudémont and Médavy arrived at Susa with almost twenty thousand men, as many French as there were Spanish. On 9 May, that is to say on the day after the final report of the Battle of Almanza was received, Médavy arrived at Marly and went to salute the King in his gardens, receiving a particularly warm welcome; after which the King took him to Mme de Maintenon's room and spent an hour with him

---

[1] Charles de Lorraine, Prince de Vaudémont, was now sharing the command of the small army left in Italy with General Médavy. Remember that there was a running fight for precedence between the Lorraines and the French dukes.

there, listening to the account of a country and a return that must have
pained him considerably. The governorship of Nivernais having fallen
vacant, the King presented it to Médavy without the asking, although he
already had that of Dunkirk, which he had paid for. He was made to return in a month's time as commander-in-chief in Savoy and Dauphiné,
with two lieutenants-general serving under him. He also received a pension of more than twelve thousand livres, which the King said was only
for the time being and because he had believed the governorship of Nivernais to be worth thirty-eight thousand livres annually, instead of the
twelve thousand which it in fact was. Contrary to what usually happens
these favours were not criticized; everyone approved them and with good
reason.

The Prince de Vaudémont did not remain long in Italy after Médavy's
departure. He stopped a few leagues from Paris at a house lent him by a
fermier-général, where his nieces Mlle de Lillebonne and Mme d'Espinay
were waiting to greet him, and to take him to the home of Mme de Lillebonne, their mother and his sister,[1] in the Rue Saint-Antoine, near the
convent of the Filles de Sainte-Marie. That house was precious to the
entire Lorraine family because it had once belonged to the infamous head
of the *Ligue* and still bore his arms and escutcheon over the door; moreover it contained the room where that last horror, the murder of Henri
III, was plotted.[2] They still call that chamber the *Chambre de la Ligue* and
have changed nothing in it, out of love and respect for the memory of its
late owner. There, on the pretext of resting, M. de Vaudémont began to
devise plans with his sister and her daughters.

He presented himself to the King, at Marly one morning, having
visited Mme de Maintenon in her room after her mass. The King received him in his study for all the world as though he had been of inestimable service both to himself and to the King of Spain—service that had
ended by the return of twenty thousand men in exchange for the whole of
Italy. A lodging was placed at his disposal at Marly, and at Versailles the
Maréchal de Tessé's apartment was lent him during the latter's absence
in Spain. The King did the honours of Marly as he had done them for the
Princesse des Ursins, and found that he was dealing with a man who
echoed, exclaimed, and admired, sometimes plainly, sometimes with the
utmost delicacy, and always with infinite tact. The master of horse was
required to provide a calèche and relays to allow him to hunt with the

[1] Vaudémont's sister Mme de Lillebonne was the illegitimate daughter of Charles IV of
Lorraine. Her husband was yet another Lorraine prince. Her elder daughter Mlle de Lillebonne
was not officially married. The younger married the Prince d'Espinay in 1691. According to
Saint-Simon, the latter 'was a man whom it filled one with repugnance to have to respect; but
one compensated for that by hating him'.

[2] A confederation of Catholics, founded 1576 by Henri de Lorraine (one of the instigators
of the massacre of St. Bartholomew) with the avowed object of defending the Catholic religion
against the Calvinists. The real object was to murder Henri III of France and put the Duc de
Guise on the throne.

King, who often drew up his own horses beside him during the checks.[1]
In a word, it was Mme des Ursins all over again, which was undoubtedly
most gratifying to Vaudémont, but needed to be used in his plans for
greater rank and wealth.

Mme de Lillebonne, his sister, was a very clever woman who, had she
lived at the time of the *Ligue*, might well have played a leading role in her
family. Her elder daughter, for all her seeming calm and indifference, and
her carefully graded civility, was full of the loftiest and most far-reaching
ambitions and possessed the knowledge and perception to make them
more than mere castles in the air. By nature she was extremely haughty,
honourable, capable of love and hatred, more given to persuasion than
dominance, and of immense perseverance. A woman of great spirit, she
was neither base nor servile, but could humble herself when necessary,
albeit with so much dignity that those of whom she asked favours perceived the cost it was to her and, far from taking offence, felt predisposed
to serve her.

Her sister Mme d'Espinay, dull, easily moulded, somewhat inclined
to be treacherous, but more from stupidity than from arrogance or want
of heart, turned her whole mind to the exercise of power, with less calculated politeness than her sister and a look of kindness that was dangerously deceptive. She served her friends and could win their devotion.
The virtue and appearance of the sisters was impressive. The elder, plain
and soberly attired, inspired respect; the beauty and graciousness of the
younger was attractive. Both were tall and vastly well-built; but for those
who possessed a nose the *Ligue* oozed from them at every pore. Neither
of them was malicious without cause, on the contrary their behaviour was
such as to disarm suspicion; but when their ambitions and interests were
at stake they were terrifying. Apart from their natural inclinations, they
had been well instructed by two close friends who of all the men at the
Court were best fitted by experience and disposition to be their mentors.
Mlle de Lillebonne and the Chevalier de Lorraine had been so closely
united throughout their lives that no one doubted but that they were
married. You have already seen what manner of man he was. He was consequently equally closely bound up with Mme d'Espinay. That is why
the sisters had become so much attached to the Maréchal de Villeroy,
the dear friend and humble servant of the Chevalier de Lorraine, and
why the King, who was deeply suspicious of all who approached Monseigneur, had placed the utmost confidence in these two ladies who were
Villeroy's friends, and showed them marked esteem even after Monseigneur's death. From that last fact we may conclude that both sisters,
or at least the younger, served the King by filling the identical secret
role *vis-à-vis* Monseigneur which the Chevalier de Lorraine had filled
towards Monsieur, whom he had ruled absolutely. That was a precedent

---

[1] After his fistula operation Louis XIV took to hunting in a light carriage with boy-postilions.

which they were well able to follow, and the Maréchal de Villeroy may sometimes have been the King's mouthpiece. It had gained them also the confidence of Mme de Maintenon, of whom I shall now relate a most alarming story, although the incident occurred somewhat later. I learned of it on the day after it happened. It will serve to demonstrate to what extent they were trusted.

Mme la Duchesse de Bourgogne was so free with the King and Mme de Maintenon that she would ferret through their papers quite openly before their eyes, reading them, and even opening private letters. It had become a joke between them, and a regular custom. One day when she was alone with Mme de Maintenon in her room she began to go through the papers on a writing-table, standing to do so only a few paces from where Mme de Maintenon was sitting, although the latter called out to her more seriously than usual to leave her things alone. That, however, only served to increase the princess's curiosity until, laughing and joking but still ploughing steadily on, she came upon a note, folded but not sealed and caught sight of her own name. Surprised, she read the first line, turned over the page, and saw the signature of Mme d'Espinay. That first line and still more the signature made her blush and hesitate. Mme de Maintenon, calmly observing her, made no effort to stop her as she might well have done had she so wished, but appeared on the contrary not ill-pleased at her discovery. 'What is the matter, my pet?' she said. 'What have you found now?' But the princess only became the more embarrassed. When she did not answer Mme de Maintenon rose and went to her side as though to see what she had discovered, and then the princess showed her the signature. 'Well!' said Mme de Maintenon, 'that is a letter to me from Mme d'Espinay. That is what comes of being inquisitive; one sometimes learns more than one bargains for.' Then, speaking in quite another tone, 'Read the whole letter, Madame, and if you are wise you will profit by it,' and she compelled her to read the whole letter from beginning to end. It was a report from Mme d'Espinay giving an account of Mme la Duchesse de Bourgogne's life in the past four or five days, word by word, place by place, hour by hour, as precise and detailed as though the writer, who was seldom in her company, had never let her out of her sight.

There was much of Nangis in the report, and much description of intrigue and imprudence. Every trivial happening was recorded, but more surprising even than the report itself was the fact of its signature, and that Mme de Maintenon had not instantly burned it or locked it away. The poor princess felt quite faint and turned all the colours of the rainbow. Mme de Maintenon gave her a very severe talking-to, pointing out that her most secret doings were known to the entire Court and warning her of the possible consequences. No doubt that she said more also, and she admitted that when she had spoken before it was with full knowledge, and that Mme d'Espinay and others were employed to watch her secretly and to deliver frequent and detailed reports. After that disturbing incident the princess could not be quick enough in returning to her own room and sending for Mme de Nogaret, whom she used to call her 'Nanny', and her 'Well of Silence'. She told all, burst into tears, and then into such a fit of rage against Mme d'Espinay as you may easily imagine. Mme de Nogaret let her finish and then gave such counsel as she thought suitable. Most of all, she warned the princess very seriously not to show anything in her conduct towards that lady, representing that she would be lost if she appeared less amiable than before. Such advice though eminently wise was hard indeed to practise. Nevertheless, Mme la Duchesse de Bourgogne, who trusted Mme de Nogaret's knowledge of the world and the Court, as well she might, tried to behave as usual to Mme d'Espinay, and succeeded so well that no one ever realized that she had learned anything. On the day after this incident Mme de Nogaret, who was a close friend of ours, told Mme de Saint-Simon and myself of the incident, word for word as I have written it down.

The disgrace of the Maréchal de Villeroy, at whose house the King had been accustomed to spend the night on his way to and from Fontainebleau, and the death of Mme de Montespan[1] together produced a novelty that had far-reaching consequences. Mme de Maintenon no longer had cause to fear the latter's son.[2] She ceased from that moment to hate him as the son of an enemy who might conceivably return to favour; whom she could not forgive for what she had been to her, for what she owed her, nor for the coin in which that debt had been paid.[3] She was now inclined to feel well-disposed to that son as being the half-brother of the bastards she so dearly loved, who had always been treated as infinitely superior to him. Now that his mother was no more, the relationship made him appear in Mme de Maintenon's eyes a proper person to be brought into the King's circle, capable of being controlled absolutely through vices so contemptible that they were in no way to be feared, but might on the contrary be used to advantage. Accordingly it was announced that the King would sleep at d'Antin's house Petit-Bourg[4] on the night of 12 September. It was marvellous to see what pains d'Antin took in the smallest details to pay his court on that flying visit, not only to the King but to his entire retinue, down to the lowest of his servants. He persuaded Mme de Maintenon's people to admit him to her apartment when she was at Saint-Cyr, and

---

[1] On 27 May, 1707.

[2] D'Antin. He had vast ambitions and vast energy. 'His daily life would have used up the strength of four ordinary men.' He was also a coward. The Prince de Conti used to greet him in the trenches, 'Hullo! d'Antin, not dead yet!'

[3] Mme de Montespan came to Mme de Maintenon's rescue when she was the destitute widow of the poet Scarron, and made her the governess of her children by Louis XIV. She persuaded him to make her Marquise de Maintenon. The latter repaid her debt of gratitude by plotting to have her separated from the King and removed from the Court.

[4] A château near Essonnes.

made a detailed plan of her rooms and furniture, everything, even including the books and the way in which they were stacked or thrown haphazard on the tables, and he had markers put in them at identical places. She found everything at Petit-Bourg precisely as it was at Versailles, an attention that was very much remarked. His consideration for all who were in favour, both masters and servants, and for the servants of such servants, was proportionate; likewise the care, courtesy, and elegance of the arrangements for others, the furnishing of the rooms, the comforts of all kinds, the abundant and delicate fare served at a vast number of tables, the profusion of all manner of refreshments, the prompt and willing service at the turn of one's head, the care, the forethought, the luxury, the charming novelties, the excellent concert, the games, ponies, and numerous decorated carriages for driving in the grounds; in a word, everything to indicate most tasteful and elegant extravagance. He managed to visit all the guests at Petit-Bourg in their rooms, even some of the valets, and to do the honours to each of them as though they had been his sole preoccupation.

The King arrived early, saw everything, and found much to praise. He afterwards had d'Antin admitted with him to Mme de Maintenon's room and was shown a plan of the entire estate. He admired everything excepting a chestnut avenue, that was vastly becoming to the gardens and landscape but quite obstructed the view from the State bedroom. D'Antin said nothing, but on the following morning when the King woke and looked out of his window he saw the most beautiful view imaginable, without the avenue, or any trace of where it had stood the night before. There was no sign of cart-ruts or disorder in the whole of its length or anywhere close by. It was as though it had never been. No one had heard noises in the night, the trees were simply gone and the land renewed for all the world as though a fairy had waved her wand over it. There was much applause to reward d'Antin for his gallant gesture, and it was noted also that the text at the King's mass well became an accomplished courtier. Indeed, he went so far that Mme de Maintenon said to him somewhat sourly, as she left next day for Fontainebleau after making the tour of his gardens, that she was glad not to have vexed the King at his house on the previous evening, since from what she had witnessed she would certainly have been put out to sleep on the hard high road. D'Antin answered like a man of spirit and thought no less well of his future, believing, as he did, that this flying visit pointed to the fulfilment of his dearest hopes. A fortnight later he felt sure of it when he applied for and was immediately granted the governorship of Orléans in which lay part of his estates. He was transported with joy and exclaimed that the ice had cracked at last and that since the King had begun to give he need no longer fear for his future. His wife, and a stupider, more foolish woman cannot easily be imagined, chattered everywhere that her husband would now go forward at a spanking pace. The Court were not edified by her delighted confidences; they had gloomily noted omens that were later more than amply fulfilled.

I went that summer to Forges,[1] in the season for drinking the waters, in an effort to be rid of a tertian fever on which quinine had had no permanent effect. I shall take the opportunity to mention by way of demonstrating the whims of doctors that Mme de Pontchartrain was also there for a persistent flow of blood, followed by water, from which she had long suffered despite all remedies. Fagon, completely at a loss, tried a novel experiment, namely to make her bathe in the most strongly mineral of the three springs, the one which people drink least and which they call the Cardinal, after Cardinal Richelieu who partook of it. No one before Mme de Pontchartrain had ever bathed in any of the springs, and she derived the very reverse of good from it.[2]

On 30 December M. le Duc d'Orléans arrived back from Spain and presented himself at the King's *lever*, after which he remained a long time alone with him in his study. The welcome given him by the King and everyone else was such as his successful and prosperous campaign had well deserved. Since he was due to return soon to that country he had left there almost all of his staff. He was well satisfied with them, and they were pleased with him. The Duke of Berwick had orders to wait for his return.

[1] Forges-les-Eaux in Normandy.
[2] Maybe Saint-Simon thought it was for that reason she died soon after.

CHAPTER XVIII

1708

Court Balls – Chamillart resigns the finances – Desmaretz is appointed controller-general – The raid on Scotland – Mgr le Duc de Bourgogne assigned to the Flanders army – Momentous conversation with the Duc de Beauvilliers – The King artfully opens the purse of Samuel Bernard – Marriage of Louville – Elopement of the Prince de Léon with Mlle de Roquelaure – The King of England serves incognito – Death of Mme de Pontchartrain, folly and falseness of her husband – I pay a visit to the Loire – Death of Mme de Châtillon – Negligence and indolence in Spain – Origin of the implacable hatred of Mme des Ursins and Mme de Maintenon for M. le Duc d'Orléans – Loss of Sardinia and Minorca – Ghent and Bruges captured by the King's troops – Battle of Oudenarde – Vendôme's insolence to Mgr le Duc de Bourgogne – Marlborough's remarkable words on the King of England – Machinations of Vendôme's cabal – Alberoni's letter and its consequences – Defence of Mgr le Duc de Bourgogne – Chamillart offers advice to Mgr le Duc de Bourgogne with bad results for both – Siege of Lille – Disquiet at the Court – I wager that Lille will fall without a battle or relief – Brilliant exploit of the Chevalier de Luxembourg – Fall of Lille – I am grossly slandered – I am warned at La Ferté by the Bishop of Chartres that I am in disgrace – Return of the Princes – Return and reception of Vendôme – Return and triumph of Boufflers – I am deeply honoured by Mgr le Duc de Bourgogne – Brilliant project to recapture Lille

THE YEAR 1708 began with grants of money, fêtes, and parties of pleasure; you will discover only too soon that it did not long continue in that way. Chamillart obtained a hundred and fifty thousand livres as a *brevet de retenue*[1] on his post of treasurer to the Order, and the Maréchal de Tessé another of two hundred thousand, as treasurer to Mme la Duchesse de Bourgogne. M. de Vendôme procured a pension of three thousand livres for his secretary Alberoni, who later, as you will see, became prodigiously wealthy and influential.[2] The King celebrated Twelfth-day in great splendour at Versailles, with numbers of ladies and the Court of Saint-Germain present. After the festival the King gave a great ball, and several others

---

[1] Meant that he or his heirs might be sure of disposing of his post for that sum at the Court.

[2] The Abbé Jules, later Cardinal, Alberoni. Wormed himself into Vendôme's confidence by making delicious cheese soup and pandering to his revolting habits. Saint-Simon says that he once exclaimed, 'Oh! Angelic bottom!', when Vendôme rose from his *chaise-percée*.

also during the winter, both masked and in court-dress, at Marly and Versailles. There were balls in Monseigneur's apartment and in that of Mme la Duchesse de Bourgogne. The ministers gave balls for her, and also Mme la Duchesse du Maine, who throughout the entire winter made a spectacle of herself by performing in comedies at Clagny before the Court and the town, quite publicly. Mme la Duchesse de Bourgogne went often to see her, and M. du Maine, although he felt the want of propriety and the enormous expense, still continued to sit by the door and do the honours.

I have already described more than once how much Chamillart, quite overwhelmed by the burden of work in his two departments, had desired to be relieved of the finances that became more difficult every day. In the end his health broke down. The vapours obliged him to lead the life of an invalid, a kind of living death; short bouts of fever, complete dejection, a general distaste for food, all work a laborious effort, a need for bed and sleep at abnormal hours; in a word, utter exhaustion and slow wasting away. In that sorry state, which compelled him often to miss the meetings of the councils and sometimes his work with the King, he felt the urgent need to be rid of the Treasury. It had to go to one of the two directors of finances[1] and his choice fell on Desmaretz. A renewal of confidence would mean no more than additional work, as Desmaretz himself said, but his future advancement now seemed assured, and he had become as much sought after as though he were already the new controller-general. Chamillart had been working to that end long since by constantly praising his work, and by handing over to him the more important affairs which he could no longer supervise. What is more he had begun to think that the King was at last aware of the desperate state of the finances and would let him resign, and to conclude, though too late, that if he deferred any longer they would be snatched away from him. At long last Chamillart was persuaded to stand up and name Desmaretz to the King as his successor, giving the King no opportunity to mention others, refuse his resignation, or delay the appointment. That happened on Palm Sunday, and I went afterwards to sup with the Duc de Chevreuse. We all tried to appear light-hearted, but when no news came everyone felt anxious and we promised to send word as soon as we learned anything.

On the Monday morning I called on the Chancellor at noon, and he told me that Desmaretz had the appointment and was now controller-general. Chamillart himself informed him of his good fortune, and after taking him to Vaucresson, a small country house belonging to the Duc de Beauvilliers, where they conferred for a long time together, they all three went to Marly so as to arrive at the end of the King's mass. Chamillart and Desmaretz then entered the study, where the King concluded the

[1] Posts created in 1701.

affair and reassured Desmaretz by personally explaining the lamentable state of the finances. This was perhaps as much to make him aware that the King knew all as to spare him the embarrassment of rendering an exact account at the start of his administration. The King said finally that things being what they were he would be obliged if Desmaretz could suggest a remedy, and not at all surprised if they continued to go from bad to worse; all of which he seasoned with the graciousness he was accustomed to show to new ministers when he installed them. Desmaretz went on to pay his respects to Mme de Maintenon, who received him with bare politeness.[1] He then returned to Paris whence he had come. He told me that the King had surprised and relieved him beyond measure by recounting so clearly the state of his finances—surprised him, because he never imagined that the King knew even a quarter of the truth, and relieved him, because it absolved him of the duty to remit a gloomy statement that would be galling for Chamillart, to whom he owed his advancement. He then gave me a brief account of his plans[2] that appeared very good to me, for, unlike Chamillart, he proposed never to make promises which he could not keep; to restore honest dealing, which is the very soul of confidence and commerce; to render to the King an exact account of his affairs each day in order to prevent his forgetting their true condition, thus exonerating himself for not working miracles and making sure of credit for any success.

Since he spoke with such entire confidence, not scrupling to hide from me his disapproval of much that Chamillart had done, I allowed myself to impress on him the debt which he owed to the latter and also to the Chancellor; and I showed him plainly that, whereas Chamillart had wished him to have the post, Pontchartrain had obtained it for him, and that together they had rescued him from his long and painful disgrace and put him once more on the path of honour and fortune by securing him his proper place in the world. I even went so far as to speak with some heat of gratitude and ingratitude. Desmaretz took all this very well; he added that if he made bad friends in the future it would be entirely his own fault, for twenty years in disgrace had taught him to distinguish them. I took the occasion to let drop a word regarding certain highly-placed persons, and discovered them to be very clear and present in his memory. I said also that since his return to the finances he must have become aware of many who were feathering their nests; that I was confident he did not include Mme de Saint-Simon and myself among them, for we abhorred such methods of money-making, and during the administrations of both

---

[1] Although she was annoyed with Chamillart for refusing an alliance with the Noailles for his eldest son, she did not want him replaced by someone less manageable.

[2] Saint-Simon had been very busy encouraging Chamillart's departure and smoothing the way for Desmaretz. He was most deeply concerned at the mismanagement of the finances and was anxious for Chamillart to resign before being dismissed.

Pontchartrain and Chamillart had refused to soil our hands in that way.[1] All I would ask of him, I said, was to have easy access to him; to be paid my emoluments,[2] and to be treated with consideration, as an old friend, in all the business that was unavoidable with the finance department since every inheritance had to be passed under review for the taxes, rates, and duties that daily increased, until now they are payable on what little remains to landlords of centuries-old tenure. He had no answer for that, but he said that there was no question of Mme de Saint-Simon and myself ever having been involved in any affairs of that kind. He then let fly at what people of high rank had amassed in the way of riches without measure or scruple, especially the Maréchale de Noailles and her daughter the Duchesse de Guiche, who continually extracted great sums, much to Chamillart's discredit. There I stopped him to explain that Mme de Saint-Simon, becoming tired of hearing Chamillart perpetually abused on the subject of those two ladies, had given him a warning, whereupon he had smilingly admitted that he had orders from the King to give both of them a profit on all their transactions, present and future, a statement that surprised Desmaretz very much. I left him then, my mind full of the changes and chances of life, but feeling very doubtful of any great and indissoluble friendship arising between him and Chamillart.

For a long time past a certain vitally important project had been knocking at every door to gain a hearing. Its hour finally came during the last visit to Fontainebleau in the previous autumn, when it was adopted. Its promoters, whose identities I had already guessed from their demeanour, confided it to me in strictest confidence, and I then learned also a secret known to very few, namely that the Duc de Chevreuse was in fact a minister of State, without appearing to be so or attending the council. I had long suspected it; by the end of that visit I was sure of it, and I said so plainly to the Duc de Beauvilliers, who asked me anxiously why I was so sure, and told me at last under the seal of secrecy. That same day I had great pleasure in confronting the Duc de Chevreuse himself, who blushed up to the whites of his eyes, grew embarrassed, and began to stammer. He then made me swear never to disclose to any other what he had been incapable of hiding from me. I thus learned from his own lips that for the past three years the ministers for foreign affairs, war, the navy, and finance had been given orders to conceal nothing from him and to confer with him on every subject.

He used often to go up to the King by the back staircase at his private hours, and had long audiences in the study, sometimes tête-à-tête when everyone else had left. Often at dinner, and nearly every evening towards

---

[1] His integrity over money was well known. In 1715 Mme de Coëtanfao left him unconditionally her entire fortune, knowing that he would hand it on intact, as she wished, to her second husband to whom the law prevented her from leaving it direct.

[2] From his governorships.

the middle of the King's supper, he appeared behind the King's arm-chair. In those days people made way for noblemen, and the King, hearing the stir, invariably looked round to see who had come. If it happened to be M. de Chevreuse a whispered conversation invariably ensued, begun either by the duke himself, or by the King speaking into his ear. For a long time I had been as puzzled as the rest of the Court, who could not imagine that regimental details of the light cavalry could possibly give rise to so much discussion.[1] Finally, I suspected other reasons, and it was at Fontainebleau that I discovered the secret. King Louis had always liked the Duc de Chevreuse, who was probably the only man of learning and intellect at the Court whom he did not fear. He found his gentleness and moderation reassuring, and his awestruck demeanour whilst in the presence was accounted a great merit. The King would have liked to have included him in the council, but Mme de Maintenon and Harcourt had forbidden that. Chevreuse had therefore to hold office *incognito*, something without precedent, to which in my opinion no other man would have agreed. It was by his advice that the raid on Scotland was seriously considered and then put into action.

The Union of Scotland with England seemed to provide a favourable opportunity, for the Jacobite party were still strong there, and determined to throw off the English yoke by restoring their rightful king to his throne. It was a sure means of creating an important diversion and depriving the Allies of the support of the English, who, fully occupied at home, would be incapable of sending reinforcements to the Archduke in Spain, or large armies anywhere else. Chamillart did no more than give his consent; worn out physically and mentally and overwhelmed with work, he was in no state to promote an enterprise of that nature. Pontchartrain[2] dared not refuse flatly, but relied on M. de Chevreuse's extreme slowness and passion for argument to bring the affair to nought. In the end, urged thereto by Mme de Maintenon and the other ministers, the King gave his grudging consent. He was disillusioned after many similar attempts[3] and only agreed to this one out of kindness, with no zest for the task. As soon as he had given the word, however, everyone went to work in earnest, for five Scottish members of Parliament, concealed in the village of Montrouge and empowered by the most important chieftains, were crying out for haste.

At Saint-Germain they took every precaution to give no sign of activity, and the few royal coaches kept in readiness for the King of England were said to be required for a hunting trip to Anet.[4] The Duke of Perth and

---

[1] His only official post was Colonel of the Light Horse.
[2] Not the Chancellor but Jérôme Pontchartrain, Secretary for the Navy.
[3] The French raid on Ireland and the defeat of James II by William III at the Battle of the Boyne, 1690.
[4] Vendôme's country house.

Lord Middleton[1] were appointed to go with him, and very few others of his countrymen. Perth was a Scot who had held for many years the post of Lord Chancellor of Scotland, the highest and most powerful office in that country. Middleton was the last secretary of State remaining with the King. His wife, governess to the English princess,[2] was a tall, well-built woman, monstrously thin, with a pinched and pious face. Both she and her husband were fiendishly spiteful and scheming; but Middleton, because he was admirably good company, mixed on equal terms with the best people at Versailles. He was a Protestant, she a Catholic, both were thoroughly worthless and the only courtiers at Saint-Germain who still received revenues from England. The late King James on his deathbed exhorted him to become a Catholic, but he was a professed and practising atheist, if such a thing can be, or at best a free-thinker, and he never pretended otherwise. This man was the only adviser given by the Queen of England to her son when he made his raid on Scotland.

The preparations reached a point when action could no longer be delayed; the news had got abroad; vast quantities of arms and coats for the Scotch were already embarked, and the activity by land and sea was plainly visible along the coast. The many deferments left no room for doubt that the English had been warned, but Admiral Leake having taken their available warships with a convoy to Spain they were reckoned incapable of interference. It was thus to everyone's dismay that news arrived on Sunday, 11 March, announcing that after being driven by contrary winds to shelter off Torbay (where in fact he had lain concealed) he had returned and was blockading the harbour of Dunkirk, where our troops had been landed with all speed. That courier also brought a letter from the King of England protesting bitterly at the disembarkation and pressing for the crossing to Scotland to be attempted at whatever cost. At Dunkirk he made so great an outcry that the English fleet was reconnoitred, and since the report gave some hope of success the troops were ordered to re-embark.

Here a totally unforeseen catastrophe occurred, even supposing that the entire enterprise was not doomed to failure from the start. The English princess had been suffering from the measles and was barely convalescent when her brother left Saint-Germain. They had prevented her from seeing him for fear of infection, but the rash broke out on him as the last troops were boarding the ships. Picture him desperate,[3] demanding to be wrapped in blankets and carried into the ship, and the doctors swearing it

---

[1] Charles Earl of Middleton, later Earl of Monmouth. Suspected at Saint-Germain of disloyalty to James II and the Pretender. He was a man of high integrity respected by the Whigs and anti-Catholic Tories. Had a restoration taken place in King William's reign, the English protestants who loathed 'Dutch William' would have trusted Middleton to see that James II's follies were not repeated.

[2] Louisa Mary Stuart.

[3] He was only twenty.

would be the death of him. Just at that moment the members of Parliament at Montrouge sent word to say that the news of his coming had aroused great enthusiasm in Scotland, which made him even more determined to be gone. Finally, recovering, but still very weak, he succeeded in embarking on Saturday, 17 March, much against the wishes of the doctors. The enemy ships were no longer visible. At six o'clock in the morning they had set sail in a high wind and fog[1] and by seven they were out of sight.

The King of England encountered a great tempest towards evening and was obliged to anchor behind the dunes of Ostend. Two days after our squadron left, twenty-seven English warships appeared off Dunkirk, and in the meantime a great number of English troops were marched to Ostend, and some Dutch to Briel[2] so as to be ready to make the crossing. Rambures, a naval lieutenant commanding a frigate, was separated from the squadron in the gale and forced to shelter on the coast of Picardy, whence as soon as he was able he made for Edinburgh, thinking that the rest of the squadron would already have arrived. He saw no ships during the voyage. As he approached the mouth of the river he saw the water covered with boats and little ships, which he greeted as friends since he could scarcely do otherwise. The captains told him that their king should have been with them, but that no news had come, and that great concourse of little vessels were going to meet him with pilots to guide him up the river to Edinburgh, where everyone was hopeful and rejoicing. Rambures was as much surprised to learn of the King of England's non-appearance as to find his coming so widely publicized. He continued towards Edinburgh surrounded by an increasing number of boats all displaying the same glad sentiments. One Scottish gentleman boarded his frigate to show him a paper signed by the greatest lords, informing him that more than twenty thousand Scots were ready to take arms and that at least one city was only waiting for the King to arrive in order to proclaim him King of Scotland.

Rambures then returned down-river in search of his squadron, being all the more concerned because what he had seen was so eminently cheering. As he neared the estuary he heard the noise of gunfire at sea, and shortly after perceived our squadron chased by twenty-six giant men-of-war and a great quantity of other vessels, but they all vanished out of his sight. He made what speed he could to join them, but was unable to do so until they were all clear of the estuary. Then after avoiding the enemy's rear-guard, he observed that the English fleet was in hot pursuit of the King of England, whose vessel was hugging the coast under cannon-fire

---

[1] The word is 'brune' but it was very early in the morning and there may well have been a 'brume'.

[2] Briel, near Rotterdam, at the mouth of the Meuse. Ostend had been in the hands of the Allies since Ramillies and under Dutch occupation.

and sometimes musketry. Rambures tried for a long time to use his frigate's speed to reach the head of the squadron, but time after time he was intercepted by enemy ships and always in danger of being captured, and he finally returned to Dunkirk, from whence he sent at once to the Court with the sad and disturbing news. The King of England himself arrived at Dunkirk on 7 April, five or six days later, with a few vessels, all of them badly damaged.

That expedition marked the first occasion on which the English king used the title Chevalier de Saint-Georges in order to pass *incognito*, and the first time that his enemies called him the 'Pretender'. Both names have clung to him ever since. He showed great courage and firmness, but spoilt all by his readiness to comply, which had been increased by a faulty up-bringing. His mother, for all that she was so pious, loved power and had been too strict and narrow in his education, either from misguided affection or because she wished to keep him obedient and fearful of her. He wrote to her from Dunkirk begging to be allowed to stay in a nearby town until the opening of the campaign, which he asked leave to serve in Flanders. This last wish was granted, but he was made to return to Saint-Germain.

It was on Friday, 20 April, that he arrived, and on the Sunday he came with the queen to Marly where the King then was. I was vastly curious to witness their encounter. The weather was marvellously fine, and the King followed by all the courtiers went out to meet him. As we descended the terrace-steps we could see the court of Saint-Germain slowly approaching us from the further end of the *Perspective*. Lord Middleton came quickly forwards to the King and embraced his thigh, which King Louis accepted graciously enough, addressing three or four remarks to him; but each time fixed him with such a stare that any other man would have been nonplussed. The King then advanced down the avenue. As the two parties approached one another they all bowed. The two kings, quickening their steps pace for pace, drew away from their courts, and with the same show of equality wrapped one another several times in a close embrace. The grief in the faces of all those unhappy people was plain to see. Afterwards they returned towards the château, making an attempt at small talk that died upon their lips. The queen with the two kings went to Mme de Maintenon's room; the princess remained in the salon with Mme la Duchesse de Bourgogne and the entire Court. The Prince de Conti, who was naturally curious, seized on Middleton, whilst the Duke of Perth drew the Duc de Beauvilliers and Torcy aside. The few remaining English received a warmer welcome than usual in an endeavour to make them talk, but nothing was extracted from them save protestations of ignorance that spoke volumes, combined with complaints at the weather and their ill-fortune. The kings were a long time alone together whilst Mme de Maintenon entertained the queen. They emerged after an hour, and a most dismal walk ensued that brought their visit to an end.

Middleton was strongly suspected of having alerted the English, who had pretended to know nothing, yet had concealed their fleet and moved all their available troops towards the Scottish border. Moreover men of proven loyalty had been sent into Scotland and Queen Anne on various pretexts had kept the Duke of Hamilton in London, who had been the moving spirit of the enterprise. She informed Parliament of the raid after all was over, and by refusing an inquiry into the complicity of individuals she most prudently avoided driving the Scots to desperate measures.[1] Such wise restraint greatly increased her authority and removed the desire for continued rebellion, especially since there was now no hope of success. Thus failed an attempt that was admirably planned and secret until the time came for putting it into action, after which it was most miserably mismanaged. Thus ended also all hopes of a revolt in the Low Countries;[2] it had become altogether impossible to think of that. I therefore decided not to interrupt this story of the abortive raid on Scotland. Let us now retrace our steps a little; in point of fact to Marly, immediately after Easter.

One sometimes learns from servants things which are believed to be closely concealed. Some of my footmen happened to be friendly with a certain coach-maker of Paris who was secretly making vehicles for Mgr le Duc de Bourgogne's use at the war. He was indiscreet enough to tell them so and to show them his work, under the promise of secrecy which he himself had not kept. They in their turn told me, which opened my eyes to an exceedingly mysterious visit paid by Chamillart to Flanders, for which he had left Versailles on the evening of Easter-Day itself. He returned to Marly on the evening of 20 April, after being absent twelve days. His sadly declining health would in itself have made this journey remarkable; what made it still more so was the timing, for the suspense regarding the Scottish raid was at its height, and the King of England returned to Saint-Germain on the same evening that Chamillart returned to Marly. I had been thinking much of a possible command for Mgr le Duc de Bourgogne, and so far as I could see it would have to be either the Rhine or Flanders. Chamillart's excursion made me plump for the latter. His reason for going, as I later discovered, was to persuade the Bavarian Elector to transfer to the Rhine, so as to leave the Flemish command to Mgr le Duc de Bourgogne at a time when great things were

---

[1] In fact there were a great number of arrests and death sentences, many of which were cancelled by Marlborough's influence.

[2] The Dutch occupation of the Spanish Netherlands in the past two years had aroused such hatred that, by comparison, even French rule seemed tolerable. A Flemish noble, Count Bergeyck, was leading a pro-French conspiracy to deliver the great fortress towns, especially Ghent and Bruges. Marlborough was well aware of this.

expected from a revolt of the Low Countries and a revolution in Scotland, even though by so doing we lost the benefits of the real affection felt for the Elector by the inhabitants of the provinces he had governed for so long. Chamillart was on the road when he received news of the King of England's mishaps during his crossing and the small hope of his success. He was so much affected that he spent part of that night motionless in his bed, quite unable to move. Next day he sent a courier to the King and continued his journey, but with very different feelings from those with which he had started out. Yet despite the entire change in the situation he orders were not cancelled.

The Elector was most unwilling to leave Flanders, where he was as of right in part of the territory remaining to him, and thus very properly commanding the French army. What is more, he was operating against the Dutch and the English, whereas on the Rhine he would be directly opposing the Imperial armies, a difficult situation for him, since sooner or later there would be peace and he did not wish to spoil his personal relations with the Emperor. His protests were many and bitter, but Chamillart, short of money though he was, resorted to bribery, and the Elector unwillingly swallowed the Rhine army. He received eight hundred thousand francs, cash down, over and above his pensions, subsidies, and all that he had extracted from King Louis; but on reflection he considered that too little and sent a courier with a retraction after Chamillart. The latter was greatly embarrassed, but the promise of a further four hundred thousand francs finally persuaded the Elector to confirm the agreement.

Berwick, having left Spain, had been appointed to the army in Dauphiné,[1] and Villars was at Strasbourg preparing to besiege Philippsburg in order to support a revolution in Belgium; but as you already know he and the Elector were not on good terms[2] and they would not serve together. Chamillart accordingly received orders to propose an exchange between Villars and Berwick, which the latter accepted. I have recorded these assignments rather sooner than they were published because I knew of them earlier. The business of buying off the Elector I learned of only later.

The weather during that Marly was perfect, and one evening M. le Duc de Beauvilliers who was anxious for a private conversation led me to the end of the gardens near the watering place,[3] where there were no hedges and we should not be overheard. I, too, wished to talk, and I broached the subject of Mgr le Duc de Bourgogne's command. He was amazed that I knew of it, and I therefore had to explain the source of my information; whereupon he told me the facts, commending the appointment as the only one possible in the circumstances. Thus it was that I

---

[1] Opposing the Duke of Savoy.
[2] Since Ramillies.
[3] The *Abreuvoir* which is still at the cross-roads in Marly village.

discovered the reason for Chamillart's excursion. I raised objections to the transfer of the Elector, but he replied that the paramount need was for Mgr le Duc de Bourgogne to be in Flanders because in the present unhappy situation strong measures, such as the presence of the heir presumptive, were needed to put fresh courage into the troops. In any case, he continued, it was unsuitable for him to be idle at home when his country was in danger and the English king going to the front. It was also high time that the Duc de Berry saw service, which he could not do whilst his elder brother stayed at home. Most important of all, in Flanders under M. de Vendôme debauchery had exceeded all bounds, and was being practised by the very men who should have prevented it; thus the only hope lay in the prince's authority. Most of our difficulties, added M. de Beauvilliers, were caused by lack of discipline; it had therefore become highly desirable to exploit the military talents shown by the prince in the only two campaigns he had fought, and give him the experience he lacked. Dauphiné and the Rhine were not sufficiently important, since little or nothing could be done there. Thus Flanders was the only possible place, and very wisely the objections had been overruled.

I concurred in all his remarks regarding the idleness of the princes and the need to train them in war, but was bold enough to question the rest. I said it was very proper in theory for Mgr le Duc de Bourgogne to command the armies, but he had missed several campaigns, during which a succession of defeats and disasters had made the troops distrust their generals and, from bad leadership, tend to break before the enemy, believing themselves beaten in advance. It was therefore a bad moment to choose. The worst objection was the presence of the Duc de Vendôme. 'There,' interrupted M. de Beauvilliers, 'you have put your finger on the precise reason why Mgr le Duc de Bourgogne is so necessary. He is the only man with sufficient authority to goad M. de Vendôme into action, overcome his obstinacy, and compel him to take those precautions which he has so often nearly ruined us by neglecting.[1] No one but Mgr le Duc de Bourgogne can brace the generals, make the officers do their duty, especially regarding debauchery, and restore the order and discipline that has been so conspicuously lacking since M. de Vendôme took over the command.' I could not refrain from smiling at such optimism from him of all people, nor from stating with conviction that nothing like this would happen, only and quite certainly the ruin of Mgr le Duc de Bourgogne. Impossible to describe M. de Beauvilliers's consternation! I allowed him to interrupt me and then begged him to be patient and give me leave to explain myself at some length.

I then said that to reach the same conclusion he had only to know the

---

[1] 'Vendôme combined military genius with heroic courage and two very dangerous faults, negligence and idleness before action, and an excess of confidence that prevented him from foreseeing dangers and taking the necessary precautions.' The Duc de Noailles, *Memoirs*.

characters of the two men chiefly concerned, to recognize the ways of the Court, and realize that when Mgr le Duc de Bourgogne arrived the army would be nothing but a court of soldiers. Fire and water, I said, were not more different nor less compatible than Mgr le Duc de Bourgogne and M. de Vendôme. The former, pious, shy, uncommunicative, apt to weigh every action, but none the less resolute, had little understanding of men, was loath to think evil of anyone, relying on their truth and virtue; his head was all too often in the clouds and too much absorbed by relatively trivial details. Vendôme, on the other hand, was impetuous, vain, arrogant, contemptuous of others, sticking to his opinions despite long experience, incapable of restraint, especially in matters concerning discipline, rude, and shut to argument, hating contradiction to the point of hurling abuse, extremely intolerant of superiors, publicly immoral in a filthy and scandalous manner which he made no attempt to hide, proud of the King's liking for him and those of his breed, and proud of the powerful cabal that upheld him at Monseigneur's court. Any means served his ambition, for he knew neither truth nor honour, and with brazen self-assurance was ready to dare all, do anything, maintain any assertion. The heights to which such qualities had raised him had confirmed in him the opinion that there was nothing beyond his powers, no one whom he had cause to fear.

The portraits I had drawn were unquestionably accurate, as would be plain to anyone who cared to examine their conduct at moments of crisis. That being so, how was it possible that they should not quarrel? The country's interests would then suffer, the blame be passed on from the one to the other, the army be divided, and the stronger nature crush the weaker. No decency, no respect would restrain Vendôme. He and his cabal would unhesitatingly destroy the young prince's reputation beyond hope of recovery, for vice and virtue never mix, and amid such a spectacle of vice the prince's virtue would appear only contemptible. Age and experience would have the advantage over youth; ruthlessness increase timidity; the sanction of licentiousness and Vendôme's skill in inspiring adoration would make censure intolerable, and the older, more selfish, more enterprising mind would snatch and retain every advantage won. The army, used to believing Vendôme glorious and powerful and the prince of no account, would abandon the latter and follow him whose audacity seemed limitless, and whose reputation froze all the ink in Italy whilst he commanded there.[1]

M. de Beauvilliers, despite his patience and goodness, had had enough and tried to speak; but I besought him to allow me to finish. 'Is it possible,' he exclaimed, 'that you have anything further to say?' 'Indeed I have,' said I, 'and if you will give me time, something of far greater

---

[1] Saint-Simon claimed that fear of Vendôme had prevented anyone but Puységur from reporting the truth of his grossly magnified victories.

moment,' and I continued that, having dealt with the army, I should proceed to embark on the Court. But to follow me here, you should recollect the situation at that time, especially regarding Mlle de Lille-bonne, Mme d'Espinay, and their uncle Vaudémont, their attachment to Monseigneur on the one hand, to MM. du Maine and de Vendôme on the other, and their influence over Chamillart and Mme de Maintenon.

I said to M. de Beauvilliers that he should reflect on the various factions at the Court and their probable actions. 'The King, Sir,' I said, 'is seventy years old and, as you are aware, the thoughts of everyone are turning to the future. At Meudon, the ruling spirits are Mlle de Lillebonne and Mme d'Espinay, who detest Mme la Duchesse de Bourgogne. Monseigneur spends most mornings alone with them in their apartment, and you may well imagine that they aspire to gain complete ascendancy over him. They and their friends form a close cabal, with the sole object of governing Monseigneur to the exclusion of all other influences, and that will continue whilst the King lives. As soon as Monseigneur comes to the throne they will vie with one another for supreme control of a sovereign too dull to form or hold opinions of his own. All these people, as you know, are M. de Vendôme's staunch allies; you had proof of that in Italy and again later. What is more, Chamillart is influenced by them and is devoted both to M. du Maine and M. de Vendôme; thus, through Vendôme, M. du Maine also is one of that cabal. That is not all. Mgr le Duc de Bourgogne is twenty-six, and his intelligence, virtue, and resolution are known throughout Europe. He is the bright hope of France. Even the Court regards him with respect although they find his piety forbidding, indeed the King himself is embarrassed by it. Such a prince, become Dauphin, will certainly be the mainspring of government. What minister, prince, or courtier would think of competing with him then? Who will not look to him for advancement? What man, considering Monseigneur's age and size, will not soon expect another reign when his son, risen to absolute power, will have all men at his mercy?

'I admit that this last consideration might be deterrent even now, but passionate and ambitious men will attempt anything when their present advancement is blocked and all their hope is in the future. Such are they of whom I have been speaking. To govern Monseigneur when he is king they must destroy his son's authority now, whilst the present King lives, and bring his name into absolute disgrace. I think, Monsieur,' I added, 'that I have given you a true picture. How can you doubt their intentions when their conduct reveals them so clearly. Moreover, it would be blind folly to deny the aspirations of those who are an abomination in the sight of God and man; for who can doubt that the bastards tremble before a prince as saintly as Mgr le Duc de Bourgogne, knowing what he must think of their birth, which is blasphemy, and of their rank which is a scandal. Such truths are too obvious to be denied. There remains therefore only one conclusion, the terrible possibility of the ruin of Mgr le Duc de Bourgogne.

'How monstrous, Monsieur,' said I finally, 'that such an idea should even enter one's mind. In the ordinary life of the Court it could not happen; but if, apart from these plots, there should be a disaster in Flanders comparable to those in Italy and Germany you will surely see M. de Vendôme emerge triumphant and Mgr le Duc de Bourgogne disgraced and ruined in the eyes of the Court, the kingdom, and the whole of Europe.'

M. de Beauvilliers, good and patient though he was, could scarcely bear to let me finish. Gravely and sternly he reproached me for giving voice to wild, impossible fancies, whose only foundation was my disgust at M. de Vendôme's vices, my loathing of his birth and rank, and my anger at the favours he received. However bad he might be, said M. de Beauvilliers, he was not mad enough to risk quarrelling with the heir presumptive, whom the King loved and esteemed despite my doubts. He then repeated, showing signs of exasperation, that my forebodings were exaggerated by my imagination and intolerance, emphasizing the nonsense (he was too gentle to name it thus but he let me read his thoughts) of thinking it possible for anyone to conceive, let alone act in a plot to ruin an eldest son of the royal line, who would in due course succeed to the throne.

I replied that although not convinced I would be advised by him, especially regarding his warning of prejudice and wild ideas; but at the same time I had felt it right to tell him my fears, since no one could hope more strongly that they were groundless.

M. de Beauvilliers at once recovered his equanimity, and we began to discuss the best way of using Mgr le Duc de Bourgogne's military talents. Thus we parted amicably. None the less, I was still so far convinced that I could not refrain from telling the Duc de Chevreuse the greater part of my forebodings, and I saw him go at once and speak to M. de Beauvilliers. Indeed, on the terms I was with them, telling one was tantamount to telling the other. I found him as hopeful for the future as his brother-in-law had been, and equally persuaded of the advantages of Flanders for Mgr le Duc de Bourgogne. He was, if possible, the more optimistic of the two because he was naturally inclined to believe everything for the best. They both of them repeated our conversations to their respective duchesses, and M. de Beauvilliers, who had been more deeply shocked than he had let me see, remonstrated with Mme de Saint-Simon. In order to appease him I gave my word not to mention the subject again, but only on condition that he promised to remember what I had said.

I must not omit a trivial affair which I witnessed on that same Easter excursion to Marly, when the King acted as guide to his gardens. At five o'clock one evening he emerged on foot and walked past all the pavilions on the Marly side. At Desmaretz's he stopped, whereupon the latter came out and presented to him the famous banker Samuel Bernard, who had been dining with him for a consultation. He was the richest man in Europe and the head of the greatest and most secure banking business. He knew his power and demanded to be treated with due respect; thus even controllers-general of finance (who had usually far greater need of his services than he of theirs) were properly deferential.[1] The King said to Desmaretz that he was pleased to see him with M. Bernard, then, turning to the latter, he remarked, 'You have probably never been to Marly before. Let me show it to you, and you shall go back later to Desmaretz.' Bernard followed him, and during all their walk the King spoke to him only, took him everywhere, and showed him everything with the charm which he could so easily assume when it suited his purpose. I marvelled, and not I alone, that the King, usually so miserly in words, should prostitute himself, or so it seemed, to a man of Bernard's quality. It was not long before I discovered the reason and I then marvelled even more at the straits to which the greatest kings sometimes find themselves reduced.

Desmaretz was at his wits' end for money; everything was lacking, every fund exhausted. He had gone hat in hand to all the bankers in Paris, but contracts of every kind had been so often and so flagrantly dishonoured and the firmest promises broken that he met with nothing but excuses and closed doors. Bernard like the rest refused to lend, and indeed he had much owing to him. Desmaretz had vainly stressed the urgent necessity and the huge profits that had sometimes accrued to him from the King's business. He had not been moved. So the King and Desmaretz were in a sorry way. Finally Desmaretz had said that taking everything into consideration Samuel Bernard was the only man capable of extricating him financially, because he undoubtedly had enormous sums at his command in all parts of the world. The question was how to persuade him to consent, and overcome the almost insolent stubbornness of his attitude. Desmaretz then made the suggestion that since he was eaten up with vanity he might possibly be induced to open his purse if the King would deign to flatter him, and in that crisis of his affairs King Louis consented. The expedient which I have described was decided on in order to give the affair a cloak of respectability and prevent any refusal. Bernard fell for the bait. He returned to Desmaretz after walking with the King, in such a state of enchantment that he straightaway said that he would rather be ruined than leave a prince in difficulties who had done him such an honour, and he proceeded to praise him to the skies. Desmaretz was quick to take advantage of that situation, by extracting far more than he had intended asking.

[1] A banker at Marly! The King's behaviour to him speaks volumes for the status of bankers in general.

Louville married at about this time. Since his return from Spain he had thought only of mending his fortunes, building comfortably but prudently on his estates at Louville, and living amongst his friends in Paris, with no regrets for his lack of advancement and as though the government of courts and kingdoms had never come his way. He thus sought to marry wisely, and decided upon the daughter of Nointel, a counsellor of State, brother of the Duchesse de Brissac and Mme de Desmaretz, who was his close friend. The wedding was celebrated at Bercy, at the home of Desmaretz's son-in-law. In addition to their respective families, the very best people attended. He had the happiness of marrying a handsome, virtuous, sensible, gay, and understanding wife, who lived with him like an angel, thinking only of her duties and entertaining his friends, although much younger than he. She was well-liked, esteemed, and respected by all.

In the December of the previous year (1707), the King had been involved, against his usual custom, in a somewhat ludicrous private quarrel between people whom he did not like and knew scarcely at all. The Duc de Rohan, who alternated with the Duc de La Trémoïlle as president of the nobles in the parlements of Brittany, had ceded that office with the King's permission to his eldest son, whom he chose to call the Prince de Léon, so as to accustom people to believe in the chimera of his royal blood.[1] He was a tall and slender lad with an ugly and most dissolute countenance, who had idled through one campaign, and then left the service on the excuse of ill-health in order to avoid a second. He was a fellow of infinite wit, ready for any expedient to gain his ends; a schemer, with all the airs and graces of high Society in which he succeeded to perfection. A great gambler, and a great spender, too, for his pleasures, he was grasping in other ways, yet was vastly agreeable, and had a particular talent for persuasion, intrigue, and underhand shifts of every kind, being full of moods, whims, and fancies, as stubborn as his father and, indeed, considering no one in the world except himself. He had fallen madly in love with Florence, an actress whom M. le Duc d'Orléans had long supported and by whom he begat the wife of Ségur, son of the Ségur I mentioned in connection with the Abbess of La Joye, M. de Beauvilliers's sister. M. de Léon spent fortunes on that woman, had children by her, and took her with him to Brittany in a coach and six, thereby creating an absurd scandal. His father lived in terror of his marrying her, even offering to pay her a pension of five thousand livres as well as caring for the children if he would leave her; but M. de Léon would not hear of it. His aunt Mme de Soubise then intervened by means of the notes that were constantly flying backwards and forwards between the King and her. The

---

[1] In 1696 the King had granted the Rohans princely rank because of their vast estates in Brittany, thus putting them on a level with the Princes de Monaco and de Bouillon. Saint-Simon claimed that there was nothing royal about any of them.

King spoke to the son, then to the father, separately, in long private audiences in the study. The son touched him at his weakest points, reverence and love, and with so much wit, grace, and eagerness to comply that the King praised him, sympathized with his stricken heart and his father's distress, and later saw the latter at even greater length in the study. But Florence was removed from the pretty little house in the lanes of Roule where the Prince de Léon had housed her and was placed in a convent. That drove him mad; he refused to see or speak to his parents, and it was thus that, at the end of December, the King sent for him and from the Duc de Rohan to confirm the separation from Florence and make him amenable to the idea of marriage.

Some months later, shortly after Easter, the Prince de Léon finally gave up hope of ever regaining his actress and announced that he was not only ready, but eager to marry. His mother and father were no less willing. They fixed on the eldest daughter of the Duc de Roquelaure, who, despite her great expectations, was humped, hideous, and past her first youth, and thus could not reasonably have foreseen so good a match as M. de Léon, who would become duke and peer with a certain income of fifty thousand écus, apart from all his other possessions. An alliance so advantageous for both sides did not take long to arrange; but at the moment of signing everything ended in anger because the Duchesse de Roquelaure imperiously demanded more money from the Duc de Rohan. He was justly offended for he had not been stingy; he and his wife took umbrage; they refused to budge, and promptly broke off negotiations. Picture the couple in despair! he thinking that his father meant to treat all marriage contracts in the same way so as to avoid giving him money; the bride terrified lest her mother's avarice leave her to rot in her convent. She was rising 25, high-spirited, resolute, adventuresome. The Prince de Léon was 28, and you already know what he was like. The Mlles de Roquelaure were at the convent of the Filles de La Croix, in the Faubourg Saint-Antoine, where M. de Léon had permission to visit his betrothed. As soon as he realized that the marriage was wrecked he rushed to the convent, told Mlle de Roquelaure everything, played the passionate, despairing lover, convinced her that they would never be allowed to marry and that she would perish in a nunnery, implored her not to be duped, swore to marry her if she would consent, and insisted that their parents had arranged the match and prevented it only by their avarice. They might be furious at first, he added, but eventually they would be mollified, and in the meantime they themselves would be man and wife and free of other people's caprices. In a word, he spoke so well that he won her, and, what is more, persuaded her that they had not a moment to lose.

Mme de Vieuville, later Mme la Duchesse de Berry's lady of the bed-chamber, was the one and only person to whom Mme de Roquelaure allowed the superior to entrust her daughters, singly or together, whenever she chose to fetch or send for them. M. de Léon, having discovered this, had a coach of the same size and shape as hers fitted up with similar trimmings and colours, with her arms upon the doors and three coats of her liveries, one each for the coachman and the two footmen. He counterfeited her seal on a note and despatched the entire outfit, with one of the footmen well briefed and bearing the letter, to the Filles de La Croix, on Tuesday morning, 29 May, at the time when Mme de Vieuville usually sent for the young ladies. Mlle de Roquelaure, forewarned, took the note to the superior, saying that Mme de Vieuville had sent for her alone, and had she any messages? Well accustomed to such happenings, neither the superior nor the chaperone troubled to inspect the note, and thus with full permission Mlle de Roquelaure and her chaperone stepped into the coach and were driven off immediately. But it stopped at the very next corner to take up the Prince de Léon, who was waiting to open the door and leap inside. Picture the coachman whipping up his horses, and the chaperone in hysterics screaming at the top of her voice, at the first sound of which M. de Léon stuffed a handkerchief into her mouth and held it firmly in place. In that way they arrived after a very short interval at Bruyères, near Ménilmontant, the country house of the Duc de Lorges,[1] M. de Léon's close friend. He was waiting for them there with the Comte de Rieux, a man whose age and conduct accorded very ill with one another, and who had come to serve as a witness with the housekeeper. A vagabond and interdicted priest, a Breton, was also there ready to marry them. He said mass and at once performed the ceremony. My brother-in-law then escorted that handsome couple to a fine bedroom. The bed and dressing-tables were all prepared;[2] they were undressed, bedded, and left alone together for two or three hours, after which they were given a good meal. They were then packed with the wretched chaperone into the coach that had brought them thither, and were driven back to the convent.

Mlle de Roquelaure calmly explained to the superior what had occurred, disregarding the shrieks of that lady and her chaperone, and went quietly to her room to write a formal letter to her mother informing her of the marriage, making excuses, and asking forgiveness. You may imagine Mme de Roquelaure's feelings. In her first paroxysm of rage, without stopping to reflect, she imagined that Mme de Vieuville had betrayed her, rushed to her house, and whilst still on the threshold, hurled violent abuse at her. Picture Mme de Vieuville completely flabbergasted, asking the matter, and amidst the sobs and howls of rage hearing and understanding nothing! At last, after a long and furious tirade, she began to see daylight, denied everything, swore that Mlle de Roquelaure had not been in her thoughts, summoned all her servants to bear witness that her

---

[1] Mme de Saint-Simon's brother.
[2] Dressing-tables were part of the ritual for putting to bed a bride and bridegroom.

carriage had not been in use, and none of her people gone to the convent. Mme de Roquelaure, still raging, swore that she was adding mockery to mortal injury, whilst her friend strove by every means to calm her. She was, however, eventually persuaded of Mme de Vieuville's innocence, after which they both set about to abuse M. de Léon and those who had abetted him. She later became even more furious with her daughter, not so much for what she had done, but for the gaiety and merry wit which she had displayed at Bruyères, and the songs with which she had entertained them at the marriage feast.

The Duc and Duchesse de Rohan were equally furious although less injured, and raised an appalling commotion. Their son again appealed to his aunt de Soubise to smooth matters with the King, and she sent him to the Chancellor's house at Pontchartrain. He arrived as the Chancellor was dressing, at five o'clock in the morning on the day after that notorious wedding, asking for help and advice, and entreating him to pacify his father, and above all Mme de Roquelaure. Hardly had they begun to talk than a message arrived to the effect that that lady herself was in her coach at the top of the hill and desired the Chancellor to come to her. She had learned on the way that the Prince de Léon was also on the road to Pontchartrain and she did not wish to meet him. The Chancellor immediately mounted his horse and went to her. He found her the very picture of rage, vowing that she had come not seeking advice but to inform him of her intentions and demand that as head of the legal profession he should give her justice. The Chancellor let her finish and then tried to speak, but when she saw that he wished to bring her to reason she lost her temper, and drove straight to Marly to find the King. Arriving there, she descended at the Maréchale de Noailles's pavilion and sent the latter to tell her woes to Mme de Maintenon, begging her to arrange a private audience. She herself appeared at the end of the King's dinner, entering by the garden-windows, through which he was accustomed to go out at that time with his following. Mme de Maintenon went to meet him, against her usual habits, whispered into his ear, and took him straight to her little room, shutting the door after them. Mme de Roquelaure flung herself at his feet, asking for exemplary justice against the Prince de Léon. The King raised her up with all the gallantry of a prince who had been once not unsusceptible to her charms, and attempted to console her; but when she still demanded justice, he asked whether she fully understood what she was asking, which was none other than the Prince de Léon's head.[1] Yet in spite of all he said she persisted until he finally exclaimed that justice she should have, and in full. He then left her with many compliments and went immediately back to his rooms looking extremely grave and speaking to no one.

Monseigneur and the princesses, with the handful of ladies who

[1] Rape was then punishable by death.

ordinarily went with him into Mme de Maintenon's little room and had
been left standing outside, could not at all understand this departure
from routine, and anxiety was added to their curiosity when they saw the
King's face as he passed. No one, as it happened, had seen Mme de
Roquelaure; thus they were still pondering when Mme de Maintenon
left her room and told Monseigneur and Mme la Duchesse de Bourgogne
what had occurred. In that ante-room, where the very cream of the Court
was assembled, a moment was spent in pitying Mme de Roquelaure;
then, some incensed by the imperious airs of that unhappy mother, but
most overcome by the absurdity of a girl, well known to be hump-backed
and hideous, being eloped with by such a villainous-looking suitor, the
entire room burst into a great gale of laughter, causing a really shocking
uproar. Mme de Maintenon was as bad as the rest, but towards the end
removed all the harm by saying that they were scarcely being kind, in a
tone not intended to reprove. She had her own reasons for considering
Mme de Roquelaure, and also for disliking her.[1] The news spread to the
salon, where it had a similar reception, but after the first merriment, reflections on a common interest, for many were fathers and mothers or
about to become so, brought everyone to Mme de Roquelaure's side, so
that despite the mockery and malice there was no one who did not sincerely pity her and excuse her first rages.

Mme de Saint-Simon and I were in Paris, and like everyone else in the
capital had learned of the elopement on the previous evening; but we
knew nothing more, especially not the place of the wedding, nor the part
which M. de Lorges had played in it. Thus, on the second day after the
adventure I was woken with a start at five o'clock in the morning to see my
windows being opened and my curtains drawn, and Mme de Saint-Simon
and her brother standing before me. They told me everything as I have
described it, or at least the essentials. A man of great intelligence and
capability who looked after our affairs then entered in his dressing-gown,
and they went off to consult with him, leaving me to dress and order the
coach. I never saw a man more terrified than the Duc de Lorges. He had
been to confess everything to Chamillart,[2] and had been sent by him to
Doremieu, a fashionable attorney, who had alarmed him even more. He
had then hurried home to us, to make us go to Pontchartrain when, as so
often arises in the gravest matters, there was a comic interlude. He began
to hammer on the door of a cubicle before the entrance of Mme de Saint-
Simon's bedroom. My daughter had been very poorly; my wife, imagining
that she was worse and that it was I who was knocking, ran to open the
door. The appearance of her brother gave her an even worse fright and
she fled back to bed, pursued by him to tell her the whole misadventure.
She rang to have her windows opened so as to see him clearly, but, as it so

happened, she had only the day before taken into her service a girl from La Ferté, aged 16, who slept in the cubicle on the other side of her room. M. de Lorges, all impatience, bade her leave the windows and go, shutting the door after her. Picture the little girl greatly troubled, snatching up her dress and petticoat, and running to wake an old housemaid above, trying to speak, not daring to, and at last stammering out that she had left Mme de Saint-Simon in bed with a handsome young gentleman, all gilded, curled, and powdered, who had sent her flying from the room. She was all of a tremble and utterly bemused. They soon discovered his identity. We heard all about it before we left, and it made us laugh, despite our anxiety.

The Chancellor described his visitations of the previous day and all that had passed. He earnestly recommended us to provide for the escape of the priest and all other possible witnesses, the removal of signed documents, and an absolute denial in answer to questions, promising us that this would ensure M. de Lorges's safety. From thence we went to L'Etang, where we found Chamillart much embarrassed by the whole unsavoury business but not unduly alarmed. The King had ordered a full report and to be informed of every step taken. It came within the jurisdiction of Pontchartrain,[1] who acted as a kind of moderator of the judges concerned; and because his wife had written to him, and perhaps even more because of the intervention of Mme de Soubise, we felt secure with him. We returned to Paris to Mme la Maréchale de Lorges's house, well persuaded that we should there find nothing but trouble, but we learned that the priest and servants had already made their escape and that the document and signatures were in process of being destroyed. Mme de Roquelaure sent a friend to impart the distressing news to her husband, at Montpellier, who was, if possible, even angrier than his wife. After an appalling rumpus, they nevertheless realized that the King, who was aware of their every action, would not allow a daughter of Mme de Roquelaure to be publicly dishonoured; still less send the nephew of Mme de Soubise to the gallows or to civil death in a foreign country. Thus they gradually came to understand that a suitable marriage of which they had originally approved might be preferable to their daughter's shame. Strangely enough the Duc and Duchesse de Rohan proved less tractable. The husband sulked; it would not have displeased him if his son, whom he had never liked, had been forced to seek his fortune in Spain. The mother much preferred the second son and would gladly have made him the eldest. They shamelessly demanded better terms, making so many difficulties that an absolute breach between the two families appeared inevitable, until the King, for the first time in his life, intervened as master. He spoke with great kindness to M. and Mme de Rohan, both together and separately, in his study, although he did not like them, and finally gave

[1] Jérôme Pontchartrain.

them the Chancellor, not as a negotiator, but as judge of the terms of the marriage-contract, saying that he absolutely insisted on the marriage being performed and celebrated before he left for Fontainebleau. He then gave permission for the Prince de Léon to thank him and ask pardon for his offences, and thus, after much scandal, anxiety, and trouble the contract was signed by the two families at the Duchesse de Roquelaure's house in an atmosphere of intense gloom. The banns were published and by permission of Cardinal de Noailles (scarcely ever given in such cases) the families met again at the chapel of the Filles de La Croix, where, since her escapade, Mlle de Roquelaure had been guarded by five or six nuns serving in relays. She entered the chapel by the convent door, and the Prince de Léon entered at the same moment by another, receiving congratulations from no one. It had been especially arranged in that way so that they should not be able to say a word to each other. The curé said mass and married them. When the ceremony was over everyone signed the register without exchanging a word. The bridal pair went off in a coach to stay at the house of a banker friend of the bridegroom, until they could find a house in Paris, where they paid for their folly in abject poverty that lasted almost for the rest of their lives, for neither long survived the Duc de Rohan and Mme de Roquelaure.

The King, who had a superstitious dislike of starting any enterprise on a Friday, felt no such scruples when he fixed the departure of his grandson Mgr le Duc de Bourgogne for 14 May. To anyone who took note of days, the anniversary of the assassination of Henri IV and the death of Louis XIII might well have seemed unpropitious for France, her kings, and their recent offspring. King Louis, however, although he could never conceive of any other King of France, must on this occasion have noticed that despite their worship of him his Court was not considering him only. The King's mass, by tradition a requiem, struck everyone with gloom and saddened the departure of the young prince. I was not myself a witness of this scene. I was at Saint-Denis, for the anniversary of him to whom, after my father, I owe my entire fortune.[1] In this I was following my father's example; a duty that comes before everything else with me and one in which I have never failed. On returning to Versailles I found everyone still profoundly depressed by the choice of that ill-omened day for the prince's departure.

Mgr le Duc de Bourgogne left an hour after noon, travelling to the war by way of Cambrai with the same strict prohibition as on his previous journey. He managed none the less to stay for a while, though only at the posting-house; but the archbishop met him there attended by all the notabilities. You may imagine the curiosity aroused by so public an audience. The young prince took his old tutor in his arms and embraced him tenderly many times, saying out loud that he never could forget all

[1] Louis XIII.

that he owed him; after which, in the same loud tones, he continued speaking almost exclusively to him. The eagerness with which he gazed straight into Fénelon's eyes and the eloquence of his glance achieved precisely what the King had forbidden, for his expression deeply moved all beholders. Thereafter, on the pretexts of bad roads or visits to friends, the court of the disgraced archbishop was swelled by the most distinguished members of Society, striving to merit present favour and future protection.

M. le Duc de Berry left on the 15th, avoiding Cambrai. He joined Mgr le Duc de Bourgogne on the evening of his arrival at Valentinois, where M. de Vendôme had set up his headquarters after leaving the Court, and where the officers were assembling. The King of England was not slow in making his appearance, shielded by an incognito so apt that it became famous.[1] Until his household arrived he ate with Mgr le Duc de Bourgogne, after which he kept his own table with sixteen covers laid. He received guests to dinner and was most gracious to all, dining with the generals also when they invited him. He had chosen his own station at the head of his countrymen, which gratified them immensely; even the English in the Allied army were pleased and allowed their satisfaction to be known.[2] He was exceedingly discreet, although he lived much in Society, endeavoured to please and succeeded, and won the respect and affection of the soldiers and generals by his keenness and goodwill; he had little chance to display other qualities.

The Imperials were slow in assembling their army, commanded by the Elector of Hanover, later King George of England, who was reckoning that Prince Eugene would join him before long. The latter left Vienna very late, however, dallied with several of the princes *en route*, stayed to muster a powerful army on the Moselle and, deaf to Hanover's protests, took from him large reinforcements by the Emperor's express command. They had great difficulty in calming him and preventing him from going home disgusted. Meanwhile Marlborough, at the head of his army in Flanders, waited with the utmost serenity. They say that he had arranged in advance with Prince Eugene to await his coming and take no step without him. At the beginning of the campaign Mgr le Duc de Bourgogne's army comprised two hundred and six squadrons and a hundred and thirty-one battalions formed into fifty-six brigades. It included the *Maison du Roi*, the gendarmerie, carabineers, and guards regiments, eighteen lieutenants-general and as many brigadiers of the line, not counting all the administrative officers.[3] The army was complete, healthy,

---

[1] 'The Chevalier de Saint-Georges.'

[2] The English cherished a sentimental affection for the heir, even though they were loyal subjects of Queen Anne and he was committing the terrible error of fighting for France against his own country.

[3] He thus had the nominal command under Vendôme of the absolute cream of the French armies.

splendidly equipped, and in excellent spirits. Never was any force more abundantly supplied or better provisioned in every way, served by a prodigious train of artillery and supply wagons. Every serving officer had hurried to his post as soon as the princes departed. All was ready; nothing now remained but to go into action.

M. de Vendôme, who gladly took root wherever he found himself comfortably installed, showed little desire to move. He was the only one so minded, but carried his opinion with an air of such superior knowledge that Puységur, foreseeing disaster, wrote at length to M. de Beauvilliers, who did not conceal his apprehensions from me. I reminded him of our conversation at Marly, but even I did not then imagine that events would go the whole course of my prediction. Let us take advantage of this time of inactivity in the first stages of the campaign to recount what was happening elsewhere. After the fighting begins we shall not be able to digress.

The King spent the night of 18 June at Petit-Bourg, arriving at Fontainebleau on the 19th. Meanwhile Mme de Pontchartrain[1] lay dying in Paris. My close friendship with the family and the more than sisterly affection existing between her and Mme de Saint-Simon kept us there also, for by that time she was seeing almost no one else. To be with my wife was her only consolation, and Mme de Saint-Simon found none excepting at her bedside. The character of that accomplished woman would take up too much space here; it would be better placed among the documents.[2] It was too fine, too remarkable, too edifying to pass unnoticed. The sad loss had long been expected. It was some woman's illness, caused by too many pregnancies too close together,[3] with so little care taken beforehand that all the usual remedies failed. Pontchartrain, who had much to reproach himself with on that account, may well have overtaxed her strength by his oppression of her, and by the savage temper, of which she constantly bore the brunt. The meekness and patience with which she endured everything took their toll at last; her blood turned acrid, and in the end could neither be cooled nor staunched.

Sincerely or otherwise, as later it seemed only too apparent, Pontchartrain felt his tragic loss to the full, and confided to me more than a year before her death that should that calamity befall him he intended to go into retirement and had his resignation ready prepared to send to the King. He proposed to stay, he said, in a small apartment owned by his father at the Institution de l'Oratoire, where he was accustomed to go for the great religious feasts, and would remain there for three or four months, until he found a place and a way of life to suit him. He begged me to keep this decision absolutely secret. It would serve no useful

---

[1] The wife of Jérôme Pontchartrain.
[2] It has been lost.
[3] Five altogether at very short intervals.

purpose to repeat the arguments I used endeavouring to dissuade a man of his age and family responsibilities from that reckless plan. I knew that I should gain nothing at the first attempt; but although there was nothing about him that was not vastly repellent, as I had better cause to know than most, for I saw him often and in intimacy, I must admit that on this occasion I was deceived into pitying him. It seemed to me that loyalty to his father, who hid nothing from me of his business and family affairs and had very often confided his disappointment regarding his son, his mother's equal confidence in me, and the close friendship between our wives, required me to do everything possible to turn him from a project likely to prove fatal for the entire family.[1] I soon realized that apart from the desire to mark his grief by some dramatic gesture he despaired of being able to hold his office without the support of his wife's high rank.[2] Such a mixture of sentiment and pride appeared monstrously hard to contend with, and I therefore thought it no disloyalty to let Mme de Saint-Simon into the secret so as to profit by her wisdom. She felt as I did, and before long Pontchartrain had opened his heart to her also.

My anxiety on his behalf caused me to leave excellent company and my building and planting works at La Ferté, where I had been since Christmas, when I learned that a mishap had occurred that seemed to herald the death of Mme de Pontchartrain. I wished to be with him in time to prevent him from sending in his resignation. Her illness, however, dragged on for another six months, which gave him the opportunity to consult Père de La Tour, the general of the Oratory and his wife's confessor, and also the Abbé de Maulévrier,[3] the King's almoner, an inveterate schemer and a clever and ambitious man, a close friend of the Jesuits and of Monsieur de Cambrai. That abbé dissuaded him from retiring to the Institution by arguing that it would vex the Jesuits, to whom Pontchartrain was as much addicted as his father was the contrary, also the risk of bringing on himself suspicions of Jansenism, which might cause trouble for Père de La Tour. Pontchartrain then decided to go to his father's country house when the blow fell, and to delay his resignation for some weeks, or even months.

When Mme de Pontchartrain died at last, on 23 June, at eleven o'clock in the morning, we had been with that tragic household almost continually for the better part of two months. The Court was at Fontainebleau and the Chancellor also, for he was unable to absent himself. His wife went to him at once and found him deeply distressed, although the death had for so long been expected. Mme de Saint-Simon, whom I had skilfully removed from the painful scene, needed succour of every kind

[1] The King considered resignation from his service as equivalent to desertion, and never forgave or forgot it.

[2] She was a Rochefoucauld-Roye.

[3] Not to be confused with the Marquis de Maulévrier, who committed suicide 1706.

despite her courage, and I wished to be with her. She, however, knew of Pontchartrain's project and realized how essential it was for his children's sake to dissuade him from it, and she pressed me so hard not to abandon him that I left her with Mme la Maréchale de Lorges, Mme de Lauzun, and my mother, on receiving an urgent summons from Père de La Tour to return to Pontchartrain's house. In brief, we then all three of us in one coach, with Bignon the intendant of finances making a fourth, drove down to his father's country house. His three sisters-in-law[1] had arrived there that same evening and little by little his friends and relatives swelled the company. A situation then developed in which the Chancellor and his wife, who thoroughly disliked the sisters-in-law, spoke only to Père de La Tour and myself, whilst Pontchartrain, still wishing to discuss his retirement, which only we knew about, constantly abandoned all his other guests to be closeted with us. I thus felt obliged to stay in order to prevent him from making any move until Bignon was ready to go to Fontainebleau, at which time the project was confided to him to reveal to the Chancellor, but he was not asked to take the resignation.

As soon as the affair was in the hands of the Chancellor I returned to Paris and Mme de Saint-Simon, and Père de La Tour to his own affairs. But not for long, for I received the most moving letter imaginable from the Chancellor, imploring me not to abandon the madman in his frenzy, swearing that he had no one to turn to except Père de La Tour and myself, and could not rest unless we were with his son. I did not, however, return at once to Pontchartrain. I then received a most urgent appeal which I found it hard to refuse; but since he instructed me at the same time to drive out the sisters-in-law and all the other guests I could not but feel that he asked too much. The facts were that even although the Chancellor had been replacing his son in his work with the King, State papers had been piling up for want of signatures, and King Louis, the last man in the world to make allowance for the troubles of others, had begun to lose patience and think himself ill-served. It also appeared that the courtiers were making mischief and calling Pontchartrain ridiculous. Truly enough, the numbers of guests at his father's house, although all were close friends or relatives, gave the appearance of a ball or party of pleasure, quite out of place there and very shocking in the circumstances. The Chancellor's state of mind may easily be imagined as he viewed the prospect of his family's ruin. A third appeal besought me to return and drag his son back to Fontainebleau. At this point Mme de Saint-Simon intervened, begging me not to refuse this great service when it was asked so pressingly.

I therefore agreed to go, but only if accompanied by Père de La Tour and preceded by the Abbé de Maulévrier, for the Chancellor had spoken

---

[1] The Saint-Simons' cronies Mmes de Blanzac, Roucy, and Roye, wives of the late Mme de Pontchartrain's three brothers.

firmly to the latter when he learned that his son had confided in him. The abbé was a man who loved meddling, especially with ministers, and he could be very hard. The Chancellor instructed him to prevail on Pontchartrain to obey his father, and to intimate to all the guests, sisters-in-law included, that they should depart. We allowed him to go on ahead of us, and Père de La Tour and I left on the following day. When we arrived we discovered that the abbé, armed though he was with parental instructions, had proved incapable of removing the guests, the sisters-in-law, or the son himself. The three ladies, knowing nothing of Pontchartrain's intentions, were intent only on comforting him. They complained bitterly of having to endure abominable treatment for love of him. Pontchartrain, who invariably resisted every attempt at paternal influence and was enjoying the society of those who had been closest to his wife, flew into a furious temper, flatly refused to budge, and easily persuaded such guests as made motions towards departure to change their minds. Père de La Tour and I swiftly perceived that the most pressing need was not so much to do what the Chancellor asked as to undo the harm caused by the Abbé de Maulévrier. Père de La Tour accordingly went to attack Pontchartrain, whilst I remained to cope with the ladies.

I had to endure a tirade from the Comtesse de Roucy, so I addressed myself next to Mme de Blanzac as being more accommodating, but she with her clever brain and deceptive meekness was far more cunning and became still more set on having her own way. I let them abuse the Abbé de Maulévrier to their hearts' content, saying merely that the Chancellor thought that his son was too happy in their company and feared that only solitude would persuade him to return to his duty. In a word, I appeased them and their husbands also. The abbé was then bundled off to Fontainebleau with a letter to be given secretly to the Chancellor. The tirades, the vapourings, the frenzies, the interminable arguments of Pontchartrain, his fury, threats, and continual outbursts against his father, descended ceaselessly and solely upon the heads of Père de La Tour and myself, leaving us empty of ideas, patience, and pity. I could hardly bring myself to believe that he was foxing us, but Père de La Tour, who was less squeamish, made that accusation and together we confirmed it. Even the sisters-in-law felt that they could detect something not entirely sincere in his vapours, howling, and transports of grief, but they mentioned that to us alone. The very servants noticed something unnatural, and they were far from silent.

We did at last manage to extract the most vital signatures from Pontchartrain, but his father was becoming sorely tried. He wrote one letter to me that was so moving, so sad regarding our mutual sorrow, so eloquent on his troubles, so indignant with his son and the sisters-in-law, so full of trust and gratitude towards me, that although he asked me to show it to Père de La Tour before burning it, I thought myself more deserving of his confidence by returning it. Finally, just as we were becoming desperate, I received a letter secretly from Pontchartrain's mother announcing that unknown to anyone but the Chancellor she had decided to come herself on the following day. That was a great relief, and with the approval of Père de La Tour I sent a trusty servant to meet her on the road two leagues from Pontchartrain, with a note explaining the present situation and the line that she should take. She has often since thanked me for my forethought, saying that my letter was most helpful.

Shortly after dinner, therefore, everyone save Père de La Tour and myself was vastly surprised to see two coaches coming over the hill, for there were no chance callers at Pontchartrain in those days. The company was even more astounded when they recognized the wife of the Chancellor. A grenade exploding would have frightened the sisters-in-law less. Père de La Tour and I managed to keep our countenances, however, and no one either then or since has ever suspected that we were forewarned. He went quietly to his own room, and I took refuge in a passage from whence I could observe their first encounter. It passed off remarkably well, at the door of the lobby leading into the courtyard. Mother and son were closeted alone at first, whilst Père de La Tour endeavoured to recall the scattered wits of the sisters-in-law. Mme de Pontchartrain then put them at their ease by announcing that she had not come to remove her son or to drive anyone away, merely to stay with him whilst he remained at her house. In the event, she managed to become so tedious to them all with her politeness and her constant presence that the absurdly protracted holiday soon came to an end, and I was at last able to return to Paris for good.

After I had gone the unhappy situation continued for a few days longer and then the sisters-in-law themselves began to urge Pontchartrain to go, to which he consented provided that his father received him kindly and that he lived in private at the Court, where he would remain, so he said, only for a year. He would have been much vexed had anyone taken him at his word. Mother and son thus returned to Fontainebleau, where the Chancellor forced himself to say a few kind words although deeply offended by what had passed. Rumours of Pontchartrain's mockery of grief had spread to the Court and was current gossip. His general behaviour, the ridiculous figure he had cut, his parade of sorrow and other theatrical displays had unmasked him completely and made him an object of derision, to the great grief of his mother and father.

Mme de Saint-Simon, more honest, and at the same time far more deeply affected, found it hard to take up her usual life at the Court; but I was particularly anxious for her to do so because the King made no allowances for suffering or absence, and was already somewhat vexed with her for having excused herself from one court-ball during Mme de Pontchartrain's last illness. At Fontainebleau, we lodged as usual in the château, with the Pontchartrains, our time being almost wholly taken up by the Chancellor, his wife, their son, and the company there assembled.

It may seem strange to have included so long and comparatively uninteresting an interlude. I should certainly not have done so but for what follows, to which it is entirely essential.

Despite my preoccupation with this death and its after-effects I had taken care to keep myself informed of many matters that seemed of first importance then, although they have since melted away like blocks of ice. Which does not prove that many weighty matters do not stem from causes equally ephemeral. I enjoyed M. le Duc d'Orléans's entire confidence. His position and his friends were such that I was the only person able to give him a true account of what happened at the Court, and I took care to tell him much else for his information and guidance. I always used a code, sending my letters by his personal couriers on their return journeys, and I sent also 'letters of straw'[1] en clair through the ordinary post and the court couriers as a diversion. I was at this time somewhat behindhand in my correspondence, and was feeling exhausted by the life I had been leading; I was therefore very ready to welcome a little distraction. It so happened that La Vrillière was going almost unaccompanied to Châteauneuf; he pressed me to go with him, I consented, and once there I shut myself up alone for an entire day from morning to evening, compiling an immensely long letter in code to M. le Duc d'Orléans and despatching it by a safe hand to be posted at Orléans, so as to preserve it from being opened. From Châteauneuf I went on to visit Cheverny and his wife at their beautiful château,[2] and I also saw Chambord, close by, of which I had heard often, but I found that I did not at all covet it. The Bishop of Blois, who came to Cheverny, invited me to Blois also, where I had been most anxious to see the salle des derniers états,[3] the prison where Cardinal de Guise and the Archbishop of Lyons were confined, and the room where Catherine de' Medici died. I learned, however, that when Gaston d'Orléans built the new château he destroyed the salle des états, and that the caretaker who now occupied the apartments of that ill-fated queen had gone away and taken the key. I also saw Ménars[4] on that excursion and was very glad to have done so because of the rare beauty of its terraces. After an eight or twelve days' eclipse I returned to Fontainebleau.

The Duchesse de Châtillon died. She had been Mlle de Royan, a niece of the Princesse des Ursins and, like her, a Trémoïlle, and had been brought up and married at her house in Paris, as I mentioned when describing my own wedding. Latterly she had become exceedingly stout, so much so indeed that the King made them entreat her never to appear at

---

[1] In the language of diplomacy, letters written to put the censor off the scent.
[2] The famous Château about fifteen kilometres from Blois.
[3] The States-general of Tours which met in the Château of Blois in 1576 and 1588. Their last meeting is famous for the assassination of the Duc de Guise.
[4] The Château on the Loire later Mme de Pompadour's country house.

the Court when Mme la Duchesse de Bourgogne showed signs of a pregnancy, or when she actually was pregnant. By dint of mimicking one of the nuns at the convent where she was first educated she had developed a twitch, so rare before her marriage as to be virtually imperceptible, but thereafter increasing to the point where every other moment her entire countenance became contorted in the most alarming fashion, though without her at all perceiving it, for it was almost continuous.

M. le Duc d'Orléans stayed longer in Madrid than he had intended. Nothing whatsoever was ready, nothing was sufficient, the negligence had been extreme. He had had to discover other sources of supply, which had not proved easy, and this had prolonged his stay. In Paris a rumour started that he had fallen in love with the queen. Monsieur le Duc and Madame la Duchesse were mainly responsible, because they were jealous of his growing reputation. This tale spread like wildfire through the Court, Paris, the provinces, even abroad; but not in Spain itself, where it was never mentioned because there was no vestige nor semblance of truth in it. M. le Duc d'Orléans was concerned with matters far more serious. Had it only pleased God to make him less provoked by the obstructions which he encountered at every turn, or had only his anxieties left him better mastery of his tongue! One evening, after a long day's work (he had done nothing since his arrival but search for means of overcoming the total lack of preparation), he sat down to dine with several of the Spanish and French nobility in his suite. Still burning with indignation, particularly against Mme des Ursins, who controlled everything and had forgotten the bare necessities for a campaign, he became more cheerful as the meal continued, indeed rather too much so. At the point when he was becoming a little tipsy, and still full of his grievances, he lifted his glass and gazing round the table said, 'Gentlemen, I give you the toast of our bitch-captain and bitch-lieutenant!' (I must apologize, but the word cannot be disguised.) That toast tickled the fancy of his guests. No one, not even the prince himself, dared to embroider it. Laughter gripped them one after another and was far stronger than their sense of danger. They drank the toast, but did not repeat the words. There was the most appalling scandal. Within half-an-hour, no more, the Princesse des Ursins had been informed, and she knew at once that the lieutenant was herself and the captain Mme de Maintenon, for if you recollect what I said on that subject you will know that it could not have been otherwise. Picture her in a frenzy of rage writing down the whole affair for the benefit of Mme de Maintenon, who fell into an equally violent passion when she read of it. *Inde iræ!* They never forgave M. le Duc d'Orléans and you shall see how close they came to ruining him completely. Mme de Maintenon until that moment had neither liked nor disliked him, and Mme des Ursins had striven in every way to charm him. That, in fact, was what had annoyed her most. To think that after what she had done to please him personally, her neglect of the army should have drawn down on her that cruel jest, which in one word had summed up her entire policy and turned it to unforgettable ridicule. From that moment they were both determined on his destruction. You may think that he had courted their hatred; but although he escaped from the immediate danger, he never ceased to feel, both during the King's life and after, by all kinds of persecution, the bitter, implacable enmity which he had aroused in Mme de Maintenon. It was a miracle that she did not in fact ruin him, but more marvellous still that she should have had the power to reduce a prince of his royal rank to a state of anxiety and confusion from which he never wholly recovered. He soon observed the change in Mme des Ursins, and it in no way assisted his plans, for from then onwards she aspired to see all his endeavours fail. Some things are unforgivable, and one must admit that his atrocious jest was supremely of such a kind. Thus M. le Duc d'Orléans made no effort to appease her, but continued about his business as usual. Indeed, I do not think that he ever repented, although he was given good cause to do so, for he found his jest so amazingly funny that he more than once vexed me by repeating his words and laughing until his sides shook. I myself felt their whole gravity and foresaw the bitter consequences; yet what annoyed me most was that even as I reproached him I could not help laughing, for in two caustic, witty terms he had summed up the tragic absurdity of petticoat government on both sides of the Pyrenees.

M. le Duc d'Orléans did finally manage to take the field, but never for more than two weeks at a stretch and not always even then with his supplies assured. At the beginning of June he captured the encampment at Ginestara, from whence he despatched Lieutenant-General Gaetano to Falcete[1] with three thousand infantry and eight hundred cavalry, taking prisoner twelve hundred infantry, four hundred horse, and a thousand of the *miquelets*.[2] He had another success near Tortosa, capturing five vessels laden with corn and salt meat. He invested that fortress on 12 June, having set up two bridges over the Ebro, one above and one below. The trench was cut on the night of the 21st, well within musket-range. The ground was almost entirely rock, which caused considerable difficulties, but the shortage of provisions caused very many more. I have heard it said that without M. le Duc d'Orléans they would never have succeeded, and that he was the best quartermaster that any army could have wished. On the night of 9 July they obtained a footing in the covered way, which the garrison defended with the utmost courage but were driven back. On the following day the defenders capitulated and surrendered the keys; four days later they were marched under escort to Barcelona. M. le Duc d'Orléans likewise had the glory of containing Starhemberg[3] and obliging

[1] Near Tarragona.
[2] Spanish bandits.
[3] The Spanish general defeated by Vendôme at Villaviciosa.

him to give ground during the remainder of the campaign, even although our army was inferior in numbers. Yet it was written that this year should be a fatal one for Spain, and that like some ancient tree worn out by the centuries her greatest limbs should fall from her one by one. Our worst calamity was not the loss of Sardinia, bad though that was,[1] for towards the end of October Sir John Leake appeared off the island of Minorca, which immediately surrendered to the Archduke.[2] The port of Mac-Mahon also surrendered after a very poor show of resistance, and with this conquest added to the taking of Gibraltar the English found themselves masters of the Mediterranean, in a position to winter entire fleets in that sea and to blockade all the southern ports of Spain. It is now time for us to return to Flanders.

Prince Eugene crossed the Moselle on the last day of June, embarked his infantry as far as Coblenz, and then marched towards Maestricht.[3] There had been some thought in our army of making a surprise attack on Brussels and four thousand ladders were assembled with that intent; but the King had first to be informed, he decided otherwise, and the project was abandoned. During the interval Bergeyck had been searching for a means by which to save some remnant of advantage from the great uprising which he had planned so skilfully that it would undoubtedly have succeeded had the Scottish raid not miscarried. The mayor of Ghent, a man of great influence in that town, quietly continued his preparations until everything was ready, whilst in Bruges Bergeyck took similar action so as to move in concert with him. Meanwhile the army of Mgr le Duc de Bourgogne appeared quite content to wait and see what the enemy would do. Artagnan was detached on 3 July with a large body of troops, ostensibly in search of supplies, and on the evening of that day Chémerault left the camp of Braine-Lalleu,[4] with two thousand cavalry and two thousand grenadiers, to forage in the direction of Tubize, but instead he continued on to Ghent, where he arrived on 6 July in the nick of time to save the mayor, and took the town without firing a shot amidst general rejoicing. The citadel fell two days later, and three hundred English marched out with the garrison. Bruges surrendered at almost the same moment. The only persons in the secret of that enterprise were Bergeyck who had planned the surprise attacks, the two princes[5] and the Chevalier de Saint-Georges, M. de Vendôme, Puységur, and at the last moment the leaders of the expeditions. The two princes with the Chevalier de Saint-Georges

[1] Sardinia surrendered to Sir John Leake in August 1708.
[2] Had been recognized by the Allies as Charles III of Spain.
[3] 150 miles. Berwick with a far stronger army was also hurrying towards Flanders. It was a race. Eugene could not hope to be more than two or three days ahead of him even with his cavalry.
[4] 19 km. east of Brussels.
[5] Bourgogne and Berry, the latter aged 23.

made a state entry into Ghent and to show confidence stopped at the
Hôtel de Ville, where they were royally entertained. There were great,
almost hysterical rejoicings at Fontainebleau, combined with prophecies
of victories to come, that went far beyond any reasonable expectations
from such easy successes. I, myself, felt great joy at so auspicious a
start, but I distrusted these raptures and could not help writing my
thoughts to M. le Duc d'Orléans.

[*The fall of Ghent and Bruges was a severe blow to the Allies. Ghent, as Berwick
said, 'was the key to all the rivers and waterways of Flanders', Bruges, only a little
less important, guarded the direct line of communication with England. Marlborough
was ill, exhausted, and very deeply depressed by the news. Prince Eugene, arriving
at his headquarters at Assche in a post-chaise, escorted by a hundred Hungarian
huzzars, four days ahead of his cavalry, found him sick and full of grave misgivings.
His comradeship encouraged and revived Marlborough, managing to persuade him
that his affairs were not in anything like so bad a state as he imagined, and he recovered sufficiently to march to Lessines in order to arrive before the French and
prevent them from investing the fortress of Oudenarde. Such deep depression before
a great victory was typical of Marlborough: it had happened to him before both
at Blenheim and Ramillies.*]

Prince Eugene's march from the Moselle to Flanders cut the Elector's
army in two. The latter came alone to spend a few days in Metz, and then
returned to Strasbourg. With the troops that remained the army of the
Rhine numbered forty-two battalions and seventy-three squadrons, of
which Berwick led thirty-four battalions and sixty-five squadrons into
Flanders.

Taking advantage of our two conquests, it appeared a simple operation
to cross the River Scheldt and burn Oudenarde, thus barring the enemy
from the country districts and making provisions of all kinds very scarce
for them and very abundant for us. M. de Vendôme agreed to that plan
and made no objections, but in order to execute it he needed to leave his
headquarters and go into camp around that fortress. The only hindrance
was the indolence of M. de Vendôme, who wished to enjoy his personal
comforts as long as possible, and persisted in maintaining that there was
no need to hurry.[1] Mgr le Duc de Bourgogne, supported by the entire
army including many of Vendôme's closest friends, tried vainly to convince him that, since he himself approved of the project, Oudenarde had
best be captured quickly; and that delay was dangerous lest the enemy be
forewarned; which he himself admitted would be the greatest misfortune.
Vendôme, however, dreaded the fatigues of a march and of changing
quarters; it upset the rhythm of his days and meant abandoning his comforts, and these considerations rated highest with him.

[1] On 10 July Eugene's cavalry were very near Brussels. Berwick's advance guard was already
at Namur.

As to Marlborough, he saw most clearly that Vendôme could discover no better plan than this, nor he than to try to prevent him. Vendôme had only to follow the chord of an arc a very short distance; to forestall him, Marlborough had to move around the whole arc on a wide curve, that is to say twenty-five leagues against Vendôme's six at the most. But the enemy marched with such astonishing speed and secrecy that they had stolen three forced marches before Vendôme had warning or any suspicion of

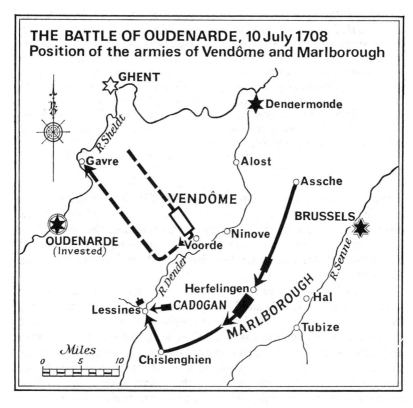

THE BATTLE OF OUDENARDE, 10 July 1708
Position of the armies of Vendôme and Marlborough

GHENT

Dendermonde

R. Scheldt

Gavre   Alost

Assche

VENDÔME   BRUSSELS

Ninove

OUDENARDE   Voorde
(Invested)

R. Dender   R. Senne

Herfelingen   Hal

Lessines ◄■ CADOGAN

MARLBOROUGH   Tubize

Miles
0   5   10   Chislenghien

their departure, though they had been very close to him at the start. When at last the news reached him he, as usual, refused to credit it, and then convinced himself that he could still outmarch them if he waited until the following morning. Mgr le Duc de Bourgogne pressed him to be gone that same evening. Those who dared spoke of the urgent need for haste. Nothing, however, would move him, although news of the enemy's swift progress kept on arriving. His indolence had been so great that work was not even begun on the bridges over a rivulet which had to be crossed almost at the head of the camp, and the engineers laboured on them all through the night.

Biron, now duke and peer and senior Maréchal de France, had hoped to be attached to the Duc de Berry in this campaign, but he had been given command of one of the flank-guards and was stationed at some distance from the main body. Orders came for him that same evening to assemble the troops around him and rejoin the army. Then, as he approached the camp, he received further orders to advance towards the Scheldt, to which our army was about to make its way, and then cross over. When he reached the rivulet where they were making bridges, as I have described, Motet, a captain of guides and very capable, gave him the news that had at last made them decide to march, and although Biron was well accustomed to M. de Vendôme he was appalled that the bridges were not yet completed or the army on the march. Being in haste to reach the Scheldt he forded the rivulet as best he could and entered the hilly country beyond. It was about two o'clock on the afternoon of 11 July, and he could see the whole of the enemy army deployed ready for action, with the feet of the columns in Oudenarde, where they had crossed the Scheldt, and the heads describing a curve and giving every appearance of being about to turn in his direction. He sent an aide-de-camp to the princes and M. de Vendôme, who had crossed the river and were dismounted and picnicking by the roadside. Vendôme, exasperated by news so different from what he had confidently predicted, at first refused to believe it. But whilst he was angrily disputing, a second officer sent by Biron arrived with confirmation, which served to make him still angrier and more contentious. A third officer then appearing, he completely lost his temper, but did at last rise from the table, or what had served him for one, and mounted his horse, swearing that the devil must have lent them wings, for such marching was impossible.[1] He returned Biron's first aide-de-camp with an order to charge the enemy, adding that he would soon be there to support him with troops. Then, telling the princes to follow gently with the main body of the army, he rode in no great haste to the head of the columns and turned them in Biron's direction.

During the interval Biron had stationed his troops as best he could in such rough and broken country, occupying with them a village and hedgerows on the edge of a deep and steep-sided ravine, after which, going to inspect his right, he perceived the advance guard of the enemy army very close indeed. At that point he would much have liked to obey Vendôme's order to charge, not with any hope of success, being so greatly outnumbered, but to protect himself from a commander who might hold him responsible for every subsequent calamity if he disobeyed an order. At that moment of perplexity Puységur arrived to lay out the camp[2] and

[1] All the French generals were surprised by the appearance of the enemy, for on the previous evening their advance guard had been reported to be at Lessines, seventeen miles further south. The Dutch deputy Goslinga wrote that Marlborough's march 'was not so much a march as a run'.

[2] For the siege of Oudenarde.

strongly advised him not to embark on so hazardous an undertaking, warning him that the ground in front of him was impassable. A few moments later the Maréchal de Matignon rode up, and after hearing the discussion forbade Biron to charge, assuming the responsibility for so doing. Biron heard fierce firing on his left, beyond the village. Galloping to the spot, he found his infantry engaged in combat and supported them to the best of his ability with the force at his command, but still further to his left the enemy gained ground. The steep ravine stopped them, however, and gave time for Vendôme to join him. The troops he led were breathless; as they arrived they flung themselves between the hedgerows, most of them in column as they had marched, and it was thus that they met an enemy attack that increased in fury without giving them respite to form a battle order. The disorder was such that only the heads of each column, in that formation and thus closely packed, came into contact with the enemy, who, deployed in order of battle, were greatly advantaged by the breathlessness and disarray of our troops and the empty spaces left at either side of the column-heads. These spaces were filled as other, equally breathless columns made their appearance. They were promptly and fiercely charged as soon as they arrived and, moreover, whilst coming into line and spreading out beside the first-comers they often disorganized them also, forcing them to rally at their rear and causing so much confusion that they could not be brought back to any kind of order.

Other misfortunes then ensued; the cavalry and the *Maison du Roi* became entangled with the infantry, increasing the confusion to such an extent that our troops failed to recognize one another. That gave the enemy time to throw sufficient fascines into the ravine to enable them to cross over and execute a wide turn around our right, in order to reach the head of the army and fall upon the flank that had been least exposed to fire, and was less disordered because the ground was by comparison more open. Near this point were the royal princes, who had been halted at the mill of Royegem, from whence they had a clear view of this unorthodox and ill-begun battle. When the troops of that right wing saw themselves suddenly attacked by a far more numerous foe they gave ground so fast that the valets of the suites of all who accompanied the princes fell back upon them with an alarm, a rapidity, and a confusion that swept them along with extreme speed and much indignity and risk towards the main battle on the left. The princes conducted themselves with great courage and composure in their most unhappy situation. They appeared in the most exposed positions, encouraged the troops, praised the officers, asked the generals what ought to be done, and told M. de Vendôme what they thought themselves.

By this time the confusion had become so great that nearly every man was parted from his troop. Cavalry, infantry, and dragoons were all higgledy-piggledy; not a battalion, not a squadron had kept together, all

were entangled and mixed one with another. When night fell an immense
amount of terrain had been lost and half the army had not yet managed
to arrive. In this desperate situation the princes consulted M. de Vendôme
to find out what should be done; but he, furious with himself for having so
grossly miscalculated, treated them all with scant courtesy. Mgr le Duc de
Bourgogne then tried to speak, and Vendôme, drunk with power and
anger, told him to hold his tongue, saying loudly in front of everyone,

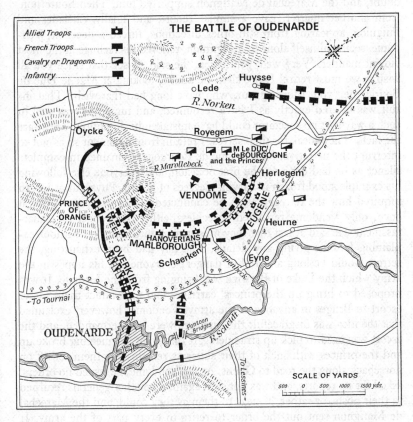

THE BATTLE OF OUDENARDE

Allied Troops
French Troops
Cavalry or Dragoons
Infantry

Huysse
Lede
R. Norken
Oycke
Royegem
M Le DUC
de BOURGOGNE
and the Princes
R. Marollebeck
Herlegem
VENDOME
PRINCE
OF
ORANGE
EUGENE
Heurne
HANOVERIANS
MARLBOROUGH
Schaerken
R. Diepenbeck
Eyne
To Tournai
OUDENARDE
Pontoon
Bridges
R. Scheldt
To Lessines
SCALE OF YARDS
500   0   500   1000   1500 yds.

'Your Highness should remember that you are with this army only on
condition of obeying me.' The enormity of those words, spoken at the
precise moment when everyone was reflecting on the terrible cost of
obedience to his indolence and stubbornness, made all his hearers tremble
with rage. The young prince to whom they had been addressed now had
to win a harder battle than any which his enemies had inflicted on him.
He knew that for him there was no middle way between the final extremity
and absolute silence, and was sufficiently master of himself to choose the
latter. Vendôme then held forth, attempting to demonstrate that all was

not lost since half the army had not been engaged. Let them, he said, spend the night in reorganizing the front, and start again on the following morning. He was heard in silence, for he clearly was in no mood to bear contradiction and had already made one example, one unpardonable, outrageous example, to deter any man brave enough to disagree with him.

Meanwhile news came from all sides of the total disorder. Puységur, arriving from the *Maison du Roi*, gave a report that left no room for doubt, and the Maréchal de Matignon supported him. Then Souternon, from another quarter, gave a similar report, and finally Chéladet and Puiguion, appearing from still other directions, forced a decision. Vendôme, seeing himself alone in his opinion, relieved his feelings in the most violent manner. 'Very well, gentlemen,' he said; 'I see that since you all wish it we must retire! Especially,' he added, looking at Mgr le Duc de Bourgogne, 'you, Monseigneur, who have long had that wish.' That insult was uttered exactly as I have recounted, and moreover was said in such a way that no spectator could have mistaken his intention. Those are the facts. They speak for themselves. I refrain from comment so as not to interrupt the narrative. Mgr le Duc de Bourgogne remained in complete silence as he had done on the first occasion, and everyone else following his example stood frozen in varying degrees of horror. Puységur at length inquired how the retreat was to be conducted. Then everyone spoke at once; only Vendôme remained speechless, either from anger or embarrassment. He said at last that they must march to Ghent, but without explaining how or giving any details. The day had been exhausting, the retreat would be long and full of danger; everyone put his hopes in the army which the Duke of Berwick was bringing from the Moselle. It was proposed to bring up the princes' carriages and to conduct them under escort to Bruges in advance of the army. Vendôme, however, exclaimed that the idea was disgraceful; the carriages were countermanded, and the escort was used to pick up stragglers. At this point the meeting broke up and the princes with such of their suites as remained to them set off on horseback along the road to Ghent. As for Vendôme, he issued no orders, asked for no reports, and was not seen again. The other generals returned to their posts, or rather, as near to them as they could, and the Maréchal de Matignon sent out the order to retire to every part of the army. It was now almost midnight; desultory fighting could still be heard in various directions, but at last, as the order came to them, the troops began their retreat.

The generals of the right wing and the *Maison du Roi*, not understanding why no orders had reached them, were holding a private council when the command to retire arrived. They then discovered that whilst they had been waiting and in suspense the Dutch had surrounded and cut them off. They were all completely amazed and were beginning to argue all over again about the best means of organizing the retreat, when the

Vidame d'Amiens, who as a newly-promoted brigadier-general had not said much, pointed out that if they talked any longer they might be hemmed in. Seeing that they still continued to argue, he urged them to follow him, and crying, 'After me!' to the light horse of which he was the colonel, he charged through a line of enemy cavalry. Behind that was a line of infantry that fired on them but opened to let them pass. The rest of the *Maison du Roi* took advantage of this brave deed and followed his troop, other troops following them, so that in the end all managed to retire in good order under cover of the night to Ghent, still led by the Vidame, whose courage and presence of mind thus saved a very large proportion of our army.

Other remnants withdrew as best they could, but in the confusion General Rosen and the cavalry of the left wing received no orders at all, and found next morning that he and his hundred squadrons had been entirely forgotten. To make a solitary retreat in broad daylight appeared to him a vastly difficult operation, but unable to remain where he was he began the march. Nangis, another recently promoted brigadier-general, perceived some scattered companies of grenadiers and other stragglers, and out of pure goodness of heart gathered together fifteen companies to form a rearguard for General Rosen's abandoned column. The enemy attacked them several times, but he fought them off vigorously in a march of some hours' duration. They made their way along by-roads which Rosen, that skilful partisan, knew from long experience, and finally arrived at the camp, after causing immense anxiety in the fourteen or fifteen hours during which their whereabouts had been unknown.

Mgr le Duc de Bourgogne passed through Ghent without stopping and continued as far as Lowendegem,[1] arriving there with the foremost troops. He set up his headquarters and the camp alongside and behind the Bruges canal, so as to rest his troops with the assurance of plentiful supplies in the rear, until fresh plans had been made and a junction with the Duke of Berwick's army effected. M. de Vendôme (I report only the bare, unvarnished facts) arrived independently at Ghent between seven and eight o'clock in the morning, as troops were entering the town. He stopped with the remnant of his suite still accompanying him, dismounted, let down his breeches, and there and then planted his stools quite close to the troops as he watched them go by.[2] He then quickly entered the town, desired no reports to be given him, flung himself into bed, and remained there for thirty hours on end, recovering from his fatigue. Only later did he learn from his staff that the army were encamped at Lowendegem. He paid no heed, but continued to take his ease, eating and

[1] Not far from Ghent.

[2] Voltaire wrote of him, 'The same lack of discipline and negligence which he allowed in the army he maintained to an astonishing degree amongst his staff and even in his personal habits. By dint of loathing all manner of ostentation, he had come to a cynical filthiness hitherto unequalled.'

sleeping more and more for several days longer, with no thought for the army only three leagues distant. The number of the casualties was as far as possible concealed, but very many were killed and wounded. Lieutenant-general Biron, Brigadiers-general Ruffey and Fitzgerald, the Duc de Saint-Aignan[1] and the Marquis d'Ancenis (the last two wounded), many officers of the gendarmerie, and a very great number of private officers were taken prisoner. Four thousand men and seven hundred officers were captured at Oudenarde, apart from those whose fate was known only later; the dispersal had been prodigious.

As soon as Mgr le Duc de Bourgogne had become established at Lowendegem he wrote a very brief report to the King, referring him to Vendôme for details. He wrote by the same courier in explicit terms to Mme la Duchesse de Bourgogne, stating that the defeat was due to Vendôme's usual over-confidence and his obstinacy in delaying their march, against his advice, until at least two days too late.[2] He continued that if such a thing should ever happen again, he would resign from the service, unless prevented by an absolute order from one to whom he owed blind obedience, for he could make no sense of the attack, the battle, or the retreat, and felt so disgusted that he would say no more. The same courier took a letter from Vendôme also as he passed through Ghent, written on a single sheet of paper before he went to bed, in an attempt to persuade the King that the result was not unfavourable. Shortly afterwards Vendôme sent another report, also very short, stating that he might have defeated the enemy in the battle had he received any support, and would certainly have been victorious on the following day if the others had not demanded a retreat, against his better judgment. For further details he referred the King to Mgr le Duc de Bourgogne. Those details, bandied from the one to the other, were never disclosed. Interest in them subsided and a mystery developed in which Vendôme had every incentive to disappear.

A third courier brought a very long dispatch, written from beginning to end by the hand of Mgr le Duc de Bourgogne, and still another from M. de Vendôme, once more excusing himself for not providing the details. The remainder of the letters were for private individuals. The King took them from the courier and read them all, some three times over, and he handed back monstrously few of them, every one opened. That courier chanced to arrive after the King's supper, and therefore the ladies-in-waiting who had followed their Princesses into the study missed

---

[1] Saint-Aignan was the Duc de Beauvilliers's brother.

[2] Fénelon on Vendôme, in a letter to the Duc de Chevreuse, 12 November, 1706, '. . . more apt to be eager and impatient than considered in his judgments of affairs, will not allow the enemy any superiority over him. He regards that as a disgrace and an insult . . . M. de Vendôme is lazy, negligent over details, believes everything to be possible without considering practical details, and rarely listens to advice. His greatest assets are his courage and judgment in battles, that make him, so they say, very capable of winning them. But he is also very capable of losing them through over-confidence.'

nothing of the readings, although the King made few comments. Mme là Duchesse de Bourgogne had another letter from her husband and a short note from M. le Duc de Berry, to the effect that M. de Vendôme had been most unfortunate and that the entire army was blaming him. When she returned to her own apartments she could not resist saying that Mgr le Duc de Bourgogne appeared to have vastly stupid people about him; but she said no more.

Biron was released on parole for a time, on condition of not returning through the army. He arrived at Fontainebleau on 25 July. His native wit did him good service in parrying indiscreet and foolish questions. The King saw him several times in Mme de Maintenon's room, not always with Chamillart present, and gave him his word to be secret, in which he was always to be trusted. Biron, however, though he told no lies, became increasingly careful of what he said, taking refuge in the fact that he had been detached before the battle and then captured, and was therefore not fully informed. He was one of my close friends and I was able to converse with him at leisure. He explained many things to me; but apart from all that he told me of the army and the battle, I learned of another event that seems worth recording.

Prince Eugene's army did not arrive in time for the battle, but he himself was present and with Marlborough's consent assumed command wherever he happened to be, for although Marlborough had the supreme authority he did not inspire the same trust and affection.[1] Biron said that he had dined at Marlborough's headquarters with many English officers on the day after the battle, and that the duke had suddenly asked him for news of the Prince of Wales, excusing himself for so naming him.[2] Biron had smiled at that, saying that there need be no embarrassment since in the French army he was known only as the Chevalier de Saint-Georges. He then went on to praise him at some length; whereat Marlborough, who had listened with keen attention, exclaimed that such praise gave him great pleasure for he could not help being vastly interested in that young prince. He then immediately changed the subject. Biron had remarked the particular gratification in the faces of Marlborough and most of his officers.

At this point you should recollect what I have said at various times of the intrigues at the Court and the aims and ambitions of the principal personages; above all my conversation with the Duc de Beauvilliers at the end of the Marly gardens, regarding the fate of Mgr le Duc de Bourgogne in Flanders. The Meudon cabal, at first stunned by the disaster, waited for enlightenment and the details, and for fear of blundering devoted all its energies to listening. They soon realized the dangers facing their hero Vendôme, and summoning up their courage dropped a word here and there to test reactions; then growing bolder they risked occasional

[1] Eugene and Marlborough were said to be 'two bodies and one soul'.
[2] Because Louis XIV recognized him as the rightful King of England.

protests. Encouraged by these experiments, for they encountered little resistance in a world so bewildered and ill-informed, they went beyond all
bounds, praising Vendôme, venturing to cast the blame on Mgr le Duc
de Bourgogne, and before long, when their earlier remarks had gone unchecked, to abusing him roundly. Only the King and Monseigneur were
in a position to silence them; but the King as yet knew nothing, and
Monseigneur was surrounded; in any case he was not the man to make a
stand. The great mass of the courtiers were completely in the dark as to
what had occurred, and living, as they did, in fear of personages of such
high rank and standing, they neither dared nor knew how to answer them,
but remained expectant and apprehensive; all of which put fresh life into
the cabal. Lacking details, which Vendôme was careful not to supply,
they ventured to print some manifestoes, so contrived, so lying, so well
aimed that they could not be construed otherwise than as a personal
assault on the prince. The first to appear was a letter from Vendôme's
secretary Alberoni, which was a tissue of lies from first to last, an out-
and-out puff for his master, the falseness and impudence of which could
be seen with half an eye.

That document, and two others equally lying and abominable, spread
like wild-fire through the Court, Paris, and the provinces.[1] I saw an example in the hands of the Duc de Villeroy, who had been lent it for a
couple of hours on his undertaking not to let it be copied, and I guessed
that Blouin, his boon companion for suppers and debauches, had provided it. Like Alberoni's letter, it was compounded of lies without a
single word of truth in it; but at the same time was so artfully presented,
so carefully and speciously worded, that it carried conviction by seeming
loath to disclose the worst. Every imaginable device was used to one purpose, namely to pin the blame for the disaster squarely on to the shoulders
of Mgr le Duc de Bourgogne, in an attack aimed at depriving him of what
men hold most dear, his honour. The enormity of this letter, compared to
which Alberoni's appeared almost restrained, made its use highly dangerous. Thus, whereas the former was passed openly from hand to hand
in order to prepare the ground and arouse interest, the other was given
into safe keeping only, to be shown to all, but with an air of confidence
and mystery that greatly added to its value. At the same time, it much
magnified, to Mgr le Duc de Bourgogne's disadvantage, the loss to the
State by not trusting M. de Vendôme, and his misfortune in being opposed
by a royal prince against whom he could not defend himself with the truth.
Thus ably manipulated the letter was read everywhere, in cafés and
theatres, in the gaming houses, on the public streets, and in the brothels.
Copies went to distant provinces and even to foreign countries, but with
infinite precautions to see that they remained in safe hands. Vaudeville

---

[1] Other letters were by Vendôme's cousin the Comte d'Evreux, Antoine Crozat, and the
dramatic poet Campistron.

ditties, fragments of verse, atrocious songs reviling the heir to the throne, with Vendôme rising a hero from his ruins,[1] spread from Paris throughout the whole of France with a speed and freedom which it was no one's concern to check. Meanwhile at the Court and in high Society the rakish and the smart applauded, crafty adventurers knowing how the land lay joined them, and the crowd swiftly followed. Within six days it had become contemptible to speak respectfully of the King's grandson in his grandfather's house; in eight it was positively dangerous to do so because the leading hounds, emboldened by success, were showing themselves in full cry and making those who dared say otherwise feel that sooner or later they would pay for it.

When the uproar first began the Duc de Beauvilliers, remembering what I had said to him in the garden at Marly, came full of grief to my room to make due apologies. I did no more than entreat him to remember that those in office gained nothing by ignoring the ambitions, intrigues, attachments, and motives of the Court, and to be willing at last to believe that my remoteness from rank, ambition, vices, and patrons did not necessarily make me fanciful. He and I and the Duc de Chevreuse had long and frequent discussions on the best means of opening the King's eyes and calming the *furore*. Not everyone at the Court had been suborned, but fear and the seeming hopelessness of trying to stem the flood kept them silent and inactive. Boufflers,[2] also, was of their number. The two dukes and I at last agreed on the best advice to give to Mgr le Duc de Bourgogne regarding his conduct in Flanders and his letters to France, and in the meantime I kept Mme le Duchesse de Bourgogne informed through Mme de Nogaret of all that I thought she should know and do. She herself had sent Mme de Nogaret to me, asking me to tell her frankly of her situation with the King and Mme de Maintenon and advise her of what she could, or could not, safely do in that direction. I believe that she had no great relish for the person of Mgr le Duc de Bourgogne and that she was not unwearied by his desire for her. I think also that she found his piety boring and envisaged a future when it would become even more so; but at the same time she realized the worth and benefit of his affection and the tremendous advantage it would be in years to come to possess his confidence. She was no less concerned for his reputation, on which all his power depended whilst the King and Monseigneur lived, and clearly saw that if this attack succeeded the worst possible disasters

---

[1] Some songs were aimed at both.

> 'They hazard neither limb nor life,
> Nor yet their honour in the strife,
> One plays at shuttlecock all day,
> The other commands from his *chaise-percée*.'

[2] Boufflers was a *grand seigneur* of the old school and thus was almost venerated by Saint-Simon, to whom he appeared to have something of the style of Louis XIII.

would follow for them both. Though gentle by nature and excessively shy the gravity of the issue gave her unusual courage. She had been deeply hurt and offended by Vendôme's public insults to her husband and the atrocious lies published by his agents, for although Mgr le Duc de Bourgogne had been most guarded in speech he had not been able to resist opening his heart to his wife in his letters. It was what he told her combined with what she had learned from other sources that finally spurred her to action.

In the event she managed so well and so tactfully that she won Mme de Maintenon over despite the veiled hints and the charm, so captivating to her, of M. du Maine, aroused her compassion, and persuaded her to speak to the King on the prince's behalf at a time when no one else cared to do so. In so doing the princess worked what was almost a miracle. Ever since the affair of M. de Cambrai when Mme de Maintenon had tried unsuccessfully to destroy the Duc de Beauvilliers she had seen the latter rarely and addressed him more seldom still in a few formal words, but never anything of a personal nature, for she regarded him as an enemy. She now invited him to come to her room for a private interview. She never in fact forgave him for keeping his office in defiance of her efforts to remove him; but on this occasion his advice and assistance were needed and she gave him her full confidence; he, too, benefited greatly from her views. In none of this was my name mentioned to her, nor did she speak of me, but I heard all that passed between them from M. de Beauvilliers and Mme de Nogaret.

The King was at first disturbed, then annoyed by Mme de Maintenon's description of the letters and the gossip. He demanded with some heat to see them at a full meeting of the council, and when Alberoni's was produced with some hesitation he had it read aloud. His first reaction was to defend Vendôme, but later he commanded Chamillart to write to him in the strongest terms, also to his Alberoni (that was his expression), Crozat, and the Comte d'Evreux, threatening to punish these last three and binding them to silence. I do not know how Campistron came to be forgotten. Such was the fear of Vendôme and his cabal that none of the ministers dared to defend their prince even at the King's council; they merely murmured their assent.

Mgr le Duc de Bourgogne accepted the Comte d'Evreux's apologies, and then appeared to go out of his way to make him forget the King's reprimand by showing him particular favour, an attitude that shocked many people and lost him the sympathies of the army and the Court. As for the cabal, they were shaken by the King's words at his council (as well they might be), but on second thoughts they concluded that since he had taken no firm action on behalf of his grandson he could not be much displeased, but was listening as usual to the advice of Mme de Maintenon. They resolved therefore to stand firm, hoping to entangle the King between his personal feeling for M. du Maine, Vendôme, bastardy in general, and his head valets on the one hand, and on the other, his habit of deferring to Mme de Maintenon, and his amused affection for Mme la Duchesse de Bourgogne. They realized moreover that their schemes would come to nothing if they behaved otherwise, and they proceeded to risk all by circulating the letters in even greater numbers and spreading even more abominable rumours. Mme la Duchesse de Bourgogne's complaints grew louder, but despite Mme de Maintenon's support of her the King was irritated, and more than once harshly reprimanded her for displaying ill-humour and chagrin. That news eventually reached Flanders, and Chamillart, influenced by Vaudémont and his nieces and infatuated with M. du Maine and Vendôme, actually wrote to Mgr le Duc de Bourgogne, venturing to suggest that he would do well to make advances to M. de Vendôme.

That letter had all the desired effect, for the prince had been confounded from the very beginning by Vendôme's contrariness and insulting behaviour. Raised, as he was, in terror of the King (fear is too weak a word), his alarms extended to all those, more especially Vendôme, who enjoyed the monarch's confidence and friendship. His virtue led him to distrust himself, his exaggerated piety had left him little time in which to know his world and narrowed and stunted his nature. Although he was very sensible of the enormity of Vendôme's treatment of him, his anger and indignation made him all the more restrained, and meanwhile M. de Beauvilliers was constantly sending him pious, temperate letters, very like those which he wrote himself. Those which his wife sent him he did not regard seriously. No one else wrote to him; he was otherwise alone in his misery and meditations and took to spending long hours shut in his office, scarcely ever showing himself in public.

Anxiety changed his expression which until then had been open and cheerful, and he now appeared grave and embarrassed. Chamillart's letter, arriving simultaneously with the news that the King was vexed with his wife, drove him still further into himself and visibly embittered him. He began to make overtures to Vendôme, who carried his head as high as usual at their interviews and took advantage of the prince's meekness to bring Alberoni in his suite; and Mgr le Duc de Bourgogne condescended to speak to him also when the occasion presented itself. This sudden retreat into solitude and display of humility had a bad effect on the army. Even those who had been strong in his defence began to take alarm, deciding that prudence demanded silence at least. They visited him less often at his headquarters and were more frequently seen at those of M. de Vendôme, with the result that the majority, seeing only the exterior, began to blame him, to use no stronger word.

Meanwhile I was much concerned on Chamillart's account. Although furious with him for being so blind I was still more alarmed, for if his office lent him power he was weak in influence compared with the bastards, Lorraines, and valets. Mme de Maintenon was already turning against him, and seemed likely to go further in view of his recent behaviour; and the anger of Mme la Duchesse de Bourgogne made me vastly apprehensive, for she could not forgive his letter to her husband. On the other hand Vendôme, for all his self-assurance, had become almost as much disquieted by reports of the activities of Mme la Duchesse de Bourgogne and Mme de Maintenon, for they were not angry with Chamillart alone, and were at all times within earshot of the King. Thus reflecting, he stooped to confiding in Mgr le Duc de Bourgogne his concern that the princess should have been so outspoken regarding him. He made no excuse nor apology, merely begged the prince to intervene on his behalf, since he dared not write to her himself. His impudence clearly shows how timidity and mistaken piety may draw contempt upon even the most godlike beings. His gesture was moreover extremely adroit for, without incurring the slightest obligation himself, he offered the princess through her much-abused husband a chance of reconciliation which she could not easily refuse, and at the same time flattered the King by making seemingly humble advances to his grandson's wife. The really amazing thing was that Mgr le Duc de Bourgogne made no difficulty about transmitting the message, which had the reception it deserved. Mme la Duchesse de Bourgogne in reply begged her husband to believe that she would never like nor respect Vendôme again. She asked him to inform the latter that she had nothing to say to him and could very well understand the reasons for his concern. She added finally that nothing would ever persuade her to forget Vendôme's conduct, and that for her part she would always regard him with loathing and contempt. We shall see in due course how courageously she kept her word. Vendôme learned from that bitter retort the kind of woman with whom he had to deal. He made no further advances to her; indeed, his vanity may already have reproached him for going even so far.

[*Berwick had reached the Sambre on the day after the battle of Oudenarde. He had marched on to Mons collecting stragglers and re-forming them into a force of 9,000 men, with whom he reinforced the garrisons of Lille, Tournai, and Mons. The defeat had been so absolute that none of these troops were fit for further service and became known as the débris of the Grande Armée. Berwick foresaw that the Allies would besiege Lille and urged Vendôme to march there with all speed so as to attack Prince Eugene, cut his supply routes and thus prevent a siege. Vendôme refused to budge from his position behind the Bruges canal. He said, 'so prudent a commander would never embark upon such a rash enterprise.'*

11 August. Eugene and Marlborough began the siege of Lille.
29 August. The armies of the Duc de Bourgogne and Berwick formed a junction at Grammont and encamped at Mons-en-Peule, 20 km. south of Lille; Berwick

refused to serve under Vendôme and became a rival adviser to the Duc de Bourgogne.

5 *September. All three spent the day reconnoitring the enemy's dispositions and the night in argument. Vendôme wished to attack, Berwick thought otherwise, the prince wrote for the King's advice. The reply came to attack at once, 'even at the risk of the misfortunes inseparable from failure, which would be less dishonourable to yourself and the army than to be mere spectators at the capture of Lille.'*

8 *September. Chamillart sent to Flanders with orders to compel the prince to obey. When he arrived he was all for the battle, but after seeing the position for himself he agreed with Berwick and the army withdrew to Tournai.*

18 September. Chamillart returned to Versailles.

Louis XIV had been fighting wars in distant parts of Europe for more than forty years. The war had now come to the frontiers of France itself; even Paris might soon be in danger. He was old and tired, but was ready for one more battle to save Lille, Vauban's masterpiece in fortification, the capital of French Flanders, the second greatest city of France. When the full account of the defeat of Oudenarde reached him he was very near breaking-point.]

At the Court the consternation was extreme, almost verging on panic. Everyone lived in the expectation of a decisive battle; everyone was tempted to hope for one in the circumstances to which we had been reduced; it seemed almost treachery to wish otherwise. The successful junction of the two armies was regarded as a sure sign of victory. Every delay was a fresh strain. Since the courier despatched from Mons-en-Peule there had been no news. Everyone was in a state of anxiety; even the King himself asked the courtiers for news, and failed to comprehend why no couriers arrived. The princes and all the nobility and courtiers in their train were absent with the army in Flanders. At Versailles one was constantly aware of the danger to loved ones and friends, and the best established families felt insecure of the future. Forty-hour services were held in the churches. Mme la Duchesse de Bourgogne spent hours in the chapel when she was supposed to be in bed and asleep, and exhausted her ladies by her vigils. Following her example, wives with husbands in the army scarcely left the churches. Gambling and even conversation had entirely ceased. Fear showed on every face and in people's remarks to a shocking extent. The sound of a horse trotting set everyone running to no known purpose. Chamillart's apartment was so inundated with lackeys that they flowed out into the street; everyone wished to know the moment a courier arrived; and this terror lasted for nearly a month, until the uncertainty was over. Paris, being further removed from the source of news, was still more disturbed and the provinces increasingly so in proportion. The King had written to bid the bishops hold public prayers, in terms that conveyed a sense of danger; and you may imagine what alarm that caused. Flattery was none the less still present, in a thousand different guises; for instance, Mme d'O went about pitying that poor Prince

Eugene, whose reputation would be ruined by his foolhardy siege; enemy though he was she could not help grieving at the disgrace of so great a commander.

The cabal grew more vociferous than ever, swearing that victory was assured, and that the relief of Lille could not miscarry with M. de Vendôme in charge. I listened with wrathful indignation, for I could not forget Oudenarde and what had happened before and after. I saw all the delays occurring at the present time, the three couriers it had needed to shift him from behind the Bruges canal, the choice of the longest route with thirteen days march, by his own reckoning, to reach Lille, always provided that he met no obstacle, and taking no account of unexpected and necessary halts. He needed, so he afterwards declared, time to reflect on where and how to set about the relief. I saw so much precious time being wasted, so much time given to Prince Eugene to secure his approaches and press the siege, and to Marlborough for making and inspecting his dispositions, deciding from which side our attack would come and meeting us with every advantage on his side. I saw also ever more clearly the workings of the plot by M. de Vendôme and his cabal, which had first dawned on me when Mgr le Duc de Bourgogne was chosen to command that army. I never believed that M. de Vendôme had any intention of relieving Lille; I was morally certain that his plan was to make the prince fail in this vital enterprise, cast all the blame upon him, and thus bring him to complete and utter ruin.

One evening, waiting impatiently for the return of a courier from Mons-en-Peule, I was at Chamillart's house talking with five or six members of his family after supper, feeling deeply penetrated by that conviction and disgusted by the boasts of a coming victory and relief which I heard from all sides, although I stifled my angry protests. They had begun to prophesy the day, even the time of the battle, when I suddenly lost my temper, and interrupting Cany,[1] I offered to wager that there would be no battle and no relief, and that Lille would be taken. Picture a vast commotion among the few assembled there at my shocking suggestion, and the stream of questions as to my reasons. I was very careful not to say the truth; I answered frigidly that such was my opinion. Cany and his father swore that apart from Vendôme's eagerness and the desire of the entire army, explicit orders had been issued for the relief. They said that I was wasting my money, simply throwing it away, and they warned me that Cany had certain knowledge. I replied with apparent calm covering my boiling feelings that I believed all they told me but that it did not change my opinion and that I would stick to my wager like an Englishman. Finally they laughed, and Cany, thanking me for my present to him, we each took four pistoles out of our pockets and paid them into Chamillart's hand. I never saw anyone more astonished.

[1] Chamillart's son.

He led me to the far end of the room, where he said, 'In heaven's name! What makes you so certain? I give you my word as a man of honour that I have sent such positive orders to attack that they cannot be disobeyed.' I murmured something of lost time and the enemy's preparations, and the impossibility of always being able to obey orders and one's own wishes. Intimate though we were, I was prudent enough to say no more to a disciple of Vaudémont and his nieces, a man obsessed by Vendôme, and at the same time too loyal and too unintelligent to be willing to think for himself.

Nothing could have been more innocent than this wager and the manner in which it was laid, in a party of friends with whom I spent almost every evening. I had expressed no sentiments, except when alone with Chamillart, of whose friendship and discretion I was assured, but a very swift and distressing recoil taught me that I could scarcely have behaved with less prudence. On the very next morning the wager had become the talk of the entire Court; no one spoke of anything else. One cannot live at courts and avoid enemies. I had no position to be envied, but my powerful friends had caused me to be regarded as someone to be reckoned with. The Lorraines did not forgive me for certain incidents which I have described, and for many others too trivial to mention. M. du Maine disliked me because I had refused his most marked advances to me, and because of my sentiments regarding his rank, and Mme de Maintenon felt as he did. I had spoken with too much freedom before the battle of Oudenarde, and Vendôme's cabal had not forgotten it. They seized upon this wager to do me harm, and my silence may have given them an inkling of whom I should hold guilty for the coming loss of Lille. Be that as it may, on the following day there was an appalling commotion, and I was accused of criticizing everything, being thoroughly discontented, and rejoicing in defeats. These suggestions were brought deliberately to the King's notice, and he was artfully persuaded of the truth of them. That reputation for being too clever and knowing too much, which had served them well after my selection for Rome, was brought freshly to his remembrance, and after two months had elapsed I found that I had long been in absolute disgrace without ever having suspected it. All I could do then was to wait for the storm to pass and say nothing, for fear of worse befalling me.

Chamillart returned to Versailles from Flanders at the hour of the King's supper, on Tuesday, 18 September. The King worked with him from the time when he rose from table until his *coucher*, and was given a report of all that he had seen and of M. de Vendôme's certain hope of cutting the enemy's supply routes and thus compelling them to abandon the siege of Lille. King Louis stood in urgent need of such crumbs of hope and comfort, for however well he might guard his words and countenance, he keenly felt his growing inability to defend himself against his enemies. What I have related of Samuel Bernard, for whom he personally did the honours of the Marly gardens so as to extract a loan which the great banker was loath to grant, is sufficient proof of that. It was moreover much remarked at Fontainebleau that when a deputation from Paris came to harangue him on Bignon's taking the oath as provost of the merchants, just at the time when Lille was invested, he was not only gracious in his reply but used the words, 'gratitude to his good city', and in speaking his face had softened; gestures which in the entire course of his reign he had never before allowed himself. On the other hand, certain lapses of mind were shocking rather than edifying. At the time of the Duke of Berwick's junction with the grand army, he observed one evening in Mme de Maintenon's apartment that Mme la Duchesse de Bourgogne appeared deeply depressed and sad. He seemed surprised and asked the reason, and then tried to cheer her with his relief and satisfaction at learning that the armies were at last united. 'And the princes your grandsons?' she retorted sharply. 'I am anxious about them,' said he, 'but I expect that all will be well.' 'I also am anxious,' she replied, 'and that is why I am low and out of spirits.'

When the Court was experiencing those agonies of fear, which I have described, waiting every hour for news of a battle, the King made them doubly miserable by his daily excursions to shoot or hunt away from Versailles, for no one was allowed to hear fresh news until after his return. As for Monseigneur, he appeared exempt from all feeling, going off to dine at Meudon as usual, saying that he would hear the news on his return, and this at a time when hope of the relief of Lille kept everyone glued to the windows, watching for couriers to arrive. He was present when Chamillart announced that the fortress had been invested and read the despatch to the King. Half way through this reading Monseigneur made as if to go, but the King called him back to hear the rest, after which he departed without saying a word. As he left he happened to see Mme d'Espinay, whose children owned great estates in Flanders and who had intended to visit Lille. 'Well, Madame!' said he giggling. 'How do you propose going to Lille now?' Such remarks were truly offensive to those who had relatives at the war. Despite this want of interest, Vendôme's cabal succeeded in endowing him with all their views. At his *coucher* one evening he praised M. le Duc de Berry to the skies and did so repeatedly, yet never once did he mention Mgr le Duc de Bourgogne. His faith in those who ruled and monopolized him passed all bounds, as I shall have occasion to show in due course; thus he swallowed all the poison that they offered him and never again viewed his eldest son with favour. But in truth he had had little liking for him or for those who educated him, and Mgr le Duc de Bourgogne's excessive piety both repelled and embarrassed him. All his heart was given to the King of Spain, and M. le Duc de Berry amused him with his pleasures and debauches. Such feelings the cabal well knew how to exploit, for their paramount interest lay in alienating Monseigneur from his heir. They did not mean to contend with the son when his father ascended the throne.

After Chamillart's return they therefore spread it abroad that had Vendôme been free he would have attacked and defeated the enemy, forced them to abandon the siege, and saved France a dozen times over. Their repeated praise of him weighed down the scales against Mgr le Duc de Bourgogne. They revived the worst that was said of the latter after Oudenarde and denied earlier favourable reports which until then no one had contradicted. Others, though apparently less violent, took a different and far more poisonous line. They did not question his courage or say anything obviously disparaging, but they spoke of his religion, saying that the thought of so much blood spilt, so many men dying unconfessed, filled him with horror, and that he could not bring himself to give battle and bear the responsibility before God. For that reason, they said, he had sent the courier from Mons-en-Peule in an attempt to throw the onus on the King. They then fell to deploring some of his admittedly trivial diversions, and others that were unfitting. They exaggerated his lengthy sessions at table, and certain parties of battledore and shuttlecock, and turned to ridicule his killing of flies and wasps, his fruit in oil, his absent-minded way of crushing grape-pips, his theories on anatomy, engineering and other abstract sciences, but more especially his too long, too frequent sessions with Père Martineau his confessor.

Monseigneur was indeed completely turned against his son, and despite Mme la Duchesse de Bourgogne and even Mme de Maintenon, the King was already half-convinced. He let slip certain remarks to his bastards and valets that were only too much like what they said to him, and they were ever on the watch to prime him with some fresh dispraise. In public he more than once protested bitterly that he failed to understand why there was no attack, even on the entrenchments. The strange thing was that he addressed such remarks almost always to Vaudémont; if anyone else, even a prince of the blood, added his word the King immediately dropped the subject, often not answering. Thus the cabal triumphed; not only did they carry with them the masses of all conditions, the smart set and Society, but even sensible people were influenced, with the result that in an incredibly short space of time it became dangerous to praise Mgr le Duc de Bourgogne in the slightest degree, whilst those who extolled M. de Vendôme at his expense might be sure of pleasing the King and Monseigneur. Meanwhile the prince's supporters did nothing. M. de Beauvilliers was more timid than he need have been, and M. de Chevreuse, all for reason and moderation, simply grieved, admitting that my prediction had been only too accurate. They saw no remedy but to wait patiently for the return of the army, when many truths would appear. When I pressed them to act they shut my mouth, saying that no one, not even Mme de Maintenon herself, could bring any change. That argument being unanswerable, I said no more. I knew all that was happening there from Mme la Duchesse de Bourgogne, with whom I still communicated through Mme de Nogaret. What little private time the princess possessed was given up to weeping and letter-writing. Indeed, she was indefatigable, full of strength and wonderfully sensible. Mme de Maintenon was most deeply affected by her sufferings, and cut to the quick that in this matter, for the first time, other people had the ascendancy over the King.

In Flanders, whilst the army recovered its breath the generals continued to search for some means of relieving Lille. Vendôme, eager as ever with rash and ill-conceived plans, was for making a vast detour so as to take Marlborough in the rear, trick him into withdrawing troops from the siege, and then quickly turn to attack him. How, being so slow in action, could he have hoped to deceive that swift and vigilant commander? Berwick and the great majority of the generals were against that hopeless project. Already they had begun to perceive that had they, after so much time wasted, thrown reinforcements into Lille instead of toying with the idea of a battle, they might have snatched victory from the enemy's grasp and, what is more, made his retreat most perilous. To that conclusion they finally came, but by then it was too late.

Prince Eugene, commanding at the siege, did not conceal his satisfaction at having to deal with the Maréchal de Boufflers. He said that he had less to fear from a man so loaded with rewards and honours than from a younger general whose entire future might depend on his defence. He soon learned his mistake; but I fail to understand how he could forget the defence of Namur, for Boufflers, who received his dukedom on that occasion, was no less a man at Lille. Forethought, exactitude and vigilance were his greatest qualities. His courage was flawless. He gave orders when under fire as coolly as though he were at home; not even the worst mishaps could ruffle his composure. His never-failing kindness and courtesy made him loved by all. When he first arrived at Lille he took infinite trouble to ration the ammunition and provisions so as to give everyone his fair share of the bread, wine, meat, and other victuals. He even presided over the distributions and saw that special care was taken for the hospitals, which made the troops and the townspeople adore him. He saw to the training of the hotchpotch of regiments that formed the greater part of the garrison, most of them escapers and stragglers from Oudenarde or townsfolk, and he made soldiers out of them not inferior to the regular battalions. He wore himself out in that service and was everywhere to be seen observing and issuing orders, and continually exposed to danger. He was sometimes reproached for courting death, but he needed to see with his own eyes, give the example, and make sure that the duties were properly performed. It was almost beyond comprehension that a man of his age, exhausted by war, could have endured such hard tests to mind and body. On one occasion he received a blow on the head that knocked him over. He was carried back to his quarters, where the surgeons wished to bleed him. He would not, however, be bled, and insisted on returning. The common soldiers at that point surrounded his house, threatening him and shouting that they would quit their posts if he reappeared during the next twenty-four hours. He was thus obliged to capitulate in that siege of his quarters, and submit to resting and being bled. When he finally emerged such joy was never seen. How much does virtue and integrity magnify and illuminate a man's character at a time of crisis!

One would need a diary to tell of all the heroism and skill in the defence at that great siege. Much fighting and many fierce sorties seriously weakened the garrison and the powder began to run short. The Maréchal de Boufflers often managed to send out messengers, and various schemes were devised to supply his needs. The Chevalier de Luxembourg,[1] then only a brigadier-general but now a Marshal of France, was charged with one attempt. With great daring he rode out from Douai and succeeded in entering the town of Lille on the night of 21 September with two thousand dragoons, each with a fusil instead of a carbine and sixty pounds weight of gunpowder behind him on the crupper. There were remarkably few casualties. The chevalier was widely admired for his brilliant feat, and was promoted to lieutenant-general on the field. In the end the fortress was captured despite all Vendôme's promises to bring relief. By 20 October the enemy had opened three breaches, drained the moat, and driven a gallery to the foot of one breach. There was no more possibility of holding out. The powder and ammunition were gone, the rations had been reduced to a bare minimum, there was almost no meat. The Maréchal de Boufflers with the consent of all the gallant defenders was obliged to sound for a parley. All that he asked was freely granted,[2] in particular the removal of the sick and wounded to other French fortresses; the safe-conduct to Douai of the eighteen hundred horses brought in by the Chevalier de Luxembourg; the safeguarding of the rights and privileges of the inhabitants of the town of Lille, and four days truce to allow M. de Boufflers to retire into the citadel. This capitulation was signed on 23 October, after two months of trench warfare, fighting every step of the way.

One most noteworthy condition made by the Maréchal de Boufflers was that the document should be sent to Mgr le Duc de Bourgogne for

---

[1] The Maréchal de Luxembourg's fourth son, made a marshal in 1734. His troops wore green branches in their helmets like the Allies, and so concealed their identity. The exploit was regarded throughout Europe as a brilliant feat of arms, and considerably annoyed Marlborough, although he pretended to think little of it.

[2] Eugene made him fix his own terms, 'Whatever you think fitting I shall agree to.'

safe-custody, if he approved it. If he did not it was to be treated as null and void. I say deliberately to Mgr le Duc de Bourgogne. Boufflers, when he embarked on his mission, obtained the King's formal permission to accept no orders from M. de Vendôme and in no way to be subordinate to him; in every circumstance he was answerable to Mgr le Duc de Bourgogne alone. Coëtquen was charged to present the capitulation to the prince at his camp near Tournai. He found him playing at battledore and shuttlecock, already aware of the sad news. It is true that the game was not interrupted, and that whilst they were finishing Coëtquen was free to speak to whom he pleased. The manner of his reception was taken much amiss, and the army with good reason was deeply shocked, which provided the cabal with fresh ammunition to use against the prince.[1]

Boufflers retired into the citadel on 26 October, having offered leave of absence to any soldier who did not wish to accompany him. Not a man accepted. On 9 November the enemy began to batter the walls with artillery and to bore into the citadel with saps. The Maréchal was slightly wounded by a bursting grenade; that, however, did not for a moment deter him, but by then everything was lacking; only twenty thousand pounds weight of powder remained and even scantier provisions. Already in the town and the citadel they had eaten eight hundred horses, and Boufflers had had them served at his own table as soon as the others were reduced to living on them. He still managed somehow to send out news, until the King dispatched orders to him in his own hand, bidding him surrender. This he did on 9 December and was treated in the most generous manner imaginable. Prince Eugene asked his leave to visit him on the day before the garrison marched out, and on the day itself the Maréchal de Boufflers, instead of riding at the head of his troops, stood beside the prince to receive the salutes of the French officers. After the march-out Prince Eugene placed him and the Chevalier de Luxembourg in his own coach on the seats of honour and insisted on taking a front seat himself. He gave his hand and a word of welcome to every one of Boufflers's officers. After dining with them he lent his own coach and many others to take them to Douai with a very large escort of cavalry, commanded (and I think this was deliberate) by the Prince d'Auverne,[2] who had orders to obey the marshal in everything and to treat him in every way as though he were Eugene himself.

I had reckoned on being able to go to La Ferté soon after the Court returned from Fontainebleau, so as to have a little of the fine weather there, but many of my important friends were anxious to dissuade me because of the great events expected in Flanders. I had been sure that

---

[1] At this point Saint-Simon does not attempt to defend him.

[2] François Egon de La Tour, Boufflers's grandson, who had deserted to the Allies in 1702, saying that the King did not pay him enough to live on. He was a major-general in the Dutch army.

nothing at all would happen and that Lille would not be relieved. More-over, I was beginning to feel defeated by the effrontery and successes of the cabal against Mgr le Duc de Bourgogne, and was longing to be away from the Court. M. de Beauvilliers, having exhausted all his arguments, appealed to me to stay a few days longer for love of the prince. He thus disarmed my impatience, and I promised to remain until he gave me per-mission to leave, although I begged him not to ask too much of my remaining strength in this wicked assault, which no one seemed able to oppose. He did so promise, and promised at the same time to tell Mgr le Duc de Bourgogne of the violence I did to my feelings for his sake. The delay did me no good, nor did it avail those who had asked for it. I was an abomination to all that cabal. They had managed to gag those who were most aware of their evil plots. Although I say it, I was the only person with sufficient courage to state my opinion, and liberate the truth. They feared me for the former, and hated me all the more for the latter because they had tamed everyone else. Not only did they spread the news of my unfortunate wager, but they had recourse to a most pernicious lie, of which they were unashamed because they had long lost sight of all truth. They began to spread it abroad that I had fallen more hardly upon Mgr le Duc de Bourgogne than anyone. Society, aware of my extreme eager-ness in his defence, merely laughed. I also felt contempt for such a mani-fest humbug, but in the end it became too much for my feelings and my longing for the calmer, fresher air of my home, and M. de Beauvilliers allowed me to go.

I had, however, not long been at La Ferté before receiving a letter from the Bishop of Chartres, dated from Saint-Cyr, warning me of malicious tales told to the King and Mme de Maintenon, and saying that some had stuck. I wrote back immediately by express messenger asking for details and telling him what I knew of the vile slanders concerning Lille and my wager. Nothing of this surprised me, but without fuller information I could not parry the blows with any certainty, and I worried because Monsieur de Chartres had returned to Chartres when my messenger reached Saint-Cyr, and afterwards he refused to say more. This affair extinguished me for more than a year, and you shall see in due course how I recovered myself. I soon returned to Versailles for I wished to be at the Court for M. le Duc d'Orléans's arrival, and especially for that of Mgr le Duc de Bourgogne.

The former appeared on 6 December and received the welcome which his glorious and difficult campaign fully deserved, although that did nothing to improve his relations with Mme des Ursins and Mme de Maintenon.

Mme la Duchesse de Bourgogne was deeply agitated as to Mgr le Duc de Bourgogne's probable reception, and the best method of seeing and instructing him before he encountered the King. I had written urging him to time his journey so as to arrive an hour or so after midnight and thus be free to go straight to her and avoid meeting anyone else. They might have had the remainder of the night together; he could have spent the morning seeing M. de Beauvilliers and perhaps Mme de Maintenon, with the added advantage of greeting the King and Monseigneur before anyone else entered their rooms, and without witnesses, save for a few valets. My advice was never given to him, or perhaps not accepted. The prince arrived at seven in the evening just after Monseigneur left for the theatre, which Mme la Duchesse de Bourgogne did not attend since she was expecting him. I do not know what made him choose to alight in the cour des princes instead of in the grand cour; but I happened to be calling on Mme de Roucy at that precise moment and we saw him from her window which overlooked that courtyard. I left her at once, and as I reached the top of the great staircase at the end of the gallery I saw him coming up between the Dukes of Beauvilliers and La Rocheguyon, who had gone to meet him at the door of his coach. Mgr le Duc de Bourgogne looked prosperous, gay, and smiling, and was chattering to them both. I made my bow at the top of the stairs. He did me the honour to embrace me, and in a manner that showed me he knew everything, and was not merely paying me the courtesy due to a duke and peer. Thereafter he talked only to me for the rest of the way, and managed to whisper that he was aware of how I had spoken and acted on his behalf. He was formally welcomed by a group of courtiers headed by the Duc de La Rochefoucauld and went with them into the great chamber of the guard instead of going to Mme de Maintenon's room by way of her daytime ante-room and the back offices, which would have been by far more direct. He walked on past the head of the grand staircase and entered her apartment by the front door.

As it happened, it was the day when Pontchartrain worked there with the King, so that he was present with them the entire time, and that very evening he gave me a description of a most momentous encounter, of which he was in fact the sole witness, because Mme la Duchesse de Bourgogne was not there for all of it, but came and went continually. To understand how this could be you must endure the tedium of some technicalities. The apartment of Mme de Maintenon was on one floor and opened upon the guardroom of the King's bodyguard. The ante-chamber was not unlike a long corridor, set crosswise, leading into another narrow ante-room of similar shape, where the captain of the guard waited. Beyond it was another large and very long room. Between the door by which one entered and the fireplace was the King's armchair with its back to the wall, a table in front, and a folding stool for the minister who worked with him. On the other side of the fireplace was an alcove hung with crimson damask, containing an armchair for Mme de Maintenon, a table in front of it and, further back, a bed in the recess. Opposite the foot of the bed was another door and five rising steps. Then came a very large drawing-room leading to the day-rooms of Mgr le Duc de Bourgogne. The first of his ante-rooms, which opened on the right into the rest of his apartment and on the left into Mme de Maintenon's great drawing-room, led down by five steps (as it does also today)[1] into the marble drawing-room that runs parallel with the landing of the grand staircase at the end of the upper and lower galleries, known respectively as Mme la Duchesse d'Orléans's, and the princes' galleries.

It was Mme la Duchesse de Bourgogne's custom to play games with the ladies who possessed that particular entrée in Mme de Maintenon's great drawing-room. She ran here, there and everywhere and as often as she pleased into Mme de Maintenon's bedroom, where the latter sat with the King. Mme de Maintenon's servants used to bring her a tray with some broth and another dish before the hour of the King's supper. She ate it, waited on by her women and a footman, still in the King's presence, while he continued to work with the minister. When she had finished they cleared her table and her ladies undressed her with great speed and put her into bed. When the King's supper was announced, he went for a moment into a closet, said a word to Mme de Maintenon, and then rang a handbell that sounded in the large drawing-room. At that point Monseigneur, if he happened to be there, Mme la Duchesse de Bourgogne, M. le Duc de Berry, and her ladies, entered Mme de Maintenon's room in procession, passed through almost to the end of it in front of the King, who then went to his supper followed by Mme la Duchesse de Bourgogne and the ladies of her household. Having said so much by way of explanation, let us return to the King's reception of Mgr le Duc de Bourgogne, all the details of which Pontchartrain carefully observed and recounted to me tête-à-tête, word for word as I relate them now, only half an hour after he had returned to his lodging.

When the bustle was heard that precedes important arrivals the King was seen to change countenance several times. Mme la Duchesse de Bourgogne seemed to be trembling, and flitted about the room trying to conceal her agitation by wondering which door the prince would use for his entry. Mme de Maintenon appeared to be in a trance. Suddenly the doors were flung wide open, and the young prince advanced towards the King who, instantly becoming more than master of himself, moved two paces to meet him, and embraced him with a sufficient show of tenderness, inquiring about his journey. He then indicated the princess and said smiling, 'Have you no greeting for her?' Mgr le Duc de Bourgogne turned and looked for a moment in her direction, answering the King respectfully but as though not daring to divert his gaze or move from his position. He then greeted Mme de Maintenon, who did very handsomely by him. Still standing, they spoke for a quarter of an hour of journeys, roads, and

[1] Alterations were made in that part of the château during the reign of Louis XV.

lodgings, after which the King dismissed him, saying that it would not be right to keep him longer from the joy of Mme la Duchesse de Bourgogne's society, and adding that there would be plenty of time for other meetings. The prince made a bow to the King, another to Mme de Maintenon, passed along the line of those few ladies who had made so bold as to advance as far into the room as the foot of the five steps, went up into the large drawing-room to embrace Mme la Duchesse de Bourgogne, greeted, that is to say kissed, the ladies present and after a few moments' conversation went alone with his wife into their apartments.

I remarked to M. de Beauvilliers with my customary freedom that I thought Mgr le Duc de Bourgogne appeared unsuitably cheerful after his disastrous campaign. He could not but agree, and by the time I left had decided to offer a warning. Indeed, the entire Court was blaming him for his ill-timed jollity. On the Tuesday and Wednesday the King was fully occupied working with his ministers, but on the Thursday, which was often a holiday for him, he was closeted with Mgr le Duc de Bourgogne for three hours in Mme de Maintenon's room. I had feared lest his piety should restrain him on the subject of M. de Vendôme, but I learned later that fortified by his wife he had spoken out and not spared him. A different, less religious man might have been more forceful, but at least he did say all, and better than could have been expected, considering who was speaking and who listening. In conclusion he had appealed urgently to be given an army to command in the next campaign, and had received from the King a firm promise to be given one.

M. de Vendôme arrived on the morning of Saturday, 15th, and made his bow as the King went from his study to dine. King Louis embraced him with such a glad look that the cabal found cause for rejoicing. He monopolized the conversation whilst the King was at table, but it was nothing but small talk, the King saying that he would grant him an audience in Mme de Maintenon's room on the following day. From thence he went to pay his court to Monseigneur, who warmly welcomed him and kept him a long time talking of nothing, from which Vendôme tried to draw some advantage by inviting Monseigneur to visit him at Anet. To his huge surprise, however, he received a vague response, which none the less made it perfectly apparent that Monseigneur had no intention of visiting him ever. Vendôme was visibly embarrassed and hurriedly left. I happened to meet him at the end of the gallery in the new wing as I was leaving M. de Beauvilliers's lodging. He was turning to go up the stairway in the centre of that gallery and was alone, without valets or torchbearers, with only Alberoni at his side and behind him a man whom I did not know. I saw him by the light of my own torches. We greeted one another civilly enough, for I had no personal acquaintance with him. He seemed to me to look vexed and was on his way to call on M. du Maine, his chief support and adviser. Next day he saw the King for less than an hour in Mme de Maintenon's room. After a week at Versailles and Meudon he departed for Anet, having never set foot in Mme la Duchesse de Bourgogne's apartments, which was no novelty for him; the mixture of grandeur and informality which he had affected for so long set him in his own eyes above such elementary courtesies. His secretary Alberoni, with unexampled impudence, made his first appearance as a courtier at the King's mass. Even before their departure Vendôme must have become aware of a decline in favour, for he stooped to asking everyone to visit him, whereas in times past he had made it a favour, inviting only the great and the rich, and not deigning to notice ordinary mortals. He certainly had cause to measure his own diminished stature, for many people sent excuses, others failed to honour their engagement, and all began to consider the distance a drawback—a journey of fifteen leagues, which in earlier years had seemed no more tiring than going to Marly. He remained at Anet until the first Marly excursion, and arrived there on the first day. He continued in that way between Marly and Meudon, never going to Versailles, until a change occurred of which I shall soon have occasion to speak.

Meanwhile the King had sent a courier to the Maréchal de Boufflers, pressing him to return. He reappeared on Sunday, 16 December, the day after M. de Vendôme, that hero trumped-up by favour and intrigue. Boufflers, on the other hand, was made a hero against his will, by general acclaim of the French nation and of their enemies. No soldier ever deserved a triumph more, nor tried with more modesty to escape one. His wife drove out early in the morning to meet him some leagues from Paris, and took him quietly home to dine with her before anyone else knew of his return. From thence they drove by night to Versailles, went straight to their apartment, and bolted the doors. The Maréchal de Boufflers sent forthwith to the Duc d'Harcourt, in residence as captain of the bodyguard, asking him to inform the King of his arrival, and the King, who had just terminated his interview with M. de Vendôme, sent word for him to come immediately to Mme de Maintenon's room. When those doors opened to admit him, he saw the King standing on the threshold with arms outstretched to embrace him, which he did three or four times over, thanking him in the most gratifying way imaginable and overwhelming him with praise. After those first moments they advanced further into the room, the doors were closed, and Mme de Maintenon, imitating the King, stepped forward to give him her congratulations.

King Louis then turned to Boufflers, saying that having deserved so well of his King and his country he might name his own reward; to which Boufflers replied that such marks of favour recompensed him beyond anything that he deserved or desired. After some argument, the King insisting that he should choose and Boufflers modestly declining, King Louis finally remarked, 'Very well! Monsieur le Maréchal, let me make you a suggestion, I will add something further if you so desire. Here and now, I create you a peer of France, present you with the reversion of the governorship of Flanders for the benefit of your son,[1] and for your own, the entrées of a first gentleman of the bedchamber.' At that time Boufflers's son was only eleven or twelve years old. The Maréchal dropped upon his knees, quite overwhelmed by a reward that went far beyond his best hopes. He also received, on his son's behalf, the reversion of the emoluments of the governorship of Lille. In its entirety, the income amounted to more than a hundred thousand livres. Of the three quite unparalleled favours the one which most pleased the maréchal was the first, for the door to new peerages had long been closed.

A few days after Mgr le Duc de Bourgogne's return, Cheverny who was an exceptionally truthful man told me something which I cannot help recording, although it almost makes me blush to do so. He said that when he and the prince were talking confidentially about the opinions expressed on the campaign, Mgr le Duc de Bourgogne had stated that he knew how often and how ardently I had spoken in his defence, and how M. le Prince de Conti also had upheld him. He had added that with the support of two such men, one did not mind so much about the rest. I was overcome to be set beside a man so far superior to me in every way; and very happy that M. de Beauvilliers had kept me to my promise when I wished to go to La Ferté.

Chamillart, who was most deeply distressed by the fall of Lille and very jealous for the welfare of the State and the personal glory of King Louis, conceived a plan for the immediate retaking of that fortress, after Eugene and Marlborough's departure from Holland and the separation of their two armies. The project was admirably reasoned and prepared; he had made the final arrangements on his last visit to Flanders, and his great desire was that the King should march with his troops to encourage them and win for himself alone the honours of a victory. Money was hard to find; the siege would be costly; Chamillart therefore decided that the train of coaches should be severely limited, and, above all, that the ladies should all be left behind, for the expense and difficulties of taking them to the frontier would otherwise be very great. In order to carry this point it was essential to hide the plan completely from Mme de Maintenon, and obtain the King's consent to keeping it secret until the last moment. Chamlay,[2] when Chamillart consulted him, warned him that he was playing with fire, and that Mme de Maintenon would never forgive him for it. He reminded him that when Louvois had made a similar plan for Mons and wished to exclude the ladies he had been utterly ruined, although far

---

[1] Boufflers was governor of (French) Flanders; this meant that his son would inherit without payment. Governorships reverted to the King and were presented elsewhere or bought back by the heir.

[2] The Marquis de Chamlay; 'had an expert knowledge of Flanders down to the smallest brooks and hamlets.'

more firmly established than ever Chamillart was. He continued that
Chamillart had witnessed that disgrace with his own eyes, and had seen
how soon it had followed on the capture of Mons. He could not have forgotten, said Chamlay, that the King himself had informed him that had
not Louvois suddenly died on the day that he did he would have been
arrested on the following. And that was true, for Chamillart had told me
so, saying that he had heard it from the King's own lips. Chamillart fully
realized the danger; but he was a brave man who loved his country and
loved the King, I may truly say, like a mistress. To him they were what
counted; his own interests were as nothing. He proceeded. When all was
ready he disclosed his plan to the King, who was delighted with it.
Boufflers was informed at once and sent back to Flanders on the pretext of
issuing orders for the winter, but in fact to make all arrangements for the
King's arrival. King Louis, however, although enraptured by the project,
was not used to hiding things from Mme de Maintenon, and he may also
have found it tiresome to work with Chamillart at unaccustomed hours in
his study. Before long he had produced urgent reasons for telling Mme
de Maintenon and persuading her with unanswerable arguments of the
need to remain at Versailles with Mme la Duchesse de Bourgogne and all
the ladies. He accordingly did so, and she had the tact and strength of will
to conceal her displeasure. She admired the plan, appeared enchanted,
entered into the details, spoke to Chamillart, praised his zeal, his industry,
his labours, above all his having conceived that brilliant exploit and made
it possible. Boufflers left on 26 December, and immediately afterwards
Berwick had a long audience of the King in Mme de Maintenon's room.
The regiments of the French and Swiss guards received their orders on
that same day and were commanded to be in readiness to march on 1
February. You shall see in the early part of the following year what became of that mighty plan and all the preparations for it.

CHAPTER XIX

1709

Plan to recapture Lille abandoned – Extreme Calamity of the great Frost – Vendôme barred from the Service – La Chastre has a Seizure – Death of Père de La Chaise – Père Tellier appointed Confessor – He makes advances to me – Death of Mme d'Heudicourt – Death of Mme de Soubise – Death of Mme de Vivonne – Remarkable agreement between the Duc de Chevreuse and myself – The Terrible Winter – Wicked Speculation in Wheat – Bankruptcy of Samuel Bernard – Death of M. le Prince de Conti – Digression on familiar Names – Disgrace of Vendôme – Death of Saumery; Character of his Son – Assignment of the armies – Chamillart is threatened – The King holds a War-council – Riots in Paris – Placards against the King – The Silver is taken to the Mint – The Armies assemble – Disgrace of Chamillart – Characters of Voysin and his Wife – The Scene at L'Etang – I intend to retire from the Court – Withdrawal of French Troops from Spain – Trouble for M. le Duc d'Orléans – More Riots in Paris – Boufflers offers to assist Villars – Battle of Malplaquet – Humiliation and disgrace of the Maréchal de Boufflers – Death of Godet, Bishop of Chartres – Character of La Chétardie – Military Destruction of Port-Royal-des-Champs – I seek an audience with the King – I propose to separate M. le Duc d'Orléans from his Mistress – Maréchal obtains an audience for me

WHILST Boufflers wore himself out in body and mind with secret preparations for the recapture of Lille, Mme de Maintenon did everything possible to frustrate his efforts. At a first glance the project had chilled her blood; later reflection had only increased her indignation, fears, and determination to put an end to it. To separate her from the King during a lengthy siege; to let him owe the glory of victory to a minister against whom (such was the King's partiality) she had not hitherto prevailed —a minister, moreover, whom she herself had sponsored, yet who had dared to ally his son with those whom she regarded as her enemies, and who without her sanction had refloated Desmaretz and overcome the King's extreme repugnance to making him controller-general of finances —any one of those offences was enough to ruin Chamillart in her eyes, but his conduct in regard to Mgr le Duc de Bourgogne and Vendôme, and this project of leaving her behind during a siege of Lille were so abominable to her that she resolved there and then to destroy him. Dealing with the worst thing first, and seizing every opportunity with enormous skill, she managed to make the plan for Lille appear less attractive to the King, then more difficult, and finally altogether too hazardous and costly. It was accordingly abandoned, and Boufflers received orders to stop everything and send back all the officers who had been made to return to Flanders. Mme de Maintenon was fortunate in the weather, for a sudden spell of bitter cold gripped the entire country at Twelfthnight and for two months was beyond living memory. In four days the Seine and every other river was frozen and, what no one had ever before seen, the sea froze hard enough to bear transport all along the coasts. Scientific observers maintained that it was as cold as in the latitudes north of Sweden and Denmark. The law-courts were closed for a longish period. What brought final disaster and a year of famine in every form of produce was that it thawed completely for seven or eight days and then re-froze as suddenly and as bitterly as before. The second bout was not so long as the first, but even the fruit-trees, and many other equally hardy varieties, as well as all the crops remained frozen. Mme de Maintenon made the most of this terrible weather, which would undoubtedly have made any siege most difficult. She added thereto every other argument that she could think of and thus succeeded in what she believed to be the most vital issue of her life, having gained merit by seeming to approve at first and finally objecting unwillingly and only for the best of reasons. Chamillart was deeply disappointed, but not much surprised. Once the secret was out and Mme de Maintenon informed, his hopes had been exceedingly dim. It was an interlude that made him thereafter dread the realization of all Chamlay's personal warnings.

Meanwhile M. de Vendôme continued to receive his pay as a serving general in command, and drew rations and billeting allowances for a staff of one hundred even although he lived at Anet and joined all the excursions to Marly and Meudon. It really began to seem as though he would serve in the next campaign; no one dared to believe otherwise and the cabal were greatly heartened. That little triumph they did not enjoy for long. M. de Vendôme came to Versailles for the ceremony of the Order at Candlemas. He was then informed that his services would not be required and that his pay would cease. It was an appalling affront; he was cut to the quick, but he manfully swallowed the pill because he feared still worse consequences which he knew were fully deserved. That was why for the first time in his life he displayed patience; making no mystery, not explaining whether or not it had been his fault, whether he were glad or sorry, simply behaving as though the news concerned a stranger, and in no way altering his behaviour, except in words, his bragging being moderated as out of season. He sold his stables.

An accident occurred to La Chastre in the theatre at Versailles on Thursday, 17 January, and brought to light other similar happenings. He was a man of quality and vastly good-looking—a fact which he allowed no one to forget—honourable and exceedingly courageous, moving in the best society, and all his life amorous and gallant. They used to call him *Le Beau Berger* and readily made fun of him. He rose to be a lieutenant-general, but had no intelligence and no capability for war or anything else. By temperament he was impulsive, and gradually this increased, leading to most distressing scenes. On the evening in question, in the middle of the play, he suddenly fell to thinking that he saw enemies on every side, drew his sword, and began to flourish it threateningly at the actors and the audience. La Vrillière, who was sitting near him, clutched him round the body saying that he himself felt ill and asking to be taken out. By that ruse he managed to get him out of the theatre, still trying to hurl himself against the enemy. It created a fearful uproar in the presence of Monseigneur and the entire Court. We afterwards learned that there had been several other occurrences. One of the earliest was in the house of M. le Prince de Conti, when he was in Paris recovering from an attack of gout. He was lying on a couch near, but some way back from the fire, and could not put foot to the ground. It so happened that La Chastre was left alone with him. He had a similar seizure and again saw enemies everywhere and wished to charge at them; then suddenly he let out a wild cry and sword in hand began to attack the chairs and screens. M. le Prince de Conti, who expected anything but that, was completely astounded and tried to reason with him, but he, shouting, 'There they go! To me! This way!' and other such cries, continued to stab and slash. M. le Prince de Conti, in absolute terror, and too far from the fireplace to ring or to arm himself with the poker and tongs, expected every minute to be mistaken for an enemy and swiftly dispatched; according to him no man ever had a worse quarter of an hour. A servant eventually appeared and managed to calm La Chastre, who came to his senses and left the room. M. le Prince de Conti swore the man to secrecy and loyally kept silence himself, but he charged him never on any account to leave him again alone with La Chastre. On the following day he asked the Duc d'Humières to call on him and as a close relative told him of the incident, promising secrecy, and asking him to warn Mme de La Chastre and to see whether between them they might take some action. There were subsequently many other such scenes in which he appeared equally wild, violent, and dangerous. People avoided his company, but he managed to keep afloat and was never removed from Society or the Court. You shall see in due course what became of him.[1]

The Court at this time witnessed the replacement of a minister, whose long service wore him down to the very marrow of his bones, but did not less please the King on that account. Père de La Chaise died on 20 January, at the Father-house of the Jesuits, in the Rue Sainte-Antoine.

---

[1] Saint-Simon never does say what happened to him.

He was the great-nephew of the famous Père Coton,[1] and nephew of the Père d'Aix,[2] who made a Jesuit of him. He distinguished himself in that society in the various teaching grades and afterwards became rector of Grenoble and Lyons; later he was made provincial of that district. He was a man of quality, and his father, who made a good marriage and acquitted himself well in the service, might have been accounted rich among his neighbours in Forez had he not had a dozen children. One of these, being very expert in the matter of hounds, horses, and hunting, for many years held the post of master of horse to that Archbishop of Lyons who was so much impassioned with hunting, and brother and uncle of the two Maréchaux de Villeroy, respectively.

Père de La Chaise and his brother were both at Lyons pursuing their various callings when, in 1674, the former succeeded Père Ferrier as the King's confessor. He thus held office for more than thirty-two years. The festival of Easter more than once caused him to be politically indisposed[3] in the days of the King's love for Mme de Montespan, and on one occasion he sent Père Dechamps in his place, who with enormous courage refused to give absolution. Père de La Chaise had not so much spirit, but he was of good character, just, upright, sensible, gentle and tolerant; a firm opponent of spies, violence, and scandal. Both he and his brother retained openly a sense of gratitude, almost of deference towards the Villeroys; but he was no one's man although much attached to his family and although it pleased him to be of noble birth and to promote their interests to the best of his ability.[4] In promotions to the episcopy he took immense pains, especially for the greater dioceses, and was content when he received full praise for them; on the other hand, when he made mistakes he readily acknowledged them and endeavoured to repair any harm which he might have caused. Withal he was a good man and a good priest, a loyal Jesuit also, but neither fanatical nor servile, for whilst he outwardly appeared one with them he knew them better than he cared to admit. Thus he never wished Port-Royal-des-Champs to be destroyed, nor acted in any way against Cardinal de Noailles, notwithstanding that the latter had achieved everything without his aid. In the same way he supported the Archbishop of Cambrai as long as it was safe to do so. He used to keep Père Quesnel's New Testament[5] on his table, the book that caused so much trouble later, and when visitors expressed surprise because of the author's reputation he would say that he loved good sound doctrine

[1] A French Jesuit, Henri IV's confessor until 1617, when he was disgraced. He is said to have made the Béarn peasantry change '*Jarnidieu!*' ('*Je ne renie Dieu—I deny God*'), their local oath, to '*Jarnicoton!*'

[2] A famous astronomer and mathematician.

[3] That incident occurred in 1675. Père de La Chaise was often stricken by such convenient indispositions, when the King despite many exhortations refused to give up Mme de Montespan.

[4] Such as obtaining invitations to Marly for his niece.

[5] *Réflexions Morales sur le Nouveau Testament.*

wherever he encountered it, and that he knew no more excellent book. As regards Mme de Maintenon, he was completely detached from her, in fact had no dealings with her, and she disliked him as much for that reason as for having opposed the proclamation of her marriage.[1] Yet she never openly took offence for she knew his high place in the King's regard.

When he reached the age of 80 with mind and body still in good order. Père de La Chaise longed to retire and made several vain attempts to do so. A general deterioration soon afterwards obliged him to renew his appeals; the Jesuits themselves, who had observed it sooner than he and feared for his shrinking reputation, urged him to make way for a younger man with the charm and zeal of a newcomer. Père de La Chaise did truly long for rest and constantly besought the King to grant it him, but all without effect; he was compelled to bear his yoke to the bitter end. Infirmity and decrepitude then bore him down, but they availed him nothing. Legs bowed, memory gone, judgment faulty, mind befuddled, all of them dreadful handicaps in a confessor, the King thought of no account. Until the very end he had the cadaver brought into his presence and despatched routine business with its assistance. At last, two days after the King's return to Versailles, he grew considerably weaker, and received the sacraments, but managed to summon even more courage than the strength required to write the King a long letter in his own hand, to which he swiftly received an affectionate reply in the King's writing. Thereafter he gave himself to God alone. Père Tellier his provincial and Père Daniel the superior of his professed house asked whether he had done what his conscience required of him, and whether he had borne in mind the honour and welfare of the Society. He replied that his mind was at rest as to the first, and they would soon find, as to the second, that he had nothing with which to reproach himself. Very shortly afterwards he died in perfect peace at five o'clock in the morning.

His two superiors brought to the King at the end of his *lever* the keys of Père de La Chaise's office, where he kept many memoirs and private papers. The King received them publicly, as befits a monarch well used to such losses, praised Père de La Chaise with particular emphasis on his kindness, and then, smiling on the two fathers, he added out loud for the benefit of the courtiers, 'He was so kind that I sometimes scolded him for it, but he always said, "It is not I who am kind, but you who are so hard." ' It is the absolute truth that the fathers and every one of his hearers were so taken aback by this remark that they lowered their eyes. The news spread in all directions, but no one blamed Père de La Chaise, who had warded off many blows in his time and suppressed many spiteful tricks and anonymous letters against people of all conditions, often giving assistance, and harming nothing except his own health. Everyone realized that his death

[1] To the King.

would mean a loss, but not the terrible, universal catastrophe that it proved to be on account of the villainy of his successor.

Maréchal, the King's first surgeon, an honourable and upright man of whom I have more than once spoken and who possessed the King's ear, related a most significant incident to Mme de Saint-Simon and myself that should not go unrecorded. He told us that, in the privacy of his study the King, whilst lamenting the death of Père de La Chaise and praising his loyalty, had mentioned a sure proof of his personal devotion. Some years back Père de La Chaise had spoken of feeling his age and of believing that the King might have to replace him sooner than he expected. His love, he had continued, drove him to ask it as a favour that the choice might fall on one of the Society. He knew that the Jesuits did not deserve all that had been said and written against them, but he none the less knew them very well and his devotion to the King's person and the preservation of his life forced him to entreat that boon most urgently. The Society, he added, was very large and contained men of widely different intellects and natures whose actions were unaccountable; if such men were driven to desperation[1] the King might incur a risk against which even he could give no guarantee, for a mortal blow was swiftly delivered and was not without precedent. Maréchal grew pale at the very thought but tried his best to conceal his dismay. It was for that reason only that Henri IV had recalled the Jesuits and loaded them with wealth. Louis XIV was not more valiant, for he was careful to remember Père de La Chaise's warning and when the time came averted all danger from the Jesuits by choosing a confessor from among their number. He enjoyed his life and liked to live in peace, and he therefore ordered the Dukes of Chevreuse and Beauvilliers to go to Paris and discover with all secrecy a Jesuit suitable for that appointment. Père Tellier, provincial of Paris, gained the entire approval of both dukes, and on their advice the King chose him. The deliberations over the selection continued for a month after Père de La Chaise's death on 20 January, and on 21 February Père Tellier was officially appointed. Like his predecessor he was also made the confessor of Monseigneur, a very severe hindrance to a prince of his advanced age.

Père Tellier was quite unknown to the King, except as a name on a list drawn up by Père de La Chaise, of four or five Jesuits suitable to succeed him. He had served in every grade of the Society, as teacher, theologian, rector, and provincial. He had been charged with the task of defending the cult of Confucius and the Chinese ceremonies,[2] and wrote a book that threatened to bring condign punishment upon himself and his family; but thanks to intrigues and his reputation in Rome it was merely

---

[1] Because of losing the King's confessional.

[2] In China the Jesuits had shown extraordinary tolerance by allowing their converts to continue for the time being to practise ancestor-worship in combination with Christianity.

placed on the index. It is really surprising that with such a blemish he should have become the King's confessor. He was equally ardent for Molinism,[1] and the overthrow of every other school, desiring only that the dogma of his Society should triumph over the ruin of all that went contrary to it, and that had been learned and taught in our Church from times immemorial. Brought up with those principles, admitted to all the inner secrets of the Society because of his brilliant intelligence, he had spent his entire time hitherto in studying such questions and forming plans to advance that cause. His sole ambition was to succeed, and in his firm opinion that aim justified any means. By nature he was hard, obdurate, ceaselessly studying, devoid of all other interests, averse to all leisure, all forms of society, all diversions, incapable of taking pleasure in his colleagues, and caring for none but those who shared his all-absorbing passion for the Jesuit cause. On that subject all moderation or indifference was anathema to him; he tolerated it only of necessity or because it served his ultimate purpose; forbearance for any other reason he regarded as shameful weakness or simply criminal. He lived austerely by habit and by preference. His only love was for steady, uninterrupted work, and in exacting the like from others he was without consideration, not understanding that one must show some regard. His head and his health were like iron; his conduct was similar; indeed, his whole nature was cruel and barbarous.

Moulded in the maxims and principles of the Society, in so far, that is, as the hardness of his nature would allow, he was basically false and deceitful, concealing his intentions beneath innumerable tortuosities, demanding all when he dared to be frank and intimidating, giving nothing away, repudiating firm promises when he no longer needed to keep them, and ruthlessly harrying those to whom they had been made. He was a man of wrath, whose aim was no less than destruction, and who after he rose to power entirely ceased to dissemble. Once in office he became inaccessible even to other Jesuits, except to the four or five who were like himself, and even they approached him in fear, not daring to go against him unless long reflection had convinced them that his proposals were contrary to their prime objective, the absolute rule of the Society and the complete overthrow not only of its enemies, but of all who would not obey it blindly. The marvel was that he had no personal ambitions, no friends nor relatives, that he was born to harm, unmoved by the slightest desire to do service, and that he rose from the gutter without ever seeking to conceal that fact. The more prudent Jesuits were alarmed by his fanaticism, the remainder, even the most ardent among them, dreaded lest he might bring them for the second time to disgrace and expulsion. His outward appearance made this seem likely, and his looks did not belie his nature. He would have been frightening to meet at the corner of a thicket.

---

[1] The doctrine of the sixteenth-century Spanish Jesuit, Luis Molina.

His face was sinister, false, terrifying; his burning, evil eyes looked angry; it was alarming to see him.

That is a true portrait of a man who gave himself body and soul to his Society, with no interest other than its deeper mysteries and no God beyond it, and whose entire life had been buried in such matters. Considering his birth and temperament no one should have been surprised to find him in other ways coarse and ill-bred, obstinate, ignorant of Society, devoid of gentleness, tolerance, prudence, or friends of any kind or condition; nor failed to realize that to him all means were good provided they achieved his ends.[1] On the first occasion that he saw the King in his study, Blouin and Fagon remained alone in a corner of the room after the presentation. Fagon, bowed over his cane, watched the interview, scrutinizing the countenance of the man, his bowing and scraping, and his replies. The King inquired whether he were related to MM. Le Tellier.[2] Père Tellier sang very small, 'I, Sire? a kinsman of MM. Le Tellier! Oh! very far from that! I am merely a peasant from Lower Normandy; my father laboured in the fields.' Fagon, closely observing, missing nothing, twisted upwards in an effort to look Blouin in the eyes. 'Zounds!' said he, indicating the Jesuit, 'Zounds! What a shark!' Then, with a shrug of his shoulders he settled back upon his cane. Time was to show that this damning judgment was not wrong. The fellow had gone through every piece of mime, every hypocritical antic to make it seem that he dreaded the thought of office and accepted only out of obedience to his Society. I have spread myself upon this confessor because he was the cause of those incredible quarrels in which Church and State, learning, doctrine, and very many worthy persons of all ranks suffered and still suffer; also because I had closer and more direct dealings with his monstrous personality than any other member of the Court.

My father and mother had early placed me in the hands of the Jesuits for religious instruction, and in so doing they were wise, for whatever may be said of them no one should deny that the Society does here and there include some saintly and enlightened men. After I grew up I continued to remain where they had placed me, although I had no dealings save with the priest to whom I applied for instruction. This Jesuit was responsible for the retreats held several times a year for laymen at their novitiate.[3] He was called Père Sanadou;[4] his work brought him into contact with his superiors, and with Père Tellier also after he was appointed confessor. That priest, unsociable by preference and temperament, knew

---

[1] Many historians agree that Pere Tellier had a disastrous influence and that there was a kind of savagery in his ardour for the Society of Jesus. Mme de Maintenon wrote: 'The King has appointed a new confessor. He is not a gentleman, but everyone speaks well of him; that is to say all who know him, for he lives the life of a recluse, wholly engrossed in study.'

[2] The late Chancellor Michel Le Tellier and the Archbishop of Rheims.

[3] Held at a house not far from Saint-Sulpice.

[4] Nicolas Sanadou, who became confessor of Saint-Cyr in 1716.

no one whom he could dispense with knowing, and in this he followed a policy, for it made him independent and better able to avoid notoriety and appeals. I was therefore greatly surprised when two or three weeks after taking office, for that it was in a very real sense, he sent Père Sanadou to me asking to be presented. Those were Père Sanadou's actual words, and the words of Père Tellier also when they came to me on the following morning. I had not met him until then and had neither visited him nor sent my compliments, but he none the less overwhelmed me with civilities and ended by asking leave to call on me occasionally, entreating me to be gracious enough to receive him. In short, he desired my friendship, and I, who had fought shy of all Jesuits, trafficking with them only because none of my own family were in the Church, vainly sought to ward him off. In the end I was overborne; he visited me more and more frequently, discussed affairs of State, sought my opinion until, in very truth, I was in two minds whether it was more dangerous to rebuff or encourage him. This forced acquaintance, in which my part was wholly passive, lasted until the death of the King. It taught me many things that will be disclosed in due course. He must have made inquiries concerning me of Père Sanadou, who had apparently informed him of my close friendship with the Dukes of Chevreuse and Beauvilliers, and perhaps of my attachment to M. le Duc d'Orléans, and to Mgr le Duc de Bourgogne, which last was then a deep secret. From that time onwards, indeed, my ears were pricked in deadly earnest, but well under cover, for although I had been involved for some time past in many important affairs, most people were not yet aware of it.

The Court was delivered from a species of familiar[1] by the death of Mme d'Heudicourt, at Versailles, at eight o'clock in the morning of 24 January. I have already mentioned her and her life-long extraordinary intimacy with Mme de Maintenon. She had grown old and hideously ugly, but in her time no one was more agreeable or better informed, more cheerful, witty, and unaffectedly diverting. On the other hand, there was no one more gratuitously, continually, and intentionally malicious, and therefore more dangerous, on account of her familiarity with the King and Mme de Maintenon. Thus everyone, favourites, nobles, officers of State, ministers, members of the royal family, even the bastards, bent the knee to that old bitch, who enjoyed doing harm and never had the faintest wish to oblige. Her apartment was a sanctuary to which by no means all were admitted. Mme de Maintenon did not leave her bedside during her last illness, was present at her death, and mourned her deeply. With her passing she and the King lost a great source of amusement, but Society at whose expense this was provided was immensely relieved, for she was a heartless creature.

[1] The familiar was also the officer of the Inquisition whose duty it was to discover and arrest suspects.

Her husband took advantage of her favour to be thoroughly insolent. He was repellently ugly, debauched, and altogether horrible, but was endured for her sake, although they never ceased tormenting one another. He was a heavy gambler and the most choleric and ill-tempered of card-players, always taking offence and furious. It was as good as a play to see him at Marly, dealing for *lansquenet*, and suddenly jerking back his *tabouret* so as to break the shins of an onlooker behind him. At other times he would turn and spit over his shoulder to catch the noses of any peeping Toms. For all her wit, his wife dreaded ghosts to such an extent that she employed women-watchers to protect her at night, and she carried that nonsense to the point of almost expiring with fright when an aged parrot, her pet for twenty years, died, and she doubled the number of 'sitters', as she called them, on that account. Her son, although in other ways no coward, suffered from a similar mania and could not bear to be by himself in a room after dark. He also was a kind of satyr, quite as evil and every bit as ugly as his father; but he was vastly obliging to the ladies and was thus made a party to all the amorous intrigues of the Court. He was addicted to drink. There are a thousand droll tales of his fear of ghosts and his drunken brawls; and he composed the funniest ditties imaginable depicting the people of the Court and their absurdities in the most subtle and irresistibly comic fashion. One in particular on his cousin the Grand Provost and his family (all of them most respectable) was so lifelike and so witty that it made one die of laughter. Someone murmured it into the ear of the Maréchal de Boufflers, as he stood behind the King at mass when the silence and decorum were extreme. On the instant, there was Boufflers, normally so solemn, grave, and dignified, a very slave to propriety, seized by a great gale of laughter and nearly bursting with the effort to control himself. The King turned once, then a second time, but wholly without effect, the laughter and the tears continued unquelled. Perfectly astounded to see the Maréchal de Boufflers of all people in such a condition, standing behind him, and at mass of all places, the King inquired rather severely as he left the chapel what had reduced him to such a state. Boufflers burst out again, replying as best he might that he could explain only in the study. No sooner had they entered than the King inquired again, the Maréchal repeated the song, and the King went into such fits of laughter that he could be heard from the ante-room. It was a long time before he could look at any of that family; it was the same with the Court, and they were finally reduced to taking a holiday. In the end Heudicourt became quite drink-sodden; but that was years after the King's death. At long last he broke his head by falling down a staircase at Versailles and died on the following day. His mother, who loved to pull people to pieces seriously or in fun, and who when she heard any-one well spoken of before the King and Mme de Maintenon always interjected a devastating *but*, was missed by no one except that lady. I used to say that she and Mme de Dangeau, the exact opposites of one another and equally privileged, were the bad and good angels of Mme de Maintenon.

Mme de Soubise was at last reaching the end of her brilliant and highly rewarding career. Her beauty cost her her life. She had lived for that and her ambitions and the uses to which she could put both. I do not believe that she had many other thoughts or was ever ready to entertain more serious considerations. Her life had been spent in rigorous dieting so as to preserve the brilliance and freshness of her complexion; veal, chickens, or capons roast or boiled, salads, fruit, some milky foods, was all that she ate without any admixture, drinking only water, occasionally tinted with wine; and she never wore her over-skirts pinned up as other women did, for fear of heating her kidneys and making her nose red. She had many children, some of whom died of scrofula despite the pretended miracle of the King's touch; the truth of which is that he touches the sick when they come from communion. Mme de Soubise, who had never asked for so much preparation,[1] fell sick of that disease when age had forced her to abandon her cooling diet. She concealed her weakness and continued to go into Society whilst she still had the strength; but in the last two years of her life she was forced to remain at home, rotting amidst the most costly furnishings imaginable in the depths of the vast palace of the Guises, which, with its purchase-money, paintings, and ornaments, must have been worth several million. Thereafter she busied herself more and more with intrigues for favour and ambition, keeping letters flying to and fro with the King and Mme de Maintenon, and managing to retain the respect and high regard of the Court. I have already described how carefully she watched over her son's advancement. She used often to say that no matter how many titles a family might acquire, nothing had any real value save the rank of duke and peer, and she always aimed at that. How it was I do not know, but by some mischance the favour which gained her such inestimable rewards never extended to that. It might have brought her within range of other important personages, whose protests and jealousy would vastly have embarrassed the King had he accorded that grace to Mme de Soubise. However that may be, she never did achieve that rank; yet although she despaired of arriving there at one bound, she still attempted to do so by degrees. Nothing came of that affair, however. Thus she had neither the pleasure of seeing her elder son made a duke, nor that of celebrating the red hat on the head of her second.[2] She died at the age of 61, on the morning of Sunday, 3 February, leaving her family more richly and splendidly situated than any other at the Court, all due to her beauty and the use to which she put it.

[1] There had been attempts to whitewash Mme de Soubise's relationship to the King.
[2] The Abbé de Rohan-Soubise, Bishop of Strasbourg, became Cardinal in 1712.

Despite such triumphs her family did not much lament her. Her husband[1] kept his wits about him. Grief did not prevent him from attempting to draw advantage from his wife's death and the location of his home by a princely act befitting not even foreign princes but only the royal blood of France. Notre-Dame de la Merci stands adjacent to his house in such a way that the great west door and his front door are directly opposite, separated only by the width of a narrow street. He had fitted up a chapel in the church long since, when he first had foreseen the death of his wife, and he was determined to have her buried there. His true intention was to have her carried straight there on the pretext of nearness and convenience, instead of taking her first to the parish church, which is customary for all save princes and princesses of the blood, who are always borne directly to their graves. Immediately after his wife's death he hurriedly arranged a splendid burial and bamboozled the curé, who could not divine the real cause, into accepting the plea of nearness and convenience. Thus Mme de Soubise was borne straight from her home to the Merci, and safely entombed before anyone had discovered the plot. Cardinal de Noailles thought very ill of the whole matter and scolded the curé, but nothing more came of it since he had been a friend of Mme de Soubise. None the less Society was alerted by the lack of scandal and at once put two and two together. It was much discussed, and for so long and so thoroughly that measures were taken against any recurrence. Indeed, when M. de Soubise died in 1712, he was taken to the parish church and from thence to the Merci. I did not want to omit this trifling event; it shows the attempts that were continually made by all kinds of underhand means to increase the rank and privileges of those who are known as foreign princes.

Mme de Vivonne, widow of the Maréchal-duc de Vivonne, died about a month later. She was a woman with a wit of such high quality that it well befitted her to marry into the Mortemarts. She was exceedingly wealthy, for the gentlemen of that family, who regularly came to ruin in generation after generation, always managed to restore their fortunes by such rich marriages. As for the couple above-mentioned, neither had cause to reproach the other, for they vied with one another in extravagance. It was as good as a play, or so I have heard from their contemporaries, to see them together; but they did not often meet and cared little for one another. The Duc de Vivonne quarrelled with his son the Duc de Mortemart, whom I remember being mourned by his brothers-in-law the Dukes of Chevreuse and Beauvilliers as a great gentleman and a man of high principles. When the son lay dying, M. de Vivonne was shamed into visiting him. He found him *in extremis* but did not approach, merely stood leaning against a table calmly observing him. The entire family were present lamenting. After a prolonged silence M. de Vivonne

---

[1] François de Rohan, Prince de Soubise.

suddenly took it into his head to remark: 'Poor fellow! He will not recover. I remember seeing his father die in just that same way.' You may imagine the scandal caused by those words, the supposed father being one of M. de Vivonne's grooms. M. de Vivonne himself appeared quite unperturbed, and after another silence left the room. He was spontaneously droll, and at the same time unendingly witty. I have heard him tell hundreds of stories to the King, each one more amusing than the last.

Mme de Vivonne was with the King at all his private times; he could not do without her company, which is not to say that he could always obtain it, for she was haughty, independent, and capricious, caring very little for favours or privileges, and seeking only her own amusement. She passionately loved cards, even in her later years, when so far as was possible with her she took to religion, after frittering away her entire fortune until nothing remained but a pension from the King and a lodging with a much depleted staff in the house of her steward. There she lived, playing *lansquenet* now and then for extremely low stakes, still retaining the regard of the Court, but missed by very few.

Meanwhile in France everything was visibly deteriorating. The nation was exhausted, the troops unpaid, disheartened by bad leadership and therefore never successful; the finances were bankrupt, the generals and ministers incapable, promotions came only by favour or intrigue, no faults were punished, no inquiries held, no councils of war. It was equally impossible to fight or to make peace. Silence and misery were everywhere, and anyone bold enough to stretch forth a hand to support the tottering Ark would instantly have been struck down.[1] I had often expressed myself strongly to the Dukes of Chevreuse and Beauvilliers on the subject of these disorders, and above all on their cause. My friends' piety and moderation had calmed my anxiety but not prevented it, for they were accustomed to the established form of government and played their parts in it; I dared not confide to them the remedies which I had been considering for a long time past. These remedies had none the less become something of an obsession with me and I had written them down, more indeed for my own satisfaction than with any hope of their leading to a practical result. No one had seen them; no one even knew of their existence, until one afternoon M. de Chevreuse called on me in the apartment which I had inherited from the late Maréchal de Lorges. He came straight upstairs to the little cupboard containing a fireplace, which one entered from the front hall and which I used as my study.[2] He was full of the

---

[1] Refers to Uzzah the Levite, who put out a hand to steady the Ark of the Lord and immediately fell down dead. II Samuel, 6.

[2] This tiny den with the unusual luxury of a fireplace was on the half-landing of Saint-Simon's first small apartment at Versailles. When the door was closed it was pitch dark. It held a table, two chairs and a cupboard. It was comfortable; better, it was private. Two men could talk there unheard, their faces almost touching (*bec-à-bec*) across the table between two lighted candles.

terrible situation throughout the kingdom; spoke with great bitterness, and finally asked whether I could suggest no remedy. I asked whether he believed that remedies were possible, not that I thought our position so desperate, but because the obstacles seemed to me invincible. Chevreuse was a man who always continued to hope and thus was always prepared for action; for action, I repeat, but action on the part of someone else. In that way his love of discussion was satisfied and no violence was done to his prudence or political feelings. That attitude of his sickened me, for I loathed castles in the air and fruitless argument. I could see the impossibility of having a wise and benevolent form of government so long as the present system continued, and I was well aware that no change would come, since the King firmly believed that the powers of the secretaries of State and the controller-general were a reflection of his own absolute authority and must thus never be restricted. Nothing, moreover, would ever persuade the King that other men than commoners might safely be admitted to his councils, with the sole exception of the head of the finance council,[1] because he had no responsibility. The notes that I had written were purely for my own satisfaction; I had long ago despaired of finding any use for them, and considered them merely as an ideal, like the republic of Plato.[2]

What therefore was my surprise when M. de Chevreuse, becoming more and more confidential, disclosed to me ideas very similar to my own. He enjoyed talking and spoke well and lucidly; it was a pleasure to listen. I accordingly listened with rapt attention and heard him unfold my own ideas, my own suggestions, my very own plan, which I had always imagined would be antipathetic to him and to M. de Beauvilliers. I was completely dumbfounded. At last, perceiving my amazement, he tried to learn my opinions, but I was far too bewildered to answer him except in monosyllables. Then he, too, was astonished because he was well used to my being frank and talking volumes in praise or disapproval, for despite the difference in our stations both dukes allowed me great freedom. Seeing me thus silent, abstracted, wrapt in thought, he exclaimed, 'Do say something! Who are you angry with today? Tell me frankly if I am talking nonsense.' At that I could contain myself no longer; I rose, and taking a key from my pocket opened the door of a small cupboard behind me, from which I took three fat little notebooks filled with my own handwriting. I gave them to him saying, 'See, Monsieur, the reason for my surprise and my silence.' He read a little, then skimmed through all, discovering therein his entire plan. I never saw a man more astonished, for there was the sketch for the selfsame administration which he had

[1] The Duc de Beauvilliers.
[2] In Saint-Simon's ideal administration the bourgeois secretaries of State were to be abolished. His plan was a Royal Council of five ministers, all of them nobles of the old *noblesse de l'épée*, and under them a series of councils for the various departments of the government.

just described to me. There were written the posts on the various councils and the names of their suggested occupants, some since deceased; and he was able to observe how well their talents harmonized with those of the ministers at their head. Everything was there inscribed, even down to the members' salaries, compared with the salaries of the present government. Such attention to detail delighted M. de Chevreuse, who approved of every name and the appropriate salary. It was a long time before we recovered our calm, but eventually we began to talk, and the more we talked the better we agreed. He begged me to lend him the note-books so that he might study them at leisure, and he gave them back to me a few weeks later. He and M. de Beauvilliers having discussed them at length had found little to alter, and that little mere trifles. The difficulty was to take action, which I had always believed impossible, on account of the King. At last they urged me to preserve my notebooks carefully until the time should come to make use of them, which would be in the reign of Mgr le Duc de Bourgogne.

As you will see, this project became the basis for those hasty, ill-considered plans for councils which were produced at the time of the King's death, and were said to have been among the papers of the late Mgr le Duc de Bourgogne. Had there been any question of implementing them I should have changed many details but not the essentials, and this project with several others might have become a reality had that prince ascended the throne.

The winter, as I have said, had been terrible, the worst within living memory. It had been so cold that bottles of Queen of Hungary water broke in the cupboards of rooms with fires and surrounded by chimneys, in several apartments of the château of Versailles. I saw some broken my-self, and once, supping with the Duc de Villeroy in his small bedroom, splinters of ice fell into our glasses from the bottles on the chimney-piece, after being brought there straight from his tiny kitchen where there was a blazing fire, on the same level as his bedroom, with only a very small ante-room between. It was the second frost that destroyed everything. The fruit trees were killed; no walnuts, olives, apples, nor vines survived, or none worth mentioning. Other kinds of trees died in great numbers, the gardens were ruined, and so was the seed planted in the ground. Impossible to form any idea of the magnitude of that national disaster. Everyone hoarded the old grain, and the price of bread rose as people despaired of a harvest. The more prudent re-sowed their corn-fields with barley; many others followed suit, and they were the lucky ones, for it saved their lives. The police, however, took it into their heads to forbid that activity and changed their minds when it was too late. Various decrees were published concerning wheat, searches were insti-tuted for hoarded grain, and commissaries were sent into the provinces three months after their arrival was announced. And all that this policy

achieved was to increase the poverty and the prices to a disastrous level
at a time when calculation showed there to have been enough wheat in
the country to feed the entire nation for two years, without reckoning
on a harvest.

Many people therefore believed that those gentry of the finances
had taken the opportunity to corner the wheat by sending agents to buy
up the corn in the markets throughout the kingdom, and re-sell it to the
King's profit, not to mention their own. A very considerable number of
barge-loads of corn purchased by the King went rotten and had to be
thrown into the Loire, which gave some weight to the rumours, for the
circumstances could not be denied. What was certain, at any rate, was
that wheat was sold at a uniform price in all the provincial markets,
whereas in Paris the commissaries kept the prices up, sometimes forcing
the vendors to raise them against their inclinations. When the people
cried out to know how long the high prices would last, some commissaries,
moved by pity and indignation—and this in a market not two yards from
my own house in Saint-Germain-des-Prés, gave this revealing answer,
'Just as long as you please,' meaning just so long as they allowed no wheat
to enter Paris except by permission of Argenson the lieutenant of police.
This prohibition had been most rigorously enforced on the bakers, and
what I am describing was taking place in the whole of France, for administrators everywhere were soon copying what Argenson did in Paris. What is
more, in all the provincial markets, the wheat left unsold at closing
time at the fixed prices was compulsorily removed, and any dealer
compassionate enough to sell at a lower price what remained was severely
punished.

Maréchal, the King's first surgeon, had the courage to tell him all that
was happening, and to warn him of the appalling conclusions to which
people were being driven, even the steadiest and least affected. The King
seemed moved by compassion and was not angry with Maréchal for
speaking out, but he did nothing. In many places huge stocks of grain
were amassed with all possible secrecy, although such hoarding was expressly forbidden by the decrees, and denouncements were ordered, but
one poor man who attempted to lay information with Desmaretz was
very roughly handled. The Parlement assembled by chambers on account
of this unrest, and then held a meeting of deputies in the great chamber. A
resolution was there passed to advise the King to send his counsellors
through the provinces at their own expense in order to inspect the stocks
of corn, give the police their instructions and punish those who disobeyed
the decrees. A list was compiled of the counsellors who were willing to go
the rounds of the various provinces. When the president informed the
King of these proposals he became extraordinarily incensed and threatened
to send back a harsh reprimand bidding the Parlement to mind its
own business and limit itself to the hearing of lawsuits. The Chancellor

dared not remind him that the advice had been perfectly correct and well within the province of the Parlement, but he did stress the love and respect with which it had been tendered, and the ministers' deep consciousness that the King alone was master and could accept or reject it. After some further argument King Louis was so far appeased that he sent no reprimand, but he absolutely insisted on the Parlement being ordered not to meddle with the wheat. The message was delivered in open council when the Chancellor was the only speaker. The other ministers preserved complete silence. What they thought was very obvious, but they took care to say nothing in a matter that touched the Chancellor's own department so nearly. In truth, although like other public bodies the Parlement was well used to snubs, it felt this one deeply and obeyed with the greatest reluctance. The public was equally distressed, for all believed that if the finance department were compelled to cease from their cruel abuses the King would be well pleased, and the Parlement do him good service by interposing itself between him and his people. It would have been made plain that the government intended no sharp practices, and the absolute, boundless authority of which the King was so supremely jealous would have been diminished in no way, either real or imaginary.

Without going into the question of who had devised or who most profited from the transactions over the wheat,[1] it may safely be said that scarcely any other age had produced a more wicked, brazen, or better organized plot, or an oppression more lasting, sure, and cruel. The fortunes made from it were countless, and countless were the numbers who died of starvation or perished later from illnesses caused by extreme poverty. Infinite numbers of families were ruined and a deluge of misfortunes followed one after another. In the meantime the taxes were raised and mutiplied, and were applied with a rigour that completed the ruin of France. Prices reached such fantastic heights that the people had not the wherewithal to buy even in the cheapest markets; yet although the cattle died because their owners were too poor to buy food for them, still more taxes were levied. Very many of those who had assisted the poor in former years found themselves reduced to a bare subsistence, and many others were driven to accepting alms in secret. No one knows how many tried to gain admission into almshouses that had been dreadful and shaming even to the poor, nor how many such houses threw back their poor upon the public charge (which meant certain death by starvation), nor yet how many good families died of hunger surrounded by their empty granaries. Again it must also be told that the sight of so much misery awakened a zeal for charity and that the sums given in alms were enormous. It will hardly be believed that at this very time when the

---

[1] Mme de Maintenon had taken to eating black bread to give the example; but Madame declared that she did this only in public and was secretly making a fortune from wheat.

poverty increased from day to day some meddlesome busybody of a philanthropist conceived the idea of a new tax and levy for the benefit of the poor. These were applied over and above the existing taxes, and with so little discrimination that numbers of people were placed in even greater need and some were provoked into curtailing their ordinary alms-giving. Thus, apart from the cost of collecting these two ill-distributed levies, the poor were left in a worse state than before. What, however, has proved far more disturbing is that these two taxes, which were originally raised to succour the needy, have been appropriated to the King's benefit in a modified but perpetual form. The officials of the finance department collect them even now as part of the royal revenues and have not troubled to change their names.

In the year 1709, however, everyone wondered what had become of all the money in France, for no one could pay because no one was paid. In country districts the people were insolvent on account of bad debts or extortions, commerce brought no return, confidence and good faith were shattered. The King was thus left with no resource but terror and the exercise of his supreme power; yet boundless though that was it often failed for want of anything to command. The circulation of money ceased en-tirely and there was no possibility of renewing it. The King could not even pay his troops, and no one could imagine what became of the millions that entered his coffers.

Such was the desperate state of affairs when Rouillé, and later Torcy, were sent to Holland to negotiate a peace. The above description is exact, true, and by no means exaggerated; for accuracy is needed if you are to have any understanding of the tragic state to which France was reduced, the enormous sacrifices which the King was forced to make in order to obtain peace, and the clear miracle performed by Him who en-compasses the sea with bounds and calls to that which is and that which is not; who saved France from the clutches of a Europe ready and willing to destroy her. In truth, our country was to emerge with great advantages, considering her wretched condition and the little hope of salvation which she had possessed.

In the meantime the reminting of the currency and its revaluation at a third above the real value brought the King some profit, but at the same time many private persons were thus ruined, and trade was thrown into such confusion that it almost entirely ceased. Lyons was destroyed by the sudden vast bankruptcy of Samuel Bernard and its disastrous effects, although Desmaretz supported him as long as he was able to do so. The cause was the issue of paper-money and its subsequent depreciation, for the famous banker had circulated notes to the equivalent of twenty millions and was in debt for almost the same amount in Lyons. He was provided with fourteen millions in good assignations in the hope that with that sum and what he could scrape together from his bank-notes he might save himself. It has since been suggested that he made a good thing out of his bankruptcy; but in fact, although no single individual of his condition ever spent or left so much, or possessed credit to the same extent throughout the whole of Europe until his death thirty years later one must except Lyons and the part of Italy adjacent,[1] for there he never recovered his credit.

M. le Prince de Conti died at nine in the morning of 21 February, after a long illness that terminated in dropsy. Gout had reduced him to a diet of milk only, which for a time had been beneficial, but eventually his stomach revolted and his doctor, by persisting, killed him. He was not 45 years old. In appearance he was most pleasing; even the defects of his body and mind[2] had immense charm, his high shoulders, his head tilted slightly on one side, his laugh, which in any other would have been called a bray, his absent-mindedness. He was gallant with the ladies, loved several at a time, and was favoured by many; he was attractive also to men, for he took pains to please everyone, cobblers, lackeys, chair-porters, ministers of State, lords, and generals alike, and his friendliness was so easy that he succeeded with them all. Thus he was a constant joy in Society and at the Court; the idol of the army and the masses; the hero of young officers, and the hope of scholars and men of science. He had an extremely good brain, enlightened, precise, and well-informed. He read much, forgot little, had studied history both general and biographical, was acquainted with genealogies real and imaginary, remembered where and in what circumstances he had been apprised of certain events, and estimated them without malice and with surprising accuracy.

In his dealings with others he was amiable, almost kindly, courteous to a degree, but ever conscious of the rank, age, and merit of those to whom he spoke; thus he robbed no one of their dignity. Monsieur de Meaux, who had watched him grow to manhood, always loved him dearly and trusted him, and so did the Dukes of Chevreuse and Beauvilliers, the Archbishop of Cambrai, and Cardinals d'Estrées and Janson. Monsieur le Prince, that great warrior, never concealed the fact that he preferred him to his own children; he was the confidant of M. de Luxembourg in the latter's declining years. In Society he was spontaneously witty and amusing; his prompt repartees were never hurtful; there was grace in everything he did, yet he was wholly unaffected, and kept a cool head amidst all the futility of the Court and the ladies' drawing-rooms. Everything seemed to come easily to him. At the war he showed heroic courage and the bearing of a hero, also a soldier's dislike of formality, although that he concealed with great art. Such a record of talents should have provided the final brush-stroke on his portrait, but like all men he had a less agreeable side, for that attractive and agreeable man cared for no one

---

[1] Saint-Simon means Savoy.
[2] He was a little deformed and was believed to drink and take drugs.

but himself. He loved his friends as others love good furniture, and despite his position was a scrounger, always taking, and allowing his wants to be known with far too much freedom. In fact, he was a miser, greedy for gain, grasping, and unscrupulous.[1]

The virtues and talents of M. le Prince de Conti had aroused no love in the hearts of Mme de Maintenon and the King, who were daily incensed by the contrast between him and M. du Maine. Moreover, the purity of his blood, the only royal blood untainted by bastardy, was an affront which they could not forgive. They hated even his friends and did not disguise their feelings. Yet despite all their servility the courtiers were glad to approach M. le Prince de Conti and were flattered to be thought part of his circle. Even in the drawing-room at Marly, he was surrounded by the best people and became the centre of such fascinating conversations that people actually forgot to go to their meals. The King was aware of this, and it did not please him; indeed he seemed not always averse to letting his annoyance be seen. None the less the courtiers could not easily dispense with M. le Prince de Conti, and the rigid control of even the smallest details in the life of the Court was lost where he was concerned. Thus the King was much relieved when he died; Monsieur le Duc[2] infinitely more so, as for the Duc du Maine, to him that death came as a deliverance. Monseigneur heard the news at Meudon as he was preparing to go hunting, but he did not change his plans.

M. le Prince de Conti had chosen to be buried at Saint-André-des-Arcs beside his virtuous mother, for whom he retained strong feelings of love and respect. He had desired all unnecessary pomps and ceremonies to be omitted. Yet I doubted whether the vanity of M. le Duc would allow him to keep within such narrow limits, and I therefore begged Desgranges, the master of ceremonies, to give me no official part in the proceedings.[3] I was right. Monsieur le Duc obtained Holy Water in the manner reserved for the first prince of the blood, for those above him, and for no others. Thus on Wednesday, 27 February, Monsieur le Duc d'Enghien,[4] robed '*en pointe*'[5] with a square cap, as representing the King, and the Duc de La Trémoïlle, appointed by the King to represent the dukes, appeared one on either side of the great courtyard at the Tuileries, where one of the King's coaches was drawn up, with pages and royal footmen, twelve members of the bodyguard, and a number of the Hundred

[1] Madame wrote: 'The late Prince de Conti was clever and brave, very good company, making himself universally popular. The worst of it was that he was false, loved no one but himself, and was utterly dissolute.'

[2] He was the Prince de Conti's brother-in-law, that prince having married Marie Thérèse de Bourbon-Condé in 1688.

[3] Another case of 'foreign princes' attempting to claim equal rank and privileges with the royal family of France.

[4] Eldest son of Monsieur le Duc.

[5] Refers to the shape of his long train. Long or short mantles worn on state occasions were a burning question in matters of precedence.

Swiss with their officers. M. de La Trémoïlle, in a long mantle, took his seat at the back of the royal coach beside the representative. Desgranges, as master of ceremonies, sat in front, with the pages riding before and behind the coach, which was undraped and drawn by one pair of horses only, between an escort of Swiss marching with their halberds, and the royal servants, also on foot, by the coach doors. The Duc d'Enghien's coach followed, containing his governor and gentlemen, and then that of the Duc de La Trémoïlle with his household. There was a mounted escort both in front and behind.

In that order they arrived at the Hôtel de Conti, which was everywhere hung with black. There Monsieur le Duc and the new Prince de Conti, accompanied by the Dukes of Luxembourg and Duras, representing the family, all four wearing long mantles with their trains borne by gentlemen also in long mantles, received the King's representative at the door of his coach and paid him the same honours as to the King himself. The Duc de La Trémoïlle's train was borne by another gentleman in a long mantle. The Abbé de Maulévrier, as the King's almoner, wearing the rochet, presented a sprinkler to the representative, and similar sprinklers were offered to the Dukes of Trémoïlle, Luxembourg, and Duras. When the service was over they departed in the same order and the return was like the arrival.

Two days later I learned that I was supposed to have resented the fact that the Duc de La Trémoïlle had been nominated in my place, and that I had said he was sure to make a blunder. That rumour had been started at Versailles in the Duc de La Trémoïlle's presence, but he had merely smiled. When someone insisted, he had taken four *pistoles* from his pocket and silenced them all by wagering that no one had actually heard me. This had confounded them, and the friendly gesture was highly gratifying, for I certainly did not think M. de La Trémoïlle capable of blunders, and even if I did I should not have said so. What is more, even had I desired to perform his functions I should have been above feeling resentment. All the same, I was very glad to have taken precautions with Desgranges; I explained that to everyone, and made him do the like. I never discovered who started the rumour, but on general principles I expressed myself strongly on whomsoever it was. No one dared to take up the challenge.

The body of M. le Prince de Conti remained exposed at his house for several days longer until everything at Saint-André-des-Arcs was in readiness. Monsieur le Duc, eager as ever to filch privileges by fair means or foul, seized the opportunity to make his upper-servants drop hints in the households of his fellow-dukes to the effect that numbers of people had come to sprinkle Holy Water and pray over the body, and that it was surprising that some had not thought fit to pay their tribute to piety and friendship, adding that long mantles were the correct attire for such funerary obligations. Nothing was easier than to ensnare the dukes, who despite long experience were completely off their guard. The Dukes of Sully and Villeroy fell into the trap, the Maréchal-comte de Choiseul, and several others. Xantrailles, who was Monsieur le Duc's first equerry and moved in the highest Society, decoyed Villeroy by citing Sully as an example. Villeroy told me so himself, adding that his father was so furious that he had sworn never again to receive Xantrailles at his house. This well-founded belief in ducal gullibility might well have set a precedent for foreign princes' funerals, had not the Maréchal de Villeroy blown the gaff and spoiled the entire plot by creating a rumpus.

Monsieur le Duc did not have the face to be angry because, apart from all the protests, it had been ludicrous of him to attempt by such a means to secure a guard of honour for the body of M. le Prince de Conti. It was a very long time since there had been a funeral for a prince of the blood, for the last Prince de Conti had succumbed at Fontainebleau in 1685, from smallpox, but a guard of honour was Monsieur le Duc's prime aim. He remembered that the Queen and the Daughters and Grand-daughters of France had been guarded by duchesses and foreign prin-cesses alternately, he remembered also that when his sister Mlle de Condé died, in 1700, they tried to have her guarded by untitled ladies, that scarcely any of them would consent, and that they had not dared to approach titled ones. What he forgot, however, was that such a guard is for princesses only, and not for princes, nor even for Kings, who are guarded by their high officers. People sneered somewhat at the few who had been duped; they made a loud outcry, and there the matter rested. But Monsieur le Duc was ready for fresh assaults. He now conceived the idea of having the body removed to Saint-André in a coach; there was much discussion regarding that. He had no chance of success in that direction and was forced to extricate himself by remembering the ban which the late prince had put on unnecessary pomp—he might indeed have remembered that earlier. When at last he perceived that the ordinary ceremonial must suffice, he positively recommended that all the dukes taking part in the procession should wear long mantles. MM. de Luxem-bourg and La Rocheguyon, intimate friends of the late prince, refused point blank; whereupon he lost his temper and began to bluster. Thus frustrated, he decided to do without a procession, on the pretext that the new M. le Prince de Conti had a cold in the head and could not take part, but he made M. le Duc d'Enghien wear a long mantle. No invitations were issued; all who came, dukes as well as others, awaited the arrival of the body at Saint-André, and they all wore simple mourning without mantles of any kind. Let us now have done with this sorry episode.

A solemn service was held at the church. Only bishops and relatives were invited, but nothing was stinted in any way. An admirable oration was pronounced by one of the officiating clergy, Père Massillon of the

Oratory, who later became Bishop of Clermont. Monsieur le Duc, M. le Duc d'Enghien, and the new M. le Prince de Conti acted as chief mourners. The bishops took offence because they were not provided with armchairs, resting their claim on their rank in the Church hierarchy and refusing to admit that a similar claim had quite recently been disallowed. Armchairs are given to bishop-peers only, who are above the rank of the ordinary clergy and set apart from them. Those bishops none the less created a rumpus, but finally consented to remain in their pews. On such occasions the rules are clear; everyone is treated as he would be in the house of the prince for whom the obsequies are held, and in every respect as though that prince were still alive. According to that rule all the dukes present should have had armchairs exactly similar to those provided for the princes of the blood; but Monsieur le Duc, ever eager to take advantage, had had them all removed. Only three remained for the princely mourners, after which was placed an ordinary bench, with other benches adjoining. When the first dukes to arrive noticed the arrangement they made a loud outcry. Monsieur le Duc pretended not to hear, but soon afterwards MM. de Luxembourg, La Meilleraye, and La Roche-guyon arrived and spoke to him. He tried to excuse himself on the grounds that there were no armchairs in the church and that he could obtain none from elsewhere. The three dukes then declared that they would leave and take the other dukes with them. This firm declaration astonished Monsieur le Duc, who had expected nothing of that nature. He had once again been trying to create a precedent, but knowing that to refuse armchairs was wholly unwarrantable he began to protest that he had intended no such slight. Perceiving, however, that the gentlemen in question were already making their bows preparatory to departing he stopped them by saying that he would do his best to content them. At this point, the whole plot was discovered, for armchairs began to appear at once from the back regions. Monsieur le Duc tried to say that there would not be enough for all the dukes present, but a compromise was soon arrived at. An armchair exactly similar to that provided for M. le Prince de Conti was placed next to it, then four or five others in the same line, and the remainder were interspaced with stools. Thus the stools appeared all to have arms and an armchair finished the row. It was obvious to all that these arrangements had been planned in case Monsieur le Duc's endeavour should fail and he with it.

No one wore a long robe except the princely mourners and their house-holds, nor did anyone dare to make that suggestion again, considering what had happened before. The foreign princes tactfully remained in the background observing all that took place without committing themselves. I have described these obsequies at some length so that you may see how, despite the lawfully high rank of the princes of the blood, they desired still greater privileges and spared neither cunning nor violence to obtain them. They were often successful in their attempts, and have constantly managed to turn their encroachments into precedents and rights.

Familiar names such as Monsieur le Prince, Monsieur le Duc, were never heard of before the intrigues of the House of Lorraine drove the Huguenots to revolt. The Prince de Condé, brother of the King of Navarre and uncle of Henri IV, became their leader. He was the only prince of royal blood on their side, and they therefore referred to him always as Monsieur le Prince. His birth and authority were their glory, their guarantee of good faith, and in many ways their strength. The custom became universally accepted, and after his death at the Battle of Jarnac, in 1569, his son was also called Monsieur le Prince. The third Prince de Condé was born posthumously and inherited the byname with his father's title. When Henri IV came to the throne, he took him from among the Huguenots, for although too young to be their leader in anything but name he was the senior prince of the blood, son of the King's first cousin, and next in the line of succession. The boy was eight years old at that time, which was towards the end of 1595. The custom having been established of referring to him as Monsieur le Prince, and there being no prince above him in rank save only the King, it endured throughout his lifetime and was passed on to his son and his grandson after him.

His paternal uncle the Comte de Soissons was a son of the original Prince de Condé's second marriage to a Longueville, which family were on the side of the Catholics. Rivalry is only too common amongst stepbrothers, especially when they are the leaders of opposing factions, and the Comte de Soissons, hearing his elder brother given an individual title, made first his servants and then his junior officers speak of him as Monsieur le Comte; his friends followed suit, and finally all the members of the House of Longueville. Nothing can equal the eagerness of a Frenchman to be in the fashion and stake a claim; in this case, since neither rank nor privilege appeared to be involved, the King let him have his way, and the familiar address was given to his son in due course. Monsieur le Prince made no objection to a member of his family sharing his particular distinction, but having conceived the idea of multiplying his prerogatives he began to speak of the Duc d'Enghien, his eldest son, as Monsieur le Duc. That also was accepted, and the style Monsieur le Duc has since gone as of right to the eldest sons of the Princes de Condé. There have been four in succession styled Monsieur le Prince and four Monsieur le Duc; but there were only two called Monsieur le Comte because the Soissons branch died out in the second generation. Louis XIV wished to revive the style for M. le Comte de Toulouse and referred to him always as Monsieur le Comte; so also did the navy, but for some reason the public did not conform, except for a few of the more servile courtiers, and even they only used the style in the King's presence.

No Dauphin before the son of Louis XIV was called Monseigneur, or addressed as such. One wrote Monseigneur le Dauphin, but said Monsieur le Dauphin or just plain Monsieur, as to the other Sons of France, and even to those beneath them in rank. The King first called him Monseigneur in jest, although I should not like to swear that this was not a sly attempt to introduce a new title to distinguish him from Monsieur, the King's brother. As though the name Dauphin were not distinction enough, quite apart from the rank, which was so far above that of Monsieur that the latter handed him his nightshirt, and his napkin at table! Be that as it may, the King never referred to him otherwise than as 'My son', or 'Monseigneur'. Madame la Dauphine, Monsieur, and Madame followed his example, and before long the entire country had adopted the habit. Those who, like M. de Montausier and Monsieur de Meaux, had attended him in his boyhood found it hard to accept the innovation. They complied so far as to say Monseigneur when speaking to him, but referred to him always as Monsieur le Dauphin. M. de Montausier, who had been his governor, used to ask him jokingly since when he had been made a bishop, for quite recently the bishops at one of the Church assemblies had made an attempt to be addressed and written to as Monseigneur, and had even taken a resolution to refer to one another by that title. They had little success with the other clergy or the laity. Everyone mocked them for it, and their effort to Monseigneurize themselves became a huge joke. They persisted none the less, and no resolution on any Church matter was ever more strictly observed.

The death of M. le Prince de Conti seemed a stroke of good fortune to the Duc de Vendôme, more especially since it removed a rival of embarrassingly high birth at the very moment when, amidst universal applause, he was about to take his place at the head of the armies. It served also to leave Vendôme in undisputed possession of Monseigneur. I have already mentioned his exclusion from holding a command, because that event could not be passed over when noting the military assignments. The downfall of that braggart prince took place in fact in three stages from the greatest height to the lowest depths. We have now arrived at the second stage; the third occurred two or three months later, but since it has no connection with any other event I shall record them both together so as to avoid repetition.

However many and excellent the reasons that had induced the King to remove M. de Vendôme from the command of his armies, I am not sure that, despite all Mme de Maintenon's gentle influence, the carefully concealed intrigues of M. du Maine, with the continual support of the valets, might not have succeeded. However that may be, an incident occurred that opened the King's eyes to the death-struggle between Vendôme, seconded by his redoubtable cabal, and the heir to the throne aided by his wife (the pride and joy of King Louis and of Mme de Maintenon who had ruled that monarch for the past thirty years), whom Vendôme had most insolently and triumphantly opposed.

You already know that on Vendôme's return from Flanders he had been granted only one audience with the King and that a short one. He had none the less found time to complain of Puységur most bitterly, proudly assuming that as usual his bare word would be enough. Puységur, whom I have mentioned more than once, was well known to the King and had a special familiarity because he served with the King's infantry regiment, which the King liked to think of as particularly his own. He had risen to be major and then lieutenant-colonel, always retaining the King's confidence and approval. He and his friend Montivel had been appointed *gentilshommes de la manche* to Mgr le Duc de Bourgogne and had become deeply attached to him and to M. de Beauvilliers also, at the time of the disgrace of the Archbishop of Cambrai. Thus because of his situation both at the Court and in the army he knew all that had passed, and had witnessed the quarrels and misunderstandings of the Lille campaign, during which he served in Vendôme's army with the rank of lieutenant-general. He had sent regular and truthful reports to the Duc de Beauvilliers at that time—if only God had ordained for him to be on the staff of Mgr le Duc de Bourgogne instead of the persons chosen! Puységur's integrity and military experience had been deeply shocked by Vendôme's conduct throughout the campaign and he had allowed his sentiments to be seen. At the junction with the Duke of Berwick's army he had become friendly with that commander and had remained so for the rest of the season, and all this had been quite sufficient to make Vendôme hate him, determined as he was to destroy Mgr le Duc de Bourgogne and all those who were loyal to him. That was the whole reason for Vendôme's complaints and for the abominable things that he said of Puységur after their return.

Soon after Vendôme's audience, the King, who had been much distressed to hear accusations against a man whom he liked and trusted, summoned Puységur to his study and there questioned him kindly and in private regarding the many trifling offences that had been laid at his door. Puységur there and then explained himself so emphatically that the King was surprised into admitting that Vendôme had been his accuser. At that name Puységur rose up in anger, seeing his opportunity. He told the King bravely and truthfully of the Duc de Vendôme's faults, follies, obstinacy, and arrogance, with so much precision and so many details that King Louis listened attentively and then proceeded to rain questions on him, demanding further enlightenment. Puységur then told all, and when he saw that the King was convinced pressed on to say that since Vendôme had shown him so little kindness he felt it not only permissible but his bounden duty to reveal that prince once and for all in his true colours. Thereupon he presented a complete portrait of M. de Vendôme, his life in the army, his physical condition,[1] his faulty judgment, his warped mind, the dangerous errors of his military strategy, his utterly irresponsible conduct of the entire campaign. Then, reverting to the Italian campaigns and the past two seasons in Flanders, he exposed the man completely, persuading the King beyond all possible doubt that, if France had not been lost a hundred times during Vendôme's command of her armies, it was purely by a series of miracles.[2] The conversation lasted more than two hours. The King, who was long acquainted with Puységur's ability and, more important, with his truthfulness, found his eyes opened to one who had so artfully been represented as the hero and saviour of his country. He felt ashamed and mortified. From that moment Vendôme was as dead to him and for ever barred from holding any command—an absolute edict that did not remain secret for long.

The end came relatively soon, as I have recounted. Vendôme, dismissed from the service, sold his equipment, and retired to Anet where the grass had already begun to grow.[3] He begged the King as a favour to allow him to pay his court at Marly only, and to pay court to Monseigneur at Meudon, where he was still bidden. This small remainder of privilege consoled him somewhat in his self-induced retirement, for it seemed to demonstrate that the King and Monseigneur were not dissatisfied with his services and conduct, despite the efforts of his all-powerful enemies. That at least was how the cabal interpreted his position, and he tried to carry off the situation with a falsely philosophical air that deceived no one. Dispirited though he was, he affected at Marly and Meudon all the arrogance of his great days, and after the first shock recovered his haughty air, his loud voice, and his habit of monopolizing the conversation. To see him there, though sparsely surrounded, one might have thought him master of the salon; indeed, from his manner with Monseigneur, and even with the King when he dared be so bold, he often appeared the most favoured person present. Mgr le Duc de Bourgogne's piety obliged him to endure Vendôme's presence and behaviour, but his staff were sorely tried, and Mme la Duchesse de Bourgogne, growing more and more indignant, said nothing but waited for her opportunity. It came on the

---

[1] He had deeply shocked the King and the Court by publicly announcing that he was taking a cure for venereal disease.

[2] Thé Duc de Bourgogne in a letter: 'I had best tell you something of him [Vendôme], which I swear will not be biased (God knows how I feel about him), nor influenced by what I learn from others, but allowing his devotion to the King, Monseigneur, and the royal family. M. de Vendôme's nature is imperious; what he wishes he believes; what he fears he thinks will never take place. He is headstrong; once an idea has entered his mind no one can shake him. He is arrogant and hasty, even with his greatest friends; moreover he is lazy, I think that his maladies may be the cause. He has a heavy body and after a long day he cannot fight off sleep. He has insufficient foresight owing to excessive confidence. He is the bravest man imaginable, perhaps too much so, for he exposes himself in battle more than the common soldiers. He has good intentions and a kind heart. That in brief is a true picture of him.'

[3] Because there were no callers to tread it down.

King's first visit to Marly after Easter. *Brelan* was then the fashion and
Monseigneur would often play in the salon during the early part of the
evening at the princess's table. They lacked a fifth,[1] and seeing Vendôme
at the end of the room he sent for him to take a hand. Thereupon Mme la
Duchesse de Bourgogne said quietly but distinctly that M. de Vendôme's
presence at Marly was sufficiently painful to her without having to play
cards with him, and she begged to be excused. Monseigneur, who until
then had not given the matter a thought, could not gainsay her; he
looked around and chose someone else. But by that time Vendôme had
arrived at the table to receive the snub before all the company assembled.
You may imagine how hard it was for that vain man to stomach the affront.
He turned sharp round on his heel and retired as swiftly as possible to his
bedroom where he could fume at leisure.

Meanwhile the young princess had had time to reflect; to be cheered by
her easy success, but somewhat concerned as to the King's reaction. As she
played her cards she decided to press on to victory or at least save herself
embarrassment, for despite her loving relations with the King she
was easily disconcerted, being by nature shy and gentle. She therefore
ran to Mme de Maintenon when the game was over and told her all,
saying that after the events in Flanders she found it most distressing even
to see M. de Vendôme, and that his perpetual haunting of the salon at
Marly, where she could not avoid him, was more than she could bear.
Their conversation was short because the King was expected to appear
at any moment. Mme de Maintenon was herself deeply offended with
Vendôme, all the more so perhaps because she had fought against him for
so long in vain. She spoke to the King that very night, and her words had
an immediate effect. The King was already incensed with him, and in any
case he disliked people with a grievance. Before retiring to bed he ordered
Blouin to inform M. de Vendôme that he should not in future solicit
for invitations to Marly.

You may imagine the latter's fury at receiving this wholly unexpected
rebuff, destroying as it did all his hopes of recovery. Yet he remained
silent for he dared not remonstrate with the King lest worse should
follow. The incident at *brelan* created a great scandal and the rumour
spread to Paris that he had been driven from Marly. That tale he scotched
by remaining, disgraced and humiliated, until the day of the King's return
to Versailles, when he departed to Anet. He never again set foot in Marly.
After the first shock he set himself to do as best he might. Blouin had said
nothing of Meudon; thus he took care to be seen there on every visit and to
boast out loud of his close friendship with Monseigneur, for all the world
like some country bumpkin. Whenever Mme la Duchesse de Bourgogne
visited Meudon there was M. de Vendôme, parading himself before her

---

[1] Another name for *brelan* was 'five heads'.

as though wishing to prove that in Monseigneur's house at least she had not prevailed against him. She, however, remembering his expulsion from Marly, quietly endured his insolence and bided her time.

Her moment came two months later when the King and Mme de Maintenon went to dine, but not to sleep, at Meudon, and she accompanied them. M. de Vendôme, there present as usual, was so tactless as to advance one of the first when they stepped down from their coach; whereupon Mme la Duchesse de Bourgogne showed less than her customary restraint, and turned her back on him after the merest sketch of a curtsey. Vendôme, noting this, pressed forward and was mad enough to follow her after dinner to her card-table. He received the same treatment there and to an even more marked degree. That cut him to the quick and put him so much out of countenance that he retired to his bedroom and remained there until very late. Meanwhile Mme la Duchesse de Bourgogne was making Monseigneur aware of his lack of consideration, and on returning to Versailles she complained openly to Mme de Maintenon and the King, pointing out that purely to spite her Vendôme was making a home for himself at Meudon in order to make up for the deprivation of Marly.

On the following day Vendôme complained bitterly to Monseigneur of persecution by the princess, but Monseigneur, having been warned, answered him so coldly that he retired, his eyes wet with tears. The day after saw the end of the affair. Vendôme was playing at *papillon* after dinner in one of the private drawing-rooms when d'Antin arrived from Versailles. He went to Vendôme's table and inquired with such a grave air when the hand would be finished that the latter asked what was the matter. D'Antin replied that he had fulfilled his commission. 'Commission?' exclaimed Vendôme, 'I gave you no commission.' 'Your pardon, Monsieur,' said d'Antin. 'You forget that I must give you an answer.' At that Vendôme left the game and accompanied him into Monseigneur's dark little privy. There, tête-à-tête, he learned that the King had ordered Monseigneur not to invite him again because his presence displeased Mme la Duchesse de Bourgogne. He was seized by a perfect transport of rage, spitting out every insult he could call to mind. The remainder of the visit was as embarrassing as it was alarming, and on the day when Monseigneur departed he fled back to Anet. He was now wholly without consolation, except such as he could find with his vices and his valets. Yet he still continued to brag of his friendship with Monseigneur and of the violence done to that prince's feelings. He relied on the faint hope that such a tale spread by his servants might persuade Society of his probable return to favour at some future date. The present had become unendurable; he dreamed of extricating himself by service in Spain and accordingly wrote to the Princesse des Ursins asking to be applied for. They needed some general there. His presence was requested, but his disgrace was still too fresh in the King's mind, and it was thought presumptuous of him to have looked in that direction for help. A flat refusal was returned.

No one gained more than Mme de Maintenon by this tremendous collapse. Apart from the joy of crushing one who, through M. du Maine, owed almost all to her and yet had dared to oppose her, she saw her influence becoming ever more formidable after such strong proof of its power. No one indeed had doubted that her hand had struck the blow. We shall discover her before long hurling other darts with no less deadly effect.[1]

On 1 May, which fell on a Wednesday, the King went to Marly. It was near the time of M. de La Rochefoucauld's retirement, and he put in no appearance although until then, though nearly blind, he had never missed the excursion. It was on that very same day that M. de Torcy went to Paris, and left immediately for Holland in the greatest secrecy imaginable. I do not know how M. de Lauzun got on to the scent of that; but I saw him buttonhole the Duc de Villeroy in the salon next morning, and several others as well, asking them whether they had seen M. de Torcy, to which they all replied no. 'Yet he returned from Paris late last night,' said Lauzun, 'and I know that there are to be marvellous dishes at his dinner. I shall not say what they are, but I am going to eat my share and I advise you to do the same.' Torcy was infinitely fastidious regarding his food; his prestige was such that no one dined with him except the best people and they did not wait to be invited. They fell for the bait and were undeceived too late because he dined late at Marly and usually worked until the moment when he was served. They found his door closed; they knocked; no answer. At last, one after the other, they realized that his lodging was empty. Picture them then cursing M. de Lauzun, furious with themselves for appearing ridiculous, and trying to find somewhere else to dine. Then, to cap all, M. de Lauzin inquired whether they had eaten well with M. de Torcy and laughed at them. That joke of his spread through Marly and allowed people to know of Torcy's journey before the King would have wished.

Old Saumery died at his house near Chambord at the age of 86. He was a tall good-looking old man, well made and of good country stock, very courageous and honourable, whom the King esteemed and had favoured. Henri IV brought amongst his other baggage two valets from Béarn. One of them was called Joanne, which may indeed have been his baptismal name since many Basques are named Joannès. When Henri IV came to the throne Joanne was made gardener at Chambord and subsequently became caretaker, but the kind of caretaker who sweeps and cleans as they do for private persons, not the kind that we now find in royal residences. His son, however, gradually rose to that footing, but was still regarded as a servant and enriched himself in that condition, which made it possible for him to marry a sister of Mme Colbert, whose father had been a citizen of

---

[1] Alluding to the coming dismissal of Chamillart on 1 June, 1709.

Blois. At the time of Saumery's marriage she was still only a very ordinary little bourgeoise, and her brother the famous M. Colbert was a little boy. When the latter rose in the service of Mazarin and became an intendant, he received his brother-in-law Saumery and found him employment in the army, where he distinguished himself, becoming eventually, thanks to Colbert's protection, governor and master of hounds at Chambord and Blois. He left two sons, the elder of whom, a very fine figure of a man with an imposing presence,[1] was wounded in the knee during one of M. de Turenne's battles. He married a daughter of Besmaus governor of the Bastille, because of whose influence, and the kindness which the King had always shown to his father, he obtained the reversion of the governorship of Chambord and the captaincy of Blois. With those two posts he might have been expected to make a fortune and live at his home, but when M. de Beauvilliers became governor of the royal princes he dug Saumery out from the banks of the Loire and made him assistant-governor. At first he appeared humble, respectful, obsequious, wholly attached to his work, but all the time he was reconnoitring the terrain, so new to him, and courting the notice of ministers and high-ranking persons. Such brains as he possessed were entirely bent on intrigue, which neither honour nor gratitude in any way restrained. He began to frequent ladies of quality and, as was said of him, to have his foot in everyone's shoes. No man ever made so many daily journeys backwards and forwards through the Château de Versailles and up and down its staircases; what is more, no man ever made so much capital out of an old wound.

In the end he persuaded himself that he was a personage. He put on airs and looked important, never perceiving that he was merely ill-bred. He whispered into people's ears or shielded his mouth with his hand, often sniggering, and then promptly disappearing, always full of gossip, always making a parade of secrecy. By skill and intrigue, and by deceiving M. de Beauvilliers, he managed to extract from the King salaries of almost eighty thousand livres for himself and his children, who had the best regiments for nothing. Withal, though he always appeared most bland he was at heart a trouble-maker. He developed a habit of never referring to anyone as *Monsieur* or *Madame*, not even those who most deserved that title of respect. His best effort was *M'sieur*, and he so termed the most eminent figures, giving them out to be his friends, and to have said such and such to him in confidence. I remember one occasion at M. de Chevreuse's house when he saw a picture of Mme la Princesse de Conti on a table. 'Hah!' said he, 'that is rather a good likeness of the Princesse de Conti.' He then proceeded to say what the poor Prince de Conti used to tell him . . . and then a sailor named Preuilly (the Maréchal d'Humières's brother). He went on to speak of Monsieur de Turenne, calling him plain Mons' Turenne, and reporting conversations between

[1] Here as so often Saint-Simon leaps a generation by mistake.

them; he, a subaltern, who would not have dared so much as to
approach a general officer, certainly not one of M. de Turenne's standing;
and he always sniggered in a patronizing way. 'The old vicomte,' he
would say; or 'the poor old vicomte'. Everyone was quite astounded when
he was discovered to mean M. de Turenne. That kind of thing was too
much of a habit with him to make news; but he so far exceeded himself
that day that we kept offering him fresh opportunities so as to mock him,
and we succeeded every time. We were dying with laughter, and there
he was never doubting but that the cause was his delightful tales which he
recounted with a marvellous mixture of authority and self-importance.

Next day Sassenage, Louville, little Renau[1] and I were at Mme de
Chevreuse's house, talking of his impertinence. Someone entered. We hid
ourselves behind a window-curtain and continued with one anecdote
after another until little Renau suddenly said out loud, 'We should be
properly trapped if M. de Saumery heard us and came and lifted the
curtain!' Hardly had he spoken before that event occurred, but instead of
being embarrassed we just shook with laughter, whilst he, who possibly
had not been listening, asked us about the joke. At that our mirth exceeded all bounds, and was taken up by all the company who realized
what it portended and that although he had caught us he remained quite
in the dark. That charlatan was akin to those rats which hasten to leave
a sinking ship, but he was not astute. It was not hard for him to foresee the rise of Harcourt or the decline of M. de Beauvilliers, to whom he
owed all. He had been personally attached to Mgr le Duc de Bourgogne but
on the pretext of his lameness he was excused war-service and went instead
to take the waters. He returned to Versailles during the Lille campaign to
find all the prospects favouring M. de Vendôme; he immediately joined the
cabal and said worse than any of them. MM. de Chevreuse and de Beauvilliers, obstinately charitable, were deaf and blind to Saumery's desertion
and continued to welcome him warmly on the rare occasions when he deigned
to visit them. They found it vastly hard to believe the tales of his remarks
concerning Mgr le Duc de Bourgogne, but eventually they could not
ignore the publicity; their manner to him then became slightly more distant, but that was all. Saumery gained M. du Maine's approval, and
through his influence was later nominated by the dying King as one of the
governors of the present monarch. In the end he became so grand a gentleman that he thought himself abominably ill-treated by not being made
chevalier of the Order. You will see that, although this sounds madness,
he was there not altogether wrong.

A few days after the assignment of the various army commanders,
the Maréchal de Villars, who was to command in Flanders[2] under

---

[1] 'Little' because of his 'exiguous stature' (*Larousse*). Exiguous indeed if Saint-Simon could
call him little!

[2] The hero of Friedlingen (1702); he had not yet been defeated by Marlborough.

16*

Monseigneur, had gone to work with the latter at Meudon, had then worked with the King, and immediately after had departed to Flanders to make everything ready. He returned at the beginning of May, made his report, and went back shortly afterwards. The troops were unpaid, and there had been no possibility of laying in stores. None the less Villars laughed and swaggered, making his usual extravagant forecasts. Nothing but a battle, he said, could save France, and he proposed to fight one on the plain of Lens at the opening of the campaign, breathing out fire and slaughter in a way that chilled the hearts of wiser men when they saw the last hope of the State committed to his hands. Yet it was not that he took his heavy responsibility lightly. He hoped rather that everyone, even the enemy who were bound to hear his remarks, might thus be deceived, the King and Mme de Maintenon heartened, and their opinion of him greatly increased.[1]

[*The campaign of 1708 had dragged on far beyond the usual time for going into winter quarters and meanwhile secret and official peace negotiations had been going on at the Hague. Rouillé, one of the French ambassadors, was sent in March to meet the Dutch plenipotentiary on the frontier. A month earlier Philip V had also sent offers of peace. On 19 April Rouillé had returned to Versailles with nothing but failure to report, for the Allies demanded the abdication of King Philip without compensation and the handing over of the whole of Spain, Italy, and the Indies to Charles the Archduke. When Louis XIV read these 'hard terms', he burst into tears before all his ministers and declared that he would be forced to agree to everything. He had been reduced to that extremity by Marlborough's seven campaigns, the terrible winter, and the famine in France, greatly increased by the cutting off of supplies of grain from Africa, the Levant, and Scandinavia by the English fleet. Torcy went to the Hague in mid-May bearing the humiliating acceptance of the Allies' terms.*

Early in May, however, King Philip's troops began to win battles. He believed that the Spanish people were loyal to him and wrote to his grandfather, 'I will only give up my crown with my life.' But the Allies now demanded a guarantee that Louis XIV would be responsible for Philip's compliance, and this new condition was what wrecked the peace, for rightly or wrongly the French interpreted this clause to mean that King Louis might be forced to drive his grandson out of Spain by armed force. On 1 June Torcy returned, having written on 28 May, 'Your Majesty is thus entirely free to reject these conditions absolutely, as I trust the state of your affairs will permit; or to accept them if you unfortunately conceive it your duty to end the war at whatever cost.' Villars's infectious optimism may have been one of the factors that decided King Louis to continue.

The campaign of 1709 opened very late and ended with the appalling slaughter of Malplaquet.]

Whilst he was in France Villars had worked many times with Monseigneur, giving him an exact account of everything, which persuaded that

---

[1] From Villars's letters it would appear that it was part of a deliberate plan to conceal the facts about the poor state of the troops.

prince that he played a role in affairs of state. Chamillart and Desmaretz also held discussions with him, on the disposition of troops and on finance. Harcourt was wiser and more prudent in refusing to command the Flanders army, alleging that he was out of practice in warfare; had commanded only small bodies of troops, and was thus without sufficient experience for large armies and important undertakings. He preferred to criticize from a safe distance and, being already on good terms with Monseigneur, he seized the chance to entice away M. de Beauvilliers's pupil, or at least divide his allegiance. He followed the example of Villars with the prince's father by working with him; but, being artful, he went even further, proposing that Mme la Duchesse de Bourgogne should be present at their sessions, and flattering them both by that means. He kept the most important matters to discuss in her presence; consulted her; admired her every word; praised her to M. le Duc de Bourgogne; prolonged their meetings; and set his entire mind to showing himself in the best possible light, so as to give them a great idea of his ability and persuade the princess of his devotion. She was indeed flattered. Harcourt had been attentive to her for some time past; he was too intimate with Mme de Maintenon and she with him for the princess not to think well of him, and she very much appreciated being consulted and sought after by men of affairs.

The various appointments were highly approved. I shared that sentiment; but I could not but deplore the fact that Chamillart had let Harcourt rejoin the hunt, and moreover had given him the chance to influence Mgr le Duc de Bourgogne. I spoke strongly to the Dukes of Chevreuse and Beauvilliers who, leaving all to God as usual and uninterested in cabals or future events, paid no attention. They were perhaps affected by the reason which Chamillart had given me, namely that he preferred to keep the Court censor at a distance. The poor fellow could not see that by removing him in appearance he actually brought him closer by giving him opportunities to meddle in everything, not only with Mgr and Madame la Duchesse de Bourgogne, but, far more dangerous, with Mme de Maintenon and the King.

More than six weeks before the assignment of the generals, there had been very strong rumours that Chamillart was about to be replaced by d'Antin. I had warned his daughter Mme de Dreux, the only member of the family to whom it was of any use speaking, for her mother never took advice, the brothers were fools, the son an ignorant boy, the two other daughters flighty, and Chamillart himself determined to discount everything and trust in the King's permanent support. Moreover, I had often warned Mme de Dreux of Mme la Duchesse de Bourgogne's resentment; she had tackled her on the subject, but as the princess had replied icily that there was nothing, she was satisfied, for want of better encouragement. I had urged her father to speak to the King concerning the rumours, and in the end he did so; but he made the vital mistake of not naming any names. The best he could do was to say that if his conduct of affairs had unfortunately displeased the King, he begged his Majesty to say so without constraint. Whereupon the King had seemed moved, had given him all manner of assurances of his continued esteem and friendship, had even praised him, and had sent him away rejoicing, seemingly more secure than ever. Such assurances did not, however, comfort me. I knew the extreme ill-will of Mme de Maintenon and Mme la Duchesse de Bourgogne and that his throat was already between the jaws of those two keen hounds. The Maréchal de Boufflers had never cared for him. He now complained bitterly of all that had been lacking at Lille, for he had discovered that Chamillart did not report all the blows which he had received, and that the King had learned of them through other channels. Being powerless to remedy, wishing not unduly to cause alarm: those were not crimes, but the Maréchal chose to consider them as such. He had said as much to me and I was unable to placate him. Sure that the burden was too great for Chamillart, and encouraged by Mme de Maintenon and Harcourt, he had no mercy on him, but spoke out his opinion like a good Frenchman as in honour bound. The Maréchal d'Harcourt skilfully shattered Chamillart's image at all his private sessions. One day, when he was holding forth against him in Mme de Maintenon's room, well knowing that she would not be displeased, she asked whom he would put in his place. 'M. Fagon, Madame,' said he coldly. She began to laugh, pointing out none the less that this was no joking matter. 'I am not joking, Madame,' he replied, 'M. Fagon is a good doctor and no soldier; M. Chamillart is a magistrate and also no soldier. M. Fagon is a man of great intelligence and good sense; M. Chamillart is neither. M. Fagon, from lack of experience, might make mistakes at the start, but he would soon correct them by wisdom and reflection. M. Chamillart has also made mistakes and goes on making them, and they will be the ruin of France; what is more he is at the end of his resources. That is why I say in all seriousness that M. Fagon would do much better.' There was no enlightened person at the Court who did not feel that Chamillart was threatened. Only he remained serene, refusing to credit the rumours, and his family shared his false sense of security. His true friends, and they were very few, trembled at his blindness. M. and Mme de Chevreuse, MM. de Beauvilliers and de Mortemart often expressed their anxiety, but it was hopeless to search for remedies when he invariably refused them.

A few weeks later the King did something, for him quite unprecedented, which set everyone agog. He interviewed the Marshals Boufflers and Villars in his study in the presence of Chamillart. That was on the afternoon of Friday, 7 May, at Marly. When they left, Villars went to Paris with orders to return on the following Sunday morning. He reappeared on the Saturday evening. People may have been surprised by that first informal meeting; they were far more so by the full-dress council of war which the King held for the first time in his life at his Court. He invited Mgr le Duc de Bourgogne, adding somewhat sourly. 'Unless you prefer to be at vespers.' Those attending were Monseigneur and Mgr le Duc de Bourgogne, the Marshals Boufflers, Villars, and Harcourt, and MM. Chamillart and Desmaretz, the former for the troops, the latter for finance. The marshals finding themselves for the first time more or less on a level with the ministers proceeded to harry them unmercifully, especially Chamillart.[1] He was already in decline, Desmaretz not yet firmly in the saddle. The King did not protect them but let Boufflers and Harcourt worry them until the normally patient and sweet-tempered Chamillart grew so upset that his angry voice could be heard in the small drawing-room, opposite to the King's bedroom where the scene was taking place. The matter concerned the withdrawal of garrisons from the fortresses and the bad condition of the troops; on which subject Desmaretz wished to be heard, but the King immediately silenced him. The bodyguard had not been paid for many months. Boufflers as captain of the guard in residence had mentioned this to the King and been snubbed for his pains. He had insisted. The King had said that he was misinformed and that they had their pay. Boufflers, taking umbrage, produced from his pocket an exact account of the amount owing to each man, which he displayed when the meeting broke up, begging the King to see that his statements were well-founded, and showing him at a glance the wretched state of the guards and the truth of his accusation. Taken by surprise the King turned on Desmaretz, asking with some harshness why this was so. Desmaretz, who was completely at a loss, mumbled something about not having known; upon which Boufflers rounded on him fiercely. The other two marshals remained in complete silence, but Chamillart could not resist putting in his dig at the controller-general, by entreating the King to believe that it was the same everywhere; that not one single regiment had been paid, and that the proofs would soon be apparent. This he said with immense feeling. The King was annoyed at his council ending on such an unexpectedly angry note. He interrupted Chamillart by telling Desmaretz severely to see that things were better organized in future, and dismissed the meeting. Immediately afterwards Villars returned to Flanders.

There had been riots in the markets of Paris,[2] which had entailed keeping at home more companies of the French and Swiss guards than was usual. Argenson, lieutenant of police, ran into trouble at Saint-Roch[3] when he went there to quell a dangerous rising by a great crowd of insolent fellows because some poor man had been trampled to death. M. de La

---

[1] There was a general inclination to blame Chamillart. His obstinacy was said to have lost the peace, and he had neglected to prepare for the new campaign.

[2] In protest against the famine and high prices.

[3] Saint-Roch, the church and the quarter of Paris near the Rue de Rivoli and the Rue Saint-Honoré. The mob had threatened to throw Argenson into the Seine.

Rochefoucauld, in his retirement at the Kennels,[1] received an appalling anonymous letter directed at the King, clearly affirming that there were still Ravaillacs[2] in France, and ending that piece of folly with praise of Brutus. The duke had thereupon rushed to Marly quite hysterical, and had interrupted the council with a message to say that he had vital information for the King. This sudden eruption of the blind recluse with his pressing need to see the King gave the courtiers much food for reflection. As soon as the council had risen the King sent for M. de La Rochefoucauld, was shown the letter, and was much displeased. Everything becomes known at courts; M. de La Rochefoucauld's mission was soon common knowledge, also that the Dukes of Bouillon and Beauvilliers had received similar epistles and had given them to the King. They, however, had been treated better because their actions were not so ostentatious. None the less, the King was deeply depressed for a few days, but after some reflection he concluded that those who threaten and advertise are usually less desirous of committing a crime than of creating a disturbance.

What most upset the King was a flood of most insolent and violent placards directed against his person, his private life, his government. For a long time these could be seen posted up on the gates of Paris and on the churches, in the public streets and, more especially, on his statues,[3] which were every night defiled in some way or other, for the marks could be seen in the morning, as well as the torn-up placards. There was also a multitude of ditties and lampoons, in which no mercy was shown him.[4] So matters stood when the procession of Sainte-Geneviève took place on 16 May. This only occurs in times of crisis, by order of the King, acts of the Parlement, and instructions from the Archbishop of Paris and the Abbé de Sainte-Geneviève. For some it was a cry for help; others saw it as a means of distracting a people dying of hunger.

Meanwhile, in Flanders especially, the armies lacked for everything. Every possible effort was made in the early part of June to send wheat, by sea from Brittany and by road from Picardy. Money and corn arrived only in small quantities, and the abandoned troops were left to forage for themselves, sometimes for long periods, on a greatly narrowed frontier. The armies in Dauphiné and Catalonia were much better off for food, and the troops were in better shape. The Duke of Berwick had long since been at his post and was constructing a fortified camp under Briançon. I have

---

[1] The old kennels behind the new Great Stables at Versailles. The Duc de La Rochefoucauld had built an enormous house on the site and lived there in retirement.

[2] Ravaillac was the assassin of Henri IV.

[3] In the Place des Victoires and the Place Vendôme.

[4] One blasphemous parody read: 'Our Father which art in Versailles unhallowed be thy name. Thy kingdom is gone. Thy will is no longer done on land or sea. Forgive our enemies who have defeated us, but not our generals who have allowed them to do so. Fall not to the temptations of the Maintenon, but deliver us from Chamillart.'

already said that I should not give any detailed account of the journeys of Rouillé and Torcy. Suffice it to say that Torcy returned to Versailles from the Hague on Saturday, 1 June, after an absence of barely a month. He brought no good news and was not well received by the King and Mme de Maintenon. The latter, especially, was highly critical of his efforts, partly because she disliked him personally, partly because she had not been informed in advance of his mission.

His return speeded the departure of all the generals. The Elector of Bavaria, whom Torcy had seen at Mons, and the Maréchal de Villars were informed of the situation. At the same time it was announced that none of the princes assigned to the armies would leave the Court, and the King sent the bâton of a Marshal of France to Bezons, who commanded in Catalonia. M. le Duc d'Orléans had long been entreating the King to let him go, but as we shall see before long his credit was not good at that time. The King explained to him that since Monseigneur and Mgr le Duc de Bourgogne were to stay at the Court, it was best to remain there also, especially since King Louis might soon find himself in the unhappy position of having to withdraw his troops from Spain.

If Mme de Maintenon's influence was disastrous in great affairs that harpy whom the Duc de Gramont had married was being equally obnoxious in lesser matters, for such is the way of jumped-up commoners. The King had commanded her to return from Bayonne, for her acquisitions by force or persuasion had become notorious; she had even managed to filch the pearls of the Queen-dowager of Spain, after showing disrespect to her in every conceivable way. She was now back in Paris, furious at not receiving the dignities and precedence that should have been hers on marriage. In the meantime, whilst the Court awaited the return of Rouillé, it was decided to arouse the patriotism of all classes by publishing the Allies' monstrous terms, say rather demands, for peace. A printed letter was accordingly despatched to all the provincial governors, bidding them make known the facts, the lengths to which the King had gone in his desire for a peace, and the failure of his endeavours. There followed an outburst of indignation coupled with cries for vengeance, and offers from people of every condition to sacrifice their worldly goods so as to continue the war, with other extravagant proposals in proof of their loyalty.

The Gramont woman perceived in that great wave of enthusiasm a means of obtaining all of which she had been deprived and so greatly desired. She persuaded her husband to go to the King and offer him his silver dinner service, hoping that the example might be followed and that she would gain credit and reward for procuring relief so swift, convenient, and acceptable. Unfortunately for her, the Duc de Gramont first spoke to his son-in-law the Maréchal de Boufflers, who thought the idea so admirable that he swiftly followed suit, presenting his own silver, which he possessed in great quantities and all very beautiful, and making a great fuss urging others to present theirs. In the event he was generally supposed to have originated the scheme and no credit was given to the Gramont or even to her husband. They thus found that they themselves had been duped, which rendered her more furious than ever. So much talk about silver created a vast commotion. No one dared to refuse it, yet no one wished to make a sacrifice. Some people had clung to their silver plates as a last resource and dreaded to part with them; others feared the dirtiness of pewter and earthenware; others again saw full well how thankless it would be to follow where only the first would receive the credit. Soon afterwards the King mentioned the silver at a meeting of the finance council, showing a strong inclination to receive plates from everyone.

The same plan had been proposed and rejected earlier, when Pont-chartrain had been the controller-general. Now that he was Chancellor he spoke against it most emphatically, stressing the small profit compared to the enormous sacrifices of the individuals concerned. He also stressed the unseemliness of the whole proceeding, which would leave the Court and nobility eating off earthenware, whilst private gentlemen in the provinces retained their silver; and if that should be made illegal, the discontent and deception that would result. He represented the loss of prestige to the government of France, which might be suspected of using this shift as a last resource; the rumours that would arise abroad, the contempt of our enemies, and the encouragement it would give to them. Lastly, he recalled the jests during the war of 1688, when the precious silver furniture in the gallery and the great and small apartments at Versailles, even including the silver throne, had been melted down. Very little, he said, was gained from that transaction, and the loss of the magnificent craftsmanship, more precious even than the metal, had proved irreparable. Despite these telling arguments the King persisted in his readiness, without using any kind of pressure, to accept free-will offerings of all the plate with which individuals might care to present him. A verbal announcement was made to that effect, and patriots were offered two alternatives. They might give their silver outright by sending it to Launay, the King's goldsmith, who would keep a record of the givers and the amounts received, which the King read attentively for the first few days at least. Otherwise, if they wished for repayment, they could send direct to the Mint, where their silver would be weighed on arrival, the names, date, and ounces written in a book, and the owners reimbursed as soon as money became available. There were many who were glad to sell, in the hope of relief from their present poverty. Inestimable harm was done, however, for much beautiful work was lost in the moulded, engraved, embossed, or carved decorations that had once adorned the silver of wealthy and tasteful persons.

When the final reckoning was made there turned out to be fewer than a hundred names on Launay's list, and the entire proceeds from gifts and conversion amounted to less than three million. The Court, Parisian Society, and a few notables had not dared to refuse; some others had followed suit hoping to gain immediate relief, but almost no one else either in Paris or the provinces. I must admit to having been one of the last to offer, for I was monstrously weary of taxes and felt very little inclined to support a voluntary levy. When, however, I found myself to be almost the only man of my rank still eating off silver I sent a few thousand pistoles' worth to the Mint, and locked the rest away. I had inherited a little undecorated silver from my father, and I regretted the loss of it less than the inconvenience and dirt. M. de Lauzun, who had a great deal of silver, all of it very fine, found that his reluctance overcame his patriotism and did not send at all. I was present with several others when the Duc de Villeroy questioned him on the subject. He answered in his customary low voice, 'I have not sent as yet; I scarcely know who would honour me by accepting it, and besides, how can I be sure that it does not go under the Duchesse de Gramont's petticoat?' I thought we should all die of laughter as he turned right-about and left us.

All the nobility took to eating off porcelain within a week, with the result that the china shops were emptied and prices rose sky high; the middle classes, however, continued to use silver. Even the King, himself, talked of going on to porcelain and sent his gold plate to the Mint. He soon discovered that most people were cheating but, although he expressed himself with unusual sourness on that score, it had no effect. He would have done far better to have spoken to the Duc de Gramont and his odious old woman, who had been the cause of this shameful and useless sacrifice. They were not hoodwinked, for they kept their good silver locked up, and she herself took their old plates to the Mint and saw to it that she was given good value. None of the donors enjoyed for long the sensation of pleasing the King. After three months had passed he had seen the futility of the whole monstrous idea and said that he was very sorry he had ever agreed to it. That is how things were managed at the Court and throughout the kingdom.[1]

The armies were mustered and the frontiers in a sadly disturbed state, yet they were more serene than the inner life of the Court, where the agitation was extreme. In all the forty-eight years during which the King

---

[1] Mme de Maintenon writing to the Duc de Noailles, 9 June: 'When it became known that the King had refused the shameful terms of peace everyone cheered and called for war, but it did not last and people soon fell back into that prostration which you saw and deplored . . . How many times have you heard it said, "Why are we allowed to keep our silver plate? It would be a pleasure if the King would take it all". . . . Now there are murmurs, people say that the King should economize first. All his spending is criticized . . . they say let him give up his horses, dogs, and servants. In brief, they want to strip him first. Where do these murmurs come from? From outside his own door. From whom? from the very people who owe all to him. As for me, they want to stone me because it is thought that I do not speak; as if he does not give his own orders!'

had reigned single-handed, that is to say since the death of Cardinal Mazarin, only two ministers had been dismissed. Fouquet, who was confined in the Château de Pignerol for the remainder of his life (no thanks to Colbert and Le Tellier that his life was spared),[1] and M. de Pomponne whose dismissal would appear to have been obtained somewhat against the King's will, since he was recalled to office immediately after Louvois's death, some twelve years later. Chamillart was the third and the last to be dismissed and was the hardest of all to expel, for although he had no other support than the King's partiality, the latter yielded most grudgingly to the mighty powers united against him.

Without repeating what I said of the errors that drew upon him the hatred of Mme de Maintenon and Mme la Duchesse de Bourgogne, I must speak of another mistake that harmed only himself. He never went out of his way to oblige Monseigneur. That prince, so nervous, so unsure, given no authority by his jealous father, scarcely ever ventured to make recommendations to the ministers, except on trifling matters when driven thereto by underlings whom he trusted. Du Mont was the man most often charged with such missions and in Pontchartrain's day he had grown accustomed to dealing with a minister who was always glad to oblige. He had an unpleasant surprise when Chamillart took over the office of controller-general, for the latter wrongly concluded that with the King and Mme de Maintenon to back him he needed no one else. He was moreover very wary of serving Monseigneur for fear of seeming to have other attachments. I had noticed for some time past that Monseigneur was not pleased with Chamillart. Some remarks of Du Mont, and others heard in passing, had set me thinking, and I had warned Chamillart's daughters. Chamillart himself would not heed me, saying that he was too old for anything beyond his immediate tasks, that the King and Mme de Maintenon were sufficient for him, and that cabals and intrigues at the Court were none of his concern.

Later, as I have mentioned already, Mme de Maintenon and Mme la Duchesse de Bourgogne conceived an aversion for him and determined to expel him, the former, at least, not then realizing the force that would be needed to detach a minister whom the King truly liked. King Louis soon grew accustomed to severe comments on his chief minister from the mouths of Mme de Maintenon, the army commanders, Mme la Duchesse de Bourgogne and her husband (by adverse remarks which she took care to repeat). It did, however, have its effect. The King's confidence was shaken, but his heart stayed firm. He had always regarded Chamillart as his own achievement, his apprentice in every post including the highest, seeing him even there as his old pupil. No other minister rode the King on so loose a rein; even after he received the supreme power he

---

[1] Turenne is reported to have said, 'I believe that M. Colbert is most eager for him to be hanged, and that M. Le Tellier is terrified lest he should escape hanging.'

did not allow him to feel the curb, but reflected on to him all the honour and all the credit. Old acquaintance before being given office, the honest return of trust by trust, willing obedience and truthful reports had successfully merged the favourite with the minister, whilst Chamillart's sincere and continual admiration, and his unaffected desire to please, had carried the King's partiality to the highest degree. It was no small token of that affection that so many thrusts, delivered in concert and increasing daily, should have been required to shake the King's faith. Shaken it was, indeed, but how strong it still remained![1]

Mme de Maintenon was aware that Monseigneur had spoken out and that the King had listened. She now persuaded him to attack again. But such powerful artillery could scarcely be brought into action without causing reverberations, and the rumour spread through the Court that either France or Chamillart must be destroyed; that his blunders had brought the nation to the verge of ruin, and that to leave him one day longer in charge was absolute folly. Some were not ashamed to abuse him openly: others spoke of good intentions and pitied failings for which the majority bitterly reproached him. Everyone admitted his honesty; but some successor, no matter who, was universally declared to be essential. Cavoye, whose long acquaintance with the Court sometimes passed for wit, said that the King's power might indeed be absolute, but even he had not the strength to uphold Chamillart against the multitude.

His smallest faults were enlarged to crimes of folly; you might almost say that he became a sacrifice which the King could no longer refuse to his people. Some stated as much in plain language, but no one produced any clear accusation. People contented themselves with vague aspersions, and although many were greatly in his debt no one volunteered to defend him. When the flood of reproaches tempted some persons to demur a higher loyalty exacted their silence. Everyone was aware that the troops lacked even bare necessities, that the garrisons were depleted, the granaries empty, but no one remembered how Chamillart had miraculously re-equipped the army on two earlier occasions, the first three weeks after Blenheim, the second a bare fortnight after Ramillies. These prodigious feats of organization twice saved France, and that is to mention those two only, because they were vitally important and known to all at the time when they occurred. No one remembered them now; a fatal sponge had been passed over them, and people turned their backs if they were mentioned.

Such were the final intimations of Chamillart's approaching downfall. I did not fail to warn him, and I begged him to speak to the King as he had

[1] 'The King was ruled by men whom he thought he ruled, but his talent was not sufficient to outweigh the incapacity, of his ministers. He even felt obliged to support them in everything and against everyone, and for their sakes deprived himself of the help of the wisest and most deserving of his subjects.' La Fare—*Mémoires*.

done once before at my urgent request, with most fortunate results for the storm clouds had passed over. But he was too noble-minded for a professional administrator; he simply replied that office was not worth the worry of a siege; that he would not want to add the anxiety of self-defence to his other labours; that whilst he still enjoyed the King's confidence he would gladly remain, but should that confidence need to be braced by intrigue he would find his position both disagreeable and untenable. He said lastly that he preferred to let matters take their course, or rather that Providence should direct them, for he was equally ready to make way for a better man, or continue his ministry with honour and peace of mind. Such noble sentiments filled me with admiration but I none the less entreated him to speak to the King. He would neither listen nor budge an inch from his opinion, and from that moment I knew that his dismissal would come very soon.

On the morning of Sunday, 9 June, Mme de Villars, who lodged next to us, came as she often did to see Mme de Saint-Simon, having earlier bidden us to supper and conversation. There would, so she said, be plenty for us to discuss. She went on to say that she was going to dine with Chamillart, which at one time would have been thought a favour, but she rather imagined that the favour was all on her side now. That was not because she had heard anything definite but because the rumours had grown stronger than ever during the past week.

It was on that same evening that the King spoke to M. de Beauvilliers before he entered the council, ordering him to go after dinner to Chamillart and to tell him that for the sake of France he must resign his office and the reversion be granted to his son. At the same time the King desired Chamillart to rest assured of his friendship and regard, and of his personal satisfaction with his past services, in token whereof he intended to continue his minister's salary of twenty thousand livres, adding to it a pension of another twenty thousand, with still another twenty thousand for his son.[1] The King said further that he wished Cany to purchase the post of master of his household, and that he would have been very glad to have seen Chamillart himself, had not the circumstances been so very painful. He must wait, said the King, until he was sent for, and would do well to leave Versailles that day; he might, however, live in Paris or wherever else he chose and once more be assured of the King's lasting affection.

M. de Beauvilliers, distressed beyond words both by the event and by his odious commission, tried vainly to shift the burden on to someone else; but the King replied that he had purposely chosen him because he was Chamillart's friend. He then immediately joined his council which was composed of the Chancellor, Torcy, Chamillart, and Desmaretz. Nothing in any way unusual occurred during the meeting, nor was there

---

[1] The Marquis de Cany.

anything at all in the King's manner or countenance to suggest something untoward. They even discussed some matter on which the King had asked Chamillart for a memorandum, and he was again told to produce one, and to bring it that evening to Mme de Maintenon's room. M. de Beauvilliers, deeply grieved and embarrassed, waited until he was alone with the King and then, speaking of his distress, entreated to be allowed to take with him Chamillart's friend the Duc de Chevreuse to share the burden. To this the King consented; but M. de Chevreuse himself thought it a great infliction.

At four o'clock in the afternoon the brothers-in-law made their way to Chamillart's house and were shown into the study, where he was alone, working. They entered with such an air of embarrassment that the unhappy minister at once realized that something had occurred, and without waiting for them to speak said calmly, 'What is it, Messieurs? If what you have to say concerns myself, pray do not be distressed. For a long time past I have been prepared to face anything.' Such gentle resolution was so touching that they could scarcely find the words to explain their errand. Chamillart listened without changing his expression and then replied in the same quiet voice, 'The King is the master. I have tried to serve him to the best of my powers; I hope that the new man will satisfy him better and be more fortunate. It is already much to be able to count on his friendship and at such a moment to receive the proof of it.' He asked if he might write to the King, and hearing that it was not forbidden he sat down to fill a page and a half with expressions of his loyalty and gratitude, which he read aloud to them because it was written in their presence. He had finished the memorandum which the King had ordered that morning, which seemed to please him, and he asked the two dukes to oblige him by giving both document and letter to King Louis. He then sealed the letter and, placing it on top of the other, handed it to them. He next wrote to Mme de Maintenon, thanking her for past kindnesses, no more; sent a verbal message to his wife to join him at L'Etang, but not saying why he went there, and put his papers in order for his successor. All this was done without tears, sighs, or a single word of complaint. He then descended his staircase, stepped into his coach with his son, and drove away to L'Etang as though nothing in the world had happened. No one else at Versailles heard of all this until long afterwards.

That same evening as I sat working in my upstairs study, writing a memorandum concerning the Blaye militia[1] (I mention this because it had serious consequences), Mme de Villars entered by the door below and asked to see me. I sent my letter to Pontchartrain and at once went down to her, finding her standing alone, because Mme de Saint-Simon had gone out. She asked whether I had heard the news; I knew

---

[1] His precious governorship of Blaye, inherited from his father, his only office, which people interfered with at their peril.

nothing, and she exclaimed, 'Chamillart is gone!' At those words I emitted the kind of groan which one utters at the death of a sick person, no matter how long his death has been expected. After some lamenting she went to the King's supper, and I, without torches, and by the inner courts so as to avoid recognition, to M. de Beauvilliers's apartment, for she had told me that he had bidden Chamillart farewell. M. de Beauvilliers was attending the King at his supper, but his wife was at home with Mme de Chevreuse, Desmaretz, and Louville. I cast a glance at the controller-general and had no difficulty in perceiving that he was a happy man though making great efforts to conceal it. I tackled Mme de Beauvilliers, but her eyes were full of tears and I could extract nothing. I therefore did not stay long but returned to my lodging, where the Maréchale de Villars joined us for supper.

Meanwhile Mme de Saint-Simon had been paying her court to Mme la Duchesse de Bourgogne in Mme de Maintenon's great drawing-room. There was great excitement and chatter, and someone whispered the news into her ear. She asked Mme la Duchesse de Bourgogne whether there was any truth in it; but the latter knew nothing because she had not been recalled to the bedroom since leaving it, and had not dared, that evening, to re-enter without a summons. Apparently the curtain was about to rise on the successor, whose name was not yet mentioned, and that was why they had left her outside. She told Mme de Saint-Simon to go to the King's supper, and that she would there tell all that she discovered in the bedroom. Mme de Saint-Simon went accordingly, and managed to be seated behind Mme la Duchesse de Bourgogne, who told her of the dismissal, the pensions, and the purchasing of Cavoye's[1] appointment. After the supper, which Mme de Saint-Simon found vastly tedious, Mme la Duchesse de Bourgogne came to her before going into the study and asked her to give Chamillart's daughters, especially the Duchesse de Lorges of whom she was fond, her love and sympathy, assuring them of her protection and assistance, so far as she was able, in their unhappy situation. M. de Lorges was anxious for the entire family. He stayed with us until very late and then went to L'Etang, resolved to do marvels for them, as he did do, constantly. I gave him a note for Chamillart, full of loving messages, asking him to send me word whether he truly wished to be alone on that first day or would allow us to visit him.

From all that has gone before you will know Chamillart's nature; kind, simple, obliging, truthful, honest, hard-working, loving the State and the King like a mistress, attached to his friends but much under-estimating them, never suspicious nor hating, pursuing his lofty course according to his lights having so little education, stubborn in the extreme, never admitting to mistakes, always supremely confident, and so infatuated as to

---

[1] The post of Master of the Household which the King wished Cany to purchase from Cavoye, who was in disgrace.

believe that by remaining honest and having the King on his side, which he never doubted, he need trim to no one save to Mme de Maintenon. He lost her regard by his son's marriage,[1] increased her aversion by his persistent support of the Duc de Vendôme against Mgr le Duc de Bourgogne (acting in this like a blindman who goes where he is led), and at last breaking with her quite unwittingly when his passion for the State, and for the King's personal glory, persuaded him to plan the relief of Lille without her knowledge. The powerful cabal that had made him see, think, and act as they pleased in the matter of Italy, and above all of Flanders, was of no assistance to him now. M. de Vendôme was ruined, M. de Vaudémont out of favour, and M. du Maine far too much in need of Mme de Maintenon to refuse her the sacrifice of Chamillart—had he not sacrificed to her his own mother?[2]

Chamillart suffered from yet another handicap most destructive to a minister; he was surrounded by people without social sense, who had never managed to acquire from the Court or Society the faintest glimmerings of understanding, and, what was even worse than such a lack of poise, whose bearing, conduct and speech were supremely ridiculous. Such were both his brothers, his cousin, Guyet his brother's father-in-law. His younger daughters, although the best creatures imaginable and the Duchesse de Lorges not unintelligent, were flighty, and so much infatuated with riches and pleasure that they scarcely restrained themselves even in disgrace. The eldest alone,[3] by her personality, good sense and conduct, made herself generally liked, esteemed, pitied, and succoured; but apart from the fact that she did not know all, she alone was not enough to check and govern the rest, nor even to advise her father, for he neither welcomed nor heeded advice from anyone. Mme de Chamillart spent her mornings between the decorators and her dressmaker, and her afternoons at the card-table, could not string two words together, knew nothing, like her husband saw no harm in anything, and by endeavouring to be civil made herself absurd, although she was the best of good women. She did not have it in her to rule her daughters or to give them an education however meagre; she was quite incapable of keeping house or household accounts, or of managing their wealth and lives; all that she left to the Abbé de La Proustière, a kinsman of theirs, who understood business matters no better than she and brought their affairs into fearful disorder.

On the Monday morning we learned that Mme de Maintenon's triumph was complete and that Voysin, her protégé who owed all his good fortune to her influence, had immediately been put in Chamillart's place. It had

---

[1] To the Duc de Mortemart's daughter. Her mother was a sister of the Duc de Beauvilliers who was out of favour with Mme de Maintenon.

[2] When he allowed Mme de Maintenon to drive out Mme de Montespan without protesting.

[3] Mme de Dreux; the two younger sisters were the Duchesse de La Feuillade and the Duchesse de Lorges (Mme de Saint-Simon's sister-in-law).

been thought latterly that he would succeed but no one had been certain until the announcement. The final decision was made only on the evening of Chamillart's dismissal, by the King and Mme de Maintenon unassisted.

Voysin had in full measure the one essential quality without which no man could, nor ever did, enter the council of Louis XIV during his entire reign (save only for M. de Beauvilliers), viz., a total lack of breeding. He was the grandson of a clerk of the criminal court of the Parlement, who lived and died in that employment. You will gather that there is no need to go further back. The brother of Voysin's father was provost of the merchants and distinguished himself greatly as a counsellor of State. He was one of those wise and modest judges of the old stock and a close friend of my father, in whose house I often saw him. He married his only daughter, a very wealthy heiress, to Lamoignon, son of the premier président and elder brother of the all too-notorious Bâville.[1] The father of our Voysin was a maître des requêtes and held various intendancies, which he was enjoying at the time of his death. His fortunate son was the only one of three brothers to make his way in the world. He married, in 1683, a daughter of Trudaine, a chief clerk of the audit office. Five years later he was made maître des requêtes, and through someone's influence, I know not whose, was sent as intendant to Hainault,[2] from whence he emerged a counsellor of State in 1694.

His wife, without aid of fashion or other embellishment, had a most charming face. She looked sweet and simple, was modest and discreet, and appeared wholly immersed in housekeeping and good works. She was in truth sensible, tactful, decorous, and appealing, and possessed to perfection the art of bringing matters her way without ever appearing to dominate. No one knew better how to manage a house, for she could be sumptuous when occasion demanded without ever offending by ostentation. The luxury of her home, still more so her attractive and polished manners, had made her extremely popular, more especially with the officers for whose comfort she worked miracles during the sieges and after the battles of Flanders, helping them with care and money and in all kinds of other ways. She became very friendly with M. de Luxembourg when for so many years he commanded the armies, and with the most distinguished of the generals, particularly M. d'Harcourt. It was M. de Luxembourg who first taught her how to please Mme de Maintenon when that lady visited the frontier, and she put his teaching to good use. She met her at Dinant,[3] where she stayed when the King was besieging Namur, curtseyed to her on arrival, took endless pains for her comfort and the furnishing of her room, had a care for even the least of her servants, and then shut herself into her own chamber, appearing only

[1] The brutal intendant of Languedoc at the time of the revolt in 1703.
[2] Now a province. of Belgium.
[3] On the Meuse.

briefly to pay respect, organizing everything from that retreat in such a way as to please the whole company, yet as though she were not living in the house. So immensely gratifying a reception predisposed Mme de Maintenon to like her hostess. Her household was equally charmed and eagerly recounted all that Mme Voysin had done since Neerwinden for the wounded officers and soldiers, praising her liberality, her well-ordered house, and extolling her for her piety and good works. One fortunate occurrence, luckily prepared for in advance, won Mme de Maintenon's heart. The weather changed suddenly from excessive heat to a damp chill that lasted for a long time. At that moment there appeared in a corner of Mme de Maintenon's bedroom a sumptuous dressing-gown modestly cut and snugly quilted, a present doubly welcome to that lady (who had brought with her no warm clothes) because of the surprise and the simplicity with which it was given. Mme Voysin's tact also enchanted her. Two whole days sometimes elapsed without her being seen at all, and she never appeared unless summoned. At such times, moreover, she could scarcely be prevailed upon to sit, appearing afraid of being a trouble and eager to find an excuse to leave. Such unaccustomed consideration was deemed a great merit and drew down upon her the playful reproach that she was the only one who could not be coaxed. She never presumed, however, not even after she had become initiated, and she managed to please Mme de Maintenon so much in that long visit that she was actually courted and bidden to call every single day when she visited Paris.

The excursion to Flanders in 1693 gave the friendship a new impulse and gained for Voysin the post of counsellor of State in the following year. After their return to Paris his wife still kept in the background, saw Mme de Maintenon very rarely, mostly on invitation, and then as she became more intimate calling occasionally of her own volition to show gratitude and affection, but at long intervals and unobtrusively. Thus, for some time their friendship was undiscovered and untainted by envy and spite. Voysin, meanwhile, went on with his work apparently quite unconcerned, until Chamillart, feeling overpressed with work, handed to him the affairs of Saint-Cyr. From that moment the eyes of the world were opened to them both and Voysin came to be considered a candidate for the highest offices.

Voysin did indeed greatly need the wife whom Providence had given him, for he remained vastly uncouth and was in other ways dry, hard, rude, tactless, and, like all intendants, utterly spoiled. He did not possess even their knowledge of the world but had in full measure their arrogance and pride. No man was ever more typically an intendant, and such he remained all his life from head to heels, using his power brutally for all kinds of purposes. That power was all in all to him, his code of law, his means, his right. What is more, he was a surly brute, knowing no one even after he had become a counsellor, and when he was made minister still incapable of doing the honours of his house.

Courtiers, nobles, officers, general and otherwise, who were used to Chamillart's informal friendliness, were shocked to find Voysin just the reverse. He was hard to approach, irritable, interrupting, giving short answers, turning his back at any rejoinder, or closing people's mouths by some terse, decisive, snubbing remark. His letters were devoid of all courtesies; they contained bare replies in masterful language, or a brief announcement of something which he officially ordained, invariably ending with 'such is the King's pleasure'. Wretched the man who had matters to treat with him depending on other laws than those which governed intendants! When he found himself out of his depth he would grow resentful and cut short the discussion! None the less he was never intentionally unjust or unkind; but he had never known any other authority than that of the King and Mme de Maintenon; their wishes were to him beyond questioning, his absolute law and sufficient reason.

In the interval before the announcement of his new appointment, Voysin went to thank his benefactress and receive her instructions. Thereafter he proceeded to Chamillart's office, possessed himself of the keys and documents, summoned the clerks, and at once took over the entire apartment and also the furniture. Thus a new face was the only change until the following Wednesday, when the King went to Marly and new furniture was installed. At some time during that evening Mme Voysin unobtrusively arrived and went straight to her old friend Mme de Caylus, without appearing at the Court. The latter immediately conducted her to her cousin, when the raptures of the protectress and the complete self-effacement of the protected were equally in evidence. Soon afterwards the King entered, embraced her twice to please his lady, and conversed with her of old times in Flanders until she felt ready to sink through the floor in embarrassment. Thereafter, managing to escape the notice of the Court, she entered her coach, and drove back to Paris to put her house in order and prepare to live continually at her husband's side, for he sorely needed her help in dealing with Mme de Maintenon.

Returning to Chamillart, La Feuillade, his much-cherished son-in-law, made no comment at Meudon after receiving a note telling him of the news. On the Monday morning, however, he waylaid the King on his way to mass, looking very jaunty and carefree, begged him to remember that he had contributed his silver, and asked for the reversion of Chamillart's lodging at Versailles. The King's only response was a cold, contemptuous nod. His behaviour was no better regarded by the public and before the morning was over he decided to go to L'Etang. I went there also when the King rose from table, accompanied by Mme de Saint-Simon and the Duchesse de Lauzun.

What a scene presented itself! A host of nervous, inquisitive visitors bursting to express condolences, the servants distracted, the family grieving, the womenfolk in tears, giving utterance between sobs, completely abandoned to their affliction. Anyone would instinctively have looked for a death-chamber and for Holy Water to sprinkle over the departed. It was truly hard to remember that there was in fact no corpse, or to avoid thinking it improper to find no funeral drapes or other pomps. It was staggering in this environment to see the dead man, for whom everyone wept, walking about and speaking kindly and quietly, with his brow serene and nothing constrained or affected in his manner. He was indeed civil to all and very much his usual self. We embraced tenderly. He thanked me, having evidently been deeply moved by my note of the previous evening. I promised never to forget the support and joy of his friendship, and I may say with truth that I kept my word faithfully both to him, and to his family after his death. His son seemed fully recovered and less affected by a downfall that left him in fragments, than relieved by deliverance from labours for which he had neither taste nor aptitude. The stupid brothers spent the time marvelling that the King could bear to be separated from Chamillart. La Feuillade hovered meanwhile, philosophizing on the instability of fortune with a cheerfulness that seemed all the more shocking after his behaviour at Versailles that same morning.

Fashion and curiosity are prime movers at the Court. For one or the other reason everyone went to L'Etang, but to see Chamillart serenely greeting them all one might well have thought him still in office and holding his usual official reception. A lawyer's ignorance of the life of the Court and Society, wherein his family gave him no assistance, a rough exterior and a rolling gait did him much harm and belied his true nature. Tuesday was much the same, or rather there were the same crowds. We spent the whole day with them, and the day following; but on the Tuesday there were so many rumours of Mme de Maintenon's annoyance at what she chose to interpret as a mark of respect,[1] blaming Chamillart bitterly for allowing himself at first to be besieged, and then opening his doors to admit the public, that, although the King had made no remark, lest worse should follow, he accepted the offer of a royal residence at Bruyères, near Ménilmontant, and departed on the Wednesday. We went with him, and M. de Lorges spared no pains to make him as comfortable there as possible.

On the Wednesday morning, the King having arranged to sleep at Marly, Cany went to make his bow. He waited among the other courtiers at the door of the study until the King's return from mass. King Louis stopped at seeing him, gave him a look of pleasure and affection, assured him of his protection and then, beginning to be moved, hurriedly entered his study. To everyone's vast surprise he reappeared a few moments later with his eyes red and swollen because he had been rubbing them. He

[1] People in disgrace were not called upon.

called Cany back to him and repeated all his assurances in even stronger terms. This is proof enough of what it had cost him to be parted from his minister, and of the powerful pressures that had been exerted. He had, in fact, yielded only after Torcy's return from Flanders, when he realized that there was no longer any hope of a peace. Voysin's reception was extremely cold, very different from the King's usual welcome to the minis-ter of his choice. That and his treatment of Cany go to show that, had Chamillart only listened to my advice and spoken earlier, the King could not have resisted him and he might have kept his post.

I stayed with him at Bruyères for several days. The master of the horse came over to dine from Royaumont and the proximity of Bruyères to Paris brought him a great number of visitors. Mme de Maintenon was excessively annoyed that his disgrace had not caused him to be shunned by all. She said as much with extraordinary bitterness, and uttered so many threats of what she would do if he did not go quite away that he felt obliged to yield to her dangerous menaces. Having no estates of his own, he was looking for somewhere in which to invest part of the price of his office, but did not know to which distant spot he should retire. He finally decided to go and visit the various estates that were offered him, so as to have a pretext for absence until he found some place in which to settle. La Feuillade made an effort and spent a night or two at Bruyères; marvellous to relate he so bewitched his father-in-law as to make him feel grateful for that brief visit. No one else, not even his worst enemies, were otherwise than indignant to hear of it.

For a long time past I had been noting that the Bishop of Chartres was only too accurate when he warned me that some people had done me a disservice with the King and had made an impression. The change in his attitude was quite remarkable, and although I still went to Marly it was clearly not for my own sake.[1] I was tired of having so many chimney-pots fall about my ears, and of being unable to trace the culprit, or con-sequently to find a remedy. I knew that through no fault of my own I had made powerful enemies, such as Monsieur le Duc and Madame la Duchesse, and the members of Vendôme's cabal, not to mention those other envious and malicious persons of whom all courts are full. On the other hand my friends, Chamillart and the Chancellor, for instance, the Maréchal de Boufflers and the Dukes of Beauvilliers and Chevreuse, were losing or had lost their influence; even with the best will in the world they could not assist me. Overcome by chagrin, I resolved once more to leave the Court and renounce all my ambitions. Mme de Saint-Simon, who was wiser, tried to persuade me of the continual and unexpected changes at the Court, those which the King's age might bring, the serious risk, not only to my fortune but to my very inheritances, and many other arguments besides. At last we decided to spend two years in Guyenne on the pretext

[1] He thought that it was for Mme de Saint-Simon.

of visiting our large estate there which we had not yet seen,[1] and thus be
absent for some considerable time without vexing the King, letting the
months slip quietly by, and then reconsidering what had best be done.

M. de Beauvilliers, who had asked for M. de Chevreuse to be present
when we consulted him, and the Chancellor to whom we spoke later,
agreed with our plan when they saw that they could by no means induce
me to remain at the Court; but they strongly advised us to mention it well
in advance so as to avoid the appearance of a grievance, or of having it
said that I had been quietly instructed to leave. One required the King's
permission to go so far and for so long. I was unwilling to speak to him
myself under those particular circumstances, and therefore my good
friend La Vrillière, in whose department Guyenne lay, spoke for me, and
the King approved.

The Maréchal de Montrevel commanded in Guyenne. I have already
mentioned what kind of man he was, at the time of his promotion to the
bâton. His new command had completely turned his head; he acted as
though he were sovereign lord of Guyenne and with many flowery compliments and civilities had usurped all my authority in my own governorship. This is not the moment to explain our quarrel;[2] suffice it to say that
it made it impossible for me to go to Blaye until I could come to terms
with that madman whom the King had favoured all his life. For
more than two years he and I had been trying to persuade Chamillart to
intervene, but that minister never had time to adjudicate in our dispute.
At last his downfall removed from him any authority to decide between us,
and from Montrevel any desire to submit to his views. Although for the
past five or six months I had been resolved to retire, Chamillart's dismissal finally decided me to do so and to hurry. A loyal friend in such high
office and favour is a continual support in fact and appearance, and leaves
a great void when he departs. What is more, I had lost the lodging of the
late Maréchal de Lorges at the château, for I was obliged to return it to
the Duc de Lorges, who had hitherto used his father-in-law's apartment,
which the King had disposed of elsewhere. To live at the Court without
a lodging, or even to frequent it, was intolerable and impossible, and
I was at that time in no position to obtain one. I had asked and been
refused ever since the Marly when the news broke of Torcy's departure
to Holland. Thus the King's hand was descending more and more hardly
upon me in trifles; wanting perhaps an occasion for something worse.

There could be no thought of going to Guyenne before the affair with
Montrevel was settled; I therefore resolved to go to La Ferté for several
years, to visit the Court only on rare occasions, not even annually, if that

---

[1] That estate included Blaye and the governorship, a house at La Cassine, and the Marais de
Saint-Simon.

[2] The quarrel was about appointing captains of the coastguards, which had been formed in
1705. Saint-Simon was determined that they came under his authority as governor.

should prove possible without neglecting my absolute duty. My devotion to Chamillart at L'Etang, Bruyères, and Paris had already been noted with displeasure. I left a month after his departure to find an estate; his daughters came to live with us at La Ferté in the meantime, and he returned there between his various excursions. That gave me an opportunity to give entertainments and diversions in his honour, which I should never have done when he was in favour and office; I had no scruples now because there was no reason to pay court to him and nothing to be gained. This he much appreciated. He remained with us for some considerable time; left his daughters still with us, and went to Paris to settle his affairs and negotiate the purchase of Courcelles, in the region of the Maine, where he finally established himself. Let us now turn to the state of the Court both before and after my departure, which was much delayed though I continued to yearn for it.

I cannot find the exact word to express my meaning. Because of the disgrace of Vendôme and Chamillart the Court had become more than ever divided. To speak of cabals is perhaps too much, but without endless hairsplitting I can think of no better term, and I shall therefore use it. Although it goes beyond the true position the sense cannot be rendered otherwise in a single word.[1] Three parties split the Court, embracing all the principal personages, very few of whom showed themselves in the open, whilst others showed certain reservations. Very few indeed had only the country's welfare at heart, although all professed that their sole concern was its precarious state. By far the greater number thought of nothing but their own advantage, with vague ambitions to secure fame, influence and, in the future, power. Some looked for wealth and office, others, more cunning or less fortunately placed, adhered to one or other of the three cabals, forming minor cliques that occasionally gave an impetus to affairs and ever contributed to the civil war of tongues. The first of the cabals existed beneath the shelter of Mme de Maintenon's wing; its principal members, their appetites whetted by the fall of Chamillart and stimulated by that of Vendôme, courted and were courted by Mme la Duchesse de Bourgogne, and were on excellent terms with Monseigneur. They bore high reputations and basked in the reflected glory of the Maréchal de

---

[1] Madame wrote to the Electress of Hanover. 'The entire Court is in a ferment. Some are trying to gain the favour of the all-powerful dame, others that of Monseigneur, others again that of the Duc de Bourgogne. He and his father do not love each other, the son despises him, has ambitions of his own, and wishes to rule. The Dauphin is completely dominated by his bastard half-sister, Madame la Duchesse. All of them are against my son, for they fear that the King may look on him kindly and arrange an alliance between his daughter and the Duc de Berry. Madame la Duchesse would prefer her own daughter to marry the latter, and she therefore monopolizes him. The Duchesse de Bourgogne wishes to rule both the Dauphin and the King; she is jealous of Madame la Duchesse and has made a pact with the Duchesse d'Orléans in order to thwart her. All this provides a very pretty play of intrigue and counter-intrigue, and I might say like the song, "If hunger does not kill us, we shall laugh ourselves to death." Meanwhile the old woman sets one against the other and rules all the stronger for it.'

Boufflers. The rest rallied round him for their own enhancement or in order to make use of him; Harcourt, away on the banks of the Rhine, was one example. Voysin and his wife were their tools and looked to them for support. In the background was the Chancellor, much chagrined by Mme de Maintenon's sudden aversion for him and by the King's coldness in consequence. Pontchartrain also supported them at a distance, as did Villeroy, who despite his disgrace had never lost his place in Mme de Maintenon's heart. His wife's lack of wit was fully compensated for by her good sense, prudence, impenetrable secrecy, and the confidence of Mme la Duchesse de Bourgogne, whom she was known to lead on a tight rein, keeping her well in hand.

On the other side, inspired by the birth, virtues, and talents of Mgr le Duc de Bourgogne and the great love which he bore him, was the Duc de Beauvilliers, a most conspicuous figure. The Duc de Chevreuse was the consolidator and inspiration of this party; the Archbishop of Cambrai, from the depths of his exile and disgrace, its pilot. Subordinate to these were Torcy, Desmaretz, Père Tellier, the Jesuits and Saint-Sulpice, who in other ways were so antagonistic towards each other. This cabal admitted no newcomers to its ranks except when absolutely essential, and then only for the emergency. They had only to play for time and, since they were already well-placed, to defend their position, not to conquer; but there was no joy in them; their piety kept them strait-laced and was eminently mockable; the gay, the fashionable, the ambitious were all on the other side either with Meudon or with Mme de Maintenon.

These two cabals regarded each other with respect. The second moving silently forward, the former making much stir and seizing every opportunity to injure the other. All the smart people of the Court and the armies belonged to the first, for exasperation with the government was increasing, and many prudent persons were attracted by Boufflers's reputation and the talents of Harcourt. The third group consisted of d'Antin, Madame la Duchesse, Mlle de Lillebonne and her sister, their uncle,[1] who was inseparable from them, and the court-circle at Meudon. Neither one of the other two cabals would have any dealings with them, they both feared and defied them but took them seriously on account of Monseigneur and Mme la Duchesse de Bourgogne's relations with him. D'Antin and Madame la Duchesse were united; both were equally discredited but led the party, d'Antin because of his private sessions with the King, which grew every day more frequent, Madame la Duchesse because of hers with Monseigneur. Not that the Lorraines did not still possess his confidence, but they had not yet recovered from the shock of Vendôme's and Chamillart's downfall. Boufflers, Harcourt, and their followers loathed Vendôme's arrogance and the supremacy which he had obtained. Chevreuse, Beauvilliers, and their supporters for similar reasons

---

[1] Vaudémont.

and especially for the sake of Mgr le Duc de Bourgogne, disliked him quite as much. Thus neither of these two parties was willing to merge with the third which was Vendôme's personal cabal, nor to deal with d'Antin who in the wild hope of superseding Chamillart had industriously worked for his dismissal. To make everything plain, let us endow these three parties with names and call them the cabal of the nobles, as it was then referred to, the cabal of the ministers, and the Meudon cabal.

The last-named were more afflicted by their failures than by Vendôme's collapse; the result of them had been the loss of Mgr le Duc de Bourgogne for reasons already explained. M. du Maine, secure in the affection of the King and Mme de Maintenon, was for himself alone, ridiculed most things, did as much harm as he was able, and was feared and known for what he was. Monsieur le Duc was indifferent, always in a smouldering temper, which made everyone avoid him as they would a live bomb. Neither the Comte de Toulouse nor the Duc de Berry played any part whatsoever. M. le Duc d'Orléans was neither anxious nor, as we shall soon see, in any condition to interfere, and Mgr le Duc de Bourgogne, deep in his prayers and his work for the council, let earthly happenings pass unheeded, following the gentle guidance of the Dukes of Beauvilliers and Chevreuse, took no action regarding either Vendôme or Chamillart, but left them to God as he had done the tribulations which they had caused him. As for Mme la Duchesse de Bourgogne, you have seen that she had already procured one dismissal, and did not spare herself to gain the other. That combined with her relationship with Mme de Maintenon to place her on the side of the nobles' cabal. There was, moreover, the additional attraction of Harcourt, the regard which she could not but have for Boufflers, and her affection for the Duchesse de Villeroy. Although she was exceedingly averse to the Dukes of Beauvilliers and Chevreuse and greatly dreaded their influence over her husband she had drawn closer to them in the Flanders troubles, which had covered such a long period that her prejudice was somewhat diminished. Regarding the Meudon cabal, which was really Vendôme's, she had no more truck with it than was consistent with prudence, on account of Monseigneur and the fact that Madame la Duchesse was the King's bastard; you will recall that they were, in any case, on bad terms personally. Only d'Antin was excepted because he had served her in Flanders, and because she hoped more from him in his private sessions with the King. D'Antin, himself, was one with Madame la Duchesse in her views, interests, vices, and haunts; they were both very wary of the Lorraines, but exchanged confidences with them and appeared outwardly friendly, a situation likely to continue during the King's life, after which they would all be at each other's throats for the sole possession of Monseigneur, then become king. The Meudon cabal rubbed shoulders with that of the nobles but was known and secretly hated for what it was, namely the one-time party of

Vendôme. As for the cabal of the ministers, they were completely hostile, save that Torcy, Madame la Duchesse, and consequently d'Antin also, had a mutual understanding with Mme de Bouzols, Torcy's sister and Madame la Duchesse's life-long boon companion in every kind of activity, who combined a hideous countenance with immense charm and the wit of twenty devils. Such was the situation at the Court in those stormy days that began with the two tremendous collapses and seemed to be preparing others for the future.

Amelot had been recalled from Spain some time since, but affairs of State had delayed his return, for he had been at the head of them all under the Princesse des Ursins, agreeing so well with her and showing himself so capable that he controlled everything. You shall soon see that his impending arrival was a terrifying moment for all the ministers. He had been at the head of affairs in Spain and had found them in the greatest chaos imaginable, with the funds entirely exhausted. He had, however, administered the finances, commerce, and the navy with such efficiency and success that despite the misfortunes of the war they were brought into excellent order and considerably increased. He had reformed and greatly improved the army, the men were now paid punctually, and the warehouses of every kind were fully stocked. That in itself was a marvellous feat; but still more wonderful was that he had managed at the same time to win the hearts of Spaniards of all ranks by his gentle, considerate and courteous manners, and still remained on excellent terms with Mme des Ursins. Everyone in Spain spoke of him admiringly and there was continual astonishment that he was not given the highest place in France, all of which was well known in France, where a great need was felt for a minister of his quality. He was spoken of for foreign affairs, for the war ministry, for the finances, even for the navy. Torcy, Desmaretz, and Pontchartrain were long on tenterhooks because his return was so often delayed.

Tournai had been invested. Surville was the lieutenant-general in command there; Mesgrigny, lieutenant-general and our best engineer after Vauban, was governor of the citadel. He had thirteen battalions, four squadrons of dragoons and seven complete companies, four hundred men altogether. Ravaillon was quartermaster, with a profusion of all kinds of munitions and food supplies. Apart from that our army in Flanders wanted for everything, and at the Court and in Paris they had reached the stage of forty-hour intercessions.[1] Spain had for some time past been regarded unfavourably and the rumour (much encouraged by the Allies) that that monarchy was the chief hindrance to peace was gaining credence. No one freely expressed an opinion on the monstrous terms offered to Torcy at The Hague; but there was a general feeling that it would be a good thing if Spain were allowed to be defeated and the chance of peace thereby

---

[1] *Prières de Quarante-heures.*

17

improved. My own feelings were quite the reverse. I had never believed that Spain was any serious obstacle to peace. I did not at all imagine that the Allies were sufficiently devoted to the Emperor and the interests of his family to exhaust themselves for his sake. I was in any case convinced that none of them wished for peace, and that hating the King and France as they did they seized upon this excuse for continuing the war so long as it suited their purpose. I concluded therefore that the only way to frustrate them was to give the King of Spain the support he needed to liberate his frontiers; then, with Spain delivered, our enemies would be reduced to negotiating a peace, when it suited them, on more generous terms.

There was still time to act, but no one was willing to look ahead at this moment when the kingdom was so far reduced by famine and disaster. People preferred to shut their eyes to any other course than to allow a throne to destroy itself that had cost us so much blood and money to uphold; and thus avoid the shame of openly siding with our common enemy by fulfilling the barbaric conditions which they demanded of us.[1] There was thus a great agitation for the return of Amelot and all the French forces in Spain, Mme des Ursins included. That was the reason for Amelot's recall, and for an order to Mme des Ursins to make her preparations for leaving. The king and queen were thrown into a panic; emitted loud complaints and begged that Amelot should at least be allowed to terminate the business in hand. Amidst this uncertainty Bezons was ordered to suspend all action, and thus although not obliged to bring his troops back to France he dared not assemble them against Count Starhemberg who was on the move.

An excursion to Marly occurred at this juncture which was most noteworthy; but to understand the whole picture you must be familiar with the background. You already know that the Duc de Chevreuse was in every way a minister of State save that he did not attend the council, and that his wife's position as one of the King's intimate circle, and of Mme de Maintenon's circle also for his sake, had remained firmly established despite a few months coolness during the affair of the Archbishop of Cambrai. The Duchesse de Chevreuse's health had for some time past prevented her from wearing a corset, and although full court-dress had been abolished at Marly, the ladies had not quite reached the stage of no stays and dressing-gowns. For that reason Mme de Chevreuse no longer went to Marly, but she invariably asked, because no one was excused from that. The King had complained, and finally desired her to appear without her stays. Thereafter, although she was never visible in the salon or at the King's table, she saw him everyday in Mme de Maintenon's room and on his private walks. M. de Chevreuse who enjoyed the solitude, privacy, and opportunity for pious retreats of his house at Dampierre, four leagues from Versailles, used the pretext of Mme de Chevreuse's ill-

[1] The guarantee that Philip V would be obliged to abdicate.

health to absent himself as much as possible. The King did not care for this and consented only grudgingly. Despite the dispensation from wearing corsets Mme de Chevreuse still did not appear and the King was annoyed; but they stayed away none the less. They did however go to this particular Marly, and their unaccustomed presence was much remarked, especially since M. de Chevreuse had attended on the last occasion and for a long time had not been seen there twice running.

The curtain was about to rise on the final decision whether or not to recall the troops in Spain. M. de Beauvilliers was most strongly in favour; Mgr le Duc de Bourgogne seconded him; even the Chancellor was not averse; but most unexpectedly Desmaretz took the opposite view as also did Voysin, though without much enthusiasm, either because of newness and inexperience or because he wished to discover how the land lay before expressing an opinion. Monseigneur, always a firm supporter of his son,[1] was excessively firm, but only on that one aspect; he was none the less overridden, and it was decided to recall the troops. The Maréchal de Boufflers at this point heard the news, for the debate had been somewhat heated; he resolved to intervene and spoke to the King, with the result that the talk at Marly was of nothing else, and the courtiers, who loved the privilege of discussing such affairs openly, became impassioned to such an extent that the maréchal summoned up the courage to see Mme de Maintenon and contend with her strongly.[2] M. le Duc d'Orléans, in agreement with Boufflers, exclaimed that he knew Spain and the Spaniards and drew a vast number of conclusions from that fact, thereby so delighting the Maréchal de Boufflers that he declared to Mme de Maintenon that the King should consult that prince's opinion on Spain, where he had distinguished himself so greatly. Alas for Boufflers! He was unaware of the fatal jest that had rendered Mme de Maintenon and Mme des Ursins the prince's mortal enemies. The King was shaken by so much emotion, and influenced by Mme de Maintenon did something quite unprecedented in an affair that had already been discussed and settled. He cancelled the orders and held a fresh meeting of his council to debate the issue once again. It was finally resolved to leave sixty-six battalions with the King of Spain so that he should not be entirely abandoned at the beginning of the campaign. That satisfied no one, but the orders were sent on the following morning. The remainder of that Marly was affected by the excitement at the beginning, and everyone noticed that the Duc de Chevreuse had an air of importance that was quite new to him.

We must now retrace our steps in order to relate without interruption the affair of M. le Duc d'Orléans's conduct in Spain, the news of which broke at this time and was the cause of all the subsequent troubles and distresses that accompanied him throughout his life, even when he was

[1] King Philip.
[2] Mme de Maintenon was for peace at any price.

most free and independent at the time when he wielded sovereign power.[1] This is not the place to go deeply into his character, suffice it here to say that his idleness, the time he wasted in improper chemical experiments and still more improper attempts to see into the future, his enslavement to Mme d'Argenton his mistress, his lechery and bad companions, his debauched appearance and lack of respect for the Court, more especially for his wife, had done him much harm in Society and still more injury with the King. Circumstances had, however, compelled the King to send him to Italy. Thereafter, when Turin fell despite his best endeavours, and he showed such determination to return to the campaign as soon as his wounds were healed, the King decided to give him the Spanish command (in 1707) as a consolation.

At that time the King wished him to live on friendly terms with the Princesse des Ursins and to restrict himself solely to matters that concerned the campaign. He obeyed that order implicitly; Mme des Ursins laid herself out to please him, and all went well between them until the start of his second season. It was then that, highly dissatisfied with the lack of preparation, and furious at losing the chance of glory because of her negligence, he let fly, as I have described, in the middle of supper, with that devastating, incomparable jest that had embroiled him in a violent but hidden quarrel with Mme des Ursins and Mme de Maintenon. He continued notwithstanding to live outwardly on good terms with Mme des Ursins, despite their frequent disputes over rations and other military supplies, but as time went on he saw that she wished to pick a quarrel and that he needed to be on his guard.

Even before the end of the first campaign he had become aware of the errors which Mme des Ursins's greed and ambition were leading her to commit, and from thence it took him little time to discover that she was both hated and feared. In the beginning it may have been merely curiosity that persuaded him to listen to the complaints of some of the leading rebels; but princes more than most men love popularity. Everywhere in Spain, and from Spain into France, his praises had travelled; men spoke of his industry, ability and courage, of his friendliness and good nature, and I am not sure that he did not mistake these tributes to his rank for the signs of genuine liking, or to what point he was led astray by them. Be that as it may, after he had seen the folly of that fatal jest, he became doubly interested in Mme des Ursins's faults, and gave ear more frequently to the grumbling of the malcontents who had begun to gather round him. He made so little mystery of that association that on his return to Madrid after his second campaign he openly defended many of them, restored some to favour, and when Mme des Ursins attacked him in the presence of the king and queen, answered that he thought he was doing

[1] During the Regency.

good service by supplying such people with a halting place between Madrid and Barcelona, to which town they might have fled had they not been restrained by promises of his support.[1] No one had found anything to say against him then, and indeed the king and queen had asked him to continue in the same way and to return to them before long; whereupon they had parted with every appearance of mutual agreement.

Towards the end of the following winter [1709] the King had inquired of M. le Duc d'Orléans whether he truly wished to return to Spain. He had replied in a way that showed his readiness to serve but no particular enthusiasm, and he failed to notice the significance of the question. When he told me about it I blamed him for his idleness, reminding him that wars end only when a peace is signed, and that unless he served in every campaign he would be likely to find himself, like other commanders before him, with all his good work forgotten and nothing remaining to him but his rank. On the other hand, if he persevered until the end, it would be very hard not to offer him some important post after the peace. Such arguments appeared to give him a more active desire to return to Spain. A few days later, however, the King asked him whether he thought he was in harmony with Mme des Ursins, and on his replying that he imagined so since he had done nothing to deserve otherwise, the King said that none the less she so much dreaded his return that she was begging for him to be detained, complaining that though she had tried in every way to please him he had become friendly with her enemies and corresponded with them through his secretary. M. le Duc d'Orléans had then expressed great surprise, saying that he had concerned himself only with military matters and had done everything in his power to convince Mme des Ursins of his desire to live at peace with her. He also described that farewell scene and their Catholic Majesties' evident satisfaction. He added finally that he had learned of errors and dangerous intrigues that if persisted in might well ruin the King and Queen of Spain and lose them their throne, and he suggested that Mme des Ursins might perhaps have discovered how much he knew and dreaded his return on that account. After a moment's reflection the King had replied that with matters at such a pass he thought it best to keep the prince away from Spain. Spain, he continued, was at present at a crisis; if King Philip were to be dethroned nothing would be gained by an inquiry into the actions of the Princesse des Ursins, if on the other hand he remained king there would be ample time for such an investigation. M. le Duc d'Orléans said nothing more.[2]

---

[1] Barcelona was in the hands of the Allies and the Archduke Charles.

[2] The King to Mme des Ursins, 29 April, 1709: 'I have spoken to my nephew. He protests that during his stay in Spain he never interfered in anything that concerned the government . . . As regards Renault the duke's secretary, he says that he employed him solely for his knowledge of Spanish, and that since his conduct has displeased you he will write immediately ordering his return. I think that you may hold him to that. As for me, I have made a pretext not to let my nephew return to Spain this year.'

When he described the scene to me he appeared only moderately angry, or so I imagined. I, myself, was far more so, for he told me that all this affair had been conducted personally by Mme des Ursins and Mme de Maintenon, and that the King had so informed him. In other words, there had been no minister concerned, and indeed, since it was a case of their joint vengeance, they did not desire one. Soon afterwards it was given out that M. le Duc d'Orléans would not be returning to Spain, because all that remained to do there was to evacuate some of the French troops, a manœuvre unfitting for one of his rank. At that point the King ordered him to have his baggage and other equipment brought home to France, advising him privately to send someone with authority who would be able to vouch for it that he had had no disloyal intentions, in case King Philip were obliged to sign a treaty renouncing his throne. The King also said that if his protestations were believed his own right to the Spanish succession would not be in question. This, at any rate, was what M. le Duc d'Orléans told me, although later many people refused to believe it. In such matters accuracy is all-important.

For the Meudon cabal the prospect of ruining the only prince of royal blood likely to figure greatly in the future was a chance too good to be missed. They started a rumour that M. le Duc d'Orléans had been attempting to form a party to place himself on the throne of Spain, after expelling King Philip on the pretext of incapacity, domination by Mme des Ursins, and his abandonment by France, symbolized by the withdrawal of French troops. They said further that he was already in treaty with Stanhope,[1] the English commander, to gain the Archduke's support on the grounds that the Dutch and English need not be concerned as to who reigned in Spain provided that the Archduke gained the Spanish possessions overseas, and that the said ruler was their man, enthroned by their act, and, no matter what his birth, an enemy of or at least completely detached from France. So much was common gossip; but there were other, more sinister rumours to the effect that he intended to have his marriage dissolved by Rome as having been forced upon him and unworthy of his birth, and thereafter to have his children proclaimed bastards in order to content the Emperor. His next move, or so they said, would be to marry the widow of Charles II and ascend the throne at her side, well knowing that she was incapable of bearing children, and finally, after her death, to marry his mistress Mme d'Argenton.[2] Alternatively, it was suggested that he meant to poison Mme la Duchesse d'Orléans so as to avoid these long and complicated manœuvres. As you may imagine, what with his alembics, laboratories, experiments in physical chemistry, and the perpetual chattering of the charlatans surrounding him, M. le Duc d'Orléans felt

[1] James Earl Stanhope (1673–1721), the English commander in Spain.
[2] Formerly Mlle de Séry. Before leaving for Italy in 1706 he was known to have attended a séance at her house, where he saw an apparition of himself wearing a crown of unknown origin.

devoutly thankful when his wife, who had been pregnant and suffering from severe attacks of colic, most fortunately recovered and still more fortunately was safely delivered of a child. That recovery served somewhat to kill the rumours; but Society was up in arms against him. The King and more especially Monseigneur treated him with a coldness which he found acutely embarrassing, and the Court, following their example, shunned him completely.

I was at that time, as I have already mentioned, somewhat in disgrace myself. I no longer went to Marly, which made my situation most disagreeably evident; thus my close attachment to M. le Duc d'Orléans was causing my friends some anxiety and they were beginning to urge me to see less of him. In truth, from my own experience of the lengths to which those who hated or feared me, particularly Monsieur le Duc and Madame la Duchesse and the Meudon cabal, were capable of going I had good reason for alarm. Yet all things considered, I still believed that a man needed honour and courage at the Court, as well as sound judgment to tell him when dangers should be faced, and I resolved neither to show fear nor to deviate in the slightest from my close friendship with M. le Duc d'Orléans, especially not at this time of his need and bitter isolation.

Later, when the news from Spain had broken, the prince confided to me that many eminent Spaniards, grandees amongst others, had convinced him that the King of Spain would not long be able to retain his throne, and that he had been strongly urged to expedite that monarch's abdication in order to replace him. M. le Duc d'Orléans told me that he had rejected this proposal with all the contempt it deserved, but that he had at the same time agreed to the possibility of his changing his mind should King Philip fall unaided, without hope of recovery. In that case, he contended, there would be no disloyalty, but great benefit to the King and to France, because the Spanish throne would be thus kept in the family—a result no less desirable for King Louis than for the prince himself. What is more, if all this could be achieved without King Louis's knowledge or participation, the latter would be relieved of the obligation to renounce his grandson in a treaty, and the Allies be willing to accept a king elected by the Spaniards themselves and independent of France; for the appearance of union and alliance would then be less obvious than under King Philip.

This confession gave me a very poor impression of the entire project and no desire to hear further details, even supposing there were more to know. Filled with misgivings, I was reduced to pointing out the folly of a scheme so nonsensical that it would be fruitless to repeat my arguments. I besought him to do his utmost to discover how much the King knew, and if he were already fully informed to confess all that he had told me. He should then ask the King's forgiveness for not having previously confided in him and taken his orders, excusing himself on the plea that there had been nothing in the scheme that was detrimental to his service of the King of Spain, and urging that had King Louis been informed his conscience might have troubled him were he obliged to renounce his grandson. I said finally that I had never heard of a worse-conceived or more crazy project, nor one more disastrous for him personally, adding that he should endeavour to extricate himself by wise conduct and a proper sense of his rank, so as to avoid the most damaging consequences, and be careful not to lose courage in the sorry situation to which he was at present reduced. He seemed to be glad of my counsel and to be already half-repenting of his folly and mistakes.

Meanwhile the King had been consulting with his family and the council. I never clearly discovered how far the plot had in fact progressed, still less how well the King had been informed; but he had certainly learned something, and he learned far more, if not the whole, when the Marquis of Villaroël, a general of the Spanish army, was arrested at Barcelona, and Don Bonifacio Manriquez seized at Madrid in a church, which in Spain is regarded as a sanctuary, only to be violated in the case of traitors. These arrests created enormous alarm, and were of the greatest assistance to Mme des Ursins, secretly backed by Mme de Maintenon, in insuring that all France was suitably shocked and horrified. Both knew very well how little substance there had been in the plot, but both wished to stir up as much of a scandal as possible, for they aimed to stampede the highest powers into taking action against a Grandson of France, the King's nephew, the uncle of the Queen of Spain and the Duchesse de Bourgogne, a prince whom it might prove most dangerous to attack unsuccessfully.

In the event they succeeded beyond their best hopes. There never was a louder outcry, nor a greater scandal, nor was there ever isolation more complete than that which M. le Duc d'Orléans was forced to endure—and for what cause?—merely for an act of folly. Had there been any criminal intentions they would certainly have come to light, for M. le Duc d'Orléans could never have managed to keep them secret. Moreover, from the fact that no one ever learned more than I have related here, I infer that neither the King, Mme de Maintenon, nor Mme des Ursins discovered anything further, since the two latter were constantly clamouring for action, and therefore very desirous of producing proofs. Amidst all this turmoil M. le Duc d'Orléans had a long interview with the King, who insisted on treating him as guilty, although he had confessed the entire project, as I have described it. That scheme, as he told the King, outrageous though it was, could not be regarded as criminal; yet the very opposite was claimed in Spain and whispered throughout France. With all diligence, by every imaginable trick, the King was impressed with the belief that M. le Duc d'Orléans's admission was nothing more than the artful device of a traitor who feels the net drawing close around him.

Against such knavery, intrigue, audacity, hatred, and jealousy M. le
Duc d'Orléans was left to defend himself alone, supported by the dis-
regarded tears of his mother, the tepid allegiance of his wife, and the
feeble good wishes of the Comte de Toulouse who, despite his cold
nature, would have helped him if he could. The King, an easy
prey to all who came on business to his study, was given no peace by Mme
de Maintenon, and Monseigneur. He was ceaselessly importuned from
Spain, and but little influenced by the eager recommendations of Mgr le
Duc de Bourgogne, who was in Flanders, or by Mme la Duchesse de
Bourgogne, who earnestly desired to help her uncle, but was reduced by
shyness, fear of Monseigneur, and an even stronger fear of Mme de
Maintenon, to the utterance of faint suggestions. Completely at a loss the
King put the matter to his council of State, but found that even there
opinion was divided. In the end he succumbed to the well-organized
chorus of accusation from his family and ordered the Chancellor to
produce a proper form of arraignment.

Immediately after that Pontchartrain was observed to stay behind on
two or three occasions after the council was dismissed, and since he had
no department and never ordinarily worked with the King, the Court and
Paris were soon hot on the scent. I had grown into the habit of going to
chat with him in his study nearly every evening, and we had discussed the
affair, which was at that time the sole topic, but only in general terms
because others had been present. One night, when I happened to arrive
earlier than usual, I found him pacing up and down his study, head bent,
hands in the pockets of his gown, as was his custom when thinking deeply.
He spoke of the outcry that daily gathered in volume, and then, trying to
broach the subject delicately, mentioned that there was talk of criminal
proceedings. He questioned me, as though idly, about the proper procedure, for he knew that I should be conversant with the matter as it was
the same for the peerage. I replied that I did indeed know the proper
forms, and quoted precedents.

He meditated for a little while longer, pacing round the study with me
beside him, neither of us uttering a word, he gazing at the floor, and I
gazing steadily at him. Suddenly he stopped dead in his tracks and turned
towards me as though waking from a dream. 'What will you do,' said he,
'if this takes place? Every peer will receive a subpoena, and you also will
be required to serve. You are M. le Duc d'Orléans's friend; how will you
manage, since I assume that he is guilty?' 'Monsieur,' I replied looking
supremely confident; 'do not wager on that or you will lose your money.'
'But seriously,' he continued, 'let us assume that he is on trial and guilty.
Now for the second time, how will you act?' 'How shall I act?' said I. 'I
see no problem. I shall attend of course; my peer's oath is quite explicit on
that point and I shall be summoned. I shall sit quietly in my place hearing
the evidence and opinions until my turn comes to speak; then I shall say

17*

that before examining the evidence we need to review the particular circumstances. This case concerns a plot, real or imagined, to dethrone the King of Spain and take his crown. Such a plot would certainly constitute a grave act of treason, but one that concerned only the Spanish king and his throne. Thus, I shall say that in my opinion the present court does not contain sufficient peers capable of adjudicating in a case of foreign treason; and I shall add that I should consider it beneath the dignity of our crown to deliver up a prince in the line of succession to any Spanish tribunal. That I believe will leave the court surprised and perplexed, and if there should be a debate I think I should have little difficulty in supporting my opinion.'

The Chancellor appeared completely dumbfounded. He gazed at me speechless for a few moments. 'You must be in league with him,' he exclaimed, stamping his foot and smiling with relief. 'I never thought of that argument; but it is sound logic.' He conversed a little longer and then dismissed me, a thing quite extraordinary at such a time, for his day's work was done and he usually had leisure for his friends. Feeling that I had made an impression I hurried away to tell all to M. le Duc d'Orléans, who embraced me warmly. I never discovered what the Chancellor did, but on the following day he once more remained after the meeting of the council, and that was for the last time. Less than twenty-four hours later the rumours had changed. It was at first whispered and then stated openly that there would be no trial. After that there was silence. The King allowed it to be understood in semi-private (so that the word should travel) that he now knew the entire affair; was surprised that so much had been made of it, and considered the malicious gossip outrageous. That ensured silence in public, but in private the affair was discussed for a long time afterwards. Everyone held his own opinion according to his lights and loyalties; but none the less the King remained permanently estranged from his nephew, and Monseigneur, who never forgave him, allowed his resentment to be seen on every public and private occasion. The Court witnessed many such scenes, and noticed also how curt and formal to him the King had become, all of which did little to change the attitude of Society. After a time of being slightly more restrained in his conduct, M. le Duc d'Orléans's distress and mortification drove him more and more often to Paris, where he was free as nowhere else and could drown his sorrows in debauchery.

The Princesse des Ursins may well have been disappointed at failing in her chief object, Mme de Maintenon and her partners also,[1] but the Meudon set were little better satisfied. They took infinite pains to widen the gulf between M. le Duc d'Orléans, the King and Monseigneur, and had it spread abroad that to visit the prince was the wrong way to pay one's court. Thus he still continued to be shunned. He minded his isolation; but, melancholy as he was because of his situation with the King,

[1] Desmaretz and d'Antin.

he did nothing to attract Society. None the less he was no longer completely deserted, as he had been when the scandal was at its height and the outcome unknown.

After so much involvement with other people's dismissals and disgraces it had become more than time for me to consider my own unhappy situation. The Maréchal de Boufflers had known everything, including my quarrel with the Maréchal de Montrevel who was under many an obligation to him; he believed that that fact combined with the high favour and influence which he then enjoyed would render him just as capable as Chamillart of ending our dispute. I accordingly gave him carte-blanche, and that is why I still remained at the Court. Montrevel, however, was so delighted to see me bereft of Chamillart that he felt he could filch everything from me, and he refused point-blank to deal either with Boufflers or with any other intermediary, which gave the former much offence. I was in no condition then to appeal to the King and I therefore left Montrevel to his own devices, determining at the same time not to go to Guyenne, but, as I have already said, to retire to La Ferté for several years. In the meantime we thought it best to take certain precautions.

Mme de Saint-Simon had never been intimate with Mme la Duchesse de Bourgogne, but she was always treated with consideration, friendliness, and respect. We had even heard that the princess wished her to fill the place of the Duchesse du Lude,[1] when that ancient and gouty lady was compelled to retire. Mme de Saint-Simon accordingly asked for a private conversation, in order to discover the cause of my disfavour, and the means of remedying it, if that were possible, before we put our plan into execution. She was received with all the kindness and sympathy imaginable—for herself, but with marked coldness when she spoke of me. The princess was quite frank as to the reason, saying that I had been reported to her as having said many exceedingly harmful things of Mgr le Duc de Bourgogne during the Flanders campaign. Mme de Saint-Simon's astonishment was considerable since she knew that Mme la Duchesse de Bourgogne was well posted on that subject by Mme de Nogaret and even by M. de Beauvilliers himself, and that Mgr le Duc de Bourgogne had not failed to tell her how much I had pleased him. She was, however, flighty and a prey to anyone; it had been easy for malicious tongues to distort during the winter all that had happened in that abominable campaign. Mme de Saint-Simon exclaimed in horror, reminded her of the true facts, and recommended her to refer to M. de Beauvilliers and M. le Duc d'Orléans also. She made an impression, and after a time that same flightiness brought the princess round to remembering all those good offices which had carefully been erased from her mind. She said finally to Mme de Saint-Simon that I had many powerful enemies, who lost no

[1] Mme du Lude had been the Duchesse de Bourgogne's lady-in-waiting from her first arrival in 1696.

opportunity to harm me; that my pride in my rank had been grossly exaggerated to the King, more especially by Monsieur le Duc, and that I was accused of blaming freely and of speaking ill of the conduct of the country's affairs; that Mme de Saint-Simon was in good favour with the King, well liked and esteemed, but that he had developed a great antipathy to me, which only time, prudence, and extreme moderation could dispel. She added that people said of me that I was cleverer, better informed, and with stronger opinions than most; that everyone feared and redoubted me; that I was seen to be attached to people in the highest offices; that they dreaded my reaching that position myself; that they could not endure my arrogance and the freedom with which I expressed my views, and that my reputation for sincerity made my words doubly hard to bear.

Mme de Saint-Simon thanked her heartily for having been so good as to be frank with her, saying with much truth that I had nothing to reproach myself with in my conduct as a whole, nor in my life; that my attackers made only vague accusations against me, as they did of anyone whom they wished to ruin, and that such criticism had only appeared since the time when I was nominated, with no canvassing on my part, for the Rome embassy; it was thus clearly designed to prevent my employment. The conversation ended with many expressions of kindness from Mme la Duchesse de Bourgogne, of sadness at the thought of losing her even for a time, and promises to take every opportunity, both she and Mme de Maintenon, to make me reconciled with the King. What is more, she spoke so earnestly to Blouin, asking him to obtain a lodging for us, that he resolved to do his best for us in order to please her; at least, that is what he afterwards said to the Duc de Villeroy and several of our friends. Mme de Saint-Simon was prudent enough not to tell me until long afterwards all that she had discovered in that conversation of the King's strong aversion to me. She did not wish to fortify my disgust with the life of the Court. I minded most of all the wicked slanders about Mgr le Duc de Bourgogne, and for that reason alone became quite determined to remove myself from such lying monsters. Thereafter I thought of nothing but of escaping to La Ferté.

I have described this conversation at some length because nothing better portrays the King and the Court than what Mme la Duchesse de Bourgogne said to my wife. It shows the King's rooted dislike and suspicion of men who were intelligent and well-informed, and that to be so considered was rated a crime in me. It was brought to his notice on every possible occasion and did me far more harm than had I been either wicked or dangerous. Even my reputation for integrity was used against me by those who wished to ruin me without just cause, for, exaggerating their praises of my wit and knowledge, they stressed the added importance that honesty gave to my casual remarks. The friendship and trust shown in me by the principal ministers and greatest nobles close in the King's confidence were made to appear another danger in his eyes, and thus what should have pleased and confirmed his good opinion of me became the chief cause of his antagonism.

Who was chiefly responsible for thus poisoning his mind? M. du Maine and d'Antin, the two most dangerous, most persistent, and most scheming of the courtiers, and known to be such. M. du Maine, the moving spirit of Vendôme's cabal, had never forgiven me for my devotion to Mgr and Mme la Duchesse de Bourgogne. He had suborned Blouin and Nyert, whose father had owed his entire fortune to mine, and together they did me all the harm they could in every possible way, although I had never merited such treatment from them. M. and Mme du Maine had not forgotten their vain attempts to win me, and thereafter they feared me for their rank. Thus my chief crime in the sight of the King was my care for my dignities; thence also arose the hatred of Mme de Maintenon, my constant and most dangerous enemy. Mme la Duchesse de Bourgogne who wished to hide that fact from us, let something slip when she said to Mme de Saint-Simon that both she and Mme de Maintenon would try to mend matters for me with the King. She knew full well that Mme de Maintenon herself was my greatest obstacle. Chamillart found that so at the time when we first became friends and he was endeavouring to have me re-admitted to Marly after leaving the service. He had had many fierce disputes with her then, when he possessed her entire confidence, and only after a very long time could he persuade her, not to change her mind regarding me, but not actually to oppose my Marlys. This I learned from his own lips, but only after the King's death, because he feared lest I become too indignant and make matters worse by my anger. I had always known that she viewed me with disfavour, although I did not rightly know why; but as for hatred, that I never realized until Chamillart asked me after the King's death what I had ever done to the old bitch to make her so detest me, and he then explained what I have just recounted.

Mme des Ursins made many changes in the councils of Spain for safety's sake, in view of all that had come to light. She kept Amelot in his place, who in truth left his colleagues only trifles to deal with and matters already decided, doing all the rest of the business himself or with the Princesse des Ursins. The reorganization provided another excuse for delaying his return to France, but when he finally appeared all the rumours and fears started again, though our ministers had done all possible to protect themselves in the interval. He may himself have assisted them, for he could have had little hope of replacing a minister already in office, and in Spain the greatest rewards which he so richly deserved were beyond his range as a man of the long robe. It then suddenly occurred to him and Mme des Ursins to marry his daughter to Chalais, son of the brother of her first husband, and thus to recompense Amelot by a grandeeship for his son-in-law. No difficulty with Spain, where they reigned supreme, nor any likely in France, for King Louis had expressed complete satisfaction with Amelot, disdained rank, would have nothing to pay, and need give him no other reward. What was their surprise to meet with resistance so strong that they could not overcome it!

While this tussle was going on, with Mme des Ursins, forewarned perhaps by Mme de Maintenon, remaining firmly in the background,[1] Amelot arrived at Paris and the Court. His reception was brilliant, but he saw the King in private for a few moments only. He called on the ministers. The Chancellor's first words to him were, 'Monsieur, we must hold fast to our posts; for you have only to desire someone's downfall, and assuredly you will have his office. But be quick to burst open the door; I warn you that if you let yourself grow cold you will never return.' He spoke truly and with full knowledge. Amelot petitioned the King for his daughter's marriage and the grandeeship. King Louis civilly put him off. A few days later he tried again with the same result. Indignant at that treatment, and still more so at not having been granted a private audience on Spain, he could not prevent his disappointment appearing; but the ministers still encouraged him. Soon afterwards Amelot realized that he was ruined, and in his bewilderment did his utmost to discover the cause. No one could have attacked his ability, integrity, or any other part of the exercise of his functions; they had therefore persuaded the King that he was a Jansenist, and on that subject to speak and convince was one and the same; the harm was done with the first hint. So it happened with Amelot. In the end he discovered the truth, but was not disturbed since never in his life had he given any cause for such a suspicion; but when he tried to clear himself all doors were shut to him, and ruined he remained, reduced to the lowly status of a mere counsellor of State, one among all the other gowns,[2] after reigning supreme in Spain and making the minister tremble for so long. He often afterwards said to the Chancellor that he realized only too well the shrewdness of his warning.

I never learned who drove that dagger into Amelot's heart, but after he was safely disposed of the Court reverted to its usual composure. At that time, the Queen of Spain gave birth to a son who did not live.

At this time the Duchess of Mantua,[3] having become thoroughly bored in her convent at Pont-à-Mousson and scarcely less so on her occasional jaunts to Lunéville to witness the pomps of the local sovereign[4] under the wing of her sister de Vaudémont, began to think that the time was ripe for a personal appearance at Paris and the Court, from whence she drew

---

[1] She must have been furious none the less.

[2] He could not wear a sword at the Court, because he was not of the *noblesse de l'épées*.

[3] Widow of Charles IV of Gonzago, Duke of Mantua, who had been given royal honours when he went to Versailles in 1704. She was the daughter of the Duchesse d'Elbeuf, one of the Lorraines, and was twenty-four years old at this time.

[4] The Duke and Duchess of Lorraine had been living there since 1702.

large sums in pensions. Mme d'Elbeuf, her mother, was equally sanguine, relying as she did on the support of Mme de Maintenon and that lady's relish for Mme de Dangeau, whose son was d'Elbeuf's nephew. She banked also on the aid of M. de Vaudémont and his nieces, and consequently on that of Monseigneur. The great decision was finally made for her arrival.

On the pretext of needing fresh air and milk, Mme d'Elbeuf obtained permission for her daughter to stay at Vincennes, in the rooms which Monsieur had been accustomed to use when the Court was in residence, and which were refurnished for her comfort together with rooms for a staff of servants, of which great numbers were required, the château having been left empty for so many years. That imposing start raised the duchess's hopes so high that she arrived at Vincennes with every intention of adopting rank equal to that of a Grand-daughter of France, that is to say offering her hand and an armchair to no one, no matter who they were, and not accompanying visitors one step towards the door. The old Maréchale de Bellefonds, who had been living at the château in pious and strict seclusion for many years past, was trapped completely. She called, and was so dumbfounded to find herself offered only a *ployant*[1] that she sat down; but when her senses returned somewhat later, she left and never again set foot inside the door. The duchess's aunt, Mme de Pompadour, did not quite dare to ask ladies of title to visit but she brought as many others as she could muster. Yet the company rapidly dwindled, leaving her to the society of her household, numerous at first, but soon much depleted for lack of victuals. During all this time Mme d'Elbeuf had been trying to obtain an allowance for her, but with remarkably little success. Mme de Maintenon had her whims and fancies, and her high and mighty airs even with friends; Mme d'Elbeuf happened to find her in a disobliging mood, and for once the King turned a deaf ear to a claimant. The Duke of Mantua was dead, childless; his lands were still occupied by the Emperor; the King had disliked the marriage in the first place, and the memory of M. de Vaudémont's intrigues to benefit the House of Lorraine still rankled. He had no wish to give the duchess any special place at Court, and so as to avoid the trouble of refusing her pretensions he decreed that she should present herself in morning dress, as for Marly, see him in Mme de Maintenon's room in the presence of Mme la Duchesse de Bourgogne, and at once return to Vincennes.

She and her mother arrived at Versailles at the hour appointed and were shown into Mme de Maintenon's room; they stayed an amazingly short time during the whole of which the King stood, and he did not kiss her which was most extraordinary. They then withdrew into the large drawing-room, following Mme la Duchesse de Bourgogne who did

---

[1] A folding stool, the lowest grade of seat at the Court; *tabourets* with fixed legs were for duchesses only.

embrace her. Mgr le Duc de Bourgogne and M. le Duc de Berry were there also; no one sat, and in less than a quarter of an hour she was dismissed and on her way back to Vincennes with her mother, without having had any private talk with Mme de Maintenon. A few days later they visited Monseigneur at Meudon, where they were received but not invited to sit nor offered anything to eat or drink, no cards, and no invitation to see the garden. Half an hour saw the end of that formality and once again mother and daughter, who never entered Meudon again, returned to Vincennes much disheartened by both encounters. The Princesse de Montauban, who owed much to Mme d'Elbeuf, was then persuaded to call at Vincennes, but she was the only titled lady to visit, and went apparently in the hope of encouraging others and to make it easier for the duchess somewhat to lower her sights. Mme d'Elbeuf, who was not easily discouraged, next tried to obtain for her a chair with a back in Mme la Duchesse de Bourgogne's drawing-room. Now the wives and daughters of reigning princes, whose ministers are recognized by all the courts of Europe, were traditionally offered chairs with backs at the late queen's receptions, but for the first visit only; thenceforward they had only *tabourets* like any one else, and no different from the French duchesses. The Duchess of Mecklenburg was granted this privilege, but the Duchess of Mantua was not, although her mother asked for it on four separate occasions.

Such rebuffs were fatal to their high ambitions, and what is more, Mme d'Elbeuf was mad enough to say that M. le Duc de Berry could scarcely be considered a good match for her daughter, which remark was I think the cause of her being refused the chair. Thus spurned by the Court, in which she never again set foot,[1] the Duchess of Mantua determined to reign in Paris with the rank of her choice. The first trial of arms was with M. and Mme de Montbazon at the second gateway of the Palais Royal. The Montbazons were alone in their two-horse coach, when the duchess's coachman rudely ordered them to pull back so as to allow her to pass. When they refused Mme d'Elbeuf, who was with her daughter, sent a gentleman to inform M. de Montbazon that the Duchess of Mantua prayed him to give her room. He replied that for himself he would have been enchanted, but that Mme de Montbazon was with him and he believed the duchess had no precedence over her. The gentleman returned to say that the Duchess of Mantua made way only for the Elector of Bavaria who was out of Paris; whereupon M. de Montbazon prudently replied that it was for his lady to decide, but that he himself had no intention of reversing. A brawl then started between the coachmen with not a few oaths, and Mme d'Elbeuf with her head out of the window beseeching them to rein back the horses, and M. de Montbazon threatening to get down and thrash any one who dared to touch them. Finally, since the arch was just sufficiently wide, the two coaches managed to

[1] She died on 16 December, 1710.

scrape past each other to the detriment of the booths lining the walls, and so ended that ridiculous encounter.

The scandal was very great, but the Duchess of Mantua was at last persuaded to cease from her endeavours, and to understand that without the hoped-for support of Mme de Maintenon she and her mother were too weak to act. She took a house in Paris and let it be known that she wished to live as though unmarried and quite undesirous of anything so illusory as rank; that she was pained to learn that others had thought differently of her, but hoped that they would find her so courteous that they would love her and seek her company. She paid visits without waiting to receive a first call, driving like everyone else in a two-horse coach. She overwhelmed with kisses and civilities the ladies whom she found at home and even paid second calls on some who did not visit her. The Duchesse de Lauzun was one of that number, and when she had made sure of the facts, she returned the call. The Duchess of Mantua received her with effusive gratitude; she was given an armchair, the hand without reserve, and when she left the duchess insisted on escorting her the entire length of three rooms, and the bastard sister[1] who acted as lady-in-waiting walked beside her to the top of the staircase. She behaved in like manner to every lady of title, and the rest she received without any pretensions and with great politeness, offering armchairs freely, and conducting most ladies as far as the door.[2]

Behaviour so different soon made her acceptable to Society. She managed to attract the crowd with large *lansquenet*-parties, which were then the height of fashion, and she conducted herself with prudence and sufficient dignity for there to be no scenes. Thus with the giving of public card-parties her grandiose aspirations to royal rank melted away, and all her schemes for being great at the Court were succeeded by the ambition to be a good hostess in Paris. None the less her downfall had been very great and was hard for her to bear, and it was made even worse by lack of funds when the needs of the army took precedence over all. Desmaretz indeed took little trouble to relieve her wants, after she had told him somewhat rashly that he might judge of the urgency since she had come in person to solicit him.

The high price of everything, more especially of bread, was causing riots in every part of the kingdom. Paris had been the scene of several, and notwithstanding that the guards had been increased by more than half to protect the markets and other suspect places, there had been dangerous disturbances and Argenson had more than once feared for his life. Monseigneur, on his way to and from the Opera, had several times been

---

[1] Saint-Simon says of this bastard that she had more wit than anyone, and possessed her half-sister's entire confidence. She was known as the Dame d'Ausselle.

[2] Seating accommodation provided problems in England also. Anne Duchess of Hamilton (1636–1717), who was descended from James II of Scotland, would have only one chair in her drawing-room, for fear of anyone sitting in her presence.

held up by mobs containing large numbers of women screaming for
bread. He had been alarmed even in the midst of his escort, who dared not
disperse the crowd for fear of worse happening. He had finally escaped by
throwing money among them and promising miracles; but since nothing
had resulted he had been too frightened to go to Paris.

The King had heard the rioters pretty plainly through the windows of
the château, for the people of Versailles were going shouting through the
streets. The speeches were insolent and frequent, and complaints against
the government and the King's person very loud and immoderate in the
streets and other public places. The poor were continually exhorted to be
patient no longer, since nothing worse could befall them than their
present poverty and imminent death from starvation. In order to appease
the rabble the poor and idle were set to remove a largish mound, part of
the old ramparts that still encumbered the boulevard between the gates
of Saint-Denis and Saint-Martin. Mouldy bread was issued to the
labourers as their sole reward, and precious little at that. On the morning
of Tuesday, 20 August, it happened that the bread ran short, and one
woman especially set up a great complaint and started off the rest. The
constables distributing the bread threatened her, but she cried all the
louder; they then very foolishly seized hold of her and stood her in a
nearby pillory. That was the signal for the entire mob to make a rush for
her, running completely wild, overturning the pillory, and looting the
bakers' and confectioners' booths. One by one the shops were shut; the
mob, ever-increasing, spread into the neighbouring streets, doing no one any
harm, but shouting for bread, and seizing it wherever they could find it.

The Maréchal de Boufflers, busy with his own affairs, happened to pass
on the way to his notary who lived in the vicinity. He was surprised at the
disturbance and learning the cause of it decided to endeavour to pacify the
mob. The Duc de Gramont,[1] who was with him, did his best to dissuade
him, but seeing that he was quite determined, went with him. About
a hundred yards from the notary's house they met the Maréchal
d'Huxelles in his coach and stopped him to ask for news because he came
from the direction of the riot. He said that it was all over, tried to prevent
them from going farther, and made off for the country with the air of one
who finds such noise distasteful and prefers not to be involved. Boufflers
and his father-in-law continued none the less and found the terror increasing as they advanced, with people calling out from their windows that
they had best go back or they would be attacked. At the top of the Rue
Saint-Denis the Maréchal de Boufflers considered that it was time to leave
their coach, and he therefore went forward on foot, still accompanied by
the Duc de Gramont. He walked straight through that angry rabble, asking what was the matter, promising bread, speaking to them gently but
firmly, and with the best eloquence at his command telling them that

[1] Boufflers's father-in-law.

theirs was not the best way to entreat. They listened to him amidst repeated cries of 'Long live M. le Maréchal de Boufflers!' as he continued to walk straight ahead through the crowd, addressing them to the best of his ability. He thus proceeded with the Duc de Gramont beside him along the entire length of the Rue aux Ours and down the neighbouring streets until they reached the heart of that minor rebellion. There the people begged him to tell the King of their sufferings and to get bread for them, which he promised to do; whereupon the mob became quiet and began to disperse, thanking him, and still crying 'Long live the Maréchal de Boufflers!' He did good service that day, for Argenson was all the time approaching with some detachments of the French and Swiss guards, and without Boufflers's efforts there might have been much bloodshed, for the musketeers were already astride their horses.

Soon after the Maréchal de Boufflers's return to his house in the Place Royale he learned that far worse rioting was going on in the Faubourg Saint-Antoine. He hurried there, still accompanied by the Duc de Gramont, and quietened that mob as he had done the other. He then again returned home, snatched a morsel of food, and set off immediately for Versailles. He refused to travel in anything except his post-chaise, with one lackey behind and no one riding beside the door, intending to cross the entire length of Paris in that way. But as he emerged from the Place Royale all the shopkeepers and the passers-by called out to him to take pity on them and to get them bread, with continued cries of 'Long live the Maréchal de Boufflers', and he was thus escorted the whole of the way as far as the Quai du Louvre.

As soon as he reached Versailles he went to Mme de Maintenon's room and found her with the King, both in great distress of mind. He explained his arrival and received many thanks, the King at once offering him the command of Paris, troops, burgesses, police, everything, and pressing him urgently to accept. The noble-minded Boufflers preferred, however, to have peace restored by the proper authority. He reminded the King that there was already one governor of Paris, whose functions should not be usurped, adding that it was disgraceful that the authority, instead of being left to him, should have been snatched away by the lieutenant of police and the provost of the merchants. He then entreated the King in this moment of danger to return the power to the Duc de Tresmes, who had lost it so completely that fresh letters patent had to be issued to him.

Thereafter the troops and burgesses were given strict orders to obey only the governor in all matters and in all places. Argenson, the lieutenant of police, and Bignon,[1] the provost, were told to report to him and to obey him implicitly, and it was the same for all the other official bodies.[2] The

---

[1] Jérôme III, one of the chief magistrates of Paris. He had once been Saint-Simon's tutor.

[2] This must have seemed to Saint-Simon a tremendous justification of his quarrel with Montrevel over the Blaye militia.

Duc de Tresmes accordingly went to Paris to exercise his authority, but with secret instructions to do nothing without the Maréchal de Boufflers's approval, and Boufflers himself was sent back to live there. The latter's modesty made him give all the credit to the Duc de Tresmes, in whose name the orders were issued. He even went so far as to go to that duke's house for their meetings, and scarcely ever allowed him to come to the Place Royale. In fact he was both master and tutor to the Duc de Tresmes, but he gave it out that he was at most an aide-de-camp, and treated him accordingly.

Very soon afterwards bread was supplied and fairly distributed. Paris was fully patrolled, rather too much so, perhaps, but there was not afterwards the smallest disturbance. Tresmes and Boufflers reported personally to the King from time to time, but did not sleep out of Paris, and gradually they went less often, until at last there was nothing to report. Boufflers's reputation, greatly enhanced by his genuine modesty, was then at its height. He was the master of Paris, the moderator in all matters of war, a paramount influence in every affair at the Court. But his lustre did not long endure; it vanished after an episode that should by rights have rendered it more glorious than ever before.

[*At the beginning of the campaign of 1709 both sides were anxious to play for time. Louis XIV forbade Villars to fight a battle and instructed him to display the utmost caution. Marlborough, Prince Eugene, and the Dutch were confident that France was on the verge of collapse from bankruptcy, famine, and demoralization. They had only to wait. After much consultation it was decided that the risk, and the expense of lives and money, of forcing a battle was unwarrantable in the circumstances.*

After the fall of Tournai, the mood of both sides and the character of the war suddenly changed. It appears as though both the Allies and the French became filled with the desire to fight it out. King Louis gave Villars permission to court a battle if he so desired. Villars did so, and on 10 September, Marlborough and Eugene attacked him in his strongly entrenched position at Malplaquet. There ensued the biggest and bloodiest battle of the entire war.]

From the very beginning of the campaign Flanders had been the chief, nay the sole focus of anxiety, and it continued to be so until the end. Prince Eugene and Marlborough, with their armies now combined, pursued their vast aims and scorned to conceal them. Their massive accumulations of troops seemed to portend sieges, and, must I confess it? in our weakness we were glad of this, for our army could be relied on only to keep itself in being. None the less, Artagnan with a detachment of eight battalions had captured Warneton without difficulty, and the Maréchal de Villars had scored a small victory on a foray. These, however, were mere trifles.

The storm-clouds had first gathered around Tournai, where Surville was in command, with Mesgrigny, another lieutenant-general, permanent governor of the citadel. The trench was cut on the night of 7–8 July. The Maréchal allowed the siege to be laid without the smallest display of opposition; he was glad enough to remain unmolested, and free to continue his cheerful, boasting utterances. In all justice, however, I must admit that food supplies were reaching him irregularly; money by slow degrees and in very small sums, and that he had every cause to fear desertions and demoralization.[1]

Surville held out for no more than twenty days and beat for a parlay on the evening of 28 July. He then sent the Chevalier de Retz back to the King, who was at Marly, to report that the garrison of four thousand and five hundred men had been reduced to three thousand to enter the citadel; that breaches thirty yards wide had been made in three attacks; that the horn-work of Sept-Fontaines was overrun; and that assaults on the citadel were about to be delivered in three simultaneous attacks. Something better than that was expected of a man so recently retrieved by the generosity of the Maréchal de Boufflers,[2] and who had been present at the siege of Lille.

The Chevalier de Retz appeared at Marly on Thursday, 1 August. Great was the astonishment when on the following Tuesday the Comte de Ravignan also arrived accompanied by Voysin, and went straight to Mme de Maintenon's room, where the King was at work. A few moments later the Maréchal de Boufflers joined them. A second, and totally unexpected, messenger from the army aroused enormous excitement at the Court. Hopes and needs combined to persuade everyone that there was a chance of peace, more especially when it was learned that Surville was being royally entertained by the victors, and that there was to be a truce until after Ravignan's return, which was fixed for the evening of the 8th. Soon afterwards, however, the mystery was solved. The enemy had proposed that this cease-fire should last during the period in which the citadel might reasonably be expected to hold out, after which time the garrison was to surrender without an assault,[3] and that meanwhile the two armies should remain at a stated distance from the fortress, without engaging in

---

[1] Marlborough wrote on 4 July: 'All the wheat is killed everywhere that we have seen or heard of. It grieves my heart to see the sad condition all the poor country people are in for want of bread; they have not the same countenances they had in other years.' And again on 11 July, 'It is not to be imagined the ill weather we have, insomuch that the poor soldiers in the trenches are up to their knees in dirt, which gives me the spleen to such a degree that it makes me very uneasy, and consequently makes me languish for retirement. . . . We shall not find forage to enable us to make a long campaign, and that is what I fear the French know as well as we. . . . The misery of all the poor people we see is such that one must be a brute not to pity them.'

[2] He had been arrested and imprisoned in 1705 for a drunken fight with another officer.

[3] Seventeenth- and eighteenth-century sieges were conducted according to a ritual of procedure. A commander was not supposed to fight to the last man and let the fortress be destroyed rather than surrender. It was the proper thing to give up when the moment came for the final assault, because neither side wanted the fortresses destroyed.

any hostile activities. Such a proposal was as monstrous as it was un-precedented, and there was general amazement that so intelligent a man as Ravignan, who had won distinction at Lille, had consented to undertake the mission. A truce with no thought of peace to follow, a given date for a fortress to surrender unassaulted, these were unheard-of suggestions, notions devised by the enemy in order to save themselves trouble, money, and ammunition, plainly showing their contempt for our army, whom they obviously regarded as incapable and unlikely to attempt a relief. Sur-ville was much blamed for countenancing the proposal, and Ravignan for bringing it; and the latter was immediately sent back with a flat refusal.

It was generally supposed that the underlying motive was the immense reputation of the fortress, which Mesgrigny, the best of our engineers after Vauban although much inferior to him, had designed according to his own ideas, and for his personal comfort since he was to be governor of the citadel. It was one of the best and the most symmetrical of all the fortresses built by the King, with excellent underground tunnels, and beneath the outworks and even under the ramparts countermines, con-trivances which, when well planted, can greatly lengthen a siege because the attackers become alarmed and discouraged when they are not sure of the ground beneath their feet. The fortress's fame was well justified, but all the admirable devices proved useless to prevent its capture, for it was surrendered on 2 September without having undergone even one assault. Such an event seemed almost impossible, and another no less incredible was that Mesgrigny, who was eighty-four years old and had scarcely left his bed during the two stages of the siege, thought it no shame to desert to the enemy for the sake of remaining governor of the citadel.

Surville returned to report and was not ill-received, which was another surprise. But the reprimand he so richly deserved for surrendering at a time when it was all-important to keep the enemy occupied descended on him for his lack of discretion. He had several times dined with Prince Eugene and the Duke of Marlborough both between the two parts of the siege and after the capitulation, and had discussed the Maréchal de Vil-lars, who claimed that they had spoken ill of him, and that Surville, drunk or eager to please, had much belittled him. The complaints were loud on either side for Surville resented the fact that Villars had made no attempt to relieve him; but eventually the former, knowing himself to be the weaker, showed a willingness to be reconciled. He was to find that he had to deal with a hot-tempered man, flushed with success, and com-pletely unforgiving.[1]

Many people were surprised that the enemy had chosen to linger over this great siege instead of attempting a penetration towards the sea. It is

---

[1] Surville retired to his house in Picardy and was never heard of again.

true that Villars had established himself at the beginning of the campaign in an excellent position to thwart that design, but he could not have parried all attempts to turn his flank, nor have been able to avoid a battle had they wished to force one upon him. Some believed that they were more concerned to advance steadily but surely on a solid front than to make hasty penetrations that might leave their rear in difficulties. Others, more hopeful and more anxious to pay their court than be guided by reason, claimed that the Dutch, who they still believed wished for peace, had chosen Tournai as a useful distraction not vital to France, and one that would last throughout the season, after which negotiations could be resumed, with the English and the Emperor easier to bring to terms because of the heavy burden of their costs. The courtiers endeavoured to allay their fears with such false hopes, and spread the report to all parts of the kingdom, being less concerned with the interests of the State than to shut people's mouths by fear or persuasion. The King often expressed himself strongly on the subject of 'speechifiers', and one became guilty of a crime, no matter what one's intentions, if one strayed ever so little from the tediousness of the *Gazette de France*[1] or the conversation of the most servile courtiers.

After the fall of Tournai, Boufflers realized the awful seriousness of the Flanders campaign. He grew anxious because only one man was in command, fearing lest sickness or accident might put him out of action with no one to replace him in such terribly dangerous times. Full of this foreboding he spoke to the King, stressing the likelihood of a battle, and explaining the risk to the army if Villars were wounded. He then offered to go himself to Villars's assistance, ignoring his own superior rank, to be there solely for the latter's support, assuming no authority except as he directed, existing for the sole purpose of replacing him in case of need. It was a noble gesture, worthy of the greatest Romans at the most sublime period of their republic, for at that time Boufflers, at the very height of his reputation, fame, and favour, had only to remain passive and enjoy his glory, despite the fact that ill-health prevented him from commanding armies in the field. Yet so far was he above any kind of self-seeking that he was willing to go to the support of a man who was a mere coxcomb, selfish, jealous, without principles, eager to steal the glory of others, to take all the credit for successes and to cast the blame for every failure on to other men's shoulders. Boufflers, moreover, knew full well what he risked. He was aware of Villars's boastful, clever, misleading talk, and the partiality of the King and Mme de Maintenon. Yet into the hands of this man, so much his junior in experience, ten years his junior as a marshal of France, the Maréchal de Boufflers proposed to place himself for the good of the State, notwithstanding that by so doing he exposed his splendid,

---

[1] Founded in 1631 by Théophraste Renaudot with the support of Cardinal Richelieu.

unblemished reputation to the certainty of envy and the probability of defeat.[1]

All this Boufflers knew, yet it did not move him. He pressed the King to let him go, but King Louis, less perceptive and still less appreciative of that magnanimous offer, praised him, thanked him, thought there was no need, and completely failed to understand the sacrifice. Ten days later, however, when Boufflers had put the matter from his mind, the King reconsidered his offer, summoned him, had him shown in by the back offices, and informed him with thanks that he might join the Flanders army in the manner suggested. Now it so happened that for the first time in his life Boufflers was suffering from a severe attack of gout and had great difficulty in dragging himself to the King's study. He none the less reiterated his willingness, received his final orders, returned to Paris and left again next day, which was Monday, 2 September, the very day on which the citadel of Tournai surrendered.

He was received by Villars with every appearance of pleasure and respect; horses and servants were placed at his service, and all the plans were confided to him. Boufflers's gout had been so painful that there had been the greatest difficulty in helping him from his coach, but he did not allow that disability to keep him for long confined to his room. Villars desired him to announce the password and issue the orders of the day, but after many compliments it was finally decided that the general in charge should give the password and receive the orders from both of them together. To all appearances there was perfect harmony between them, and no one could tell what were Villars's private thoughts at the sudden descent upon him of a second-in-command of such a quality, and for whom he had not applied. Whether he felt vexed or hindered, or whether in the critical circumstances he was glad of the assistance, no one has ever discovered. Be that as it may, the two commanders appeared to be united, and Boufflers, faithful to his promise, was ever on the watch not to seem a critic, deferring in everything to Villars, never opposing him, and showing a readiness to serve that must have been vastly reassuring.

The enemy had marched away towards Mons immediately after the capture of Tournai. Villars recalled his detachments, and the King of England under his incognito of the Chevalier de Saint-Georges, serving voluntarily as in previous years, arrived in haste with the remnants of a fever, showing no concern for his health. The garrison of Tournai, although prisoners of war, were escorted to Condé; they were permitted to take their arms and baggage and the enemy made the gallant gesture of

---

[1] Saint-Simon was unfair to Villars. Boufflers was his beau-ideal of what a nobleman should be; Villars's jovial expansiveness was to Saint-Simon's mind anything but *noblesse de l'épée* quality, and when he was subsequently made a ducal-peer Saint-Simon almost refused to recognize such a bounder as his equal.

allowing Surville to retain two pieces of cannon. They still numbered three thousand and were assigned for exchanges with enemy prisoners. Surville and Ravignan were freed, on condition that if we captured officers of comparable rank we would return them without requiring an exchange.

The enemy crossed the Scheldt on the night of 3 September, reached the Maine above Mons on the 5th, and continued their advance. Our army, led by both marshals, moved on 4 September, and at nine o'clock on the morning of the 9th took up a strong position at Malplaquet, the right and left flanks resting upon two woods, and a belt of trees and low bushes screening the centre. Between these three areas of woodland there were two gaps or corridors. Villars placed his artillery on some rising ground, stationed his infantry in the outskirts of the woods, alongside the gaps and within half-range of his cannon, and dug trenches to protect them. Marlborough and Prince Eugene moved swiftly in that direction and arrived at the same spot by mid-morning of the 10th. The firing began almost at once and continued without interruption throughout the day, doing little damage, except to Coëtquen, whose leg was blown off as he rode from one part of the field to another. It was from the courier sent to inform his family that we first learned that the armies had met.

The first essential for Marlborough and Prince Eugene was to reconnoitre our position and decide the best arrangement for themselves. To do this with the maximum of leisure and safety and allow time for their rearguard to join them they devised a ruse which proved wholly successful. They sent some apparently junior officers up to the trenches which our infantry was strengthening, with orders to get into conversation with the sentries and advance further on parole. There is every reason to believe that these young officers were carefully picked, for they fulfilled their mission with extraordinary skill. They approached to the very edge of the entrenchments, attracted the attention of some of our younger officers, began to chat with them, and asked to speak to the captains and corps-commanders. When a colonel of Charost's brigade appeared, they told him that a group of high-ranking officers whom they could see some way off contained General Cadogan,[1] and that he would much like to have a word with one of our generals, if he would care to approach. These conversations had been going on for some considerable time, but it was at this point that they were first noticed by Count Albergotti as he rode round the outposts. He inquired what was happening and arrived on the spot just as the Marquis de Charost,[2] who had been alerted, was ordering away the enemy officers and calling back our own. Albergotti was not so particular; he sent word to Cadogan that he was present, indicated a place

[1] William Cadogan (1675-1726), an Irish general, made Earl Cadogan in 1718. He was Marlborough's close friend.
[2] Duc de Charost, later still Duc de Villeroy and governor of Louis XV.

to which he might advance on parole, and went there himself with a very small following of officers. Cadogan joined him; he was Marlborough's friend and confidant and in the way of disinterested loyalty was the Puységur of their army. He span out the civilities and flowery compliments for a very long time, whilst Albergotti listened with his usual icy calm, finally saying that had the Maréchal de Villars been on the spot he would have been glad to talk of peace, and might have shown that it would not be hard to make. That provided sufficient excuse for a parlay and for prolonging it. The group of officers around them grew larger, rumours of peace spread swiftly through the trenches and before long reached the entire army. Villars, who had received no report of all this from Albergotti, thought that the holding of such a conference without his permission was highly irregular. He rode forward and ordered Albergotti to return at once; thus everything ended in mutual hopes for peace and the expression of empty courtesies.

The generals moved slowly away, but the other officers persisted in hanging around our trenches on the pretext of exchanging names and embraces with such of our officers as they had greeted without previous acquaintance. At last threats were made of firing on them, and one or two shots were actually discharged into the air before they could be made to retire. During all this time, however, a very small group of the most experienced officers, and some of their best generals, on horseback, but only very few for fear of arousing suspicion, and a larger number of engineers and draughtsmen had been taking advantage of the absurd situation to note down the details of our position and to make sketches of the main features of the terrain, so as to site their artillery with greater advantage, which information they used only too well. We were told of this ruse later by the prisoners of war.

Albergotti defended his actions with spirit and the air of unconcern that never deserted him. Villars feared him at the Court because he had powerful supporters. Boufflers liked him also, and not regarding himself as the general in command felt that it would be best to keep him for the following day, beyond which the battle could clearly not be postponed. Thus nothing was done to him. Villars merely emitted vague threats against the subalterns for their irresponsible conduct, after which all thoughts were turned to the coming attack. It was a quiet night, and the darkness was prolonged by a thick fog until six o'clock next morning. Prince Eugene and Marlborough had made their dispositions that same day and thus, on the morning of the eleventh, they were prepared to fall upon the King's army.

As I have already mentioned, our right and left wings rested on two woods, and there was another wood in the centre with a gap on either side. Now you must also know that facing the centre and the two gaps lay a small expanse of open ground with a wood beyond. That wood we did not hold. It served to screen the movements of our centre from the enemy, but served them far better because they were able to hide troops among its bushes monstrously close to our centre and fall upon us unperceived. Villars did not make a straight line but one curved crescent-shaped, so that the tips of his two wings were much further advanced than the centre, and consequently much more easy to encircle and break through than with the usual straight line of battle. He decided also that his left was less secure than his right and therefore chose that station, giving the right to Boufflers. By seven in the morning the fog had lifted and the enemy columns were observed marching and deploying; and under light gunfire both wings of our army were simultaneously attacked by their infantry. They had taken the precaution of keeping their cavalry some distance away, almost in column formation, so as to protect them from our cannon; whereas ours, which was filling the two gaps in support of our infantry, was raked by artillery at half-range for six hours on end, with many and profitless losses. Meanwhile the attack was being pressed fiercely on our left, the enemy making every possible use of their prior knowledge of the terrain. They rightly supposed that attacks on both our wings at once would absorb all the Maréchal de Villars's thoughts and that at a pinch he would weaken his centre to support them, confident that the open ground in front would give him notice of any trouble brewing there. That was the whole cause of our defeat. The enemy was repulsed in the first attack on our left wing, and then, launching a second with a very great force of infantry, succeeded in breaking through. Thereupon Villars, as they had expected, sent for all the infantry of his centre, leaving only the French and Swiss guards and Charost's brigade; but even with that reinforcement he could not restore the situation.

At that point the enemy, perceiving that their ruse had been successful, brought from the wood facing our centre still another large body of infantry, which they had concealed there unobserved, and with these fresh troops fell upon the brigades of guards, who put up a very poor show of resistance, or so it is said, and almost immediately were thrown back by vastly superior numbers. During the confusion the Maréchal de Villars received a severe wound on the knee and Albergotti another, which put them both out of the battle, and after that the defeat of the left wing, already almost complete, became a fact despite the efforts and example of King James of England. The fighting on the right had been very fierce. The Maréchal de Boufflers, after valiantly repelling the attacking infantry and the cavalry charge that came after, gained a large expanse of ground. He served in the same way other bodies of cavalry that charged him, throwing them back three times with equal success. It was at this moment when he was intent on following up this small victory that he learned of the defeat of the centre, the disaster on the left wing, the removal of the wounded Villars, and the fact that the entire responsibility for restoring the perilous situation into which Villars had precipitated them rested on his shoulders. Maddened at seeing victory snatched from his grasp, and what is more by French hands; sick with anguish at what, judging by the army's condition, he took to be the death-struggle of France, he set himself to inspire his wing to superhuman efforts by short exhortations as he rode through the lines. Then, giving free rein to his personal valour, he showed an example of that heroism in despair that sometimes turns defeat to victory. Indeed, his reckless disregard of danger as he charged at the head of his squadrons and battalions made men think that he had a charmed life; not for years had the soldiers seen a general who cared so little for himself, and they responded to him magnificently. After a time, however, he began to fear lest this stupendous effort should separate him from the rest of the army and therefore attempted to drive diagonally so as to come nearer the centre. He there discovered that a single regiment of ours had managed to take the enemy in the rear and had driven them back into the wood and that our cavalry had crossed the trenches in pursuit of them. Unfortunately, as they approached the wood they had encountered such an intense bombardment that they had been compelled to retire under a murderous cross-fire.

During the cannonade, the enemy had continued to force us back and had completed the break-through on our centre. The conduct of the guards and the household regiments was said to have been very bad at that moment, for they allowed the trenches to be overrun almost without resistance. There the enemy halted whilst they sent for their cavalry, which until then had not been seriously engaged, and with these fresh troops, charging at full gallop, they forced twenty squadrons through the intervals in our lines. Our own squadrons waited too long before attacking the ever-increasing numbers of cavalry, then made a feeble charge and returned at once. That was the gendarmerie; the household cavalry supporting them did little better, for their courage and great efforts had reached their limit. A few moments later the musketeers arrived with Coëtenfao leading the red troops of the *Maison du Roi*, and together they stopped and threw back the enemy cavalry, but finding several more lines drawn up one behind the other, and the remainder of the pursued cavalry able to rally beyond them, they were forced to stop. There then appeared the four companies of lifeguards, who broke the enemy lines one after another, but exhausted by so many charges they eventually gave ground which was retaken by fresh bodies of enemy cavalry, who thus snatched victory out of defeat. That renewal of the fighting lasted a long time and was contested horse to horse, until at last our men had to yield to superior numbers and leave the battle-field to the enemy. It was the final struggle of that fateful day.

At four o'clock in the afternoon the Maréchal de Boufflers formed the whole army into four columns and slowly began the retreat, placing himself in the last of all the rearguards. The enemy gave him no trouble at all in the entire course of his march. All the cannon were saved, excepting one or two. As for baggage, there was none because everything had been sent to the rear when our army marched out to meet the enemy. In this good order the River Ronelle was reached, and the army encamped behind it between Valenciennes and Le Quesnoy. The wounded were taken to those two towns and also to Maubeuge and Cambrai. The Allied armies spent the night on the field of battle amid twenty-five thousand dead. They frankly admitted to having lost more than we in dead and wounded, including generals and other officers, flags and trophies. In fact their losses amounted to seven lieutenants-general killed or wounded, five other generals, about eighteen hundred officers, and more than fifteen thousand men killed or put out of action in other ways. They also freely expressed their admiration of the valour of the greater part of our army, and their commanders-in-chief did not conceal their view that had we been better led we should have beaten them.

The Maréchal de Villars's ideas in courting a battle are extraordinarily hard to comprehend. Why, for instance, did he march so great a distance in order to be attacked, when there were two whole days in which he might himself have struck with far less trouble—or at least a day and a half, to be strictly accurate? If it be argued that he mistook a very powerful advance guard for their entire army, the answer is that he should have been better informed. In any case he could never have won a battle on such unfavourable terrain, and, on examination, his dispositions proved to have been no better than his choice of ground, especially not the posting of his cavalry under the fire of the batteries for no purpose whatsoever. Finally, what need had he to fight at all after allowing Tournai to be taken unopposed? and if he intended to protect Mons it would have been far better either to have stopped them much sooner, or better still to have let them lay the siege and then weakened them by attacks on their trenches and outposts. It would seem that of all times and places during the entire campaign, the time and place selected by Villars was the worst possible. Such, indeed, was the view of both the armies, but you shall see that the King and Mme de Maintenon were of a different opinion.

Immediately after the battle Boufflers despatched a courier to the King. His letter was truthful, clear, modest and concise, but full of praise of Villars, who was at Le Quesnoy in no condition to attend to business. On the following day Boufflers wrote at greater length, allowing his sense of all that had been inflicted on the troops and his devotion to the King to exceed all bounds. He was, in fact, so bent on consoling the King and extolling the nation that he appeared almost to be announcing a victory and predicting others to follow. The first courier brought the full, shocking news of the disgrace; but at that time the Court was so hardened to defeat and its disastrous consequences that a battle lost in this way appeared a semi-victory. Boufflers's second letter, exaggerating in every way, fulsome in praise of Villars and the valour of the soldiers, with its confident hope for the future designed to console the King, appeared so outrageous when it was published that it did him irreparable harm. D'Antin, who was Villars's friend, seized on its absurdity in order to belittle him to the King, with subtle mockeries verging on contempt, until Society blinded by their disgust at his letter almost forgot Lillè and the heroism that had led him to go to Villars's aid. Such was the rock on which that pattern of virtue was shattered, with the help of rascally and jealous men. It produced, as you shall see, another cause for bringing down this godlike figure to the level of ordinary mortals.

In the meantime the Allies proceeded to besiege Mons, and the King's army, destitute of all supplies, looked on powerless to intervene. Boufflers, who had been completely absorbed in the ever-increasing problems of subsistence, now slowly became aware that Villars was rated his equal for having fought and lost a crucial but wholly unnecessary battle, although he, Boufflers, had saved France by preserving the army despite Villars's mistakes. As for the latter, he was less conscious of his wound, now rapidly healing, than of the enormous honour,[1] for which he had to thank the King's partiality that had rescued him from the very brink of ruin, and of the arrival of Maréchal the chief surgeon, who never ordinarily left the King but was now despatched to him with orders to remain until he could be transported back to France. Taking advantage of these favourable omens, and making the most of his invalid state, Villars used his friends to strike at the Maréchal de Boufflers, questioning and criticizing his actions, whilst that hero, knowing that he had saved France, and sure of his great reputation, ignored such pinpricks. At last, however, their increasing number persuaded him that there was some malice in Villars's behaviour and he began to suspect a plot. He was somewhat disturbed, but not to the extent of changing his attitude, or of ceasing to be lavish with praise and compliments. So matters rested for a time, with the one continually attacking and the other bearing his injuries with increasing annoyance but showing no outward sign.

Boufflers's excess of zeal caused him to weigh every detail when making recommendations for advancement or rewards, and he was thus more than ordinarily slow in providing the King with candidates for the vacant posts. It was not in fact until two weeks after the battle that he sent in his list. Picture his indignation when he received that same evening a complete account of all the promotions and honours, signed and sealed, his first intimation that the King had not intended to consult him. That was his first recompense for the services he had rendered, notwithstanding

---

[1] He was elevated in one bound to be duke and peer. Saint-Simon's prejudice may have blinded him to the fact that after Malplaquet France was no longer in danger of invasion, and that the King might have thought that deserving of a great reward.

that the King continually repeated, even in public, that God had certainly inspired him to send Boufflers to the army, for without him all would have been lost. He suffered the added humiliation of knowing that every man in that army knew what had occurred, and that he was probably the first commander to be treated with such marked contempt.

Truth, for in such matters it is vital to be accurate, compels me to admit that Boufflers's fall did not distress me so much as the reasons responsible for it. There were three altogether, and the most deplorable was the evidence of his foolish letters. They were indeed monstrously fulsome, but although they betrayed his stupidity they also showed him at his most generous in his attempts to conceal Villars's mistakes, dispel the prevailing gloom, and, from sheer loyalty and devotion, to cheer and comfort the King. The second was the determination of Villars and Voysin, from the army and the war ministry, each acting separately, to be rid of him as a mentor. The former supplied the ammunition, the latter used it to good effect. The villains in the King's intimate circle added all that they could devise in order to bring down this honest man who had forced his way into the King's cabinet, and whom they feared even in their safe refuge. Thus it has often happened in very many kingdoms that those whose noble, disinterested service is above reward are destroyed by envy; for jealous men will combine to bring down a paragon whose unquestioned superiority is regarded by all as a right, and rightly earned. Few are the monarchs who can let justice triumph over pride; few to whom the appearance of a subject too noble for rewards does not become at first oppressive and finally abominable.

It was, however, the third cause that did Boufflers the vital injury. All three causes are beyond question, and I am at a loss only for the actual time of the last. He plainly resented Villars being made his equal by sudden elevation to a ducal peerage, in a manner vastly different from his own slow rise. That, in the particular circumstances, may have turned his brain, for it was then that he first aspired to so inconceivably august a title that had anyone dared to suggest it as the reason for his going to Flanders he would have flatly denied it. Be that as it may, the sword of High Constable of France fired his imagination and he began to think it not beyond his merit, especially since Villars had been made a peer, and so for the present at least his equal in rank. He argued that his functions of moderator of Paris and adviser to Voysin were those of the first officer of the crown, and he saw no other man great enough to dispute his claim, no prince of the blood to feel overshadowed, for M. du Maine had long since fallen out of the race, and M. le Duc d'Orléans after his latest escapades would scarcely dare to show offence. Men are prone to self-flattery; Boufflers sincerely believed that his past services provided ample proof of there being no danger in reviving that supreme and all-powerful office for his benefit, and that the abuse of it by past holders would be thought impossible in his case. That and the magnitude of Villars's reward were sufficient answer to his mind against the risk of making a subject too mighty that had caused the office of High Constable to become obsolete a hundred years earlier.

All the above is certain, and I myself have positive assurance of it. What I do not know is the exact moment when Boufflers dropped the first hint. Whether it was done by letter from Flanders written in the heat of the moment to Mme de Maintenon, or perhaps to the King himself; whether, on the other hand, he waited until after his return is something which I have never discovered. That he did hint, broadly, and more than once as I believe, is past all doubt, and that is what finally and completely destroyed him.

After the surrender of Mons the Allies separated their armies. Boufflers dispersed his own, and then returned to the Court. He received a welcome less warm than that of an ordinary general returning from an uneventful campaign. No audience with the King; not so much as a passing word concerning Flanders; nothing but silence, avoidance, and coldness, with now and then a casual greeting; no more at all. His troubles during the past campaign had combined with his grievances to raise an impenetrable barrier between him and the King. Mme de Maintenon, who was still his friend, laboured in vain to comfort him. Even Monseigneur and Mgr le Duc de Bourgogne endeavoured to rally him, but he was too noble to find comfort in the thought of the King's old age and approaching death, and far too proud to unsay his words. His courage allowed him to appear outwardly the same as usual; but a canker was slowly devouring him, for he could reconcile himself neither to the change in his position, nor to the refused honour which he truly thought he had well-deserved. He used often to open his heart to me, not in self-pity, nor abandoning the narrow path of virtue, but with a wounded heart for which neither time nor reflection could find a cure. Thereafter he dwindled, and though not bed-ridden nor house-bound lived no longer than two or three years.

Villars returned in triumph. The King desired him to take up residence at Versailles so that Maréchal might continue to care for his wound; and because his own apartments were very small and on the top floor he was lent the magnificent suite of rooms belonging to the late M. le Prince de Conti, on the ground floor of the new wing, where it was easier to carry him. What a contrast! What difference in service, merit, birth, and rank between these two men! What an inexhaustible source of meditation!

The famous Cardinal Portocarrero, whom I have often mentioned, died at this time after outliving his day by many years. He left Mme des Ursins more powerful than ever, feeling delivered from a ghost who, though no longer an obstacle, had made her feel uncomfortable. He had turned wholly to religion after his dismissal, and had died in a noble and edifying manner at Madrid, which is in the diocese of Toledo. He had desired to be buried beneath one of the aisles of his own cathedral of Toledo, in front of the entrance to the chapel dedicated to 'The New Kings', which chapel is in itself a great church, with its own chapter and services. He asked that his tomb should not be raised or enriched in any way, but that people should walk upon it, and he desired also that the words, *Hic jacet cinis, pulvis, et nihil*,[1] be engraved there as his only epitaph. His wishes were exactly obeyed. I myself have seen his tomb at Toledo[2] where he is greatly venerated. There are neither his arms upon it nor anything else; it is all perfectly flat, on a level with the floor. All that has been added is an inscription on the wall of the chapel, near the door, with his arms and titles, the position of his tomb, and the fact that all was done as he desired.

The Bishop of Chartres also died about this time, worn out by work and study. He was of no possible account in respect of his birth, but had close connections by marriage that did him much honour. Monsieur de Chartres, Godet by name,[3] was one of the first pupils of Saint-Sulpice, and perhaps the one who shed most lustre and profit on that seminary, which has since become a nursery for bishops. When Mme de Maintenon removed her academy from Noisy to Saint-Cyr, which is in the diocese of Chartres, she was inevitably brought into communication with the bishop, and developed such a liking for him that she made him its superior and spiritual director, and her own director as well, who in very truth had the guidance of her heart and conscience, for she kept nothing secret from him. So far as was possible she brought him to the notice of the King, in order to provide a counter-weight in the distribution of benefices to balance that of Père de La Chaise and the Jesuits, for whom she had no love; and she managed to advance him to the point of being consulted by them both in respect of their marriage. He spoke and wrote of it freely to the King, and often congratulated him on his admirable choice.[4] I never saw these letters myself, but his nephew and successor[5] read them because they contained other matters, and many times told me of their contents long after they all were dead.

The death of Monsieur de Chartres set two men upon candlesticks[6] whom he had strongly recommended to Mme de Maintenon. The first of these was Bissy, Bishop of Meaux, later of Toul and soon after made a cardinal, who inherited her absolute confidence in matters concerning the Church, out of which he made his fortune and far worse. The second was La Chétardie, curé of Saint-Sulpice, a priest of enormous holiness, but

---

[1] 'Here lie ashes, dust, and nothingness.'
[2] In 1721, when he went to Spain as ambassador-extraordinary.
[3] Godet des Marais.
[4] 'You have a most excellent wife, full of God's spirit and understanding,' he wrote in one of his letters to the King.
[5] His great-nephew the Abbé de Mérinville, Charles François des Moustiers.
[6] Refers to the parable, St. Mark IV, 21. 'Is a candle brought to be put under a bush or under a bed and not to be set on a candlestick?'

the stupidest and most commonplace man imaginable.[1] The latter gained
Mme de Maintenon's confidence in personal matters; he became her
confessor, her spiritual director, and thus to some extent the director also
of Saint-Cyr. What was really astounding to those who knew the man was
that before long Mme de Maintenon, for all her shrewdness, was keeping
nothing secret from him, in the same way that she had been in the habit
of telling all to Monsieur de Chartres. She constantly wrote to him for his
advice on public affairs, or to inform him of them; but what was almost
inconceivable was that this simpleton, who beside his extensive parish was
also superior of the convent of the Visitation of Sainte-Marie of Chaillot,
took her letters and read them aloud to the youngest nuns. One of Mme
de Saint-Simon's sisters[2] who was a nun at that convent and many times
its superior, a woman of great piety but also vastly intelligent and full of
worldly knowledge, often nearly swooned with terror at the secrets being
unfolded to the other nuns. Indeed, many things came to light because of
these readings, although no one at that time could imagine how, and so
long as he lived, which was very long, no one could persuade Mme de
Maintenon to part with him. He interfered in everything with great want
of tact, caused many important matters to go awry, supported many that
were unworthy, had not the first notion of anything, and quite blatantly
used his advancement to collect around himself a little circle of admirers.
As for Bissy, we shall soon see him taking wing for the topmost heights.

Mme de Moussy, sister of Premier Président Harlay, and a noted professional pietist with all the attendant accessories, died at this time
without issue. She had always been on very loving terms with her brother
and his son,[3] and had lived with them nearly always. She none the less
disinherited her nephew for no reason whatsoever, leaving the latter
utterly dumbfounded when he discovered that she had bequeathed all she
possessed to the hospitals.

She was the widow of the last of the Bouteillers. I am speaking of that
noble family that for many years included the Comtes de Senlis, who were
known as the Bouteillers, or the Bouteillers de Senlis, because they so
often held the once high office of Chief Butler of France. We find their
signatures and witnessed presences on the ancient royal charters, together with those of the *dapifer*[4] which comprised the Grand-master (or
as he was then entitled the King's steward), the Grand-chamberlain, the
Constable, who was no more than the Master of the Horse, and last of all
the Chancellor. In the still more remote past the holder of the first of these

---

[1] Joachim Trotti de La Chétardie. 'Idiot!' exclaimed Saint-Simon of him on one occasion.
Fénelon said that his mind was deformed.
[2] Marie Louise Gabrielle de Lorges; entered the convent of the Visitation at Chaillot on
30 January, 1702.
[3] Achille IV de Harlay (1669–1717).
[4] The officers of the household who served the king at his meals.

posts was called the Seneschal and was sometimes promoted to be steward of the palace or merely major-domo; indeed that officer could bear any one of these titles for the self-same post.

This autumn was the last on which the famous Abbey of Port-Royal-des-Champs could be seen standing. For a very long time it had been the quarry of the Jesuits; it at last became their prey. I shall not expatiate on the origin, progress, outcome, and events of a disputation and quarrel with which everyone is familiar, nor on the opposing sides, Molinist and Jansenist, for their doctrinal and historical writings are enough to form an ample library, and their views have been aired for many years past in Rome and at our Court. It will suffice if I give a very short explanation, enough to make you aware of the powerful influences that set in motion such mighty energies, for one must not omit events that are part of the history of that time. The ineffable, incomprehensible mystery of Grace, which is as far removed from our understanding as that of the Trinity itself, has been a cause of quarrels within the Church since the doctrine of Saint Augustine on that mystery was first disputed by the priests of Marseilles almost immediately after it was published. Saint Thomas[1] upheld Saint Augustine; the Church, more especially the Church of Rome and the Popes, adopted it in its synods and councils; yet despite such august rulings sects holding the opposite doctrine continued to exist, using various disguises for their better concealment. In later times, when the Jesuits made themselves masters of the courts through the confessionals of almost every Catholic sovereign, and masters of the public by the instruction of children, their talents and arts were of vital importance to Rome in advancing claims on the revenues of princes and on dominion over their souls, by which means they destroyed the powers of the bishops and Church-councils. They became most formidable because of their great influence, the wealth which they used to promote their intrigues, and the authority lent them by their scholarship and their presence in every department of life, for they made themselves pleasant by a smoothness and a charm never before encountered in penitential sessions, and were especially favoured by Rome because of a fourth vow of obedience to the Pope, which is peculiar to their Society and most efficacious in extending papal supremacy. People revered them also for the austerity of their lives, devoted as they were to learning, the defence of the Church against heresy, and the sanctification of their Society and its early founders. Even more redoubtable were their subtle internal politics, directed to no other end than their own power, supported by a rule in which sovereignty, authority, rank, influence, secrecy, uniformity of views, and infinite variation in methods are the very soul.

The Jesuits, I say, after various trials, especially after capturing the schools beyond the Alps and, so far as they dared, undermining them

---

[1] Saint Thomas Aquinas.

everywhere on this side, risked the publication of a book by their own Père Molina,[1] offering a doctrine on Grace utterly contrary to that of Saint Augustine, Saint Thomas, the early fathers, the Popes, or the Church of Rome, which last was many times on the brink of pronouncing it anathema, but always in the end refrained. The Church of France, in particular, opposed a seductively novel theory that was gaining many adherents by offering easy salvation and appealing to human vanity. The Jesuits thus found themselves in an awkward dilemma, but before long they had discovered a means of sowing discord among the French theologians. By the use of many artful devices, by persuasion and bullying, and finally by the support of our Court, they succeeded in turning the tables on their opponents by the invention of a new heresy, without originator or sect, which they affirmed to having discovered in a book by Cornelius Jansen, Bishop of Ypres, who had died in the bosom of the Church and in the odour of sanctity. They thus became the accusers, not the defendants in their quarrel, and forced their late attackers on to the defence. That is how the terms Molinist and Jansenist first came to be used to distinguish the opposing sides. There were great and lengthy debates in Rome on this purely imaginary heresy, which the Jesuits had manufactured, or rather invented, for the sole purpose of cutting the ground beneath the feet of Molina's antagonists. At last Pope Paul, who had a decree of anathema already prepared against the Molinist doctrine, thought it more prudent not to publish. He therefore refrained from anathematizing, and though he could not quite give their doctrine his blessing he did everything possible to content the Jesuits in respect of this supposed Jansenist heresy which no one upheld, but which they could use to great advantage.[2]

At that time many saints and scholars lived in pious retirement at the Abbey of Port-Royal-des-Champs, some to write books, others to collect disciples, whom they instructed in religion and the sciences. The greatest works on moral science, those universally acclaimed as shedding light on the principles and practice of religion, were written by them. These learned men possessed friends and connections, who also entered the quarrel against Molinism, which was enough to turn the Jesuits' earlier suspicions to implacable hatred, ending in the persecution of the Jansenists of the Sorbonne, of M. Arnauld who was regarded as the leader of them all, and finally in the dispersal of the hermits of Port-Royal. The next event in the dispute was a move by the Jesuits to introduce a formal statement of doctrine (something that has so often proved fatal, so often been banned in the Church) by which the so-called heresy was not only proscribed, which might have gained acceptance, but was explicitly stated

[1] Père Luis Molina (1536–1600). Died at Madrid.
[2] Saint-Simon's hatred for the Jesuits and for the fruit of royal bastardy such as Vendôme made him strangely blind to any of their great qualities.

to occur in the book entitled *Augustinus*, by Cornelius Jansen, Bishop of Ypres. Moreover, the formula proposed to demand an oath of inward and literal belief in its contents. The sanctioning, that is to say the proscription of five heretical propositions in which no one believed did not present the slightest difficulty; the statement as a tenet of faith that they were contained in Jansen's book created much, for not one of them could be found there, either then or afterwards. The excuse given was that they were disseminated throughout the work, yet no one was ever able to demonstrate how or where. To swear in the name of God and one's salvation that one believes in something that one does not think is founded on fact, so that it cannot be demonstrated what one believes, appeared abominable to all upright men. A great wave of indignation greeted the publication of the formula; and what appeared still more outrageous was that in order to destroy Port-Royal, whose inmates would certainly refuse to swear, it was offered to every nun in the kingdom for her signature.[1] Now to require people to swear an oath that something was contained in a book which they had not read, and for the most part were incapable of reading since it was in Latin, of which they were ignorant, did unparalleled violence to their principles, and filled the country districts with exiles, and the prisons and monasteries with captives.

At the Court no efforts were spared to assist the Jesuits, who were helping to make the *Ligue* and its consequences forgotten by spreading a belief that the Jansenists were revolutionaries, as much opposed to the King's authority as they were to that of the Pope, whom the Jesuits called 'the Church', and who had approved and later required the signing of the formula. A distinction between the general and the particular anathema was suffered for a time, but was later forbidden as rebellion against the Church, notwithstanding that the Church had not pronounced on the subject and had never been accustomed to demand implicit belief in facts determined at the general councils and the councils of bishops; many facts so determined continue to be doubted and disputed without its being considered either reprehensible or criminal. The benefices assigned for the protection of the Jesuits, distributed as they were by the King's confessor, the high esteem or the disrespect, to say no worse, with which prelates were regarded according to whether they pleased or displeased the Court and the Jesuits, fanned the persecution to the point of deprivation of the Sacraments, even of the last. Such excesses finally stirred up certain bishops to write to the Pope and thereby to risk dethronement, for the relevant documents were already in preparation when a great number of their colleagues came to the rescue by supporting the same cause. Rome and the Court then intervened, fearing a schism; other prelates came forward, including Cardinal d'Estrées, then Duke-bishop of Laon, made

---

[1] The formula was prescribed by the clergy on 17 March, 1675.

cardinal four or five years later. Negotiations resulted in what has come to be known as the Peace of Clement IX, Rospigliosi,[1] a document that stated categorically that the Holy See did not then, nor ever had claimed that signature of the formula implied belief that the five banned propositions were present either explicitly or implicitly in Jansen's book, but only that they were to be condemned in whatever book they were discovered. Thus freedom and the Sacraments were restored to those who had been deprived of them, and the doctors and other dismissed persons were given back their posts. I shall say no more. This brief history will suffice to explain what follows and henceforward I shall use the terms Jansenist and Molinist without further remark.

The Jesuits and their followers were outraged by that Peace, which all their efforts in France and Rome had been powerless to prevent. They cunningly distracted attention from Molinism by taking the offensive, and from having to defend their doctrine became the aggressors. The Jansenists, whilst protesting against the five propositions, which they found easy to condemn since no one had ever upheld them, still continued to attack the doctrine of Molina and the excesses resulting therefrom; which, as the famous Pascal makes clearly evident, do very palpably exist in the doctrine and practice of the casuistical Jesuits, and which he mocks in his brilliant letters to a Provincial, now so celebrated under the title of *Lettres Provinciales*.[2] The hatred and bitterness increased and was made permanent in documents, and meanwhile the Jesuits continued to strengthen their position at the Court, endeavouring to destroy their opponents by driving them from every high office in the Church and the schools. When Père Tellier appeared on the scene the bitter dispute was at its height. He was, as I have already said, a fanatic whose God was Molinism and the advancement of his Society. He found the perfect opportunity for so doing with a King who was completely ignorant in Church matters and had heard only the Jesuit side, a king, moreover, who had readily let himself be persuaded that the Jansenists were his personal enemies and longed to be rid of them, who cared little for religion, and all his life had been willing to do penance on the backs of others, especially Huguenots and Jansenists, who, he believed, were alike in many ways and almost equally heretical. That King, what is more, was surrounded by people almost as ignorant as himself and equally prejudiced, Mme de Maintenon, for instance, MM. de Beauvilliers and de Chevreuse, and the clergy of Saint-Sulpice, not to mention the courtiers and head-valets who knew no better or were intent on making their fortunes. The priesthood, long ago ruined, had become increasingly so by Monsieur de Chartres's

---

[1] 1668.

[2] Pascal's *Lettres Provinciales* were published anonymously between January 1656 and March 1657. Saint-Simon's bare reference to this famous work may seem extraordinary, but although he did have an appreciation of literature history was his passion.

doing, for he had filled the episcopy with ignorant nobodies straight from the gutter, who thought the Pope God Almighty, and abhorred the maxims of the Church, tradition being unknown to them and history of no meaning. As for the Parlement, it had been shorn of its responsibilities and long since reduced to servitude, such of its members as ability and office had made fit to speak were hungry for favour and advancement alone.

One or two persons none the less still seemed a danger to the Jesuits, or rather to their ambitions, such men for example as Cardinals d'Estrées, Janson,[1] Noailles, and the Chancellor. But the last, as I have already mentioned, was worn out, as Père Tellier well knew; d'Estrées was old and a courtier; Janson the same and also in failing health. Noailles, however, was different, and, what is more, was on terms of intimacy with Mme de Maintenon and a powerful influence at the Court because of the King's partiality for him, his family connections, unblemished reputation, and the veneration with which he was regarded in his diocese and the priesthood, of which he was the head in France. As soon as Père Tellier had become firmly anchored, he therefore set himself to embroil Cardinal de Noailles with the King on the one hand and the Jansenists on the other, with the further intention of completing the work so long in preparation, the total destruction of the Abbey of Port-Royal-des-Champs. Its nuns had been restored to their convent after the Peace of Clement IX, for Père de La Chaise had been content to forbid them novices, believing that by that means they would become extinct without further violence. You already know how Maréchal visited them, how the King permitted, nay ordered that visit, how he repented for driving them too hard and subsequently regarded them as being on the whole a very saintly band of women. Père Tellier soon changed that opinion. He remembered a Constitution which had been issued from Rome three or four years earlier,[2] in an effort to satisfy the incessant demands of the Molinists, whom the Vatican pampered as the champions of its trans-Alpine claims to which so many nations have been sacrificed. This Constitution had more or less condemned Jansenism, but in such general terms that it offered no danger to those who still clung to the Peace of Clement IX. In fact it had served no purpose whatsoever.

Père Tellier, for want of a better weapon, proposed to make use of it in the hope at least of injuring Port-Royal and of embarrassing Cardinal de Noailles when he should receive the King's order to see that it was signed. Since the above-mentioned Constitution did not affect the Peace of Clement IX in any fundamental way the cardinal was loath to refuse, and he therefore proceeded to obtain easy signatures first of all and later those which might prove harder to secure. This method was so successful

---

[1] Cardinal de Janson (1630–1713) Bishop of Beauvais.
[2] The Bull *Vineam Domini Sabaoth* issued by Clement XI in 1705.

that even Gif,[1] the sister-house of Port-Royal and accustomed to act in union with her, consented to sign. Armed with that signature Cardinal de Noailles felt sure of Port-Royal. Never was he more mistaken. The nuns, who so often before had been cruelly abused, were suspicious of new documents presented to them for signature in their closely watched retreat, which no one entered without danger of exile, or even of imprisonment. They had no one to turn to whose advice they could trust, and thus they would not sign, and no other signatures could persuade them to change their minds, not even that of Gif. The cardinal vainly exhorted them, explaining that what was required in no way affected the Peace of Clement IX or the truths to which they clung. Nothing served to calm the fears of their saintly and over-scrupulous souls. They would not be persuaded that this new signature did not conceal some venom, was not an overture to a fresh attack, and their courage did not fail them at the thought of what refusal might entail. All had now happened as the Jesuits hoped. Cardinal de Noailles was committed, and they were free to proceed towards the destruction of that hated convent, whose obliteration they had for so many years desired. They were terrified lest the remaining nuns should survive the King, and be allowed after his death once again to accept novices, for then indeed they would have been powerless to prevent the resurgence of what they chose to regard as the centre and headquarters of Jansenism.

Cardinal de Noailles had feared trouble for Port-Royal but not its total destruction, which at that time was inconceivable. He pleaded again and again with the nuns through his agents and personally, for he many times visited them, but all to no purpose. The King harassed him, egged on by his confessor, and at last he was overborne and deprived Port-Royal of the Sacraments. Père Tellier seized upon this to malign the nuns, affirming in the King's mind the picture of a band of revolutionaries standing out alone against a Constitution which all the rest of the Church had accepted as orthodox, and persuading him that he would have no peace so long as their rebellious house remained standing. The cunning confessor so tormented and goaded the King that the irons were heated for the burning.

Port-Royal in Paris was a mere annex of Port-Royal-des-Champs, whose nuns had long ago[2] been removed to that city, leaving the old house little better than a farm. In the ensuing years the nuns were divided between the two houses in the various persecutions. Those who submitted formed the Paris house, the rest were sent to Port-Royal-des-Champs where they found no greater enemies than their sisters in Paris, who had been endowed with nearly all their funds in the hope of reducing

[1] The Abbey of Notre-Dame-du-Val-de-Gif, Benedictine, founded by Maurice de Sully in 1140.
[2] At the time of the *Fronde*.

them by famine; they had, however, managed to keep themselves alive
by hard work, economy, and alms. When the time came for destruction
Voysin, then only a counsellor of State but ready to do anything for profit,
was commissioned to judge the claims of Les Champs. I leave you to
imagine how impartial he would have been; but at that point to everyone's
amazement the nuns regularized their position by appealing to Rome
and gaining a hearing. Since the Bull or Constitution *Vineam Domini
Sabaoth* had never been intended to undermine the Peace of Clement IX,
the nuns were not found to have been obstructive when they refused to
sign it unless the words 'without prejudice to the Peace of Clement IX'
were added. Thus what had appeared a crime in France, deserving of
obliteration and the most dire punishment of the individuals concerned,
was seen in Rome as perfectly innocent, for the nuns had submitted to the
bull in the spirit in which it was drawn up, and nothing more than that
was required of them. That made the Jesuits quickly change their tune
for the wicked use which they had intended to make of the Bull was now
plain to all and now that Rome, on whom they relied, had ceased to support them they were obliged to think again. They feared moreover
lengthy inquiries in Paris and Rome by special commissaries of the Vatican. It was a Gordian knot that appeared to them easier to cut than undo.

They accordingly acted on the principle that there was only one Port-
Royal, which had been divided into two houses for the sake of convenience. Now that it was proposed to restore the old order it seemed
better to retain the Paris house rather than the other, which was poverty-
stricken, starving, in an unhealthy locality, and inhabited only by a few
obstinate old sisters who for years past had been banned from receiving
novices. A warrant was then issued, by means of which, on the night of
28 October, the abbey of Port-Royal-des-Champs was quietly surrounded by detachments of the French and Swiss guards. Towards noon
on the 29th, d'Argenson entered the convent with the constables of the
watch. He flung open the gates, summoned the community to the Chapter, showed them the warrant, and after giving them no more than a
quarter of an hour's grace removed the entire body. He had brought with
him a number of private coaches, each of them containing an elderly
chaperone, amongst which he distributed the nuns according to their
different destinations, situated ten, twenty, thirty, forty, even fifty leagues
distant, sending them away, each coach escorted by mounted constabu-
lary, for all the world as though they were whores arrested in a bawdy
house. I shall pass over in silence all the accompaniments of that moving scene; entire books have been written on the subject.

After they had gone, d'Argenson searched the convent from attic to
cellar, seized whatever he thought might be of profit, and returned to
report to the King and Père Tellier on his glorious exploit. The treatment
meted out to the nuns in their various prisons in an effort to force them

18*

to sign became the subject of other writings that were soon known to everyone despite the vigilance of the tyrants. There followed an outburst of indignation so violent that the Court and even the Jesuits were discomfited; but Père Tellier was not the man to give up half-way. It will be best to end this matter here and now, although it dragged on into the early months of the following year. Arrests and *lettres de cachet* came thick and fast. Families with relatives buried at Port-Royal-des-Champs were ordered to exhume and rebury them elsewhere; all the rest were thrown into the cemetery of a neighbouring parish with every imaginable indignity. They next proceeded to raze the abbey to the ground, chapel, outhouses, everything, exactly as they serve the dwellings of kings' assassins. At the end no stone was left standing. All the building materials were sold and the site was ploughed and sown with grass. In very truth, no compunction was shown, they were quite ruthless. The scandal was extreme even at Rome.

I shall confine myself to this bald account of a most odious and almost military enterprise. Cardinal de Noailles realized the full horror of it when, from lack of foresight, he had rendered himself powerless to prevent it. He was on no better terms afterwards with the Molinists, and on far worse ones with the Jansenists, which was exactly as the Jesuits had intended. His tranquillity never returned after that fatal day; by which I mean that he came under almost incessant attacks, and was little by little driven to the last extremities until the day of his death.

The above-mentioned happenings delayed our departure to La Ferté until the end of September. Chamillart's daughters came with us and he joined us in the interval between his journeys to find a suitable estate. I endeavoured to entertain him even better than if he had been in office and favour and to divert him with such pleasures as the country could provide. After ten or twelve days he returned to Paris to conclude the purchase of Courcelles. His daughters followed him soon after, except for the Duchesse de Lorges, who remained with us and other company. Her father and the rest of the family were not long in establishing themselves at Courcelles and I took my sister-in-law to them a few days later. I am not saying that everything possible was not done to dissuade me, for the visit was far from prudent in the circumstances, but it seemed to me that friendship demanded that much. I spent the mornings with Chamillart, who opened his heart to me, and explained many of the mysteries surrounding his time in office. Had I not already realized the fickleness of Mme de Maintenon's mind, regard, and affections, for no other reason than her changing whims, I should have been made fully aware of it then, as well as of the effects that so often meant the failure of the best-laid plans because of her continual changes of mood.

The rest of that visit was spent in diversions and outings. Chamillart remained serene, good-humoured, alert, but almost never wished to be alone, as though he were afraid and trying to fill the void with distractions. He talked well but did not care to discuss the news and adroitly changed the subject whenever it was mentioned. The neighbours called and were made welcome, and his family endeavoured to amuse him, and themselves at the same time. Two things happened when I was with them that I cannot help recounting. The great college of La Flèche is only two leagues from Courcelles; we went to see it. The Jesuits laid themselves out to give him a splendid reception; Chauvelin, the intendant of the Province, was there to do him honour. Tessé had given one of his daughters in marriage to La Varenne, who was the lord of La Flèche; she was a widow and lived there; Chamillart thought that it would be civil to call on her and asked me to accompany him. I felt it right to tell him that she was Tessé's daughter, since the marshal had helped to cause his dismissal, and had not minded his tongue during the final days. That did not stop Chamillart, and I said no more. We called. The house was very meagrely staffed, and so ill-ordered that we were kept waiting alone in an anteroom for nearly a quarter of an hour. In that room there was a huge old-fashioned chimney-piece on which one could read in enormous letters the Latin words:

CUM FUERIS FELIX MULTOS NUMERABIS AMICOS
TEMPORA SI FUERINT NUBILA SOLUS ERIS[1]

I noticed this, and was most careful to pretend otherwise, but during our long wait Chamillart had every opportunity to read it for himself. When I saw him do so I walked away so as to conceal from him that I also had observed it, and to give him no reason to speak of the inscription. The other affair was more tedious. The church at Courcelles is small, at some distance, and reached by a very bad road. We had been there to high mass on All Saints' Day and therefore thought we might go to vespers at a convent, named La Fontaine-Saint-Martin, only half a league further. We greeted the abbess at the grille and the ladies entered. Chamillart and I were hoping to avoid a dull sermon, but the abbess informed us that the Bishop of Le Mans having heard of our proposed visit had asked the Jesuits to send their best preacher, who might feel hurt if we absented ourselves. We were thus forced to comply. At his first words I began to shiver. He took for his text the difference between the bliss of the saints in heaven and the greatest happiness that one may enjoy on earth, the eternal duration of the one, and the continual uncertainty of the other; the troubles that are inseparable from great wealth, the danger of rejoicing in prosperity, the regrets and distresses of losing it. The Jesuit, enlarging on all this, made it appear very vivid and unanswerable. Had he kept to generalities, the day he was solemnizing might have excused his lack of

[1] 'While you continue to prosper you will have many friends; if the clouds gather you will be alone.'

taste; but after waxing very eloquent on the whole subject, he produced
an example so perfectly adapted to Chamillart that no one could mistake
or fail to be embarrassed by it. He spoke of no other kind of good fortune
or happiness save that of gaining the favour and trust of a great king, of
managing his affairs, and the government of his kingdom. He entered in
detail into all the errors which such men are prone to put down to ill-
luck; he did not omit one particular. He came then to disgrace, dismissal,
emptiness, and downfall. He affirmed that a prince might well count it a
priceless boon to a dismissed minister not to require of him an account of
his ministry. He ended his sermon with an exhortation to those so reduced
in status to make pious use of their distresses so as to win greater and everlasting treasure in heaven. If he had addressed his words to Chamillart
by name he could not have made it more manifest that he preached at
him in particular, for nothing in his sermon applied to any other person.
Everyone left in a state of acute embarrassment. Only Chamillart appeared
unmoved. After the service we returned to the convent-parlour; he praised
the preacher, and gave him a courteous greeting when he came to meet
the company, adding his compliments on the sermon. At that point a
collation fortunately appeared, which gave us a chance to talk of other
things. We returned to Courcelles, and were able to say what we really
thought of that astounding lapse which the Jesuit seemed to think in
excellent taste. A few days later I returned to La Ferté after a month's
absence.

The company had all departed, and thus Mme de Saint-Simon and I
were able to sit down at leisure and discuss my plans for the future. I still
felt that my only course was to leave the Court. I was accused of all manner of crimes, yet I could not see that I had been in any way at fault; thus
I had nothing to justify or defend, nor any hope that by doing so successfully I might restore my fallen fortunes. They said that I was too clever,
too well-informed, and took advantage of the King's fear of such qualities
to put me out of his favour. My friendships with great nobles, ministers,
and ladies of influence were other matters supposed to make me undesirable; they feared lest these friends should advance me and I make
use of their support. No one wished me to rise and, for the first time
in the history of the Court, the King was persuaded to think it a crime
for a man to win the esteem, affection and trust of those for whom he felt
the same, and whom he had promoted on that account.[1] How could I
possibly disclaim cleverness and knowledge of affairs when the King had
been maliciously persuaded to the contrary? How explain a ruse that took
advantage of his own weaknesses? How excuse myself for making use of
my clever brains when no one had accused me of so doing, and my position had never allowed me to profit by them? Finally, how defend myself
for possessing friends so high in reputation, merit, and office that their

[1] He was thinking of Beauvilliers, Chevreuse, and Pontchartrain.

friendship did me honour? In any other man the King would have regarded such attachments as a guarantee of merit.

It was strange that no one had thought of turning my friendship with
M. le Duc d'Orléans against me, although it was well known and very little
disguised and he so much out of favour. Nothing gave better proof of
my enemies' intentions. They did not fear my friendships but only the
support which friends could give me. In face of all this I did not see how I
could recover the King's good opinion, for he had been warned that I was
highly dangerous, although no facts could be proved against me. The
cause for such intense ill-feeling was the jealousy and malice of those
whom I had not spared during the siege of Lille. They feared lest I be
revenged at some future date and therefore did their utmost to destroy me
permanently. My activity in matters of rank, my outspoken intolerance of
encroachments, the knaves of all sorts and conditions on whom I had expressed myself somewhat freely, my small acquaintance with the young,
whose triviality and debauches did not at all attract me, made a total of
complaints beneath which I was sinking, and my highly-placed friends
were not strong enough to rescue me. My wager on Lille was another
matter that had given Vendôme's cabal ammunition to use against me,
for they had spread that tale and convinced the King that I was blaming
his government, with every embellishment most likely to enrage him.
How could I defend myself there? How tell the King of the plot against
his grandson, when it involved so many powerful courtiers, including
some whom he esteemed and favoured, believing them to be truly attached
to him? My ills appeared to be beyond remedy, if only because there was
no substance on which to work a cure. I could neither endure to swallow
continual insults at the Court nor adopt a servile pose which I despised
and moreover believed not only unlikely to assist me, but far more likely to
bring me to absolute ruin.

Mme de Saint-Simon, thinking only of me, reminded me gently of the
dangerous consequences; the deadly effects of resentment, the tedium of
idleness, the barrenness of walks and reading for a man like myself whose
mind needed stimulation and who was accustomed to an active life. My
irritation at wasting my time, so she said, would increase in the long
future ahead of me; my children's introduction into Society would be
embarrassing and distressing, and the care of my patrimony required my
constant presence at the Court, for there would always be the possibility
of its being removed from me in anger.[1] Lastly, she encouraged me with
the thought of changes in the future and of the difference in age that
would inevitably bring them. At that point I had still the firm intention of
spending the four winter months of every year in Paris and the remainder

---

[1] Louis XIV expected all his courtiers to be in attendance at Versailles all the time. 'I never
see him!' he would say of absentees, and feel justified in disallowing their claims to reversions
or hereditary posts.

at La Ferté, visiting the Court only when need arose, and giving Mme de Saint-Simon full freedom to be less long in the country if she so pleased; but we suddenly learned of the death of our agent, who had served us ably and faithfully for more than thirty years,[1] and that misfortune speeded our return.

Mme de Saint-Simon proposed that we spend the night at Pontchartrain, and she secretly arranged for our journey to take place during a Marly, when the Chancellor would be at home. She also informed him in advance of all our conversations, so that he was lying in wait for me and I, suspecting no evil, fell into the trap. We arrived on 19 December. Next morning the Chancellor led me to his wife's sitting-room, where Mme de Saint-Simon already was, and carefully closed the door behind us. He asked how I had progressed since we last met, and whether reflection had calmed my mind. I then told him all, exactly as I have related it here, and he let me proceed uninterrupted. He took up my points one by one with all the humour and sagacity that was so natural in him and tried to upset all my reasoning, using the same arguments as Mme de Saint-Simon. After which he reproached me, but with the most touching gentleness and affection. He showed me that the enemies I complained of had good cause to hate me and to strive to be rid of me before I could harm them, since, with the intolerance of youth, I took very little heed of their feelings even in public. I was right in saying that I spoke rarely, and sometimes not at all, but the violence of my words, even at ordinary times, made people fear me, and my silence at certain moments was scarcely less eloquent. He said that there was no cause for me to do anything spectacular or unbecoming, but only to show by using more restraint that I was not incapable of reflection and improvement. He promised me that there was no great matter in the Lille wager and that it would soon be forgotten; that it was one error to suppose myself ruined, and another to believe that a man like myself could not be retrieved by care and patience. He produced several examples of men whose good fortune had provoked envy, and showed me that they had all weathered periods as seemingly disastrous, adding that servility would not help to reinstate me but only prudence and good behaviour. Thence he turned to my present afflictions, comparing them with those I should suffer in retirement, and he maintained that it was less honourable and less courageous to leave my enemies to enjoy their triumph than to oppose them and try my best to restore my fortunes. Like Mme de Saint-Simon, he ended by contrasting my age with that of the men whom I needed to convince. His wife joined in at that point, and they continued both together. I shall not repeat what they said of my capabilities and what I might one day become, because in their love for me they grossly exaggerated.

[1] Guillaume Le Vasseur, Abbé de Notre-Dame d'Aubepierre.

At last they said that the greatest trouble for me at that moment was that I had no lodging at Versailles, for not only did that entail the fatigue of journeys to and from Paris, but it curtailed the social activities that imperceptibly brought one great advantage. Here the Chancellor reminded me that I had been so sure of keeping the late Maréchal de Lorges's apartment at the château that I had never applied for one myself. No blame, he said, attached to my brother-in-law for wanting to take back his father's lodging and I ought not to be vexed with him on that account. Then, returning to this handicap, they offered me all that they had to spare, a fine large room and a privy in their own apartment. It had been their brother's[1] lodging, but since his apoplexies[2] he had never quitted his house in Paris. They argued that even if I did not wish to sleep there I might use it in the day-time, that Mme de Saint-Simon would have somewhere to change her dress, and that we could entertain our friends. They continued to press me until I felt acutely embarrassed; but Mme de Saint-Simon was silent, as she had been throughout the entire conversation, that had lasted nearly three hours. The Chancellor finally begged me to say nothing then but to think the matter over, if only to please them, and in due course it would be seen whether they had made any impression on me. On the following day they spoke to me of Mme de Saint-Simon, depicting the dreariness of her life in retirement and proceeding thence to urge the great assistance that she might be to me at the Court, where she was universally loved, respected, and admired, not least by the King himself.

I stayed three nights at Pontchartrain and seized the occasion to inquire concerning M. le Duc d'Orléans's circumstances. They could scarcely have been worse, a most marked estrangement from the King and an incomparably greater one from Monseigneur, discomfiture, obvious ill-health, complete isolation even in the public rooms, and on the rare occasions when he made an advance he was soon left standing by himself. He appeared to be entirely preoccupied with his mistress Mme d'Argenton and the low company that frequented her house in Paris. I was told that only a few weeks earlier she had acted as hostess at a great banquet which he had given for the Elector of Bavaria. Everyone, it seemed, had been shocked and the King was much annoyed. In a word no one of his age had ever ruined himself more completely. I had indeed expected nothing good, but not such a desperate situation and it gave me much to think of. I saw that I should have to return to Versailles, for a time at least.

On Saturday 21 December, when the King returned from Marly, we all dined at the Chancellor's apartment and Mme de Pontchartrain

---

[1] Jean Phélypeaux, once Intendant of Paris.
[2] You were supposed to have three attacks; 1. To slow you down, 2. To convert you, 3. To deliver you.

showed us the room she wished to offer us. She was supremely tactful in persuading us, trying to make us feel that she would be hurt and offended if we refused. They showed even more generosity by offering to provide meals for us and for our friends. In short, they persisted until I was brought to bay like a hunted stag, and quite powerless to refuse them. I did, however, manage to remain firm about the meals, for that I could never have allowed. It is impossible to describe the tact and affection with which they both behaved, but notwithstanding that, I was not at all happy, though I was affected by their reasoning and still more by their affection. I made a wry face to find myself back at Versailles with a lodging at the other end of town and only this refuge at the château, and very ill-pleased at the thought of enduring further disgrace and humiliations in a situation from which I saw no issue.

That same evening, however, when the Court returned, I found myself surrounded by friends, both men and women; Chevreuse, Beauvilliers, Levis, Saint-Géran, Nogaret, Boufflers, Villeroy, and many others gathered round me, all in their different ways pressing me with the same familiar arguments, a kind of incantation aimed to frustrate my plans, of which some had heard and others had guessed from my prolonged absence. They also set about me in relays, for all the world as though they were conspiring to give me no peace. Mme la Duchesse de Bourgogne sent for Mme de Saint-Simon the moment she knew of her return and overwhelmed her with kindness, and Mgr le Duc de Bourgogne did the same with me. The warmth of this welcome took me completely by surprise. I was deeply touched by the loyalty and affection of so many eminent persons at a time when I was in disgrace and very conscious of being powerless to serve anyone, even should my fortunes improve. I therefore resolved to stake everything on a chance of settling my life once and for all, either by a success that would reaffirm me at the Court, or by having to leave it forever, which would at least secure me from persecution.

I accordingly went to Maréchal, who, as you will recollect, was an honest fellow and greatly attached to me. Indeed, he was one of those who had most strongly pressed me not to throw in my hand, and had written to me at La Ferté in urgent terms, bidding me hasten my return. I found him at his house. Our conversation turned at once to my unhappy situation and the difficulty of my being accused of no particular crime but of a whole host of trivial failings, magnified and envenomed until they were destroying me more completely than any single offence. After some further talk I said suddenly that the worst trouble was having to deal with an unapproachable sovereign, for could I but speak to him at leisure I thought I might succeed in exposing the knavish tricks that were being employed to discredit me. I then added that I would ask a service of him that was not beyond his power to grant. I had good reason, I added, to trust in his friendship and goodwill, and being so persuaded, I begged him to say frankly if my request embarrassed him. I then asked him to choose a moment to tell the King that I was in despair from thinking that I had displeased him without knowing the cause; that only for that reason I had been absent four months and should still be in the country if our agent had not died and obliged me to return; that I could not rest until I had spoken to him freely and at ease, and that I implored him to give me a hearing. I asked Maréchal to say further that if the King refused me an audience I should know that all was over, but that if he consented I might believe that some hope remained. Maréchal reflected for a while and then looked me in the face. 'I will do it,' he said heartily. 'It is indeed the only hope. You have spoken to him several times already and have always pleased him. He knows that he need not fear what you will say. I cannot vouch for his consenting if he is set against you, but I will do my best and choose my own time.' We then arranged that he should send word by express messenger to Paris as soon as he had spoken.

When I left him I went straight to tell all to the Chancellor and Mme de Saint-Simon, explaining at the same time that as a result of their badgering I had resolved to make this one last effort, and if it failed to depart for ever. The Chancellor feared only that if the King had nothing positive against me he might refuse me an audience. Mme de Saint-Simon was far more despondent because from something said by Mme la Duchesse de Bourgogne she was persuaded that the King intensely disliked me, a piece of information which she judiciously kept to herself. Meanwhile they all decided that we could but wait and hope.

Whilst I was thus heating the irons for my own purposes I did not forget M. le Duc d'Orléans. He had gone straight from Marly to Paris; I was therefore unable to see him at Versailles, and in Paris I never visited him. Stricken as I was by the immensity of his ruin I could see only one way to restore him, most painful for him, most dangerous to urge unsuccessfully, and very hard for him to decide to take; that, however, did not intimidate me. I resolved accordingly to make him part with his mistress, never to see her more. I realized all the difficulty and all the risk of such an undertaking, but so necessary did it seem that I determined to proceed. None the less, I dared not embark alone on an adventure so beset with dangers and I thought of Bezons[1] who, though I scarcely had any acquaintance with him, was the only man able and perhaps willing to assist. He was deeply attached to M. le Duc d'Orléans, who had great confidence in him and had strongly supported his promotion. He was a rough sort of a fellow, often brutal, without much perception, and what he had entirely devoted to his own advancement. He possessed, however, good commonsense, with the head of a Rembrandt or Van Dyck, thick eyebrows and a

[1] The Maréchal-comte de Bezons had been on the Duc d'Orléans's staff in Spain but had not distinguished himself there. He was only of the *noblesse de robe* and had four daughters and three sons.

vast periwig that gave him credit for far more. An able general, especially of cavalry, he was only mediocre in commanding armies for despite his physical courage he feared every danger in the task entrusted to him. All in all he was a blunt, honest man with excellent principles and a somewhat high standard where others were concerned, which he slackened a little for himself, for he felt his want of wealth, breeding, and good connections; moreover he had a large family to support and a keen desire to advance them. M. le Duc d'Orléans's friendship had been of the greatest service to him, he had therefore every reason to deplore the prince's disgrace and to wish to see him reinstated. This, combined with the fact that Bezons was the only man in the prince's confidence whom I could make use of at that juncture, persuaded me to associate with him.

Without revealing my plot to anyone I therefore approached Bezons in the great drawing-room during the King's mass and spoke to him of M. le Duc d'Orléans's desperate situation. He, knowing that I was a friend, at once opened his heart, depicting the circumstances as even worse than the Chancellor had supposed, and adding that according to the servants he was the only man to cross the prince's threshold in the past month, not the only gentleman, but positively the only person apart from members of the household. He said that it made him wretched to witness his tragic and unjust desertion, but that he saw no remedy for it. I then looked him straight in the eye and said that I, on the contrary, did have a remedy, the only possible one, swift and sure, but terribly hard to swallow and most dangerous to administer; that I dared not act alone, but that since he was capable of advising and assisting me I had resolved to consult him. In brief, I said that if he agreed we should each separately speak frankly to M. le Duc d'Orléans, and then both together advise him to part with Mme d'Argenton, who was the main cause of his troubles and offences. If she vanished all his faults would be forgiven by the King, who knew from bitter personal experience to what lengths blind passion can drive a man. The public would follow suit and the royal family also, for everyone copied the King. It was his only chance, and by delaying he risked the King's anger turning to permanent dislike. I asked Bezons to consider well and to join me if he thought good. He at once consented, although he fully realized the danger; but just at that moment d'Antin passed close by us; we looked at one another, struck by the same thought, and decided to separate immediately and to meet again on Christmas afternoon at my house in Paris, in order to make our plans and arrange for their prompt execution.

Full of these weighty matters I returned with Mme de Saint-Simon to Paris and informed both her and my mother of my plans. They were both excessively alarmed and tried to dissuade me, saying that M. le Duc d'Orléans would never summon enough strength to dismiss his mistress or keep from telling her of our intervention. She was, they said, a malicious, insolent hussy, a close friend of Mme de Ventadour[1] and the Meudon cabal, and a boon companion of the most vicious women in Paris. She would be bound to turn on me, they added, and set me quarrelling with the prince, and finally that it was no business of mine and I should do far better to mind my own affairs and be somewhat more distant in future with M. le Duc d'Orléans. Their advice appeared very wise to me and I was sorely tempted to abide by it. Bezons kept our rendezvous on Christmas Day, but was considerably less enthusiastic, as indeed I was myself; and when I spoke of my doubts, instead of encouraging him, he said that there were truly great risks. Thus without absolutely changing our minds we decided to say nothing to M. le Duc d'Orléans unless an opportunity presented itself in the conversation, in which case whoever happened to be with him should open the subject tactfully, mentioning the other one, even saying that we two had formed a plan, but all with the greatest caution.

On the penultimate day of the year, as I was dining alone with Mme de Saint-Simon, I received an express letter from Maréchal to say that he had done what I asked, that it had not been ill-received, and that I might speak when I so wished. He none the less thought it best that I should see him first. This cheered us up considerably, for we thought it a great advance to be granted an audience. The problem now was how to ensure that it was not too long delayed nor obstructed. We accordingly decided to go to Versailles on the following day so as to look eager, and to remain there careful not to appear importunate, but waiting until it pleased him to hear me. I asked Mme de Saint-Simon to accompany me, in order to have her advice at this moment on which our entire future and that of our children depended.

We arrived on the last day of the year and I went at once to Maréchal. He told me that on the previous day he had chanced to find the King less surrounded and in a better humour than usual. He had returned to speak confidentially, out of earshot of the servants on duty at that time, and had tested the King's mood with some small matter within his sphere of duty. On receiving a favourable answer he had added that there was something else that meant far more to him personally. The King asked very kindly what was the matter, and Maréchal then proceeded to tell him that he had found me in despair because I thought I had displeased His Majesty. He took the opportunity to praise me and to stress my love of the King and my constant presence at his Court. The King did not exactly frown, but became distinctly chilly, remarking that he had nothing against me and was at a loss to understand why I thought otherwise. Thereupon Maréchal had increased the pressure, begging him to grant me an audience as the thing I most desired on earth, and one which would give him personally the greatest possible joy. The King did not reply as to the audience,

[1] Noted for her piety, and therefore a strange friend for Mme d'Argenton.

but exclaimed, 'What can he want to say? There is nothing wrong. It is true that I have heard one or two trifles about him, but nothing very grave. Tell him not to be disturbed, for I have nothing against him.' Maréchal none the less persisted in begging for an audience, imploring him to grant me one since without one I could not be easy, but to do so when he had the leisure and not at any stated time, provided only that I might see him alone in his study. At that point the King had replied with apparent unconcern, 'Very well! I agree, whenever he wishes.'

Maréchal further assured me that although the King had been cold he was not angry. He said that he thought I should have an unhurried and private audience, and advised me to explain my conduct once and for all, and not to mind taking my time about it, for the matter concerned trifles that must be discussed in detail. He urged me to speak freely and frankly, to mix some affection with my respect, and especially to keep well within range of his eye so as to allow him to choose his own time. Our talk ended with gratitude from me in proportion to the great service he had rendered me, the magnitude of which may be gauged from the fact that none of my other friends, nobles, ministers, or men in office, had felt sufficiently secure to attempt it on my behalf. That may seem amazing, but it is true, and it clearly shows how little the King trusted anyone, with the sole exception of his personal attendants. Maréchal asked me to tell no one, save only Mme de Saint-Simon and the Chancellor, and I kept faith with him. He did not so much mind people knowing that I had been granted an audience—they would know that in any case after the event; what he feared was their learning that he had obtained it for me. So ended the year 1709.

[*The end of the year 1709 marked the lowest ebb in the fortunes both of France and of Saint-Simon himself. Thereafter the great and victorious Alliance became increasingly disunited. The war on the northern frontiers still lingered on, but by 1711 France had miraculously recovered and Louis XIV was able to claim better terms at the Peace of Utrecht, 1713, than would have appeared even remotely possible in 1709. As for Saint-Simon, he obtained his audience and emerged from disgrace. His wife received the unwelcome honour of being appointed lady-in-waiting to the new Duchesse de Berry; he himself, after Monseigneur's death in 1710, became, through the good offices of the Duc de Beauvilliers, the confidential assistant of the heir-apparent, the Duc de Bourgogne, in the very centre of affairs of State. In 1711 for all too brief a time 'a brilliant and not far-distant future opened before my eyes'.*]

INDEX

Saint-Simon is profuse in his mention of both persons and places; lack of space unfortunately makes necessary the omission of some of these from this index— e.g. persons named simply as battle casualties and places noted as on the route of/or near journeys or near military movements when they play no vital part in the thread of Saint-Simon's narrative. It is hoped that their omission will not inconvenience the reader.

19